Beginning
SQL Server™ 2005 Administration

Beginning
SQL Server™ 2005 Administration

Dan Wood

Chris Leiter

Paul Turley

Wiley Publishing, Inc.

Beginning SQL Server™ 2005 Administration

Published by
Wiley Publishing, Inc.
10475 Crosspoint Boulevard
Indianapolis, IN 46256
www.wiley.com

Copyright © 2007 by Wiley Publishing, Inc., Indianapolis, Indiana

Published simultaneously in Canada

ISBN-13: 978-0-470-04704-0
ISBN-10: 0-470-04704-6

Manufactured in the United States of America

10 9 8 7 6 5 4 3 2 1

1B/QW/RR/QW/IN

Library of Congress Cataloging-in-Publication Data:

Wood, Dan, 1962-
  Beginning SQL server 2005 administration / Dan Wood, Chris Leiter, Paul Turley.
    p. cm.
  ISBN-13: 978-0-470-04704-0 (paper/website)
  ISBN-10: 0-470-04704-6 (paper/website)
  1. SQL server. 2. Database management. I. Leiter, Chris, 1975- II. Turley, Paul, 1962- III. Title.
  QA76.9.D3W6642 2007
  005.75'85--dc22

                    2006030328

For my Best Friend, Cheerleader, and Bride, Sarah

This project, like everything else in my life, would be empty, meaningless, and most likely incomplete without your constant unconditional love, support, and the occasional kick to get me moving again. I can't begin to express my love and gratitude.

— Dan Wood

About the Authors

Dan Wood (Silverdale, WA) is the Operations Manager and Senior DBA for Netdesk Corporation, a Microsoft Gold Partner for Learning Solutions in Seattle. At Netdesk, he spends most of his time training corporate IT professionals in the fine art of SQL Server administration and development. Dan was a contributing author of *Beginning Transact-SQL with SQL Server 2000 and 2005* (Indianapolis: Wiley, 2005). He contributed Chapters 1, 2, 3, 4, 5, 7, 9, and 10.

Chris Leiter (Kent, WA) is a Network Engineer for Sagem Morpho, Inc., an industry leader in biometric technology in Tacoma, WA. He has more than 12 years experience in Systems Administration and Security, primarily for technologies such as Active Directory, Internet Security and Acceleration Server, Internet Information Services, and SQL. He has worked for companies in the telemarketing, IT professional training, and online gaming industries. His experiences with both small and large organizations have given him insight into what most businesses need to help get the most out of their IT investment. He has been a Microsoft Certified Professional since 1997, and a Trainer since 2001. He currently holds his Microsoft Certified Systems Engineer (MCSE): Security, Cisco Certified Network Associate (CCNA), Microsoft Certified Trainer (MCT), Microsoft Certified Database Administrator (MCDBA), and Microsoft Certified IT Professional (MCITP): Database Administrator certifications. Chris lives in the Puget Sound area with his wife, Bridget, and their cat, Cosmo. He contributed Chapters 6, 8, 11, 13, 14, 15, and 16.

Paul Turley (Seattle, WA) is a Senior Consultant for Hitachi Consulting, where he architects and develops database systems. He has been a Microsoft Certified Professional and Trainer since 1996, and lead author of *Beginning Transact-SQL with SQL Server 2000 and 2005* (Indianapolis: Wiley, 2005), *Professional SQL Server Reporting Services* (Indianapolis: Wiley, 2006), and other Wrox database titles. He contributed Chapter 12.

Credits

Executive Editor
Robert Elliott

Development Editor
Kevin Shafer

Technical Editor
John Mueller

Production Editor
Pamela Hanley

Copy Editor
Kim Cofer

Editorial Manager
Mary Beth Wakefield

Production Manager
Tim Tate

Vice President and Executive Group Publisher
Richard Swadley

Vice President and Executive Publisher
Joseph B. Wikert

Graphics and Production Specialists
Carrie A. Foster
Denny Hager
Barbara Moore
Lynsey Osborn
Heather Ryan
Alicia B. South

Quality Control Technician
Christy Pingleton

Project Coordinator
Ryan Steffen

Proofreading and Indexing
Techbooks

Acknowledgments

Dan Wood: My heartfelt thanks and praise to Lukas, Tessa, and Caleb for being the great kids they are, even when the answer was, "Sorry, I can't... I have to work on the book."

Thank you to the Netdesk team, especially Todd Shelton and Lance Baldwin. Your support and encouragement during this project have been awesome.

A special thanks to Chris Leiter for pulling me out of the fire and contributing way more than he signed up for. It was truly a blessing to work with such a talented and knowledgeable professional. Dinner at the Met!

A heartfelt thank you goes to my friend Paul Turley for introducing me to Wiley publishing and for providing a developer's perspective to the book.

Thanks to everyone at Wiley Publishing, especially Bob Elliott for his undying patience (you were patient, right?) and to Kevin Shafer for all his hard work in editing the writing of three prima donnas. Huge thanks to John Mueller for an absolutely top-notch job of technical editing. Your comments and suggestions were invaluable. Long live the semicolon!

A very special thank you goes to my son, Kyle. I am constantly inspired by your talent, your wit, your wisdom, and your love. Your personal sacrifice to the defense of our country and to all the free people of the world is remarkable. I can't think of anyone I trust more for the job. Thank you for restful sleep.

Chris Leiter: I would like to thank everyone who helped me in one way or another with this book, which includes (but is not limited to) the following people: Dan, for bringing me on board, and then making me do more work than I originally agreed to; Kevin and John for putting up with prima donna writers (this one, anyway); Paul, for not holding the $25 I owe him over my head; the staff at Netdesk, for continually supporting and encouraging me; Thierry, Jeff, and Albert at Morpho, for giving me a great opportunity to give my skills a real workout; Rick Kingslan, for being a friend, a mentor, and who I want to be when I grow up; the Banz and Leiter families, for putting up with me working through the holidays; and, of course, my wife, Bridget, without whom I wouldn't be where I am today.

Contents

Introduction   **xxi**

   Who This Book Is For   **xxiii**
   What This Book Covers   **xxiii**
   How This Book Is Structured   **xxiv**
   What You Need to Use This Book   **xxiv**
   Conventions   **xxiv**
   Source Code   **xxv**
   Errata   **xxvi**
   p2p.wrox.com   **xxvi**

Chapter 1: Introducing SQL Server 2005   **1**

   What Is SQL Server 2005?   **1**
      Database Engine   2
      Analysis Services   3
      Reporting Services   3
      Integration Services   4
      Notification Services   4
      Service Broker   4
      Data Tier Web Services   4
      Replication Services   4
      Multiple Instances   5
      Database Mail   5
   SQL Server 2005 Editions   **5**
      SQL Server 2005 Mobile Edition   6
      SQL Server 2005 Express Edition   6
      SQL Server 2005 Workgroup Edition   7
      SQL Server 2005 Standard Edition   7
      SQL Server 2005 Enterprise Edition   7
   SQL Server 2005 Architecture   **8**
      SQL Server 2005 Communication   8
      SQL Server 2005 Services   9
   SQL Server 2005 Database Objects   **12**
      Server   12
      Database   12

Contents

Schema   13
Object Names   13
SQL Server 2005 Databases   **14**
System Databases   14
User Databases   16
Distribution Databases   16
SQL Server 2005 Database Storage   **17**
Data Files and Filegroups   17
Log Files   18
SQL Server Security   **18**
Windows Authentication Mode   18
SQL Server and Windows Authentication Mode (Mixed Mode)   19
A (Very) Brief History of SQL Server   **19**
In the Beginning   19
The Evolution of a Database   19
Microsoft Goes It Alone   19
Summary   **20**

Chapter 2: Installing SQL Server 2005   **21**

SQL Server Installation Planning   **21**
Hardware Considerations   22
Processor Considerations   23
Memory Considerations   23
Storage Considerations   23
Minimum Software   27
SQL Server Setup Application   **28**
System Configuration Checker (SCC)   29
Installation Options   31
Installing to a Windows Cluster   38
Configuring the Virtual Server Name   39
Post-Installation Considerations   41
Installation Review   **43**
Summary   **44**

Chapter 3: SQL Server 2005 Tools   **45**

SQL Server Management Studio   **46**
Tool Windows   47
Toolbars   56
SQL Server Management Studio Configuration   71
Log File Viewer   **77**

SQL Server Business Intelligence Development Studio   **78**
SQL Server Profiler   **80**
  SQL Server Trace   80
  Trace Properties   80
Database Engine Tuning Advisor   **84**
  General Tab   84
  Tuning Options Tab   86
SQL Server Configuration Manager   **87**
Reporting Services Configuration Manager   **87**
Command-Line Tools   **89**
  SQLCMD   89
  BCP   91
Summary   **94**

Chapter 4: SQL Server 2005 Storage Architecture   **95**

The Resource Database   **96**
  The SYS Schema   96
SQL Server Database Physical Structure   **97**
  Physical Storage Data Types   98
  Other Data Types   101
  SQL Server Database Files   102
  Data Files   102
  Transaction Log   105
Summary   **111**

Chapter 5: SQL Server 2005 Databases   **113**

System Databases   **113**
User Databases   **113**
Database Planning   **114**
  Capacity Planning   114
Creating Databases   **116**
  Getting Started   116
  Creating a New Database   116
  Schemas   132
  Tables   135
  Table Keys and Constraints   155
Database Diagrams   **163**
Views   **164**
  System Views   164
Synonyms   **165**

Contents

Programming Objects   **166**

- Stored Procedures   167
- Functions   167
- Database Triggers   167
- Assemblies   169
- Types   170
- Defaults   172
- Rules   172

Summary   **172**

Chapter 6: SQL Server 2005 Security   175

SQL Server Authentication Modes   **175**
- Changing the Authentication Mode from Management Studio   176
- Using the xp_instance_regwrite Extended Stored Procedure   177

Principals   **178**
- Logins   179
- Credentials   185
- Server Roles   186
- Database Users   188
- Fixed Database Roles   192

Permissions   **198**
- Server Permissions   202
- Database Scope Permissions   206
- Schema Scope Permissions   209
- Using SQL Server Management Studio for Managing Permissions   211

SQL Server Encryption   **213**
- Encryption Tools   216

Best Practices   **224**

Summary   **226**

Exercises   **226**

Chapter 7: Configuring SQL Server Network Communication   229

SQL Server 2005 Network Protocols   **229**
- Shared Memory   230
- Named Pipes   230
- TCP/IP   230

SQL Native Client Configuration   **232**

SQL Server Endpoints   **233**
- Default TSQL Endpoints   234
- TSQL TCP Endpoints   236

Database Mirroring Endpoints 238
SOAP Endpoints 240
Service Broker Endpoints 245
Securing Endpoints 246
Summary **251**

Chapter 8: Automating Administrative Tasks **253**

Database Mail **254**
How It Works 254
How to Configure Database Mail 255
Configuring Database Mail Options 259
Managing Profiles and Accounts 260
Guidelines for Deleting Mail Objects 269
Sending Mail 269
Managing Messages 274
Event Notifications **275**
SQL Server Agent **276**
Configuring the Agent Service 276
Agent Security 282
Creating Jobs 283
Creating Schedules 294
Creating Operators 301
Creating Alerts 304
Creating Proxies 313
Multi-Server Jobs 316
Maintenance Plans **318**
Maintenance Plan Wizard 318
Maintenance Plan Designer 319
Best Practices **321**
Summary **321**
Exercises **322**

Chapter 9: Disaster Prevention and Recovery **323**

Preparing the SmallWorks Database **323**
Database Recovery Models **325**
Full Recovery Model 325
Bulk-Logged Recovery Model 326
Simple Recovery Model 326
SQL Server 2005 Database Backup **327**
Backup Devices 327
How SQL Server Database Backups Work 328

Contents

SQL Server 2005 Backup Types   **329**
  Full Backup   330
  Differential Backup   330
  File/Filegroup Backup   330
  Transaction Log Backup   331
  Partial Backup   332
  Copy Only Backup   332
Backup Options   **332**
  Backup Stripe   332
  Mirrored Backup   333
  WITH Options   333
Backup Strategies   **335**
  Full Backup Only   336
  Full Backup with Differential   336
  Full Backup with Transaction Log   337
  Full and Differential Backup with Transaction Log   337
  File and Filegroup Backup   338
  Filegroup with Differential   338
  Partial Backup   339
  Backup Summary   339
Restoring Databases   **339**
  Restore Process   339
  RESTORE Command   340
  RESTORE DATABASE database_name   341
  FROM Options   342
  WITH Clause   342
  Database Restore Preparation   345
  Restoring User Databases   347
  Recovering System Databases   353
  Database Restore Summary   355
Database Snapshots   **355**
  Database Snapshot Limitations   358
  Disaster Recovery and Database Snapshots   358
Summary   **360**

Chapter 10: Monitoring SQL Server for Performance   **361**

Monitoring and Optimization Overview   **361**
  Optimization Strategy   362
  Creating a Baseline   363
Tools and Techniques for Monitoring Performance   **369**
  Log File Viewer   370
  Activity Monitor   371

System Stored Procedures 373
Using Profiler 379
Using the Database Tuning Advisor (DTA) 386
Monitoring Files 393
Monitoring Database Modifications **396**
Data Definition Language (DDL) Triggers 396
Summary **399**

Chapter 11: SQL Server High Availability **401**

Introduction to Availability **401**
Failover Clustering **402**
Windows Clustering — A Quick Primer 403
Clustering Components 404
Active/Passive Clustering 405
Active/Active Clustering 405
Considering Clustering 406
Log Shipping **406**
Preparing for Log Shipping 407
Configuring Log Shipping with SQL Management Studio 407
Configuring Log Shipping with Transact-SQL 413
Configuring Failover 418
Database Mirroring **419**
Client Redirection 420
Database Mirroring Modes 420
Configuring Database Mirroring 422
Monitoring Database Mirroring 428
Managing Database Mirroring 430
Summary **433**

Chapter 12: Administering SQL CLR Programming Objects **435**

Databases and Programming **435**
Is the SQL Language a Relic? **436**
.Net and the CLR **437**
Assemblies 437
SQL Server CLR Objects **438**
Enabling SQL CLR 439
Creating a SQL CLR Assembly 439
Adding an Assembly 444
Compatible Data Types 444
User-Defined Functions 445
CLR Stored Procedures 446

Contents

Triggers 447
User-Defined Types 448
User-Defined Aggregates 452
Code-Generation Features in Visual Studio **454**
Programming Support **457**
Threading 457
Impersonation 458
Security Options **458**
.NET Security 458
Securing SQL CLR 459
SQL Server CLR Permission Sets 459
Summary **461**

Chapter 13: Introduction to SQL Server 2005 Integration Services   463

About SSIS **463**
Integration Service 464
Integration Services Object Model 465
Integration Services Run-time 465
Integration Services Data Flow 466
Importing and Exporting Data **466**
Transforming Data with SSIS **472**
Understanding the Development Environment 473
Package Elements 475
Creating a Simple Package 482
Summary **487**

Chapter 14: Introduction to SQL Server 2005 Notification Services   489

Overview **489**
Introduction to the Notification Services Architecture **490**
Subscription Management 490
Event Collection 491
Subscription Processing 495
Notification Formatting and Delivery 495
Installing a Notification Services Application **496**
The Notification Services Instance 497
The Notification Services Application 499
Creating the Instance 504
Summary **505**

Contents

Chapter 15: Introduction to the Service Broker   507

Service-Oriented Architecture   **507**
Service Broker Overview   **508**
Service Broker Elements   **508**
   Conversations   509
   Contracts   510
   Queues   511
   Services   511
   Routes   511
Security Considerations for Service Broker   **512**
   Dialog Security   512
   Transport Security   513
Creating a Sample Application   **513**
   Preparing the Database   514
   Creating the Service Broker Objects   514
   Creating Objects for the TicketInputService   516
   Creating Objects for the TicketNotifyService   519
   Testing the Application   522
Summary   **525**

Chapter 16: Introduction to Replication   527

Replication Overview   **527**
SQL Server Replication Agents   **528**
   Snapshot Agent   529
   Log Reader Agent   529
   Distribution Agent   529
   Merge Agent   529
   Queue Reader Agent   529
SQL Server Replication Types   **529**
   Distributed Transactions   530
   Transactional Replication   531
   Snapshot Replication   532
   Merge Replication   532
   Oracle Replication   533
SQL Server Replication Models   **533**
   Single Publisher / Multiple Subscribers   534
   Multiple Publishers / Single Subscriber   534
   Multiple Publishers / Multiple Subscribers   534

Contents

Replication Tools   **534**

Filtering   535

New Publication Wizard   536

New Subscription Wizard   538

Replication Monitor   540

Summary   **541**

Appendix A: Exercise Answers   **543**

Index   **547**

Introduction

I feel kind of like Sid in the movie *Toy Story* when his rocket came in the mail—"It came it finally came!" I remember anticipating SQL Server 7 when working with SQL Server 6.5 and hoping for an improvement. I wasn't disappointed. SQL Server 7 left far behind all the baggage of OS/2 and the UNIX environment from which SQL Server initially emerged. It was truly a new and innovative release. When SQL Server 2000 was announced, I was hoping for some even more dramatic improvements, and I wasn't disappointed. Although the changes in the product from SQL Server 7.0 to SQL Server 2000 were not of the magnitude of the changes between SQL Server 6.5 and SQL Server 7.0, they were still impressive. SQL Server was easier to program against, and easier than ever to manage. That was five long years ago.

Shortly after the release of SQL Server 2000, I heard about a new database system, code-named "Yukon," that was in development at Microsoft. The information I received made it sound like it was going to be the most significant release ever, and I became "cautiously optimistic."

The company I was working with was invited to join Microsoft's Yukon Ascend program when the product was in its Beta 1 stage. The Ascend program was designed to get Microsoft partners and key customers up on the product before it shipped in order to help spread early adoption. The Microsoft Developer Evangelists and Technical Evangelists were gearing up to spread the news about this new release, and my company was hired on to help "spread the good news." What I encountered after joining the Ascend team was intriguing, even exciting. The possibilities this new release seemed to create were incredible. Still, the product was in very early Beta. I withheld judgment, waited, and explored the product, encountering many "This feature not yet implemented" messages along the way.

When Yukon finally graduated to Beta 2 and its name was officially announced as SQL Server 2005, my excitement overcame my caution. From that day, I became a little obsessed with the product. I read everything I could find about it, I played with it, and I migrated several development applications to it. I was impressed with what I saw. The possibilities this new release offered seemed almost endless. However, trouble loomed on the horizon as the dates for Beta 3 kept slipping. Many people started calling it "SQL Server 2006," or joked that the release date would be December 14, 2005.

Enter Paul Flessner, Executive Vice President, Microsoft Corporation. Flessner announced at the Microsoft TechED conference that the release date for SQL Server 2005, Visual Studio 2005, and BizTalk 2006 would all be on November 7, 2005. In addition, he also announced that there would be no Beta 3. For the last few months of the product's development cycle, only the interim builds (known as "Community Technical Previews") would be released. Flessner told an attentive crowd that "the SQL team loves SQL Server 2005 so much they don't want to let it go." He was cutting the apron strings. SQL Server 2005 would ship in 2005. Was it really ready? Only time would tell.

For me, November 7 couldn't come fast enough. I was very excited not to have to wait until the official launch, and was installing the RTM version of SQL Server 2005 within hours of it becoming available on the MSDN Subscriber Web site on the last day of October 2005. I immediately started putting it through its paces to see if it was all that Microsoft's marketing claimed it would be. Because I had worked with the beta and CTP releases for more than two years, I wasn't surprised with what I encountered with the final release. I was, however, impressed with the stability and thoroughness of the 2005 release.

Introduction

As I'm writing this, eight months and a service pack have passed since the initial release. I and my colleagues have had good opportunity to explore the many facets of this latest version. We have deployed it to support large enterprise applications. We have consulted with organizations and helped them design new SQL Server 2005 implementations as well as upgrade their existing SQL Server 2000 installations. Along the way, we have learned a great deal and have encountered countless database administrators who were anywhere from slightly perplexed to outright intimidated and confused about this new release, and how to manage it with the new tool set. This book is a result of those experiences.

With more and more applications being created that require a robust and scalable data store, SQL Server databases are finding their way into all levels of the information technology infrastructure. Six years ago, I worked with a small company with about 30 employees that had one SQL Server 7.0 installation with two databases to support their Web site and customer management software. That same company today is using four SQL Server installations to support almost 20 different applications from the original customer management software and Web site to SharePoint, Project Server, Microsoft Operations Manager, and several third-party applications. I have also worked with a large health care insurance company that has gone from no SQL Server installations six years ago to more than 50 today.

Along the way, both these companies discovered the same thing. Someone had to be hired or trained to manage these systems. Without proper management and administration, database servers get unruly and unresponsive. Transaction logs can fill up disk arrays, and, without a comprehensive backup plan, a disk failure can mean a huge loss in data and revenue.

Since you are reading these words, chances are that you are either one of those people who have been selected to manage a SQL Server 2005 installation, or you are hoping to be one of those people. Congratulations! I often joke with my non-database administrator colleagues that IT is a great deal like the solar system where many planets revolve around the all-important sun. But in the IT system, SQL Server is the sun, and all the other applications are the suns and moons that are bathed in its light. Welcome to the sun, a place where data is the queen, but the data manager is the king.

This book, as the title suggests, is all about database administration. But what is database administration? Database administrators are more and more often being called upon to perform duties that are not strictly "administrative" in nature. Along with typical administrative duties such as backups, database maintenance, and user management, database administrators are increasingly being asked to perform tasks such as building complex data transformations for data import, building distributed data solutions, and, with the release of SQL Server 2005, maintaining the security and integrity of the database while enabling the integration of managed code into the database engine.

In a nutshell, for many organizations, the database administrator has become the one-stop shop for all things related to data storage. This makes the job of being a database administrator much more complicated and difficult than in the past because of the scope and power of each subsequent release.

As a result of the database administrator's increasingly broadening role in the enterprise, it is impossible for one book to adequately cover every facet of this critical skill set. This book lays the foundation by covering in detail the most common database administrative tasks. It also introduces you to many of the more advanced areas that enterprise database administrators need to be familiar with. Read these pages carefully, and apply what you learn. From here, move on to more complex jobs and tasks. The opportunities for talented and hard-working database administrators are virtually unlimited.

It's an exciting time to be in the business of developing and maintaining databases. With the explosive growth of databases and the applications that depend on them, the demand for skilled database administrators has never been greater. As mentioned previously, this book lays an important foundation. That foundation is built upon by several different books offered by Wrox. In addition to this book Wrox has a follow-up book titled *Professional SQL Server 2005 Administration* (Indianapolis: Wiley, 2006), a book devoted to integration services titled *Professional SQL Server 2005 Integration Services* (Indianapolis: Wiley, 2006), a book on reporting services titled *Professional SQL Server2005 Reporting Services* (Indianapolis: Wiley, 2006), and one on the Common Language Runtime titled *Professional SQL Server 2005 CLR Stored Procedures, Functions, and Triggers* (Indianapolis: Wiley, 2006).

Who This Book Is For

There you are, standing in front of the book rack at your favorite book store, leafing through these pages, wondering if this is the one you are looking for. Go ahead; look around to see if I'm watching you. I'll wait.... OK, the coast is clear. So, did we write this book for you?

Since you're reading this, it's very likely. Our primary audience is IT professionals (both developers and administrators) who have found themselves responsible for the management and maintenance of a SQL Server 2005 database. You may have been responsible for a SQL Server 2000 database and were just getting used to that when your company decided to move to SQL Server 2005. The new features and new tool set can be intimidating.

We wrote this book for you. You may be thinking, "I'm a senior DBA and this book's title is *Beginning SQL Server 2005 Administration*. I am *not a beginner*." I understand. However, we also wrote this book for you. SQL Server 2005 is a dramatic departure from its predecessors and, even if you are an expert on SQL Server 2000 or SQL Server 7, you will find a great deal of very useful information in this book. Go ahead, flip through the pages, and check it out for yourself. I believe you will find what you're looking for.

Assumptions

Even though we made no assumptions about prior SQL Server experience in this book, we did make a couple of other assumptions. This book assumes that you are familiar with relational database concepts. It also assumes that you are comfortable with navigating a Windows Server 2003 or Windows XP Professional operating system. Probably the biggest assumption is that you are at least marginally experienced with the Structured Query Language (SQL). The examples in this book are all clearly defined, but there will be times when you will be required to alter the provided scripts to work in your environment. A basic knowledge of SQL will be invaluable in this case. *Beginning Transact-SQL with SQL Server 2000 and 2005* (Indianapolis: Wiley, 2005) is a great resource if you need some help in this area.

What This Book Covers

As much as we would like to have included everything that any database administrator might need for any given circumstance, there just isn't enough time or paper to cover it all. We have made every attempt to cover the main areas of SQL Server 2005 administration. Inside this book, you will find detailed information about how to maintain and manage your SQL Server 2005 installation. Most of the day-to-day tasks of the DBA are described within the pages of this book. Installation, configuration, backups, restores, security, availability, performance monitoring, and the tools to manage these areas are all covered. Our intent, our goal, and our sincere desire are to provide you with the information necessary to be a competent and successful database administrator.

How This Book Is Structured

When putting this book together, we made a conscious effort to cover the material in a logical and sequential order. The first four chapters cover the overall structure of SQL Server 2005, as well as the installation process. Once that foundation is laid, we move on to the administration process of building and securing databases in the next two chapters, followed by three chapters on specific administrative tasks and high-availability solutions. The last five chapters are dedicated to introducing you to the SQL Server 2005 services, and features including the Common Language Runtime (CLR), SQL Server Integration Services (SSIS), Notification Services, and the Service Broker. As mentioned, we tried to follow a logical order in the structure of this book, but like most technical books, it is not absolutely essential to read it in any particular order. However, if you are fairly new to SQL Server, you may want to read through Chapter 1 first to get an overall picture of the product before diving into the remaining chapters.

What You Need to Use This Book

To take full advantage of this book, you will need to have an edition of SQL Server 2005 installed along with the AdventureWorks sample database. To perform all the steps outlined in the following chapters, the Developer Edition (with its full support of the Enterprise Edition feature set) is highly recommended. In order to duplicate the examples in Chapter 12, "Administering SQL CLR Programming Objects," you will also need to have either Visual Basic 2005 or Visual C# 2005 installed.

Conventions

To help you get the most from the text and keep track of what's happening, we've used a number of conventions throughout the book.

Examples that you can download and try out for yourself generally appear in a box like this:

Example title

This section gives a brief overview of the example.

Source

This section includes the source code:

```
Source code
Source code
Source code
```

Output

This section lists the output:

```
Example output
Example output
Example output
```

Try It Out

The "Try It Out" is an exercise you should work through, following the text in the book.

1. It usually consists of a set of steps.

2. Each step has a number.

3. Follow the steps through with your copy of the database.

> Boxes like this one hold important, not-to-be forgotten information that is directly relevant to the surrounding text.

Tips, hints, tricks, and asides to the current discussion are offset and placed in italics like this.

As for styles in the text:

❑ We *highlight* important words when we introduce them.

❑ We show keyboard strokes like this: Ctrl+A.

❑ We show file names, URLs, and code within the text like so: `persistence.properties`.

❑ We present code in two different ways:

In code examples we highlight new and important code with a gray background.

```
The gray highlighting is not used for code that's less important in the present
context, or has been shown before.
```

Source Code

As you work through the examples in this book, you may choose either to type in all the code manually or to use the source code files that accompany the book. All of the source code used in this book is available for download at `http://www.wrox.com`. Once at the site, simply locate the book's title (either by using the Search box or by using one of the title lists) and click the Download Code link on the book's detail page to obtain all the source code for the book.

Because many books have similar titles, you may find it easiest to search by ISBN; for this book the ISBN is 0-470-04704-6.

Once you download the code, just decompress it with your favorite compression tool. Alternatively, you can go to the main Wrox code download page at `http://www.wrox.com/dynamic/books/download.aspx` to see the code available for this book and all other Wrox books.

Errata

We make every effort to ensure that there are no errors in the text or in the code. However, no one is perfect, and mistakes do occur. If you find an error in one of our books, like a spelling mistake or faulty piece of code, we would be very grateful for your feedback. By sending in errata you may save another reader hours of frustration and, at the same time, you will be helping us provide even higher-quality information.

To find the errata page for this book, go to http://www.wrox.com and locate the title using the Search box or one of the title lists. Then, on the book details page, click the Book Errata link. On this page you can view all errata that has been submitted for this book and posted by Wrox editors. A complete book list including links to each book's errata is also available at www.wrox.com/misc-pages/booklist.shtml.

If you don't spot "your" error on the Book Errata page, go to www.wrox.com/contact/techsupport .shtml and complete the form there to send us the error you have found. We'll check the information and, if appropriate, post a message to the book's errata page and fix the problem in subsequent editions of the book.

p2p.wrox.com

For author and peer discussion, join the P2P forums at p2p.wrox.com. The forums are a Web-based system for you to post messages relating to Wrox books and related technologies, and interact with other readers and technology users. The forums offer a subscription feature to e-mail you topics of interest of your choosing when new posts are made to the forums. Wrox authors, editors, other industry experts, and your fellow readers are present on these forums.

At http://p2p.wrox.com, you will find a number of different forums that will help you not only as you read this book, but also as you develop your own applications. To join the forums, just follow these steps:

1. Go to p2p.wrox.com and click the Register link.
2. Read the terms of use and click Agree.
3. Complete the required information to join, as well as any optional information you wish to provide, and click Submit.
4. You will receive an e-mail with information describing how to verify your account and complete the joining process.

You can read messages in the forums without joining P2P, but to post your own messages, you must join.

Once you join, you can post new messages and respond to messages other users post. You can read messages at any time on the Web. If you would like to have new messages from a particular forum e-mailed to you, click the Subscribe to this Forum icon by the forum name in the forum listing.

For more information about how to use the Wrox P2P, be sure to read the P2P FAQs for answers to questions about how the forum software works, as well as many common questions specific to P2P and Wrox books. To read the FAQs, click the FAQ link on any P2P page.

Introducing SQL Server 2005

To help you become familiar with SQL Server 2005, this chapter focuses on the key ingredients of the software. This chapter also outlines differences between different editions of the software before diving into particulars on the topics of architecture, database objects, databases, database storage, and server security. The chapter concludes with a brief look at the historical evolution of SQL Server.

What Is SQL Server 2005?

As you most likely know, SQL Server 2005 is primarily thought of as a *Relational Database Management System (RDBMS)*. It is certainly that, but it is also much more.

SQL Server 2005 can be more accurately described as an *Enterprise Data Platform*. It offers many new features, and even more enhanced or improved features from previous editions of the product. In addition to traditional RDBMS duty, SQL Server 2005 also provides rich reporting capabilities, powerful data analysis, and data mining, as well as features that support asynchronous data applications, data-driven event notification, and more.

This book is primarily focused on the administration of the Database Engine. However, as mentioned, SQL Server 2005 includes many more features than just the relational engine. In light of that, it is important to start with some point of common reference. This section introduces the features of SQL Server 2005. It is not meant to be all-inclusive, but it will provide the context for the remainder of the book.

Later chapters go into greater detail and delve into the technologies behind each feature and how they affect you, the database administrator. SQL Server 2005 is such an enormous product that no one book could possibly cover every feature in detail, so some features will only be covered briefly as an introduction, while the core administrative features will be described in greater detail.

Database Engine

The Database Engine is the primary component of SQL Server 2005. It is the Online Transaction Processing (OLTP) engine for SQL Server, and has been improved and enhanced tremendously in this version. The Database Engine is a high-performance component responsible for the efficient storage, retrieval, and manipulation of relational and Extensible Markup Language (XML) formatted data.

SQL Server 2005's Database Engine is highly optimized for transaction processing, but offers exceptional performance in complex data retrieval operations. The Database Engine is also responsible for the controlled access and modification of data through its security subsystem. SQL Server 2005's Database Engine has many major improvements to support scalability, availability, and advanced (and secure) programming objects:

❑ *Physical partitioning of tables and indexes* — Tables and indexes can now be physically partitioned across multiple file groups consisting of multiple physical files. This dramatically improves the performance of data retrieval operations and maintenance tasks that are executed against very large tables. (See Chapter 5 for more information.)

❑ *Data Definition Language (DDL) triggers* — DDL triggers can be used to execute commands and procedures when DDL type statements are executed. In the past, modifications to the database could go undetected until they caused an application to fail. With DDL triggers, a history of all actions can be easily recorded or even prevented. DDL triggers can be placed at the server or database level.

❑ *Enhanced variable-length data types* — A new MAX keyword has been added to varchar, nvarchar, and varbinary data types that allow the allocation of up to 2GB of space for large object variables. One of the chief advantages of this addition is the ability to use large value types in the declaration and use of variables.

❑ *XML data type* — The new XML data type enables the storage of well-formed and schema-validated XML data. It also brings rich support in the form of XML data type methods, along with enhancements to OPENXML and FOR XML T-SQL commands.

❑ *Multiple Active Result Sets (MARS)* — MARS allows for clients to maintain more than one data request per connection. For example, in the past, if a connection was opened in an application, only one data reader could be opened to retrieve data from the database. To open another data reader, the first one had to be closed. With MARS, this limitation is removed.

❑ *Structured error handling* — T-SQL now includes the ability to perform structured error handling in the form of TRY and CATCH commands that remove the necessity of repeated checks for errors in scripts, and the ability to elegantly handle any errors that do occur.

❑ *Common Table Expressions (CTE)* — Microsoft has extended the American National Standards Institute (ANSI) compliance of T-SQL by including the ability to use the CTE object. CTEs are extraordinarily useful in the creation of efficient queries that return hierarchical information without the need for using lengthy and complicated recursive sub-queries.

❑ *Security enhancements* — SQL Server's security architecture has been enhanced considerably with the ability to enforce account policies on SQL Server logins. Other additions to SQL Server's security architecture include the control of execution context and the ability to create encryption keys and certificates to control access and guarantee the integrity of database objects through the use of digital signatures. See Chapter 6 for more information.

❑ *Common Language Run-Time (CLR) integration* — One of the most exciting additions to SQL Server is the integration of the CLR. It is also possibly the most misunderstood. The CLR provides a hosted environment for managed code. No longer is it necessary to make calls to external Application Programming Interfaces (API) via hard-to-manage extended stored procedures written and compiled utilizing unmanaged code to perform advanced and programmatic functions. Because the CLR is integrated in the Database Engine, database developers can now create secure and reliable stored procedures, functions, triggers, aggregates, and data types utilizing advanced C# and/or VB.NET features in the .NET Framework. The CLR in no way makes T-SQL obsolete, because T-SQL still out-performs managed code in the traditional manipulation of relational data. Where the CLR shines is in instances that require complex mathematical functions or that involve complex string logic. For an introductory look at the CLR see Chapter 12.

For complete coverage of the CLR check out the book, Professional SQL Server 2005 CLR Stored Procedures, Functions, and Triggers *by Derek Comingore (due for release by Wrox Press in the Fall of 2006).*

Analysis Services

Analysis Services delivers Online Analytical Processing (OLAP) and Data Mining functionality for business intelligence applications. As its name suggests, Analysis Services provides a very robust environment for the detailed analysis of data. It does this through user-created, multidimensional data structures that contain de-normalized and aggregated data from diverse data sources (such as relational databases, spreadsheets, flat files, and even other multidimensional sources).

The Data Mining component of Analysis Services allows the analysis of large quantities of data. This data can be "mined" for hidden relationships and patterns that may be of interest to an organization's data analyst. An example of this could be the online book store that analyzes your searches and purchases, comparing them to previous customers' search and purchase patterns to offer you suggestions or targeted advertisements. It could also be the cancer research group comparing health records and demographic data of patients to find some common pattern to the emergence of a particular form of cancer.

For a very detailed look at SQL Server 2005 Analysis Servers, check out the book, Professional SQL Server Analysis Services 2005 with MDX, *by Sivakumar Harinath and Stephen R. Quinn (Indianapolis: Wrox Press, 2006).*

Reporting Services

Reporting Services is a Web service–based solution for designing, deploying, and managing flexible, dynamic Web-based reports, as well as traditional paper reports. These reports can contain information from virtually any data source. Because Reporting Services is implemented as a Web service, it must be installed on a server with Internet Information Services (IIS). However, IIS does not have to be installed on a SQL Server. The Reporting Services databases are hosted on SQL Server 2005, but the Web service itself can be configured on a separate server.

For a detailed description of SQL Server 2005 Reporting Services and information about how to implement and extend SQL Server 2005 reports, check out an excellent book written by four very talented developers and personal friends, Professional SQL Server 2005 Reporting Services (Indianapolis: Wrox Press, 2006). *Paul Turley, Todd Bryant, James Counihan, and Dave DuVarney are amazing guys who I have had the great pleasure of working with over the past few years. You will not be disappointed.*

Integration Services

SQL Server Integration Services (SSIS) is Microsoft's new enterprise class data Extract, Transform, and Load (ETL) tool. SSIS is a completely new product built from the ashes of SQL Server 2000's Data Transformation Services (DTS). SSIS offers a much richer feature set and the ability to create much more powerful and flexible data transformations than its predecessor. This huge improvement, however, is not without a cost. SSIS is a fairly complex tool and offers a completely different design paradigm than DTS. Database administrators adept at the former tool are very often intimidated and frustrated by the new SSIS. Their biggest mistake is in thinking that Integration Services would just be an upgrade of Data Transformation Services. As stated previously, this simply isn't the case. More research, preparation, and training will be crucial to effectively utilizing SSIS. For an introductory look at SSIS, see Chapter 13.

> For a very thorough discussion of this new feature of SQL Server 2005, read the excellent book, Professional SQL Server 2005 Integration Services (Indianapolis: Wiley, 2006).

Notification Services

Notification Services is used to build and deploy applications that support the generation and sending of data-driven notifications. Notification Services' applications provide the mechanism for subscribers to create a subscription for a specific event, which could be a database, file system, or some other programmatic event. The notification can take the form of an email or other custom delivery methods. For more information on Notification Services, see Chapter 14.

Service Broker

Service Broker provides the framework and services to enable the creation of asynchronous, loosely coupled applications. Service Broker implements a Service Orientated Architecture (SOA) in the data tier. It provides more controlled transaction-based communications than traditionally available in other SOA implementations such as Microsoft Message Queuing (MSMQ). Service Broker allows the developer to create database applications that focus on a particular task and allows the asynchronous communication with other applications that perform related (yet disconnected) tasks. For more information, see Chapter 15.

Data Tier Web Services

SQL Server 2005 provides support for creating and publishing data tier objects via HTTP without the use of an Internet Information Services (IIS) server. SQL Server 2005 can listen and respond to an HTTP port allowing developers to create applications that interact with a database across the Internet or through a firewall by using a Web service. For more information, see Chapter 7.

Replication Services

SQL Server 2005 Replication Services provides the ability to automate and schedule the copying and distribution of data and database objects from one database or server to another, while ensuring data integrity and consistency. Replication has been enhanced in SQL Server 2005 to include true Peer-to-Peer replication, replication over HTTP, the ability to replicate schema changes, and, very interestingly, the ability to configure an Oracle server as a replication publisher.

Multiple Instances

SQL Server 2005 provides the capability of installing multiple instances of the database application on a single computer. Depending on the edition of SQL Server being installed, up to 50 instances can be installed. This feature allows for one high-performance server to host multiple instances of the SQL Server services, each with its own configuration and databases. Each instance can be managed and controlled separately with no dependency on each other.

Database Mail

In the past SQL Server relied on a Messaging Application Programming Interface (MAPI) mail client configured on the server to facilitate email and pager notification for administrative and programmatic purposes. What this essentially meant was that to fully utilize administrative notifications, the administrator needed to install Outlook or some other MAPI-compliant client on the server, and then create a mail profile for the service account to use.

Many organizations wanted to take advantage of the SQL Server Agent's ability to send job and event notification via email but were unwilling to install unnecessary and potentially risky software on production server assets. The SQL Server 2005 Database Mail feature removes this requirement by supporting Simple Mail Transfer Protocol (SMTP) for all mail traffic. In addition, multiple mail profiles can be created in the database to support different database applications. For more information about Database Mail, see Chapter 8.

SQL Server 2005 Editions

SQL Server 2005 comes in six different flavors, and each has its specific place in the data management infrastructure with the probable exception of the Enterprise Evaluation Edition, which is only useful for short-term evaluation of the product (180 days). At the top of the list is the Enterprise Edition that supports absolutely everything that SQL Server 2005 has to offer. On the other end of the spectrum is the Express Edition, which offers very limited (but still exciting) features.

The following table contrasts the major differences between all but the Developer and Evaluation Editions. As discussed later in this section, the Developer Edition supports the same functionality as the Enterprise Edition, and the Evaluation Edition is the Enterprise Edition with a time-limited and restricted license.

Feature	Enterprise Edition	Standard Edition	Workgroup Edition
Failover Clustering	Yes	2-node	No
Multi-Instance Support	50	16	16
Database Mirroring	Yes	Limited	No
Enhanced Availability Features	Yes	No	No
Table and Index Physical Partitioning	Yes	No	No

Table continued on following page

Feature	Enterprise Edition	Standard Edition	Workgroup Edition
Analysis Services Support	Yes	Yes	No
Data Mining	Yes	Limited	No
Reporting Services	Yes	Limited	Very Limited
Notification Services	Yes	Limited	No
Integration Services	Yes	Limited	Very Limited
Replication Services	Yes	Limited	Limited

For a complete list of supported features consult SQL Server 2005 Books Online under the topic "Features Supported by the Editions of SQL Server 2005."

SQL Server 2005 Mobile Edition

SQL Server Mobile is the replacement for SQL Server CE first offered in SQL Server 2000. The Mobile Edition enables the installation of a small SQL Server database on a mobile device to support a CE or Windows mobile application. SQL Server Mobile also enables the support of a database that is replicated from a database hosted on a Windows Server.

This ability creates a world of opportunity for collecting data in a remote scenario and synchronizing that data with a land-based database. For example, consider an overnight delivery service that must maintain a record of a delivery truck's inventory, including packages delivered and picked up. The truck inventory could be uploaded via replication to a mobile device, where a mobile application kept track of the deliveries and new packages picked up at delivery locations. Once the truck came back to the delivery center, the mobile device could be synchronized with the central database via replication or data upload.

SQL Server 2005 Express Edition

SQL Express is at the lowest end of functionality and scalability, but I am very excited about this particular edition. SQL Express replaces the Microsoft Desktop Edition (MSDE) and has a similar price index — it's free. For its very low price (you can't beat free), it still contains a great deal of functionality.

The reason this edition excites me is that it is perfect for many of my customers who are starting or running small businesses. They have a genuine need for a centralized managed database, but aren't ready to pay for a more scalable and robust solution. At the risk of offending my friends in the Open Source community, most of my customers are not very technically savvy, and so very flexible and viable solutions like MySQL running on Linux or Windows is just not appropriate when a Database Engine with an intuitive and free graphical management tool exists.

One of the most exciting improvements to Microsoft's free version of its database system is that it comes with a graphical management environment. It also supports databases up to 4GB in size and contains much of the same functionality as the other editions.

SQL Express is a big step up from MSDE, its predecessor and is a very viable solution for standalone applications that require a managed data-store or even distributed applications with a minimal number of connections.

SQL Express can be installed on any Microsoft desktop or server operating system from Windows 2000 and beyond, so a very small company can still leverage the database technology without making a large investment. Once the company starts to grow, it will inevitably need to make the move to one of the more robust editions, but the upgrade process from SQL Express to its bigger siblings is a piece of cake because the data structures are nearly identical.

SQL Server 2005 Workgroup Edition

The Workgroup Edition replaces the SQL Server Personal Edition. It contains all the functionality of SQL Server 2005 Express Edition and then some. This edition is targeted to those small companies that have either outgrown the Express Edition or needed a more flexible solution to begin with, and yet do not need all the features of the Standard or Enterprise Edition.

The Workgroup Edition is very flexible and contains many of the features of the more expensive editions. What the Workgroup Edition doesn't provide is support for more advanced business intelligence applications, because SQL Server Integration Services and Analysis Services are not included in this edition. The Workgroup Edition also has a reduced feature set in regard to Reporting Services, but the Reporting Services features supported should satisfy most small organizations.

Like the Express Edition, the Workgroup Edition can be installed on both desktop and server operating systems, with the exception of Windows XP Home (which is not supported).

SQL Server 2005 Standard Edition

Most of the capabilities of SQL Server 2005 are supported in the Standard Edition, which makes it the ideal data platform for many organizations. What the Standard Edition does not provide are many of the features designed for the support of large enterprise databases. These features include many of the high-availability and scalability enhancements, such as Partitioned Tables and Parallel index operations. It also lacks some of the more advanced business intelligence features and Integration Services.

SQL Server 2005 Enterprise Edition

The Enterprise Edition is the full-meal deal. Nothing is held back. Parallel operations, physical table partitioning, complete business intelligence, and data mining support — you name it, the Enterprise Edition has it.

If you require an easy-to-implement-and-maintain platform that can support millions of transactions a second, 64 terabytes (TB) of RAM, and 64-bit processors, this release is for you. It is also an appropriate solution if you just require advanced business analytics, and not necessarily the millions of transactions a second that this edition offers.

Enterprise Edition is performance. Although the feature set between the Enterprise Edition and the Standard Edition is not huge, the differences in performance between the two editions can be. The Enterprise Edition fully optimizes read-ahead execution and table scans, which results in marked improvement in read and scan performance.

SQL Server 2005 Architecture

It is the job of SQL Server to efficiently store and manage related data in a transaction-intensive environment. The actual theories and principles of a relational database are beyond the scope of this book, and hopefully you already have some of that knowledge. What is pertinent to this book is the way SQL Server manages the data, and how it communicates with clients to expose the data. The following discussion describes the communication architecture utilized by SQL Server 2005, the services SQL Server 2005 utilizes, and the types of databases SQL Server uses. This section also discusses how those databases are stored and accessed, but you can find a detailed description of SQL Server 2005 storage architecture in Chapter 4.

SQL Server 2005 Communication

To adequately plan for a SQL Server database application, it is important to understand how SQL Server 2005 communicates with clients. As mentioned previously, SQL Server 2005 is more of a data platform than just a relational database server. Because the SQL Server 2005 platform offers several different data services, it also must provide different ways of accessing that data.

SQL Server 2005 ships with the ability to communicate over different protocols. By default, SQL Server will accept network connections via TCP/IP. The local Shared Memory protocol is also enabled by default to enable local connections without having to incur the overhead of a network protocol.

In addition to the TCP/IP, Named Pipes, and Shared Memory protocols, the Virtual Interface Adapter (VIA) protocol is available for VIA Storage Area Network (SAN) implementations.

With the exception of HTTP endpoints (described in Chapter 7), SQL Server utilizes a communication format called *Tabular Data Stream* (TDS). The TDS packets utilized by SQL Server are encapsulated in the appropriate protocol packets for network communication.

The task of wrapping the TDS packets is the responsibility of the SQL Server Network Interface (SNI) protocol layer. The SNI replaces the Server Net-Libraries and the Microsoft Data Access Components (MDAC) that were utilized in SQL Server 2000. SQL Server creates separate TDS endpoints for each network protocol.

Although TDS is the primary method for connecting to and manipulating data on a SQL Server, it is not the only method available. In addition to TDS communication, SQL Server 2005 supports native Data Tier Web services (see Chapter 7). By utilizing SQL Server Web services, connections can be made to SQL Server via any client application that supports HTTP and Simple Object Access Protocol (SOAP).

Supported Languages

SQL Server 2005 supports the following five different languages to enable data manipulation, data retrieval, administrative functions and database configuration operations:

❑   *Transact-Structured Query Language (T-SQL)* — This is Microsoft's procedural language extension to the Structured Query Language (SQL) standard established by the American National Standards Institute (ANSI). T-SQL is entry-level compliant with the ANSI-99 standard. T-SQL is the primary and most common method for manipulating data. For more information about T-SQL, consult *Beginning Transact-SQL with SQL Server 2000 and 2005* (Indianapolis: Wiley, 2005).

- ❑ *Extensible Markup Language (XML)* — This is fully supported in SQL Server 2005, as well as language extensions to XML that enable the retrieval and modification of data by utilizing XQuery syntax or native XML methods.

- ❑ The *Multidimensional Expressions (MDX)* — This language is used to query against multidimensional objects in SQL Server 2005 Analysis Services.

- ❑ *Data Mining Expressions (DMX)* — This is a an extension of Transact-SQL that enables the creation of queries against a data mining model implemented in SQL Server 2005 Analysis Services.

- ❑ *Extensible Markup Language for Analysis (XMLA)* — This can be used to both discover metadata from an instance of SQL Server 2005 Analysis Services and to execute commands against an instance of SSAS. XMLA commands are generally limited to the creation or modification of SSAS objects. Actual retrieval of SSAS data is done with MDX queries.

SQL Server Programming Object Models

Most of the administrative activity that must be done on SQL Server 2005 can be done using the provided tools, but sometimes it may be necessary to build custom administrative tools, or to be able to programmatically build and manipulate database objects. Three new object models have been created to support this need:

- ❑ *SQL Management Objects (SMOs)* — SMOs enable developers to create custom applications to manage and configure SQL Server 2005, SQL Server 2000, or SQL Server 7.0 Database Engines. It is an extensive library that provides full support for virtually all aspects of the relational store. The SMO library makes it possible to automate administrative tasks that an administrator must perform through custom applications, or with command-line scripts using the SMO `scripter` class.

- ❑ *Replication Management Objects (RMOs)* — RMOs can be used along with SMOs to implement and automate all replication activity, or to build custom replication applications.

- ❑ *Analysis Management Objects (AMOs)* — AMOs, like SMOs and RMOs, represent a complete library of programming objects. AMOs enable the creation of custom applications or automation of Analysis Server management.

SQL Server 2005 Services

SQL Server runs as a service. In fact, it runs as several services if all the different features of the product are installed. It is important to know what service is responsible for what part of the application so that each service can be configured correctly, and so that unneeded services can be disabled to reduce the overhead on the server and reduce the surface area of SQL Server.

MSSQLServer (SQL Server)

The MSSQLServer service is the database engine. To connect and transact against a SQL Server 2005 database, the MSSQLServer service must be running. Most of the functionality and storage features of the database engine are controlled by this service.

The MSSQLServer service can be configured to run as the local system or as a domain user. If installed on Windows Server 2003, it can also be configured to run under the Network System account.

SQLServerAgent (SQL Server Agent)

This service is responsible for the execution of scheduled jobs such as scheduled backups, import/export jobs, and Integration Services packages. If any scheduled tasks require network or file system access, the SQLServerAgent service's credentials are typically used.

The SQLServerAgent service is dependent on the MSSQLServer service. During installation, the option is given to configure both services with the same credentials. Although this is by no means required, it is common practice. A frequent problem encountered by database administrators is that jobs that work perfectly when run manually fail when run by the agent. The reason for the failure is because the account that is used when testing the job manually is the logged-in administrator, but when the job is executed by the agent, the account the agent is running under does not have adequate permissions.

MSSQLServerADHelper (SQL Server Active Director Helper)

Very often, the MSSQLServer service and the SQLServerAgent service are configured to run with a domain account that has local administrative rights on the server SQL Server is installed on. Although this configuration offers a great deal of flexibility to what the two services can do locally, it doesn't give them any permission to Active Directory.

In order for the MSSQLServer service to register its respective instance of SQL Server, it must be either running as the local system account (which significantly reduces the flexibility of the service), or be a member of the domain admin group (which grants it way too much access, violating the principle of least privilege).

To enable SQL Server to register itself in the domain, but not limit its functionality, the MSSQLServerADHelper service was created. The MSSQLServerADHelper service runs under the local system account of the domain computer SQL Server is installed on, and is automatically granted the right to add and remove objects from Active Directory. The MSSQLServerADHelper service only runs when needed to access Active Directory and is started by the MSSQLServer service when required. Regardless of the number of installed instances there is only one MSSQLServerADHelper service per computer.

MSSQLServerOLAPService (SQL Server Analysis Services)

MSSQLServerOLAPService is the service that Analysis Services runs under. Analysis Services provides the services and functionality to support all of SQL Server 2005's OLAP needs, as well as the new data mining engine included with SQL Server 2005.

SQLBrowser (SQL Server Browser)

The SQLBrowser service is used by SQL Server for named instance name resolution and server name enumeration over TCP/IP and VIA networks.

The default instance of SQL Server is assigned the TCP port 1433 by default to support client communication. However, because more than one application cannot share a port assignment, any named instances are given a random port number when the service is started. This random port assignment makes it difficult for clients to connect to it, because the client applications don't know what port the server is listening on. To meet this need, the SQLBrowser service was created.

On startup, the SQLBrowser service queries the registry to discover all the names and port numbers of installed servers and reserves UDP port 1434. It then listens on UDP port 1434 for SQL Server Resolution Protocol (SSRP) requests and responds to the requests with the list of instances and their respective port assignments so that clients can connect without knowing the port number assignment. There are definite security considerations to this arrangement, so it is very important that no unauthenticated traffic on UDP port 1434 be allowed on the network, because the service will respond to any request on that port. This creates the potential of exposing more information about the server instances than some organizations find acceptable.

If the SQLBrowser service is disabled, it will be necessary to specify a static port number for all named instances of SQL Service and to configure all client applications that connect to those instances with the appropriate connection information. For a full list of what features are affected by disabling the SQLBrowser, consult SQL Server 2005 Books Online.

MSFTESQL (SQL Server Full-Text Search)

The Microsoft Full-Text Engine for SQL Server (MSFTESQL) is used to support full-text indexing and full-text queries against text data stored in the database. The text data can be of several different data types including char, nchar, varchar, nvarchar, text, and ntext. In addition, full-text indexes can be created on binary formatted text such as Microsoft Word documents.

The chief advantage of the MSFTESQL service and associated engine is that it allows much more flexible and powerful searches against text data than the Transact-SQL LIKE command, which is limited to exact match searches. The MSFTESQL engine can perform exact match, proximity, linguistic, and inflectional searches. It will also exponentially outperform comparative Transact-SQL LIKE searches against large (millions of rows) tables. For a more complete discussion on both the Transact-SQL LIKE command and Full-Text search see *Beginning Transact-SQL with SQL Server 2000 and 2005* (Indianapolis: Wiley, 2005).

MSDTSServer (SQL Server Integration Services)

The MSDTSServer service provides management and storage support for SSIS. Although this service is not required to create, store, and execute SSIS packages, it does allow for the monitoring of SSIS package execution and displaying of a hierarchical view of SSIS packages and folders that are stored in different physical locations.

ReportServer (SQL Server Reporting Services)

The ReportServer service is the process in which Reporting Services runs. The service is accessible as a Web service and provides for report rendering, creation, management, and deploying. For more information on Reporting Services, see *Professional SQL Server 2005 Reporting Services* (Indianapolis: Wiley, 2004).

SQLWriter (SQL Server VSS Writer)

The SQLWriter service allows for the volume backup of SQL Server data and log files while the SQL Server service is still running. It does this through the Volume Shadow Copy Service (VSS). SQL Server database backups are typically performed through SQL Server's backup program or through third-party applications that communicate with SQL Server's backup program.

Normal system backups of volumes containing SQL Server log or data files will normally fail, because as long as SQL Server is running, the files are open. The SQLWriter service overcomes this limitation by allowing you to perform the backups with the VSS service. It is still recommended, however, to perform regular backups through SQL Server's backup program.

MSDTC (Distributed Transaction Coordinator)

The MSDTC service is used to manage transactions that span more than one instance of SQL Server or an instance of SQL Server and another transaction-based system. It utilizes a protocol known as Two-Phased Commit (2PC) to ensure that all transactions that span systems are committed on all participating systems.

SQL Server 2005 Database Objects

SQL Server 2005 database objects are defined and exist within a defined scope and hierarchy. This hierarchy enables more control over security permissions and organization of objects by similar function. SQL Server 2005 objects are defined at the Server, Database, and Schema levels.

Server

The server scope encompasses all the objects that exist on the instance of SQL Server, regardless of their respective database or namespace. The database object resides within the server scope.

One of the more confusing terms when working with SQL Server 2005 is the term *server*. When you hear the term "server," you often think of that piece of hardware taking up space on a *server* rack in the *server* room. Where the confusion arises is that you can install multiple instances of SQL Server on a single *server* (huh?).

What would probably be clearer is to say that the capability exists to install multiple instances of the SQL Server 2005 Data Platform application on a single computer running a Windows operating system. Though this might be more descriptive, it doesn't make for very interesting marketing material.

What is left is the fact that, when it comes to SQL Server 2005 and you read "server," it is important to check the context to make sure that it means an instance of SQL Server 2005 or the physical computer that SQL Server is installed on.

When it comes to the server scope and SQL Server 2005 database objects, the term "server" actually refers to the SQL Server 2005 instance name. In the majority of the examples in this book, the instance name is AUGHTFIVE, which is also the name of the server used in the writing of this book. So, the instance name AUGHTFIVE is the default instance installed on the Windows Server 2003 named AUGHTFIVE.

Database

The database scope defines all the objects within a defined database catalog. Schemas exist in the database scope.

The ANSI synonym for "database" is "catalog." When connecting to an instance of SQL Server 2005, it is generally desired to specify an Initial Catalog, or Initial Database. An instance of SQL Server 2005 can contain many databases. A typical database application is constrained within one database that contains all the data objects required to provide the functionality the application requires. This is not always the case, but it is the most common.

Schema

Each database can contain one or more schemas. A schema is a namespace for database objects. All data objects in a SQL Server 2005 database reside in a specific schema.

SQL Server 2005 implements the ANSI schema object. A database schema is a defined namespace in which database objects exist. It is also a fully configurable security scope. In previous releases of SQL Server, the namespace was defined by the owner of an object. In SQL Server 2005, the ownership of an object is separated from an object's namespace. An individual user may be granted ownership of a schema, but the underlying objects belong to the schema. This adds greater flexibility and control to the management and securing of database objects. Permissions can be granted to a schema, and those permissions will be inherited by all the objects defined in the schema.

Object Names

Every object in a SQL Server 2005 database is identified by a four-part, fully qualified name. This fully qualified name takes the form of `server.database.schema.object`. However, when referring to objects, the fully qualified name can be abbreviated. By omitting the server name SQL Server will assume the instance the connection is currently connected to. Likewise, omitting the database name will cause SQL Server to assume the existing connection's database context.

Omitting the schema name will cause SQL Server to assume the namespace of the logged-in user. This is where some confusion can be created. Unless explicitly assigned, new users are assigned the default schema of dbo. (See Chapter 6 for user and login management information.) As a result, all references to database objects not explicitly qualified will be resolved to the dbo schema.

For example, the user Fred logs in to the server AUGHTFIVE and his database context is set to AdventureWorks. Because Fred was not assigned a user-defined schema, he exists in the default dbo schema. Fred wants to retrieve the contents of the Contact table, so he executes the following query:

```
SELECT * FROM Contact;
```

Fred's query will resolve to `AUGHTFIVE.AdventureWorks.dbo.Contact`. Unfortunately, that table does not exist. The fully qualified name for the contact table is `AUGHT5.AdventureWorks.Person.Contact`. In order for Fred's query to work, one of two things will have to happen. The query will have to be rewritten to reference the appropriate schema scope, like the following example:

```
SELECT * FROM Person.Contact
```

Or, Fred's default schema can be changed to the Person schema so that his query will be properly resolved with the following command:

```
USE AdventureWorks;
GO
ALTER USER Fred WITH DEFAULT_SCHEMA=Person;
GO
```

Now, take a look at a different scenario. The user Fred is created and assigned the default schema of Production. Fred wants to retrieve the contents of a table called dbo.HourlyWage so he executes the following:

```
SELECT * FROM HourlyWage
```

SQL Server first resolves this query as AUGHTFIVE.AdventureWorks.Production.HourlyWage because Fred's default schema is Production and he did not explicitly tell SQL Server what schema to work with. Because the HourlyWage table does not exist in the Production schema, the initial resolution fails, but SQL Server then falls back to the dbo schema and resolves the name as AUGHTFIVE .AdventureWorks.dbo.HourlyWage. The resolution succeeds and Fred is returned the data he wanted.

SQL Server will always search the assigned schema first, then the dbo schema if the initial resolution fails. Care must be taken when creating objects so that the proper namespace is referenced. It is completely possible to create a table with the same name in two different schemas (for example, a dbo.HourlyWage and a HumanResources.HourlyWage). When this happens and an application is created to expose the contents of the HourlyWage table, the possibilities for inconsistencies and confusion are endless. If the schema is not referenced in the applications query, some users will invariably get their results from the table in the dbo schema, whereas others will end up getting results from the HumanResources version of the table. As a best practice, all objects should be referenced by a two-part name to avoid this confusion.

SQL Server 2005 Databases

There are two types of databases in SQL Server: system databases and user databases. The *system databases* are used to store system-wide data and metadata. *User databases* are created by users who have the appropriate level of permissions to store application data.

System Databases

The system databases are comprised of Master, Model, MSDB, TempDB, and the hidden Resource database. If the server is configured to be a replication distributor, there will also be at least one system distribution database that is named during the replication configuration process.

The Master Database

The Master database is used to record all server-level objects in SQL Server 2005. This includes Server Logon accounts, Linked Server definitions, and EndPoints. The Master database also records information about all the other databases on the server (such as their file locations and names). Unlike its predecessors, SQL Server 2005 does not store system information in the Master database, but rather in the Resource database. However, system information is logically presented as the SYS schema in the Master database.

The Model Database

The Model database is a template database. Whenever a new database is created (including the system database TempDB), a copy of the Model database is created and renamed with the name of the database being created. The advantage of this behavior is that objects can be placed in the Model database prior to the creation of any new database and, when the database is created, the objects will appear in the new database. For example, it has always bugged me that Transact-SQL does not contain a `Trim` function to truncate both leading and trailing spaces from a string of characters. Transact-SQL offers an `RTRIM` function that truncates trailing spaces and an `LTRIM` function that removes leading spaces. The code to successfully implement a traditional trim operation thus becomes the following:

```
LTRIM(RTRIM('character string'))
```

To reduce my irritation level and the number of characters I needed to type to successfully trim a character string, I created my own `TRIM` function in the `Model` database with the following code:

```
USE Model
GO
CREATE FUNCTION dbo.Trim (@String varchar(MAX))
RETURNS varchar(MAX)
AS
BEGIN
  SELECT @String = LTRIM(RTRIM(@String))
  RETURN @String
END
```

After creating this function in the `Model` database, it will be propagated to all databases created after adding it to the `Model` database and can be utilized with the following simplified code:

```
dbo.TRIM('character string')
```

I know it's only a saving of two characters, but those two characters are open and close parenthesis characters, which are often the source of annoying syntax errors. By reducing the nested functions, the overall complexity of the function call is also reduced.

Almost any database object can be added to the `Model` database so that they are available in subsequently created databases. This includes database users, roles, tables, stored procedures, functions, and assemblies.

The MSDB Database

I mostly think of the `MSDB` database as the SQL Server Agent's database. That's because the SQL Server Agent uses the `MSDB` database extensively for the storage of automated job definitions, job schedules, operator definitions, and alert definitions. The SQL Server Agent is described in greater detail in Chapter 8, but for now, just know that the Agent is responsible for almost all automated and scheduled operations.

The SQL Server Agent is not the only service that makes extensive use of the `MSDB` database. Service Broker, Database Mail, and Reporting Services also use the `MSDB` database for the storage of scheduling information. In addition to automation and scheduling information, SQL Server Integration Services (SSIS) can also utilize the `MSDB` database for the storage of SSIS packages.

The TempDB Database

The `TempDB` database is used by SQL Server to store data — yes, you guessed it, temporarily. The `TempDB` database is used extensively during SQL Server operations, so careful planning and evaluation of its size and placement are critical to ensure efficient SQL Server database operations.

The TempDB database is used by the Database Engine to store temporary objects (such as temporary tables, views, cursors, and table-valued variables) that are explicitly created by database programmers. In addition, the TempDB database is used by the SQL Server database engine to store work tables containing intermediate results of a query prior to a sort operation or other data manipulation. For example, if you wrote a query that returned 100,000 rows and you wanted the results sorted by a date value in the results, SQL Server could send the unsorted results to a temporary work table where it would perform the sorting operation and then return the sorted results to you. The TempDB database is also used extensively to support new connection options such as SNAPSHOT ISOLATION or Multiple Active Result Sets (MARS). If online index operations are performed, the TempDB database will hold the index during the build or rebuild process.

Another important aspect to keep in mind about the TempDB database is that all database users have access to it and have the ability to create and populate temporary objects. This access can potentially create locking and size limitation issues on SQL Server, so it is important to monitor the TempDB database just like any other database on SQL Server.

The Resource Database

The last system database is the Resource database. The Resource database is a read-only database that contains all the system objects used by an instance of SQL Server. The Resource database is not accessible during normal database operations. It is logically presented as the SYS schema in every database. It contains no user data or metadata. Instead, it contains the structure and description of all system objects. This design enables the fast application of service packs by just replacing the existing Resource database with a new one. As an added bonus, to roll back a service pack installation, all you have to do is replace the new Resource database with the old one. This very elegant design replaces the older method of running many scripts that progressively dropped and added new system objects.

User Databases

User databases are simply that: databases created by users. They are created to store data used by data applications and are the primary purpose of having a database server. During installation, you have the option of installing two sample user databases: AdventureWorks and AdventureWorksDW.

The AdventureWorks database is an OLTP database used by the fictitious Adventure-Works Cycles Company, which sells mountain bikes and mountain-biking-related merchandise.

The AdventureWorksDW database is an OLAP database used for data analysis of historical Adventure-Works Cycles data. Most of the sample code and examples provided in Books Online use these two sample databases.

Distribution Databases

One or more distribution databases can be configured to support replication. Some SQL Server professionals describe the distribution databases as system databases, and yet others describe them as user databases. I don't think it makes much difference. What is important is what the database or databases do.

The distribution database stores metadata and transactional history to support all types of replication on a SQL Server. Typically, one distribution database is created when configuring a SQL Server as a replication Distributor. However, if needed, multiple distribution databases can be configured.

A model distribution database is installed by default and is used in the creation of a distribution database used in replication. It is installed in the same location as the rest of the system databases and is named distmdl.mdf.

SQL Server 2005 Database Storage

All system and user databases (including the Resource database) are stored in files. There is always a minimum of two files: one data file and one transaction log file. The default extension for data files is .mdf, and the default for transaction log files is .ldf.

The default location for the system database files is <drive>:\Program Files\Microsoft SQL Server\MSSQL.X\MSSQL\Data\, where <drive> is the installation drive and X is the instance number (MSSQL.1 for the first instance of the database engine). The following table lists the names and default locations for system database files associated with the first instance of SQL Server.

System Database	Physical Location
Master	<install path>\MSSQL.1\MSSQL\Data\master.mdf
	<install path>\MSSQL.1\MSSQL\Data\mastlog.ldf
Model	<install path>\MSSQL.1\MSSQL\Data\model.mdf
	<install path>\MSSQL.1\MSSQL\Data\modellog.ldf
MSDB	<install path>\MSSQL.1\MSSQL\Data\msdbdata.mdf
	<install path>\MSSQL.1\MSSQL\Data\msdblog.ldf
TempDB	<install path>\MSSQL.1\MSSQL\Data\tempdb.mdf
	<install path>\MSSQL.1\MSSQL\Data\templog.ldf
Resource	<install path>\MSSQL.1\MSSQL\Data\Mssqlsystemresource.mdf
	<install path>\MSSQL.1\MSSQL\Data\Mssqlsystemresource.ldf

When it comes to the system databases, the following guidance is given: *Don't mess with them.* Your ability to manipulate the system databases in SQL Server 2005 has been extremely limited by the developers at Microsoft. Overall, this is a good thing. Generally speaking, the only thing you are permitted to do with system databases is back them up or move them to faster, more reliable disk arrays if they prove to be a performance bottleneck. The ability to modify the data contained in system tables through ad hoc updates that existed in prior releases has been almost completely removed from SQL Server 2005. To modify the system catalog, the server must be started in Single-User mode and even then, activity is restricted and is not supported by Microsoft.

Data Files and Filegroups

When a user database is created, it must contain at least one data file. This first data file is known as the *primary data file*. The primary data file is a member of the default *Primary filegroup*. Every database has one Primary filegroup when created and is made up of at least the primary data file. Additional data files can also be added to the Primary filegroup. More filegroups can also be defined upon initial creation of the database, or added after the database is created. Chapter 4 describes the storage architecture of files in greater detail, and Chapter 5 explains the advantage of filegroups. For now, it is sufficient to know that all of the data objects in a database (such as tables, views, indexes, and stored procedures) are stored within the data files. Data files can be logically grouped to improve performance and allow for more flexible maintenance (see Figure 1-1).

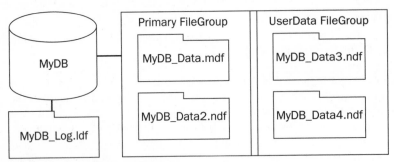

Figure 1-1: Data files and filegroups

Log Files

Upon initial creation of a database, one transaction log must be defined. The transaction log is used to record all modifications to the database to guarantee transactional consistency and recoverability.

Although it is often advantageous to create multiple data files and multiple filegroups, it is very rarely necessary to create more than one log file. This is because of how SQL Server accesses the files. Data files can be accessed in parallel, enabling SQL Server to read and write to multiple files and filegroups simultaneously. Log files, on the other hand, are not accessed in this manner. Log files are serialized to maintain transactional consistency. Each transaction is recorded serially in the log in the sequence it was executed. A second log file will not be accessed until the first log file is completely filled. You can find a complete description of the transaction log and how it is accessed in Chapter 4.

SQL Server Security

Chapter 6 provides a thorough discussion of SQL Server 2005 security features. However, to select the proper authentication model during installation, it is important to have a basic understanding of how SQL Server controls user access.

SQL Server 2005 can be configured to work in either the Windows Authentication Mode or the SQL Server and Windows Authentication Mode, which is also frequently called Mixed Mode.

Windows Authentication Mode

In Windows Authentication Mode only logins for valid Windows users are allowed to connect to SQL Server. In this authentication mode, SQL Server "trusts" the Windows, Windows Domain, or Active Directory security subsystem to have validated the account credentials. No SQL Server accounts are allowed to connect. They can be created, but they cannot be used for login access.

SQL Server and Windows Authentication Mode (Mixed Mode)

In SQL Server Mode and Windows Authentication Mode or Mixed Mode, valid Windows accounts and standard SQL Server logins are permitted to connect to the server. SQL Server logins are validated by supplying a username and password. Windows accounts are still trusted by SQL Server. The chief advantage of Mixed Mode is the ability of non-Windows accounts (such as UNIX) or Internet clients to connect to SQL Server.

A (Very) Brief History of SQL Server

How did we get here? Where did SQL Server 2005 come from? Without spending a great deal of time discussing the complete history of SQL Server, I thought it would be of some interest to give a very brief overview of SQL Server's roots. I often joke with colleagues and customers that some day I'm going to write a "Trivial Pursuit, Geek Edition." This short description may help you get the yellow history wedge, so pay close attention!

In the Beginning

Microsoft's foray into the enterprise database space came in 1987 when it formed a partnership with Sybase to market Sybase's DataServer product on the Microsoft/IBM OS/2 platform. From that partnership, SQL Server 1.0 emerged, which was essentially the UNIX version of Sybase's DataServer ported to OS2.

The Evolution of a Database

After a number of years, the developers at Microsoft were allowed more and more access to the Sybase source code for test and debugging purposes, but the core SQL Server application continued to be a product of Sybase until SQL Server 4.2 was released for Windows NT in March of 1992.

SQL Server 4.2 was the first true joint product developed by both Sybase and Microsoft. However, the database engine was still pure Sybase. Only the tools and database libraries were developed by Microsoft. Up to that point, SQL Server had been developed to run primarily on the OS/2 platform, but with the release of Windows NT, the developers at Microsoft essentially abandoned any OS/2 development and focused on bringing a version of SQL Server to Windows NT.

Microsoft Goes It Alone

With the growing success of Sybase in the UNIX market and Microsoft in Windows, the two companies found themselves competing for market share on a product essentially developed by Sybase. As a result, in 1994, the two companies terminated their joint development agreement, and Sybase granted Microsoft a limited license to use and modify Sybase technology exclusively for systems running on Windows.

A year later, in June 1995, Microsoft released the first version of SQL Server developed exclusively by Microsoft developers—SQL Server 6.0—but the core technology was still largely Sybase code-base. Less than a year later, more changes were made and Microsoft released SQL Server 6.5 in April of 1996.

Meanwhile, the developers on the SQL Server team were beginning work on a new database system code-named "Sphinx." The Sybase code-base was rewritten almost from scratch for Sphinx, and only a handful of code remained to indicate SQL Server's humble beginnings in OS/2.

In December of 1998, Sphinx was officially released as SQL Server 7.0. The changes from SQL Server 6.5 were readily apparent from the first second a database administrator launched the new Enterprise Manager. Finally, there was a robust and reliable database system that was easy to manage, easy to learn, and still powerful enough for many businesses.

As SQL Server 7.0 was being released, the next version was already in development. It was code-named "Shiloh." Shiloh became SQL Server 2000 and was released in August of 2000. The changes to the under-lying data engine were minimal, but many exciting changes that affected SQL Server's scalability issues were added (such as indexed views and federated database servers), along with improvements like cas-cading referential integrity. Microsoft's enterprise database server was finally a true contender in the marketplace.

Back at Microsoft, the SQL team was working on an even more powerful and exciting release code-named "Yukon," which is now SQL Server 2005. After more than five years in development, a product that some were calling "Yukon the giant (Oracle) killer" was finally released. It is indeed a very signifi-cant release, and only time will tell how successful Microsoft is with it.

So, now, without further delay, the remainder of this book will be dedicated to introducing you to this very exciting and capable database management system.

Summary

This chapter introduced the basic structure and purpose of SQL Server 2005, along with a brief explana-tion of the various features available in this release of Microsoft's database application. Subsequent chapters delve into the technologies and features exposed in this chapter so that the database adminis-trator can better understand and implement each feature introduced.

In Chapter 2, you learn how to plan and perform a SQL Server 2005 installation. Included in the discus-sions are prerequisite hardware and software configurations, as well as service and security considera-tions. A thorough installation plan will always reap enormous benefits when it comes to post-installation modifications. Understanding what to install (and how to install it) is invaluable.

Installing SQL Server 2005

The first step in administering a SQL Server database is quite often the installation process. Although installing SQL Server is a fairly straightforward process, it is of critical importance to have a thorough plan prior to ever breaking the seal on the installation media and accepting the licensing agreement. The installation wizard does a good job of identifying all the prerequisite objects that should exist prior to installation, and then installing almost everything you will need for a successful setup. However, successful planning and pre-configuring all the requisite support objects will make for a much smoother and successful installation.

SQL Server Installation Planning

"There is never enough time to do it right, but always enough time to do it twice." Sound familiar? I hated it when my Dad would raise his eyebrows and throw that old cliché out when I was rushing through a job. However, Dad was right. To avoid having to do it twice, you need to create a thorough plan. Too often installations are rushed and then must be uninstalled when technical issues arise. The questions that must be asked range from collation settings and named instances to the separation of log and data files. Will SQL Server be installed in a cluster? How about Storage Area Networks (SAN) or Network Attached Storage (NAS)? There are many questions and it is very important that answers (and, more importantly, the reasons for those answers) are documented. The "why" is very often just as important as the "how" when it comes to technology issues.

In addition to the "how" and "why," there are the "who," "when," and "what" questions that make up the five questions that must be answered to create an adequate plan. The "who" is most likely going to be the DBA, but other individuals will need to be included in the installation plan as well, because there are network and storage considerations to account for. The "what" question can be a bit more complex. The first "what" is "what features will be installed?" However, more "what" questions could include "What constitutes a successful installation?" or "What resources are required?" The "when" question is also imperative. "When will the installation be started and when will it be complete?"

It would be impossible to cover all the possible variations that could arise during a SQL Server installation, so this chapter covers only the essentials. Remember, when it comes to technology, the answer to almost every question is, "It depends." There are almost always "best practices," but best practices sometimes have to be left behind in favor of practicality and budget.

For example, as a best practice, transaction logs should be placed on a RAID 1 array as opposed to any striped array configuration because of how the transaction log is accessed by SQL Server. However, if the only available fault-tolerant storage is a RAID 5 striped array, then by all means it should be used to store and protect the log data. I have encountered and managed many databases where this was the exact case. The only storage available because of budget and hardware constraints was a single RAID 5 array where both the transaction log and data files were hosted. In a large enterprise solution, this would be completely unacceptable; but for a small to medium business implementation, it may be the only choice. The key point I am trying to make is that it is very important to know what the "best" solution is, but also keep in mind that compromises are often necessary to meet deadlines and budgetary constraints.

Hardware Considerations

Minimum requirements are exactly that: minimum. SQL Server will run on a system with minimum hardware, but the performance is not going to be stellar. Even the "recommended" hardware is to be exceeded whenever practical.

Upgrading almost any hardware object on a server hosting SQL Server 2005 will result in improved performance, but all things being equal, you should probably increase the amount of RAM available to SQL Server first. However, an underpowered processor or slow disk system will cause just as many performance problems as insufficient RAM, but RAM limitations will often cause processor and disk issues to be exacerbated.

I remember several years ago taking a certification exam that had a series of questions where I had to choose how to allocate different limited resources across different types of servers. I was presented with a file server, domain controller, and database server, and had to determine where to place the faster CPU, the better disk array, and the new RAM. I remember hating those questions. Obviously, the best place to put all the resources was on the database server, but I knew that wasn't what the test designers were looking for, so I grudgingly went along with their twisted view of the enterprise and managed to pass the exam. However, because more and more the database is becoming the center of the information technology universe, I still maintain my viewpoint that the database server needs all the upgrades first.

I know that my viewpoint as a DBA seems self-serving, but it is actually based on the needs of every organization I have worked with in the past few years. For example, at one company I worked with, we had several mission-critical applications that we used. These applications included our Web site with an e-commerce component, a customer management application, Microsoft SharePoint Server, Microsoft Project Server, an accounting application, Microsoft Operations Manager, Microsoft Systems Management Server, and several other support applications. Without exception, these applications utilized SQL Server as a data store. Optimizing the server running SQL Server would have an immediate positive impact on a majority of the applications used for the key line of business activities, as well as many support applications.

Processor Considerations

Microsoft sets the minimum processor at a 600 MHz Pentium III or compatible processor but recommends at least a 1 GHz processor. SQL Server utilizes the processor extensively during the compilation and execution of query plans. Your server can have an extraordinarily fast disk array and plenty of RAM, but if it has an underpowered processor, it is all for naught. As the workload of the server increases and more and more transactions are executed against it, the processor will have to schedule and handle the multitude of query execution plans and programmatic manipulation of data.

Chapter 10 discusses the ways to monitor SQL Server to ensure that the CPU is not a bottleneck, but from the outset SQL Server should be given plenty of processor power. In addition, SQL Server is very adept at utilizing multiple processors to execute parallel operations, so adding a second processor will often pay larger dividends than upgrading a single processor. However, if your license is per processor, the cost may be prohibitive to adding additional processors.

Memory Considerations

The minimum amount of RAM, according to Microsoft, is 512MB. I personally find this minimum requirement a bit on the ridiculous side. I wouldn't set up a Windows server running any multi-user application with only 512MB of RAM, let alone a RAM-hungry application like SQL Server. Would 512MB be sufficient for a desktop machine running SQL Server 2005 Developer Edition? Maybe, as long as no serious load was put on the server.

That's not to say that SQL Server wastes memory, or that it consumes a bloated footprint. The simple fact is that SQL Server likes memory — *a lot*. It attempts to place as much data as possible in RAM so that the data is readily available for processing. It also tries to keep the data in RAM as long as possible.

SQL Server creates and maintains different memory pools for various database operations. For example, there is a *buffer cache* that is used to store data pages retrieved from the disk; a *procedure cache* that is used to store compiled stored procedures, triggers, functions, views, and query plans; and even a *log cache* for transaction log operations.

Having sufficient RAM on hand allows SQL Server to minimize the amount of page swapping required and enables the data to be pre-fetched for fast processing. If you want to keep SQL Server happy, feed it RAM. What you will get in return is a hard-working database server that efficiently and effectively utilizes that RAM to service your requests as fast as possible.

Storage Considerations

An often overlooked hardware aspect of SQL Server installations is the disk subsystem. Many smaller organizations end up installing the operating system, SQL Server, and all the database files on the system partition. Although this will work, it is not anywhere near the best arrangement. The question on how to best place the application and database files is answered with a definite "it depends."

It depends on a few factors like what existing hardware can be leveraged? How important is fault tolerance? How much money is the organization willing to spend on the database solution? How much disk space will be needed? How busy is the existing disk system? An optimal installation of SQL Server could look something like Figure 2-1.

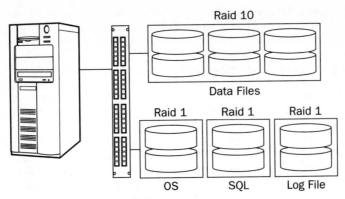

Figure 2-1: Optimal installation

Notice that the application is installed on a separate set of spindles than the operating system. This reduces contention for disk resources and makes the application more efficient. The term "spindle" may be new to you. The reason it is used instead of "drive" or "disk" is that it leaves no room for interpretation. Physical disk drives have one spindle, which is loosely analogous with the center of a spinning top. In the case of Figure 2-1, the two spindles that host the log file on a RAID 1 array will actually look like a single drive to the operating system, when, in reality, there are two physical disks or spindles.

In addition to the application existing on a separate set of spindles, the data files and the log files are on yet another set. The idea here is not to keep the hard disk industry in business, but to maximize efficiency, fault tolerance, and recoverability. Placing the operating system, application, and database all on the same spindle is putting all your proverbial eggs in one basket. If the basket is dropped, you will lose all of your eggs. Likewise, if the spindle fails, you will lose your operating system, application, and databases. Your recovery time in this instance is tripled.

It is definitely a best practice to separate the data files of a database from the log file. If the database is corrupted or damaged, the most recent backup can be used to recover it, and then the existing transaction log can be used to recover all the transactions since the last backup. Likewise, if the transaction log is lost, it can be re-created with minimal data loss from the database. If both data files and the log file are on the same spindle, a catastrophic failure of the spindle will result in all data since the last backup being lost.

The separation of the different components of SQL Server is just part of the equation. When choosing a disk system, it is also important to know what type of disk is best for each part of the database. Notice in Figure 2-1 that the operating system is installed on a RAID 1 array. The same goes for the SQL Server application and the database log file, while the data files are placed on a striped array. It is possible to place all the SQL resources on one or more RAID 10 or RAID 5 arrays, and many organizations do just that. However, when it comes to the transaction log, a RAID 1 configuration is more appropriate than a RAID 5. A transaction log placed on a striped array will actually decrease the performance of SQL Server. This is because of the inherent hit in write performance on a RAID 5 array, and also because of the way SQL Server writes serialized data to the log. Log files, by their nature, are mostly written to, which means that often RAID 1 (or RAID 10 if you have the budget) is the best choice for performance. RAID 1 or RAID 10 is also better because of the sequential and serial nature of the transaction log as compared to the parallel friendly nature of data files.

Each transaction is written to the transaction log before it is written to memory. This puts the transaction log in the position to become a possible bottleneck. A fast duplexed array will help prevent the log from becoming a performance liability.

SAN and NAS vs. Local Disk Storage

Another decision to be made during a SQL Server installation is that of storage architecture. There are many vendors in the marketplace with hundreds of possible configurations for sale. Many larger organizations have placed much of their corporate data on local and remote SANs. At the same time other organizations have chosen NAS, and still others (mostly smaller organizations) have chosen to place all their data on local attached disk arrays. Although a complete discussion of these different technologies is beyond the scope of this book, a brief explanation is useful in describing the utilization of these technologies in database implementations.

Storage Area Network (SAN)

For SANs, the network infrastructure is typically Fibre Channel, although some organizations use Gigabit Ethernet as well. The data transfer mechanism used by SANs is block Small Computer Systems Interface (SCSI). This is well-suited to SQL Server, because the database application expects block access to data, which is not easily supplied using NAS. Utilizing SAN software, multiple volumes can be created and "presented" to the servers, utilizing the storage space on the SAN, as shown in Figure 2-2.

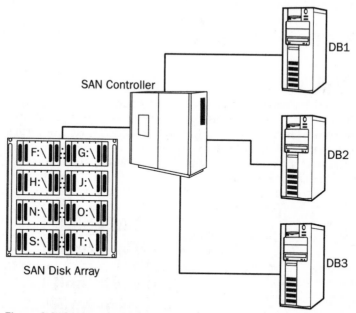

Figure 2-2: Storage Area Network

Network Attached Storage (NAS)

The NAS network infrastructure is Gigabit Ethernet or Fast Ethernet, but the storage type is file-based via traditional file sharing protocols. Volumes are not presented to the servers that utilize a NAS; instead, files are accessed through Universal Naming Convention (UNC) shares, as shown in Figure 2-3.

File-based access degrades SQL Server performance considerably, which is why NAS storage should be avoided. By default, databases cannot be created with a UNC location, but this behavior can be changed. However, if the database is going to be used for any serious I/O scenarios, you will find that NAS will not be able to provide an adequate response.

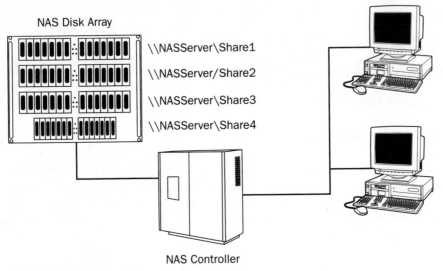

Figure 2-3: Network Attached Storage

Local Attached Disk Array

There is a lot to be said for sharing storage resources among multiple servers on a high network, but some organizations (for a variety of reasons) have chosen to dedicate local attached storage to their database implementations (see Figure 2-4). In reality, the only difference between local attached disk arrays and SANs is that the volumes created on the local array are only accessible to the server the array is attached to and that SAN controllers can optimize data transfer. Local arrays are typically connected via a high-speed SCSI cable or Fiber Channel.

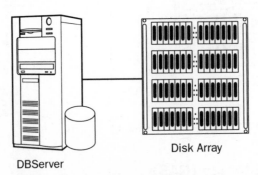

Figure 2-4: Local attached directory

Minimum Software

Minimum software requirements come in a couple of variations. The first is what software components are required to support the various features of SQL Server 2005. The System Consistency Checker (SCC) does a very thorough job of ensuring all requisite services and dependent components are present before allowing the setup program to run. The SCC will prevent installation from continuing in the case of an error, but it will allow installations to continue if warnings are reported. It is up to the DBA to evaluate the warning to ensure that it is acceptable to continue the installation. For example, if Internet Information Services (IIS) are not installed on a server, a warning may appear, but IIS is not required for a successful installation, so this warning can be ignored in many instances. The second variation is operating system levels (which is what operating system is required for the different editions of SQL Server 2005). The following table describes the different operating systems required for each edition of SQL Server 2005.

Operating System	SQL Server Edition				
	Enterprise Edition	Standard Edition	Workgroup Edition	Developer Edition	Express Edition
Windows 2000 Professional Edition SP4				X	X
Windows 2000 Server SP4	X	X	X	X	X
Windows 2000 Advanced Server SP4	X	X	X	X	X
Windows 2000 Datacenter Edition SP4	X	X	X	X	X
Windows XP Home Edition SP2				X	X
Windows XP Professional Edition SP2				X	X
Windows XP Media Edition SP2		X	X	X	X
Windows XP Tablet Edition SP2		X	X	X	X
Windows 2003 Server SP1	X	X	X	X	X
Windows 2003 Enterprise Edition SP1	X	X	X	X	X
Windows 2003 Datacenter Edition SP1	X	X	X	X	X
Windows 2003 Web Edition SP1					X

Table continued on following page

Operating System	SQL Server Edition				
	Enterprise Edition	Standard Edition	Workgroup Edition	Developer Edition	Express Edition
Windows Small Business Server 2003, Standard Edition SP1	X	X	X	X	X
Windows Small Business Server 2003,					
Premium Edition SP1	X	X	X	X	X
Windows 2003 I64 Datacenter Edition SP1					
Windows 2003 I64 Enterprise Edition SP1					
Windows 2003 X64 Standard Edition SP1	X	X	X	X	X
Windows 2003 X64 Datacenter Edition SP1	X	X	X	X	X
Windows 2003 X64 Enterprise Edition SP1	X	X	X	X	X

SQL Server Setup Application

SQL Server 2005 setup is very straightforward. If you are accessing the installation files directly from the CD-ROM, the auto-start feature may very well launch the splash screen for setup. If not, the installation can be launched from the SETUP.EXE file located in the Servers folder of the installation media.

There are actually two different folders defined for installation. If your installation media is a DVD, then these folders are most likely on the same disk. If you have obtained a set of CD-ROMs you will find one CD-ROM contains the Server folder and the other contains the Tools folder. This may be a trifle obvious, but the Server folder contains all the files necessary to install an instance of SQL Server, whereas the Tools folder contains only the files required to install the management and development tools for SQL Server. When using the CD-ROMs you will need both to complete the installation if you choose to install the tools as well as the server.

When the SETUP application is launched from the Server folder of the installation media, the first thing the SQL Server installation process does is prompt you to read and acknowledge the license agreement. If you have never actually read the agreement, you should do so. It contains some very interesting language and limitations about how the software can be used.

Many organizations are not aware that any component of SQL Server installed on a server requires a license. For example, if the Database Engine is installed on one server and the Reporting Services engine is installed on a different server, a separate license is required for each installation. This is a major area of confusion for many DBAs. Common sense would say that a purchase of a SQL Server license that included the Database Engine, Reporting Services, Integration Services, and Analysis Services would give an organization the right to spread these services across as many servers as necessary, as long as only one instance of each service was used. Common sense, in this instance, may get you into trouble with the licensing police. If you haven't read the licensing agreement, do so, or have your lawyer read it for you.

After the license agreement is agreed to, the setup application checks for software prerequisites and will install them if they are not present (see Figure 2-5).

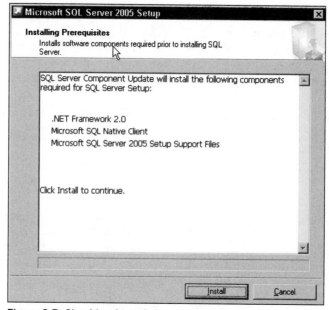

Figure 2-5: Checking for software components

System Configuration Checker (SCC)

Once the prerequisites have been successfully installed, the SQL Server setup utility launches the SCC. The SCC scans the system prior to actually installing the SQL Server to ensure that an installation can succeed. The SCC also provides information on how to overcome check failures. The SCC returns errors and/or warnings. An error will block the setup application from continuing, but a warning will not. For example, if Internet Information Services (IIS) are not installed, the SCC will return a warning, but not block setup. The following table describes the areas that the SCC examines. Figure 2-6 shows the desired outcome of the SCC.

Component	Description
Windows Management Instrumentation (WMI) service requirement	WMI service must be available. A failed check on this item will block setup.
Microsoft XML Core Services (MSXML) requirement	MSXML is required for some SQL Server 2005 components. If required, it will be installed by SQL Server setup.
Operating System minimum level requirement	The SCC checks the operating system for minimum requirements.
Operating System version and service pack (SP) level requirement	Windows 2000 SP4, Windows XP SP2, or Windows Server 2003 is required. Any unsupported operating system blocks setup.
SQL Server compatibility with operating system requirement	The operating system type must support the given SQL Server edition. For example, SQL Server Enterprise Edition can only be installed on Windows 2000 or later. A failed check on this item will block setup.
Minimum hardware requirement	Hardware must satisfy minimum CPU and memory requirements. A failed check on this item will block setup.
Feature availability	The SQL Server feature selection tree will check for prerequisites before displaying SQL Server components available to install.
Pending reboot requirement	SQL Server setup cannot run if files required by setup are locked by other services, processes, or applications. A failed check on this item will block setup.
Performance monitor counter requirement	The SCC checks registry key values to verify proper incrementing for installation of SQL Server Performance Counters. A failed check on this item will block setup.
Default installation path permission requirement	The SCC will verify drive formatting and read/write permissions. Setup also requires that SQL Server be installed to an uncompressed drive. A failed check on this item will block setup.
COM+ catalog requirement	The SCC will verify the current COM+ catalog configuration.
System administrator privilege requirement	The user running setup must have administrator privileges on all destination computers: local, remote, and all cluster nodes where SQL Server will be installed.
Enable default administrative share directory requirement (Remote/Cluster only)	All cluster nodes must have the default administrative share `admin$` enabled.

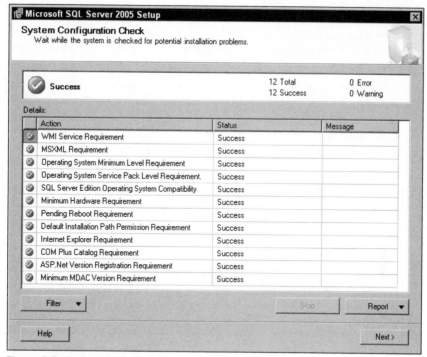

Figure 2-6: Desired SCC results

Installation Options

Once the SCC completes the check of the system, as long as there are no errors that will block the installation of the server, the Registration Information screen appears and asks for your 25-character product key. After entering the product key, you will be presented with the installation option screen (see Figure 2-7). Here is where you will choose what aspects of SQL Server you want to install. For a more detailed feature selection list click the Advanced button for a typical Microsoft Office–like installation option screen.

Instance Options

After choosing what features of SQL Server are to be installed, the setup utility asks for instance information. You can install either a named instance or a default instance. The *default instance* takes on the name of the machine where SQL Server is being installed. There can be only one default instance. However, SQL Server 2005 supports up to 50 instances of SQL Server to be installed on a single machine. If there is a default instance, a maximum of 49 named instances can be configured. If no default instance is installed, 50 named instances can be configured.

Named instances are referenced by the server name followed by the instance name. For example, the server name used to write this book is named AughtFive. The default name of the SQL Server 2005 installation is the same as the server name. However, the named instance on AughtFive is called Dagobah (I am a big Yoda fan). To connect to the Dagobah instance of SQL Server it must be referenced as AughtFive\Dagobah. In addition to the name, any client accessing a named instance must utilize the SQL Server 2000 or SQL Server 2005 connection objects. Legacy ODBC and old OLEDB drivers will be unable to enumerate a named instance of SQL Server 2005.

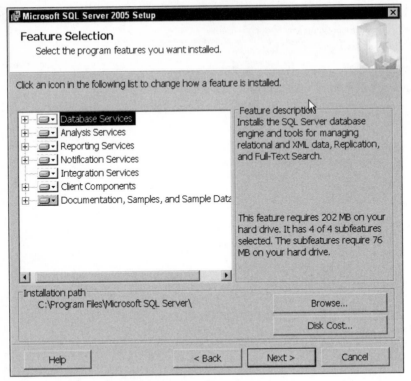

Figure 2-7: Feature Selection screen

Service Options

After the instance configuration is completed, the service accounts that SQL Server will utilize must be specified. Chapter 1 describes the various services that SQL Server may need to run depending on what features were installed. When configuring the security credentials for these services, you have a choice to make. Does the service require the ability to authenticate and connect to external resources? If so, the local system account will not be appropriate.

Best practice security guidelines recommend that the local system account not be used because it may provide too much privilege to various services. An additional problem created with using the local system account for services is that it prevents the service from accessing external resources.

A very useful feature of SQL Server is the ability to utilize the SQL Server Agent's scheduling options to run unattended jobs. If the ability to schedule SQL Server jobs that require access to external resources is desired, then at a minimum, the SQL Agent account will need to be configured to utilize a domain account so that the respective account can be granted permissions to the appropriate resource.

The ability to configure each installed SQL Server service individually is provided (see Figure 2-8), which is also a security best practice, but it does increase the administrative complexity of the system.

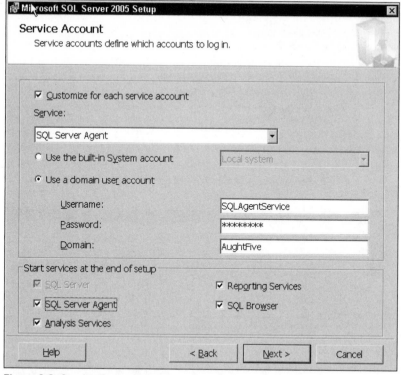

Figure 2-8: Service Account screen

In addition to the security information for each individual service, each service can be configured for automatic or manual startup during installation.

Authentication Modes

The authentication mode configuration screen appears after the service configuration. Authentication and security are covered in great detail in Chapter 6. However, a brief explanation is appropriate at this point.

If the default "Windows Only" configuration is chosen, only connections that have been authenticated by the local Windows security subsystem (or by the domain security subsystem) are allowed to be made to SQL Server. In this scenario, SQL Server validates that the login exists and has been authenticated, but no password verification takes place because SQL Server "trusts" that the login has been validated. A frequent connection error that occurs on servers configured for "Windows Only" is one that says that the connection failed because the login was not associated with a "trusted SQL Server connection" (see Figure 2-9).

This is admittedly a vague response to a login request and is not the most intuitive message in the world. "Login Failed because it is not a valid Windows account and the server is configured for Windows Only authentication" or something a bit more informative would have been more useful. The message can be even more cryptic, given the fact that the respective SQL login may, in fact, exist. Being in "Windows Only" does not prevent the database administrator from creating SQL Server login accounts. However, any attempt to connect with a valid SQL Server login when the server is in "Windows Only" will result in the vague "trusted SQL Server connection" error.

With "Mixed Mode Authentication," SQL Server can authenticate Windows logins as well as logins that have been created locally on the SQL Server. Local SQL Server logins are validated by username and password verification. The username and an encrypted version of the password are stored in the Master database. When a SQL login connection is requested, the SQL Server security subsystem encrypts the provided password, compares it to the stored password, and allows or refuses the connection based on the credentials provided.

Invalid credentials (either bad login name or bad password) result in the same "Login failed" message (see Figure 2-10) when SQL Server is configured for "Mixed Mode" security.

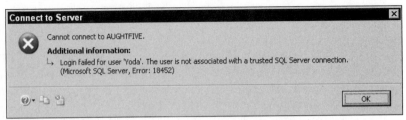

Figure 2-9: "Trusted" SQL Server connection error message

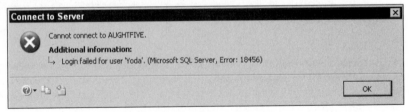

Figure 2-10: Bad login or bad password error message

Collation Settings

After setting the authentication mode of SQL Server, the installation application asks what collation will be used on the server. The first question many people have is, "What is collation?" The dictionary definition of "collation" is "assembling in proper numerical or logical sequence." Collation settings have two significant effects on your database: the sorting of your character-based data and the searching of your character-based data. Several options are available for collation, as shown in Figure 2-11.

A different collation can be set for both the SQL Server and Analysis Services, but Analysis Services only supports Windows collation, whereas SQL Server can support both Windows and SQL collation. SQL collation support is included for backward compatibility, however, and it is recommended to configure the server collation with Windows collation.

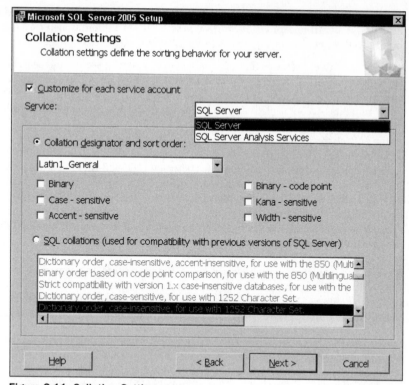

Figure 2-11: Collation Settings screen

Choosing Windows collation by selecting the Collation Designator provides a greater level of control and more choices when it comes to customizing the collation settings for the server. The collation setting affects what data will be returned when searching on character data, and in what order the data will be returned. It also determines what characters will be supported.

The default collation for an installation is determined by the locale that Windows was configured with. For example, the default collation the SQL Server installation application chooses when being installed on a Windows server configured for the United States is SQL_Latin1_General_CP1_CI_AS. A brief definition of this underscore-delimited name is definitely in order:

❑ SQL_Latin1_General_CP1 indicates that characters from the Latin Code Page One (CP1), which is equivalent to the 1252 character set, are supported. These characters provide support for the storing, sorting, and searching of character data in any Latin-derived language. These languages include Western European, English, and Latin American languages. However, it is important to note that sort orders can be different between Latin-derived languages. For example, in German the ö character comes before z, but in Swedish, the opposite is true (z comes before ö). Therefore, small discrepancies can occur from language to language.

The number 1252 represents the character set identifier as assigned by the Organization for International Standards (ISO).

❑ CI (Case Insensitive) indicates that the character data is to be sorted and searched in dictionary order without regard to capitalization. As this setting infers, there is also a CS (Case Sensitive) setting as well.

❑ AS (Accent Sensitive) indicates that the character data is to be sorted and searched in dictionary order with preference to accent marks. As a result, a search for a German "spatlese" wine will not return the correct spelling of this sweet late harvest wine, which is "spätlese" if it is stored with the umlauts. Accent sensitivity can be turned off by specifying AI (Accent Insensitive).

These are not the only character settings that can be set. Character data can be set to be stored with sensitivity to width with the designation of WS (Width Sensitive) or WI (Width Insensitive). Width sensitivity applies to Unicode character data and differentiates between UTF-8 (8-Bit Unicode Text Format) and UTF-16 (16-Bit Unicode Text Format). There is also a setting for Kana sensitivity: KS (Kana Sensitive) and KI (Kana Insensitive). Kana sensitivity essentially controls the sorting and searching of Asian Unicode characters (Japanese, Chinese, and so on) that can represent the same words using different script. For example, when Japanese kana characters Hiragana and Katakana are treated differently, it is called *Kana sensitive*; when they are treated the same it is *Kana insensitive*.

Character data can also be sorted by their binary value. Binary sorting and searching is actually faster than dictionary sorting and searching, but is not as user friendly. For example, the following script creates a table with two columns. The first column is assigned a character data type with case-sensitive dictionary collation. The second column is assigned a character data type with binary collation:

```
USE TempDB
CREATE TABLE MySortTable
(DictionarySort varchar(10) COLLATE Latin1_General_CS_AS NULL)
 BinarySort varchar(10) COLLATE Latin1_General_BIN)
GO
```

Once the tables are created, you can populate both of them with the same six rows: Alpha, Bravo, Charlie and alpha, bravo, charlie by executing the following command:

```
USE TempDB
INSERT MySortTable
 VALUES ('Alpha','Alpha')
INSERT MySortTable
 VALUES ('Bravo','Bravo')
INSERT MySortTable
 VALUES ('Charlie','Charlie')
INSERT MySortTable
 VALUES ('alpha','alpha')
INSERT MySortTable
 VALUES ('bravo','bravo')
INSERT MySortTable
 VALUES ('charlie','charlie')
GO
```

Now that the tables are created and populated you can query them. Notice the different order of results using an identical query:

```
SELECT DictionarySort
FROM MySortTable
ORDER BY DictionarySort ASC

DictionarySort
--------------
alpha
Alpha
bravo
Bravo
charlie
Charlie

(6 row(s) affected)


SELECT BinarySort
FROM MySortTable
ORDER BY BinarySort ASC

BinarySort
----------
Alpha
Bravo
Charlie
alpha
bravo
charlie

(6 row(s) affected)
```

As you can see, server collation can have a profound effect on how your data is stored and retrieved, so careful planning is essential when deciding on a server collation. Fortunately, collation can also be set at the database and column level, so multiple collations are supportable.

As a word of caution, though, be careful when implementing non-compatible collations on a single server. Issues may arise when the server collation is set to a collation that is not compatible with a database collation. This is because the TempDB database is set to the default server collation. When temporary objects are created in TempDB from a user database that utilizes a non-compatible collation, errors can occur.

Final Steps

The last configuration screen is the error reporting screen where you can choose to send information to Microsoft about your SQL Server experience. Then, a final summary screen appears that provides you with a list of the services and features that will be installed. Clicking "Next" launches the SQL Server installation and a Setup Progress screen appears (see Figure 2-12). The setup progress screen gives summary information about all the different features required by SQL Server and shows when each individual feature is finished installing.

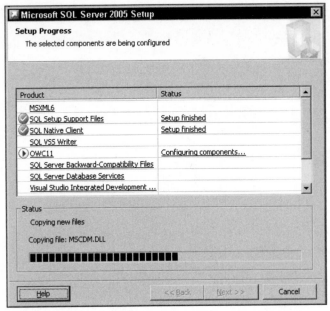

Figure 2-12: Setup Progress screen

Installing to a Windows Cluster

The most difficult part about installing SQL Server to a cluster is configuring the Windows cluster, which is beyond the scope of this book. However, it is very important that adequate planning and research is completed for the Windows cluster to ensure a smooth and faultless installation of SQL Server on to the cluster. Once the Windows cluster is installed and configured, the installation of SQL Server to the cluster has some very significant differences from installing to a single server. One of the first things you will most likely notice is that when the SCC runs, it detects the cluster and scans both nodes to make sure that they meet all the requirements for a SQL Server install (see Figure 2-13). An important note on cluster installations is to ensure that no one is logged in to the secondary server's console when the installation is started. If a console session is in progress on the passive node, installation will fail.

After the SCC completes its checks, it is once again time for the component select screen. However, in a cluster installation, the option to "Create a SQL Server Failover Cluster" is not disabled. Checking this box and clicking Next will start the failover installation. Because the setup utility has detected the presence of a cluster and the failover option has been selected, the installation will be slightly different than previously described for a single server installation. After choosing to install the failover cluster, the Instance Name Configuration screen appears. SQL Server 2005 supports multiple instances in a cluster, as well as in standalone scenarios.

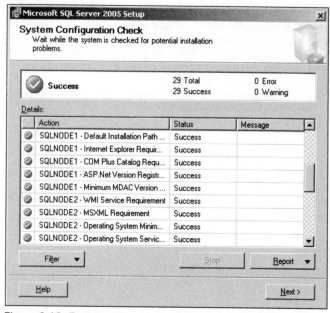

Figure 2-13: Ensuring the requirements are met for the install

Configuring the Virtual Server Name

The least-intuitive part of installing a SQL Server Failover Cluster is the naming configuration. When the Windows cluster was originally installed, a virtual name was designated for the cluster. However, a virtual name must also be specified for the SQL Server installation, and it cannot be the same as the virtual name used for the cluster. For my test cluster, I installed Windows Server 2003 on two computers and configured the two servers as nodes in a Windows Failover Cluster. During the SQL Server installation, the setup utility will prompt for the SQL Server Instance information. Choosing either the default instance or a named instance will still result in the setup utility prompting for a Virtual Server name.

If you choose a named instance, the instance name will be `VirtualServer\InstanceName`. If you choose a default instance, the name of the SQL Server will be the Virtual Server name.

After choosing a virtual server name, an IP address for your server must be chosen, and then a valid cluster group must be designated for the SQL Server installation files. A *cluster group* is a collection of shared resources that are available to both nodes of the cluster (such as physical disks and shared networks). Typically, the cluster administrator will create a resource group just for SQL Server that contains a shared SCSI array, a network name, and a network IP address. As shown in Figure 2-14, after the appropriate cluster group is selected, the Cluster Node Configuration screen appears, where any available nodes can be added to the SQL cluster.

After the desired nodes are added to the cluster, the setup utility prompts for a domain account that has administrative privileges, and then the Service Configuration screen appears. Unlike a standalone installation, in a cluster the service account must be a domain account. It is not possible to run both nodes under the local system account, so that option is disabled. Choose an existing domain account. On the next screen, you will be asked what security groups to place the service account into, as shown in Figure 2-15.

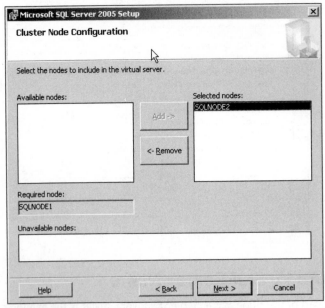

Figure 2-14: Cluster Node Configuration screen

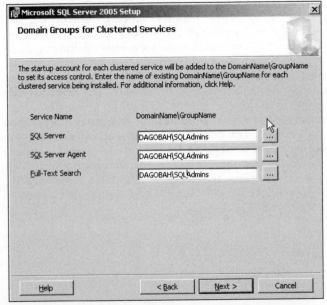

Figure 2-15: Domain Groups for Clustered Services screen

The Domain Groups for Clustered Services configuration screen is the last dialog that is different from a standalone installation. The summary screen is presented after the services screen, and then the installation begins. During the installation, the SQL Server setup utility will install SQL Server to all the nodes in the cluster as shown in Figure 2-16. So, setup only has to be run once.

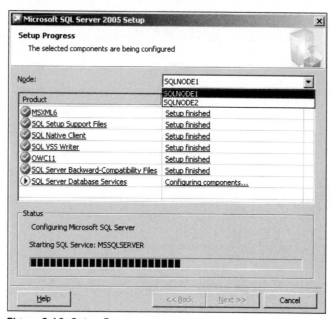

Figure 2-16: Setup Progress screen

Once SQL Server is successfully installed, it can be controlled just like any other SQL Server instance. The only difference is the ability of SQL Server to fail over to the second node automatically in the case of fault tolerance, or manually for scheduled maintenance events.

Post-Installation Considerations

Although the opportunity to configure services to auto-start and specify appropriate security principals to service accounts is provided during SQL Server setup, a very useful tool for post-installation configuration is provided by Microsoft. The tool is the SQL Server Surface Area Configuration tool.

SQL Server Surface Area Configuration

The SQL Server Surface Area Configuration tool enables the database administrator to configure SQL Server to only use the features and services required to support necessary database operations. It does this through two separate sub-tools, as shown in Figure 2-17: the Surface Area Configuration for Services and Connections and the Surface Area Configuration for Features.

The Services and Connections tool provides the database administrator with the ability to control how each service starts, and whether a service starts at all. It also allows for the enabling and disabling of remote connections to each instance of SQL Server as shown in Figure 2-18.

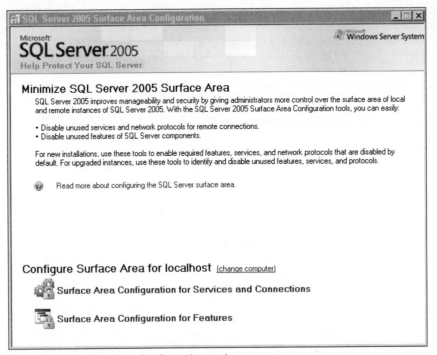

Figure 2-17: Surface Area Configuration tool

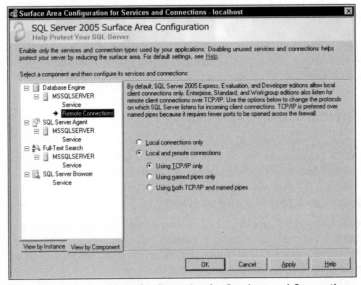

Figure 2-18: Surface Area Configuration for Services and Connections

The Features tool (see Figure 2-19) provides a centralized tool to enable and disable many of the advanced features available with SQL Server 2005 such as CLR integration, Dedicated Administrator Connections, and more.

The purpose of the Surface Area Configuration tools is to allow the administrator to either enable or disable any feature and service in order to minimize any potential security risk.

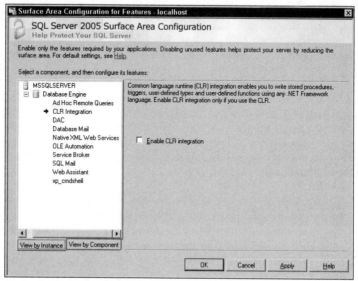

Figure 2-19: Surface Area Configuration for Features

Installation Review

I spent 20 years in the United States Navy's Submarine Service working on various computer systems. These systems ranged from 10-ton analog computers to state-of-the-art weapons guidance systems, not to mention the traditional network and server systems I was responsible for. The relentless training that occurs on a submarine and the shore-based centers that support them has left an indelible mark on everything I do.

The part of that training that has a great deal of significance for this particular chapter is the first lesson that is taught to all new commissioned and non-commissioned officers alike: "You get what you inspect—not what you expect."

My point is that after installing SQL Server, it is important to review the installation to "inspect," or ensure that what you expected to happen, indeed actually happened. Did the services get installed with the proper credentials? Are they configured to auto-start? Are the program files and database files where they were expected to be? This may seem to be a little overkill, but like my Mom liked to say, "An ounce of prevention is better than a pound of cure."

Summary

Careful planning prior to the installation process prevents the need to uninstall and start over. It also prevents a continuous struggle with an installation that is "not quite right." In later chapters, the optimization process, disk and memory access, as well as disaster recovery are discussed in great detail, and the connection to a well-designed infrastructure for installation will become increasingly evident. An important aspect of installing SQL Server is understanding the questions and options presented during the installation. Too many times new administrators click through a configuration screen without fully understanding the ramifications of their actions. A good example of that is the collation configuration screen. I have encountered very few DBAs who really understood what effect different collation settings had on the sorting and searching of data—not to mention the impact of supporting different database solutions.

This chapter spent a little time describing physical storage options, which is a big part of any database configuration. By placing SQL data files and log files on separate physical disks, you decrease the chance of a major disaster and increase the speed of recovery. By placing SQL Server's assets on separate controllers and arrays, you also increase the performance of SQL Server by reducing resource conflicts and maximizing database throughput. A modest investment, then, of storage hardware will pay great dividends for database availability and performance.

When it comes to availability, keep in mind that Microsoft worked very hard to make SQL Server "cluster friendly." It is fairly easy to configure a failover cluster, but keep in mind that a full discussion of the Windows cluster was not provided. A number of very good resources are available on the Web and in print that cover the topic of clustering in great detail. It is strongly recommended that you research them thoroughly prior to any SQL Server cluster installation.

Chapter 3 takes a look at the tools used to administer, manage, monitor, and maintain SQL Server 2005. The new and enhanced tools provided with SQL Server 2005 are well designed and easy to use—once you learn how to use them.

SQL Server 2005 Tools

SQL Server 2005 includes some new and very versatile tools. The venerable SQL Server Enterprise Manager with its clunky, but intuitive, Microsoft Management Console (MMC) interface has been put to pasture. Accompanying Enterprise Manager into retirement are Query Analyzer and almost all of the remaining SQL Server toolset. SQL Server Profiler alone managed to keep its name, but with significantly improved functionality and a better interface.

Most database administrators (DBAs) fall into one of two distinct groups. The first group is made up of database administrators whose background is system and network administration. The second group is made up of application and database developers who have become responsible for the administration of a SQL Server infrastructure. When existing database administrators from the first group encounter the new tools in SQL Server 2005, their first response is often "What is Microsoft trying to do, make me a developer?" The only answer is, "Yes, that is exactly what Microsoft is trying to do and I wholeheartedly agree with the goal."

A database administrator must be about half system administrator and half developer in order to be completely successful. A few years ago, when Microsoft announced its Microsoft Certified Database Administrator (MCDBA) certification, it was no real surprise that the required exams were both from the administrative side of database administration and the programming side. Microsoft's intent was clear. To be a database administrator worth his or her salary, it would be absolutely imperative to understand database design and database application development. The tools used to manage SQL Server 2005 were developed with this point of view clearly in mind.

There is no doubt that Microsoft considers database administrators to be, at least marginally, developers. However, this does not mean that the tools are not intuitive and easy to use, because they are both! What it does mean is that the functionality that developers have become used to, such as source control, solution files that manage multiple related files, and a fully functional Integrated Development Environment (IDE), are now available for the database administrator.

If you have experience with SQL Server 2000 or SQL Server 7 and you really like Enterprise Manager, you may be intimidated by the new tools at first glance, but give them a chance. If you are anything like hundreds of other database administrators, you will soon be won over. To put it simply — these tools rock!

SQL Server Management Studio

SQL Server Management Studio completely replaces Enterprise Manager and Query Analyzer. In addition, it also replaces some of the functionality formerly found in Analysis Manager. It does an excellent job of both replacing the old tools and exceeding them in almost every possible way.

The SQL Server Management Studio interface looks a lot like the Visual Studio IDE and is, in actuality, a Visual Studio shell. The Visual Studio shell brings many very useful tools and features to the creation and organization of database objects, as well as the full feature set of the old tools.

When the SQL Server Management Studio is first launched, the default view is a great deal like the old Enterprise Manager with a slight Query Analyzer influence (see Figure 3-1).

Because there are many different windows that can be viewed in the Management Studio, the management of screen real estate becomes critical. Most of the windows have the capability to either be pinned open or configured to fly out when the mouse pointer is placed over the menu bar, or auto-hide when the mouse cursor is placed elsewhere. If you are familiar with the Visual Studio Integrated Development Environment (IDE), this will all be very familiar; if not, it may take a little while to get used to.

If you are unfamiliar with the Visual Studio interface, the following bit of instruction is offered: Any window that supports the pinned and unpinned option will have a pin at the top right of the window. When the window is pinned, the pin will appear vertically oriented. When the window is unpinned, it will be horizontal (see Figure 3-2), and the toolbar will auto-hide or fly out, depending on the mouse cursor location.

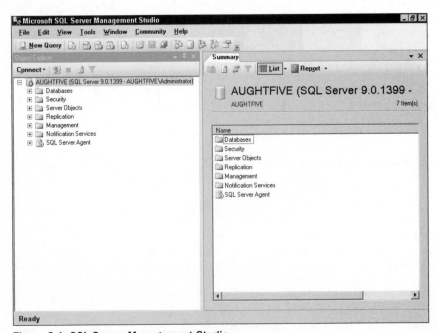

Figure 3-1: SQL Server Management Studio

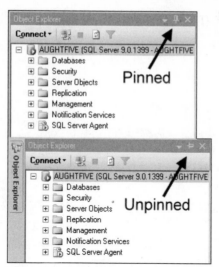

Figure 3-2: Object Explorer with a pinned and unpinned window

As mentioned before, the Visual Studio interface takes a little getting used to, but once you do, it is hard to imagine any interface that works as well. It offers the advantage of being able to hide windows when you don't need them, but make them visible when you do, without having to reconfigure the interface. This conserves a great deal of screen real estate without having to click several menus to expose the features you want.

Tool Windows

SQL Server Management Studio offers many different tool windows that facilitate the development and modification of database objects, as well as the effective management of SQL Server. The various views are accessible from the View menu as well as the Standard toolbar. Each window can be configured as Dockable, which is the default, but can also be configured as a Tabbed Document or a Floating Window.

A *dockable window* means that the window can be dragged and docked at almost any location in the studio. If you don't like the Object Explorer window on the left of the studio, just drag it to the right, top, or bottom, and dock it there. When dragging a tool window, a navigation cross will appear in the center of the screen representing the dockable areas. Dragging the window over one of the area representations (see Figure 3-3) will cause a shadow to appear in that area, indicating the window can be docked there by releasing the mouse button.

Changing a windows property to Tabbed Document mode changes the window into a tab on the main window. The Floating Window option specifies that the tool window is not anchored anywhere and can be moved around the main interface.

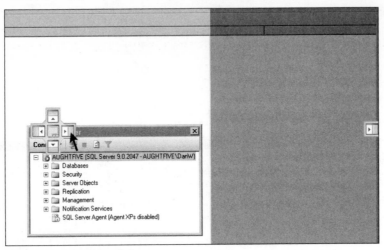

Figure 3-3: Dockable window

Object Explorer

The Object Explorer (see Figure 3-2) is more than just a way to explore the database objects on a server. The Object Explorer is also the tool that will be used in most of the database management tasks. It is arranged in a standard tree view with different groups of objects nested in folders.

The Object Explorer's functionality is exposed through the context menu. Right-clicking any object or folder within Object Explorer exposes the list of available options, from creating tables and users to configuring replication and database snapshots. The context menu also presents the ability to create scripts that manipulate. For example, right-clicking a table exposes a context menu that allows the user to either view or modify the table structure through the graphical interface, or create scripts to perform actions against the table or its data. This functionality exists for virtually every object that is visible in the Object Explorer.

Another great feature of SQL Server Management Studio that is exposed through the Object Explorer and other areas of the Studio interface is the ability to create scripts based on actions performed in the graphical designers. For example, right-clicking the table folder and choosing to create a new folder launches a graphical interface where the table structure can be defined. Once the table design is complete you can either save the table (which creates it), or you can click the Generate Change Script button on the Table Designer toolbar (which will write the appropriate T-SQL to complete the task).

Likewise, when working with other objects in Management Studio, a Script button will appear at the top of the respective designer, which will cause the actions performed in the designer to be scripted to a new editor window. This feature is especially useful when several different objects of the same type are to be created. The first one can be designed in the designer, the script generated for it, and that script modified to create the remaining objects. It is also very useful to learn the syntax for creating and modifying objects.

Try It Out   Creating a Script

In the following example, you use the Object Explorer to create a script for a new database called TestDB:

1. In Object Explorer, right-click Databases. In the context menu that appears, click New Database.

2. The New Database dialog appears (see Figure 3-4).

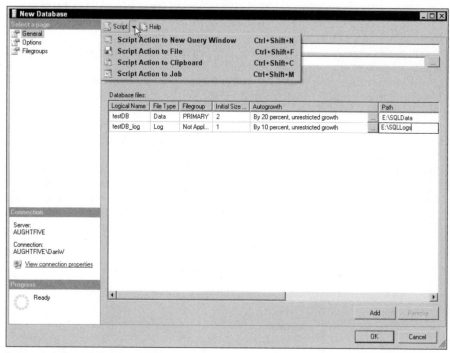

Figure 3-4: New Database dialog

3. Enter **TestDB** for the name of the database.

4. Click the Script button at the top of the New Database dialog.

5. The Script button causes the appropriate T-SQL code to be written to a new query window.

Clicking the down arrow to the right of the Script button (Figure 3-4) gives you the option of sending the script to a variety of locations.

6. Click Cancel. (Clicking OK will cause the database to be created.)

7. The script remains, but the database is not created unless the script is executed.

Code Editor

SQL Server Management Studio's Code Editor provides the ability to open, edit, or create new queries. The types of queries supported by the Editor are Database Engine queries, data mining queries, multidimensional queries, XML for Analysis (XMLA) queries, and SQL Server Mobile queries.

Database Engine queries are written in Transact-SQL (T-SQL). *Data mining queries* are created by using extensions to the Structured Query Language (SQL) called Data Mining Extensions (DMX). DMX queries are written to return information from data mining models created in SQL Server 2005 Analysis. *Multidimensional queries* are written using Multidimensional Expressions (MDX). MDX queries are used to retrieve information from multidimensional cubes created in Analysis Services.

The Code Editor is essentially a word processor. It provides color coding of syntax, multiple query windows, and partial code execution by highlighting the desired code and clicking the Execute button or pressing F5. SQL Server 2005 documentation refers to the Code Editor as the Query Editor, Text Editor, or simply the Editor, depending on what aspect of SQL Server you are reading about.

The basic functionality that the Code Editor brings is the same for all the possible types of queries it supports. However, more complete functionality is provided for specific languages. For example, when creating MDX, DMX, or XMLA queries, the Code Editor provides basic IntelliSense functions such as those found in Visual Studio. When it comes to T-SQL queries, there is, unfortunately, no IntelliSense. What almost (but not quite) makes up for the lack of IntelliSense is the direct access to the graphical query builder. Right-clicking the Code Editor window, when that window is associated with a Database Engine query, results in a context menu that includes the Design Query in Editor option (see Figure 3-5). The Query Designer is also available from the SQL Editor toolbar described later. The Query Designer is very useful when writing queries against databases that are not familiar to the query writer.

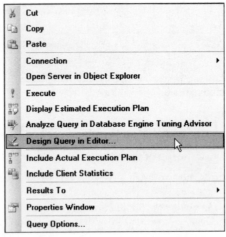

Figure 3-5: Query window context menu

Solution Explorer

In the past, organizing queries and object definitions was a completely left to the DBA or database developer. The ability to organize and group scripts together or to check them in to a source control system was completely manual. SQL Server Management Studio takes full advantage of Visual Studio's solution system by providing the means of grouping various connection objects and scripts into a single solution called a SQL Server Management Studio Solution. Each solution can have one or more projects associated with it. For example, if you are developing several objects for a new application that includes both Database Engine and Analysis Engine objects, you can create a new solution that links them all together by creating a new SQL Server Management Project (see Figure 3-6).

If no solution is currently open, the Management Studio will create a new one. As you can see in Figure 3-6, there are three types of projects to choose from. *SQL Server Script* projects contain T-SQL Database Engine queries; *Analysis Services Script* projects contain MDX, DMX, and XMLA analysis queries; and, obviously, *SQL Mobile Script* projects contain SQL Mobile queries.

The solution is managed through a SQL Server Management Studio Solution (SSMSSLN) file with an .ssmssln extension. The example shown in Figure 3-6 created a new solution folder called Adventure WorksWebApp that contains a project folder called ProductCatalog. By default, the solution folder and the first project folder will have the same name, so it is generally a good idea to change the name of the solution. The "Create directory for solution" option can also be cleared and a solution folder specified. In this way, only a project folder will be created in the specified directory. If a solution is already opened, creating a new project can add the project to the solution, or be configured to create a whole new solution and close the open one. Solutions can contain many projects. For example, a project called Sales Procedures can be added to organize the files for the sales piece of the solution (see Figure 3-7).

Figure 3-6: Associating projects and solutions

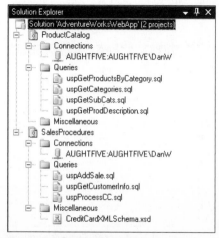

Figure 3-7: Multiple projects

Projects contain three folders: Connections, Queries, and Miscellaneous. The Connections and Queries folders are self-explanatory. The Miscellaneous folder can be used to store just about any other file that is pertinent to the project. This may be project documentation, XML files, or even the .NET assemblies used to create managed code procedures.

The solution folder contains two files. One file is the *solution file*, which, in this case, is called `AdventureWorksWebApp.ssmssln`. This contains a list of all the projects in the solution and their locations. The second file is the *SQL Solution Options* file `AdventureWorksWebApp.sqlsuo`. The solution options file contains information about the options that customize the development environment.

The solution folder will contain a project folder for every project added to the solution. The project folder contains all the project files, including the project definition file. The project definition file, or SQL Server Management Studio SQL Project (SSMSSQLPROJ) file, is an XML file with the `.ssmssqlproj` extension. In the previous `ProductCatalog` project example, this file is called `ProductCatalog.ssmssqlproj`. The project definition file contains the connection information, as well as metadata about the remaining files in the project.

Properties Window

The Properties window is linked to the Solution Explorer and simply displays the properties for the currently selected item in the Solution Explorer window. Editable properties will be bolded.

Registered Servers

Multiple servers can be registered and managed with the Management Studio. Right-clicking anywhere in the Registered Servers window (see Figure 3-8) will expose a context menu that allows for the addition of new server registrations. It also allows for the creation of server groups. The Registered Servers window is not visible by default. To open it, use the View menu and select Registered Servers or press Ctrl+Alt+G.

If you have multiple servers in your organization, server groups can be very useful. For example, server registrations can be segregated so that all the test and development servers are in one group, and the production servers are in another, or servers could be grouped based on function or department. Instances of the Database Engine, Analysis Services, Reporting Services, Integration Services, and SQL Mobile can be registered in the Registered Servers window. Once registered, the Registered Servers window provides the ability to manage the associated services, or launch other SQL Server tools associated with the respective instance.

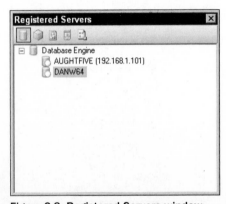

Figure 3-8: Registered Servers window

Bookmark Window

When working with very large scripts in the Code Editor, it is very useful to be able mark a location in the script. Bookmarks enable this functionality. The Bookmark window is made visible with the View menu and is enabled when working with any SQL Server script type. Any number of bookmarks can be created and then renamed with an intuitive name that identifies the bookmark (see Figure 3-9). If the script is part of a solution, the bookmarks are saved with the solution in the solution options file. Bookmarks can be organized into multiple folders for each project.

```
UPDATE [HumanResources].[Employee]
SET [Title] = @Title
    ,[HireDate] = @HireDate
    ,[CurrentFlag] = @CurrentFlag
WHERE [EmployeeID] = @EmployeeID;

INSERT INTO [HumanResources].[EmployeePayHistory]
    ([EmployeeID]
    ,[RateChangeDate]
    ,[Rate]
    ,[PayFrequency])
VALUES (@EmployeeID, @RateChangeDate, @Rate, @PayFrequency);

COMMIT TRANSACTION;
END TRY
BEGIN CATCH
    -- Rollback any active or uncommittable transactions before
```

Connected.		AUGHTFIVE (9.0 SP1) AUGHTFIVE\DanW (53) Advent

Bookmarks

Bookmark	File Location	Line Number
☑ ☐ **InsertPayHistory**	C:\SQLServerSolutions\uspUpdateEmployee.sql	31

Figure 3-9: Bookmark window

Toolbox

The Toolbox (see Figure 3-10) contains Maintenance Plan tasks that can be dragged to the Maintenance Plan designer, which is described in Chapter 8.

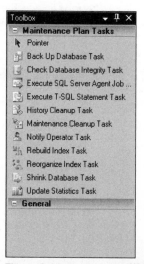

Figure 3-10: Toolbox window

Summary Window

The Summary window is displayed by default and is a great deal like the list or detail view in Windows Explorer. However, the Summary window also provides a very useful reporting feature. This feature allows the rendering of various server and database reports. The report feature is enabled when selecting an object in the Object Explorer or in the Summary window that has reports associated with it. The following table contains a list of all the supported reports and where they can be found.

Report Object	Reports
Server	Server Dashboard
	Configuration Changes History
	Schema Changes History
	Scheduler Health
	Memory Consumption
	Activity — All Blocking Transactions
	Activity — All Cursors
	Activity — Top Cursors
	Activity — All Sessions
	Activity — Top Sessions
	Activity — Dormant Sessions
	Activity — Top Connections
	Top Transactions by Age
	Top Transactions by Blocked Transactions Count
	Top Transactions by Locks Count
	Performance — Batch Execution Statistics
	Performance — Object Execution Statistics
	Performance — Top Queries by Average CPU Time
	Performance — Top Queries by Average IO
	Performance — Top Queries by Total CPU Time
	Performance — Top Queries by Total IO
	Service Broker Statistics
	Transaction Log Shipping Status
	Disk Usage
	Backup and Restore Events

Report Object	Reports
	All Transactions
	All Blocking Transactions
	Top Transactions by Age
	Top Transactions by Blocked Transactions Count
	Top Transactions by Locks Count
	Resource Locking Statistics by Objects
	Object Execution Statistics
	Database Consistency History
	Index Usage Statistics
	Schema Changes History
	User Statistics
Service Broker	Service Broker Status
Full Text Catalogs	Active Full Text Catalogs
Management	Tasks
	Number of Errors
Notification Services	General
	Job Steps Execution History
	Top Jobs

Web Browser

An Internet Explorer window can be launched from within SQL Server Management Studio if desired to minimize the number of open applications, and to allow direct access to Internet content from within the Management Studio application. The Web Browser window is made visible in the View menu and has two options: Home and Search. The Home command opens the SQL Server home page at Microsoft in a Management Studio browser window. The Search command opens the MSDN site.

The benefit of having a browser window in Management Studio is that it allows tabbed browsing of content or newsgroups that may be pertinent to the current solution. You can search or ask questions without having to switch back and forth between the Management Studio and Internet Explorer. Keep in mind that the Web Browser window is just an instance of Internet Explorer embedded in Management Studio. The behavior of the Web Browser window is the same as Internet Explorer, and the security configuration of Internet Explorer is in full effect in the Web Browser window.

Template Explorer

The Template Explorer (see Figure 3-11) contains hundreds of SQL Server, Analysis Server, and SQL Mobile scripts. Each script is grouped into folders based on their function. The template scripts can be opened by being dragged onto an open query window. If no query window is open, the templates can be opened by double-clicking with a mouse, using the Edit menu, or right-clicking a context menu, all of which cause a new query window to open.

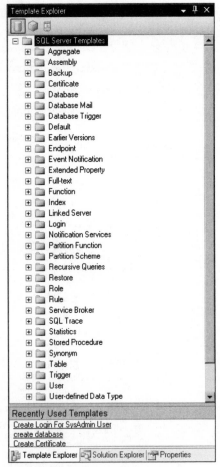

Figure 3-11: Template Explorer

Once a template is open in the Query Editor, the parameters of the template can be replaced with actual values by launching the Specify Values for Template Parameters dialog (see Figure 3-12). This dialog can be launched from the SQL Editor toolbar or through the Query menu.

Toolbars

SQL Server Management studio provides 11 different toolbars that expose features from various menus. Each toolbar can be displayed or hidden by using the View → Toolbars menu (see Figure 3-13). Toolbars can also be customized to display only the buttons that are most often used, or you can create a new toolbar that has just the commands you typically use.

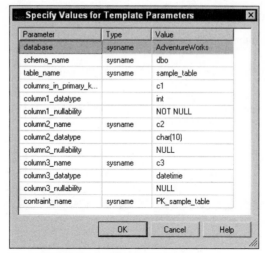

Figure 3-12: Parameter replacement

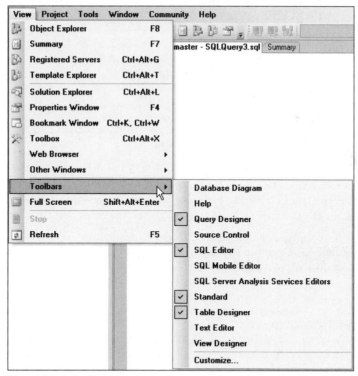

Figure 3-13: Toolbars menu

Try It Out   Creating a Custom Toolbar

To create a new custom toolbar complete the following steps:

1. Select the Customize command on the View → Toolbars menu. This will launch the Customize window.

2. On the Customize window, click the New button (see Figure 3-14), give your toolbar a new name, and click OK. A new empty toolbar will appear.

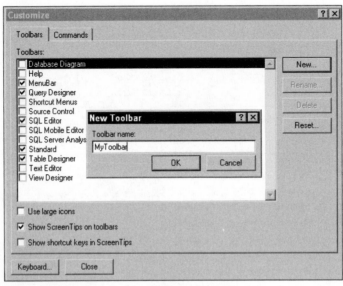

Figure 3-14: Custom toolbar window

3. Select the Commands tab on the Customize window. Two panes are visible on the Commands tab: Categories and Commands. Each category contains commands specific to that category. For example, the File category contains commands such as Open File, Save Project, and so on.

4. Select the Edit Category and drag several commands to the new custom toolbar created in Step 2 (see Figure 3-15). Once you have all the commands that you want on the new toolbar, you can drag it and dock it in a desired location.

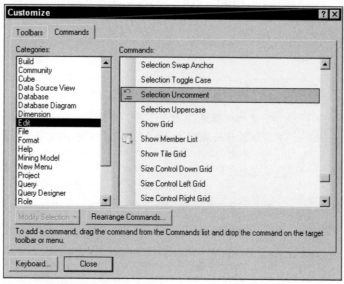

Figure 3-15: Custom edit toolbar

Creating new toolbars or customizing existing ones is an excellent way of conserving screen real estate by only showing commands that you frequently use.

Database Diagram Toolbar

The Database Diagram toolbar (see Figure 3-16) exposes a great deal of functionality for use on database diagrams.

Figure 3-16: Database Diagram toolbar

The toolbar is not used just for diagramming the database, but also for modifying or creating database objects from within the diagram interface. The Database Diagram toolbar features are described in the following table.

Feature	Purpose
New Table	Enables the creation of new tables from within the database diagram.
Add Table	Adds an existing table from the database to the diagram.
Add Related Tables	By selecting a table in the database diagram and clicking the Add Relate Tables button, all the tables that are related by a declarative Foreign Key constraint will be added to the diagram.
Delete Tables From Database	Not only removes the table from the diagram, but deletes the table and its contents as well.
Remove From Diagram	Removes the selected table from the diagram.
Generate Change Script	Any changes made to database objects in the diagram (such as creation, deletion, or modifying of attributes) can be sent to a script. If changes are made to underlying objects and the diagram is saved, a prompt is shown asking to confirm changes to the underlying objects.
Set Primary Key	Sets or changes the primary key assignment to the selected column.
New Text Annotation	Adds a textbox for annotation to the database diagram.
Table View	Enables the changing of table presentation in the diagram, including a customized view to configure exactly what aspects of the table are displayed.
Show Relationship Labels	Displays or hides the name of the foreign key constraints.
View Page Breaks	Displays or hides page break lines to enable the organization of diagrams for printing.
Recalculate Page Breaks	Re-centers table objects onto as few pages as possible after being manually arranged on the diagram.
Arrange Selection	Arranges selected tables so they do not overlap and are viewable in the diagram.
Arrange Tables	Arranges all tables so they do not overlap and are viewable in the diagram.
Zoom	Increases or decreases the zoom factor on the displayed diagram.
Relationships	Launches a dialog that displays existing foreign keys defined on a selected table and enables the defining of additional foreign keys.
Manage Indexes and Keys	Launches a dialog that displays existing primary and unique keys defined on a selected table and enables the defining of additional keys.
Manage Full-Text Indexes	Launches a dialog that displays existing full-text indexes on a selected table, and enables the defining of additional full-text indexes on full-text index-enabled databases.
Manage XML Indexes	Launches a dialog that displays existing XML indexes on a selected table, and enables the defining of additional XML indexes.
Manage Check Constraints	Launches a dialog that displays existing Check Constraints on a selected table, and enables the defining of additional Check Constraints.

Help Toolbar

The Help toolbar (see Figure 3-17) provides a very easy and convenient mechanism for consulting online help articles while using the Management Studio.

Figure 3-17: Help toolbar

The Help toolbar's commands are described in the following table.

Command	Purpose
Web Browser Back Web Browser Forward	If the Web Browser window is opened in Management Studio, the Web Browser Back and Forward commands can be used to move from a viewed Web page to the previously viewed Web page, and vice versa.
Web Browser Stop	Stops the loading of a Web page in a Web Browser window.
Web Browser Refresh	Refreshes the current Web Browser window.
Web Browser Search	Launches the MSDN Web site in a new Web Browser window.
Font Size	Changes font size of the Web Browser window. Clicking this repeatedly will cycle the font size from Smallest, Smaller, Medium, Larger, and Largest.
How Do I	The How Do I command launches SQL Server Books Online and loads up the How Do I section, which allows the user to navigate through articles that explain how to perform a myriad of actions with SQL Server 2005.
Search	Launches the search feature of SQL Server Books Online.
Index	Launches the SQL Server Books Online index.
Contents	Launches the SQL Server Books Online Table of Contents.
Help Favorites	Launches SQL Server Books Online and opens the Help Favorites window for navigating any saved favorites.
Add to Help Favorites	Adds the currently viewed help page to the Help Favorites.
Save Search	Saves the current search in SQL Server Books Online search page to the Help Favorites.
Sync With Table of Contents	If the SQL Server Books Online Table of Contents is visible, this button will navigate to the location in the Table of Contents that the current article window is opened to.

Table continued on following page

Command	Purpose
Ask a Question	Opens the Search Community Forums home page at the MSDN Web site. Here you can create a profile and ask questions of other SQL Server professionals, or answer other people's questions.
Check Question Status	Once you have a MSDN Community Forum account, your questions are associated with your account, so you can easily check back to see if anyone has replied to your question.
Send Feedback	The Send Feedback command allows you to provide feedback to the SQL Server product team about SQL Server 2005.

Query Designer Toolbar

The Query Designer toolbar (see Figure 3-18) is enabled when a table is opened with Object Explorer.

Figure 3-18: Query Designer toolbar

To open a table, follow these steps:

1. Right-click the table you want to open in Object Explorer.
2. Click Open Table.

If the Query Designer was not visible, it will be when the table is opened. If it was visible, it will now be enabled. Although opening a table in a test and development environment is probably acceptable, opening a table in this manner in a production environment is not recommended. Opening a table with the Object Explorer dumps the data from the table in to an updatable scrollable cursor. What this means is that while the table data is exposed in the results window any change to the displayed data is also made to the underlying data in the table. There is no Confirm message or warning. The data is just modified. This can be very dangerous. Displaying the entire contents of the table can also consume a great deal of server resources if the table is large. As a general rule, if the entire contents of a table need to be exposed, the best way is to write a query with no filters, such as the following:

```
USE AdventureWorks
GO
SELECT * FROM Person.Address
```

This exposes the same information as opening the table, but does not populate an updatable cursor, so the results are read-only. If the data in that table needs to be updated, an update command is more appropriate than modifying the data in an open table results window.

The Query Designer toolbar features are described in the following table.

Feature	Purpose
Show Diagram Pane	Displays or hides the Diagram Pane, which can be used to add or remove tables from the query, add derived tables, and configure table join criteria.
Show Criteria Pane	Displays or hides the Criteria Pane, which can be used to alias column names, establish sort orders, and configure filter criteria.
Show SQL Pane	Displays or hides the SQL Pane, which displays the resultant SQL syntax from the Diagram Pane. The SQL syntax can also be manipulated in the SQL Pane, resulting in changes to the Criteria and Diagram Panes.
Show Results Pane	Displays or hides the results of the query if it has been executed.
Change Type	Allows changing the type of query from SELECT to INSERT, DELETE, or UPDATE.
Execute SQL	Executes the query against the database.
Verify SQL Syntax	Validates the syntax of the query, but does not execute it.
Add/Remove Group By	Adds a GROUP BY expression and formats the query so that non-aggregated columns in the SELECT list are present in the GROUP BY list.
Add Table	Adds an existing table to the Diagram Pane and SQL Pane.
Add New Derived Table	Adds an empty table to the Diagram Pane and the shell syntax for creating a derived table subquery to the SQL Pane.

Source Control Toolbar

The Source Control toolbar (see Figure 3-19) is enabled when working with scripts and a Source Control plug-in has been configured such as Visual Source Safe 2005. The addition of source-control functionality to SQL Server projects is a great step forward in recognizing the need for a structured solution environment in the development of database solutions.

Figure 3-19: Source Control toolbar

The following examples use Visual Source Safe 2005 as the source-control tool, but there are other source-control applications available that will interact with SQL Server Management Studio. In addition, a full description of Visual Source Safe 2005 configuration and use is beyond the scope of this book, so it will be limited to just the interaction with SQL Server Management Studio.

To configure Management Studio to use source control, use the File menu, select the Source Control menu item, and click Launch Microsoft Visual Source Safe. The Add Visual Source Safe Database wizard will launch.

Click Next on the Welcome screen. The Database Selection screen will appear, asking for the location of an existing Source Safe database. If you or your organization has already configured a source-control database, select the "Connect to existing database" option. If this is a new installation, check the "Create a new database" option (see Figure 3-20).

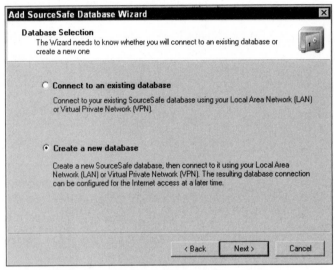

Figure 3-20: Source-control database selection

The next step is either to choose an existing source control share location or to create one. After choosing to either use an existing share or to create a new one, the summary screen for the wizard will appear. Clicking Finish on the wizard will launch the Visual Source Safe Explorer. The Visual Source Safe Explorer can be used to create and manage project folders for both SQL Server Management Studio and Visual Studio solutions.

In a previous example, I created a Management Studio solution called `AdventureWorksWebApp`. Now that Visual Source Safe is configured for use with Management Studio, I can add the solution to the source-control database to control the modification of the included files, and to provide structured version control.

Much of the functionality of the Source Control toolbar is only enabled if the current project has already been added to the source-control database.

To add a solution to source control, right-click the solution in Solution Explorer and select Add Solution to Source Control. After logging in to the source control Web site, choose a location for the solution (see Figure 3-21) and click OK.

Now that the solution has been added to source control, the Source Control toolbar is fully enabled for managing the solution.

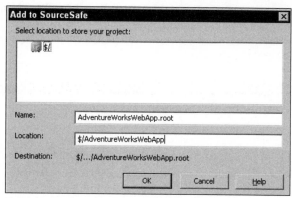

Figure 3-21: Add solution to source control

The features available on the Source Control toolbar are described in the following table.

Feature	Purpose
Change Source Control	Displays a dialog that enables the linking of new and existing items in the Solution Explorer to a source-control database folder.
Get Latest Version	Opens the latest version of the item or items selected in the Solution Explorer.
Get	Returns a list of all versions of the selected item and allows the selection of a particular version.
Check Out for Edit	Opens the selected items for editing and marks its status in the source-control database as "Open for Edit," preventing other users from editing it at the same time.
Check In	Saves changes and marks the selected item in the source-control database as "Checked In" and allows editing by other users.
Undo Checkout	Discards any changes and marks the selected item in the source-control database as "Checked In" and allows editing by other users.
View History	Displays the history of a project, which includes a list of everything done to the project from creation to deletion.
Refresh Status	Queries the source-control database for the most recent status of all project items.
Share	Allows for a single item to be shared in multiple projects. Changes made to shared items are reflected in all the projects that use the item.
Compare	Compares an item to a previous version to expose the changes made.
Properties	Displays detailed status information on the selected item.
Source Control Manager	Launches the associated source control application as identified in the Management Studio options settings.

As I am writing this, a new product, "Visual Studio 2005 Team Edition for Database Professionals," is in development at Microsoft. This application will add new functionality and the ability to control and manage the development of data tier solutions, including databases and associated database objects.

SQL Editor Toolbar

The SQL Editor toolbar (see Figure 3-22) becomes visible (or is enabled if already visible) when a new SQL query window is opened. It provides the most common features used by SQL programmers and DBAs.

Figure 3-22: SQL Editor toolbar

The supported features available on the SQL Editor toolbar are described in the following table.

Feature	Purpose
Connect	Queries can be written without being connected to a database, so when it comes time to execute the query or validate its syntax against a database, the Connect button displays a server connection dialog that enables the selection of the applicable server and database.
Disconnect	In certain instances, it is not advantageous to be actively connected to a database while creating SQL queries. The Disconnect button disconnects the active query window from its current database and server.
Change Connection	Enables changing the connected server. A script can be created and tested on a test and development server and then the connection changed to the production server for execution.
Available Databases	Drop-down list box for selecting the database context for the query.
Execute	Executes the SQL in the current window against the selected database.
Parse	Checks the SQL in the current window for valid structure and syntax. It does *not* check to ensure that referenced objects actually exist.
Cancel Executing Query	Terminates the present query.
Display Estimated Execution Plan	Displays a graphical execution plan for the current window. It does not actually execute the query, but simply checks the metadata of the referenced object and builds a query plan based on current information.

Feature	Purpose
Analyze Query in Database Engine Tuning Advisor	Launches the Database Engine Tuning Advisor (see the section "Database Engine Tuning Advisor," later in this chapter), which can analyze the present query and recommend changes in the underlying database to optimize the performance of the query.
Design Query in Editor	Launches the graphical Query Editor.
Specify Values for Template Parameters	Displays a dialog that enables the replacement of template parameters with defined values.
Include Actual Execution Plan	A graphical query plan used during execution is returned along with the results of the query.
Include Client Statistics	Client statistics including statistics about the query, network packets, and the elapsed time of the query are returned, along with the query results.
SQLCMD Mode	SQLCMD replaces OSQL as the command-line SQL tool. SQLCMD Mode allows the editing and testing of command-line scripts in the editor.
Results to Text	Formats the results of any query executed in the Query Editor as text.
Results to Grid	Query results are returned in a grid. By default grid results cannot exceed 65,535 characters.
Results to File	When a query is executed a Save Results window will appear, prompting for a filename and location.
Comment Out Selected Lines	Adds in-line comment marks to comment-out the selected lines.
Uncomment Selected Lines	Removes in-line comment marks.
Decrease Indent	Decreases the indent of selected text.
Increase Indent	Increases the indent of selected text.

SQL Mobile Editor Toolbar

The SQL Mobile Editor toolbar (see Figure 3-23) becomes visible (or is enabled if already visible) when a new SQL Mobile query window is opened. The tools on the SQL Mobile toolbar are a subset of the SQL Editor tools that are applicable for SQL Mobile queries.

Figure 3-23: Mobile Editor toolbar

SQL Server Analysis Services Editor Toolbar

The Analysis Services toolbar (see Figure 3-24) also becomes visible (or is enabled if already visible) when a new Analysis query is opened or created. The tools on this toolbar are also a subset of the SQL Editor tools, but contain only those tools applicable to Analysis Services queries (DMX, MDX, XMLA).

Figure 3-24: Analysis Services toolbar

Standard Toolbar

The Standard toolbar (see Figure 3-25) provides buttons to execute the most common actions such as opening and saving files. It also provides buttons that will launch new queries and expose different tool windows.

Figure 3-25: Standard toolbar

The commands available on the Standard toolbar are described in the following table.

Feature	Purpose
New Query	The New Query command launches a new Database Engine query window by default.
Database Engine Query	Opens a new Database Engine query window.
Analysis Services MDX Query	Opens a new MDX query window.
Analysis Services DMX Query	Opens a new DMX query window.
Analysis Services XMLA Query	Opens a new XMLA query window.
SQL Server Mobile Query	Opens a new SQL Server Mobile query.
Save	Saves the currently selected window.
Save All	Saves all open and changed files.
Registered Servers	Displays the Registered Servers window.
Summary	Displays the Summary window.
Object Explorer	Displays the Object Explorer window.
Template Explorer	Displays the Template Explorer window.
Properties Window	Displays the Properties window.

Table Designer Toolbar

The Table Designer toolbar (see Figure 3-26) becomes visible (or is enabled if already visible) when a new table is created using Table Designer or an existing table is modified using the Table Designer. The Table Designer is launched by right-clicking the table node in the Object Explorer and choosing New Table from the context menu, or by right-clicking an existing table in the table node of Object Explorer and choosing Modify.

Figure 3-26: Table Designer toolbar

The following table describes the toolbar.

Feature	Purpose
Generate Change Script	Table creation or modification done with the Designer can be sent to a query window for later execution.
Set/Remove Primary Key	Sets the selected column of the table as the primary key column, or removes the key if it has already been set.
Relationships	Enables the creation of foreign key constraints.
Manage Indexes and Keys	Enables the creation of unique keys and indexes.
Manage Fulltext Index	Launches a dialog that enables the creation of full-text catalogs and full-text indexes.
Manage XML Index	Launches a dialog that enables the creation and management of Primary and Secondary indexes.
Manage Check Constraints	Launches a dialog that enables the creation and management of check constraints.

Text Editor Toolbar

The Text Editor toolbar (see Figure 3-27) offers additional shortcuts to those provided in the other language-specific editors.

Figure 3-27: Text Editor toolbar

The features are described in the following table.

Feature	Purpose
Display an Object Member List	When editing DMX, MDX, or XMLA scripts, invokes an IntelliSense window that displays a list of possible script members. IntelliSense features are not available when working with SQL scripts.
Display Parameter Info	Displays the parameter list for system-stored procedures and functions used with Analysis Services.
Display Quick Info	Displays declaration information for XML objects created or referenced in an XMLA script.
Display Word Completion	Displays possible words to complete a variable, command, or function call. If only one possible option exists, it is implemented.
Decrease Indent	Decreases the indent of selected text.
Increase Indent	Increases the indent of selected text.
Comment Out Selected Lines	Adds in-line comment marks to comment out the selected lines.
Uncomment Selected Lines	Removes in-line comment marks.
Toggle a Bookmark on the Current Line	Adds or removes a bookmark to the current script at the position of the cursor.
Move the caret to the previous bookmark	Moves the cursor to the previous set bookmark in the current script project.
Move the caret to the next bookmark	Moves the cursor to the next set bookmark in the current script project.
Move the caret to the previous bookmark in the current folder Bookmark window.	Moves the cursor to the previous set bookmark in the currently selected bookmark folder of the
Move the caret to the next bookmark in the current folder	Moves the cursor to the next set bookmark in the currently selected bookmark folder of the Bookmark window.
Move the caret to the previous bookmark in the current document	Moves the cursor to the previous set bookmark in the current script window.
Move the caret to the next bookmark in the current document	Moves the cursor to the next set bookmark in the current script window.
Clear all bookmarks in all files	Removes all configured bookmarks from the current project.

View Designer Toolbar

The View Designer toolbar (see Figure 3-28) is almost exactly like the Query Designer toolbar, with the exception of being limited to writing SELECT queries. In addition, queries written with the View Designer are saved as views and not just query scripts. For information about the function of the buttons on the View Designer toolbar, consult the table in the earlier section "Query Designer Toolbar."

Figure 3-28: View Designer toolbar

SQL Server Management Studio Configuration

Management Studio's look and feel can be customized through the Tools → Options menu (see Figure 3-29), which is accessed by selecting Tools on the main menu and clicking Options.

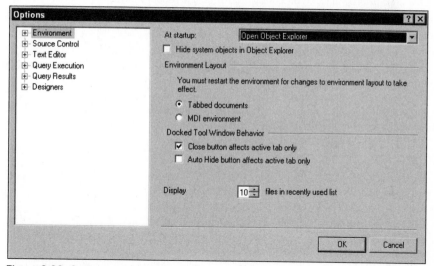

Figure 3-29: Options menu

The Options dialog enables the customization of the Management Studio IDE. The configuration options are divided into the following six areas.

Environment

The Environment configuration section is broken down into four sub-areas:

❑ *General* — Startup options and environment layout (such as tabbed windows versus MDI windows) and how the windows behave.

❑ *Fonts and Colors* — The fonts and colors used in the text editor are extraordinarily customizable in this area. The color and font used for reserved words, stored procedures, comments, and background colors are just a sampling of what can be changed.

❑ *Keyboard* — For those database administrators who are used to Query Analyzer's keyboard shortcuts, this configuration area enables the setting of the keyboard shortcuts to the same ones used in Query Analyzer. The keyboard configuration area also allows for the addition of custom keyboard shortcuts.

❑ *Help* — The Help area enables the integration of Help into a Management Studio window or launching Help externally. It also allows for customizing local and online help resources.

Source Control

The Source Control configuration section allows for the integration of a source-control plug-in such as Visual Source Safe 2005. The Source Control section is broken down in to three different areas:

❑ *Plug-In Selection* — Here, the specific plug-in can be chosen (such as Visual Source Safe 2005, or Visual Studio team System).

❑ *Environment* — The Environment section allows for the configuration of the Source Control Environment settings supported by the configured source-control plug-in. For Visual Source Safe 2005, there are three preconfigured settings: Visual Source Safe, Independent Developer, and Custom. These settings determine the automatic Check-In and Check-Out behavior of source-control projects.

❑ *Plug-In Settings* — The Plug-In Settings section provides the ability to customize the source-control actions (such as what to do with unchanged files that have been checked out, and how to manage file comparisons and timestamps).

The features available in the Source Control section are dependent on the application used. Consult the documentation of the applicable program for more information.

Text Editor

The Text Editor section enables the customization of the various text editors and is divided into the following four sub-areas:

❑ *File Extension* — File extensions for all the possible script and configuration files can be configured in the File Extension area. Known file extensions such as `.sql`, `.mdx`, `.dmx`, and `.xml` are not listed, but are automatically associated with their respective editors. They can be reassigned with a "with encoding" option so that Management Studio will prompt for specific language encoding every time an associated file type is opened. Custom file extensions can also be added.

❑ *All Languages* — The All Languages area is divided in to two parts, General and Tabs, and provides configuration settings for IntelliSense features, word-wrap, line numbers, and indentation for all script languages. Keep in mind that IntelliSense options have no impact on SQL scripts.

❑ *Plain Text* — Configuration settings for plain-text documents not associated with a particular scripting language.

❑ *XML* — Configuration settings for XML documents. These settings consist of the same settings from the All Languages area, as well as XML-specific settings such as automatic formatting and schema download settings.

Query Execution

The Query Execution section provides configuration options for how queries are executed, as well as connection properties and timeout settings. The Query Execution section is divided into two sub-areas:

❑   *SQL Server* — The SQL Server area has configuration options that control the maximum row count and the maximum amount of text or Unicode text that is returned to the Management Studio results window. This area also has options to specify a batch delimiter other than GO and to specify query execution timeout settings. There are also Advanced and ANSI areas that provide for the configuration of specific connection level options described in the following table.

Option	Description
SET NOCOUNT	Suppresses the *X* number rows message from being returned on the connection.
SET NOEXEC	Configures the Query Processor to only parse and compile SQL batches, but not to execute them.
SET PARSEONLY	Configures the Query Processor to only check the validity of SQL batches, but not to compile or execute them.
SET CONCAT_NULLS_YIELDS_NULL	Configures the Query Processor to return a NULL for any string concatenated with a NULL. This Setting is selected by default.
SET ARITHABORT	Configures the Query Processor to terminate the query if an arithmetic error, overflow, divide-by-zero, or a domain error is encountered.
SET SHOWPLAN_TEXT	Configures the Query Processor to only return the query plan in text format, but not to actually execute the query.
SET STAISTICS TIME	Configures the Query Processor to return the amount of time spent in the parse, compile, and execution of a script.
SET STATISTICS IO	Configures the Query Processor to return the amount of scans, physical reads, logical reads, and read-ahead reads required to execute a script.
SET TRANSACTION ISOLATION LEVEL	Provides the option of configuring the isolation level of SQL scripts. The default is READ COMMITTED.
SET DEADLOCK_PRIORITY	Configures the deadlock priority of SQL scripts to either Normal or Low. The default is Normal.
SET LOCK TIMEOUT	Configures the time a connection will wait until terminating a query that is being blocked by a lock. The default setting is -1, which means forever.
SET QUERY_GOVERNOR_COST_LIMIT	Configures the Query Processor to prevent any query from executing that is calculated to take longer than the configured limit. The default value is 0, which disables the time limit.

Table continued on following page

Option	Description
Suppress provider message headers	Configures the Query Processor to suppress messages returned by data providers such as OLEDB or SQLClient. This setting is enabled by default.
Disconnect after the query executes	Disconnects the active query window from the database after execution. This setting is disabled by default.
SET ANSI_DEFAULTS	Sets all ANSI connection settings to On.
SET QUOTED IDENTIFIER	Configures the Query Processor to allow double quotes as legitimate object delimiters.
SET ANSI_NULL_DFLT_ON	Specifies that columns created in a CREATE TABLE or ALTER TABLE statement default to allowing NULLs if NOT NULL is not defined in the script.
SET IMPLICIT_TRANSACTIONS	Configures the Query Processor to begin, but not commit a transaction any time an UPDATE, INSERT, or DELETE statement is executed outside an explicit transaction.
SET CURSOR_CLOSE_ON_COMMIT	When set to ON, causes any open Cursor to be closed on a COMMIT TRANSACTION statement or ROLLBACK TRANSACTION statement not associated with a save point.
SET ANSI_PADDING	When set to ON, causes trailing spaces to be added to any fixed-length character string, or trailing zeros to be added to fixed-length binary strings. Trailing spaces or trailing zeros explicitly added to variable-length strings are not trimmed.
SET ANSI_WARNINGS	When set to ON, causes a warning to be returned if any aggregate function encounters a NULL or an arithmetic function fails.
SET ANSI_NULLS	When set to ON, equality or inequality operations executed against a NULL value will return an empty set.

❑ *Analysis Services* — Configuration setting to control the execution timeout setting for Analysis Server queries.

Query Results

The Query Results section provides configuration options for how query results are formatted and is also divided into the same two sub-areas as the execution settings.

❑ *SQL Server* — The SQL Server section has configuration options to specify the default location for query results: to a grid, as text, or to a file, as well as the default location for results sent to a file. The grid settings are described in the following table.

Option	Description
Include the query in the result text	The query executed is returned as part of the result. This setting is off by default.
Include column headers when copying or saving results.	Results copied to the clipboard or saved to a file include the column header names. This setting is off by default.
Discard results after execution	Queries are executed, but results are immediately cleared from the results window. This setting is off by default.
Display results in a separate tab	etting is off by default, but if selected, the option to automatically switch to the result tab is enabled.
Maximum Characters Retrieved	Grid results are limited to a specified number of characters. By default, this limit is 65,535 characters for non-XML data and 2MB of XML data.

The text settings are described in the following table.

Option	Description
Output format	The default text output format is column aligned. Comma, tab, space, and custom delimiters are available.
Include column headers in the result set.	Column headers are returned in the text results by default.
Include the query in the result text	The query executed is returned as part of the result. This setting is off by default.
Scroll as results are received	The results window scrolls to expose the last set of rows returned that will fit in the results window.
Right align numeric values	This option is only available when the column aligned output format is selected and is disabled by default.
Discard results after execution	Queries are executed, but results are immediately cleared from the results window. This setting is off by default.
Display results in a separate tab	Results are sent to a separate tab instead of a results window beneath the query window. This setting is off by default, but if selected, the option to automatically switch to the result tab is enabled.
Maximum characters displayed in each column	Configures the maximum length of any column returned in text format. The default is 256 characters.

❑ *Analysis Services* — Configuration settings for Analysis Services query results include showing grids in separate tabs and playing the default Windows beep when the query completes. Both settings are disabled by default.

Designers

The Designers section provides configuration options for the graphical designers used in Management Studio. The Designers section is divided into three sub-areas:

❑ *Table and Database Designers* — The Table and Database Designers area allows for the configuration of specific designer behavior. The following table describes the Table options.

Option	Description
`Override connection string time-out value for table designer updates`	Changes the default connection string timeout. When modifying the structure of large tables, more time is often required than the default of 30 seconds. Enabling this option also enables a text box for entering the new time-out value.
`Auto generate change scripts`	When this option is enabled, Management Studio will automatically generate a change script and prompt for a location to save the file any time designer modifications are saved. The applicable modifications are executed, as well as a script being generated.
`Warn on null primary keys`	A primary key placed on a column that allows `NULLs` will cause an error when the option is enabled. If this option is not enabled, the designer will automatically clear the `Allow Nulls` attribute from the column designated as a primary key without raising an error.
`Warn about difference detection`	When selected, Management Studio will raise a warning dialog if the changes made conflict changes made by any other user.
`Warn about tables affected`	Management Studio will raise a warning and confirmation dialog if changes to a table affect any other table in the database.

The following table describes diagram options.

Option	Description
Default table view	Used to select the default way tables are represented in database diagram tool. Possible views are:
	Standard — Shows the table header, all column names, data types, and the `Allow Nulls` setting.

Option	Description
	Column Names — Shows the column names only.
	Key — Shows the table header and the primary key columns.
	Name Only — Shows only the table header with its name.
	Custom — Allows you to choose which columns to view.
Launch add table dialog on new diagram	When the database diagram designer is opened, Management Studio automatically prompts for the selection of existing tables to be added to the diagram when this option is selected.

❑   *Maintenance Plans* — The Maintenance Plan Designer options determine the way new shapes are added to the maintenance plan design area.

❑   *Analysis Designers* — The Analysis Designers options page provides options to set the connection timeout for the Analysis designers and the colors for the Data Mining Model viewer.

Log File Viewer

The Log File Viewer (see Figure 3-30) is launched from within SQL Server Management Studio. To open it, follow these steps:

1.   Expand the Management node in Object Explorer.

2.   Expand SQL Server Logs.

3.   Right-click a log and select View SQL Server Log.

The great thing about the Log File Viewer is that almost all the logs that the DBA would want to view are available in it. SQL Server logs and the Operating System logs can be opened in the same window for easy correlation of system and SQL Server events.

When viewing multiple logs in the Log Viewer, it is often very helpful to filter the view so that only the information that is of interest is shown. For example, the filter settings allow the specification of a start date and an end date. Filter settings can also be set to display only those events from a certain subsystem. Applying appropriate filters reduces the problem of "Information Overflow" in trying to sift through thousands of log entries.

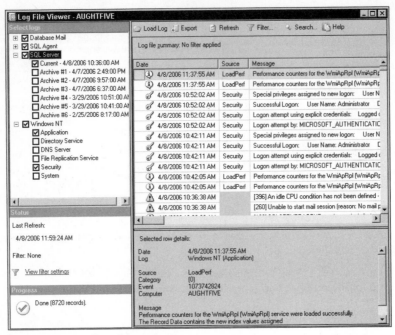

Figure 3-30: Log File Viewer

SQL Server Business Intelligence Development Studio

The SQL Server Business Intelligence Development Studio (BI Studio) is actually Visual Studio 2005. Many DBAs are surprised to find Visual Studio installed on their workstation after installing the SQL Server tools, but this is exactly what happens. If Visual Studio is launched from the All Programs, SQL Server 2005 menu as BI Studio, or from the All Programs, Visual Studio menu as Visual Studio, it launches the exact same application. If the full Visual Studio suite has not been installed, the only available project templates will be business intelligence projects. However, if the full suite is installed all the installed features and templates will be available.

A complete discussion of the Visual Studio IDE is beyond the scope of this book, but a very brief description is definitely in order.

Microsoft has divided business intelligence into three distinct pieces: Integration, Analysis, and Reporting. These three parts of the business intelligence package are implemented through SQL Server Integration Services, SQL Server Analysis Services, and SQL Server Reporting Services. Correspondingly, the BI Studio provides business intelligence project templates that focus on these three areas. The templates are available when creating a new project from the BI Studio (see Figure 3-31) by selecting File → New → Project from the main BI Studio menu.

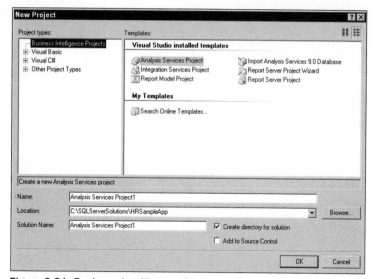

Figure 3-31: Business Intelligence Studio

Once a template is selected from the New Project screen, the template loads with the appropriate tools for the project. The available templates are briefly described in the following table.

Template	Description
Integration Services Project	Integration Services projects are used to create robust Extract-Transform-Load (ETL) solutions to enable the moving and transforming of data.
Analysis Services Project	Analysis Services projects are used to create SQL Server 2005 Analysis Services databases that expose the objects and features of Analysis Cubes used for complex data analysis.
Import Analysis Services 9.0 Database	The import project enables the creation of an Analysis Services project from an existing SQL Server 2005 Analysis Services database. It essentially reverse-engineers the project from an existing database.
Report Server Project	Report Server projects are used to create and deploy enterprise reports for both traditional (paper) and interactive reports.

Table continued on following page

Template	Description
Report Server Project Wizard	The Report Server Project Wizard offers the same functionality as the Report Server Project, but starts the development of the project in a step-by-step process that guides the user through the various tasks required to create a report. Like many wizards, this one leaves the project in a skeleton phase, which will require more detailed finalization.
Report Model Project	Report Model projects are used to create and deploy SQL Server Reporting Services 2005 report models, which can, in turn, be used by end users to create reports using the Report Builder tool.

SQL Server Profiler

The SQL Server Profiler is an absolutely essential tool for both DBAs and developers alike. The Profiler provides the ability to monitor and record virtually every facet of SQL Server activity. It is actually a graphical interface for SQL Trace, which is a collection of stored procedures and functions that are used to monitor and record server activity. SQL Server Profiler can be launched from the Tools menu of SQL Server Management Studio, or from the All Programs → Microsoft SQL Server 2005 → Performance Tools menu.

SQL Server Trace

The Profiler can be used to create and view SQL Server Traces. When creating a new trace, the Profiler will prompt you for the server on which you will be running the trace. Remember that the Profiler is just a graphical interface for SQL Trace, and what is occurring in the background is the execution of stored procedures and functions on the server you connect to. If the server is very busy and is operating at the edge of its capabilities, the additional load of running SQL Trace on it may well put it over the edge. Profiler and SQL Trace procedures are discussed in greater detail in Chapter 10.

Trace Properties

When creating a new trace, the Trace Properties dialog is shown (see Figure 3-32). The Trace Properties dialog has two tabs on it by default: the General tab and the Events Selection tab. A third tab, Events Extraction Settings, will be enabled if any XML SHOWPLAN event is selected in the Events Selection tab.

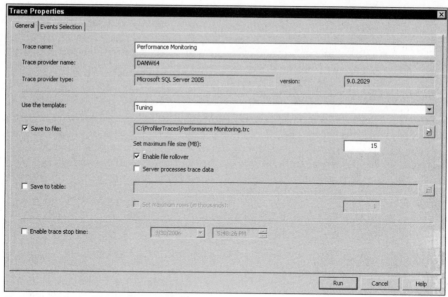

Figure 3-32: Trace Properties dialog

General Tab

The General tab provides the ability to set the basic structure of the trace (such as the trace name, trace template, saving options, and trace stop time). It also displays the provider name and type, because SQL Server Profiler is not limited to the Data Engine. It can also be used to trace SQL Server 2005 Analysis Services.

❑ *Use the template* — This drop-down list contains several pre-built trace templates. Each template is a predefined set of events and filters that provide for the monitoring of SQL Server for particular purposes. These templates can be a good place to start when creating traces to monitor SQL Server. It is also possible to create your own templates, and it is strongly recommended that you do. The provided templates are fine, but you will undoubtedly want to collect different information than the templates provide. To avoid having to create the same custom trace over and over again, create and save a template to capture the information you are interested in.

❑ *Save to file* — Selecting this checkbox will display a dialog prompting for a file location to save the trace data to. The filename defaults to the name assigned to the trace with the .trc extension. However, the name can be changed if desired. The default maximum file size for a trace file is 5MB, but it can be set to virtually any size. When the "Save to file" option is selected, two additional options are enabled: the "Enable file rollover" option and the "Server processes trace data" option.

❑ *Enable file rollover* — This option causes a new file to be created every time the maximum file size is reached. Each file created is named the same as the original file with a sequential number added to the end of the name. Each sequential file is linked to the preceding file, so that each file can be opened in sequence, or they can all be opened in a single trace window.

❑ *Server processes trace data* — This option causes the server that the traces are running on to also process the trace information. By default, the Profiler application processes the trace information. During high-stress operations, if the Profiler processes the data, it may drop some events and even become unresponsive. If the server processes the trace data, no events will be dropped. However, having the server process the trace data and run the trace puts an additional load on the server, which can have a negative impact on server performance.

❑ *Save to table* — Trace data can also be saved to a table instead of a file by selecting the "Save to table" option. This is very useful if the trace data is going to be analyzed by an external application that requires access to the data stored in a relational format. The down side is that large traces will generate huge amounts of data that will be inserted into the storage table. This can also cause server performance issues. If saving trace data to a table, the maximum amount of rows to be stored can be also be assigned.

❑ *Enable trace stop time* — Traces can be started and configured to automatically stop at a predefined time by enabling the "Enable trace stop time" option and assigning a stop time.

Events Selection Tab

The Events Selection tab provides the ability to choose what SQL Server events are to be traced (see Figure 3-33). Events are grouped in 21 SQL Server event groups with a total of 171 distinct SQL Server events, including 10 user-definable events. There are also 11 Analysis Services Groups with 41 distinct events. SQL Server Books Online has an excellent reference that describes each group and event. Search for the titles of "SQL Server Event Class Reference" for SQL Server events and "Analysis Event Classes" for Analysis Services Events.

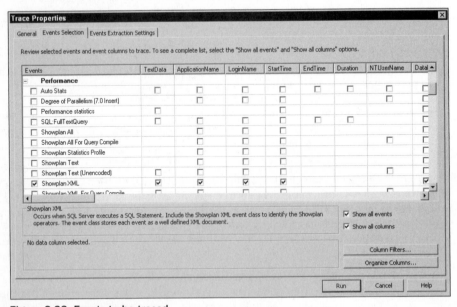

Figure 3-33: Events to be traced

❑ *Column Filters* — Also in the Events Selection tab is the option to filter the events that are traced (see Figure 3-34). The ability to filter the data is incredibly useful. For example, if you are troubleshooting a particular application, you can filter on just the events generated by the application of interest, and avoid having to sift through all the events generated by SQL Server and other applications.

❑ *Organize Columns* — The Organize Column button enables you to place the trace columns you are most interested in so that they are easily seen when viewing the trace. Because a great deal of data can be returned, it may very well be that the column you are most interested in is off the screen to the left. The Organize Columns button helps prevent this.

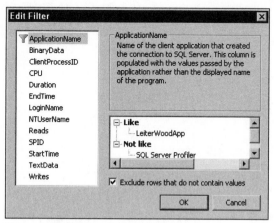

Figure 3-34: Filtering traced events

Events Extraction Settings Tab

The Events Extraction Settings tab (see Figure 3-35) is enabled when one of the SHOWPLAN XML events are chosen from the Performance event group. This tab is divided into two group boxes. The first provides the ability to save SHOWPLAN information. All SHOWPLAN information can be saved to a single file, or multiple XML files that can be opened in SQL Server Management Studio. When opened, they are displayed as graphical execution plans, which are described in detail in Chapter 10. The second group is used for saving graphical deadlock information. Because deadlocks are automatically detected and killed by SQL Server, they are often hard to troubleshoot. SQL Server Profiler provides the ability to trace deadlocks and graphically represent the sequence of events that led to the deadlock.

Chapter 10 describes how to use the SQL Server Profiler to gather pertinent SQL Server data and how to use the profile traces to troubleshoot and optimize SQL Server performance.

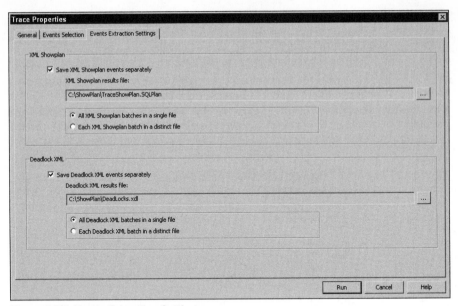

Figure 3-35: Events Extraction Settings

Database Engine Tuning Advisor

The Database Tuning Advisor (DTA) can analyze SQL Server scripts or SQL Server Profiler traces to evaluate the effective use of indexes. It can also be used to get recommendations for building new indexes, indexed views, or for creating physical table partitions.

Chapter 10 describes how to use the DTA to help optimize SQL Server databases, so this section is limited to describing the tool and its features.

When the DTA is started, it prompts for a server to connect to, and then automatically creates a new session. The session is displayed in two tabs: a General tab and a Tuning Options tab.

General Tab

The General tab (see Figure 3-36) is used to define the session name, the workload for analysis, and the database(s) to tune.

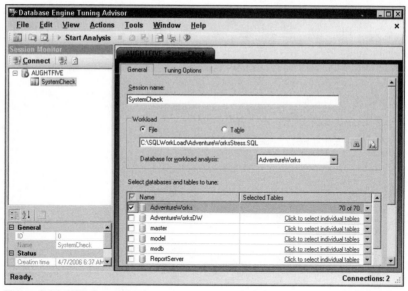

Figure 3-36: DTA General tab

Following are some options found under this tab:

❑   *Session name* — By default, the session name is the name of the logged-on user combined with the current date and time, but it can be changed to a more descriptive name.

❑   *Workload* — The Workload section provides the ability to retrieve trace information from either a file or a table. The table designated must have been previously created by a SQL Server Profiler trace, and the table must be located on the same server the DTA is running on. The file can be a SQL script, a Profiler trace (.trc) file, or a Profiler trace saved as XML.

❑   *Database for workload analysis* — This option just sets the initial connection information for the DTA.

❑   *Select databases and tables to tune* — In this section, you can designate the database or databases to be tuned. Keep in mind that the more objects chosen to monitor, the bigger performance impact on the server being monitored. The DTA doesn't actually rerun all the activity from the trace, but it does retrieve a great deal of metadata about the objects contained in the workload, along with any available statistics. This activity alone generates a lot of server activity. Both SQL Server Profiler and DTA activity should be as specific as possible for performance reasons, and the fact that the more specific the monitoring is, the better the results will be. Another reason for being specific about choosing the right tables to tune is that if the DTA sees no activity for a table that was selected for monitoring, it will recommend dropping any indexes on that table not associated with a constraint.

Tuning Options Tab

The Tuning Options tab (see Figure 3-37) contains the controls used to configure how the DTA analyzes the workload and what kind of recommendations it will return. At the bottom of the tab is a description box that both describes the individual options and provides feedback for incompatible settings.

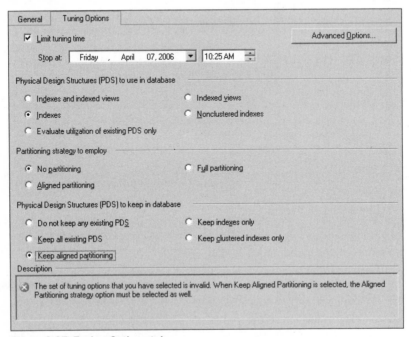

Figure 3-37: Tuning Options tab

❑ *Limit tuning time*—Large workloads can take a very long time to fully analyze, and can be very expensive in CPU and Database Engine resources. Limiting the amount of time the DTA spends analyzing the workload will cause it to return any recommendations generated with the amount of workload it was able to analyze in the time allocated. For the best results, the DTA should be allowed unlimited time, so this option should be cleared. Once analysis has started, it can be stopped by clicking the Stop Analysis button on the DTA toolbar.

❑ *Physical Design Structures (PDS) to use in database*—This option group allows the configuration of the type of PDS recommendations the DTA will return. Options include the returning recommendations for the creation of all indexes and indexed views, indexes only, nonclustered indexes only, and indexed views only. There is also an option for the DTA to only evaluate the effectiveness of current PDS structures, but not recommend the creation of additional structures.

❑ *Partitioning strategy to employ*—This option group is used to configure the type of physical table partitioning to employ: no partitioning, full partitioning, and aligned partitioning. Physical partitioning is described in Chapter 4.

❑ *Physical Design Structures (PDS) to keep in database*—When the DTA analyzes workloads, if it determines the PDS structure is not beneficial, it will recommend dropping the structure from the database. This option group is used to configure what PDS structures the DTA will not recommend dropping. The DTA can be configured to recommend dropping any non-beneficial PDS structure, to keep indexes only, to not recommend dropping any PDS, to keep clustered indexes only, and to keep any aligned partitioning structure.

❑ *Advanced Options* — The Advanced Options dialog is used to configure the maximum amount of disk space to use for recommendations, the maximum amount of table columns to include per individual index, and online indexing recommendations.

SQL Server Configuration Manager

The SQL Server Configuration Manager is a Microsoft Management Console (MMC) snap-in and is used to manage all the services and protocols used by an instance of SQL Server. It combines the functionality of SQL Server 2000's Service Manager, Client Network Utility, and Server Network Utility. Each instance of SQL Server is divided into three nodes:

❑ *SQL Server 2005 Services* — The Services node offers the same functionality as the Services applet in the Administrative tools set. However, because it only shows SQL Server services, it is much easier to both control and monitor the status of SQL Server 2005 services.

❑ *SQL Server 2005 Network Configuration* — The Network Configuration node displays and enables the configuration of all the available server protocols. The protocols available for use with SQL Server 2005 are Shared Memory, Named Pipes, TCP/IP, and Virtual Interface Adapter (VIA).

❑ *SQL Native Client Configuration* — The SQL Native Client Configuration node displays and enables the configuration of the client protocols used to connect to an instance of SQL Server 2005. The configurations only affect the computer that the Configuration Manager is running on. In addition to protocol configuration, the Native Client Configuration node enables the configuration of server aliases.

Reporting Services Configuration Manager

In SQL Server 2000 Reporting Services, changing the SMTP server or the Reporting Services database server was a tedious exercise of manually configuring XML configuration files. SQL Server 2005 drastically improves this error-prone method by providing a graphic interface for complete control and modification of the Reporting Services installation.

The Reporting Services Configuration Manager provides an intuitive interface that shows the status of each Reporting Services area. Each area is shown as Configured, Not Configured, Optional Configuration, or Recommended Configuration (see Figure 3-38).

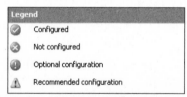

Figure 3-38: Reporting Services Configuration Manager interface

For a thorough discussion of SQL Server 2005 Reporting Services check out Professional SQL Server Reporting Services, Second Edition *(Indianapolis: Wiley, 2006).*

Each has its own configuration areas, including the following:

❑ *Server Status* — The Service Status area allows you to monitor the status, and stop and start the Reporting Services service. Although this area is called Server Status, it is really only the status of the Reporting Services service.

❑ *Report Server Virtual Directory* — The Report Server Virtual Directory configuration area enables the viewing or changing of the virtual directory on the Internet Information Server (IIS) that is used to display reports to users. The default virtual directory name is ReportServer, which may not be the most intuitive name to use, especially since the default directory for the administrative interface is Reports. The default names can be a bit strange and so, when you install and configure Reporting Services, you should typically name the Report Server Virtual Directory, which hosts the reports accessed by users, Reports and the administrative virtual directory ReportManager.

❑ *Report Manager Virtual Directory* — This area is where the virtual directory for the administrative interface, Report Manager, is viewed or configured. As described previously, the default name of Reports for the Report Manager is less than intuitive, because it is not really where the reports are viewed from; it is where the reports are configured.

❑ *Windows Service Identity* — This area is used to configure which account the Reporting Service runs under. If Reporting Services is installed on Windows Server 2003, the recommended configuration is using the built-in Network Service. In other installations, the use of a domain account is recommended. Local system and local service accounts will not work very well, unless SQL Server and Reporting Services are installed on the same computer.

❑ *Web Service Identity* — This area is used to configure the account used by the Reporting Service Web service. IIS 5 is automatically configured to use the ASP .NET machine account. IIS 6 installations can be configured to use a specific application pool.

❑ *Database Setup* — The Database Setup area is used to create or configure SQL Server 2005 Report Server databases. It can also be used to upgrade SQL Server 2000 Report Server databases. The Report Server databases provide storage of report definitions, report connections, and intermediately rendered reports.

❑ *Encryption Keys* — During the installation of Reporting Services, the installation program automatically generates a symmetric key that is used to encrypt security credentials stored in the Report Server database. To preserve access to this encrypted information, it is critical to back up and restore the key during certain Report Server maintenance procedures. For example, if the database is moved to a different server or the service accounts are changed, the key will have to be restored to preserve access to the encrypted information. The Encryption Keys configuration area provides an easy-to-use graphical interface to back up and restore the keys. It also provides the ability to delete all encrypted content, in which case all the stored security credentials would have to be re-entered. In the past, this functionality was provided only through the RSKEYMGMT command-line utility, which is still available.

❑ *Initialization* — The Initialization tool is used to generate the symmetric key used by the Web service to access and store encrypted data in the Report Server database. When setting up a load-balancing environment with multiple Web servers accessing a single Report Server, each additional Web server will need to be initialized.

❑ *Email Settings* — The SMTP Server settings are very straightforward and simple. However, using the Reporting Services Configuration tool, you can only specify the SMTP server to use and the sender's address. Additional configuration to the email settings must be done manually by editing the Report Server configuration file.

❑ *Execution Account* — The Execution Account is used when a report needs resources that are not locally available (such as a graphic stored on a remote server). It can also be used to connect to resources that do not require credentials.

Command-Line Tools

SQL Server 2005 comes with plenty of great graphical tools to accomplish almost everything you could ever need to do, but there also comes a time when a simple command-line tool is the best tool for the job. The two tools used most frequently are SQLCMD and BCP, but there are many more. This section describes just the BCP and SQLCMD utilities, because they are the ones that most DBAs use on a regular basis. For more information about all the command-line tools supported by SQL Server 2005 check out SQL Server Books Online under the topic "Command Prompt Utilities."

SQLCMD

The SQLCMD utility replaces OSQL as the utility used to execute Transact-SQL statements, Stored Procedures, and SQL script files from the command prompt. OSQL is still available for backwards compatibility, but SQLCMD is a more full-featured tool. SQLCMD utilizes OLE DB to connect to SQL Server and execute Transact-SQL batches.

The SQLCMD utility includes the ability to use variables, connect to servers dynamically, query server information, and pass error information back to the calling environment. Access to the Dedicated Administrator Connection (DAC) is also provided by the SQLCMD utility. The DAC is a special diagnostic connection that can be used by the DBA to connect to a SQL Server when all other connection types fail to diagnose and correct server problems.

SQLCMD supports several arguments that change the way it behaves and connects to an instance of SQL Server. An abbreviated list is included in the following table. For a complete list of the argument options, consult SQL Server Books Online under the topic "SQLCMD Utility." SQLCMD command line arguments are case-sensitive.

Argument	Description
-S	Specifies the SQL Server Instance name for SQLCMD to connect to.
-E	Configures SQLCMD to use a trusted connection.
-U	Specifies a user name to use when connecting with a SQL Server login.
-P	Specifies the password to use when connecting with a SQL Server login.
-i	Specifies the Transact-SQL script input file to run.

Table continued on following page

89

Argument	Description
-o	Specifies the output text file to return the results of a SQLCMD execution.
-v	Specifies the parameter(s) to pass to a SQLCMD script execution.
-A	Designates the SQLCMD connection as a DAC

The SQLCMD utility is typically used to execute saved Transact-SQL scripts in batch processes. This functionality is further enhanced by the ability of SQLCMD to accept scripting parameters. The following code is an example of a SQLCMD script that accepts a parameter called DBName to back up a designated database to a file named DatabasenameDB-Month-Year-Day.BAK to the C:\SQLBackups folder:

```
DECLARE @BackupDest AS varchar(255)
SET @BackupDest = 'C:\SQLBackups\'
+ '$(DBName)'
+ 'DB-'
+ DATENAME(m,GETDATE())
+ '-'
+ DATENAME(dd,GETDATE())
+ '-'
+ DATENAME(yy,GETDATE())
+ '.BAK'
BACKUP DATABASE $(DBName)
TO DISK = @BackupDest
```

If the preceding script is saved to a file called BackupDBs.SQL in the C:\SQLBackups folder, it could be executed to back up the Master database on a server called AughtFive using Windows authentication with the following command line:

```
SQLCMD -E -S AughtFive -i C:\SQLBackups\BackupDBs.SQL -v DBName="Master"
```

SQL Server Management Studio makes the creation of SQLCMD scripts even easier with its SQLCMD Mode. The BackupDBs.SQL script can be written and tested with Management Studio by selecting SQL-CMD Mode on the SQL Editor toolbar. However, to fully test it in the Query Editor, the following command must be inserted in the beginning of the script:

```
:SETVAR DBName="Master"
```

The SETVAR command can also be used in the execution of SQLCMD from the command line, but it usually makes more sense to use the -v variable argument.

Multiple variables can be set with the SETVAR command, as well as passed in to a SQLCMD script with the -v argument. The following example shows how to use multiple SETVAR commands:

```
USE AdventureWorks
GO
:SETVAR ColumnName "LastName"
:SETVAR TableName "Person.Contact"

SELECT $(ColumnName)
FROM $(TableName)
```

If the preceding example is saved to a file called `GetContacts.SQL` with the `SETVAR` commands omitted, it would look like the following example:

```
USE AdventureWorks
GO

SELECT $(ColumnName)
FROM $(TableName)
```

This script could be executed with the SQLCMD utility using the following command line:

```
SQLCMD -E -S AughtFive -i C:\GetContacts.SQL -v ColumnName="LastName" TableName =
"Person.Contact"
```

Dedicated Administrator Connection (DAC)

SQLCMD is particularly useful for creating batch scripting jobs for administrative purposes. However, as an emergency utility to diagnose and hopefully correct server problems, it has no peer. With the -A argument, the SQLCMD utilizes an exclusive connection to SQL Server. If no other connection is possible, the SQLCMD -A command is the last and best hope for diagnosing server problems and preventing data loss. By default, only local DACs are allowed because the DAC components only listen on the loopback connection. However, remote DACs can be enabled using the SQL Server Surface Area Configuration Tool, or the `sp_configure` stored procedure by changing the `'remote admin connections'` option to `true` as the following code illustrates:

```
sp_configure 'remote admin connections', 1
RECONFIGURE
```

BCP

The BCP utility is mainly used to import flat-file data into a SQL Server table, export a table out to a flat file, or export the results of a Transact-SQL query to a flat file. In addition, it can be used to create format files that are used in the import and export operations.

The syntax of the BCP utility is as follows:

```
usage: bcp {dbtable | query} {in | out | queryout | format} datafile
  [-m maxerrors]    [-f formatfile]  [-e errfile]   [-F firstrow]    [-L lastrow]
  [-b batchsize]    [-n native type] [-c character type] [-w wide character type]
  [-N keep non-text native] [-V file format version] [-q quoted identifier]
  [-C code page specifier] [-t field terminator] [-r row terminator] [-i inputfile]
  [-o outfile]     [-a packetsize]  [-S server name] [-U username]   [-P password]
  [-T trusted connection] [-v version] [-R regional enable] [-k keep null values]
  [-E keep identity values] [-h "load hints"] [-x generate xml format file]
```

BCP format files can be created in two separate formats: XML and non-XML. These files can then be referenced in the import and export of data. The BCP is well-documented in Books Online, but the following examples show the most common usage of BCP.

Non-XML Format File Example

This example shows how to begin an interactive BCP session to create a non-XML format file based on an existing table. The BCP utility will prompt for a column data type, a prefix length, and a field delimiter. It is usually best to accept the defaults provided for the data type and the prefix length, because these values are determined by the table being referenced in the BCP command. The delimiter value can be any character, but defaults to "None."

The following command uses BCP to create a format file based on the CreditCard table in the AdventureWorks database and Sales schema of the local default instance of SQL Server:

```
BCP AdventureWorks.Sales.CreditCard format nul -T -f C:\BCP\CreditCard.fmt
```

It is often better to provide the –S switch and specify the server name. The format argument tells BCP that the desired output is a format file. The absence of an –x switch specifies that the output file is not XML. The nul argument sends a NULL as the username, because the –T switch was used indicating that BCP should use a Windows trusted connection. If –T is not used, the –U username switch is required followed by the –P password switch. If nul is not used, BCP will fail with the error that a username was not provided.

The result of the preceding command, accepting the defaults for the field data type and prefix length, but entering a comma as the field delimiter, is as follows:

```
9.0
6
1   SQLINT       0   4    ","   1   CreditCardID       ""
2   SQLNCHAR     2   100  ","   2   CardType           SQL_Latin1_General_CP1_CI_AS
3   SQLNCHAR     2   50   ","   3   CardNumber         SQL_Latin1_General_CP1_CI_AS
4   SQLTINYINT   0   1    ","   4   ExpMonth           ""
5   SQLSMALLINT  0   2    ","   5   ExpYear            ""
6   SQLDATETIME  0   8    ","   6   ModifiedDate       ""
```

The 9.0 at the top of the results designates the version of BCP. 9.0 is SQL Server 2005, 8.0 would be SQL Server 2000. The number 6 under the 9.0 specifies how many columns are in the file. Following the column number is the SQL Server data type of the column, followed by the number of bytes needed by the prefix length. The prefix length of a column depends on the maximum number of bytes, whether the column supports NULLs, and the storage type.

If the BCP command is supplied a data format argument (–c or –n), it will output a format file with all columns mapped to the supplied format without any interaction.

XML Format File Example

This example shows how to use the BCP command to generate an XML format file:

```
BCP AdventureWorks.Sales.CreditCard format nul -x -T -f C:\BCP\CreditCard.xml
```

As you can see, the syntax is identical, except that the –x switch is used to specify an XML output. The result is as follows:

```
<?xml version="1.0"?>
<BCPFORMAT xmlns="http://schemas.microsoft.com/sqlserver/2004/bulkload/format"
xmlns:xsi="http://www.w3.org/2001/XMLSchema-instance">
 <RECORD>
  <FIELD ID="1" xsi:type="NativeFixed" LENGTH="4"/>
  <FIELD ID="2" xsi:type="NCharPrefix" PREFIX_LENGTH="2" MAX_LENGTH="100"
COLLATION="SQL_Latin1_General_CP1_CI_AS"/>
  <FIELD ID="3" xsi:type="NCharPrefix" PREFIX_LENGTH="2" MAX_LENGTH="50"
COLLATION="SQL_Latin1_General_CP1_CI_AS"/>
  <FIELD ID="4" xsi:type="NativeFixed" LENGTH="1"/>
  <FIELD ID="5" xsi:type="NativeFixed" LENGTH="2"/>
  <FIELD ID="6" xsi:type="NativeFixed" LENGTH="8"/>
 </RECORD>
 <ROW>
  <COLUMN SOURCE="1" NAME="CreditCardID" xsi:type="SQLINT"/>
  <COLUMN SOURCE="2" NAME="CardType" xsi:type="SQLNVARCHAR"/>
  <COLUMN SOURCE="3" NAME="CardNumber" xsi:type="SQLNVARCHAR"/>
  <COLUMN SOURCE="4" NAME="ExpMonth" xsi:type="SQLTINYINT"/>
  <COLUMN SOURCE="5" NAME="ExpYear" xsi:type="SQLSMALLINT"/>
  <COLUMN SOURCE="6" NAME="ModifiedDate" xsi:type="SQLDATETIME"/>
 </ROW>
</BCPFORMAT>
```

Export a Table to a Flat File Example

Once the format file is created, it can be used to control data export and import operations. To export data to a delimited flat file using the XML format file created in the preceding example, execute the following code:

```
BCP AdventureWorks.Sales.CreditCard OUT C:\BCP\CreditCard.dat -T -f
C:\BCP\CreditCard.XML
```

Import Flat File Example with a Format File

To test a BCP import, first create a copy of the CreditCard table with the following script:

```
USE AdventureWorks
GO
SELECT * INTO Sales.CreditCard2
FROM Sales.CreditCard
TRUNCATE TABLE Sales.CreditCard2
```

Once the destination table exists, the flat file and XML format file can be utilized to import the data to the new CreditCard2 table with the following code:

```
BCP AdventureWorks.Sales.CreditCard2 IN C:\BCP\CreditCard.dat -T -f
C:\BCP\CreditCard.xml
```

Summary

This chapter described the tools most often used by the DBA. A few tools were either briefly mentioned or omitted, because they are used on a much less frequent basis by database and business intelligence developers and not necessarily database administrators. At this point, you should have a good idea about the tools you will use on a daily basis to manage SQL Server 2005.

The biggest and best of these tools is the SQL Server Management Studio. In the past, it was always a question on whether to use Enterprise Manager or Query Analyzer. Do you write code or use the graphical interface? Now the question is pretty moot, especially because the functionality of both tools has been encapsulated in the Management Studio. However, because Management Studio's graphical interface can be used to create almost any script the question now becomes, "Do you use the graphical tools to write the code, or do you write the code yourself?" Admittedly, there are still some tasks that can only be accomplished by writing the code yourself, so a thorough knowledge of Transact-SQL is still imperative for the DBA, but that is the topic of a different book.

In the coming chapters, you will be using the tools described in the preceding pages to learn the fine art of administering a SQL Server 2005 database. It's going to be fun, so let's get started!

Chapter 4 describes how SQL Server stores its data physically and logically. It describes the physical architecture of data and log files, as well as how SQL Server manages these files. Understanding how SQL Server stores and accesses data will be invaluable in the administration and troubleshooting of any SQL Server problem that may occur.

SQL Server 2005
Storage Architecture

I had just spent the better part of the day describing the storage architecture to a group of about 30 new database administrators when one of them approached me while the class was on break and asked me pointedly, "Why do I need to know this stuff? I mean, who cares how SQL Server stores data as long as it does it?" They were valid questions. After all, I have no idea how the fuel injection system on my car works, but I drive it anyway. The key difference is that when my car needs service, I take it to a mechanic. If your database doesn't work, who are you going to take it to? Understanding the mechanics of the SQL Server storage will help you make informed decisions on where the data is stored, how the data is indexed, and how to troubleshoot an ailing database.

Retrieving information about data storage requires digging into the inner storage structures of SQL Server. For SQL Server 2005, Microsoft has made some fairly dramatic changes to how metadata and system information is stored and accessed. Understanding these changes, or if you are brand new to SQL Server with this release, just the overall storage architecture is critical to understanding how SQL Server accesses and retrieves data.

For years, SQL Server database administrators have grown accustomed to having unrestricted access to system objects. This ability gave the DBA incredible power for both good and for evil. For example, a database administrator could turn on ad hoc updates to the system tables and then modify any value, including password hashes. This ability was certainly useful for correcting some system errors; more damage was just as likely, however.

In the past, Microsoft strongly recommended that system objects not be accessed directly, while sometimes offering solutions to database problems that required directly updating system tables. This apparent contradiction is now at an end. Unless Microsoft (or a mysterious third party) releases some hidden secret handshake that unlocks system objects to modification, they are completely inaccessible for updates by the DBA. Read-only access to the system tables has been restricted and can only be accomplished through the Dedicated Administrator Connection (DAC), and even that allowance is made with the disclaimer *"Access to system base tables by using DAC is designed only for Microsoft personnel, and it is not a supported customer scenario."*

To Microsoft's credit, they certainly did their homework. They researched the primary reasons DBAs performed ad hoc updates to system tables, and provided mechanisms to perform those actions in a controlled manner without compromising the integrity of the system catalog.

In this chapter, you learn how SQL Server 2005 stores and organizes data. This knowledge will be very helpful in any effort to optimize and tune SQL Server, as well as troubleshoot performance issues.

The Resource Database

A big reason for the locking away of the system objects is because they all have a common source now called the Resource database. The Resource database is the physical repository for all system objects and is inaccessible during normal operations of SQL Server. Although the system objects are physically stored in the Resource database, they are logically presented as the SYS schema in each database. Microsoft strongly recommends that the Resource database be left alone, but it can be accessed if SQL Server is started in single-user mode. Even this access, however, is read-only, as is access to any objects in the SYS schema. Any attempt to modify a system object will result in an error, even if ad hoc updates to the system catalog is enabled.

Persisting all the system objects in the Resource database allows for rapid deployment of service packs and upgrades to SQL Server 2005. When installing a service pack, the process is simply one of replacing the Resource database with a new version and executing whatever modifications are required to the operating system objects. This dramatically reduces the amount of time it takes to update SQL Server.

Even though the Resource database isn't accessible during normal SQL Server operations, information about the database can be retrieved using system functions and global variables. The following code returns the build number of the Resource database:

```
SELECT SERVERPROPERTY('ResourceVersion')
```

To return the date and time the Resource database was last updated, the following code can be executed:

```
SELECT SERVERPROPERTY('ResourceLastUpdateDateTime')
```

The SYS Schema

As previously mentioned the system objects stored in the Resource database logically appear in the SYS schema of each database. The SYS schema contains views that can be utilized by the DBA to retrieve information about the objects in a database. Most (but not all) of the information the DBA typically needs access to is available through the use of system functions and stored procedures that return metadata from the system objects. Sometimes, however, it is beneficial to retrieve the metadata directly from the system objects. The views in the SYS schema are provided for this reason.

If you have ever used SQL Server 2000 system tables, you will find that almost all of the old system table names have been preserved, but now are persisted as views. However, these views are only provided for backward compatibility. They do not expose any SQL Server 2005–specific metadata. Any future operations should be based on the new SQL Server 2005 system views.

A word of caution is needed here. As a general rule, any scripts or applications created to consume system metadata directly from system objects should be built with the knowledge that they may not work in future releases of SQL Server. There is nothing really new about this. Microsoft has cautioned against formalizing processes that directly access system objects for years and has warned that the system objects could be altered by future upgrades and service packs.

Dynamic Views and Functions

In addition to the traditional system objects that can be used to view system metadata, new dynamic views and functions in the SYS schema expose some very useful information about SQL Server processes and database activity. The dynamic views and functions are grouped into the following functional categories:

- ❑   Common Language Run-time Related Dynamic Management Views
- ❑   I/O Related Dynamic Management Views and Functions
- ❑   Database Mirroring Related Dynamic Management Views
- ❑   Query Notifications Related Dynamic Management Views
- ❑   Database Related Dynamic Management Views
- ❑   Replication Related Dynamic Management Views
- ❑   Execution Related Dynamic Management Views and Functions
- ❑   Service Broker Related Dynamic Management Views
- ❑   Full-Text Search Related Dynamic Management Views
- ❑   SQL Server Operating System Related Dynamic Management Views
- ❑   Index Related Dynamic Management Views and Functions
- ❑   Transaction Related Dynamic Management Views and Functions

Many of the new dynamic views and functions replace previous system-stored procedures and Database Consistency Checker (DBCC) commands. Most of the old stored procedures and DBCC commands still exist, but they are provided only for backwards compatibility and do not expose new SQL Server 2005 objects and processes. The new views and functions provide much more detailed information and return relational result sets that can be used with ease in custom monitoring applications.

In later chapters, many (but by no means all) of the views and functions are used and explained in the context of describing database maintenance and monitoring tasks. For a complete description of each system view and function, check out SQL Server Books Online under the topic "Dynamic Views and Functions."

SQL Server Database Physical Structure

SQL Server stores all of its data in files. These files are divided up into substructures that SQL Server manages to maintain the integrity, structure, and logical organization of the data contained with them. Although this book is meant to be a beginner's guide to SQL Server 2005 database administration, it is still very important for the new DBA to understand such advanced topics as physical database architecture. Knowing how SQL Server stores and maintains data will give you a better understanding of how changes to the data affect performance, and will allow you to more effectively diagnose database problems.

Physical Storage Data Types

Before getting started on the physical storage of data, it is important to have a good understanding about the types of data that SQL Server stores. SQL Server 2005 Books Online groups data types into the following seven functional groups:

❑ Exact numerics

❑ Approximate numerics

❑ Date and time

❑ Character strings

❑ Unicode character strings

❑ Binary strings

❑ Other data types

Though the functional grouping of data types makes perfect sense when looking at data types from a usability viewpoint, what is relevant to this discussion is how the data is stored. SQL Server data types can essentially be grouped into three storage type groups: Fixed-length data types, variable-length data types, and Large Object data types. In certain circumstances, Large Object data types can also act like variable-length types, which is explained later. The data types described in this section are only data types that can be assigned table column data types for the physical storage of the associated data. This precludes the cursor and table data types that are described later in this chapter.

Fixed-Length Data Types

Fixed-length data types are exactly that—fixed. The amount of space used to store them in memory or on disk does not change. Following is a list of fixed-length data types:

❑ bit—The bit is an integer data type that supports a value of 0 or 1. Contrary to what its name implies, the bit data type actually consumes a byte of space for 8 or less bit data types used.

❑ tinyint—The tinyint data type uses 1 byte of storage space to store an unsigned integer value between 0 and 255.

❑ smallint—The smallint data type uses 2 bytes of storage space to store a signed integer between –32,768 and 32,767.

❑ int—The int data type uses 4 bytes of storage space to store a signed integer between –2,147,483,648 and 2,147,483,647.

❑ bigint—The bigint data type uses 8 bytes of storage to store a signed integer between –9,223,372,036,854,775,808 and 9,223,372,036,854,775,807.

❑ decimal and numeric—The decimal and numeric data types are functionally identical. For clarity, you should typically use decimal, because it is more descriptive of the data it is used to store. The decimal data type can be set to consume different fixed amounts of storage space based on how it is used. When using the decimal data type you have the option of specifying the precision (p) and scale (s) of the data to be stored. This is expressed by decimal(p,s). The precision and scale are specified with positive integer values between 0 and 38. However, the scale value must be less than or equal to the precision value, and can only be specified if a precision value is specified. Storage space is dependent on the value of precision, as described in the following table.

Precision	Storage Bytes
1–9	5
10–19	9
20–28	13
29–38	17

❑ smallmoney — The smallmoney data type stores monetary values between –214,748.3648 and 214,748.3647. The smallmoney data type is accurate to a ten-thousandth of whatever currency unit is being stored and consumes 4 bytes of space.

❑ money — The money data type stores monetary values between –922,337,203,685,477.5808 and 922,337,203,685,477.5807. The money data type is accurate to a ten-thousandth of whatever currency unit is being stored and consumes 8 bytes of space.

❑ real — The real data type is a floating-point number, so its value is approximate. The values supported by real are negative numbers between –3.40E+38 and –1.18E-38, 0 and positive numbers between 1.18E-38 and 3.40E+38. The real data type consumes 4 bytes of space.

❑ float — The float data type is a floating-point number, so its value is also approximate. The range of values supported by float and the resultant storage space required is dependent on the specified precision of the float. The precision is expressed as float(n), where (n) is the number of bits used to store the mantissa of the number in scientific notation. Allowable precision values are between 1 and 53. Precision values from 1 to 24 require 4 bytes of storage space, and precision values of 25 to 53 require 8 bytes of storage space. With the default precision of 53, the range of values supported by float are negative numbers between –1.79E+308 and –2.23E-308, 0, and positive numbers between 2.23E-308 and 1.79E+308.

❑ smalldatetime — The smalldatetime data type is used to store dates between January 1, 1900 and June 6, 2079. It is accurate to the minute and consumes 4 bytes of space. Internally, SQL Server stores smalldatetime data as a pair of 2-byte integers. The first 2 bytes are used to store the number of days since January 1, 1900, and the second 2 bytes are used to store the number of minutes since midnight.

❑ datetime — The datetime data type is used to store dates between January 1, 1753, and December 31, 9999. It is accurate to 3.33 milliseconds and consumes 8 bytes of space. Internally SQL Server stores datetime data as a pair of 4-byte integers. The first 4 bytes are used to store the number of days since January 1, 1753, and the second 4 bytes are used to store the number of milliseconds (rounded to 3.33) since midnight.

❑ char — The char data type is used to store a fixed amount of non-Unicode data between 1 and 8,000 characters, and is expressed as char(n), where (n) is the number of characters to store. Each character requires 1 byte of storage space.

❑ nchar — The nchar data type is used to store a fixed amount of Unicode data between 1 and 4,000 characters, and is expressed as char(n), where (n) is the number of characters to store. Each character requires 2 bytes of storage space. Unicode types are appropriate if multiple languages must be supported.

❑   binary — The binary data type is used to store a fixed amount of binary data between 1 and 8,000 bytes, and is expressed as binary(n), where (n) is the number of binary bytes to store.

❑   rowversion or timestamp — rowversion is the data type synonym for timestamp and consumes 8 bytes of storage space. rowversion should be specified instead of timestamp whenever possible, because it more accurately reflects the true nature of the data type. The timestamp data type has nothing to do with time. It is actually an 8-byte binary string that is used to define a versioning value to a row. When a timestamp or its synonym rowversion is specified as a table column's data type, every insert or update to that table will cause a new value to be generated by SQL Server and placed in the appropriate field.

❑   uniqueidentifier — The uniqueidentifier data type is stored as a 16-byte binary string represented by 32 hexadecimal characters. uniqueidentifiers can be generated by SQL Server with the NEWID() function or existing uniqueidentifiers inserted and stored in a uniqueidentifer column.

Variable-Length and Large Object Data Types

Variable-length data types are used when the exact amount of space required by data cannot be predicted (such as a column that holds a last name of a person). The varchar, nvarchar, and varbinary data types fall into this category.

However, when the (MAX) option is specified for the length of the character or binary string, these variable data types can be treated as Large Object data types. The primary difference is in how the data is stored. Large Object data is stored outside the data row in separate physical structures by default, whereas variable-length data is stored in the data row.

This is explained in the following descriptions:

❑   varchar — The varchar data type is used to store a variable amount of non-Unicode data between 1 and 8,000 characters, and is expressed as varchar(n), where (n) is the maximum number of characters to store. Each character requires 1 byte of storage space. The actual storage space used by a varchar is the value of (n) plus 2 bytes. The varchar data type also supports an optional (MAX) length specification. When using varchar(MAX), the maximum amount of characters supported is 2,147,483,647 consuming up to 2GB of storage space. When the (MAX) option is specified, SQL Server will store the varchar data in the data row, unless the amount of data exceeds 8,000 bytes, or doing so would exceed the maximum row size of 8,060 bytes. In these cases, SQL Server will move the varchar data out of the row and into a separate Large Object storage space (see the section "Data Pages" later in this chapter).

❑   nvarchar — The nvarchar data type is identical to the varchar data type, except it is used to store Unicode data. Each Unicode character requires 2 bytes of storage, resulting in the maximum number of characters supported being 1,073,741,824.

❑   varbinary — The varbinary data type is also very similar to the varchar data type, except that it is used to store binary data and not character data. Other than that, the storage and use of the (MAX) option works identically.

❑   text — The text data type is a Large Object data type, and is very similar to the varchar(MAX) data type in that it can also be used to store up to 2GB of character data. The primary difference is that text data is stored out of the data row by default, and the text data type cannot be passed as a parameter in SQL Server functions, stored procedures, or triggers.

❑ ntext — The ntext data type is identical to the text data type, except that it is used to store Unicode data. As a result, the 2GB of Unicode character data represents only 1,073,741,824 characters.

❑ image — The image data type is a Large Object data type and is very similar to the varbinary(MAX) data type. It can also be used to store up to 2GB of binary data, but is always stored outside the data row in separate Large Object data pages.

❑ XML — The XML data type is a Large Object type that is used to store XML (Extensible Markup Language) in its native format. Up to 2GB of XML data can be stored per data row.

❑ sql_variant — A sql_variant data type can be utilized in objects when the actual data type of a value is unknown. The sql_variant data type can be used to store almost any value that consumes less than 8,000 bytes. The type of data that is incompatible with the sql_variant type is text, ntext, image, timestamp, cursor, varchar(MAX), and nvarchar(MAX).

In-Row Data

By utilizing the 'large value types out of row' table option, the DBA can specify that all of the varchar(MAX), nvarchar(MAX), and varbinary(MAX) data is treated as Large Object data, and is stored outside the row in separate Large Object data pages. The option can be set to 'ON' or 'OFF', as shown here:

```
sp_tableoption 'tablename', 'large value types out of row', 'ON'

sp_tableoption 'tablename', 'large value types out of row', 'OFF'
```

Likewise, if the DBA wants to keep text or ntext data in the row unless it exceeds a specified size, the table option 'text in row' can be specified. This option allows the DBA to specify a range of data to keep in the row. The supported range is from 24 to 7,000 bytes. Instead of specifying a limit, the word 'ON' can be passed resulting in a default value of 256 bytes. To turn the option off, the word 'OFF' is passed:

```
sp_tableoption 'tablename', 'text in row', 'number of bytes'

sp_tableoption 'tablename', 'text in row', 'ON'

sp_tableoption 'tablename', 'text in row', 'OFF'
```

Other Data Types

As previously noted, SQL Server 2005 has three data types that are not used to store data physically on the disk by being part of a table or index definition. The following data types are used in programming objects to manipulate data:

❑ table — The table data type is used to store a set of rows in memory. It is primarily used with Table-Valued Functions, but can be used in any programming object to return an organized result set that has most of the properties of an actual table. A table variable can be declared and instantiated with a set of columns, a specified primary key, check constraints, and a default constraint.

❑   cursor — Transact-SQL performs best with sets of data, but occasionally it is necessary to manipulate data one row at a time. The cursor data type is used for this type of requirement. A cursor holds a complete set of rows from a query and can then be manipulated to return single rows at a time. For a complete discussion on cursors and their uses, check out the book *Beginning Transact-SQL with SQL Server 2000 and 2005* (Indianapolis: Wiley, 2005).

SQL Server Database Files

SQL Server stores data in data files and transactional records in transaction log files. These files, when grouped together under a logical database name, *are the database.* A SQL Server database can have many data files and multiple transaction log files, although one transaction log file is usually sufficient.

When a database is first created, it will have one primary data file with the default file extension of .mdf. It can also optionally have secondary data files with the default extension of .ndf. These data files can be grouped together in a logical grouping called a *filegroup,* which is explained in Chapter 5. The database will also have, at a minimum, one transaction log file with the default extension of .ldf. The file extensions for SQL Server databases are not enforced, so you can use anything you want, but the default extensions are typically used because they readily identify the file's purpose. The following sections are limited to a description of the physical storage structure of the data and transaction log files. For a complete description of the database creation process and how files are created and used, see Chapter 5.

Data Files

The database master data file (.mdf), or primary data file, and any secondary data files (.ndf) that are part of the database, have identical structures. Both files are used to store data, as well as all the metadata that allows SQL Server to efficiently find, read, modify, and add data to the database. All the data from tables and indexes and the metadata that describes that data is organized in storage objects called *extents* and *pages.*

Extents

Extents are a SQL Server file storage structure that is 64KB in size. Extents are comprised of eight contiguous 8KB pages. There are two types of extents: mixed extents and uniform extents. *Mixed extents* contain pages from more than one object. For example, a mixed extent might contain data pages from Table A, an index page from indexes on Table B, and still more data pages from Table C. Because there are eight pages in an extent, it is possible for eight different objects to share an extent. *Uniform extents* contain eight contiguous pages that belong to the same object. The differences are illustrated in Figure 4-1.

When data is retrieved or written to disk during database operations, the extent is the basic structure for data retrieval. SQL Server always allocates space in 64KB increments. This maps very nicely to the way data is organized in memory and on a NT File System (NTFS) formatted partition. As previously noted, however, SQL Server can store pages from different objects in a single extent to maximize the efficiency of the storage process.

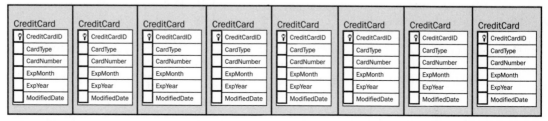

Mixed Extent

Uniform Extent

Figure 4-1: Mixed extents and uniform extents

Pages

Every data file begins with a mixed extent containing pages that are used to track information about the data file. The first page on the first extent of a data file contains a File Header page. This page contains descriptive information about the data file, such as its logical name, physical name, max size, growth increment, and filegroup membership.

All data and metadata in a SQL Server 2005 database are stored in pages. Unlike extents, pages always store data from the same object. This includes rows from tables, rows from indexes, and Large Object data. Pages are 8KB in size and are organized on 64KB extents, which are made up of eight contiguous 8KB pages. Every page has a 96-byte header that contains information about the page, such as the page number, the type of data stored on the page, the amount of free space available on the page, and what object owns the page. SQL Server contains several different types of pages that are used to both store data and to manage data.

Data Pages

Data pages contain data rows from tables. These rows cannot span pages. Because of the page header and row offset information, the maximum row size is limited to 8,060 bytes. Row sizes are determined by the number of columns in the row and the data type defined on each column. To maximize performance, table and index rows should be kept as narrow as possible. For example, if a single table row was 4,100 bytes in width, only one row could be stored on each data page leaving almost 4,000 bytes of unusable space. Resulting reads from a table with this structure would require 8KB of data retrieval for only 4,100 bytes of data. This is obviously very inefficient. Physical data page structure is illustrated in Figure 4-2.

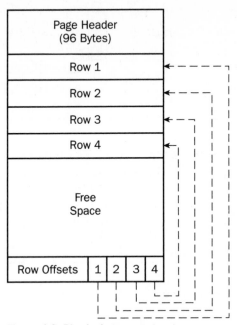

Figure 4-2: Physical storage structure

Each row-offset block consumes 2 bytes of space for every row stored on a page. Rows from tables are physically arranged differently than their logical definition in order to optimize storage space. When a row is stored on a data page, the row is identified with a 4-byte header, which uniquely identifies the row on the page, followed by the fixed-length data columns, a Null block, a variable block, and then all the variable data columns at the end of the physical row, as shown in Figure 4-3.

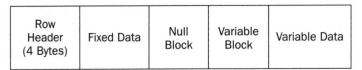

Figure 4-3: Header identifying a row

The *Null block* contains a 2-byte block that indicates how many columns in the row can contain nulls, followed by a bitmap that indicates whether the nullable column is null. The size of the null bitmap is equal to 1 bit per column, rounded up to the nearest byte. One to eight nullable columns require a 1-byte bitmap. Nine to 16 columns require a 2-byte bitmap and so on.

The *variable block*, like the Null block, contains 2 bytes that indicate how many variable-length columns are present, followed by a bitmap that indicates what the maximum length of each variable column is. Unlike the Null block, the variable column bitmap contains 2 bytes per column that points to the end of each variable-length column, so that all the variable data can be stored contiguously at the end of the row. If no columns are defined as variable length, the variable block is omitted.

Index Pages

Index pages contain rows from indexes. They have the same structure and limitations as data pages.

Text/Image Pages

When a column is defined with a Large Object data type, SQL Server places a 16-byte pointer in the actual data row and places the Large Object data on separate data pages. This data includes those defined as `text`, `image`, `varchar(MAX)`, `nvarchar(MAX)`, `varbinary(MAX)`, and `XML`.

Global Allocation Map (GAM) and Secondary Global Allocation Map (SGAM) Pages

The *GAM* and *SGAM pages* are allocation pages that manage extents on a file-by-file basis. The second page of every data file is a GAM page, and the third page of every data file is a SGAM page. SQL Server will add additional GAM and SGAM pages as necessary, because each GAM and SGAM page can track only 63,904 extents. The GAM and SGAM pages form a bitmap that indicates whether an extent is a uniform or mixed extent. The GAM and SGAM bitmap also indicates whether the extent is full, empty, or has free data pages.

Page Free Space (PFS) Pages

PFS pages record the status of each page, whether or not a page has been allocated, and the amount of free space on each page.

Index Allocation Map (IAM) Pages

The *IAM page* contains information about the extents that a table or index uses. The IAM page contains the location of the eight initial pages of an object, and a bitmap representing the extents that are in use for that object. Every IAM page can track up to 512,000 data pages. SQL Server utilizes the IAM and PFS pages to find and allocate new pages for data.

Bulk Changed Map (BCM) Pages

The *Bulk Changed Map pages* contain the location of extents that were modified by bulk operations since the last transaction log backup. Bulk operations include `UPDATETEXT`, `WRITETEXT`, `SELECT INTO`, `BULK INSERT`, and image operations. BCMap pages are used primarily for transaction log backup operations when the database is in `BULK-LOGGED` recovery mode (see Chapter 9 for a full explanation of the `BULK-LOGGED` recovery mode).

Differential Changed Map (DCM) Pages

The *Differential Changed Map pages* contain the identifier of any extent that has been modified since the last database backup. The DCM pages are used when performing differential backups.

Transaction Log

The purpose of the transaction log is to maintain a physical record of all transactions that have occurred on a SQL Server database during a specific interval. The specific interval depends on the database recovery mode.

In the default database configuration, the transaction log keeps a record of all database modifications and is never cleared unless it is backed up or explicitly truncated by a database administrator.

The transaction log is a binary file. It is not simply a traditional log file that can be opened and viewed with a log viewer or Notepad, so its contents are not readily available to the database administrator. There are a couple of third-party products that can be used by the database administrator to open and view the contents of the transaction log. These products can be used to audit database modifications, and also can be used to create scripts that will reverse the effects of an unwanted transaction.

The transaction log is maintained on disk as one or more physical files. In most cases, one transaction log file is sufficient, because any additional log files will not be used until the first is completely full and has reached its maximum size. Internally, the physical transaction log file is divided into multiple virtual logs. The number and size of the virtual log files that a physical file or files are divided into is configured dynamically by SQL Server and is not configurable. When SQL Server configures the transaction log internal structure, it tries to keep the number of virtual logs small.

To help SQL Server maintain a smaller number of virtual logs, the initial size of the transaction log should be set to accommodate all expected transactions that may occur between transaction log backups. If the log is configured to auto-grow, the growth increments should be fairly large to avoid small repetitive growths that will cause the creation of multiple small virtual logs.

Transactions

All data modifications occur within a transaction and are recorded in the transaction log. A *transaction* is a single unit of data operations that can be controlled so that either all the modifications in a transaction occur, or none occur. SQL Server has three ways of executing transactions: Implicit Transactions, Explicit Transactions, and Auto-Commit Transactions. Implicit and Auto-Commit Transactions are mutually exclusive.

Auto-Commit

By default SQL Server connections use *Auto-Commit Transactions*. Any INSERT, UPDATE, or DELETE statement executed alone or in a batch will automatically be applied to the database. An example of this type of activity is as follows:

```
USE AdventureWorks
GO
DECLARE @ContactID AS int, @CreditCardID as int

INSERT Person.Contact
(NameStyle,Title,FirstName,LastName,EmailAddress
,EmailPromotion,Phone,PasswordHash
,PasswordSalt,rowguid,ModifiedDate)
VALUES
(0,'Mr.','Fred','Flintstone','fredf@slategravel.com'
,2,'101-555-1212','F295DC2A87C7FD93151A2BC232BEAFF1133F95A2'
,'TVGHbhY=', NEWID(),GETDATE())

SET @ContactID = @@IDENTITY --Capture the auto incremented primary key value

INSERT Sales.CreditCard
```

```
(CardType, CardNumber, ExpMonth, ExpYear, ModifiedDate)
VALUES
('BedrockGold','01234567891012',12,2010,GETDATE())

SET @CreditCardID = @@IDENTITY --Capture the auto incremented primary key value

INSERT Sales.ContactCreditCard
(ContactID, CreditCardID, ModifiedDate)
VALUES
(@ContactID, @CreditCardID, GETDATE())
```

Each of the three modifications in this example are transactions. In Auto-Commit mode, they will be applied to the database independently of each other. If the first two inserts succeed, but the third fails, there will be no way to link the new credit card information to the new contact, and no way to roll back the changes to the Contact and CreditCard tables, short of performing another modification to delete one or both of the orphaned records.

Implicit

The ANSI standard for the Structured Query Language specifies that no modifications should be made to data unless explicitly committed. SQL Server supports this specification through a connection property called IMPLICIT_TRANSACTIONS. When IMPLICIT_TRANSACTIONS is set to ON, any data modification will implicitly begin a transaction, but will not close the transaction. The transaction will remain open until it is explicitly committed or rolled back. An example of this is as follows:

```
SET IMPLICIT_TRANSACTIONS ON

BEGIN TRY

  DECLARE @ContactID AS int, @CreditCardID as int

  INSERT Person.Contact
    (NameStyle,Title,FirstName,LastName,EmailAddress
    ,EmailPromotion,Phone,PasswordHash
    ,PasswordSalt,rowguid,ModifiedDate)
  VALUES
    (0,'Mr.','Fred','Flintstone','fredf@slategravel.com'
    ,2,'101-555-1212','F295DC2A87C7FD93151A2BC232BEAFF1133F95A2'
    ,'TVGHbhY=', NEWID(),GETDATE())

  SET @ContactID = @@IDENTITY --Capture the new primary key value

  INSERT Sales.CreditCard
    (CardType, CardNumber, ExpMonth, ExpYear, ModifiedDate)
  VALUES
    ('BedrockGold','01234567891012',12,2010,GETDATE())

  SET @CreditCardID = @@IDENTITY --Capture the new primary key value

  INSERT Sales.ContactCreditCard
    (ContactID, CreditCardID, ModifiedDate)
  VALUES
```

```
     (@ContactID, @CreditCardID, GETDATE())

  COMMIT TRANSACTION

END TRY

BEGIN CATCH

  ROLLBACK TRANSACTION

END CATCH
```

In this example, if any error occurs during data modification, the CATCH block will be called to roll back the transaction. If no errors occur, the transaction will be committed. In Auto-Commit mode this same logic would not work, because there was no implicit or explicit transaction to commit or roll back. Turning on IMPLICIT_TRANSACTIONS turns off Auto-Commit.

Explicit

An explicit transaction requires a BEGIN TRANSACTION to begin the transaction and an explicit COMMIT TRANSACTION or ROLLBACK TRANSACTION to close the transaction, as shown in the following example:

```
BEGIN TRANSACTION

BEGIN TRY

  DECLARE @ContactID AS int, @CreditCardID as int

  INSERT Person.Contact
    (NameStyle,Title,FirstName,LastName,EmailAddress
    ,EmailPromotion,Phone,PasswordHash
    ,PasswordSalt,rowguid,ModifiedDate)
  VALUES
    (0,'Mr.','Fred','Flintstone','fredf@slategravel.com'
    ,2,'101-555-1212','F295DC2A87C7FD93151A2BC232BEAFF1133F95A2'
    ,'TVGHbhY=', NEWID(),GETDATE())

  SET @ContactID = @@IDENTITY --Capture the new primary key value

  INSERT Sales.CreditCard
    (CardType, CardNumber, ExpMonth, ExpYear, ModifiedDate)
  VALUES
    ('BedrockGold','01234567891012',12,2010,GETDATE())

  SET @CreditCardID = @@IDENTITY --Capture the new primary key value

  INSERT Sales.ContactCreditCard
    (ContactID, CreditCardID, ModifiedDate)
  VALUES
```

```
      (@ContactID, @CreditCardID, GETDATE())

   COMMIT TRANSACTION

END TRY

BEGIN CATCH

   ROLLBACK TRANSACTION

END CATCH
```

In this example, like the implicit transaction example before it, any error can be used to immediately roll back the transaction, ensuring data integrity.

Much of the documentation available on SQL Server states that a transaction is a "single unit of work that most accomplish entirely, or not at all." However, even if the data modifications are placed in a transaction, this does not guarantee that the transaction will accomplish entirely. Without the TRY and CATCH blocks, an implicit or explicit transaction will work just like the Auto-Commit example. Any successful modifications will be made to the database, and any failed ones will not. Proper error handling is critical to managing transactions.

Recording Transactions

Now that you know what a transaction is, take a look at how SQL Server records them on the disk.

Data modifications are never made directly to the database data file. When a modification is sent by an application, SQL Server finds the data page that contains the data, or, in the case of an insert, a page with enough space in it to accommodate the data in the buffer cache. If the page is not located in the cache, SQL Server will read the page from disk and place it in the buffer cache and then modify it there. At the same time, SQL Server records the data modification on disk in the transaction log. When the page was initially read into the buffer cache, it was a "clean" page. Once the page was modified by the transaction, the page became "dirty."

SQL Server periodically issues an event called a CHECKPOINT. When a CHECKPOINT is issued, all dirty pages in the buffer cache are written to the data file on disk. The purpose of checkpoints is to reduce the amount of dirty data stored in the cache to minimize the amount of time required for SQL Server to recover from a failure. Consider the following sequence of events:

```
BEGIN TRANSACTION 1
UPDATE ...
INSERT ...
UPDATE ...
COMMIT TRANSACTION 1

BEGIN TRANSACTION 2
INSERT ...
UPDATE ...

***CHECKPOINT***

BEGIN TRANSACTION 3
```

```
DELETE ...
UPDATE ...
COMMIT TRANSACTION 3

BEGIN TRANSACTION 4
UPDATE ...
***Server Power failure***
```

When SQL Server restarts after the power failure, it will read the transaction log to find the last CHECKPOINT issued. Everything from the last CHECKPOINT to the beginning of the log has been safely written to the disk. However, the only record of data modifications after the CHECKPOINT is in the transaction log. Because Transaction 3 was successfully committed, the calling application was notified of its success, and should expect to see all the modifications that were submitted. In light of this, SQL Server will roll the entire Transaction 3 forward and commit the changes to disk. Transaction 2, on the other hand, was never successfully committed, even though the first two modifications were written to disk by the CHECKPOINT. SQL Server will use the information in the transaction log to undo, or roll back the modifications. Transaction 4 was also never successfully committed, but neither was it written to the disk. Transaction 4 data modifications will essentially be deleted from the transaction log.

Transaction Log Physical Characteristics

The transaction log is implemented as a serialized, sequential, rotary write-back log. As data modifications are written to the log, they are given a Log Sequence Number (LSN). Because the transaction log is used to record more and more transactions, it will eventually fill up. If the transaction log has been set up to auto-grow (see Chapter 5), SQL Server will allocate additional file space to accommodate storage of transaction records. This behavior will continue until the transaction log's maximum size has been reached, or the disk that contains the transaction log fills up. If the transaction log becomes completely full, no data modifications will be allowed on the database.

To keep the transaction log from becoming completely full, it is necessary to periodically remove old transactions from the log. The preferred method of clearing the log is by backing up the transaction log (see Chapter 7). By default, once the transaction log has been successfully backed up, SQL Server will clear the inactive portion of the transaction log. The inactive portion of the transaction log is from the LSN of the oldest open transaction to the earliest LSN in the transaction log. This clearing of the transaction log does not reduce the size of the transaction log, but it does free up space in the log for additional transaction records.

The inactive portion of the transaction log can also be manually cleared, but this is strongly discouraged because doing so deletes all record of data modifications since the last database backup.

As previously noted, the transaction log is a rotary file. Once the end of the physical log is reached, SQL Server will loop back and continue writing the current logical log at the beginning of the physical log, as shown in Figure 4-4.

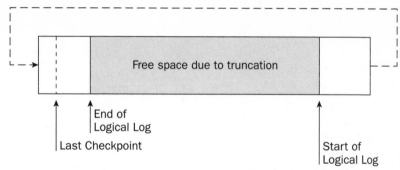

Figure 4-4: Looping back and continuing to write the current logical log

Summary

This chapter examined how SQL Server physically stores data and transaction records on disk. Although this information may seem a bit esoteric in nature, it will become increasingly valuable as your SQL Server skills advance and you encounter more complex troubleshooting and optimization issues that require a deep understanding of how SQL Server stores and retrieves data. Keep in mind that this chapter just scratched the surface when it comes to the deep inner workings of the database engine. For a complete discussion of the database engine internals, consult SQL Server 2005 Books Online.

The database is the heart of SQL Server, and Chapter 5 exposes and describe all the parts and pieces that SQL Server uses to manage, modify, and organize the data stored within it. This includes everything from the tables used to store the data to the programming objects used modify the data, and everything in between.

SQL Server 2005 Databases

In one of his comedy routines about being a parent, Bill Cosby commented on a very profound question that one of his kids asked. The question was, "Why is there air?" Cosby's answer was instantaneous: "To fill up basketballs." What other answer would be appropriate, if not "to fill up footballs"? I wish I had a glib and funny answer for the question "What is a SQL Server 2005 database?" But, like the question "Why is there air?," there is no real quick and easy answer. The database is at the heart of SQL Server 2005 and touches on every aspect of this very large and very powerful release of Microsoft's enterprise data-management platform.

Previous chapters discussed the SQL Server installation process and the internal structure of the files that make up a SQL Server 2005 database. This chapter delves into the databases created during installation, along with the parts and pieces of user-created databases.

System Databases

As mentioned in Chapter 1, when SQL Server 2005 is installed, five system databases are created to store system information and support database operations. Four of the system databases (Master, Model, MSDB, and TempDB) are visible during normal database operations, but the fifth (the Resource database, as described in Chapter 4) is not. Distribution databases can be created if the SQL Server instance is configured to be a Distributor for SQL Server Replication.

User Databases

User databases are those databases that are created by any Master database user. There are no user databases created by default, but during installation, the optional AdventureWorks sample databases that are briefly described in Chapter 1 can be installed if desired.

Database Planning

One of the key responsibilities of the database administrator is the management of database creation. All too often, a company will purchase an application from a vendor that requires a SQL Server back-end without fully planning the data tier support. The vendor many times will be more than happy to come out and install the SQL Server instance and create the necessary databases to support the application. In other cases, the application vendor will create setup programs that install and configure the database automatically. I have seen many of these installations and, with just a few exceptions, the configuration of the supporting databases was either inefficient or flat out wrong.

This is not to say that the application developers from software vendor companies don't know what they are doing. The problem is much more complex. First, it is almost impossible to accurately predict the hardware platform, database usage, and the amount of data stored for every installation of a database application combination, so default values are almost always wrong. Second, and this comes from a lot of experience, many application developers have no idea how SQL Server really works. They think of it only as a place to stick data. The idea of leveraging the power of the data tier or optimizing the data tier doesn't occur to very many application developers.

A good friend of mine (and a brilliant programmer) has accused me of having one tool in my toolbox: a SQL Server sledgehammer. He says that some business requirements are finishing nails and others are ten-penny nails, but I want to drive them all in with my SQL Server sledgehammer. My friend may be right, but at the same time, he still sees SQL Server as just someplace to store data. He doesn't spend a great deal of time worrying about such things as data integrity, inefficient space allocation, and fragmented indexes.

Database administrators should worry about how and why a database is performing the way it is. The best time to start managing a database is before it is created. Whether a data application is developed internally or purchased from a software vendor, it is imperative that the database administrator be intimately involved in the planning and creation of the supporting database. With that in mind, here's a closer look at the database creation process and the configuration options available during database creation.

Capacity Planning

One of the first things that must be determined when planning a new database is how much disk space will be required to support the database. The idea is to both ensure that there is sufficient disk space available for data expansion and to reduce the amount of data and log file growths that are performed to accommodate the data expansion to improve database efficiency.

If the database is being built to support an application purchased from a vendor, the capacity planning for the database may be very easy. However, the simplicity depends on the software vendor providing detailed documentation. The documentation must describe the average size of the database after periodic intervals where a defined number of users and transactions were supported. If the documentation is provided, you will have a good idea of what to expect from the database and can configure it accordingly. If the vendor did not provide the information, your job as a database administrator becomes a bit more complicated, and, like Mr. Spock in *Star Trek IV* (every technical book needs at least one reference to *Star Trek*), you may just have to guess. However, like Mr. Spock, it must be an educated guess based on as much information as you are able to collect. The difficulty is often in the fact that you may not know how the vendor is storing and retrieving data, so the database must be monitored for growth trends to adequately predict the amount of storage space.

If the database is being designed and built internally, there are established techniques in determining how big the data files will need to be. These techniques work because you know how much data is added for every transaction, whereas in a vendor-provided database, that information may not be available.

One such technique that I am sure you will encounter is calculating a database size requirement by calculating table sizes. It looks like this:

1. Add up the total number of bytes used by the fixed-length columns in the table.

2. Average the total number of bytes used by the variable-length columns in the table.

3. Add the number from Step 1 to the number calculated in Step 2.

4. Divide 8092 (the maximum amount of data bytes in a page) by the number calculated in Step 3, and round down to the nearest whole number. This is number of rows that will fit on a single page. Remember that rows cannot span pages, which is why you round down.

5. Divide the total number of expected rows by the number of rows per page calculated in Step 4. This is the total number of data pages expected to support the table.

6. Multiply the number calculated in Step 5 by 8192 (the size of data page). This is the total number of bytes required for the table.

7. Repeat the process for every table in the database.

Sounds like fun doesn't it? Here's a tip: *Don't do it*. The results from this algorithm are misleading at best. The calculation doesn't take into account variables that affect storage space, such as the number of indexes, the fill-factor used on the indexes, and data fragmentation, just to name a few. So, why did I even bother to explain the process? Because it does give insight to size considerations and because, as I mentioned earlier, you will most likely encounter this technique and I wanted to make sure you knew its limitations.

There is a more realistic method of determining how big to make a data file. The idea is to take the database prototype (or the test and development version of the database) and fill it with an appropriate amount of test data. After the test database has been populated, check the size of the data file on disk and then multiply it by 1.5. The resulting file size should be sufficient to accommodate the initial data load of the new database with some room to spare. This technique is by no means perfect, but it is a great deal easier than the first technique, and typically much more accurate.

Once the database is put into production, it will become extremely important to monitor the size of the database files in order to analyze growth trends. This will allow you to increase the size of files when necessary, but also to increase them in sufficient percentages so that the increases are seldom executed.

Planning the size of the transaction log file is much more complicated. To accurately plan the log size, you will need to know how big the average transaction is that will be executed on the database, as well as how often the transactions will take place and what the physical structure of the tables being modified is. For example, an insert executed on a table stored in a heap with a row size of 800 bytes and a non-clustered index on a integer column will increase the amount of data in the transaction log by approximately 820 bytes. This is because the new row is recorded in the transaction log along with the new index row. The size of the transaction log is also dependent on the recovery mode of the database, and how often the database transaction log is backed up. Recovery modes are introduced later in this chapter, as well a complete description of indexes. Transaction log backups and their effect on the transaction log are described in Chapter 9.

Creating Databases

Databases are usually created either by writing and executing Transact-SQL code, or through the graphical interface. In either case, the only required information during the database creation process is the name of the new database, so the following code will create a database called SampleDB:

```
CREATE DATABASE SampleDB
```

Executing this Transact-SQL will cause SQL Server to create a single database data file and one transaction log file in the default location for files specified during the SQL Server 2005 installation process. For a typical installation of a default instance of SQL Server 2005, this code, when executed, will create the following file system objects:

```
C:\Program Files\Microsoft SQL Server\MSSQL.1\MSSQL\Data\SampleDB.mdf
C:\Program Files\Microsoft SQL Server\MSSQL.1\MSSQL\Data\SampleDB_log.ldf
```

The first file is the database data file and the second file is the database transaction log file. Although this default behavior is very convenient, it is usually better not to take advantage of it because all databases are not created equal, besides the fact that the system partition is hardly the recommended destination for data and log files. The database creation process allows for the specification of data file(s), transaction log file(s), and database options.

Getting Started

Before creating a database, it is important to understand all the available settings and options. This section explains the process of creating a database with the graphical interface, and examines each configuration setting and option, as well as how it affects the database creation process. Once you have gone through the entire process, I'll show you how to turn all the work into a script that can be run again and again by specifying different values for the database name, filenames, and file locations.

Creating a New Database

Creating a database graphically with SQL Server Management Studio is very easy and intuitive. The first step is to open SQL Server Management Studio from the Start menu and connect to the Database Engine of your SQL Server.

Right-click the Databases node and click New Database. The New Database screen appears as shown in Figure 5-1.

In the "Database name" field, enter the name of the new database. When specifying a database name, keep in mind that it can be a maximum of 128 characters long. SQL Server Books Online also states that a database name must start with a letter or underscore, and then subsequent characters can be a combination of letters, numbers, and some special characters, but this requirement is not enforced. However, data applications may be unable to make the connection to a database if the name does not conform to accepted standards, so it is a very good idea not to deviate from them. As a best practice, database names should be as descriptive as possible, but also kept as short as possible. Embedded spaces in object names are also problematic, because they can cause unexpected problems when the database is accessed programmatically.

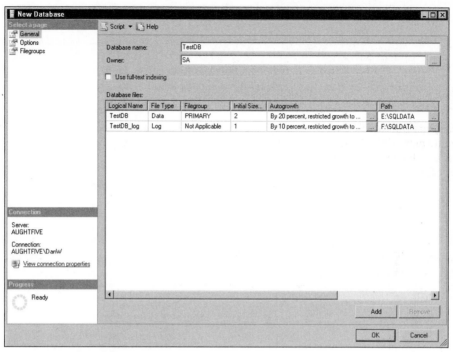

Figure 5-1: New Database screen

In the "Owner" field you should typically specify SA, which is the built-in SQL Server System Administrator account. The default owner is the login account that performs the database creation. The owner of the database gains complete control of the database. Database ownership can be modified by executing the `sp_changedbowner` stored procedure and specifying any valid login as shown in the following example:

```
USE AdventureWorks
GO
sp_changedbowner  SA
```

To retrieve information about databases (such as who the owner is), the `sp_helpdb` stored procedure can be used. To retrieve information about a specific database, the database name is passed with the stored procedure, as demonstrated in the following example:

```
USE Master
GO
EXEC sp_helpdb AdventureWorks
```

The results of the stored procedure when executed with the database name are shown in Figure 5-2.

Results | Messages

	name	db_size	owner	dbid	created	status	compatibility_level
1	AdventureWorks	215.13 MB	sa	6	Jul 9 2006	Status=ONLINE, Updateability=READ_WRITE, UserAcc...	90

	name	fileid	filename	filegroup	size	maxsize	growth	usage
1	AdventureWorks_Data	1	E:\SQLData\AdventureWorks_Data.mdf	PRIMARY	180992 KB	Unlimited	16384 KB	data only
2	AdventureWorks_Log	2	E:\SQLData\AdventureWorks_log.LDF	NULL	39296 KB	Unlimited	10%	log only

Figure 5-2: `sp_helpdb` **results with database name**

To retrieve basic information about all databases the `sp_helpdb` stored procedure can be executed alone. The following example and results shown in Figure 5-3 demonstrate the differences between the two methods of retrieving database information:

```
USE Master
GO
EXEC sp_helpdb
```

Results | Messages

	name	db_size	owner	dbid	created	status	compatibility_level
1	ActivityTracker	6.75 MB	AUGHTFIVE\danw	7	Jul 23 2006	Status=ONLINE, Updateability=READ_WRITE, UserAcc...	90
2	AdventureWorks	215.13 MB	sa	6	Jul 9 2006	Status=ONLINE, Updateability=READ_WRITE, UserAcc...	90
3	AdventureWorksDW	84.99 MB	sa	5	Nov 3 2005	Status=ONLINE, Updateability=READ_WRITE, UserAcc...	90
4	library	65.00 MB	AUGHTFIVE\danw	12	Feb 1 2006	Status=ONLINE, Updateability=READ_WRITE, UserAcc...	90
5	master	4.75 MB	sa	1	Apr 8 2003	Status=ONLINE, Updateability=READ_WRITE, UserAcc...	90
6	model	1.69 MB	sa	3	Apr 8 2003	Status=ONLINE, Updateability=READ_WRITE, UserAcc...	90
7	msdb	9.06 MB	sa	4	Oct 14 2005	Status=ONLINE, Updateability=READ_WRITE, UserAcc...	90
8	Northwind	9.75 MB	AUGHTFIVE\danw	11	May 31 2006	Status=ONLINE, Updateability=READ_WRITE, UserAcc...	90
9	ReportServer	11.31 MB	AUGHTFIVE\danw	9	Dec 21 2005	Status=ONLINE, Updateability=READ_WRITE, UserAcc...	90
10	ReportServerTempDB	23.13 MB	AUGHTFIVE\danw	10	Dec 21 2005	Status=ONLINE, Updateability=READ_WRITE, UserAcc...	90
11	SampleDB	2.94 MB	AUGHTFIVE\danw	15	Jun 26 2006	Status=ONLINE, Updateability=READ_WRITE, UserAcc...	90
12	tempdb	8.75 MB	sa	2	Jul 23 2006	Status=ONLINE, Updateability=READ_WRITE, UserAcc...	90

Figure 5-3: `sp_helpdb` **results without database name**

To avoid any potential issues the database owner should almost always be SA. See Chapter 6 for more information about the SA account.

Leave the "Use full-text indexing" box unchecked. Full-text indexing can be enabled at any time, not just at database creation. Full-text indexing allows for the use of more flexible string-matching queries than Transact-SQL strictly allows, and is managed through the Microsoft Full-Text Engine for SQL Server (MSFTESQL) service. Though full-text indexing offers some very flexible and useful tools, it is not always necessary, and should only be turned on when needed.

Database Files

In the "Database files" section of the New Database dialog, notice that the Logical Name of the first data file, as well as the Logical Name for the first log file, have been given names automatically. The first data file is named the same as the database and the log file is given the name of the database with `_log` appended to the end. The *logical names* are the names the files can be referred to programmatically. Multiple files can be specified in the creation process. Every file contains its own configuration settings (such as for initial size and growth behavior). The file type is automatically populated and cannot be changed once the file has been added to the database.

Click the Add button at the bottom of the New Database dialog. A new row for an additional file is added to the "Database files" section. The new row defaults to a data type file, but it can be changed.

Type in a Logical Name for the new data file and then in the Filegroup column, click the drop-down list and choose <new filegroup>. The New Filegroup dialog displays as shown in Figure 5-4.

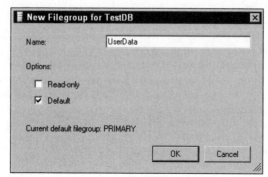

Figure 5-4: New Filegroup dialog

Filegroups

Databases are created on files that are organized in *filegroups*. The only required filegroup is the one called *Primary*. Filegroups are a logical grouping of data files that will hold the database objects defined for the database. The Primary filegroup contains all the system references for the database. This is where the objects defined in the `Resource` database are presented for user databases, as well as any system-created objects. The Primary filegroup also contains all the object definitions for user-defined objects. In addition to the Primary filegroup, more user-defined filegroups can be created as needed.

In my opinion, one of the biggest advantages of filegroups (and, more specifically, user-defined file-groups) boils down to one word: *control*. With user-defined filegroups, the database administrator has complete control over what data is in what location. Without user-defined filegroups, all data is stored in the Primary filegroup, so the flexibility and scalability of the database is reduced dramatically. Although this may be perfectly acceptable for smaller databases, once the database grows to a large size, it will become increasingly unacceptable to have all the user and system data grouped into the same filegroup.

I wish I could tell you exactly when it becomes necessary to segregate data, but like almost all questions in technology, the answer is, "It depends." It depends on the hardware the SQL Server is running on, and how the database is being accessed; there is no hard-and-fast rule. Discussions on how to make the decision on data partitioning are also beyond the scope of this particular book, which is most keenly focused on the "how" of SQL Server 2005 with some pertinent discussions of the "why," but even the "why" changes from one implementation to the next. For more information about data segregation and the use of filegroups check out *Professional SQL Server 2005 Administration* (Indianapolis: Wiley, 2006).

Type in a name for the new filegroup, select the Default checkbox, and click OK. This sets the new user-defined filegroup as the default. All user objects created will be created by default in the new filegroup. This essentially segregates system data from user data, and allows for more control of the database structure.

The Read-only checkbox sets the filegroup as read-only. This can be very advantageous when organizing the different objects in a database. The objects that change can be placed in an updatable filegroup, whereas those that never (or seldom) change can be placed in a read-only filegroup. This segregation of objects can reduce the amount of data required to be backed up and restored, which is a useful option with very large databases.

Maintenance or Performance?

Should filegroups be implemented to optimize performance or optimize maintenance tasks? Why not both? Filegroups provide the ability to improve both the performance and the maintainability of a database by separating data across multiple physical files in groups of tables.

The maintenance advantage comes from the ability to back up and restore individual files and filegroups as opposed to backing up entire databases. (File and filegroup backups are described in Chapter 9.) This ability is useful with very large databases separated into multiple filegroups, and even more useful when some of the filegroups are marked as read-only. This segregation of data that changes from static data enables the database administrator to back up only the data that is subject to modification, which can minimize backup and restore time of large databases. This ability, however, does not come without a cost. File and filegroup backup strategies can become quite complex. The complexity of the maintenance plans can quickly outweigh the flexibility that is gained.

Performance advantages that are delivered with filegroups are primarily divided into three areas. The first is parallel read and write operations that are made possible by separating the data files across multiple physical devices. However, the same performance gain can be achieved in a single filegroup with many physical files in it. The second is the ability to move non-clustered indexes and Large Object data off of the filegroup reserved for the regular data space. Separating non-clustered indexes from the data enables the database engine to seek row locations from the index and retrieve the rows from the tables simultaneously using separate threads. Separating infrequently accessed Large Object data from transaction-intensive relational data can improve scan performance in some instances. The third (and most significant) advantage filegroups enable is the ability to physically partition large tables across multiple filegroups. (Indexes and physical table partitioning are described later in this chapter.)

When it comes to performance, filegroups will only offer a small increase in performance to most databases, with the exception of very large databases that can fully exploit physical table partitioning. The best way to improve disk access to data is to implement a robust Redundant Array of Inexpensive Disks (RAID) environment. The primary reasons for using filegroups for most database administrators is the control it offers in the storage of the data, and the ability to segregate system and user data, which equates to maintenance concerns.

File Size

In the Initial Size (MB) column (see Figure 5-1), a value should be assigned based on how big the file is expected to be within the first few weeks (and maybe even months) of operation. When looking for a house and planning a large family, it would be inadvisable to buy a one-bedroom house and then have to remodel it every time a new child was born. It makes much more sense to buy the largest house possible. The same goes for database files. If a file is expected to hold 1GB of data within the first few months of its existence, it only makes sense to allocate 1GB of space to that file. As a best practice, file size modifications should be kept to a minimum, so allocating enough contiguous disk space to accommodate all the expected data plus a percentage of space for growth is recommended.

Auto Growth

Click the ellipsis button on the right of the Autogrowth column (see Figure 5-1) for the primary data file. The Change Autogrowth dialog displays, as shown in Figure 5-5. The Change Autogrowth dialog enables the configuration of the maximum size and file growth setting for each individual file. Ensure the Enable Autogrowth checkbox is checked. Clearing this checkbox sets the `filegrowth` property to zero.

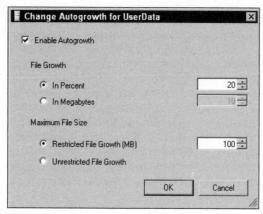

Figure 5-5: Change Autogrowth dialog

File growth can be set at a fixed allocation size or a percentage of the existing file size. As a best practice the Autogrowth option should be set to a sufficiently large enough increment to minimize the number of file-growths required to accommodate data growth. Frequent file-growths are detrimental to both data and log file performance.

Restrict the size of the file by selecting the Restricted File Growth (MB) option button and specifying a maximum size. This size cannot be exceeded by automatic or manual file-growth operations. It is generally a best practice to set a maximum file size to safeguard against any errant process that may attempt to insert millions of rows (instead of just a few) and also to maintain control of database growth. The maximum size property can be changed and additional space allocated. The size selected should be the maximum amount of data expected for that file in a determined period of time. This operation should be performed on every file in the database.

Path

Either click the ellipses button on the right of the Path column of the New Database dialog (see Figure 5-1) for each data file and select a destination folder for each individual file, or simply type in the correct path in the Path column. When placing files, keep in mind that data files and log files should never be on the same physical disk; doing so puts the data at high risk of loss caused by disk or controller failure.

Now that all the general settings of your new database are complete, it is time to configure the database options.

Database Options

Click Options in the "Select a page" section in the upper-left of the New Database dialog, as shown in Figure 5-6. The Options window displays, enabling the setting of several database options.

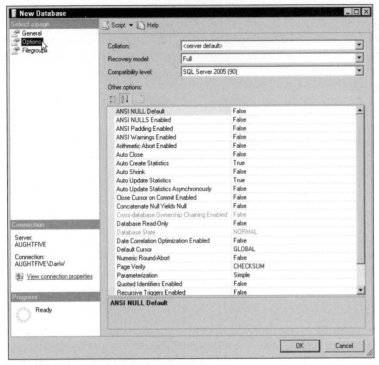

Figure 5-6: Enabling database options

Collation

Click the Collation drop-down list and review the different collation settings that are available, but leave the setting set to <server default>.

As noted in Chapter 2, an instance of SQL Server is assigned a default server collation that determines what characters are supported on the server by default, and how those characters are searched and sorted. Collation settings can also be assigned to the database as well. As a result, just because a SQL Server instance has been configured to use the Latin character set doesn't mean that a database built to support Korean characters cannot be created on the same instance. However, also as previously described, collation incompatibilities in the TempDB database may occur.

Recovery Model

Click the "Recovery model" drop-down list and review the available choices. The available models that can be set are Full, Bulk-Logged, and Simple. If the Model database has not been set otherwise, the default recovery model for new databases is Full. Recovery models are explained in complete detail in Chapter 9, so for now an abbreviated explanation will suffice.

For all intents and purposes, there are really only two recovery models, Full and Simple. The Bulk-Logged model is meant only as an accessory to the Full recovery model for use during bulk operations. This is because in Full recovery model all modifications to the database are fully logged. Although this recovery model offers the greatest level of protection from data loss, it comes at a cost. Because all modifications to a database are fully logged, the transaction log can grow very rapidly to large sizes during certain operations (such as bulk loading of data or table index maintenance operations). The Bulk-Logged recovery model is also known as minimal logging and was developed so that the database could be temporarily set to Bulk-logged during those operations that could cause the transaction log to rapidly swell and then be set back to Full recovery once those operations were complete.

The Simple recovery model used to be called "Truncate Log on Checkpoint" back in the days of SQL Server 7.0 and the database option "trunc. log on chkpt." is still supported for backward compatibility. Setting this database option has the same impact as setting the recovery model to Simple and, in fact, does set the recovery model to Simple. In Simple recovery model, the transaction log is cleared of all inactive content every time a checkpoint is issued. Checkpoints were described in Chapter 4. The repercussion of the Simple recovery model is that the transaction log cannot be backed up or used for database restore operations. The transaction log is only used for transactional consistency, but no long-term storage of transactional history is completed.

Compatibility Level

Click the "Compatibility level" drop-down list and review the possible choices. Unless you have specific reasons to change the compatibility level, it should be set to SQL Server 2005 (90). The compatibility level option changes the behavior of some database operations, and is only necessary if an instance of SQL Server 2005 is sharing database responsibilities with a previous release of SQL Server. SQL Server Management Studio only allows for the selection of compatibility levels of 70, 80, and 90, which, as the drop-down list indicates, correlates to SQL Server 7.0, SQL Server 2000, and SQL Server 2005, respectively. However, programmatically, the compatibility level can be set to 60 and 65 as well, which corresponds to SQL Server 6.0 and SQL Server 6.5. The 60 and 65 settings have been marked as deprecated and will be removed in a future release. For a complete discussion of all the differences between compatibility levels, there is an excellent description in SQL Server Books Online under the topic *"sp_dbcmptlevel (Transact-SQL)."*

> *Databases upgraded from SQL Server 2000 or 7.0 are configured for a compatibility mode respective of their original version. For example, a SQL Server 2000 database upgraded to SQL Server 2005 will have a compatibility level of 80.*

Other Options

By default, the "Other options" section of the New Database screen organizes the options categorically. For purposes of this discussion the options are sorted alphabetically. For this exercise, leave all the options in their default configurations. Each one is described in the following sections. Some of the database options are also connection options. Where this is the case, the commands to set the database option and the connection-level options are both shown. It's important to know that connection-level options, if specified, will override database-level options. When they are not specified, the database option will be in effect.

Click the Alphabetical sort button, which can be identified by an A and Z with a vertical arrow pointing down. The available options are now listed alphabetically, as shown in Figure 5-6.

ANSI NULL Default

The ANSI NULL Default setting specifies whether or not the default for columns added to a table during a CREATE TABLE or ALTER TABLE operation is to allow nulls. When the ANSI NULL Default setting is set to False, Columns added will not allow nulls unless explicitly specified to do so. When connecting to SQL Server with SQL Server Management Studio, the connection setting for new queries defaults to setting ANSI NULLS ON, which overrides the database setting. To set it at the connection level or database level, the following commands are used:

```
--Connection Settings
SET ANSI_NULL_DFLT_ON OFF --ANSI NULL Default False
SET ANSI_NULL_DFLT_ON ON  --ANSI NULL Default True

--Database Options
ALTER DATABASE AdventureWorks SET ANSI_NULL_DEFAULT OFF
ALTER DATABASE AdventureWorks SET ANSI_NULL_DEFAULT ON
```

ANSI NULLS Enabled

This setting controls the behavior of comparisons to NULL values. When set to True, any comparison to a NULL value results in an unknown. When set to False, comparisons to NULL will return True if the values are null. To set it at the connection level or database level, the following commands are used:

```
--Connection Settings
SET ANSI_NULLS OFF
SET ANSI_NULLS ON

--Database Options
ALTER DATABASE AdventureWorks SET ANSI_NULLS OFF
ALTER DATABASE AdventureWorks SET ANSI_NULLS ON
```

ANSI Padding Enabled

When set to True, this dictates that trailing spaces for character data and trailing zeros for binary data are appended to the end of columns for fixed-length character or binary columns. Variable-length character and binary columns are not padded, but trailing spaces or trailing zeros are not trimmed either. When set to False, fixed-length binary and character columns set to NOT NULL behave the same as when ANSI Padding Enabled is True. However, nullable fixed-length character and binary columns are not padded, and any trailing spaces or trailing zeros are trimmed. Variable-length columns behave the same as nullable fixed-length columns when ANSI Padding Enabled is False. To set it at the connection level or database level, the following commands are used:

```
--Connection Settings
SET ANSI_PADDING OFF
SET ANSI_PADDING ON

--Database Options
ALTER DATABASE AdventureWorks SET ANSI_PADDING OFF
ALTER DATABASE AdventureWorks SET ANSI_PADDING ON
```

ANSI Warnings Enabled

When set to True, warnings will be raised by the database engine whenever an aggregate function encounters a null. When set to False, no warnings are raised. To set it at the connection level or database level, the following commands are used:

```
--Connection Settings
SET ANSI_WARNINGS OFF
SET ANSI_WARNINGS ON

--Database Options
ALTER DATABASE AdventureWorks SET ANSI_WARNINGS OFF
ALTER DATABASE AdventureWorks SET ANSI_WARNINGS ON
```

Arithmetic Abort Enabled

Any statement or transaction that encounters an arithmetic overflow or divide-by-zero error will terminate when set to `True`. When set to `False`, a warning is raised, but the statement or transaction will not be terminated. To set it at the connection level or database level, the following commands are used:

```
--Connection Settings
SET ARITHABORT OFF
SET ARITHABORT ON

--Database Options
ALTER DATABASE AdventureWorks SET ARITHABORT OFF
ALTER DATABASE AdventureWorks SET ARITHABORT ON
```

Auto Close

When a database is first accessed, it is opened. When Auto Close is `True`, the database will be closed when the last user connected to it closes the connection. This setting is off by default because the act of opening and closing the database on a server platform is unnecessary, and produces unneeded overhead. The exception to this rule is SQL Server Express Edition, because SQL Express is designed to run on a desktop system where resources are more restricted and an open database consumes resources. If no user is connected, those resources can be returned to the system.

Auto Create Statistics

When set to `True`, the Database Engine will generate statistics for columns that are missing statistics when those columns are referenced in a `WHERE` clause, or the `ON` clause of a `JOIN` operation. Statistics are used by the Database Engine to determine the selectivity and distribution of data in a column. If set to `False` it will be up to the database administrator to create statistics manually wherever needed.

Auto Shrink

When set to `True`, the Database Engine will periodically examine the total size of all database files and compare it to the amount of data being stored. If there is more than 25 percent total free space remaining, the Database Engine will perform file-shrink operations on database files to reduce the total free space to 25 percent. This option is set to `False` by default, except for the SQL Express edition and, apart from the rare instance that a database will increasingly get smaller, it should be left set to `False`.

Auto Update Statistics

When set to `True`, the Database Engine will automatically update statistical information on columns to maintain the most efficient query plans possible. This typically takes place when a query is executed and the Query Processor discovers the out-of-date statistics. If set to `False`, it will again be up to the database administrator to manually keep column statistics up to date.

Auto Update Statistics Asynchronously

When set to `True`, statistics that are discovered to be out-of-date during queries will be updated, but the query that was being executed when the discovery was made will not wait for the new statistics. Subsequent queries will take advantage of the new statistics. When set to `False`, query compilation will not occur until after the statistics are updated.

Close Cursor on Commit Enabled

When set to `True`, cursors contained in a transaction will be closed after the transaction has been committed or rolled back. When this setting is `False`, cursors will remain open when the transaction is committed. However, rolling back a transaction will close any cursors except those defined as `INSENSITIVE` or `STATIC` when set to `False`. To set it at the connection level or database level, the following commands are used:

```
--Connection Settings
SET CURSOR_CLOSE_ON_COMMIT OFF
SET CURSOR_CLOSE_ON_COMMIT ON

--Database Options
ALTER DATABASE AdventureWorks SET CURSOR_CLOSE_ON_COMMIT OFF
ALTER DATABASE AdventureWorks SET CURSOR_CLOSE_ON_COMMIT ON
```

Concatenate Null Yields Null

When a character string is concatenated with a `NULL`, it will return `NULL` when this setting is `True`. When set to `False`, a character string concatenated with a `NULL` will return the character string. To set it at the connection level or database level, the following commands are used:

```
--Connection Settings
SET CONCAT_NULL_YIELDS_NULL OFF
SET CONCAT_NULL_YIELDS_NULL ON

--Database Options
ALTER DATABASE AdventureWorks SET CONCAT_NULL_YIELDS_NULL OFF
ALTER DATABASE AdventureWorks SET CONCAT_NULL_YIELDS_NULL ON
```

Cross-database Ownership Chaining Enabled

This option is not settable in the Options dialog and only indicates what the value is set to. When `True`, it indicates that the database can participate in a cross-database ownership chain. To set this option, execute the `ALTER DATABASE <DBName> SET DB_CHAINING ON|OFF` command.

Database Read Only

This option specifies that no modifications are allowed to the database when set to `True`. Exclusive access to the database is required to set this option, except for the `Master` database.

Database State

This option is not configurable in SQL Server Management Studio, and, for the most part, is not directly configurable at all. The exception is the `ONLINE`, `OFFLINE`, and `EMERGENCY` states. Database State will indicate different values based on what is occurring on the database. The following table describes the various states the database can be in.

State	Description
ONLINE	The database is online and available
OFFLINE	The database is unavailable. Databases are set offline by executing the command ALTER DATABASE <DBName> SET OFFLINE. This can be done if the database administrator wants to move a database file from one location to another. In this case, the database would be set OFFLINE, then the ALTER DATABASE <DBName> MODIFY FILE command would be executed, followed by changing the database back to ONLINE.
RESTORING	One or more files are being restored. The database is unavailable.
RECOVERING	The database is being recovered. Except in the case of database mirroring, this is a transient state that occurs during the automatic or manual recovery process. The database is unavailable.
RECOVERY PENDING	A database will be in this state if SQL Server encounters a resource-related error during recovery. The database will be unavailable until the database administrator resolves the resource error and allows the recovery process to be completed.
SUSPECT	One or more database files have been marked as suspect because of a data access or read error. This may occur if a TORN PAGE has been detected during database read operations. If a database has been marked as SUSPECT, the database is unavailable until the error has been resolved.
EMERGENCY	The database will be in this state when the database administrator has set the status to EMERGENCY. In this state, the database is in single-user mode and may be repaired or restored. If the database has been marked as SUSPECT, this is the first step in correcting the problem, short of a database restore. Only members of the sysadmin fixed server role can set a database to the EMERGENCY state.

Date Correlation Optimization Enabled

When this option is set to True, it indicates that the Database Engine will maintain date statistics between two tables with datetime columns joined by a foreign key constraint to optimize queries between those two tables where the datetime field is a filter.

Default Cursor

Unlike local and global variables whose scope is based on connections, cursors are always local to the connection in which they are declared. When this option is set to Global, it specifies that a declared cursor can be referenced by any batch, stored procedure, or trigger executing on the same connection. If set to Local, the cursor can only be referenced inside the batch, stored procedure, or trigger in which the cursor was declared.

Numeric Round-Abort

When this option is set to `True`, it means that any numeric rounding that occurs will generate an error. For example, if Numeric Round-Abort is set to `True`, the following code will generate an error:

```
DECLARE @Num1 AS decimal(4,3)
SET @Num1 = 7.00004 / 2.84747
SELECT @Num1 AS Answer
```

```
RESULTS:
-----------------------------------------------------------------
Msg 8115, Level 16, State 7, Line 2
Arithmetic overflow error converting numeric to data type numeric.
```

The error is caused because the decimal variable was declared with a scale of 3. Remember that the scale specifies how many digits are supported to the right of the decimal place. To perform this calculation, SQL Server must round the number. If Numeric Round-Abort is set to `False`, this code will succeed:

```
DECLARE @Num1 AS decimal(4,3)
SET @Num1 = 7.00004 / 2.84747
SELECT @Num1 AS Answer
```

```
RESULTS:
-----------------------------------------------------------------
Answer
--------
2.458
```

Page Verify

The Page Verify option enables the database administrator to set different options for page write verification. The available options are Checksum, Torn_Page_Detection, and None. As far as performance goes, the best option is None. However, with None set, pages corrupted during disk write operations (or by some other disk anomaly after the page is written to disk) will not be discovered.

With the Checksum option, SQL Server will calculate a checksum value and store it in the page header. This checksum value is very much like the Cyclic Redundancy Check (CRC) values created when files are written to disk by the operating system. When a data page is read, SQL Server will recalculate the checksum and compare it to the one stored in the page header. If the values match, the page is good. If the values do not match, the page is considered corrupted, an error will be raised, and the database status is changed from `ONLINE` to `SUSPECT`.

In a typical configuration only 512 bytes of data are written to the disk with each pass of the disk under a write head. Therefore, it takes 16 passes to write an 8KB page. The Torn_Page_Detection option configures SQL Server to write an error bit in the page header at the end of every write cycle. If the error bit is absent when the page is later read, an error is raised and the database status is changed from `ONLINE` to `SUSPECT`.

Choosing an appropriate Page Verify setting depends on the degree of acceptable risk and CPU utilization. As mentioned earlier, the best option for performance is setting Page Verify to None, but this setting exposes your database to the risk of undetected data corruption. The Checksum option offers the best protection from undetected corruption because any modification to the data on disk during or after data write operations will be detected by the checksum verification. However, the Checksum option costs the most CPU cycles. The Torn Page option is a lower-cost method of detecting corrupted pages, but it will only detect page corruption that occurs during the write operation. The recommended setting is Checksum because of its high degree of data integrity verification.

Parameterization

This is a very interesting, but advanced new option for SQL Server 2005. By default, the Database Engine auto-parameterizes some queries so that the query plans created and compiled can be reused even when different values are defined in the WHERE clause. For example, consider this code:

```
USE AdventureWorks
GO
SELECT * FROM Person.Contact
WHERE LastName = N'Flintstone'
```

If you type this code in a query window and then click the Display Estimated Execution button on the SQL Editor toolbar, you will find that the Database Engine compiles the query with the search criteria of LastName = N'Flintstone' (see Figure 5-7) when the Parameterization option is set to Simple. This is because SQL Server decides what queries to parameterize and what ones not to when Simple is set, and for this particular query, it determines it is not worth the extra cost.

When the option is set to Force, SQL Server will parameterize all queries that can be parameterized, and the same query will result in a parameterized query plan instead (see Figure 5-8). Forcing auto-parameterization can improve performance in some instances, but careful monitoring should be done to ensure that it doesn't have a negative impact on performance.

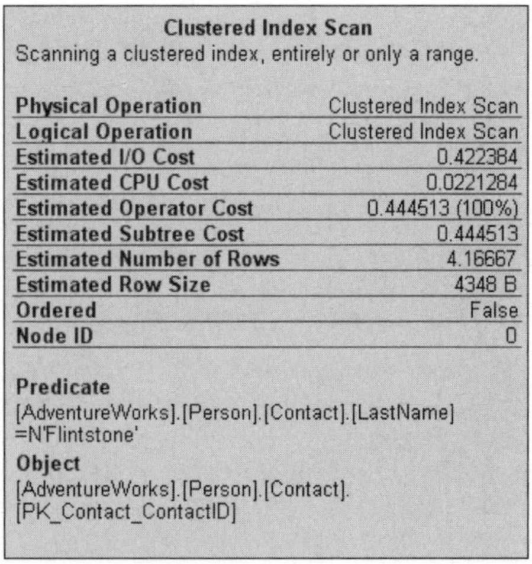

Clustered Index Scan	
Scanning a clustered index, entirely or only a range.	
Physical Operation	Clustered Index Scan
Logical Operation	Clustered Index Scan
Estimated I/O Cost	0.422384
Estimated CPU Cost	0.0221284
Estimated Operator Cost	0.444513 (100%)
Estimated Subtree Cost	0.444513
Estimated Number of Rows	4.16667
Estimated Row Size	4348 B
Ordered	False
Node ID	0

Predicate
[AdventureWorks].[Person].[Contact].[LastName]
=N'Flintstone'
Object
[AdventureWorks].[Person].[Contact].
[PK_Contact_ContactID]

Figure 5-7: Simple parameterization

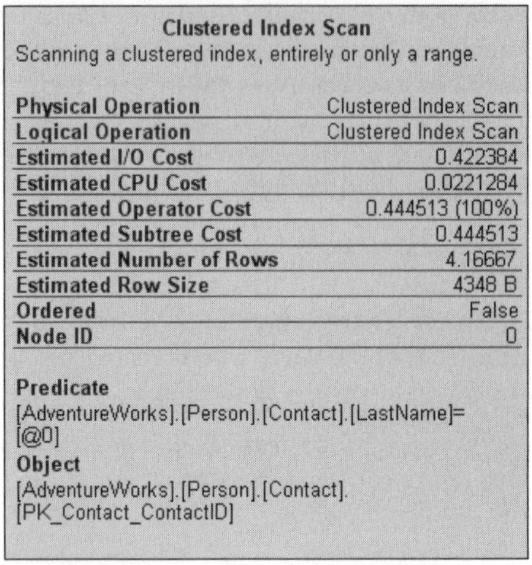

Clustered Index Scan	
Scanning a clustered index, entirely or only a range.	
Physical Operation	Clustered Index Scan
Logical Operation	Clustered Index Scan
Estimated I/O Cost	0.422384
Estimated CPU Cost	0.0221284
Estimated Operator Cost	0.444513 (100%)
Estimated Subtree Cost	0.444513
Estimated Number of Rows	4.16667
Estimated Row Size	4348 B
Ordered	False
Node ID	0

Predicate
[AdventureWorks].[Person].[Contact].[LastName]=
[@0]
Object
[AdventureWorks].[Person].[Contact].
[PK_Contact_ContactID]

Figure 5-8: Forced parameterization

Quoted Identifiers Enabled

By default, SQL Server uses square brackets ("[ ]") to delimit objects. Delimiting objects is only required if the object name contains an embedded space or a reserved word. The ANSI standard delimiter is the double quotation marks. The following examples show how to create and reference an object with an embedded space with both square brackets and double quotation marks.

Following is an example for the ANSI double quote delimiter:

```
USE AdventureWorks
GO
CREATE TABLE "Sales.USA Customers"
( AcctNumber int IDENTITY(1,1) NOT NULL
, "Last Name" varchar(75) NOT NULL
, "First Name" varchar(75) NOT NULL)

SELECT AcctNumber, "Last Name", "First Name"
FROM "Sales.USA Customers"
```

Following is an example of the default square bracket delimiter:

```
USE AdventureWorks
GO
CREATE TABLE [Sales.USA Customers]
( AcctNumber int IDENTITY(1,1) NOT NULL
, [Last Name] varchar(75) NOT NULL
, [First Name] varchar(75) NOT NULL)

SELECT AcctNumber, [Last Name], [First Name]
FROM [Sales.USA Customers]
```

When the Quoted Identifiers option is `True`, both square brackets and double quotation marks are accepted. If the Quoted Identifiers option is set to `False`, only square bracket delimiters will be accepted. To set this option at the connection level or database level, the following commands are used:

```
--Connection Settings
SET QUOTED_IDENTIFIERS OFF
SET QUOTED_IDENTIFIERS ON

--Database Options
ALTER DATABASE AdventureWorks SET QUOTED_IDENTIFIERS OFF
ALTER DATABASE AdventureWorks SET QUOTED_IDENTIFIERS ON
```

On a completely editorial note, I personally believe that embedded spaces in object names are wrong and should never be used. They typically introduce nothing but problems to your database and application design for the negligible benefit of a natural language name.

Recursive Triggers Enabled

Recursive triggers are considered an advanced programming technique that allows the same trigger to fire more than once, in sequence, in the same transaction. When set to `False`, this action is not allowed and is the default configuration.

Restrict Access

The Restrict Access option enables the database administrator to restrict access to a database to a defined set of logins. The default value of this option is `MULTI_USER`, which allows multiple non-privileged users to access the database. Two other options exist to restrict access: `SINGLE_USER` and `RESTRICTED_USER`.

When the `SINGLE_USER` Restrict Access option is set, only one user account is allowed access to the database at a time.

If the `RESTRICTED_USER` Restrict Access option is set, only members of the `db_owner`, `dbcreator`, or `sysadmin` roles can connect to the database.

Trustworthy

The Trustworthy option indicates whether or not the instance of SQL Server trusts the database to access external or network resources. Database programming components created with managed code, or database components that need to execute within the context of a highly privileged user, are not allowed access to any resource external to the database by default. This is the Trustworthy setting of `False`. In those instances, when one of those two situations is required, the Trustworthy option can be set to `True`. The Trustworthy option cannot be set in the Options screen of SQL Server Management Studio. To change the Trustworthy option, execute the `ALTER DATABASE <DBName> SET TRUSTWORTHY ON|OFF`.

Generating Database Creation Scripts

Now that you have gone through all the steps and options of creating a database, take a look at how you can script this process so that you don't have to go through the process again.

At the top of the New Database dialog is a button called "Script," as shown in Figure 5-9.

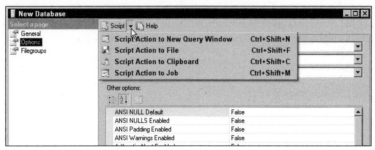

Figure 5-9: Script button

Click the down arrow to the right of Script and it will expose the scripting options available. If you have followed along with the last few pages, then clicking any of the Script Action options will generate a script that will duplicate all the settings you specified in the graphical interface. This script can then be used to create new databases with the same options simply by changing the logical and physical names of the database and associated files. The Script Action options are also great for exploring the actual syntax for creating or modifying database objects. Almost every configuration screen for creating or modifying database objects includes the Script Action option.

Another option for reusing scripts is to replace the actual names of objects and files with parameters. The parameters can then be passed in using the Query Editor or with the SQLCMD utility. The only tricky part in creating Data Definition Language (DDL) scripts is having to use dynamic SQL because parameters can't be passed directly to a DDL script. The following example demonstrates how to use dynamic SQL to create a new database:

```
DECLARE @DBName AS nvarchar(255)
SET @DBName = N'SlateGravel'
EXECUTE (
'CREATE DATABASE ' + @DBName +
' ON  PRIMARY
( NAME = ''' + @DBName + '''
, FILENAME = ''S:\SQLDataFiles\' + @DBName + '_data.mdf''
, SIZE = 20MB
, MAXSIZE = 100MB
, FILEGROWTH = 30%)
, FILEGROUP UserData
( NAME = ''' + @FGName + '''
, FILENAME = ''S:\SQLDataFiles\' + @FGName + '_data1.ndf''
, SIZE = 2048KB , FILEGROWTH = 20%)
 LOG ON
( NAME = ''' + @DBName + '_log''
, FILENAME = ''T:\SQLLogFiles\' + @DBName + '_log.ldf''
, SIZE = 100MB
, FILEGROWTH = 20%)')
```

Schemas

SQL Server 2005 implements the database schema as defined in the ANSI standard. Every object in SQL Server 2005 exists within a defined schema. A *schema* is a named collection of database objects that forms a namespace. The namespace is owned by a single user. Within the namespace, objects cannot have duplicate names. However, objects can have the same name if they exist in different namespaces, or more specifically, different schemas.

For example, if a table called `MyTable` is created in the schema `Sales` on the server `AughtFive`, its name becomes `AughtFive.Sales.MyTable`. An additional table called `MyTable` can still be created in the `Marketing` schema and its name would be `AughtFive.Marketing.MyTable`.

Schemas also form a security scope that can be used by the database administrator to control access to all objects within the schema namespace. This covered in detail in Chapter 6.

Database objects fall within the scope of a schema and are essentially owned by the schema. In SQL Server 2000, the schema was implemented as the owner namespace that was associated with every user. Essentially, every user was also a schema namespace in SQL Server 2000. Therefore, every user could independently own objects and the namespace in which the objects existed. This created issues when it came time to delete a user that owned multiple objects, as well as causing unpredicted errors in database applications because SQL Server 2000's name resolution was poorly understood.

Name resolution issues can still occur in SQL Server 2005, so it is important to understand how the schema implementation affects object name resolution. However, individual users no longer own database objects, with the exception of the schema.

In SQL Server 2005, a user is assigned ownership of a schema, and that schema owns the constituent objects such as tables, views, stored procedures, and functions. If a user who owns a schema needs to be deleted, ownership of that schema will have to be assigned to a different user first. In SQL Server 2000, to reduce complexity, the recommendation was for the `dbo` user to own all objects. Likewise, in SQL Server2005, the easiest solution is to have the `dbo` user own all the schemas. The `dbo` user is a built-in user that is mapped to any member of the fixed server role `sysadmin`. The `dbo` user always exists, and cannot be dropped, so it is a perfect candidate for schema ownership. For more information about the `dbo` user, fixed server roles, and SQL Server 2005 security, see Chapter 6.

Schemas and Name Resolution

Because schemas are, in fact, namespaces, it is important to set the context of object references when calling on database objects in SQL Server 2005. Every user is assigned a default schema. When they log in to a SQL Server and call on database objects, this default schema will play a distinct role in how the objects must be referenced.

For example, a user named `FredF` is created in the `AdventureWorks` database and assigned the default schema of `Sales`. If Fred logs in and executes the query `SELECT * FROM CreditCard`, the `CreditCard` table will be resolved to `AdventureWorks.Sales.CreditCard` because Fred's default schema is `Sales`. The `Sales.CreditCard` table exists, and so the contents of the `CreditCard` table will be returned.

If Fred executes the query `SELECT * FROM Contact`, the table `Contact` will be resolved to the `Sales` schema as `AdventureWorks.Sales.Contact`, a table that does not exist. Because SQL Server is unable to find the `Contact` table in Fred's default schema, it will default to the `dbo` schema and look for the `AdventureWorks.dbo.Contact` table, again with no success. SQL Server will then return the error `"Invalid Object Name"`.

Schema Creation

To group objects in a common namespace, new schemas can be created. To create a schema, the only required information is the name of the schema. The ownership of the schema defaults to the user that runs the creation script, but any valid database user can be specified as the owner. The simplest approach is to designate dbo as the owner of the schema, but there are situations in which it may be desirable to designate a regular user as the owner. The syntax and an example of the CREATE SCHEMA statement are as follows:

```
CREATE SCHEMA Schema_Name [ AUTHORIZATION owner ]
```

```
USE AdventureWorks
GO
CREATE SCHEMA Operations AUTHORIZATION dbo
```

Any schema-scoped statements that follow the CREATE SCHEMA statement will fall in to the scope of the schema just created, as the following example illustrates:

```
USE AdventureWorks
GO
CREATE SCHEMA Operations AUTHORIZATION dbo

    CREATE TABLE BrontoDriver
    (DriverID int IDENTITY NOT NULL
    ,LName varchar(75) NOT NULL
    ,FName varchar(75) NOT NULL)

    GRANT SELECT ON BrontoDriver TO FredF
```

Even though the schema was not specified in the CREATE TABLE statement, this script sets the schema for the BrontoDriver to Operations, and the GRANT SELECT still succeeds, even though the schema was again not designated because the CREATE SCHEMA statement set the scope of the schema for the remaining statements in the batch. If the script is changed slightly so that the GRANT SELECT statement is in a different batch, the GRANT SELECT will fail.

```
CREATE SCHEMA Operations AUTHORIZATION dbo

CREATE TABLE BrontoDriver
(DriverID int IDENTITY NOT NULL
,LName varchar(75) NOT NULL
,FName varchar(75) NOT NULL)

GO

GRANT SELECT ON BrontoDriver TO FredF
------------------------------------------------------------------------

Msg 15151, Level 16, State 1, Line 1
Cannot find the object 'BrontoDriver', because it does not exist or you do not have
permission.
```

The GO keyword placed the GRANT SELECT statement outside of the batch that created the schema, and so the execution context reverted to that of the user executing the script. As a best practice, the schema of an object should always be specified to avoid any unexpected results.

```
CREATE SCHEMA Operations AUTHORIZATION dbo

CREATE TABLE Operations.BrontoDriver
(DriverID int IDENTITY NOT NULL
,LName varchar(75) NOT NULL
,FName varchar(75) NOT NULL)

GRANT SELECT ON Operations.BrontoDriver TO FredF
```

Remember that schema scope resolution always starts at the user's default schema, and will revert to the dbo schema if a referenced object is not scope-qualified.

Schema Maintenance

If a schema contains objects it cannot be dropped:

```
DROP SCHEMA Operations

------------------------------------------------------------------------

Msg 3729, Level 16, State 1, Line 1
Cannot drop schema 'Operations' because it is being referenced by object
'BrontoDriver'.
```

If the object in the schema is still required, it can be transferred to a different schema with the ALTER SCHEMA statement:

```
ALTER SCHEMA Production TRANSFER Operations.BrontoDriver
```

This example alters the schema Production by moving the table BrontoDriver from the Operations schema to the Production schema. Because that was the last object in the schema, it can now be dropped. Be advised, however, that transferring an object from one schema to another clears any permissions set on the object.

A user that owns a schema cannot be dropped from the database, which is one of the reasons why you may decide to have the dbo user own all schemas. To change the ownership of a schema, the AUTHORIZATION property of the schema is altered. The following example changes the ownership of the Operations schema to Fred:

```
ALTER AUTHORIZATION ON SCHEMA::Operations TO Fred
```

Tables

SQL Server 2005, like all relational database management systems, stores data in objects called *tables*. As mentioned in Chapter 1, this book makes the assumption that you are at least familiar with relational database concepts, so I won't spend much time explaining what a table is or how to create them. What is pertinent to the SQL Server 2005 database administrator is how to maintain and secure tables to optimize the performance and security of the database. Security is discussed in detail in Chapter 6, so for this chapter, the discussion is limited to the maintenance of data tables, but first a little background information is required.

Table Architecture

Tables are a collection of rows and are stored in either a heap or a clustered index. By default, tables are stored in unorganized heaps. As the data is inserted, it is added to the next available row on a data page. There is no attempt to keep the data organized or sorted. Although this arrangement works great for adding data to a table, it is less than an optimum solution when trying to find a particular row or set of rows in a table.

Think of a library. If you managed a library that put all the books on shelves as they came in with no regard to genre, author, or title, it would take very little effort to shelve the books as they came in. However, when it came time to find a particular book you would be forced to scan through all the shelves looking for the one book you wanted. At first, all the books may indeed be sorted, but only through happenstance. They will be in inserted order, but after removing a book for checkout, and adding new books, the order will soon be scrambled.

This is exactly how SQL Server works as well. The next section examines methods to organize the data physically, or aid in the location of data through the use of indexes.

Table Indexes

As noted previously, SQL Server tables are stored as heaps by default. A heap is a table that does not have a clustered index. A table stored as a heap has no enforced physical order, but a clustered index does. As data is added to a table stored as a heap, it will be in inserted order at first as described in the library example.

Heaps work very well for storing data, and are very efficient in handling new records, but they are not so great when it comes to finding specific data in a table. This is where indexes come in. SQL Server supports two basic types of indexes: *clustered* and *non-clustered*. It also supports XML indexes, which are discussed later in this chapter, but they are quite different from the regular relational indexes that will be used to locate the majority of the data in database tables.

The key difference between clustered and non-clustered indexes is the leaf level of the index. In non-clustered indexes the leaf level contains pointers to the data. In a clustered index, the leaf level of the index is the actual data.

Clustered Indexes

As I mentioned before, a table with a clustered index is not stored as a heap. Heaps and clustered indexes are thus mutually exclusive. A *clustered index* is a collection of organized table rows.

The white pages of the phone book are a perfect example of a clustered index. All the rows of the white pages are clustered on the combination of last name and first name. When scanning the white pages looking for a phone number, you are scanning both the index and the data. When the indexed value is found, so is the rest of the pertinent data.

This is also true of SQL Server clustered indexes. Clustered indexes can be created to sort the data by a particular attribute, or column, of the row. Going back to the library example, libraries organize most of the books in a clustered index based on genre and/or topic, and then break that organization down further by author. When clustered indexes are created on columns that have duplicate values, SQL Server generates an internal number to uniquely identify duplicate clustered index keys. The non-leaf level of the clustered index when using the phone book analogy can be thought of as the names at the top of the page. The leaf level of a clustered index is the actual data row, not just a pointer to the data.

Non-Clustered Indexes

Non-clustered indexes are more like the indexes in the back of a book. When the indexed value is found, so is a pointer that tells the location of the actual data. Non-clustered indexes can be built on a heap or a clustered index. The leaf level of a non-clustered index contains the indexed column (or columns) and a pointer to the actual data to which the indexed value refers. When the non-clustered index is built on a heap, the pointer is a physical location of the data. When it is built on a clustered index, the pointer is the clustered index key value.

Non-Clustered Indexes on Heaps

When a non-clustered index is built on a table organized as a heap, the indexed column or columns are sorted along with a pointer to the physical location of the data.

For example, let's go back to the library analogy. If the physical location of every book that came into this unorganized library were recorded in an index as it was placed on the shelf, that index could be referenced to find the location of a book instead of scanning all the shelves. The downside of this technique is that similar records (or, in the library analogy, similar books) could be located in completely different places. For example, searching for books on SQL Server 2005 could return several books; each one located in opposite ends of the library. Retrieving the books may take more effort than would be required if all the SQL Server books were clustered together.

Whether to create a clustered index or leave the records in a heap is a design decision that is typically driven by how the data is accessed. When data from a table is primarily accessed by a predictable attribute or column, then it may be useful to cluster the rows of the table on that specific column. However, if the column is based on a large data type, creating a clustered index on it will be costly as far as storage and index maintenance.

In a simple one-column index built on a heap table, the index itself is a great deal like a two-column table. The first column records the indexed value and the second column records the physical location of the row in which the indexed value can be found. The physical location is essentially an identifier that specifies the Extent ID, Page ID, and Row ID of the indexed value on the page.

Non-Clustered Indexes on Clustered Indexes

When a non-clustered index is built on a clustered index, the pointer value in the index is a representation of the clustered index key value.

For example, in the phone book analogy, you learned that the white pages of the phone book are just like a clustered index in SQL Server. I live in a small town west of Seattle and my phone book contains an interesting additional index just after the white pages. I call them the "slightly off-white pages." These off-white pages contain every published phone number in town listed in sorted order, along with the last name and first name of the phone number's holder. This is a perfect example of a non-clustered index built on a clustered index. The phone number can be used to discover the last name–first name combination, and then the last name–first name combination can be used to find the address, if it is listed. (You can't believe how useful that index was when I would find a phone number written on my daughter's homework or school folder!)

XML Indexes

A third type of index supported on tables in SQL Server 2005 is XML indexes. With SQL Server 2005's ability to store native XML in tables comes the ability to build indexes on that XML to help locate and retrieve specific data within the XML text. XML data is stored as a Binary Large Object (BLOB) in the SQL database. To search for specific elements, attributes, or values in the XML document, SQL Server must first open the BLOB and then shred its contents. The act of shredding is what SQL Server does to create a list of XML objects that it can then navigate. It essentially extracts the XML data structure and stores it in temporary relational structures.

XML indexes, like their relational counterparts, come with some overhead, but XML index overhead is more significant than regular indexes. For this reason, XML indexes should be reserved for columns in which the XML data is seldom modified.

It is typically much more efficient to have the database applications store and retrieve complete XML documents, rather than inserting and modifying parts and pieces of the document, which results in shredding. However, there are business cases that call for just this type of functionality, so the ability to create XML indexes was included to avoid the necessity of shredding complete documents.

XML indexes are essentially pre-shredded sections of the XML data linked to the unique key of the table. There are four types of XML indexes. The first XML index must be a *primary XML index*. In addition to the primary index, three *secondary indexes* can be created that build on the primary. Each additional index type will improve XML query performance, but will also adversely affect XML data modification.

Primary XML Indexes

The primary XML index isn't strictly an index. It is a clustered index on an internal table known as the *node table* that is directly linked to the clustered index of the table where the XML index is being created. To create an XML index, the table with the XML column must have a clustered index on its primary key. The node table created to support the primary XML index is not directly accessible, but information about it can be exposed through the use of system views. The primary XML index stores a relational representation of the XML field, and assists the query optimizer in creating efficient query plans to extract data from an XML field. An example of the syntax to create a primary XML index is as follows:

```
USE AdventureWorks
GO
CREATE PRIMARY XML INDEX PXML_Illustration
ON Production.Illustration (Diagram)
```

Primary XML indexes can also be graphically created in Management Studio. To create a new set of XML indexes, first create a table to use. To create a copy of the Person.Contact table that contains an XML column, execute the following code that creates the MyContact table and then creates a clustered index on the primary key, which is required to create XML indexes:

```
USE AdventureWorks
GO
SELECT * INTO dbo.MyContact FROM Person.Contact
GO
ALTER TABLE dbo.MyContact
ADD CONSTRAINT PK_MyContact_ContactID
PRIMARY KEY CLUSTERED (ContactID)
```

Now that you have a table to play with, expand the AdventureWorks database in the Object Explorer, expand Tables, and then expand the dbo.MyContact table.

You may have to refresh the Tables node to get the MyContact table to appear.

Right-click the MyContact table and click Modify. The table structure will appear to the right of the Object Explorer, and the Table Designer toolbar will appear.

Click the AdditionalContactInfo column and then click the Manage XML Indexes button on the Table Designer toolbar (see Figure 5-10). If the Table Designer toolbar is not visible, select it on the View → Toolbars menu.

Figure 5-10: Manage XML Indexes button

On the XML Indexes dialog (see Figure 5-11) click Add and then change the name of the new primary XML index to PXML_AddContactInfo, and give it a short description such as "Primary XML Index."

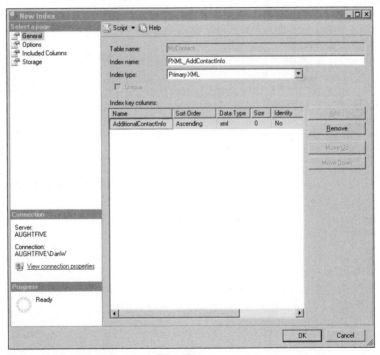

Figure 5-11: XML indexes configuration

Notice that the Is Primary property is set to Yes and cannot be changed. Because this is the first XML index, it must be a primary index.

Primary XML indexes can also be created through the new index dialog by right-clicking the Indexes node in Object Explorer, clicking New Index, and then choosing Primary XML from the list in the "Index type" drop-down box. However, secondary indexes cannot be created this way.

Secondary XML PATH Indexes

XML PATH indexes can improve the performance of XML queries that specify path expressions on XML columns. PATH secondary indexes (like all other secondary XML indexes) are built on the nodes provided by the primary XML index. An example of the syntax to create a secondary PATH index is as follows:

```
USE AdventureWorks
GO
CREATE XML INDEX XML_Path_MyContact
  ON dbo.MyContact(AdditionalContactInfo)
  USING XML INDEX PXML_AddContactInfo
  FOR PATH
```

Creating secondary indexes graphically is the same as the primary index, except that the secondary index type can now be chosen from the Secondary Type drop-down list. To create a Secondary XML index, click the Add button again on the XML Indexes configuration window. Now that a Primary XML index has been added, the next index type defaults to Secondary, the Is Primary property is set to No, and a new Secondary Type drop down list appears (see Figure 5-12).

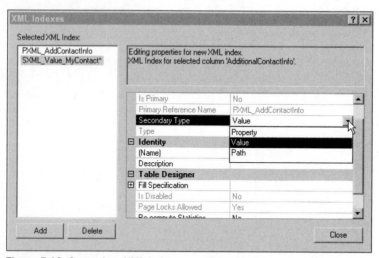

Figure 5-12: Secondary XML indexes configuration

To commit the changes to the table and actually create the indexes, the table must be saved after closing the XML Indexes configuration window.

Secondary XML VALUE Indexes

The secondary VALUE indexes are designed to support XML queries where the path is not fully specified, or where a value is being searched by a wildcard. An example of the syntax for creating a secondary VALUE index is as follows:

```
CREATE XML INDEX XML_Value_MyContact
   ON dbo.MyContact(AdditionalContactInfo)
   USING XML INDEX PXML_AddContactInfo
   FOR VALUE
```

Secondary XML PROPERTY Indexes

XML PROPERTY indexes are used to optimize queries that return values from XML documents using the .Value XQUERY method and are created with the following command:

```
CREATE XML INDEX XML_Property_MyContact
   ON dbo.MyContact(AdditionalContactInfo)
   USING XML INDEX PXML_AddContactInfo
   FOR PROPERTY
```

Table Collation

As discussed earlier in this chapter, when creating a database, collation support can be configured that is different from that of the server. This is also true for table columns that contain character data. Each column can be defined with a different collation setting. For example, The AdventureWorks Cycles Company wants to enable customers from all over the world to browse and search the product catalog in their own languages. To enable this functionality, a GlobalProductDescription table is built with the following script:

```
USE AdventureWorks
GO
CREATE TABLE Production.GlobalProductDescription(
   ProductDescriptionID int IDENTITY(1,1) NOT NULL,
   EnglishDescription nvarchar(400) COLLATE SQL_Latin1_General_CP1_CI_AS NULL,
   FrenchDescription nvarchar(400) COLLATE French_CI_AS NULL,
   ChineseDescription nvarchar(400) COLLATE Chinese_PRC_CI_AI NULL,
   ArabicDescription nvarchar(400) COLLATE Arabic_CI_AS NULL,
   HebrewDescription nvarchar(400) COLLATE Hebrew_CI_AS NULL,
   ThaiDescription nvarchar(400) COLLATE Thai_CI_AS NULL,
   ModifiedDate datetime NOT NULL)
```

Each column is now sorted and searchable using the native language collation settings as defined in the business requirement. Now, don't let me mislead you. SQL Server definitely is not some kind of universal translator (more *Star Trek*). SQL Server just provides the framework for storing multiple languages. You will have to arrange for the proper translation of the descriptions and place them in the appropriate columns and handle any collation incompatibilities that arise because of TempDB's collation.

Table Partitions

As previously noted, SQL Server 2005 stores table data in heaps or clustered indexes. SQL Server physically stores these heaps or clustered indexes in partitions. Unless specifically separated, tables are stored in a single partition defined on a single filegroup. However, SQL Server provides the ability to separate large tables into smaller manageable chunks by horizontally partitioning the tables across multiple files managed by filegroup definitions.

The Table Partitioning feature is available only in the Enterprise and Developer editions of SQL Server 2005.

For example, a transaction table with millions of rows can be physically partitioned so that all the transactions for the current year are separated from previous years. In this way, only the subset of the table will need to be scanned to select, insert, or update current-year transactions.

To illustrate the advantages of physical table partitioning and demonstrate how to implement them, you must first build a table that is a candidate for partitioning. Using the following script, create the dbo.Transactions table that will hold of your test data. The Transaction table has the same basic structure as the Production.TransactionHistory and Production.TransactionHistoryArchive tables, along with a clustered index on the TransactionID column.

```
USE AdventureWorks
GO
CREATE TABLE dbo.Transactions(
   TransactionID int NOT NULL,
   ProductID int NOT NULL,
   ReferenceOrderID int NOT NULL,
   ReferenceOrderLineID int NOT NULL,
   TransactionDate datetime NOT NULL,
   TransactionType nchar(1) NOT NULL,
   Quantity int NOT NULL,
   ActualCost money NOT NULL,
   ModifiedDate datetime NOT NULL,
CONSTRAINT PK_TransactionID PRIMARY KEY CLUSTERED (TransactionID))
```

To populate the new Transactions table, insert all the rows from the TransactionHistory and TransactionHistoryArchive tables by using a UNION operator:

```
USE AdventureWorks
GO
INSERT dbo.Transactions
SELECT * FROM Production.TransactionHistory
UNION ALL
SELECT * FROM Production.TransactionHistoryArchive
```

Now that you have a nice size table to work with, run a query against it to see the performance before partitioning. The table contains a total of 202,696 rows. Of the transaction rows in the table 12,711 took place in 2001, 38,300 in 2002, 70,599 in 2003, and 81,086 took place in 2004.

```
--Pre Partition Statistics
USE AdventureWorks
GO
SET STATISTICS IO ON
DECLARE @BeginDate AS datetime, @EndDate AS datetime
SET @BeginDate = '2002-01-01'
```

```
SET @EndDate = '2002-12-31'

SELECT SUM(Quantity) AS TotalQuantity, SUM(ActualCost) AS TotalCost
FROM dbo.Transactions
WHERE TransactionDate BETWEEN @BeginDate AND @EndDate
```

The script turns on statistic reporting with the SET STATISTICS IO ON option, and then queries the dbo.Transactions table to return the total sales amount and total quantity of products sold in 2002.

The results of the query are as follows.

```
TotalQuantity TotalCost
------------- ---------------------
1472494       16427929.3028

(1 row(s) affected)

Table 'Transactions'. Scan count 1, logical reads 1414, physical reads 0, read-
ahead reads 0, lob logical reads 0, lob physical reads 0, lob read-ahead reads 0.


(1 row(s) affected)
```

As you can see, to satisfy the query, SQL Server had to scan the table, which is implemented as a clustered index. To find the 38,300 rows that met the criteria of the WHERE clause SQL Server had to scan through 202,696 rows. This scan resulted in 1,414 logical reads.

Now, let's see what happens when you physically divide the table into multiple files by partitioning the table so that all the transactions are divided by year.

In a perfect world, you would know that you wanted to physically partition a table before you ever populated it with data, but perfect worlds are rare. In this case, you have decided to physically partition the Transactions table after it has been built. Having a clustered index makes this much easier. If the data were stored in a heap, you would have been forced to create a new partitioned table and move the data to it, then drop the original table.

The first step in partitioning the table is to create the filegroups that will hold the data files to be used to store the partitions of the table. Remember from the previous discussion on filegroups that tables cannot be assigned to a particular file, only to a filegroup. In this example, each filegroup will contain only one file. This is by no means a requirement. Partitions can be defined to exist on multiple files, as well as just one.

The following script adds four new filegroups with one file per filegroup to contain this partitioned transaction table. As the names suggest, you will be partitioning the Transaction table by date:

```
USE MASTER
GO
ALTER DATABASE AdventureWorks
ADD FILEGROUP FGPre2002
GO
ALTER DATABASE AdventureWorks
ADD FILE
  ( NAME = 'AworksPre2002'
```

143

```
     , FILENAME = 'E:\SQLData\AworksPre2002.ndf'
     , SIZE = 20MB
     , FILEGROWTH = 20% )
TO FILEGROUP FGPre2002
GO
ALTER DATABASE AdventureWorks
ADD FILEGROUP FG2002
GO
ALTER DATABASE AdventureWorks
ADD FILE
    ( NAME = 'Aworks2002'
    , FILENAME = 'E:\SQLData\Aworks2002.ndf'
    , SIZE = 20MB
    , FILEGROWTH = 20% )
TO FILEGROUP FG2002
GO
ALTER DATABASE AdventureWorks
ADD FILEGROUP FG2003
GO
ALTER DATABASE AdventureWorks
ADD FILE
    ( NAME = 'Aworks2003'
    , FILENAME = 'E:\SQLData\Aworks2003.ndf'
    , SIZE = 20MB
    , FILEGROWTH = 20% )
TO FILEGROUP FG2003
GO
ALTER DATABASE AdventureWorks
ADD FILEGROUP FG2004AndAfter
GO
ALTER DATABASE AdventureWorks
ADD FILE
    ( NAME = 'Aworks2004AndAfter'
    , FILENAME = 'E:\SQLData\Aworks2004AndAfter.ndf'
    , SIZE = 20MB
    , FILEGROWTH = 20% )
  TO FILEGROUP FG2004AndAfter
GO
```

This script assumes the presence of an "E" drive and a SQLData *folder. To run it in your environment, you may have to change the drive letter assignment.*

The next step in partitioning this transaction table is to create a *Partition Function*. Partition Functions specify what data type is used to horizontally partition the index or table and will map to a column in an index or table. The function will also determine the range of values for each partition. For example, if an integer data type is chosen as the partitioning data type, the Partition Function will specify what the range of values are as in 1 through 100,000, and 100,000 through 1,000,000, and so on. Keep in mind that when specifying a partitioning data type and corresponding column, you can only define one. However, you can create as many Partition Functions as you want.

In this example, you will be partitioning the data by date to group together the data in accordance to the most frequent queries run against the table. Run the following script to create a Partition Function that partitions a table or index into four groups of dated records. The first group is from NULL to 12/31/2001. The second group is from 1/1/2002 to 12/31/2002. The third group is from 1/1/2003 to 12/31/2003, and the last group is from 1/1/2004 to INFINITY.

```
CREATE PARTITION FUNCTION YearFunction (datetime)
AS RANGE RIGHT FOR VALUES ('1/1/2002','1/1/2003','1/1/2004')
```

When creating a Partition Function, the option RANGE RIGHT or RANGE LEFT can be used. When using a RANGE LEFT Partition Function, the first value will act as an upper boundary in the first partition. The RANGE RIGHT option specifies that the first value will act as a lower boundary in the second partition. I personally find this counter-intuitive, but that is how it works.

Once the function is created to define the data types that will be used for partitioning, a *Partition Scheme* must be created. A Partition Scheme is used to bind the Partition Function to the filegroups in a database. Run the following script to create a Partition Scheme that binds the YearFunction to the filegroups that you created earlier:

```
CREATE PARTITION SCHEME YearScheme
AS PARTITION YearFunction
TO (FGPre2002,FG2002,FG2002,FG2004AndAfter)
```

All that is left to do is move the Transactions table to the partition. This is made easier because the table has a clustered index. SQL Server 2005 allows for the dropping of a clustered index and provides the ability to move the information from the clustered index (which you know is the actual data from the table) to a different location.

When creating Partition Functions and Partition Schemes, remember that they can be used to partition as many tables and indexes as needed. The YearFunction and YearSchema can be used to partition any table in the AdventureWorks database that has a datetime column in it.

Run the following script to drop the primary key constraint and associated clustered index, and move the clustered data to the partition based on the datetime column of TransactionDate:

```
ALTER TABLE dbo.Transactions
DROP CONSTRAINT PK_TransactionID
WITH (MOVE TO YearScheme(TransactionDate))
```

This script moves the data, but it also drops the primary key that was defined on the table, which is probably *not* what you want. However, for the time being leave it that way. To see if you have improved the performance of your query, run the same query that you ran before on the Transactions table. Be sure to verify that the "Include Actual Execution Plan" option is still set.

```
--Post Partition Statistics
SET STATISTICS IO ON
SELECT SUM(Quantity) AS TotalQuantity, SUM(ActualCost) AS TotalCost
FROM dbo.Transactions
WHERE TransactionDate BETWEEN '1-1-2002' AND '12-31-2002'
```

The results of the query are as follows:

```
TotalQuantity  TotalCost
-------------  --------------------
1472494        16427929.3028

(1 row(s) affected)

Table 'Transactions'. Scan count 1, logical reads 266, physical reads 0, read-ahead
reads 0, lob logical reads 0, lob physical reads 0, lob read-ahead reads 0.

(1 row(s) affected)
```

Now that the table is physically partitioned the logical reads required to retrieve the results went from 1,414 to 266. The decrease in IO cost will also result in a decrease in CPU cost resulting in a much more efficient query. Keep in mind that the savings in performance are on a table with only 202,696 rows. Imagine the savings if the table contained 10 years of data comprised of millions of rows and the partitions were defined on each year. The savings when querying a specific year would be much more dramatic.

When you moved the data from the clustered index to the partition, you dropped the primary key constraint to do it. One of the limitations of partitions is that if the table has a unique index (which almost all tables should), and that index is on a column that is not the column chosen for partitioning, then the unique index cannot be partitioned with the data. The only way around this is to define the primary key or unique index on the column chosen for partitioning *and* the unique column. For example, the primary key of the dbo.Transactions table could be created on the TransactionID column and the TransactionDate column.

Indexes that are partitioned with the table are "Aligned Indexes." Because you want to enforce uniqueness on the TransactionID column, but partition on the TransactionDate column, your primary key unique index will not be aligned with the partition unless you create the index across both the TransactionID and TransactionDate columns. Because you have decided not to create a composite, primary key the key will have to be created on a single filegroup and defined as a non-clustered index. SQL Server will let you define a unique clustered index on the partitioned table in a separate filegroup, but doing so will move the data off of the partition scheme and back to a single filegroup, defeating the purpose of the partitioning.

To enforce uniqueness on the TransactionID column, you will re-create the primary key constraint on the TransactionID column. However, the index used to ensure uniqueness will not be a clustered index, because you have already distributed the actual data based on the TransactionDate column. Run the following script to create a primary key constraint on the TransactionID column:

```
ALTER TABLE dbo.Transactions
ADD CONSTRAINT PK_TransactionID PRIMARY KEY NONCLUSTERED (TransactionID)
ON [Primary]
```

Any filegroup can be specified when adding the constraint, but the Partition Scheme cannot. For simplicity, the script places the non-clustered index on the Primary filegroup. If the table is partitioned on the primary key, this isn't an issue, and the table and unique index can be fully aligned. After adding the primary key, rerun the query. You will see that it had no impact on the query performance. The adding of the primary key has no impact on the performance of the query.

Maintaining Tables

Now that you have a better idea of how data is organized in tables, look at how you can keep the data optimized for quick retrieval and modification. Table maintenance falls in to three basic categories:

❑   The building and optimizing of indexes

❑   The creation and maintenance of index statistics

❑   The partitioning of large tables to optimize scan performance

We have already discussed partitioning, so now take a look at maintaining table indexes and statistics.

Index Fragmentation

One of the leading causes of poor query performance is poorly maintained indexes. As indexes are updated, they become fragmented. This occurs because indexes are a collection of contiguous, sorted data. To maintain the sorted order of indexes SQL Server must split full data pages to make room for more data.

For example, Extent 72 (see Figure 5-13) contains a clustered index defined on the LastName column of the fictitious Slate.Employee table. Each data page in the extent is completely full.

EXTENT 72

Page 110	Page 111	Page 112	Page 113	Page 114	Page 115	Page 116	Page 117
Deniut	Donovan	Edwards	Fakhouri	Foster	Garcia	Givens	Gray
Desai	Drury	Ellerbrock	Farrell	Frank	Garza	Glimp	Greer
Dewer	Dudenhoef	Elson	Feng	Friedland	Gates	Gode	Grisso
Diaz	Duff	Eminhizer	Ferrier	Friske	Gehring	Goktepe	Groth
Dickson	Dulong	Entin	Finley	Funk	German	Goldstein	Guo
Dillon	Duncan	Ersan	Flood	Gage	Gibson	Gonzales	Gustafson
Dobney	Dyck	Estes	Fluegel	Galos	Gilbert	Gottfried	Guzik
Dodd	Eaton	Evans	Ford	Ganio	Gilliat	Graham	Hagege

Figure 5-13: Full data pages

The code in the following example is shown for illustration purposes only and is not intended to be executed.

The following batch is executed to insert a new row in to the Slate.Employee table:

```
INSERT Slate.Employee
(LastName, FirstName, Title, EmailAddress, Phone, ModifiedDate)
VALUES
('Flintstone','Fred','Mr.','fredf@slategravel.com','123-456-7890',GETDATE())
```

An immediate page split occurs. This is because there is no room on the data page for a new record. To maintain the order of the rows, SQL Server splits Page 113 and moves approximately 50 percent of the rows to a new unallocated data page (see Figure 5-14).

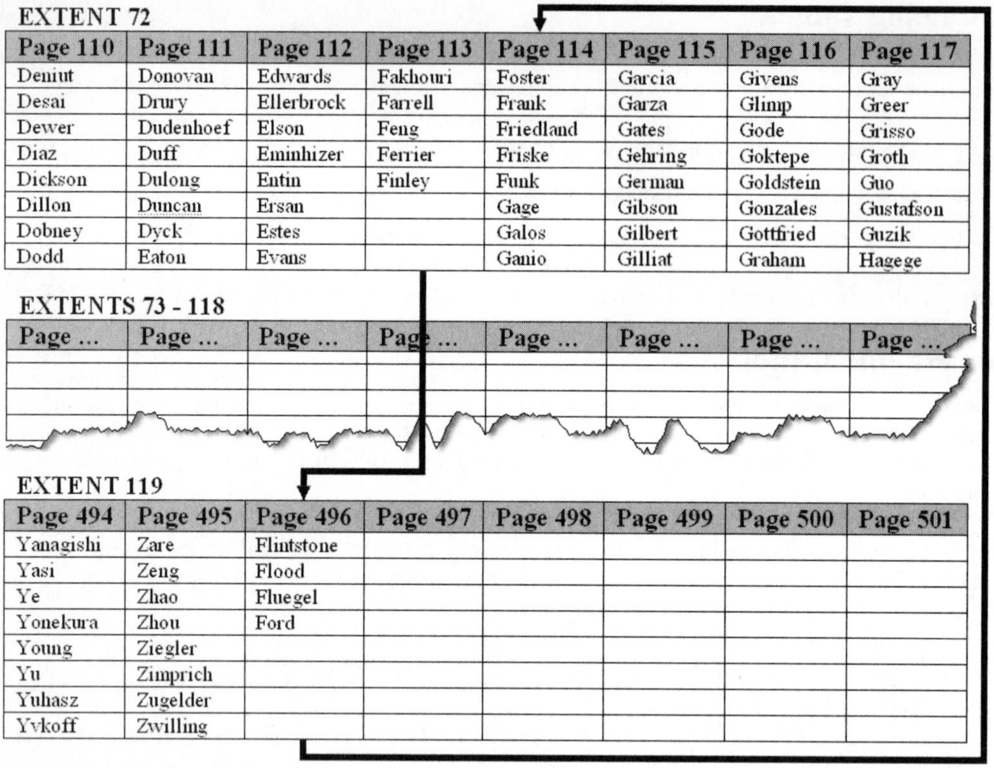

EXTENT 72

Page 110	Page 111	Page 112	Page 113	Page 114	Page 115	Page 116	Page 117
Deniut	Donovan	Edwards	Fakhouri	Foster	Garcia	Givens	Gray
Desai	Drury	Ellerbrock	Farrell	Frank	Garza	Glimp	Greer
Dewer	Dudenhoef	Elson	Feng	Friedland	Gates	Gode	Grisso
Diaz	Duff	Eminhizer	Ferrier	Friske	Gehring	Goktepe	Groth
Dickson	Dulong	Entin	Finley	Funk	German	Goldstein	Guo
Dillon	Duncan	Ersan		Gage	Gibson	Gonzales	Gustafson
Dobney	Dyck	Estes		Galos	Gilbert	Gottfried	Guzik
Dodd	Eaton	Evans		Ganio	Gilliat	Graham	Hagege

EXTENTS 73 - 118

Page ...	Page ...	Page ...	Page ...	Page ...	Page ...	Page ...	Page ...

EXTENT 119

Page 494	Page 495	Page 496	Page 497	Page 498	Page 499	Page 500	Page 501
Yanagishi	Zare	Flintstone					
Yasi	Zeng	Flood					
Ye	Zhao	Fluegel					
Yonekura	Zhou	Ford					
Young	Ziegler						
Yu	Zimprich						
Yuhasz	Zugelder						
Yvkoff	Zwilling						

Figure 5-14: Splitting Page 113

As a result of this page split, when SQL Server reads the data pages to retrieve the contents of the `Slate.Employee` table, it will have to switch from Extent 72 to Extent 119, and then back to Extent 72 again to continue the scanning of rows. After many more employees are added, additional page splits will occur. These page splits cause index fragmentation. The fragmentation of the indexes will eventually cause SQL Server to perform an excessive amount of reads to retrieve data, resulting in poor query performance.

To check for fragmentation on all the indexes of a table or specific indexes, the dynamic management function `sys.dm_db_index_physical_stats` is used. This function returns a great deal of information about the indexes on a table, including the amount of data on each data page, the amount of fragmentation at the leaf and non-leaf level of the indexes, and the average size of records in an index.

When querying this table-value function, the data I am most often interested in are the levels of fragmentation and the average percentage that each page is full. The fragmentation level will let me know if the indexes need to be rebuilt, and the amount of fullness of the data pages will tell me how soon I can expect more page splits to occur. To query the `sys.dm_db_index_physical_stats` dynamic management view, the following syntax can be used:

```
SELECT {* | column list} FROM
sys.dm_db_index_physical_stats
({database_id | NULL}
```

```
,{object_id | NULL}
,{index_id | NULL | 0}
,{partition_number | NULL}
,{mode | NULL | DEFAULT}
```

As the syntax indicates, the `sys.dm_db_index_physical_stats` function requires five parameters to be passed to it when retrieving index information. The following table describes the parameters.

Parameter	Description
database_id	The integer ID value assigned by SQL Server to the database. If this is unknown, the output of the DB_ID() function can be passed. For example, the value DB_ID(AdventureWorks) can be provided in lieu of the integer. If NULL is passed, the information for all indexes in all databases will be returned. If NULL is specified, you must also specify NULL for object_id, index_id, and partition_number.
object_id	The integer ID value for the table hosting the indexes to be examined. If the object_id value is unknown, the output of the OBJECT_ID() function can be passed. For example, the value OBJECT_ID(Person.Contact) can be provided. If NULL is passed, the information for all tables will be returned. If NULL is provided for object_id, you must also specify NULL for the index_id and partition_number.
index_id	The integer value of the index on the table. If NULL is passed, the information for all indexes will be returned. If NULL is provided as the value, you must also specify NULL for partition_number. Finding the value of index_id requires querying the sys.indexes catalog view. For example, finding the name and index_ids of the indexes on the Person.Contact table would require the following query.
	USE AdventureWorks
	GO
	SELECT name, index_id FROM sys.indexes
	WHERE object_id = OBJECT_ID('Person.Contact')
Partition_number	The integer value of the index partition number if the index is partitioned. Non-partitioned indexes have a partition number of 1. Because partitions are stored on separate physical files, their fragmentation can be different on each partition. If NULL is provided as the value for partition_id, all partitions will be returned. To discover the partition numbers that an index are on, the following query can be used.
	USE AdventureWorks;
	GO
	SELECT * FROM sys.dm_db_partition_stats
	WHERE object_id = OBJECT_ID('Person.Contact')

Table continued on following page

Parameter	Description
mode	Mode specifies what level of index analysis is performed (LIMITED, SAMPLED, or DETAILED). The default value is LIMITED.
	LIMITED mode is the fastest, but it only scans the index pages above the leaf level, which makes it the least accurate.
	SAMPLED mode samples 1 percent of the index or heap pages to return the analysis information. If there are fewer than 10,000 pages, SQL Server will use DETAILED instead.
	DETAILED mode scans all pages.

To practice examining and maintaining indexes, run the following command to create the MyContacts table that is used in the next few examples:

```
USE AdventureWorks
GO
SELECT ContactID, LastName, FirstName, Title, EmailAddress, Phone, ModifiedDate
INTO dbo.MyContacts
FROM Person.Contact
CREATE CLUSTERED INDEX clLastName ON dbo.MyContacts (LastName)
```

To query the sys.dm_db_index_physical_stats view to return all the possible data in relation to the MyContacts table, the following query can be used:

```
DECLARE @dbID smallint, @objectID int
SET @DbID = DB_ID('AdventureWorks')
SET @ObjectID = OBJECT_ID('dbo.MyContacts')

SELECT *
FROM sys.dm_db_index_physical_stats(@DbID, @ObjectID, NULL, NULL , 'DETAILED')
```

However, running this query returns more information than is generally needed. Because I am more particularly interested in just the fragmentation of the leaf level of the index and the fill percentage of the data pages, I can limit the amount of data returned. The reason I am less concerned about the non-leaf level is that the non-leaf level is typically very small. It can indeed get very fragmented, but the fragmentation of the non-leaf level of the index does not have anywhere near as much impact on performance as leaf-level fragmentation.

To reduce the information returned by the sys.dm_db_index_physical_stats query, it can be limited to just the columns of interest and the leaf level of the index, as follows:

```
DECLARE @dbID smallint, @objectID int
SET @DbID = DB_ID('AdventureWorks');
SET @ObjectID = OBJECT_ID('dbo.MyContacts')

SELECT avg_fragmentation_in_percent, avg_page_space_used_in_percent
```

```
FROM sys.dm_db_index_physical_stats(@DbID, @ObjectID, NULL, NULL , 'DETAILED')
WHERE index_level = 0
```

```
Results:
-----------------------------------------------------------------
avg_fragmentation_in_percent      avg_page_space_used_in_percent
----------------------------      ------------------------------
0                                 98.9996046454164
```

This query only returns the fragmentation level and page space used for the leaf level of the index, which is where the worst fragmentation (as far as performance is concerned) will occur.

The precise definition of fragmentation as a measurement is the percentage of pages where the next physical page is not the next logical page, as shown in Figure 5-14.

Now, insert some more records in the MyContacts table. The MyContacts table contains 19,972 rows. The following script inserts 3,994 additional records, which constitutes a 20 percent increase in rows:

```
INSERT dbo.MyContacts
(LastName, FirstName, Title, EmailAddress, Phone, ModifiedDate)
SELECT LastName, FirstName, Title, EmailAddress, Phone, ModifiedDate
FROM Person.Contact WHERE ContactID % 5 = 4
```

Querying the sys.dm_db_index_physical_stats dynamic management view now returns some very interesting data:

```
DECLARE @dbID smallint, @objectID int

SET @DbID = DB_ID('AdventureWorks');
SET @ObjectID = OBJECT_ID('dbo.MyContacts')

SELECT avg_fragmentation_in_percent, avg_page_space_used_in_percent
FROM sys.dm_db_index_physical_stats(@DbID, @ObjectID, NULL, NULL , 'DETAILED')
WHERE index_level = 0
```

```
RESULTS:
-----------------------------------------------------------------
avg_fragmentation_in_percent      avg_page_space_used_in_percent
----------------------------      ------------------------------
74.7980613893376                  70.6283172720534
```

Because of the additional rows that have been added to the MyContacts table almost 75 percent of the time when SQL Server was reading the data pages, the next physical page was not the next logical page. In addition to the fragmentation, the data pages are now only 70 percent full.

The combination of the fragmented indexes and the partially filled data pages causes SQL Server to read 470 logical extents, when only about 80 logical extent reads should have been required. This information is available through a deprecated Database Command Console (DBCC) command called DBCC SHOWCONTIG. DBCC. SHOWCONTIG will be removed in a future release of SQL Server, but for now, see what it tells you about the MyContacts table:

```
USE AdventureWorks
GO
DBCC SHOWCONTIG('dbo.MyContacts')
```

```
RESULTS:
-----------------------------------------------------------------------
- Pages Scanned...............................: 619
- Extents Scanned.............................: 79
- Extent Switches.............................: 470
- Avg. Pages per Extent.......................: 7.8
- Scan Density [Best Count:Actual Count].......: 16.56% [78:471]
- Logical Scan Fragmentation .................: 74.80%
- Extent Scan Fragmentation ..................: 5.06%
- Avg. Bytes Free per Page....................: 2377.3
- Avg. Page Density (full)....................: 70.63%
```

The DBCC SHOWCONTIG command shows you that SQL Server scanned 79 extents to retrieve all the data in the MyContacts table, but to scan those 79 extents, it had to switch between them 470 times!

It has already been established that SQL Server uses indexes to find rows in data tables for reading, updating, or deleting. However, if all you ever did was insert data in tables, you would not need an index. The general rule is that indexes help data read performance and hurts data insert performance. Here is an analogy and a confession.

I am a home improvement organizational slob. I am just incapable of putting things back where they belong. As a result, when I am finished with a particular home project, I invariably grab all the tools I have used and throw them on my workbench. Putting stuff away never takes me very long. However, as I start the next project, I invariably spend a huge amount of time just trying to find my hammer. Out of desperation, I sometimes just go buy another one. The home improvement stores love me. If I just spent the extra time required to put things back where they belong, I could save time and money.

The same goes for databases. Planning and building indexes takes time and effort; so does maintaining the indexes once they are built. However, even the most insert- and update-intensive database can usually be found to perform five reads for every write. That means that maintaining indexes at peak performance is going to pay off five-fold. With that firmly in mind, take a look at how to mitigate index fragmentation and correct it once it has occurred.

Mitigating Fragmentation with Fill Factor

To mitigate fragmentation caused by page splits, the database administrator can design or rebuild the indexes so that they are not completely full. This option is called *fill factor*. When building or rebuilding the index, a fill factor percentage can be specified. If an index page is only filled 90 percent of the way, it will take more inserts to the index to cause page splits and fragmentation to occur. Taking a look at the previous example, take a look at what impact filling the data pages to 90 percent would have (see Figure 5-15).

As you can see, now that the data pages are not completely full, adding additional contacts will not cause the pages to split as quickly. The fill factor is only effective when the indexes are built or rebuilt. After a few inserts, the indexes will again fill and page splits will occur. However, the page splits will not occur immediately, and the amount of time between index rebuilds can be lengthened.

Page 110	Page 111	Page 112	Page 113	Page 114	Page 115	Page 116	Page 117
Deniut	Dobney	Dulong	Elson	Fakhouri	Fluegel	Funk	Gates
Desai	Dodd	Duncan	Eminhizer	Farrell	Ford	Gage	Gehring
Dewer	Donovan	Dyck	Entin	Feng	Foster	Galos	German
Diaz	Drury	Eaton	Ersan	Ferrier	Frank	Ganio	Gibson
Dickson	Dudenhoef	Edwards	Estes	Finley	Friedland	Garcia	Gilbert
Dillon	Duff	Ellerbrock	Evans	Flood	Friske	Garza	Gilliat

Figure 5-15: Impact of filling the data pages

The index fill factor option has a down side (you just knew it would). Only filling up the index pages partially increases the amount of page reads required to retrieve the data. As a result, there is a definite point of decreasing returns when setting a fill factor. I personally believe that the fill factor of indexes should rarely be less than 90 percent. On heavily updated and queried tables, this percentage might go as low as 85 percent, but keep in mind that at an 85 percent fill factor, SQL Server will have to perform 15 percent more reads than is strictly required to retrieve the records at a 100 percent fill factor. As a result, a 10 percent fragmentation level may have about the same effect as a 90 percent fill factor.

Removing Fragmentation

To remove fragmentation, the indexes can be dropped and re-created, rebuilt in place, or reorganized. Each method has its advantages and disadvantages. The drop and re-create option is used with the CREATE INDEX command. The rebuild and reorganize options are used with the ALTER INDEX command.

Create Index with Drop Existing

The main advantage of dropping and re-creating an index is that almost everything about the index can be changed. For example, the columns that the index is defined on can be changed, the FILLFACTOR of the index can be modified, or the index can be changed from a non-clustered index to a clustered index, if a clustered index does not already exist. However, when using the DROP_EXISTING option with the CREATE INDEX command, a specific index must be specified. When using the rebuild or reorganize options of the ALTER INDEX command, all the indexes on a table can be specified at once.

Rebuilding an index with the DROP_EXISTING option removes index fragmentation by rebuilding all the index pages in indexed order. It also compacts the index pages so that empty space created by page splits is filled. Both the leaf level and the non-leaf level of the indexes are rebuilt.

Following is an example of the syntax for dropping and re-creating an index with the CREATE INDEX command:

```
CREATE UNIQUE CLUSTERED INDEX PK_Address_AddressID
    ON Person.Address(AddressID)
    WITH (FILLFACTOR = 90, DROP_EXISTING = ON)
```

Rebuilding Indexes

When an index is rebuilt using the ALTER INDEX command, SQL Server actually drops and re-creates the index much like the CREATE INDEX command. The difference is that the columns of the existing index cannot be changed, nor can the type of index. However, the FILLFACTOR can be modified as well as the very useful ability to execute the command only once on an entire table to rebuild all the indexes on that table.

Another very useful feature is the ONLINE option. If ONLINE is on, SQL Server will not place any long-term locks on the table being indexed, resulting in a much lower impact on user performance. The ONLINE option, however, is only available with the Enterprise Edition of SQL Server.

Like the DROP_EXISTING option, the REBUILD option of ALTER INDEX rebuilds both the leaf and non-leaf levels of the index.

The following is an example of rebuilding an individual index and then all the indexes on a table with a FILLFACTOR of 90 percent and the ONLINE option on:

```
USE AdventureWorks
GO

ALTER INDEX IX_Address_StateProvinceID ON Person.Address
REBUILD WITH (FILLFACTOR=90,ONLINE=ON)

USE AdventureWorks
GO

ALTER INDEX ALL ON Person.Address
REBUILD WITH (FILLFACTOR=90,ONLINE=ON)
```

The ONLINE indexing option leverages the TempDB database for index creation and maintenance. Indexes are created or rebuilt in the TempDB database, and then moved to the appropriate database. This decreases the impact on users in the database, but it can cause unanticipated growth of the TempDB database. The ONLINE index option is only available with the Enterprise and Developer editions of SQL Server.

Reorganizing Indexes

Reorganizing indexes consumes the least amount of system resources, but doesn't do as thorough a job as an index rebuild. When SQL Server reorganizes an index, it rearranges and compacts the data pages so that their logical order matches their physical order. Index reorganization only affects the leaf level of the index.

The guideline on when to perform index reorganization versus when to perform a rebuild is the 30 percent fragmentation level. If the level of fragmentation is less than or equal to 30 percent, a reorganization will take less time than an index rebuild, and consume much less system resources. If the fragmentation is greater than 30 percent, index reorganization will most likely take longer than a rebuild, but it will still consume less resources.

In general, if the indexes are rebuilt periodically with an appropriate FILLFACTOR, the need for index reorganization between those periods is reduced. However, intervals of high transaction activity may necessitate an intervening reorganization to prevent fragmentation from exceeding 30 percent, and potentially causing performance issues.

Statistics

Statistics are used by SQL Server to find the most efficient means of retrieving data from database tables by storing information about the selectivity of data in a column, as well as the distribution of data in a column. They can be created manually and automatically. Chapter 10 describes statistics in greater detail.

Table Keys and Constraints

As mentioned in previous chapters, the assumption of this book is that you are at least marginally familiar with database theory, so I will not expound on the purpose of primary and foreign keys to maintain data integrity. Instead, what is covered in this section is how to create these constraints, as well as other database objects that are used to maintain the integrity and consistency of data.

Primary Keys

A table can have only one *primary key* that is used to uniquely identify every row in the table. The primary key can be made up of more than one column if it takes more than one column in combination to uniquely identify each row. It is critical that you understand how SQL Server enforces uniqueness of the key values specified in a primary key definition. It does so by creating a unique index on the column or columns participating in the key.

It would be very inefficient to try to enforce uniqueness without sorting the data. The problem with SQL Server in this respect is that it defaults to a unique clustered index if a clustered index does not already exist. Decisions on what column or columns participate in a primary key and what ones define the physical structuring of the table's data are completely different. It should not be assumed that a primary key will also be the table's cluster key. Remember that all the table's non-clustered indexes will be built on top of the clustered index. If the primary key length is large, this will prove to be very detrimental to non-clustered index storage and retrieval.

Primary keys can be created by selecting the column or columns in the table designer window, and then clicking the Set Primary Key button on the Table Designer toolbar, or by using Transact-SQL in a CREATE TABLE or ALTER TABLE command. The following are examples of setting a primary key on tables during and after creation.

This first example shows how to create a primary key with the CREATE TABLE command and specify the name of the index:

```
USE AdventureWorks
GO
CREATE TABLE Sales.MyCreditCard(
    CreditCardID int IDENTITY(1,1) NOT NULL,
    CardType nvarchar(50) NOT NULL,
    CardNumber nvarchar(25) NOT NULL,
    ExpMonth tinyint NOT NULL,
    ExpYear smallint NOT NULL,
    ModifiedDate datetime NOT NULL,
  CONSTRAINT PK_MyCreditCard_CreditCardID
  PRIMARY KEY NONCLUSTERED (CreditCardID))
```

This next example also creates a primary key constraint in the CREATE TABLE command, but does not specify a key name. The key that results from this is named PK_TableName, so, in this, case it is PK_MyCreditCard2:

```
CREATE TABLE Sales.MyCreditCard2(
     CreditCardID int IDENTITY(1,1) NOT NULL PRIMARY KEY NONCLUSTERED,
     CardType nvarchar(50) NOT NULL,
     CardNumber nvarchar(25) NOT NULL,
     ExpMonth tinyint NOT NULL,
     ExpYear smallint NOT NULL,
     ModifiedDate datetime NOT NULL)
```

This last example shows how to add a primary key constraint to a table after the table has been created by using the ALTER TABLE command:

```
CREATE TABLE Sales.MyCreditCard3(
     CreditCardID int IDENTITY(1,1) NOT NULL,
     CardType nvarchar(50) NOT NULL,
     CardNumber nvarchar(25) NOT NULL,
     ExpMonth tinyint NOT NULL,
     ExpYear smallint NOT NULL,
     ModifiedDate datetime NOT NULL)
GO
ALTER TABLE Sales.MyCreditCard3
ADD CONSTRAINT PK_MyCreditCard3 PRIMARY KEY NONCLUSTERED (CreditCardID)
```

Remember that if the keyword NONCLUSTERED is not used, SQL Server will create a clustered index to enforce the key. Be sure this is what was intended.

Unique Keys

Whereas only one primary key is allowed on a table, many *unique keys* (or, more accurately, *unique constraints*) can be specified. For example, a delivery company that employs drivers may want to record information about its drivers in a table like the following example:

```
CREATE TABLE dbo.Driver(
   DriverID int IDENTITY(1,1) NOT NULL PRIMARY KEY NONCLUSTERED
  ,LastName varchar(75) NOT NULL
  ,FirstName varchar(75) NOT NULL
  ,MiddleInitial varchar(3) NULL
  ,SocSecNum char(9) NOT NULL
  ,LicenseNum varchar(25) NOT NULL)
```

In this example, the employer would probably want to ensure that both the Social Security number and the driver's license number were unique in addition to the primary key. You may be thinking, "Why don't we just use the Social Security number or driver's license number as the primary key?" There are actually two reasons why these columns are not good candidates for a primary key.

When it comes to the Social Security number both reasons apply: security and efficiency. Because most primary keys are also used as foreign keys, the Social Security number would be duplicated in several places. Given the sensitivity placed on private information, this would become a management nightmare. The other reason applies to both the Social Security number and the driver's license number.

Because both these numbers are not numbers at all, but rather strings of characters, they are not the best values to use to enforce referential integrity, because the join criteria would be large instead of a more efficient integer value.

To create a unique constraint, you can either add a unique index or a unique constraint to the table. A unique index behaves like a unique constraint, and SQL Server will create a unique index to enforce a unique constraint. It is almost a case of "What comes first: the chicken or the egg?"

To create unique indexes or keys graphically, first open the table for modification by right-clicking the table name and clicking Modify.

On the Table Designer toolbar, click the Manage Indexes and Keys button (see Figure 5-16).

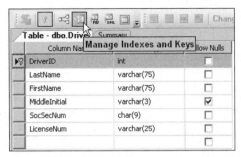

Figure 5-16: Manage Indexes and Keys button

On the Indexes/Keys dialog (see Figure 5-17), click Add and then specify the properties of the new index or key. Notice in the Type property that either Index or Unique Key can be chosen. If the Is Unique property is set to True, then either Index or Unique Key will have the same effect.

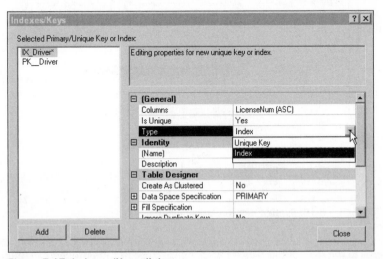

Figure 5-17: Indexes/Keys dialog

To enforce uniqueness on the `LicenseNum` column, one of the following commands can be used. They both have the same effect:

```
ALTER TABLE dbo.Driver
ADD CONSTRAINT UK_LicenseNum UNIQUE NONCLUSTERED (LicenseNum)

CREATE UNIQUE NONCLUSTERED INDEX IX_UK_LicenseNum
ON dbo.Driver (LicenseNum)
```

Foreign Keys

Foreign keys are created to guarantee referential integrity between tables. To create a foreign key on a table, the column or columns defined in the foreign key must map to column or columns in a primary key table, where the columns are designated as either primary keys or unique keys (both unique constraints and unique indexes qualify).

The following examples are based on the dbo.`Driver` table created earlier and the dbo.`DriverRecord` table, which can be created with the following script:

```
CREATE TABLE dbo.DriverRecord (
  RecordID int IDENTITY (1,1) NOT NULL PRIMARY KEY NONCLUSTERED
 ,DriverID int NOT NULL
 ,InfractionID int NOT NULL
 ,RecordDate datetime NOT NULL)
```

To create a foreign key with the graphical tools, expand the table in Object Explorer. Right-click the Keys node and click New Foreign Key. The Foreign Key Relationships dialog will display (see Figure 5-18).

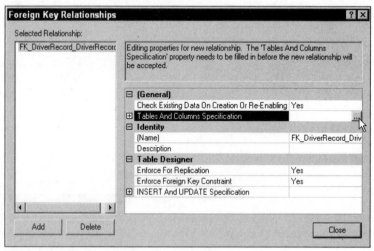

Figure 5-18: Foreign Key Relationships dialog

Click the ellipsis to the right of the Tables and Columns Specification property to select the primary key and foreign key columns.

In the resulting Tables and Columns dialog (see Figure 5-19), change the name of the relationship to FK_DriverRecord_Driver. Then choose Driver as the primary key table and DriverID as the column in both the primary key and foreign key tables.

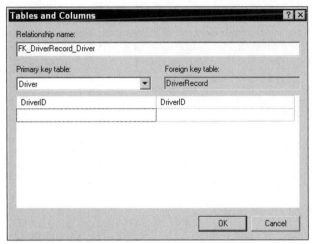

Figure 5-19: Tables and Columns dialog

Foreign Key Options

Foreign key constraints have a number of advanced options that change the way they behave during creation and after creation that are described in the following sections. These options can be set in the General and Table Designer sections of the Foreign Key Relationships dialog, or through Transact-SQL. Examples of the code necessary to create foreign keys and set their options are given with each description.

The following examples all use the same constraint name. To execute the examples in succession, it will be necessary to drop the existing constraint prior to re-creating it. Constraints can be deleted using SQL Server Managements Studio's Object Explorer, or by executing the script ALTER TABLE dbo.DriverRecord DROP CONSTRAINT FK_DriverRecord_Driver.

WITH CHECK

This is the default setting when adding a foreign key. This setting specifies that any existing data in the foreign key table is validated to conform to the key:

```
ALTER TABLE dbo.DriverRecord WITH CHECK
ADD CONSTRAINT FK_DriverRecord_Driver FOREIGN KEY (DriverID)
    REFERENCES dbo.Driver (DriverID)
```

WITH NOCHECK

This setting specifies that existing data is not validated to conform to the new key. This option can make the creation of the key more efficient when you know that any existing data already conforms to the constraint, but it is important to keep in mind that any non-conforming records will be ignored during the key creation process. However, during subsequent updates to the non-conforming row, the key will be enforced, resulting in an error.

```
ALTER TABLE dbo.DriverRecord WITH NOCHECK
ADD CONSTRAINT FK_DriverRecord_Driver FOREIGN KEY (DriverID)
    REFERENCES dbo.Driver (DriverID)
```

Cascading Constraints

Foreign keys prevent the updating or deletion of parent values (primary or unique values) by default. However, there are times when this is not desirable. SQL Server provides the option of specifying what action is taken if a parent record is deleted or updated.

ON DELETE NO ACTION and ON UPDATE NO ACTION are the default settings for foreign keys. These settings specify that any attempt to delete a row or update a key referenced by foreign keys in existing rows in other tables will fail.

In addition to the default NO ACTION setting, the options CASCADE, SET NULL, and SET DEFAULT are possible, which allow for deletions or updates of key values to cascade in a defined manner to the tables defined to have foreign key relationships.

ON DELETE CASCADE

This option specifies that any child record will be deleted when the parent row is deleted. If the child record also has child records, the foreign key options on those tables will be enforced and either cascade or fail, as the case may be.

```
ALTER TABLE dbo.DriverRecord WITH NOCHECK
ADD CONSTRAINT FK_DriverRecord_Driver FOREIGN KEY (DriverID)
    REFERENCES dbo.Driver (DriverID)
    ON DELETE CASCADE
```

ON UPDATE CASCADE

When a parent key is updated, the update will cascade to any child records that reference the parent keys.

```
ALTER TABLE dbo.DriverRecord WITH NOCHECK
ADD CONSTRAINT FK_DriverRecord_Driver FOREIGN KEY (DriverID)
    REFERENCES dbo.Driver (DriverID)
    ON UPDATE CASCADE
```

ON DELETE SET NULL

With this setting, any child record's foreign key will be set to NULL if the parent row is deleted. The foreign key column must allow nulls for this option to work.

ON UPDATE SET NULL

Any child record's foreign key will be set to NULL if the corresponding parent key is updated. All foreign key columns of the child table must be nullable.

```
ALTER TABLE dbo.DriverRecord WITH NOCHECK
ADD CONSTRAINT FK_DriverRecord_Driver FOREIGN KEY (DriverID)
    REFERENCES dbo.Driver (DriverID)
    ON DELETE SET NULL
    ON UPDATE SET NULL
```

ON DELETE SET DEFAULT

When a parent record is deleted, the corresponding child key value will be set to the value specified by any DEFAULT constraint defined on that column. If no DEFAULT constraint exists, the value will be set to NULL as long as the foreign key column is nullable. The value specified in the DEFAULT constraint must have a corresponding row in the parent table.

ON UPDATE SET DEFAULT

When a parent key value is updated, any corresponding child records will be updates to the value specified in the DEFAULT constraint defined on the foreign key column. Like the previous option, the default value must exist in the parent table. If there is no DEFAULT defined, and the foreign key column is nullable, the child value will be set to NULL.

```
ALTER TABLE dbo.DriverRecord WITH NOCHECK
ADD CONSTRAINT FK_DriverRecord_Driver FOREIGN KEY (DriverID)
    REFERENCES dbo.Driver (DriverID)
    ON DELETE SET DEFAULT
    ON UPDATE SET DEFAULT
```

The cascade setting can be combined and mixed. For example, the cascade for a DELETE can be set to CASCADE, but NO ACTION for an UPDATE.

Check Constraints

Check constraints are used to ensure that the data in a field conforms to a defined expression. The check constraints can be created graphically by following these steps on the dbo.Driver table that was created earlier:

1. Expand the dbo.Driver table in Object Explorer.

2. Right-click the Constraints node and click New Constraint. This will launch the Check Constraints dialog.

3. In the Check Constraints dialog (see Figure 5-20), change the name of the constraint to CK_DriverSocSecNum in the Identity section and change the description to "Enforces numeric values for SSN's."

4. Edit the expression for the constraint by typing in the following expression:

```
(SocSecNum LIKE '[0-9][0-9][0-9][0-9][0-9][0-9][0-9][0-9][0-9]')
```

This expression ensures that any Social Security numbers added to the table will be nine contiguous integers with no dashes.

Here is the Transact-SQL command to create the same constraint:

```
ALTER TABLE dbo.Driver ADD CONSTRAINT
  CK_DriverSocSecNum
  CHECK (SocSecNum LIKE '[0-9][0-9][0-9][0-9][0-9][0-9][0-9][0-9][0-9]')
GO
```

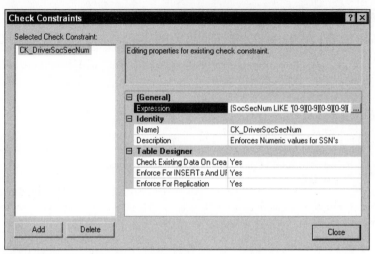

Figure 5-20: Check Constraints dialog

Default Constraints

Default constraints specify a value to be inserted in a table if no value is specified. They can be specified on a table when the table is created or being modified. To create a default constraint with the graphical tools, specify a default value or binding in the Column Properties window of the Table Designer, as shown in Figure 5-21.

Figure 5-21: Creating a default constraint

Bindings are links to a Database Default or Rule and are discussed later in the chapter.

For this example, specify the string '000000000' as the default value to assign to any Social Security number not provided in a table insert command.

The Transact-SQL command for accomplishing this same task is as follows:

```
ALTER TABLE dbo.Driver ADD CONSTRAINT
    DF_Driver_SocSecNum DEFAULT '000000000' FOR SocSecNum
GO
```

DML Triggers

Data Manipulation Language (DML) triggers are stored Transact-SQL or managed code objects that are executed as a result of a DML command (INSERT, UPDATE, DELETE). There are two types of DML triggers in SQL Server 2005: After triggers and Instead Of triggers.

Traditional triggers are known as *After* triggers because they execute *"after"* the DML statement is executed on the table with the defined trigger. The code in the trigger is implicitly part of the transaction that caused the trigger to execute. Any ROLLBACK command in the body of the trigger will cause the trigger and the associated transaction to be rolled back.

Instead Of triggers are so named because the commands in the trigger are executed *"instead of"* the actual transaction that caused the trigger to be executed. Instead Of triggers were created primarily as a method of sending updates to tables referenced in views containing a UNION operator, because these views cannot be directly updated. For information about Instead Of triggers and these partitioned views check out *Beginning Transact-SQL with SQL Server 2000 and 2005* (Indianapolis: Wiley, 2005).

Database Diagrams

Once the database and its objects have been created, it is often convenient to be able to create entity relationship diagrams that are linked to the underlying structures. That way, any changes that must be made (especially the creation of foreign key constraints) can be made and applied to the database in a convenient graphical environment. The database diagram feature in SQL Server Management Studio provides this functionality. The database diagram feature, however, is not a replacement for full-fledged database design tools. It is more often used in the test and development phase of database deployment.

The database diagram feature is accessed in the Object Explorer of SQL Server Management Studio in the individual database node. The first time the Database Diagram node is selected, an informational message will display notifying you that "One or more support objects" are missing, and ask whether or not you want to install them. Selecting "Yes" will cause SQL Server to create a system owned table called dbo.sysdiagrams that will contain the definitions of any new diagrams created.

The following steps will guide you through the creation and modification of a database diagram:

1. Expand the Databases node and then the AdventureWorks database node. Right-click the Database Diagrams node in AdventureWorks and click New Database Diagram. The database diagram pane will appear, as well as an Add Table dialog that alphabetically lists all the user tables in the database.

2. Select the `Address(Person)` table. Click Add to add the `Person.Address` table to the diagram and then click Close on the Add Table dialog.

3. Right-click the `Address(Person)` table and then click Add Related Tables. This causes all tables that have a defined relationship to the `Person.Address` table to be added to the diagram. This feature comes in very much handy when you are unfamiliar with the structure of the database.

Notice that all the tables are just piled on top of each other in the diagram. You can manually reorder them, or just right-click an empty space on the diagram and click Arrange Tables. SQL Server arranges the tables neatly on the diagram pane so that the tables and their relationships are easily viewed.

Because there is limited space in the diagram, you can create multiple diagrams that divide the database into functional areas, or you can display page breaks on the diagram and divide a large diagram into many pages. To display page breaks, right-click an empty space on the diagram and click View Page Breaks.

Right-clicking any table provides the option of changing the way the table is displayed on the diagram, deleting the table from the database, removing the table from the diagram, as well as several table modification options normally available from the Table Designer toolbar.

Views

SQL Server 2005 views are simply saved named queries that can be managed independently of the tables they reference. They are very much like the tables they reference, except that they are, by default, logical objects and not physical objects. The one exception to this is when a clustered index is created on a view, causing the view to be "Materialized." Views are typically created to abstract complex database design, to simplify permissions by granting access to one view instead of multiple tables, and to arrange data for export to other data stores.

The creation of views and other programming objects is unfortunately beyond the scope of this book. For more information on how to create views and why to create views, check out *Beginning Transact-SQL with SQL Server 2000 and 2005* (Indianapolis: Wiley, 2005). For information about securing views read Chapter 6.

System Views

System views, as noted in Chapter 4, are the database administrator's view of system objects. There are too many system views to describe here, and all are documented in SQL Server 2005 Books Online. System views can be divided up into four categories:

❑ *Information Schema Views* — Information Schema views are predefined views that belong to a special schema known as `INFORMATION_SCHEMA`. Information schema views provide a consistent view of SQL Server metadata that is generally stable from one release to another.

❑ *Static System Views* — The static system views are another method for retrieving metadata from SQL Server, but it is recommended not to build objects that directly query these views, because they are not as stable from release to release as the Information Schema views. They do provide a great deal of useful information, however, that can be utilized in the troubleshooting and maintenance of SQL Server 2005. Just use caution if building permanent scripts or objects that reference these views.

❏ *Dynamic System Views* — Dynamic System views return server state information that can be used to monitor SQL Server processes, diagnose problems, and tune performance. They are briefly described in Chapter 4.

❏ *Backward Compatibility System Views* — Because the system tables from SQL Server 2000 are no longer available, SQL Server 2005 provides many views that carry the same name as the previous system tables. These views return only the features of SQL Server 2005 that are compatible with SQL Server 2000, and are provided strictly for use with objects and scripts designed on SQL Server 2000. Future development work should use the new system views that return SQL Server 2005–specific information.

Synonyms

Although Books Online states that "Microsoft SQL Server 2005 introduces the concept of a synonym," there is nothing really new about synonyms. It is just that Microsoft SQL Server has not used them in several releases. *Synonyms* are a very good tool used to give names to SQL Server database objects that can be used by database applications instead of their defined two-part, three-part, or four-part schema-scoped names. For example, a database application that references a table on one server and a table on another server would typically need to be configured to access the tables using a four-part name. Defining a synonym essentially presents an alias that maps directly to the table without having to fully qualify the table.

Try It Out   Creating a Synonym

To fully understand the synonym, it will be better to create one, and then explore how to use it.

In Object Explorer expand the `AdventureWorks` database, right-click the Synonyms node, and click New Synonym.

In the New Synonym dialog, enter or select the following values in each of the fields:

❏ Synonym name: Products

❏ Synonym schema: dbo

❏ Server name: *The name of your server.* (In my case, it's AughtFive.)

❏ Database name: AdventureWorksDW

❏ Schema: dbo

❏ Object type: Table

❏ Object name: DimProduct

Your configuration should be similar to Figure 5-22.

Click OK.

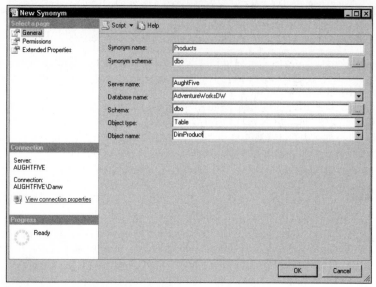

Figure 5-22: New Synonym dialog

This will create a synonym called `Products` in the `AdventureWorks` database that references the `dbo.DimProduct` table in the `AdventureWorksDW` database.

Now that you have a new synonym, open a new query window and type in the following code:

```
USE AdventureWorks
GO
SELECT ProductKey, EnglishProductName, StandardCost
FROM dbo.Products
```

Notice that the query returns 606 rows from the `AdventureWorksDW` database without having to qualify the object name, like the following example:

```
USE AdventureWorks
GO
SELECT ProductKey, EnglishProductName, StandardCost
FROM AdventureWorksDW.dbo.DimProduct
```

Synonyms can be created that reference views, tables, stored procedures, and functions on any database, or a linked server to simplify the application data access.

Programming Objects

As previously noted, the creation and logic behind programming objects is beyond the scope of this book, but the purpose of the objects and their basic use is pertinent. The database administrator needs to understand how programming objects can impact the behavior of the database. The most important aspect is typically security, which is addressed in Chapter 6.

Stored Procedures

A *stored procedure* is a named collection of Transact-SQL or managed code that is stored on the server in a database. SQL Server stored procedures are very similar to procedures from other programming languages in that they are used to encapsulate repetitive tasks. They support user-declared variables, conditional execution, and many other programming features.

Stored procedures can be written in traditional Transact-SQL or in a .NET managed language such as C# or VB.NET. Chapter 12 discusses the advantages of using managed code to create complex stored procedures that would push the limits of Transact-SQL.

The major purpose of stored procedures is to encapsulate business functionality and create reusable application logic. Because the stored procedures are stored on the server, changes to the business logic can be accomplished in a single location.

Stored procedures also provide controlled modification of data in the database. Giving users permission to modify data in database tables is typically a very bad idea. Instead, stored procedures can be created that perform only the modifications that are required by the application. Users can then be given the permission to execute the stored procedure to perform the required data modification.

User-created stored procedures are more efficient than ad-hoc Transact-SQL, and much more secure. They drastically reduce the number of network packets needed to query and modify databases, and are compiled and cached for long periods of time for efficient re-use.

In addition to user-created stored procedures, SQL Server provides literally hundreds of *system-stored procedures*. These system-stored procedures are used to retrieve system information, as well as make changes to the underlying system objects. They range from simple stored procedures that return a list of all the logged-in users, to complex stored procedures that create database maintenance jobs. Some of these stored procedures are covered in later chapters as they apply to the topic at hand.

Functions

SQL Server 2005 provides support for three types of user-defined functions: scalar functions, table-valued functions, and aggregate functions. SQL Server functions are very similar to functions in other programming languages. They accept parameters, perform some action based on the input parameter, and return a value. Table-value functions always return a table data type. Scalar and aggregate functions can return any data type except text, ntext, and image.

User-defined functions can be created with Transact-SQL or managed code with the exception of aggregate functions, which are always created in managed code. User-defined functions offer many of the same benefits as stored procedures as far as efficiency and security are concerned.

System functions are separated into categories in the Object Explorer of SQL Server Management Studio. Some functions are used to manipulate user data (such as aggregate and string functions), whereas others are used to retrieve or manipulate system information (such as security and metadata functions).

Database Triggers

SQL Server 2005 provides the ability to create triggers at the table, database, and server scope. Table triggers were discussed previously and are also called Data Manipulation Language (DML) triggers.

Database and server scope triggers are also known as *Data Definition Language (DDL) triggers*. They offer the same functionality — the ability to execute a procedure when a database or server DDL level event occurs. DDL Level events are primarily CREATE, ALTER, and DROP commands, but can also include commands such as UPDATE STATISTICS. DDL triggers provide the ability to audit or prevent database and server modifications.

The following example demonstrates how to create a database-level DDL trigger to audit modifications made to the database.

First, you create a table to record all the DDL events that occur on the database. Do this by running the following script:

```
USE AdventureWorks
GO
CREATE TABLE AuditDDL (
   EventID     int IDENTITY(1,1) NOT NULL
  ,LoginName   varchar(75) NOT NULL
  ,EventTime   datetime NOT NULL
  ,DDLEvent    varchar(100) NULL
  ,Eventdata   xml NOT NULL)
GO
```

Next, create a trigger that will execute whenever any DDL level event is executed. This trigger uses a system function called EVENTDATA that returns an XML resultset containing all the information about the DDL event. In the trigger are XQUERY commands to shred the XML data into a relational resultset to be inserted into the audit table.

```
USE AdventureWorks
GO

CREATE TRIGGER RecordDDL
ON DATABASE
FOR DDL_DATABASE_LEVEL_EVENTS
AS
DECLARE @data XML
SET @data = EVENTDATA()
INSERT AuditDDL
  (LoginName, EventTime,DDLEvent,EventData)
VALUES
  (SYSTEM_USER
  ,GETDATE()
  ,@data.value('(/EVENT_INSTANCE/TSQLCommand)[1]', 'nvarchar(2000)')
  ,@data)
RETURN
GO
```

Now, test the trigger by creating and dropping a table called TriggerTest, and then querying the audit table to see if you captured the information you wanted:

```
USE AdventureWorks
GO

CREATE TABLE TriggerTest (
```

```
    Column1 int
  ,Column2 int)

DROP TABLE TriggerTest

SELECT * FROM AuditDDL
```

You should get two rows that look similar to Figure 5-23 (of course, your `LoginName` and `EventTime` will vary).

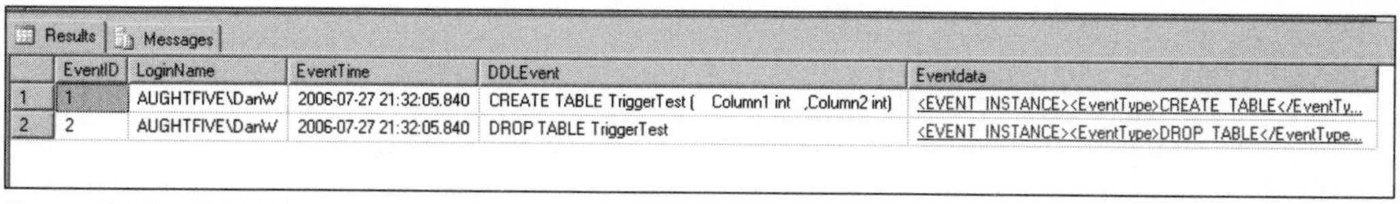

	EventID	LoginName	EventTime	DDLEvent	Eventdata
1	1	AUGHTFIVE\DanW	2006-07-27 21:32:05.840	CREATE TABLE TriggerTest (Column1 int ,Column2 int)	<EVENT_INSTANCE><EventType>CREATE_TABLE</EventTy...
2	2	AUGHTFIVE\DanW	2006-07-27 21:32:05.840	DROP TABLE TriggerTest	<EVENT_INSTANCE><EventType>DROP_TABLE</EventType...

Figure 5-23: DDL Trigger Audit results

To ensure that this trigger does not interfere with other exercises later in the book, you may want to drop it by executing the command DROP TRIGGER RecordDDL.

Assemblies

Assemblies are database programming objects created with Visual Studio 2005. They can include stored procedures, functions, triggers, aggregates, and types written in a managed language such as C# or Visual Basic.NET. They are directly accessible with the integration of the Common Language Runtime (CLR) and the Database Engine. Assemblies offer a significant advantage over traditional Transact-SQL programming objects in certain situations such as those that require intensive and recursive mathematical operations or complex string manipulation. Chapter 12 describes CLR objects and integration in more detail.

As inferred in Chapter 12, there is a definite tension between database administrators and developers. Often, this tension is exacerbated by the database administrator's lack of programming skills. With the integration of the CLR and the Database Engine, it is more important than ever that the database administrators understand programming, and communicate with the developers who interact with their systems.

CLR assemblies can be imported into the database with Visual Studio 2005, Transact-SQL, or with the Assembly Assisted Editor in Management Studio. This discussion focuses on just Transact-SQL and the Assembly Assisted Editor.

To launch the Assembly Assisted Editor, expand Databases, expand `AdventureWorks`, expand Programmability, right-click Assemblies, and click New Assembly.

In the New Assembly dialog (see Figure 5-24), browse to the assembly, specify an assembly owner, and set the permissions for the assembly.

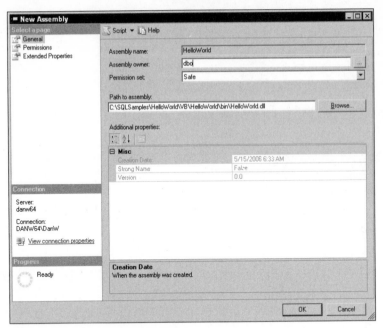

Figure 5-24: New Assembly dialog

The permission set defines how much access the assembly is given to perform the contained actions. Safe limits the assembly to the current database and connection. External Access enables the assembly to interact with the operating system, network, and file system. Unsafe allows the assembly all the privileges of External Access, as well as the ability to make calls to unmanaged code. Assembly permission sets are discussed in more detail in Chapter 6 and Chapter 12.

Now that the assembly has been added to the database, a stored procedure, function, trigger, type, or aggregate can be added to the database that links to the assembly. (For this exact process, check out Chapter 12.)

Types

Types are a collection of system data types, user-defined data types, and user-defined types, as well as any XML schema collections used in the database. System data types were described in an earlier chapter.

User-Defined Data Types

User-defined data types are aliases to define system types that exist only within the database they are created in. User-defined data types are most often used to provide an intuitive data type name and maintain data type consistency across different tables.

For example, I ask five different database developers to create a table that stores information about an individual. The table will contain the individual's last name, first name, address, and phone number. The chances are that the five different database developers would provide at least three differing data types to store any one of the fields specified. For example, one developer may use a varchar(13) to represent a phone number, thinking that phone numbers would be represented as (111)111-1111. Another developer may decide to think globally and provide for international codes as well, and specify a phone number of `varchar(25)`. To avoid possible type conflicts later, you can specify user-defined data types be used.

To create a user-defined data type graphically, expand Databases in the Object Explorer, expand `AdventureWorks`, expand Programmability, expand Types, right-click "User-defined data types," and click "New User-defined data type."

Figure 5-25 illustrates the creation of a `ZipCode` data type in the `dbo` schema that is based on the system type `char(5)`. User-defined data types can also be bound to database defaults and rules by specifying them in the appropriate text boxes. Defaults and rules are described later in this chapter.

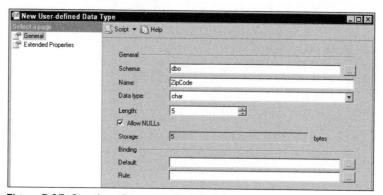

Figure 5-25: Creation of a `ZipCode` data type

The drawback of user-defined data types is that they are not transparent to database applications. For example, an application programmer would not be able to instantiate a variable in the application layer that utilized the `ZipCode` data type. The programmer would have to know that the base type was a `char(5)`. In addition to the application-layer visibility, user-defined data types only exist in the database they are created in. For example, a `ZipCode` data type in the `AdventureWorks` database may not be the same as a `ZipCode` data type in the `AdventureWorksDW` database.

User-Defined Types

User-defined types (UDTs) are very similar to user-defined data types, except that they are created using managed code and defined in a custom class that can be imported into a SQL Server database. UDTs can be very complex and can define custom data types that have no parallel system type. For example, a UDT could be created to define a complex single value that represented a map coordinate of latitude and longitude, or something like a true Social Security number data type that really was stored as a number, but didn't truncate leading zeros.

The other advantage of UDTs is that they are visible from the application layer as well. Because they are defined in a class, that class can be referenced in a database application so that parameters could be instantiated using the native UDT. User-defined types are also troublesome when it comes to cross-database application, because even the UDT is database-specific. However, if the same CLR assembly is referenced in the creation of the UDT in each database, this limitation is reduced. As previously noted,

Chapter 12 contains more information about CLR assemblies, and the database objects that can be created with them, including UDTs. For even more information on the CLR, consult *Professional SQL Server 2005 CLR Stored Procedures, Functions, and Triggers* (Indianapolis: Wiley, 2006).

Defaults

Instead of creating a default constraint on a column in a table, a standalone *default* can be created at the database level, and then bound to any table column in the database. Defaults have been marked for deprecation, and it is recommended that you do not use them in any new development work. They are found in the Programmability node of databases in Object Explorer, but must be created with Transact-SQL. The following example demonstrates how to create a default Social Security number, and then bind it to the SocSecNum column on the dbo.Driver table:

```
USE AdventureWorks
GO
CREATE DEFAULT dfltSocSecNum AS '000000000'
GO
sp_bindefault 'dfltSocSecNum', 'dbo.Driver.SocSecNum'
```

Rules

Rules, like defaults, have been deprecated. A *rule* is like a check constraint. However, it is created once at the database level and then bound to any column that matches the data type specified. The following example demonstrates how to create a rule that enforces numeric data on a character-based column, and then how to bind that rule to the SocSecNum column:

```
USE AdventureWorks
GO
CREATE RULE AllNumRule AS
@value LIKE '[0-9][0-9][0-9][0-9][0-9][0-9][0-9][0-9][0-9]'
GO
sp_bindrule 'AllNumRule','dbo.Driver.SocSecNum'
```

Summary

This chapter has covered a great deal of information, and some of the topics covered were only briefly described. An entire book could be written on just the SQL Server database and all the features it includes. This, however, is not that book. The purpose of this chapter was to expose you to many, but not all, of the objects that can be found in a SQL Server database and how to create or manage them. Future chapters explain how to use all the features of SQL Server 2005 from the database administrator's perspective.

If you have read the chapters in order, you should have a pretty good understanding of how SQL Server organizes data, and how to access the various parts of a SQL Server database. From this point forward, Chris, Paul, and I will show you how to administer this powerful new database server, as well as provide the background information necessary to understand exactly what it is you are administering. So press on my young Padawan, press on. (OK, not just a *Star Trek* reference, but a *Star Wars* reference as well. Is this not the ultimate geek book?)

In Chapter 6, you learn how to secure a SQL Server 2005 server, database, and all the associated objects that comprise SQL Server. SQL Server security is more configurable than ever before, and there are many new features. Chapter 6 describes these new features (such as SQL Server certificates, credentials, and encryption) in detail. It also covers the core security features, and explains how to ensure that your server is as secure as it possibly can be.

SQL Server 2005 Security

Security is a double-edged sword. As an administrator, you want your servers to be as secure as possible, but often don't want to sacrifice functionality or have to pay an outrageous amount of money to secure your infrastructure. Unfortunately, many administrators have been victims of the belief that "it won't happen to me." With the increasing number of threats, you must ensure that you apply due diligence to protect your servers as much as possible. You are never going to be able to say with absolute certainty that your SQL Servers are invulnerable. It is a fact that regardless of how much money you spend, and how many rights and privileges you limit your users to, you will still be attacked.

Security isn't about guaranteeing a completely attack-proof system. It's about mitigating and responding to risk. It's about ensuring that you take the necessary steps to minimize the scope of the attack. This chapter takes a look at SQL Security from the outside in. You will learn about the different types of accounts and principals that are available. You will see how to control access to database objects, and how you can use some new tools to encrypt and protect your data. This chapter also includes some guidelines for providing a secure solution for deploying and managing your SQL Server.

It is important to note that the concepts discussed and examples given in this chapter have been tested to work in Windows XP and Windows Server 2003. As of this writing, the Windows Vista beta introduces a number of new security features that can change the way some of these tasks are performed. Regardless of which operating system you use, you should be familiar with its security features.

Also, many of the examples used in this chapter refer to the server `AughtFive`. Remember to replace `AughtFive` with your own server name.

SQL Server Authentication Modes

Microsoft SQL Server 2005 offers two options for authenticating users. The default mode is Windows Authentication Mode, which offers a high level of security by using the operating system's authentication mechanism to authenticate credentials that will need access to the server. The other, SQL Server and Windows Authentication Mode (also known as Mixed Mode), offers the ability to allow both Windows-based and SQL-based authentications. Although Windows Authentication Mode provides greater security than SQL Server and Windows Authentication Mode, the application your database supports may not be able to use Windows authentication.

Windows Authentication Mode allows you to use existing accounts stored in the local computer's Security Accounts Manager (SAM) database, or, if the server is a member of an Active Directory domain, accounts in the Microsoft Windows Active Directory database. The benefits of using the Windows Authentication Mode include reducing the administrative overhead for your SQL or Database Administrators by allowing them to use accounts that already exist, and the ability to use stronger authentication protocols, such as Kerberos or Windows NT LAN Manager (NTLM).

Mixed Mode authentication allows you to create logins that are unique to the SQL Server, and do not have a corresponding Windows or Active Directory account. This can be helpful for applications that require users who are not part of your enterprise to be able to authenticate and gain access to securables in your database. When SQL logins are used, the SQL Server authenticates these credentials.

When deciding on the authentication method, identify how users will be connecting to the database. If your SQL Server and your database users are all members of the same Active Directory forest, or even different forests that share a trust, using Windows authentication can simplify the process of creating and managing logins. However, if your SQL Server is not in an Active Directory domain, or your database users are not internal to your organization, consider the use of SQL-based logins to create a clear distinction between security contexts.

In Chapter 2, you learned how to install Microsoft SQL Server 2005, and you selected which authentication mode to use. If you wish to change the authentication mode after the installation, be aware that this will require you to restart the SQL Service.

Changing the Authentication Mode from Management Studio

To change the authentication mode from the Management Studio, follow these steps:

1. Launch SQL Server Management Studio.

2. In Object Explorer, select your server.

3. Right-click your server and select Properties (see Figure 6-1).

4. Under the "Select a page" pane, select Security.

5. Under the heading "Server authentication," select or review the appropriate authentication mode.

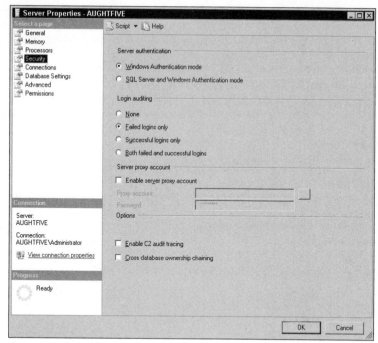

Figure 6-1: Server Properties screen

Using the xp_instance_regwrite Extended Stored Procedure

You can also change the authentication mode using the xp_instance_regwrite extended stored procedure, as long as you have administrative permissions on the local server. The following example shows you how to change the authentication mode to SQL Server and Windows Authentication Mode:

```
USE master
EXEC xp_instance_regwrite N'HKEY_LOCAL_MACHINE',
N'Software\Microsoft\MSSQLServer\MSSQLServer', N'LoginMode', REG_DWORD, 2
```

You can also change the authentication mode to Windows Authentication Mode by changing the DWORD value to 1, as shown in this example:

```
USE master
EXEC xp_instance_regwrite N'HKEY_LOCAL_MACHINE',
N'Software\Microsoft\MSSQLServer\MSSQLServer', N'LoginMode', REG_DWORD, 1
```

When you installed SQL Server, if you selected Windows Authentication Mode, the sa account is disabled by default. If you are changing the authentication mode from Windows Authentication Mode to SQL Server and Windows Authentication Mode, the account remains disabled with a blank password. Blank passwords are never a good idea, but you cannot enable the sa account without setting one. And, quite frankly, using the sa account in a production environment can increase your security risk because you lose the ability to associate an action with a specific person.

Principals

The term *principal* is used to describe individuals, groups, and processes that will interact with the SQL Server. The resources available to a principal are dependent on where the principal resides. Microsoft SQL Server supports several different types of principals defined at three different levels: the Windows level, the SQL Server level, and the database level. Each type of principal is identified here, and the way they are used. To prepare for some of the exercises in this chapter, you will want to create some local Windows accounts as follows:

1. From the Start Menu, right-click My Computer and select Manage.

2. In the Computer Management window, expand Local Users and Groups (see Figure 6-2).

3. Right-click the Users folder and select New User.

4. In the User Name box, enter **Bob**.

5. In the Password and Confirm Password boxes, enter **P@ssw0rd**.

6. Clear the check next to the "User must change password and next login" box.

7. Click Create.

8. In the User Name box, enter **CarolStreet**.

9. In the Password and Confirm Password boxes, enter **P@ssw0rd**.

10. Clear the check next to the "User must change password and next login" box.

11. Click Create.

12. In the User Name box, enter **Alice**.

13. In the Password and Confirm Password boxes, enter **P@ssw0rd**.

14. Clear the check next to the "User must change password and next login" box.

15. Click Create.

16. Click Close.

17. Right-click the Groups folder and select New Group.

18. In the Group Name Box, enter **G NorthWest Sales**.

19. Click Create.

20. Click Close.

21. Close the Computer Management window.

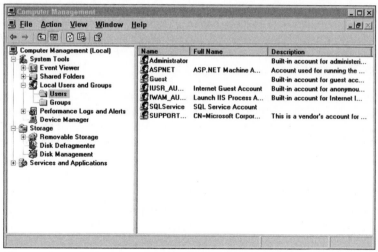

Figure 6-2: Computer Management screen

Logins

Microsoft SQL Server 2005 offers two kinds of logins for authentication. Windows logins are associated with user or group accounts stored in Active Directory or the local Security Accounts Manager (SAM) database. SQL logins are used to represent an individual or entity that does not have a Windows account, and, therefore, must rely on the SQL Server for storage and management of account information.

Windows logins, whether they represent an individual or a group, are bound by the password policy of either the domain or the SAM in which the account exists. When a login is created for a Windows user or group, no password information is stored in the SQL Server. The password for a Windows login is usually NULL, but even if this field is populated, the value is ignored. Windows logins are also authenticated prior to connecting to the SQL Server. This means that Active Directory or the operating system will have already verified the principal's identity.

When a Windows login is created for a group, all members of that group have the ability to authenticate against the SQL Server without having to create separate logins for each user.

SQL Server logins, however, must authenticate against the SQL Server. This makes the SQL Server responsible for verifying the user's identity. SQL stores the login and password information in the Master database. It is important that passwords for SQL logins adhere to security best practices, such as enabling complexity requirements, prohibiting non-expiring passwords, and requiring passwords be changed regularly. In fact, new options in Microsoft SQL Server 2005 allow you to enforce requirements for password complexity and expiration for SQL logins based on your Windows or Active Directory policies. Complex passwords are defined as having a combination of at least three of the following four criteria:

- ❏ Uppercase alpha characters
- ❏ Lowercase alpha characters
- ❏ Non-negative integers (0–9)
- ❏ Special characters ($, %, *, &)

If the SQL Server is a member of an Active Directory domain, the password policy is usually defined in a Group Policy object linked to the domain container. For SQL logins, or logins based on a local Windows account, this may be superseded by a Group Policy object linked to an Organizational Unit. If the SQL Server is not a member of an Active Directory domain, the password policy is defined in the Local Group Policy object.

SQL Server 2005 automatically creates logins for the [BUILTIN\Administrators] group, which allows anyone with local administrative rights on the server to log in to the SQL Server. A SQL login, sa, is also created. The sa account has full administrative access to all SQL functions. If you install SQL Server using Windows Authentication Mode, the sa account is disabled. Even if you switched to Mixed Mode authentication, the account remains disabled until you set a secure password, and choose to enable the account.

Creating Logins in Management Studio

To create logins from Management Studio, follow these steps:

1. From the Object Explorer, expand your server.

2. Expand the Security folder.

3. Right-click Logins and select New Login.

4. In the New Login dialog box (see Figure 6-3), either type the Login name you want to add, or click the Search button to browse for a Windows account.

5. If you are creating a SQL Login, select the "SQL Server authentication" radio button.

6. Also, when you select "SQL Server authentication," you can choose to not enforce the password policies.

7. You may also want to change the user's default database and language.

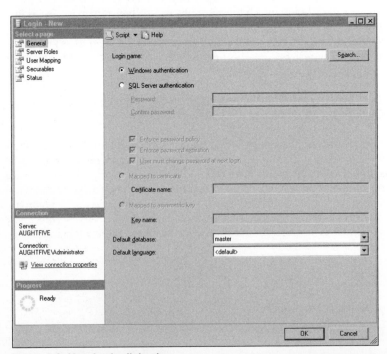

Figure 6-3: New Login dialog box

Although the dialog box lists options to map the login to a certificate or asymmetric key, these are not selectable through the New Login window. However, you can use this to view the login mapping information.

Create a New Login for Alice

To create a new login for Alice, follow these steps:

1. From the Object Explorer, expand your server.
2. Expand the Security folder.
3. Right-click Logins and select New Login.
4. In the New Login dialog box, click Search.
5. In the Select User or Group dialog box, type **Alice** and click OK.
6. Select AdventureWorks as the default database.
7. Click OK.

Creating Logins Using T-SQL

Alternatively, you can use the CREATE LOGIN statement. CREATE LOGIN allows you to create either Windows or SQL logins. This statement replaces two stored procedures that were used in previous versions of SQL, sp_grantlogin and sp_addlogin. Both of these stored procedures are still available in SQL 2005, as of this writing, but they have been deprecated and will be removed in a future version of SQL. Use the following format for the CREATE LOGIN statement:

```
CREATE LOGIN [name] {WITH <options> | FROM <source>}
```

The following table shows the options available with this statement.

Option	Description
PASSWORD = 'password'	Creates a new password for SQL logins. If this value is already hashed, use the HASHED option. Passwords are case-sensitive. See the "Best Practices" section in this chapter for more information on password guidelines.
HASHED	When a password is created for a SQL login, the password is stored in the database using a one-way hashing algorithm. This provides several benefits. Because the password is not stored in plaintext, it cannot be read by simply querying a system view. Because the hashing process is one-way, the password cannot be extrapolated from the hash value. This also secures the password in transmission, because the SQL Authentication process will send the hashed value of the password, not the actual plaintext password.
MUST_CHANGE	Requires the user to change his or her password at the next login. This is valid for SQL logins only. CHECK_POLICY and CHECK_EXPIRATION must be set to ON for this to work.

Table continued on following page

Option	Description
CREDENTIAL = credential_name	Maps an existing credential to a login. Credentials are discussed later in this chapter.
SID = sid	Allows you to manually specify a SID (Security Identifier) for a new user. If this value is left blank, the SID will be automatically generated.
DEFAULT_LANGUAGE = language	Assigns the default language for the login. If not specified, the default language of the server at the time the login was created will be used. This will not change if the server's default language is changed.
CHECK_POLICY = { ON	OFF }	This is often a favorite option for the CREATE LOGIN statement. It allows you to apply your Windows-based password policies to SQL logins. When Microsoft SQL Server 2005 is installed on Microsoft Windows Server 2003, this is ON by default.
CHECK_EXPIRATION = { ON	OFF }	A complement to the CHECK_POLICY option, this allows your Windows-based password expiration policy to also apply to SQL logins. If CHECK_POLICY is ON, then this will default to ON. Otherwise, the default value is OFF.

Sources	Description
WINDOWS	Identifies a login will be created based on an existing Windows user or group.
CERTIFICATE certname	Associates a pre-existing certificate with a login. Certificates are discussed later in this chapter.
ASYMMETRIC KEY asym_key_name	Associates a pre-existing certificate with a login. Certificates are discussed later in this chapter.

SQL Server will automatically hash a password before storing it in the database. Be careful about using the HASHED option unless you are sure that the password you are supplying has already been hashed by SQL Server. For example, if you type the following statement:

```
CREATE LOGIN Alice WITH PASSWORD 'P@ssw0rd' HASHED
```

SQL will assume that P@ssw0rd is a hash of another value. So, when Alice tries to log in with P@ssw0rd, the authentication will fail. You can use the loginproperty function to obtain the hashed value of an existing user's password, as shown in the following example:

```
SELECT LOGINPROPERTY(alice,'passwordhash')
```

Managing Logins

SQL Server Management Studio includes several property sheets to configure logins, which are addressed later in this chapter. In addition to the general property sheet, you should also be familiar with the Status page, which allows you to enable or disable the login, unlock the login, and specifically grant or deny access to connect to this SQL Server.

From the General property sheet, you can change the following attributes:

- ❏ Password
- ❏ Password Policy
- ❏ Password Expiration
- ❏ Force the user to change the password at the next login
- ❏ Default Database
- ❏ Default Language

Logins can also be managed using the ALTER LOGIN statement. In addition to many of the options listed previously for the CREATE LOGIN statement, the ALTER LOGIN statement uses the following format:

```
ALTER LOGIN name {<status> | WITH <options>}
```

The following table shows the options available with this statement.

Option	Description
Status {Enable | Disable}	Enables or disables the login as needed.
OLD_PASSWORD = 'oldpassword'	Specifies the current password when changing the password for the login.
NAME = login_name	Allows you to rename a login. If renaming a Windows-based login, the SID of the Windows object must match the SID for the login in SQL Server. SQL Server–based logins must not contain a backslash (\) character.
NO CREDENTIAL	Removes the mapping between the login and a server credential.
UNLOCK	A SQL Server login may become locked out after too many invalid password attempts. If that occurs, this option can remove the lock.

Also, note that the HASHED option is not available when using the ALTER LOGIN statement. New passwords provided using ALTER LOGIN should not be pre-hashed.

CREATE LOGIN

To create a new login in Transact-SQL, use the CREATE LOGIN statement. The following example creates a new login for a user account named Bob on the AughtFive server:

```
CREATE LOGIN [AughtFive\Bob] from Windows;
GO
```

To create a new login for a Windows group, use the following example:

```
CREATE LOGIN [AughtFive\G NorthWest Sales] from Windows;
GO
```

To create a new SQL Server login for Carol, use the following syntax (you must be in SQL Server and Windows Authentication Mode):

```
CREATE LOGIN Carol
WITH PASSWORD = 'Th1sI$|\/|yP@ssw0rd';
GO
```

To change Carol's password to use the all lowercase "newpassword," use the following command:

```
ALTER LOGIN Carol WITH PASSWORD = 'newpassword',
CHECK_POLICY=OFF;
GO
```

To remove an exising login, use the DROP LOGIN statement. For example, if you want to remove Bob's login (remember, Bob has a Windows-based login), use the following:

```
DROP LOGIN [AughtFive\Bob];
GO
```

For More Information

For backward compatibility, Microsoft SQL Server 2005 supports the stored procedures for managing logins listed in the following table. Because these stored procedures have been deprecated, you should use the CREATE LOGIN and ALTER LOGIN statements.

Stored Procedure	Description
sp_grantlogin:	Creates a new Windows-based login.
sp_revokelogin:	Removes a Windows-based login.
sp_addlogin:	Creates a new SQL Server login.
sp_droplogin:	Removes a SQL Server–based login.

Credentials

Microsoft SQL Server 2005 includes a new feature for mapping SQL Server logins to external Windows accounts. This can be extremely useful if you need to allow SQL Server logins to interact with the resources outside the scope of the SQL Server itself (such as a linked server or a local file system). They can also be used with assemblies that are configured for EXTERNAL_ACCESS.

Credentials can be configured as a one-to-one mapping, or a many-to-one mapping, allowing multiple SQL Server logins to use one shared Windows account for external access. Logins, however, can only be associated with one credential at a time.

Creating a New Credential

To create a new credential, follow these steps:

1. In Object Explorer, expand your server.

2. Expand the Security folder.

3. Right-click Credentials and select New Credential.

4. Type a name for the credential (see Figure 6-4).

5. Either type the name of a Windows account, or click the "..." button to browse for an account.

6. Enter the password for the account.

7. Re-enter the password to confirm.

8. Click OK.

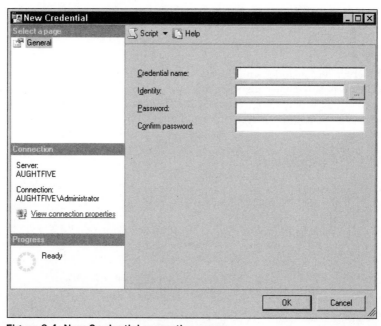

Figure 6-4: New Credential properties screen

Using Transact-SQL

You can use the CREATE CREDENTIAL statement as an alternative means to create a new SQL credential object. The syntax is as follows:

```
CREATE CREDENTIAL name WITH IDENTITY = 'identity_name'[, SECRET = 'secret']
```

Likewise, the ALTER CREDENTIAL statement can be used to alter the name of the credential, the identity it's associated with, and the password. Once the credential is no longer needed, it can be removed with the DROP CREDENTIAL command, as follows:

```
DROP CREDENTIAL name
```

Try It Out   Create a New Credential for a Windows Account

Earlier in the chapter, you created a Windows account named CarolStreet with a password of P@ssw0rd. You will now create a new credential named StreetCred for that user. When running the following script, replace AughtFive with your own server name:

```
USE master
CREATE CREDENTIAL StreetCred
WITH IDENTITY = 'AughtFive\CarolStreet',
SECRET = 'P@ssw0rd';
GO
```

You can then associate Carol's SQL Server login with the StreetCred credential:

```
ALTER LOGIN Carol WITH CREDENTIAL = StreetCred;
GO
```

Server Roles

Microsoft SQL Server 2005 includes a number of server-level roles that are available to simplify management (and the delegation of management) for SQL logins. These are often referred to as fixed server roles because membership is the only thing you can really change about these roles. The fixed server roles are designed to allow you to automatically assign a common set of permissions to a login, based upon the purpose of the role.

The following table shows the fixed server roles.

Role	Description
sysadmin	Members have full administrative access to the SQL Server, and can perform any action. By default, this includes the BUILTIN\Administrators group.
serveradmin	Members can change server-wide configurations and shut down the server.
securityadmin	Members can manage SQL logins, including changing and resetting passwords as needed, as well as managing GRANT, REVOKE, and DENY permissions at the server and database levels.

Role	Description
dbcreator	Members can create, drop, alter, and restore any database for the server.
diskadmin	Members can manage disk files for the server and all databases.
processadmin	Members can manage and terminate processes on the SQL Server.
setupadmin	Members can add and remove linked servers.
bulkadmin	Members of this role can execute the BULK INSERT statement for any database on the server.

To add a login to a fixed server role, use the sp_addsrvrolemember stored procedure. The stored procedure uses the following format:

```
sp_addsrvrolemember [ @loginame= ] 'login' , [ @rolename = ] 'role'
```

Simply provide the login name and the role name. To add Ted to the securityadmin role, use the following command:

```
USE master
CREATE LOGIN Ted WITH PASSWORD = 'P@ssw0rd';
GO
EXEC sp_addsrvrolemember 'Ted', 'securityadmin';
GO
```

Use sp_dropsrvrolemember to remove a login from a fixed server role. The syntax is similar to the sp_addsrvrolemember stored procedure, as shown in the following example:

```
USE master
EXEC sp_dropsrvrolemember 'Ted', 'securityadmin';
GO
```

For More Information

You can query the Security Catalog Views to find out more information about principals at the server scope. The following table shows views that identify server-level principals.

View	Description
sys.server_principals	Returns information about all server-level principals.
sys.sql_logins	Returns information about SQL Server logins.
sys.server_role_members	Returns the role ID and member ID for each member of a server role.

Database Users

Database users are another component of the security model employed by Microsoft SQL Server 2005. Users are granted access to database securables, either directly or through membership in one or more database roles. Users are also associated with ownership of objects such as tables, views, and stored procedures.

When a login is created, unless it is a member of a fixed server role with database administrative privileges, that login has no explicit permissions within the various databases attached to the server. When this happens, the login is associated with the guest database user, and inherits the permissions of that user account.

When managing database users in SQL Server Management Studio, you have several options from which to select. On the General property sheet (see Figure 6-5), you will be able to create a name for the user, and associate the user with an existing login. Note that the user name does not have to match the login name. For ease of administration, it is a best practice to try to use a consistent naming convention, but it is not required. Also, note that there are radio buttons that show whether the user is mapped to a login, a certificate, a key, or without any association. Through the Graphical User Interface (GUI), you can only create a user mapped to a login. In the next section, you see how to create users with other mappings.

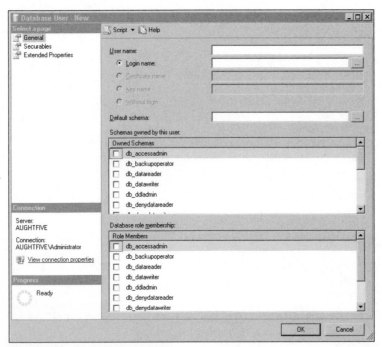

Figure 6-5: General property page

Other options you can configure from the General page include specifying the user's default schema, any schemas owned by this user, and to which database roles the user belongs. In the Securables page, you can list all the securable items the user has permissions to, and what permissions they have. Finally, you have the Extended Properties page, which allows you to designate or view additional metadata information about this user.

Try It Out   **Create a New User and Default Schema**

For this example, you will create a new database user in the AdventureWorks database for Carol, and set her default schema to the Sales schema.

1.   In Object Explorer, expand Databases.

2.   Expand AdventureWorks (see Figure 6-6).

3.   Expand Security.

4.   Right-click Users and select New User.

5.   Type **Carol** in the User Name box.

6.   Type **Carol** in the "Login name" box, or select her login using the "..." button.

7.   Type **Sales** in the "Default schema" box.

8.   Click OK.

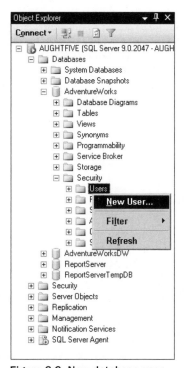

Figure 6-6: New database user

Now that Carol has a database user account in the AdventureWorks database, she has inherited the permissions granted to the public database role. Database roles and permissions are covered later in this chapter.

CREATE USER

The CREATE USER statement can also be used for creating new database users. CREATE USER offers more options over how the user is created than the GUI allows. For example, you can create a user based on an existing certificate or key, or even create a user that is not associated with a login. Although reasons for implementing these types of users will be limited, they can have access to database objects without being associated with a specific login. They can be used to access resources that have specific security requirements. For example, a stored procedure might contain the EXECUTE AS clause, in which case the stored procedure runs as the user associated with a particular certificate, or asymmetric key. The caveat, though, is that these users are valid only in the database in which they were created. If they attempt to access resources in another database, they will access the other database as guest. If the guest user is disabled in the other database, then they will be denied access.

Each database has two users created by default. The dbo user (also known as the *database owner*) has all rights and privileges to perform any operation in the database. Members of the fixed server role, sysadmin, as well as the sa account, are mapped to dbo. Any object created by a sysadmin is automatically owned by dbo. The dbo user is also the owner of the default schema, also called dbo. The dbo user cannot be deleted.

The guest account is also present in every database, but is disabled by default. The guest account is commonly used when a person has login access to the SQL Server, but no user access to a database. If the database has a guest account, and it is enabled, then the login will connect to that database with guest access. guest is a member of the public role, and has all of the permissions assigned to that role, but can be granted explicit permissions to securables as well.

You may also notice two other "users," sys and INFORMATION_SCHEMA. Although they are not users in the conventional sense, they do own objects in the database, primarily for storing and retrieving metadata. These users are not mapped to any login, and cannot be managed.

Following is the syntax and the options for the CREATE USER statement:

```
CREATE USER name [{{FOR | FROM} source | WITHOUT LOGIN]
    [WITH DEFAULT_SCHEMA = schema_name]
```

The following table explains the options that are available.

Source Options	Description
Login login_name	This option specifies the login name to associate with this user. If this value is not present, SQL Server assumes the user you are trying to create is using the same name as an existing login. If there is not a login with the same name as the user, the operation will fail.
CERTIFICATE cert_name	This option allows you to create a user that is associated with a certificate, rather than with a login. The certificate must already exist in this database for the operation to succeed. Certificates are discussed later in this chapter.
ASYMMETRIC KEY key_name	This option allows you to create a user associated with an asymmetric key, rather than with a login. The asymmetric key must already exist in the database. Keys are discussed later in this chapter.

Other Options	Description
WITHOUT LOGIN	This option allows you to designate that the user is created without any association to a login, or other objects such as asymmetric keys or certificates.
WITH DEFAULT_SCHEMA = schema	This option lets you specify the schema in which the user will operate. The benefit to users is that whenever they create or access an object within their default schema, they can use the object name by itself. The users may still be able to access objects in other schemas, as long as they have they correct permissions, by using the schema.object naming convention.

Try It Out   Create a New User

So, take a look at the CREATE USER statement in action. In an earlier example, you created a new SQL Server login called Carol, and an associated user in the AdventureWorks database. If you wanted to create a user for Carol in the tempdb database, you could execute the following statement:

```
USE tempdb;
CREATE USER Carol;
GO
```

That's all there is to creating a new user. Look at another example. If you executed the DROP LOGIN [Aughtfive\Bob] statement earlier, you'll need to re-create his login. In this example, you'll create a database user named BillyBob that will be mapped to Bob's login, and set BillyBob's default schema to the Sales schema:

```
USE master;
CREATE LOGIN [AughtFive\Bob] FROM WINDOWS;
USE AdventureWorks;
CREATE USER BillyBob FOR LOGIN [AughtFive\Bob]
WITH DEFAULT_SCHEMA = sales;
```

The last example shows creating a new user from an existing certificate. Certificates are covered later in this chapter, but for this example, create the certificate first, and then create the user:

```
USE AdventureWorks;
CREATE CERTIFICATE SalesCert
    ENCRYPTION BY PASSWORD = 'P@ssw0rd'
    WITH SUBJECT = 'Sales Schema Certificate',
    EXPIRY_DATE = '12/31/2010';
GO
CREATE USER SalesSecurity FOR CERTIFICATE SalesCert;
GO
```

You can also use the ALTER USER statement to make changes to a user account. This is another example where the Transact-SQL gives you greater flexibility than the Management Studio. ALTER SCHEMA lets you modify both the name property and the DEFAULT_SCHEMA property. Both are illustrated in the following examples:

```
USE AdventureWorks
ALTER USER SalesSecurity
WITH NAME = SalesSchemaSecurity;
GO

USE AdventureWorks
ALTER USER BillyBob
WITH DEFAULT_SCHEMA = Production;
GO
```

Finally, once a user has outlived its usefulness, use the DROP USER statement to remove it from the database. The DROP USER statement is straightforward, as seen in the following example:

```
USE AdventureWorks
DROP USER BillyBob;
GO
```

One of the benefits of using Microsoft SQL Server 2005 versus previous versions is the separation of the owner object and schema context. This helps to minimize orphaned objects when a user is dropped by keeping those objects part of a schema that may be owned by a role or a Windows group. Although it was easier to manage objects that were all owned by dbo as seen in previous versions, using schemas helps provide a more logical, hierarchical security design.

Fixed Database Roles

Every SQL database has a list of fixed database roles that allow you to delegate permissions to users as necessary. As with the fixed server roles, membership is the only thing you can change about these roles. It is important to know how and when to use these roles.

The following table shows the fixed database roles.

Role	Description
db_accessadmin	This role can add or remove access for Windows logins, Windows groups, and SQL Server logins.
db_backupoperator	This role has the right to back up the database.
db_datareader	Members of this role can read data from all user tables.
db_datawriter	Members of this role can write data from all user tables.
db_ddladmin	This role can execute data definition language (DDL) statements for any object in the database.
db_denydatareader	This role is explicitly excluded from being able to read from any user table with the database.
db_denydatawriter	This role is explicitly excluded from being able to write to any table in the database.

Role	Description
db_owner	Members of this role can perform any activity within the database. New to SQL Server 2005 is the ability for this role to drop the database from the server. The dbo user is automatically a member of this role.
db_securityadmin	This role can manage permissions and role membership within the database.
public	Membership in the public role is automatic. Permissions that apply to the public role apply to everyone who accesses the database.

Note that the fixed database roles include db_denydatareader and db_denydatawriter. These roles explicitly deny read or write access to user tables in the database, and should be used sparingly. Deny permissions are authoritative and cannot be overridden.

User-defined database roles offer greater control over managing permissions and access to resources within a database. Frequently, when using a role-based security model, you may find that built-in principals (such as groups in Windows or roles in SQL) may offer either too much access, or not enough. In this case, you can create user-defined roles that allow you to control access to securables for an entire collection of users at once. Database roles are very similar in concept to Windows groups. You can create a database role to identify a group of users, all of whom need access to a common set of resources, or you can use roles to identify the permissions being granted to a securable in the database. Regardless of the purpose of your role, its function should be clearly identified by the name of the role.

Creating a New User-Defined Database Role in Management Studio

In the New Role dialog box, you are prompted to provide a name for the role, as well as identifying an owner for the role. The owner of the role can modify it at any time. You can also select existing schemas that will be owned by this role, and add users as members to this role. In addition to the General property sheet, you also have the Securables page and the Extended Properties page, which you can use to assign permissions or set additional attributes, respectively.

In this example, you can create a new database role called ProductionRole and then add Carol as a member:

1. In Object Explorer, expand Databases.
2. Expand AdventureWorks and then expand Security.
3. Expand Roles and then expand Database Roles.
4. Right-click Database Roles and select New Database Role.
5. In the Role Name box, type **ProductionRole** (see Figure 6-7).
6. Under the list of members of this role (which should be empty) click Add.
7. Enter **Carol** in the window and click Check Names. This should resolve her name. Click OK.
8. In the Database Role - New window, click OK.

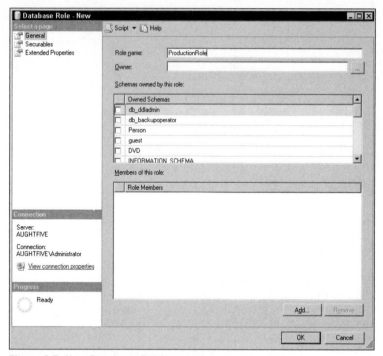

Figure 6-7: New Database Role properties screen

CREATE ROLE

CREATE ROLE is the Transact-SQL equivalent for creating a new user-defined database role. When using the CREATE ROLE statement as shown here, you can also specify the owner of the role. Note that if you are assigning a user as the owner of a role, you must have the IMPERSONATE permission, and if you're assigning another role as the owner, you must either be a member of that role or have ALTER permission on the role.

```
USE AdventureWorks
CREATE ROLE SalesStaff
AUTHORIZATION Ted;
GO
```

The ALTER ROLE statement is fairly limited, allowing you to change only the name of the role:

```
USE AdventureWorks
ALTER ROLE SalesStaff
WITH NAME = SalesStaffRole;
GO
```

DROP ROLE rolename will let you remove a role from the database once it is no longer needed:

```
USE AdventureWorks
DROP ROLE SalesStaffRole;
GO
```

As with fixed server roles, database roles (both fixed and user-defined) can have users added to them either through the SQL Server Management Studio, or through a stored procedure. The stored procedure for database roles is `sp_addrolemember`. Unlike the stored procedures for adding and dropping members from server roles, `sp_addrolemember` and `sp_droprolemember` identify the role as the first variable, and the user as the second.

The following example adds the database user Ted to the `db_datareader` role:

```
USE AdventureWorks
EXEC sp_addrolemember 'db_datareader', 'Ted';
GO
```

To remove Ted from the `db_datareader` role, use the following stored procedure:

```
USE AdventureWorks
EXEC sp_droprolemember 'db_datareader', 'Ted';
GO
```

Application Roles

Another type of role that can be used to help secure the database environment is the application role. Application roles are quite different from standard role types. They do not have members, and they can (and should) be configured to authenticate with a password. Application roles are typically used when database access must be the same for all users who run a particular application. Rather than depending on the individual user to have the appropriate access for the application to work properly, the application can instantiate the application role without prompting the user to provide a username and password.

You can create a new application role from SQL Server Management Studio, from the Application Roles folder. The dialog box for creating a new application role is very similar to the standard database role dialog, with the exception of the password field, and the lack of a members list.

Try It Out   **Create an Application Role**

In this example, you create a new application role named `PurchasingOrderEntry`, with a password of `POEpass1`:

1.   In Object Explorer, expand Databases.

2.   Expand AdventureWorks and then expand Security.

3.   Expand Roles and then expand Application Roles.

4.   Right-click Application Roles and select New Application Role.

5.   Type **PurchasingOrderEntry** for the Role name (see Figure 6-8).

6.   Set the Default schema to Purchasing.

7.   Enter **POEpass1** in the Password and Confirm password boxes.

8.   Click OK.

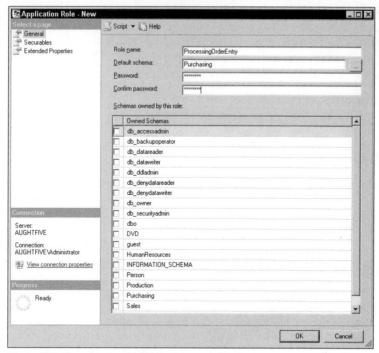

Figure 6-8: New Application Role Properties screen

In the next section, you see how to instantiate that role.

CREATE APPLICATION ROLE

The CREATE APPLICATION ROLE does what the name suggests. When using this statement, specify the name of the application role, a password for the application role, and, optionally, a default schema for the application role. The following example creates an application role named SalesApp:

```
USE AdventureWorks
CREATE APPLICATION ROLE SalesApp
WITH PASSWORD = 'P@ssw0rd',
DEFAULT_SCHEMA = Sales;
GO
```

To use an application role, you can execute the sp_setapprole stored procedure. This can be called from an application, or you can test it from your query window. The stored procedure includes options to activate the application role by providing an encrypted password, creating a cookie, and setting information in the cookie. The following command activates the SalesApp application role and then returns the username:

```
USE AdventureWorks
GO
DECLARE @cookie varbinary(8000);
EXEC sp_setapprole 'SalesApp', 'P@ssw0rd'
    , @fCreateCookie = true, @cookie = @cookie OUTPUT;
GO
SELECT USER_NAME();
```

Once you've executed the preceding script, all activity performed from that connection operates under the application role. When you close the connection, the application role session ends.

With the ALTER APPLICATION ROLE statement, you can change the name of the application role, the password, and the default schema. The following example changes the SalesApp role to OrderEntry and sets a new password:

```
USE AdventureWorks
ALTER APPLICATION ROLE SalesApp
WITH NAME = OrderEntry,
PASSWORD = 'newP@ssw0rd'
```

If you intend to run the ALTER APPLICATION ROLE script listed previously, ensure that you don't do it while connected as that application role. Opening a new query window under your own credentials will prevent errors.

DROP APPLICATION ROLE rolename will remove an application role from the database. Ensure that you do not have any applications still using the application role; otherwise, the application will be unable to connect to the database.

For More Information

The following Security Catalog Views can be used to identify which principals exist in your database, and their role membership.

View	Description
sys.database_principals	Returns information about all database-level principals.
sys.database_role_members	Returns the ID of each database roles and its members.

For backward compatibility, Microsoft SQL Server 2005 supports the following stored procedures. Because these stored procedures have been deprecated and will be removed from future releases, you should use the appropriate statements listed in this chapter.

Stored Procedure	Description
sp_adduser	Creates a new database user.
sp_grantdbaccess	Creates a new database user.
sp_dropuser	Removes a database user.
sp_revokedbaccess	Removes a database user.
sp_addrole	Creates a new user-defined database role.
sp_droprole	Removes a user-defined database role.
sp_addapprole	Creates a new application role.
sp_approlepassword	Changes the password for an application role.
sp_dropapprole	Removes an application role from the database.

Permissions

Permissions are at the heart of security in SQL Server 2005. In the previous section, you looked at the different types of objects that can be created to help manage security by identifying to whom you can grant access. In this section, you look at permissions that can be applied to the different resources in SQL Server.

To begin with, you should understand there are essentially three permission states that exist: GRANT, GRANT_W_GRANT, and DENY. In addition, when a principal does not have an explicit permission defined, the permission is considered "revoked." The following table shows the different permission states.

Permission	Description
GRANT	This state means that you have been given the right to perform this action, or interact with this resource based on what the actual permission is.
GRANT_W_GRANT	Not only can you perform this action, but you also have the right to give others the ability to perform this action.
DENY	You cannot perform this action. This is also known as an "explicit deny," because nothing will allow you to perform this action.
REVOKE	This is not really a permission state as much as it is the absence of a permission state. Revoked permissions will not show up in a sysprotects table or sys.sysprotects view, and are considered an "implicit deny." The idea is that if you haven't been granted this permission, either directly or through membership in a role with that permission, it is safe to assume you shouldn't be doing that. Therefore, you will not be doing that.

To control permission states, you can use the Object Explorer or Transact-SQL. The three commands that you can use to control permission states are GRANT, REVOKE, and DENY, which are described in the following table.

Command	Description
GRANT	This command allows you to grant the right to perform and action or interact with an object in a specific way. The GRANT statement includes the WITH GRANT OPTION option, which also allows the grantee the ability to become a grantor of this permission.
REVOKE	This command removes any explicit permission granted to the grantee, either grant or deny. Revoked permissions will remove the ability to perform that task. Remember that if the user is a member of another role, they may still have the ability to perform the action, unless an explicit deny is specified.
DENY	This command creates an entry that will prevent the user from performing the action. Denied permissions cannot be overridden by grant permissions.

The following table shows a general list of the actions you can grant, deny, or revoke, and the types of objects on which you can grant them. A short description is provided for each.

Action	Description	Securable
INSERT	Controls the ability to add a new row to a table or view.	Synonyms
		Tables and columns
		Views and columns
DELETE	Controls the ability to remove data rows from a table or view.	Synonyms
		Tables and columns
		Views and columns
EXECUTE	Controls the ability to launch programmability objects.	Procedures
		Scalar and aggregate functions
		Synonyms
RECEIVE	Controls the ability to retrieve one or more messages from a queue.	Service Broker queues
VIEW DEFINITION	Controls the ability to return metadata information about objects.	Procedures
		Service Broker queues
		Scalar and aggregate functions
		Synonyms
		Tables
		Table-valued functions
		Views
ALTER	Controls the ability to change all the properties of an object except ownership. ALTER ANY can also be used when assigning permissions to all objects of a specific type at the server scope.	Procedures
		Scalar and aggregate functions
		Service
		Broker queues

Table continued on following page

Action	Description	Securable
		Tables
		Table-valued functions
		Views
TAKE OWNERSHIP	Controls the ability to take ownership of an object. Object owners can change permissions of the object.	Procedures
		Scalar and aggregate functions
		Synonyms
		Tables
		Table-valued functions
		Views
CONTROL	Controls the ability to have full control of an object. This is similar to the ALTER permission, but includes TAKE OWNERSHIP.	Procedures
		Scalar and aggregate functions
		Service Broker queues
		Synonyms
		Tables
		Table-valued functions
		Views

Now that you understand the permissions and permission states, take a look at the specific permissions available. SQL Server 2005 uses a hierarchical security model that allows you to specify permissions that can be granted at the server, database, schema, or object levels. You can also assign permissions within tables and views for selected columns.

The next section examines the scopes in which the different securables reside, and how you can use them to control access to your database resources. Microsoft and other vendors are encouraging role-based administrative models to simplify the process of creating a secure environment, not only for your databases and database servers, but for all of your operations.

The strategy you should employ when granting permissions is known as the *principle of least privilege*. This strategy mandates that you give your users appropriate permissions to do their jobs, and nothing more. By keeping such tight constraints on our database environment, you can offer a solution that minimizes the attack surface of your servers, while maintaining operational functionality.

When evaluating the different securables within SQL, you should have a good understanding of where and how permissions apply, and how you can use some of the native features of the hierarchical model to your advantage. Permission applied to a specific class of objects at a higher level in the hierarchy allows for permission inheritance. For example, if you want Ted to be able to update any row on every table within the `Sales` schema, you could simply use the following command:

```
USE AdventureWorks
GRANT UPDATE ON SCHEMA :: Sales to Ted;
GO
```

Alternatively, if you wanted Ted to have the ability to update any object in the database, you could use the following:

```
Use AdventureWorks
GRANT UPDATE TO Ted;
GO
```

Take a quick look at the different levels in your security hierarchy. Figure 6-9 outlines the different levels of security you need to manage. At the Windows scope, you create Windows users and groups, manage the files and services needed by the SQL Server, as well as the behavior of the server itself. In the server scope, you manage logins, endpoints, and databases. In the database scope, you work with users, keys, certificates, roles, assemblies, and other objects. Also in this scope are schemas, which contain your next set of securables. Finally, within the schema scope, you have data types, XML schema collections, and objects. These objects include your tables, views, stored procedures, and more.

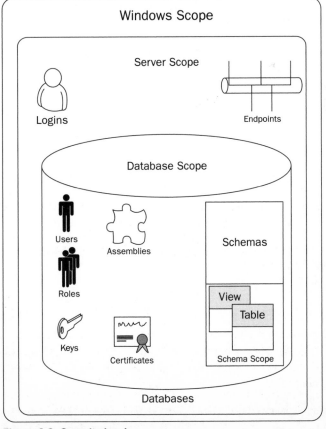

Figure 6-9: Security levels

Server Permissions

Server control permissions can be managed by simply specifying the permission and the login the permission will be assigned to. For example, to grant permissions to create databases to the login Ted, you could use the following statement:

```
USE master
GRANT CREATE ANY DATABASE TO Ted;
GO
```

If you also wanted Ted to be able to have the permissions to alter logins, and to allow others to alter logins, you could use the following statement:

```
USE Master
GRANT ALTER ANY LOGIN TO Ted
WITH GRANT OPTION;
GO
```

To remove Ted's ability to alter logins, you could use the following statement:

```
USE master
REVOKE ALTER ANY LOGIN TO Ted CASCADE;
GO
```

The CASCADE keyword is required because you gave Ted the GRANT_W_GRANT permission. If you had not used GRANT OPTION, the CASCADE keyword would have been optional.

Note that the preceding example revokes a permission that had been previously granted to Ted. If Ted were a member of the securityadmin fixed server role, he would still have the ability to alter logins for that server.

Now, if you want to prohibit Ted from being able to create a new database, you could use the DENY statement as follows:

```
USE master
DENY CREATE ANY DATABASE TO Ted;
GO
```

Unfortunately, the DENY permission state isn't always the end-all be-all answer to whether or not a login or user will be able to perform a certain action. If a login is a member of the sysadmin fixed server role, that login has complete control over the SQL Server and its resources, and it wouldn't make a lot of sense to prevent that login from being able to access any object on the server. Even if the DENY permission statement were successfully executed on an object, the sysadmin role can always change the permissions on that object.

Also, if the GRANT OPTION was specified in the GRANT statement, you will need to ensure that you use the CASCADE option.

The following table identifies the permissions that can be used to control the server, as well as granting blanket permissions to any resource of a particular type on the server. You can control access by using the following statement:

```
{GRANT | REVOKE | DENY} action on securable to principal WITH {options}
```

Action	Securable
ADMINISTER BULK OPERATIONS	None
ALTER	ANY CONNECTION
	ANY CREDENTIAL
	ANY DATABASE
	ANY ENDPOINT
	ANY EVENT NOTIFICATION
	ANY LINKED SERVER
	ANY LOGIN
	RESOURCES
	SERVER STATE
	SETTINGS
	TRACE
AUTHENTICATE SERVER	
CONNECT SQL	
CONTROL SERVER	
CREATE	ANY DATABASE
	DDL EVENT NOTIFICATION
	ENDPOINT
	TRACE EVENT NOTIFICATION
EXTERNAL ACCESS ASSEMBLY	
SHUTDOWN	
UNSAFE ASSEMBLY	
VIEW	ANY DATABASE
	ANY DEFINITION
	SERVER STATE

Endpoints are server-level objects that use a slightly different syntax than server permissions when granting, revoking, or denying as necessary. The following example creates an endpoint named ServiceBroker that will be used for a Service Broker application (endpoints are covered in Chapter 7, and Service Broker is introduced in Chapter 15), and then grants the ALTER permission for that endpoint to Ted:

```
CREATE ENDPOINT ServiceBroker
STATE = STARTED
AS TCP( LISTENER_PORT = 5162 )
FOR SERVICE_BROKER (AUTHENTICATION=WINDOWS);
```

```
GO

USE master
GRANT ALTER ON ENDPOINT :: ServiceBroker TO Ted;
GO
```

The following table lists the permissions you can grant for endpoints.

Action	Description
ALTER	Modify all properties of an endpoint, except ownership.
CONNECT	Connect to an endpoint.
CONTROL	Modify all properties of an endpoint, including ownership.
TAKE OWNERSHIP	Take ownership of an endpoint.
VIEW DEFINITION	View metadata about an endpoint.

The next server-level object you can set permissions for are logins. The syntax for setting permissions on logins is similar to the syntax for setting permissions on endpoints. For example, to give Carol the ability to alter Ted's login, you would use the following statement:

```
USE master
GRANT ALTER ON LOGIN :: Ted TO Carol
WITH GRANT OPTION;
GO
```

The following table shows how you can control these permissions for logins.

Action	Description
ALTER	Change any property of an existing login except ownership.
CONTROL	Change all properties of an existing login including ownership.
IMPERSONATE	Perform an action as that login.
VIEW DEFINITION	View metadata information about that login.

Finally, the last object type at the server level is the database object. Unlike logins and endpoints, database permissions are specified for database users. This keeps the security of the database within the database itself. Additional options may be available based on whether you are granting, denying, or revoking. The following table lists permissions that can be granted on the database object.

Action	Securable
ALTER	(alter can be used by itself)
	ANY DATABASE EVENT NOTIFICATION
	ANY APPLICATION ROLE

Action	Securable
	ANY ASSEMBLY
	ANY ASYMMETRIC KEY
	ANY CERTIFICATE
	ANY CONTRACT
	ANY DATABASE DDL TRIGGER
	ANY DATASPACE
	ANY FULLTEXT CATALOG
	ANY MESSAGE TYPE
	ANY REMOTE SERVICE BINDING
	ANY ROLE
	ANY ROUTE
	ANY SCHEMA
	ANY SERVICE
	ANY SYMMETRIC KEY
	ANY USER
AUTHENTICATE	
BACKUP	DATABASE
	LOG
CHECKPOINT	
CONNECT	
CONNECT REPLICATION	
CONTROL	
CREATE	AGGREGATE
	ASSEMBLY
	ASYMMETRIC KEY
	CERTIFICATE
	CONTRACT
	DATABASE (Master database only)
	DATABASE DDL EVENT NOTIFICATION
	DEFAULT
	FULLTEXT CATALOG

Table continued on following page

Action	Securable
	FUNCTION
	MESSAGE TYPE
	PROCEDURE
	QUEUE
	REMOTE SERVICE BINDING
	ROLE
	ROUTE
	RULE
	SCHEMA
	SERVICE
	SYMMETRIC KEY
	SYNONYM
	TABLE
	TYPE
	VIEW
	XML SCHEMA COLLECTION
DELETE	
EXECUTE	
INSERT	
REFERENCES	
SELECT	
SHOWPLAN	
SUBSCRIBE QUERY NOTIFICATIONS	
TAKE OWNERSHIP	
UPDATE	
VIEW	DEFINITION
	DATABASE STATE

Database Scope Permissions

In the database scope, there are additional permissions you can assign based on the different types of securables that you have. Permissions assigned to an object class allow you to perform the defined action on all members of that class. However, an object can be explicitly identified by declaring the class and then the object name. The syntax for assigning permissions to database securables is as follows:

```
{GRANT | REVOKE | DENY} action ON class :: object TO principal
```

In the following example, you can grant the CONTROL permission for the Sales schema to the user BillyBob:

```
CREATE USER Alice FOR LOGIN [AughtFive\Alice]
WITH DEFAULT_SCHEMA = SALES;
GO

USE AdventureWorks
GRANT CONTROL ON SCHEMA :: Sales TO Alice;
GO
```

The following table lists the various permissions and the database objects and classes to which you can assign them.

Action	Securable
ALTER	ASSEMBLY
	ASYMMETRIC KEY
	CERTIFICATE
	CONTRACT
	FULLTEXT CATALOG
	MESSAGE TYPE
	REMOTE SERVICE BINDING
	ROLE
	ROUTE
	SCHEMA
	SERVICE
	SYMMETRIC KEY
	USER
CONTROL	ASSEMBLY
	ASYMMETRIC KEY
	CERTIFICATE
	CONTRACT
	FULLTEXT CATALOG
	MESSAGE TYPE

Table continued on following page

Action	Securable
	REMOTE SERVICE BINDING
	ROLE
	ROUTE
	SCHEMA
	SERVICE
	SYMMETRIC KEY
	USER
DELETE	SCHEMA
EXECUTE	ASSEMBLY
	SCHEMA
IMPERSONATE	USER
INSERT	SCHEMA
REFERENCES	ASSEMBLY
	ASYMMETRIC KEY
	CERTIFICATE
	CONTRACT
	FULLTEXT CATALOG
	MESSAGE TYPE
	SCHEMA
	SYMMETRIC KEY
SELECT	SCHEMA
SEND	SERVICE
TAKE OWNERSHIP	ASSEMBLY
	ASYMMETRIC KEY
	CERTIFICATE
	CONTRACT
	FULLTEXT CATALOG
	MESSAGE TYPE
	REMOTE SERVICE BINDING
	ROLE

Action	Securable
	ROUTE
	SCHEMA
	SERVICE
	SYMMETRIC KEY
UPDATE	SCHEMA
VIEW DEFINITION	ASSEMBLY
	ASYMMETRIC KEY
	CERTIFICATE
	CONTRACT
	FULLTEXT CATALOG
	MESSAGE TYPE
	REMOTE SERVICE BINDING
	ROLE
	ROUTE
	SCHEMA
	SERVICE
	SYMMETRIC KEY
	USER

Schema Scope Permissions

Finally, within the scope of a schema, there are additional permissions you can assign to objects, data types, and XML schema collections. When granting permissions to schema-level objects, the syntax is similar to what you saw earlier:

```
{GRANT | REVOKE | DENY} action ON class :: securable TO principal
```

When the class is an OBJECT, you can omit OBJECT :: as long as the schema name is included with the object name, as in the following example:

```
Use AdventureWorks
GRANT SELECT, UPDATE ON Person.Contact to Alice;
GO
```

Schema objects include the following:

❑ Aggregates

❑ Constraints

- ❑ Functions
- ❑ Procedures
- ❑ Queues
- ❑ Statistics
- ❑ Synonyms
- ❑ Tables
- ❑ Views

The following table lists the schema classes and the permissions that can be set for each of them. Remember that not all permissions are valid for every object type. You can't expect to grant EXECUTE on a table, or SELECT on a stored procedure.

Class	Permissions
OBJECT	ALTER
	CONTROL
	RECEIVE
	TAKE OWNERSHIP
	DELETE
	EXECUTE
	INSERT
	REFERENCES
	SELECT
	UPDATE
	VIEW DEFINITION
TYPE	CONTROL
	TAKE OWNERSHIP
	EXECUTE
	REFERENCES
	VIEW DEFINITION
XML SCHEMA COLLECTION	ALTER
	CONTROL
	TAKE OWNERSHIP
	EXECUTE
	REFERENCES
	VIEW DEFINITION

Using SQL Server Management Studio for Managing Permissions

You can also use the Object Explorer in SQL Server Management Studio to set or view permissions on objects. In this section, you learn how to use the GUI to control access to SQL resources.

The first thing to look at is auditing permissions on the objects themselves.

For the next example, create a new login, a new database user for the AdventureWorks database, and then grant control permissions to the Sales schema for this new user. Use the following code:

```
USE master
CREATE LOGIN Chris WITH PASSWORD = 'P@ssw0rd',
DEFAULT_DATABASE = AdventureWorks;
GO

USE AdventureWorks
CREATE USER Chris WITH DEFAULT_SCHEMA = Sales;
GO

GRANT CONTROL ON SCHEMA :: SALES TO Chris;
GO
```

Now, use the Object Explorer to see what permissions have been granted to Chris. First, look at the database itself:

1. Expand your server.
2. Expand Databases.
3. Right-click AdventureWorks and select Properties.
4. Select Permissions.
5. In the Users or Roles page, select Chris.

Under "Explicit permissions for Chris," scroll down until you find "connect." Note that the user who granted the permission is also listed.

Above the list of explicit permissions for this user, there is an Effective Permissions button. Clicking this button will give you a list of the permissions the user has for this resource, including those that were granted through membership in a role or group. This new feature can really help simplify the process of auditing your security settings, or troubleshooting why a user is having problems accessing a resource.

Because you granted control of the Sales schema to Chris, take a look at what permissions have actually been assigned to that schema, and the objects within it. To do this, you open the property sheet for Chris's user account in the AdventureWorks database (see Figure 6-10):

1. Close the Database Properties — AdventureWorks window by clicking OK or Cancel.
2. In Object Explorer, expand AdventureWorks.
3. Expand Security.

4. Expand Users.

5. Right-click Chris and select Properties.

6. Select the Securables page and click Add.

7. Select Specific Objects... and click OK.

8. In the Select Objects dialog, click Object Types.

9. Select Schemas from the list and click OK.

10. Enter **Sales** in the object name box and click OK.

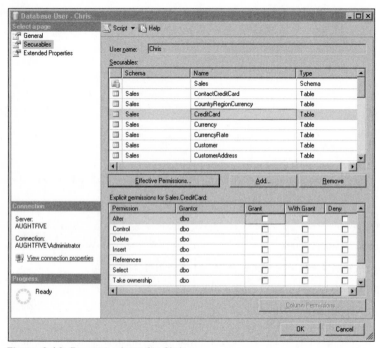

Figure 6-10: Property sheet for Chris

If you look at the list of explicit permissions on the Sales schema, notice that Chris only has CONTROL permissions. Clicking the Effective Permissions button will show you that the user has full access to any object in the schema. Click OK or Cancel to exit the Effective Permissions dialog.

Now, take a look at specific objects in the Sales schema:

1. On the Securables page, click Add.

2. In the Add Objects dialog, select "All objects belonging to the schema" and select Sales from the drop-down list.

3. Click OK.

4. Select CreditCard in the list of Securables.

Look at the list of explicit permissions for `Sales.CreditCard` (see Figure 6-11) and notice that Chris has no explicit permissions on this table. Clicking the Effective Permissions button will show you that the user has full access to any column in this table.

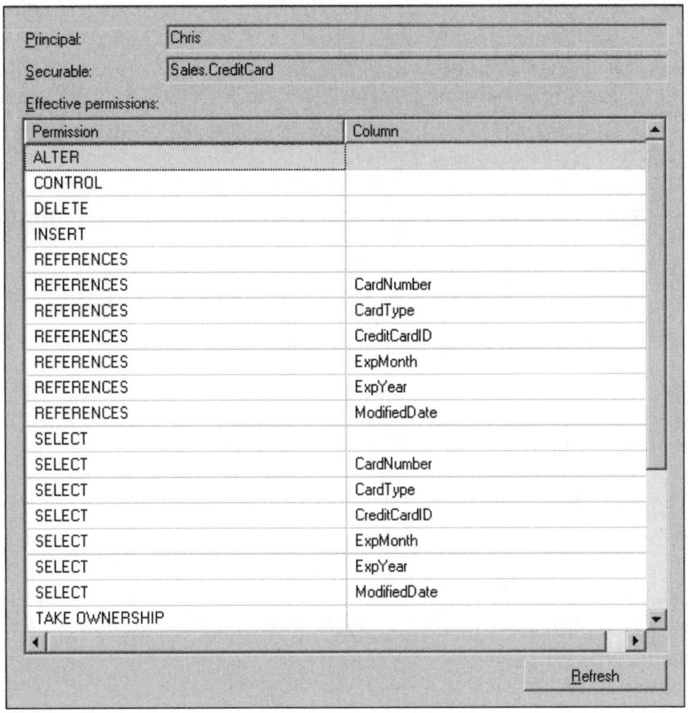

Figure 6-11: `Sales.CreditCard` **permissions**

You now have a user with full access to the `Sales` schema, but no access to resources outside of it. Any attempt to query a view in another schema will result in the following error:

```
SELECT * FROM HumanResources.vEmployee
-------------------------------------------------------------------------------

Msg 229, Level 14, State 5, Line 1
SELECT permission denied on object 'vEmployee', database 'AdventureWorks', schema
'HumanResources'.
```

Also note that you can add permissions for database objects from here as well. You can use the Management Studio to assign permissions by editing the properties of the securable, or by editing the properties of a principal.

SQL Server Encryption

Protecting data, both in storage and during transmission, is important for the integrity of your applications and services. Microsoft SQL Server 2005 offers several options for both. In this section, you see some of the tools available for protecting your data.

First of all, whether you're using symmetric keys, asymmetric keys, or certificates, there are two main components to encrypting data: the encryption algorithm and the key value. The *encryption algorithms* available include Data Encryption Standard (DES), Triple Data Encryption Standard (3DES), RC4, and Advanced Encryption Standard (AES_256). The algorithm is simply a mathematical formula that dictates how to turn the data from plaintext into ciphertext. The key is a value that is used within that formula to determine the actual output based on the input. It's not unlike basic algebra where you take a statement like $x + y = z$. In this case, x is the plaintext value, y is the encryption key, and z is the ciphertext. Fortunately, the encryption algorithms are significantly more complex than that, but you get the idea.

Keys come in two flavors: symmetric and asymmetric. *Symmetric keys* use the same data key value to both encrypt and decrypt data. This is actually very good for encrypting large amounts of data, but has a relatively low level of security. *Asymmetric keys* use one key value for encrypting data, and a different value for decrypting data. This provides a higher level of security than symmetric keys, but is a costly operation, and not good for large amounts of data. A well-designed encryption method encrypts data using symmetric keys, and encrypts the symmetric keys using asymmetric keys. Certificates use asymmetric keys, but have additional functionality that can be used for authentication or non-repudiation.

Now, take a look at how SQL provides encryption services. Figure 6-12 shows a high-level overview of the encryption hierarchy used by SQL Server 2005. At the top level is the Windows layer, which includes the Windows Data Protection API (DPAPI). The DPAPI is responsible for encrypting the server's service master key using the server's local machine key. The *service master key* is the top of the encryption food chain within the SQL environment. The service master key is automatically generated the first time a lower-level key is created.

Beneath the service master key is the *database master key*. The database master key can protect the private keys of all certificates and asymmetric keys within a database. It is a symmetric key that is encrypted using the 3DES algorithm and a password. Copies of the key are encrypted using the service master key, and are stored in both the master database and the database for which it was created. If the database is moved to another server, the database master key can be decrypted by using the OPEN MASTER KEY statement and providing the password used to encrypt it.

Also in the database scope are symmetric and asymmetric keys you can create for encrypting data, as well as certificates that can also be used for digital signing and non-repudiation. Creating and managing the different key types are discussed in the next section.

One of the first steps you should take is creating the database master key. Remember that the database master key is a symmetric key that encrypts all private key data within the database. This is helpful if you are using asymmetric keys or certificates, in that they can be created without having to supply a password or other mechanism to protect the private keys associated with both. To create a new master key for the AdventureWorks database, you can execute the following command:

```
USE AdventureWorks
CREATE MASTER KEY
ENCRYPTION BY PASSWORD = 'P@ssw0rd';
GO
```

Creation of a master key requires CONTROL permission on the database. Also, if you already have a master key created, you must drop the existing one if you need to create a new master key. An existing master key cannot be dropped if it is being used to encrypt a private key in the database.

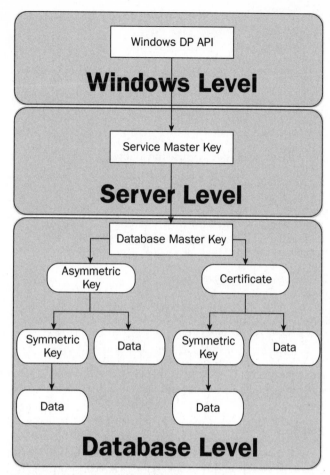

Figure 6-12: Encryption hierarchy

Once you've created your master key, you can query the sys.databases catalog view to see if the database master key has been encrypted using the service master key by looking at the value of the is_master_key_encrypted_by_server column. This column uses a Boolean value to indicate whether the database master key is encrypted with the service master key. The value may be 0 if the database master key was created on another server.

Before continuing on to the subject of working with other keys to encrypt database information, let's look at the topic of backing up your service master key and database master keys. This can be extremely valuable in case you have to perform a disaster-recovery operation, and need to recover data that had been protected or encrypted with one of these keys. The syntax for both keys is similar, but an additional step is required to back up an encrypted database master key.

Let's start with the service master key first. Quite simply, use the BACKUP SERVICE MASTER KEY statement with a file path, which can be a local or UNC path, and a password that meets your password-complexity requirements. Using a password on the backup file prevents someone from being able to restore your master key on another server, and then being able to decrypt your database master keys.

```
BACKUP SERVICE MASTER KEY TO FILE = 'C:\KeyBackups\ServiceMasterKey'
ENCRYPTION BY PASSWORD = 'c@MplexP@ssw0rd';
GO
```

If you need to restore the service master key, you can issue the following statement:

```
RESTORE SERVICE MASTER KEY FROM FILE = 'C:\KeyBackups\ServiceMasterKey'
DECRYPTION BY PASSWORD = 'c@MplexP@ssw0rd';
GO
```

To back up and restore a database master key, use the following examples:

```
--Backup the database master key
USE AdventureWorks;
OPEN MASTER KEY
 DECRYPTION BY PASSWORD = 'P@ssw0rd'
BACKUP MASTER KEY TO FILE = 'C:\KeyBackups\AWorksMasterKey'
ENCRYPTION BY PASSWORD = 'dn9e8h93ndwjKJD';
GO
--Restore the database master key
USE AdventureWorks;
RESTORE MASTER KEY FROM FILE = 'c:\KeyBackups\AWorksMasterKey'
DECRYPTION BY PASSWORD = 'dn9e8h93ndwjKJD'
ENCRYPTION BY PASSWORD = 'P@ssw0rd'
GO
```

Note that when you use the RESTORE MASTER KEY statement, you need to provide a new password for encrypting the database master key. The command will fail without this step.

Encryption Tools

Now that you understand some of the basics of encryption, take a look at creating and managing encryption tools. Each of the objects in this section serves a specific purpose. After you learn how to create symmetric keys, asymmetric keys, and certificates, you will learn how to use them.

Symmetric Keys

As mentioned earlier, symmetric keys offer an efficient model for being able to encrypt large amounts of data. The resource overhead is minimized by using the same keys for both encryption and decryption. Here's the syntax for generating symmetric keys:

```
CREATE SYMMETRIC KEY name [AUTHORIZATION owner] WITH options
ENCRYPTION BY mechanism
```

The following table shows the arguments that can be used.

Argument	Description
AUTHORIZATION owner	Identifies who the owner of the key is.
KEY_SOURCE pass phrase	Identifies a pass phrase used to derive the key.

Argument	Description
ALGORITHM	Choose one of the following: DES, TRIPLE_DES, RC2, RC4, RC4_128, DESX, AES_128, AES_192, AES_256.
IDENTITY_VALUE pass phrase	Used to generate a GUID for identifying data that has been encrypted with this key.
ENCRYPTION BY mechanism	One or more of the following methods for encrypting the symmetric key:
	CERTIFICATE certificate_name
	PASSWORD = 'password'
	SYMMETRIC KEY symmetric_key_name
	ASYMMETRIC KEY asym_key_name

Try It Out   Create a Symmetric Key

The following example creates a new symmetric key named SalesKey1, which uses the 56-bit data encryption standard algorithm:

```
USE AdventureWorks
GO
--Create Symmetric Key
CREATE SYMMETRIC KEY SalesKey1
    WITH ALGORITHM = DES,
    KEY_SOURCE = 'The quick brown fox jumped over the lazy dog',
    IDENTITY_VALUE = 'FoxAndHound'
    ENCRYPTION BY PASSWORD = '9348hsxasnA@B';
GO
```

You can add or remove methods for encrypting the key with the ALTER SYMMETRIC KEY statement, and you can remove a symmetric key by using the DROP SYMMETRIC KEY keyname statement.

In this example, use the SalesCert certificate created in the earlier section, "Database Users," to encrypt the symmetric key, and remove the password encryption from the previous example:

```
--Open the symmetric key
OPEN SYMMETRIC KEY SalesKey1
 DECRYPTION BY PASSWORD = '9348hsxasnA@B'
--Add encryption using the certificate created earlier
ALTER SYMMETRIC KEY SalesKey1
 ADD ENCRYPTION BY CERTIFICATE SalesCert
--Remove the password encryption
ALTER SYMMETRIC KEY SalesKey1
 DROP ENCRYPTION BY PASSWORD = '9348hsxasnA@B'
--Close the symmetric key
CLOSE SYMMETRIC KEY SalesKey1
```

Asymmetric Keys

Asymmetric keys use a pair of keys rather than a single one. These keys are often referred to as the *public key* and *private key*. One key is used for encryption, and the other is used for decryption. It doesn't really matter which key is used for encryption, but the data cannot be decrypted without the corresponding key.

When creating an asymmetric key pair, you can specify the owner of the key pair and the key source (which is either a strong-name file, an assembly, or an executable assembly file). Alternatively, you can use an algorithm that determines the number of bits used by the private key, selecting a key length using 512, 1024, or 2048 bits. You can also use the ENCRYPTION BY PASSWORD option to encrypt the private key. If you do not specify a password, the database master key will encrypt the private key.

```
USE AdventureWorks
CREATE ASYMMETRIC KEY HumanResources
    WITH ALGORITHM = RSA_2048;
GO
```

You can use the ALTER ASYMMETRIC KEY statement to change the properties of a key pair. You can use the REMOVE PRIVATE KEY option to take the private key out of the database (make sure you have a backup of the private key first!), or you can change the way the private key is protected. For example, you can change the password used to encrypt the private key, and then change the protection from password to database master key, or vice versa.

For example, use the following code to encrypt the private key from the HumanResources key pair created in the earlier example using a password:

```
USE AdventureWorks
ALTER ASYMMETRIC KEY HumanResources
    WITH PRIVATE KEY (
    ENCRYPTION BY PASSWORD = 'P@ssw0rd');
GO
```

In the next example, you can change the password used to encrypt the private key by first decrypting it, and then re-encrypting it with a new password:

```
USE AdventureWorks
ALTER ASYMMETRIC KEY HumanResources
WITH PRIVATE KEY (
DECRYPTION BY PASSWORD = 'P@ssw0rd',
ENCRYPTION BY PASSWORD = '48ufdsjEHF@*hda');
GO
```

Certificates

Certificates (also known as *public key certificates*) are objects that associate an asymmetric key pair with a credential. Certificates are objects that can be used not only for encryption, but for authentication and non-repudiation as well. This means that not only can you obfuscate data that would normally be in plaintext, but you can provide a means of guaranteeing the source, or the trustworthiness of that source.

The details of a certificate identify when the certificate was created, for how long the certificate is valid, who created the certificate, and what the certificate can be used for. It also identifies the public key associated with the certificate, and the algorithm that can be used for digitally signing messages.

The ability to create and use certificates is a feature that is new to SQL Server 2005, and one that even experienced DBAs may have trouble grasping at first. Certificates are part of the bigger scope of application security and identity, and the functionality extended to SQL Server 2005 is no different than how you would use certificates with other applications and services. This topic is almost like opening a Pandora's box, but once you understand the basics of how certificates work, and how they can be used to protect your services and data, you will appreciate their flexibility.

Certificates also have a feature that let you trace the genealogy of the certificate, its "family tree," if you will (see Figure 6-13). This certificate hierarchy identifies not only what *Certification Authority* (CA) issued the certificate, but what CA generated the certificate used by the CA to generate the certificate you have. This is known as the *certificate chain*. The certificate chain can be used to identify either a common Root CA (the highest authority in a chain) that can be trusted for authentication, or another Root CA that is considered a trustworthy source. Many applications and operating systems include a list of commercial CAs that are automatically trusted. When the certificate from a Root CA is trusted, it is assumed that any certificates that can trace its genealogy back to that root are also trusted. If the certificate is not from a trusted certificate chain, the user may be warned that the certificate is not trusted, and should proceed with caution. Commercial CAs are often used to obtain Server Authentication and SSL certificates, simply because many Web browsers already trust the most popular Root CAs.

Many organizations have developed their own *Public Key Infrastructure* (PKI). These companies have found it necessary to deploy and use certificates for a variety of reasons. Some might use certificates with Smart Cards for logging in to their computers. Some may use certificates for encrypting data on the NTFS file system, using Encrypting File System (EFS). Some organizations may use certificates for digitally signing applications and macros, so that their users know where the application came from, or that it hasn't been modified. These organizations often have their own CA hierarchy. They may have a Root CA they manage themselves, or they may have the ability to generate their own certificates that are part of a third-party certificate chain.

Figure 6-13: Certificate information

Microsoft SQL Server 2005 has the ability to create its own self-signed certificates. In a way, SQL can be its own CA! But don't expect these certificates to be automatically trusted outside of the SQL instance. The certificates generated by SQL Server conform to the X.509 standard, and can be used outside of the SQL Server if necessary, but they are not part of a trusted hierarchy. A more common approach is to use a certificate generated by another CA and import that into SQL Server. Certificates can be just as widely used in SQL Server as they can outside of SQL. You can use them for server authentication, encryption, and digital signing.

On the subject of encryption, public key certificates operate in the same way as asymmetric keys. The key pair, however, is bound to this certificate. The public key is included in the certificate details, and the private key must be securely archived. Private keys associated with certificates must be secured using a password, the database master key, or another encryption key. When encrypting data, the best practice is to encrypt the data with a symmetric key, and then encrypt the symmetric key with a public key.

When creating a certificate that will be self-signed, you can use the CREATE CERTIFICATE statement. You can choose to encrypt the private key using a strong password, or by using the database master key. You can also use the CREATE CERTIFICATE statement to import a certificate and private key from a file. Alternatively, you can create a certificate based on a signed assembly.

Once the certificate has been created, you can modify the certificate with the ALTER CERTIFICATE statement. Some of the changes you can make include changing the way the private key is protected, or removing the private key from the SQL Server. Removing the private key should be done only if the certificate is used to validate a digital signature. If the public key had been used to encrypt data or a symmetric key, the private key should be available for decryption.

It is a good idea when creating certificates to make a backup of the certificate and the associated private key with the BACKUP CERTIFICATE statement. You can make a backup of the certificate without archiving the private key, and use the public key for verification or encrypting messages that can only be decrypted with the private key.

Once a certificate is no longer needed, you can get rid of it with the DROP CERTIFICATE statement. Be aware that the certificate can't be dropped if it is still associated with other objects.

Try It Out Create a New Certificate

In the following example, create a new certificate named PersonnelDataCert, which you will use later to encrypt data. After creating this certificate, back up the certificate to the file system (you can either change the path in the example, or create a new folder on your C: drive called certs). Once that is done, the last step is to import the certificate into the TempDB database.

```
-- Create the Personnel Data Certificate
USE AdventureWorks;
CREATE CERTIFICATE PersonnelDataCert
    ENCRYPTION BY PASSWORD = 'HRcertific@te'
    WITH SUBJECT = 'Personnel Data Encryption Certificate',
    EXPIRY_DATE = '12/31/2009';
GO

--Backup the certificate and private key to the file system
Use AdventureWorks
BACKUP CERTIFICATE PersonnelDataCert TO FILE = 'c:\certs\Personnel.cer'
    WITH PRIVATE KEY (DECRYPTION BY PASSWORD = 'HRcertific@te',
```

```
     FILE = 'c:\certs\Personnelkey.pvk' ,
     ENCRYPTION BY PASSWORD = '@notherPassword' );
GO


--Import the certificate and private key into the TempDB database
USE tempdb
CREATE CERTIFICATE PersonnelDataCert
    FROM FILE = 'c:\certs\Personnel.cer'
     WITH PRIVATE KEY (FILE = 'c:\certs\Personnelkey.pvk',
    DECRYPTION BY PASSWORD = '@notherPassword',
     ENCRYPTION BY PASSWORD = 'TempDBKey1');
GO
```

In the next example, change the password used to encrypt the private key using the ALTER CERTIFICATE statement:

```
Use tempdb
ALTER CERTIFICATE PersonnelDataCert
    WITH PRIVATE KEY (ENCRYPTION BY PASSWORD = 'P@ssw0rd789',
    DECRYPTION BY PASSWORD = 'TempDBKey1');
GO
```

Now, you can remove the private key from the AdventureWorks database. Because the certificate and the private key are backed up, you can perform this action safely.

```
Use tempdb
ALTER CERTIFICATE PersonnelDataCert
    REMOVE PRIVATE KEY
GO
```

Finally, clean up the TempDB database:

```
USE tempdb
DROP CERTIFICATE PersonnelDataCert;
GO
```

Encrypting Data

Now that you've seen the different objects that can be used for encryption or non-repudiation, take a look at how you can actually use them. First of all, not everything needs to be encrypted. Because the process of encrypting and decrypting data can be resource-intensive, you should be mindful of what data you need to encrypt. Data that should be kept confidential (such as credit card or Social Security numbers) would fall into this category. An employee's middle name, no matter how embarrassing it might be, would not. Also note that not every data type can be encrypted with the encryptbykey function. The valid data types are nvarchar, char, wchar, varchar, and nchar.

Prior to encrypting data, you must open the key that will perform the encryption process. Again, data is commonly protected with a symmetric key, which is in turn, protected with an asymmetric key pair. If the symmetric key is protected with a password, then any user with ALTER permissions on the symmetric key and the password can open and close the symmetric key. If the symmetric key is protected by an asymmetric key or certificate, the user also needs CONTROL permissions on the asymmetric key or the certificate.

| Try It Out | **Create an Encrypted Column** |

Use the following sample code to create an encrypted column in the `Sales.CreditCard` table. In this example, use the symmetric key `SalesKey1` and the certificate `SalesCert`, both created earlier in this chapter:

```
ALTER TABLE Sales.CreditCard
    ADD EncryptedCardNumber varbinary(128);
GO

OPEN SYMMETRIC KEY SalesKey1 DECRYPTION BY
 CERTIFICATE SalesCert WITH PASSWORD = 'P@ssw0rd'

UPDATE Sales.CreditCard
SET EncryptedCardNumber
    = EncryptByKey(Key_GUID('SalesKey1'), CardNumber);
GO

CLOSE SYMMETRIC KEY SalesKey1;
GO
```

Because the symmetric key was used to encrypt the data, it will also be used for decryption. Using the preceding example as a template, you could use the following commands to create another new column that stores the decrypted data. A SELECT statement is included that allows you to view the original data, the encrypted data, and the decrypted data columns:

```
ALTER TABLE Sales.CreditCard
    ADD DecryptedCardNumber NVARCHAR(25);
GO

OPEN SYMMETRIC KEY SalesKey1 DECRYPTION BY
 CERTIFICATE SalesCert WITH PASSWORD = 'P@ssw0rd';
GO

UPDATE Sales.CreditCard
SET DecryptedCardNumber
    = DecryptByKey(EncryptedCardNumber);
GO

CLOSE SYMMETRIC KEY SalesKey1;
GO

Select TOP (10) CreditCardID, CardNumber AS Original, EncryptedCardNumber AS
Encrypted, DecryptedCardNumber AS Decrypted
FROM Sales.CreditCard;
GO
```

You don't have to create a whole new column to view the decrypted data, though. The DECRYPTBYKEY function can be executed in a SELECT statement to view the unencrypted data. The following example shows you how:

```
OPEN SYMMETRIC KEY SalesKey1 DECRYPTION BY
 CERTIFICATE SalesCert WITH PASSWORD = 'P@ssw0rd';
```

```
GO

SELECT CreditCardID, CardNumber,EncryptedCardNumber
    AS 'Encrypted Card Number',
    CONVERT(nvarchar, DecryptByKey(EncryptedCardNumber))
    AS 'Decrypted Card Number'
    FROM Sales.CreditCard;
GO

CLOSE SYMMETRIC KEY SalesKey1;
GO
```

Digital Signatures

Digital signatures provide authentication and non-repudiation. Often, with public key pairs, the private key is used to digitally sign a message (or, in the case of a code-signing certificate, an application or assembly). Take a look at how digital signing works in with email messages as an example.

Bob sends Alice a message, and his email client is configured to automatically add his digital signature to all outgoing messages. In this case, while the message is being prepared for delivery, a key is generated and passed to a hashing algorithm for a one-way transformation of the data into a hash value. The hash value is attached to the message, and the key that was used to generate the hash is encrypted with Bob's private key.

The message is delivered to Alice, who receives the message in plain text, as well as receiving the hashed version of the message. Alice, who has access to Bob's public key, uses it to decrypt the key that was used to generate the hash. The key is then passed through the hashing algorithm, and a new hash is generated. If the new hash matches the hash that was sent with the message, Alice can feel confident that the message hasn't been changed during delivery. If the hash values do not match, then the message may have been altered since it was transmitted and should not be trusted.

In a similar vein, you can use digital signatures to sign SQL Server components (such as stored procedures) to associate the stored procedure with a hash value. If the stored procedure changes by a single bit, then the hash values will differ; and you'll know that someone must have used an ALTER PROCEDURE statement on it!

You can use both asymmetric keys and digital certificates to sign stored procedures, functions, or DML triggers in SQL Server. The following code creates a simple stored procedure called Sales.DisplaySomeVendors. You can then add a signature to that stored procedure using the SalesCert certificate from earlier. The private key will need to be decrypted to digitally sign the stored procedure.

```
CREATE PROCEDURE Sales.DisplaySomeVendors AS
    SELECT TOP (20) * FROM Purchasing.Vendor;
GO

USE AdventureWorks;
ADD SIGNATURE TO Sales.DisplaySomeVendors
    BY CERTIFICATE SalesCert WITH PASSWORD = 'P@ssw0rd';
GO
```

If you look at the properties of the stored procedure, you can now see that the stored procedure has been digitally signed, and it was signed by the `SalesCert` certificate (see Figure 6-14). You can also query the `sys.crypt_properties` catalog view. This view will show any objects that have been digitally signed. In the next example, you can query the `sys.crypt_properties` view to see the digital signature assigned to the `Sales.DisplaySomeVendors` stored procedure. Then you can alter the procedure, query the view again, and note that the procedure is no longer digitally signed.

```
SELECT * FROM sys.crypt_properties

ALTER PROCEDURE Sales.DisplaySomeVendors AS
  SELECT TOP (10) * FROM Purchasing.Vendor

SELECT * FROM sys.crypt_properties
```

Current connection parameters	
Database	AdventureWorks
Server	AUGHTFIVE
User	AUGHTFIVE\Administrator
Description	
Created date	1/31/2006 8:54 PM
Execute as	Caller
Name	DisplaySomeVendors
Schema	Sales
System object	False
Options	
ANSI NULLs	True
Encrypted	False
For replication	False
Quoted identifier	True
Recompile	False
Signatures	
SalesCert	SIGNATURE BY CERTIFICATE

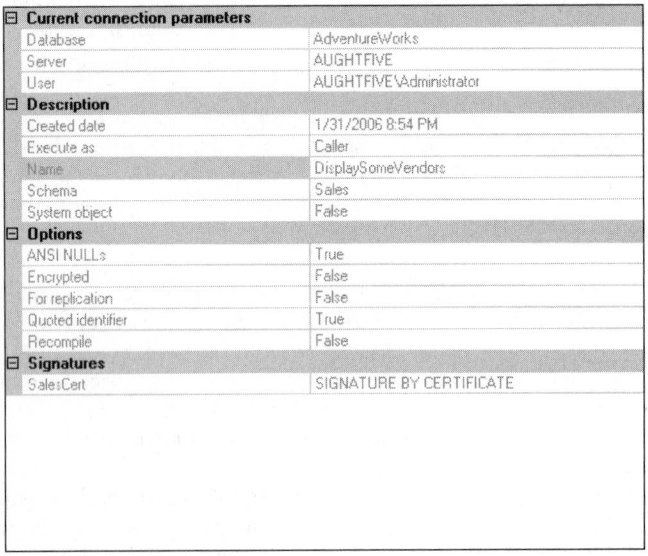

Figure 6-14: Digital signature

Best Practices

Like any other application or server product, there are a few guidelines you should follow to help increase the level of security in place. Remember that you will never be able to plan for and protect against every possible threat, but you can make it more difficult for malicious users to gain access to your data.

❑　*Rename the* sa *account* — A general rule of thumb about account security is that if a malicious user knows your login ID, the intruder has half of what is needed to gain access to your system. By renaming the sa account, you can minimize the likelihood of someone obtaining full access to your SQL Server.

❑ *Use strong passwords* — As mentioned earlier in this chapter, you should take advantage of the password policies, and require users to create complex passwords that get changed regularly. You should educate your users about the importance of strong passwords. While password policy enforcement for SQL Logins is managed at the server, you should provide an application or tool that allows users a way to change their passwords and be notified when their passwords are about to expire.

❑ *No one should log on as* sa — The sa account should rarely (if ever) log in. To provide more accurate auditing information, users should be forced to use their own logins (or login through the membership in a group) in order to track what users are performing which actions. If everyone has the sa password, and everyone is able to log in as that account, nothing would stop them from being able to steal or destroy your data. You wouldn't be able to hold that person accountable, because you may not know who that person is!

❑ *Use least-privilege accounts for SQL Services* — Apply the principle of least privilege, and use accounts that have exactly the rights and permissions needed by the services, and nothing else. While it might be tempting to make the SQL Server account or the SQL Server Agent account a member of an administrative group, it may not be necessary. Identify what resources outside of the SQL Server each of these accounts will be interacting with, and assign only the required permissions.

❑ *Audit principals regularly* — A diligent administrator will know what accounts have been created, who is responsible for these accounts, and identify what steps must be taken to disable or remove superfluous accounts.

❑ *Disable or remove any unused network protocols* — In the SQL Configuration Manager you have the ability to enable or disable protocols used by the SQL Server. Additionally, consider disabling the NetBIOS protocol for your network adapter, if NetBIOS will not be used by your server or applications.

❑ *Use on-the-wire encryption to protect your data in transit* — It's not enough for you to protect the data while it sits idly on the server. As a database administrator, you should use technologies like Secure Sockets Layer (SSL) and Internet Protocol Security (IPSec) to protect the data while it's moving from server to server.

❑ *Do not place the SQL Server in a location with poor physical security* — There is a well-known article published by the Microsoft Security Response Center known as the "Ten Immutable Laws of Security." The first law dictates that if a malicious user has physical access to your computer, it's no longer your computer. Unless you can provide the means to control access to the hardware, your data can easily be stolen, compromised, damaged, or destroyed. Hardware locks, secure server rooms, and security personnel can all be instrumental in helping to protect your data.

❑ *Minimize the visibility of the server* — SQL Servers should never be publicly available. The Slammer worm should never have been a problem, had application architects and database administrators taken the necessary precautions to protect against that type of attack. Slammer was able to propagate so much, so fast, because few organizations recognized the harm in publishing SQL connectivity through their firewalls. A well-designed database application will use a robust and secure front-end, minimizing the exposure to the database engine.

❑ *Remove or disable unnecessary services and applications* — You should minimize the attack surface of your SQL Server as much as possible by turning off services and features that will not be used. Typically, it's a good idea to avoid running other services such as IIS, Active Directory, and Exchange on the same machine as SQL. Each one of these services can be a potential entry point for a malicious user to exploit, thereby granting the user access to your data.

❑   *Use Windows Authentication whenever possible* — Windows and Kerberos authentication are inherently more secure than SQL Authentication, but this is a design decision that you, your application developers, and security team must address.

❑   *Understand your role in the company's security policy* — Most organizations have a documented security policy that defines acceptable use for the network, and expectations for server or service behavior. As a database administrator, your responsibilities to configure and secure your servers may be documented as part of the overall security policy. What is expected of you, and of your servers, must be unambiguous. Your liabilities should also be clearly stated.

Summary

In this chapter, you learned about many of the security features available to you in SQL Server 2005. You should have a good understanding of the way security is applied to SQL Server from the top down, including:

❑   How to configure the different authentication modes

❑   How to create and manage server and database principals

❑   How to assign and control permissions

❑   How to protect your data on the server

You should also be able to apply some of the best practices discussed in this chapter to your own environments. You should never be overconfident of your security design, because complacency leads to sloppiness, which leads to *ginormous* holes in your security design, but you should feel confident about the skills you picked up.

In Chapter 7 you learn about creating and managing SQL endpoints, and how you can enable access to database resources using alternative connection methods.

Exercises

1.   Use the CREATE LOGIN statement to create a new SQL login for yourself, using your own name. Ensure that your password meets the password policy's complexity requirements, but don't require the password to expire. Set your default database to the AdventureWorks database. Then, in the AdventureWorks database create a user account for your login; but assign the user a different name. Set your default schema to the HumanResources schema, and grant your user permissions to query and update any object in the HumanResources schema.

2.   Create a new certificate named HRCert. The certificate should expire on 1/31/2016, and it should have the subject "HR Certificate." The private key should be protected by the password HRPassw0rd. Then, create a new symmetric key named HRDataKey using the AES_128 algorithm. Protect the key with the HRCert certificate. Make sure your user has CONTROL permissions on the certificate, and ALTER permissions on the symmetric key. To prepare for the next exercise, create a new column named EncryptedSSN in the HumanResources.Employee table that will store the data in the instructions in an encrypted format. The data type should be varbinary(128).

3. Use a new query window to log in using your new SQL login. In this window, create a script that will use the `HRDataKey` symmetric key to write an encrypted copy of the data from the `NationalIDNumber` column into the `EncryptedSSN` column.

4. Write a `SELECT` statement that will display the columns in the `HumanResources.Employee` table, but display the `EncryptedSSN` in a plaintext format.

Configuring SQL Server Network Communication

SQL Server 2005 is a client-server application designed to efficiently exchange data and instructions over one or more network connections. Understanding the network connections and how they can be configured is a big part of the database administrator's job. SQL Server 2005 has made part of the DBA's job easier by reducing the number of protocols that can be used to connect to SQL Server, but at the same time, the job of the DBA is made more complex by the ability to configure multiple connection types with each protocol with the new endpoint server object. This chapter discusses the different endpoints that can be configured, as well as the protocol configurations that the endpoints rely on. The chapter also takes a brief look at the client configurations that can be configured with SQL Server 2005.

SQL Server 2005 Network Protocols

SQL Server 2005 provides support for four protocols:

- ❑ Shared Memory
- ❑ TCP/IP
- ❑ Named Pipes
- ❑ Virtual Interface Adapter (VIA)

By default, the only network protocols enabled for most editions of SQL Server are TCP/IP and Shared Memory. The Developer and Enterprise Evaluation editions are configured with all protocols except Shared Memory disabled during installation, but the remaining protocols can be enabled if required. If a protocol is not enabled, SQL Server will not listen on an endpoint that is configured to utilize that protocol.

The SQL Server Configuration Manager is used to configure server protocols. With this tool, each supported protocol can be enabled, disabled, and configured as required. The configuration options of the network protocols are not completely clear, so they require a little explanation.

Opening the SQL Server Configuration Manager displays a node for configuring SQL Server services, SQL Server network protocols, and SQL Native Client protocols. To configure the Server protocols, expand the SQL Server 2005 Network Configuration node and select the instance to be configured. The right-hand pane shows all four of the supported protocols and their status. To display the configurable properties of any of the protocols, double-click the protocol, or right-click the protocol and select Properties to launch the corresponding Properties window.

Shared Memory

The Shared Memory protocol can only be used by local connections, because it is a shared memory and process space used for inter-server communication. It has only one configurable property: Enabled. The Enabled property can be set to Yes or No, resulting in a status of Enabled or Disabled.

Named Pipes

Named Pipes uses Inter-Process Communication (IPC) channels for efficient inter-server communication, as well as local area network (LAN) communication. The Named Pipes protocol has some enhancements in SQL Server 2005 including support for encrypted traffic, but because of the excessive overhead of Named Pipes when connecting across networks or firewalls, and the additional port that Named Pipes requires to be opened (445), it is generally a good idea to leave the Named Pipes protocol disabled. However, there are many applications that take advantage of the Named Pipes protocol because they were designed for local network implementations. Named Pipes provides easy access to Remote Procedure Calls (RPC) within a single security domain, and so is advantageous to these applications. If you need to support one of these applications, and the SQL Server is not exposed to external traffic, the risk of enabling the Named Pipes protocol and corresponding endpoint is minimal.

Named Pipes has two configurable properties: Enabled and Pipe Name. The Enabled property works the same as the Shared Memory protocol. The Pipe Name specifies the inter-process pipe that SQL Server will listen on. The default pipe is \\.\pipe\sql\query.

TCP/IP

The TCP/IP protocol is the primary and preferred protocol for most SQL Server installations. It is configured on two separate tabs on the TCP/IP Properties window: the Protocol tab and the IP Addresses tab, as shown in Figure 7-1.

The Protocol tab has the following four configurable properties:

- ❑ Enabled—This works the same as the other protocols.
- ❑ Keep Alive—This specifies how many milliseconds SQL Server waits to verify an idle connection is still valid by sending a KEEPALIVE packet. The default is 30,000 milliseconds.
- ❑ Listen All—This specifies whether SQL Server will listen on all IP addresses configured on the server.
- ❑ No Delay—This option specifies whether the TCP protocol queues small packets to send out larger packets. This queuing is typically undesirable in transaction-based systems, and so it should be left in its default configuration of No.

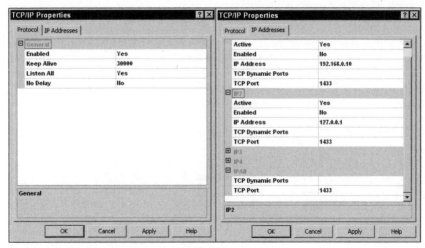

Figure 7-1: Tabs for configuring the TCP/IP protocol

As you can see in Figure 7-1, the IP Addresses tab contains configuration settings for each configured IP address on the server and one section for the configuring of all IP addresses. On my system, there are four IP addresses. Three are associated with a network adapter and one is associated with the 127.0.0.1 loopback address. As a result, there are five IP sections: IP1, IP2, IP3, IP4, and IPALL. The settings for IP3 and IP4 are collapsed as indicated by the "+" symbol to the left of the section header. Clicking the "+" symbol will expand the address configuration. The IPALL section can be used to configure all the IP address settings instead of individually configuring them.

IP address settings are described in the following table.

Setting	Description
Active	Specifies whether the individual address is active and available on the server. This setting is not available for the IPALL configuration (shown in the bottom of the right-hand pane in Figure 7-1).
Enabled	If the Listen All property on the Protocol tab is set to No, this property indicates whether SQL Server is listening on the IP address. If the Listen All property on the Protocol tab is set to Yes, the Enabled property is ignored. This setting is not available for the IPALL configuration.
IP Address	Specifies the IP Address for individual configuration, not available for the IPALL configuration.
TCP Dynamic Ports	Specifies whether the TCP port will be dynamically generated at start up. If left blank, dynamic assignment is disabled. A setting of 0 (zero) specifies that dynamic assignment is enabled.
TCP Ports	Specifies the TCP port to be used for all addresses if in the IPALL section, or the port for a specific address in an individual IP address section. If dynamic port assignment is enabled, this property will display the value of the dynamically configured port.

SQL Native Client Configuration

The same four server-side protocols are supported for the SQL Native Client and, again, the SQL Server Configuration Manager is used to enable, disable, or configure these protocols. In addition to the configuration of the client protocols, the binding order of the protocols can also be set. You can do this by expanding the SQL Native Client Configuration node and selecting Client Protocols. In the right-hand pane, right-click a protocol and select Order to set the order of all enabled protocols, as shown in Figure 7-2.

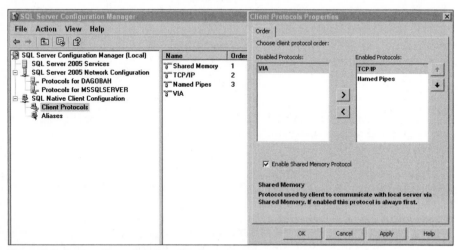

Figure 7-2: Setting the order of enabled protocols

As Figure 7-2 shows, if the Shared Memory protocol is enabled, it is always first in the binding order. It is not available for manual ordering.

Aliases can be created using the SQL Native Client Configuration. Aliases are very useful in enabling clients to connect to a server even though the name of the server does not match that in the client's connection string. For example, a standby server may be brought up to take the place of a failed server that serves an application with a hard-coded connection string. Without an alias, either the application's connection string would need to be changed, or the server name would have to be changed. By specifying an alias, client requests can be directed to the server without changing the server name. Aliases can also be used to replace a complicated named instance name.

Figure 7-3 shows the alias YODAHOME being configured for the named instance AUGHTFIVE\DAGOBAH. To launch the New Alias dialog, right-click the Aliases node shown in the left-hand pane of Figure 7-3 and select New Alias. Once the alias has been created, new connections can be created by referencing the alias name in lieu of the instance name.

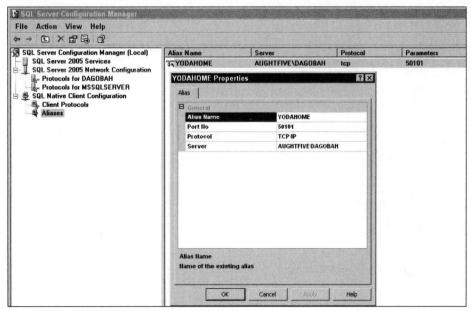

Figure 7-3: Configuring the alias YODAHOME

SQL Server Endpoints

"SQL Server what?" That's a common response when I introduce this topic during SQL Server 2005 workshops and training classes. However, endpoints are not really all that new. An *endpoint* after all, is just a point of termination on a network, or to be perfectly precise, an endpoint is the name for the entity on one end of a transport layer connection. In previous releases of SQL Server, the default network endpoints were UDP port 1434 for the SQL Server Resolution Service and TCP port 1433 for the default instance of SQL Server. Additional TCP ports could be configured for the default and/or any additional named instances. Most database administrators didn't really think of the server listener as an endpoint, but that's what it was, and that's what it remains. The primary difference in SQL Server 2005 is that now connection objects are actually called endpoints and they are more manageable, along with the fact that there are additional endpoint types as well. SQL Server 2005 can listen on different ports, using different transport protocols for different services.

SQL Server provides four different types of endpoints:

- ❑ TSQL (both default and TCP)
- ❑ Database Mirroring
- ❑ SOAP
- ❑ Service Broker

Each endpoint provides separate functionality and can be uniquely configured to control access to the database engine and associated services.

Default TSQL Endpoints

TSQL endpoints are essentially the same as the standard endpoints that existed in SQL Server 2000. During installation, five TSQL endpoints are created:

❑ TSQL Default TCP

❑ TSQL Default VIA

❑ TSQL Named Pipes

❑ TSQL Local Machine

❑ Dedicated Admin Connection (DAC)

The TSQL endpoints are created to provide connection services for the four supported protocols (TCP, VIA, Named Pipes, and Shared Memory). These protocols correspond to the Default TCP, Default VIA, Named Pipes, and Local Machine endpoints. The fifth endpoint created to support the DAC listens on a dedicated TCP port that is configured at startup to support an administrative connection. The configured port is logged in the current SQL Server log file. (SQL Server log files are described in Chapter 10.)

Regardless of the condition of the network protocol, TSQL endpoints have two states: *started* and *stopped*. If the network protocol is enabled and the endpoint is started, SQL Server will listen and accept connections on that endpoint. A stopped endpoint still listens, but actively refuses new connections. If the corresponding protocol is disabled, the TSQL endpoint will not listen and will not respond to client requests.

TSQL endpoints are also known as Tabular Data Stream (TDS) endpoints. TDS has been around since Sybase created it in 1984 to support its fledgling relational database engine. Microsoft inherited the protocol during its joint venture with Sybase, and has since made many changes to the protocol to make it more efficient and secure. It remains the primary protocol for transmitting data from SQL Server to clients via the TCP, Named Pipes, VIA, and Shared Memory protocols.

TSQL Default TCP

The TSQL Default TCP endpoint is created during the installation of a SQL Server instance, and is automatically configured to listen on port 1433 for default instances. Named instance TSQL Default TCP endpoints are randomly assigned a TCP port every time the named instance starts up. However, the port number for named instances can be configured with the SQL Server Configuration Manager. Configuring a static port can simplify client access and reduce the dependency on the SQL Browser service that enumerates named instances.

To statically configure the port that a named instance of SQL Server will listen on, open the SQL Server Configuration Manager, expand the SQL Server 2005 Network Configuration node, and select the instance to configure. Double-click the TCP/IP protocol in the right-hand pane, or right-click it and click Properties to launch the TCP/IP Properties window. By default SQL Server is configured to listen on all available IP addresses, and so the only place that the static port needs to be set is in the IPALL section of the IP Addresses tab on the TCP/IP Properties window (see Figure 7-4). This behavior can be changed by setting the `Listen All` property to `No` on the Protocol tab and individually configuring each IP address.

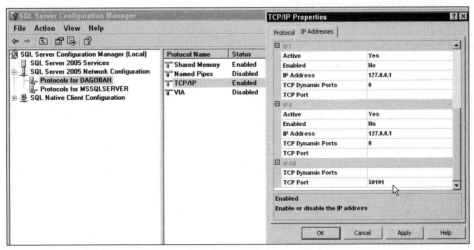

Figure 7-4: The IPALL section of the IP Addresses tab

Figure 7-4 shows the TCP port for the named instance DAGOBAH being statically set to port 50101. When configuring ports for named instances, it is a best practice to choose a port above 50000, because many ports below 50000 are associated with other applications. To retrieve a list of reserved and well-known ports, visit the Internet Assigned Numbers Authority (IANA) Web site at `http://www.iana.org/assignments/port-numbers`.

Keep in mind that the supported protocols are separate from endpoints and multiple endpoints can be configured for each protocol.

By default, all users have access to the Default TCP endpoint. However, access to the endpoint can be more tightly controlled with the `GRANT CONNECT` | `DENY CONNECT` | `REVOKE CONNECT` commands.

The status of any endpoint can also be changed with the `ALTER ENDPOINT` command, as shown in the following example:

```
USE Master;
GO
ALTER ENDPOINT [TSQL Default TCP]
STATE=STOPPED;
```

```
USE Master;
GO
ALTER ENDPOINT [TSQL Default TCP]
STATE=STARTED;
```

TSQL Default VIA

The VIA protocol is used to support VIA hardware devices such as VIA Storage Area Network (SAN) devices. The VIA protocol is dependent on vendor implementations, so a discussion of the VIA endpoint is somewhat difficult without seemingly endorsing one hardware vendor over another. The VIA configurations are usually very straightforward and only require a port assignment. If you are using a VIA hardware implementation for your SAN configuration, make sure you get all the technical documentation you can from your supplier.

TSQL Named Pipes

The Named Pipes endpoint is created to support Named Pipes protocol connections. The Named Pipes protocol was described earlier in this chapter.

TSQL Local Machine

The TSQL Local Machine endpoint allows connections to occur using the Shared Memory protocol. Shared Memory is only accessible on the local machine, hence the TSQL Local Machine designation for this endpoint. Installations of the Enterprise Evaluation and Developer editions of SQL Server 2005 use this endpoint exclusively, unless additional protocols are enabled.

Dedicated Admin Connection (DAC)

The Dedicated Admin Connection (DAC) endpoint is used to support limited administrative actions when other connections are unavailable or unresponsive. It utilizes its own memory area, dedicated TCP port, and CPU scheduler. By default, the DAC endpoint only listens for local connections. Remote DAC connections can be enabled using the Surface Area Configuration tool, or by executing the following code:

```
USE Master;
GO
sp_configure 'remote admin connections', 1;
GO
RECONFIGURE;
GO
```

DAC connections are facilitated through the SQLCMD command-line tool.

TSQL TCP Endpoints

In addition to the default TCP endpoints created automatically, additional TSQL TCP endpoints can be created. These TSQL TCP endpoints can be created to support special security or application requirements. However, an important fact to keep in mind is that when a new TSQL TCP endpoint is created, SQL Server automatically revokes all connect permissions to the default endpoint. If connection support is still required for the default endpoint, explicit GRANT CONNECT permissions will be necessary to utilize the default endpoint. SQL Server helps you remember this important fact by always returning a message informing you of the impact of creating a new TCP endpoint, as shown in the next example.

If an additional TSQL TCP endpoint is needed, it can be created using T-SQL. The following example creates an additional TSQL TCP endpoint that is configured to listen on port 50102 and all IP addresses, and shows the resulting message warning about permissions:

```
USE Master;
GO
CREATE ENDPOINT DagobahEP
STATE = STARTED
AS TCP
    (LISTENER_PORT = 50102, LISTENER_IP = ALL)
FOR TSQL();
GO
```

```
RESULTS:
---------------------------------------------------------------------------
Creation of a TSQL endpoint will result in the revocation of any 'Public' connect
permissions on the 'TSQL Default TCP' endpoint.  If 'Public' access is desired on
this endpoint, reapply this permission using 'GRANT CONNECT ON ENDPOINT::[TSQL
Default TCP] to [public]'.
```

If a single IP address is needed, the LISTENER_IP argument can be set to a specific value inside parentheses, as the following example illustrates:

```
USE Master;
GO
CREATE ENDPOINT DagobahEP
STATE = STARTED
AS TCP
    (LISTENER_PORT = 50102, LISTENER_IP = (192.168.1.101))
FOR TSQL();
GO
```

IPV6 is also supported by SQL Server 2005. The address can be configured by passing in the hexadecimal IPV6 address as a binary string in single quotes enclosed in parentheses, as the following example illustrates:

```
USE Master;
GO
CREATE ENDPOINT DagobahEP
STATE = STARTED
AS TCP
    (LISTENER_PORT = 50102
    , LISTENER_IP = ('5F05:2000:80AD:5800:0058:0800:2023:1D71'))
FOR TSQL();
GO
```

In a previous example, the TCP/IP protocol was configured for the named instance DAGOBAH to listen on port 50101. With the additional endpoint and associated port, it will necessary to add the port to the TCP/IP protocol with the SQL Server Configuration Manager. This is done by simply adding another port to the port assignment delimited by a comma, as shown in Figure 7-5.

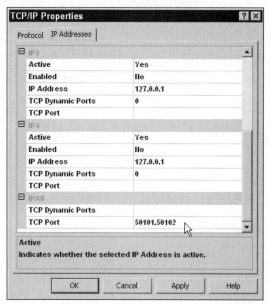

Figure 7-5: Adding another port to the port assignment

Database Mirroring Endpoints

SQL Server 2005 uses a mirroring endpoint for exclusive use of the server that is configured to participate in a database mirroring configuration. In mirroring, which is described in Chapter 11, each instance
of SQL Server is required to have its own dedicated database mirroring endpoint. All mirroring communication uses this database mirroring endpoint, but client connections to a database configured with a
mirror use the standard TDS endpoint.

The configuration of an exclusive mirroring endpoint ensures that database mirror process communication is handled in a separate process from all other database activities. The easiest way to configure mirroring endpoints is to run the mirroring wizard as explained in Chapter 11. To create and configure a
mirroring endpoint manually, and enforce secure encrypted communication over the endpoint, the following code can be utilized:

```
CREATE ENDPOINT AughtFiveDagobahMirror
   AUTHORIZATION SA
   STATE=STARTED
   AS TCP (LISTENER_PORT = 5022, LISTENER_IP = ALL)
   FOR DATA_MIRRORING
   (ROLE = PARTNER, AUTHENTICATION = WINDOWS NEGOTIATE
   ,ENCRYPTION = REQUIRED ALGORITHM RC4);
```

This example can be used to create the mirroring endpoint on either the principal or mirror server. It
assumes that the same domain account is used for the SQL Server service on both the principal and the
mirror. For the witness server, the ROLE argument would need to be changed to WITNESS.

If different accounts are used for each MSSQLSERVER service on the servers, logins that are mapped to the service accounts from each server will need to be granted the CONNECT permission to the other servers participating in the mirroring configuration. The following script can be run to ensure encrypted authenticated communication between the three servers configured to take part in a mirroring relationship. AughtFive is the principal server, Dagobah is the mirror server, and Tatooine is the witness server. In this example, all three instances are running on the same physical server, which is why each endpoint is configured with a different port number. In the case of separate physical servers, the port numbers could be configured consistently.

```
--Run on AughtFive
USE Master;
GO
CREATE ENDPOINT AughtFiveDagobahPrincipal
 AS TCP (LISTENER_PORT = 5022)
 FOR DATA_MIRRORING (ROLE = PARTNER, ENCRYPTION = REQUIRED ALGORITHM RC4);
GO
CREATE LOGIN [AughtFive\DagobahSQL] FROM WINDOWS;
CREATE LOGIN [AughtFive\TatooineSQL] FROM WINDOWS;
GO
GRANT CONNECT ON ENDPOINT::AughtFiveDagobahPrincipal
 TO [AughtFive\TatooineSQL];
GRANT CONNECT ON ENDPOINT::AughtFiveDagobahPrincipal
 TO [AughtFive\DagobahSQL];

--Run on Dagobah
USE Master;
GO
CREATE ENDPOINT AughtFiveDagobahMirror
  AS TCP (LISTENER_PORT = 5023)
  FOR DATA_MIRRORING (ROLE = PARTNER, ENCRYPTION = REQUIRED ALGORITHM RC4);
GO
CREATE LOGIN [AughtFive\AughtFiveSQL] FROM WINDOWS;
CREATE LOGIN [AughtFive\TatooineSQL] FROM WINDOWS;
GO
GRANT CONNECT ON ENDPOINT::AughtFiveDagobahMirror
TO [AughtFive\AughtFiveSQL];
GRANT CONNECT ON ENDPOINT::AughtFiveDagobahMirror
TO [AughtFive\TatooineSQL];

--Run on Tatooine
USE Master;
GO
CREATE ENDPOINT AughtFiveDagobahWitness
  AS TCP (LISTENER_PORT = 5024)
  FOR DATA_MIRRORING (ROLE = WITNESS, ENCRYPTION = REQUIRED ALGORITHM RC4);
GO
CREATE LOGIN [AughtFive\AughtFiveSQL] FROM WINDOWS;
CREATE LOGIN [AughtFive\DagobahSQL] FROM WINDOWS;
GO
GRANT CONNECT ON ENDPOINT::AughtFiveDagobahWitness
TO [AughtFive\AughtFiveSQL];
GRANT CONNECT ON ENDPOINT::AughtFiveDagobahWitness
TO [AughtFive\DagobahSQL];
```

The preceding commands set up the communication framework for mirroring, but do not actually initialize mirroring. See Chapter 11 for more information on how to configure and monitor mirroring.

SOAP Endpoints

Simple Object Access Protocol (SOAP) is a platform-independent protocol that defines how to use XML and HTTP to access services, objects, and servers. SOAP endpoints are created to publish SQL Server programming objects over data tier Web services without the use of IIS as a Web server. Creating data tier Web services with SOAP endpoints requires Windows Server 2003 or Windows XP Professional.

Data tier Web services provide a very powerful alternative to XML Web services, and provide the means of exposing stored procedures and functions over HTTP the same as conventional Web service architecture. In addition to stored procedures and functions, SOAP endpoints can be configured to allow ad hoc queries, but as a general rule, ad hoc access should be avoided.

The potential of SOAP endpoints is very exciting, but the potential for exploitation because of poorly configured and secured endpoints is almost as great. It is imperative that the DBA understand the ramifications and the security features included in SOAP endpoints to successfully and securely employ this new feature.

SOAP endpoints return SOAP messages consisting of an XML document with a header and a body. SOAP messages are essentially one-way transmissions from a sender to a receiver. SOAP does not define any application semantics such as a programming model or implementation-specific details. Web services, on the other hand, require a request/response model. The solution is to send SOAP messages within the body of an HTTP request and response. This solution provides the required model for Web services, and SOAP endpoints provide the structure to accomplish the communication.

The following syntax is used for creating a SOAP endpoint:

```
CREATE ENDPOINT endPointName [ AUTHORIZATION login ]
STATE = { STARTED | STOPPED | DISABLED }
AS HTTP (
PATH = 'url'
 , AUTHENTICATION =( { BASIC | DIGEST | INTEGRATED | NTLM | KERBEROS }
   [ ,...n ] )
 , PORTS = ( { CLEAR | SSL} [ ,... n ] )
 , [ SITE = {'*' | '+' | 'webSite' }]
[, CLEAR_PORT = clearPort ]
[, SSL_PORT = SSLPort ]
[, AUTH_REALM = { 'realm' | NONE } ]
[, DEFAULT_LOGON_DOMAIN = { 'domain' | NONE } ]
[, COMPRESSION = { ENABLED | DISABLED } ]
  )

FOR SOAP (
  [ { WEBMETHOD [ 'namespace'.] 'method_alias'
  (   NAME = 'database.schema.name'
  [ , SCHEMA = { NONE | STANDARD | DEFAULT } ]
  [ , FORMAT = { ALL_RESULTS | ROWSETS_ONLY | NONE} ]
  )
  } [ ,...n ] ]
```

```
[   BATCHES = { ENABLED | DISABLED } ]
[ , WSDL = { NONE | DEFAULT | 'sp_name' } ]
[ , SESSIONS = { ENABLED | DISABLED } ]
[ , LOGIN_TYPE = { MIXED | WINDOWS } ]
[ , SESSION_TIMEOUT = timeoutInterval | NEVER ]
[ , DATABASE = { 'database_name' | DEFAULT }
[ , NAMESPACE = { 'namespace' | DEFAULT } ]
[ , SCHEMA = { NONE | STANDARD } ]
[ , CHARACTER_SET = { SQL | XML }]
[ , HEADER_LIMIT = int ]
```

Because syntax specifications can be a bit arcane, the following example is provided to demonstrate the creation of a SOAP endpoint. The example creates a SOAP endpoint called AWSales that uses Windows integrated security to control access to a Web service that is published at the location http://AughtFive/AdventureWorks/Sales. The endpoint exposes the stored procedure AdventureWorks.dbo.uspGetBillOfMaterials as the Web method GetBillOfMaterials. The SOAP document that is created by this Web service can be viewed by opening Internet Explorer and navigating to the Web service URL and appending a Web Service Descriptive Language (WSDL) query to the end of the URL:

```
http://AughtFive/AdventureWorks/Sales?wsdl
```

Keep in mind that you will most likely have to change the server name in your environment.

```
USE Master;
GO
CREATE ENDPOINT AWSales
STATE = STARTED
AS HTTP(
        PATH = '/AdventureWorks/Sales'
        ,AUTHENTICATION = (INTEGRATED)
        ,PORTS = ( CLEAR )
        ,SITE = 'AughtFive')
FOR SOAP(
  WEBMETHOD 'GetBillOfMaterials'
        (NAME='AdventureWorks.dbo.uspGetBillOfMaterials'
        ,FORMAT=ROWSETS_ONLY)
       ,WSDL = DEFAULT
       ,DATABASE = 'AdventureWorks'
       ,NAMESPACE = 'http://AdventureWorks/'
    );
GO
```

Although Internet Explorer can be used to view the SOAP document, the real use for data tier Web services are for applications that are created to connect to and consume XML Web services. Later in this chapter you will see how to do this.

The HTTP arguments available for configuration in a CREATE ENDPOINT statement are described in the following table.

Argument	Description
PATH	Specifies the path of the Web service. An analogous setting would be the virtual directory name in IIS. Thus, the PATH setting specifies what comes after the http://Servername, as specified in the SITE argument.
AUTHENTICATION	The AUTHENTICATION argument is used to specify what type or types of authentication are allowed for the endpoint. One or more of the following settings can be configured: BASIC, DIGEST, NTLM, KERBEROS, or INTEGRATED. Multiple settings can be specified by comma delimiting the settings.
PORTS	Specifies whether HTTP or HTTPS is used with the endpoint. When CLEAR is specified, HTTP is used. SSL specifies that requests must use HTTPS. Both CLEAR and SSL can be configured concurrently, enabling communication with either HTTP or HTTPS.
SITE	The SITE argument specifies the host name used along with the PATH configuration. Possible choices are '*', '+' or 'website'.
	The asterisk ('*') specifies that the endpoint will listen to all available hostnames that are not reserved.
	The plus sign ('+') specifies that the endpoint will listen to all configured hostnames.
	WebSite is used for a specific server name (for example, 'AughtFive').
CLEAR_PORT	Specifies the clear port to use. The default is 80.
SSL_PORT	Specifies the SSL port to use. The default is 443.
AUTH_REALM	AUTH_REALM defaults to NONE, but when the AUTHENTICATION argument is DIGEST, AUTH_REALM can be used to return the digest realm hint to the client.
DEFAULT_LOGON_DOMAIN	When AUTHENTICATION is set to BASIC, this setting specifies the default login domain. The default is NONE.
COMPRESSION	When set to ENABLED, SQL Server will honor requests where gzip encoding is accepted and return compressed responses. The default setting is DISABLED.

The configurable SOAP arguments are described in the following table.

Argument	Description
WEBMETHOD	The published method that will be exposed through a HTTP SOAP requests to an endpoint. More than one WEBMETHOD clause can be defined to publish multiple SQL Server functions and stored procedures. In the preceding example, the WEBMETHOD was GetBillOfMaterials.
(WEBMETHOD) NAME	The physical name of the function or procedure published as the Web method, as in AdventureWorks.dbo.uspGetBillOfMaterials.
(WEBMETHOD) SCHEMA	Determines whether inline XSD schema will be returned for the Web method in SOAP responses. The possible choices are NONE, STANDARD, and DEFAULT.
	NONE omits the Web method from the schema if a schema is returned.
	STANDARD specifies that a XSD schema is not returned.
	DEFAULT specifies that the endpoint SCHEMA option setting is to be used.
(WEBMETHOD) FORMAT	Specifies the format of data returned by the endpoint. The possible choices are ALL_RESULTS, ROWSETS_ONLY, and NONE. The default is ALL_RESULTS.
	ALL_RESULTS specifies that a result set, row count, and any error message or warnings are returned.
	ROWSETS_ONLY specifies that just the result set is returned without errors, warnings, or row count information.
	NONE configures the endpoint not to return any SOAP-specific formatting with the result. If this option is used, the stored procedure or function is responsible for proper formatting of the result set as well-formed XML.
BATCHES	The BATCHES argument specifies whether ad-hoc batches can be sent to the endpoint. It can be set to ENABLED or DISABLED. The default setting is DISABLED.
WSDL	WSDL stands for Web Services Description Language. The WSDL setting is used to determine how a SOAP endpoint responds to a WSDL request. The possible configuration settings are NONE, DEFAULT, or the name of a stored procedure that returns the desired WSDL information.
	NONE specifies that the endpoint will not return any information to a WSDL request.
	DEFAULT specifies that basic metadata about the published Web method will be returned to a WSDL request. This information includes any possible parameters and the type of data returned.

Table continued on following page

Argument	Description
	`"Proc_Name"` is a procedure created to return a custom WSDL document to a WSDL request.
SESSIONS	When set to ENABLED, allows multiple SOAP request/response message pairs in a single SOAP session. The default is DISABLED.
LOGIN_TYPE	Specifies which type of Login authentication is supported by the endpoint. The choices are WINDOWS and MIXED. The choices correspond to the server authentication mode. If WINDOWS is specified, only Windows logins will be allowed. If MIXED is specified, both Windows and SQL Server logins are allowed.
SESSION_TIMEOUT	Specifies how long a session will stay open without activity. The value is an integer and specifies the number of seconds to wait before closing a session. Subsequent requests that utilize an expired session ID will return an exception.
DATABASE	Specifies the database context that the Web method will be executed in.
NAMESPACE	Specifies an XML namespace to be used with the endpoint. If no namespace is specified, or if the DEFAULT option is used, the namespace will be configured as `http://tempuri.org`.
SCHEMA	Like the WEBMETHOD SCHEMA argument, this option specifies whether inline XML Schema Definition (XSD) data is returned. The possible choices are NONE and STANDARD.
	NONE configures the endpoint not to return inline XSD data with the SOAP response.
	STANDARD specifies that inline XSD data is returned with the SOAP response. If the SCHEMA setting is omitted in the WEBMETHOD section, the Web method will use the setting specified here.
CHARACTER_SET	Specifies what to do with result data that is not valid in an XML document. The two choices are XML and SQL.
	XML specifies that all characters are returned as XML or delimited XML, and is the default setting.
	SQL specifies that non-XML characters are encoded as character references, and are returned with the XML data.
HEADER_LIMIT	Configures the maximum size of the header section in the SOAP envelope. The default size is 8K. If the SOAP headers are larger than the configured size, a parsing exception will be thrown.

Reserving a URL Namespace

When creating the SOAP endpoint, SQL Server will reserve the URL that is created by the combination of the SITE and PATH arguments of the CREATE ENDPOINT command, but this URL reservation is only held for as long as the SQL Server service is running. To permanently reserve the URL namespace the stored procedure sp_reserve_http_namespace is used, as the following example shows:

```
sp_reserve_http_namespace N'http://AughtFive:80/HRWebService'
```

By running this stored procedure, SQL Server prevents any other process from creating a published URL with the same name. For example, if IIS is installed alongside SQL Server on a physical server, it could be possible to publish a virtual directory with the same name as the SOAP endpoint's URL if the SQL Server service was stopped at the time. Running the sp_reserve_http_namespace system stored procedure stops this conflict from occurring by writing the URL to the registry.

Service Broker Endpoints

As described in Chapter 15, Service Broker is a new and powerful feature of SQL Server 2005 that enables database applications to asynchronously communicate with other database applications in a Service Oriented Architecture (SOA). Service Broker endpoints are only required if the two instances of the broker service are located on separate instances of SQL Server. They are created in much the same way as SOAP endpoints. The basic CREATE ENDPOINT command is used, but instead of the FOR SOAP clause that defines the endpoint as a SOAP endpoint, the FOR SERVICE_BROKER clause is used. The syntax for creating a Service Broker endpoint is as follows:

```
CREATE ENDPOINT endPointName [ AUTHORIZATION login ]
STATE = { STARTED | STOPPED | DISABLED }
AS TCP (
  LISTENER_PORT = listenerPort
  [ [ , ] LISTENER_IP = ALL | ( 4-part-ip ) | ( "ip_address_v6" ) ]
)
FOR SERVICE_BROKER (
   [ AUTHENTICATION = { WINDOWS [ { NTLM | KERBEROS | NEGOTIATE } ]
   | CERTIFICATE certificate_name
   | WINDOWS [ { NTLM | KERBEROS | NEGOTIATE } ] CERTIFICATE certificate_name
   | CERTIFICATE certificate_name WINDOWS [ { NTLM | KERBEROS | NEGOTIATE } ]
} ]
   [ [ , ] ENCRYPTION = { DISABLED | { { SUPPORTED | REQUIRED }
      [ ALGORITHM { RC4 | AES | AES RC4 | RC4 AES } ] }
   ]
   [ [ , ] MESSAGE_FORWARDING = { ENABLED | DISABLED* } ]
   [ [ , ] MESSAGE_FORWARD_SIZE = forward_size ]
)
```

An example of this syntax put in use to create a Service Broker endpoint is as follows:

```
USE Master;
CREATE ENDPOINT MyEndpoint
STATE = STARTED
AS TCP ( LISTENER_PORT = 50001 )
FOR SERVICE_BROKER ( AUTHENTICATION = WINDOWS );
```

In all likelihood, when creating Service Broker or mirroring endpoints, certificates will be used to ensure authenticated and encrypted traffic between endpoints, especially if the endpoints are located on different physical servers. For more information on the workings of Service Broker, take a look at Chapter 15. For security configurations, see Chapter 6.

Securing Endpoints

A critically important aspect of all endpoints is securing them so that only connections that are authorized can enumerate and call the Web methods or other services that the endpoint provides. The key permission for endpoints is the CONNECT permission. Only those logins that have been explicitly granted the CONNECT permission will be able to expose the functionality behind the endpoint. In addition, the login will need permissions to the underlying objects that the endpoint provides access for.

Try It Out   **Data Tier Web Services**

To re-create this exercise requires that you have Visual Studio 2005 installed, as well as SQL Server 2005. As described in Chapter 2, the SQL Server 2005 installation installs a piece of Visual Studio, but it does not install everything you need to create database applications. The following examples and descriptions assume that you have installed either C# or VB.NET (or both). If you haven't, the information is still very useful, but you will not be able to practice or re-create it. The examples using Visual Studio may seem to be a bit out of context in this book. However, it is next to impossible to describe the use of SOAP endpoints without using a Visual Studio application to demonstrate the purpose of data tier Web services.

Create the Endpoint

The first step is to create the endpoint that will publish the two stored procedures you want to make available via a data tier Web service where they can be used by any SOAP-compliant application. Execute the following code to create the SOAP endpoint HRWebService that publishes the uspGetEmployeeManagers and uspGetManagerEmployees stored procedures as the GetEmployeeManagers and GetManagerEmployees Web methods:

```
USE Master;
GO
CREATE ENDPOINT HRWebService
STATE = STARTED
AS HTTP(
        PATH = '/AdventureWorks/HR'
        ,AUTHENTICATION = (INTEGRATED)
        ,PORTS = ( CLEAR )
        ,SITE = 'AughtFive')
FOR SOAP(
        WEBMETHOD 'GetEmployeeManagers'
          (NAME='AdventureWorks.dbo.uspGetEmployeeManagers'
          ,FORMAT=ROWSETS_ONLY)
        ,WEBMETHOD 'GetManagerEmployees'
          (NAME='AdventureWorks.dbo.uspGetManagerEmployees'
          ,FORMAT=ROWSETS_ONLY)
        ,WSDL = DEFAULT
        ,DATABASE = 'AdventureWorks'
        ,NAMESPACE = 'http://AdventureWorks/'
    );
GO
```

Once the endpoint has been created to make the procedures visible through the Web service, a SOAP-compliant application will be able to enumerate and reference the Web methods specified in the endpoint.

Start Visual Studio 2005 and create a new VB.NET or C# Windows Application Project by clicking the File menu, selecting New, and then Project.

In the New Project window, select either Visual Basic or Visual C# from the Project Types pane, and then choose Windows Application from the Templates pane, as shown in Figure 7-6.

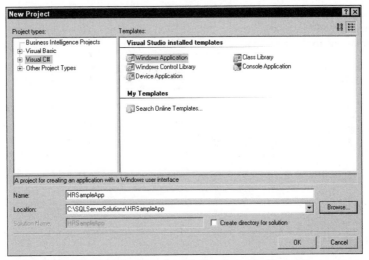

Figure 7-6: Selecting Windows Application from the Templates pane

Give the project a name such as HRSampleApp. Choose a folder for the solution to be created in and click OK. A design window showing a blank windows form will appear.

From the toolbox (to the left of the form designer by default), select and drag a button control to the upper-left-hand side of the form. Then, drag a text box and place it to the right of the button. Lastly, drag a datagridview control on to the form and place it under the button and text box controls, as shown in Figure 7-7. If the toolbox is not visible, it can be launched by pressing Ctrl+Alt+X, or by selecting it from the View menu.

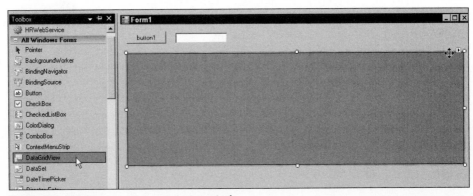

Figure 7-7: Placing a datagridview control

After creating the form, right-click the project name in the Solution Explorer window, and select Add Web Reference, as shown in Figure 7-8.

Figure 7-8: Selecting Add Web Reference

The Add Web Reference window will display where the data tier Web service can be added as a Web reference to the project.

In the URL drop-down text box, type in the appropriate address for your server, followed by a WSDL query command. In my case, the URL and query takes the form of http://AughtFive/ Adventureworks/hr?wsdl.

Click the GO button to query the SQL Server for information regarding any Web methods published at that location. You should see results similar to those shown in Figure 7-9.

In the "Web reference name" field, type in the name **HRWebService** and click the Add Reference button.

Now that all the foundation work has been completed, it is time to write the code that will call on the Web methods made available with the SOAP endpoint.

Double-click the button1 button on the form designer. This will launch the code editor window and create the basic code to handle the button click event. In the button click event handler, type in the code shown in the next example. There is one set of code for a VB.NET application, and another for Visual C# application.

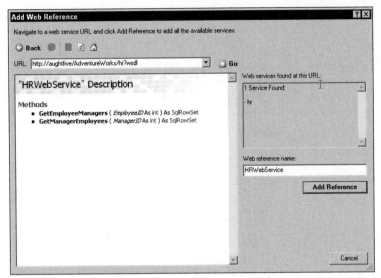

Figure 7-9: Viewing the results of a query for information regarding Web methods

Following is the Visual C# code:

```csharp
private void button1_Click(object sender, EventArgs e)
{
  DataSet dsEmployees;
  HRWebService.AWHumanResources proxy =
      new HRSampleApp.HRWebService.AWHumanResources();
  proxy.Credentials = System.Net.CredentialCache.DefaultCredentials;

  try
  {
   Int32 intMgrID;
   intMgrID = Convert.ToInt32(textBox1.Text);
   dsEmployees = proxy.GetManagerEmployees(intMgrID);
   dataGridView1.DataSource = dsEmployees;
   dataGridView1.DataMember = dsEmployees.Tables[0].TableName;
  }
  catch (Exception ex)
  {
   MessageBox.Show(ex.Message);
  }
}
```

Following is the Visual Basic.NET code:

```vbnet
Private Sub button1_Click(ByVal sender As System.Object, _
ByVal e As System.EventArgs) Handles btnGetEmployees.Click

  Dim Proxy As New HRWebService.AWHumanResources
```

```
    Proxy.Credentials = System.Net.CredentialCache.DefaultCredentials

    Try

      Dim dsEmployees As DataSet = Proxy.GetManagerEmployees(textBox1.Text)
      dataGridView1.DataSource = dsEmployees
      dataGridView1.DataMember = dsEmployees.Tables(0).TableName

    Catch
      MsgBox(Err.Description)
    End Try

  End Sub
```

Notice that the amount of code required to consume the Web service is actually very small. Not counting error-handling code, there are only five lines of code for VB.NET and eight lines for Visual C#. This is one of the features that makes consuming Web services so attractive; most of the work has been done at the Web service side.

Once the code has been entered in to the button click event, press F5, or click the green triangle on the menu to start the application debugging process. If everything goes well, what you should see is the windows form created earlier.

Enter the number **109** in the text box and click button1. Your results should look like those in Figure 7-10.

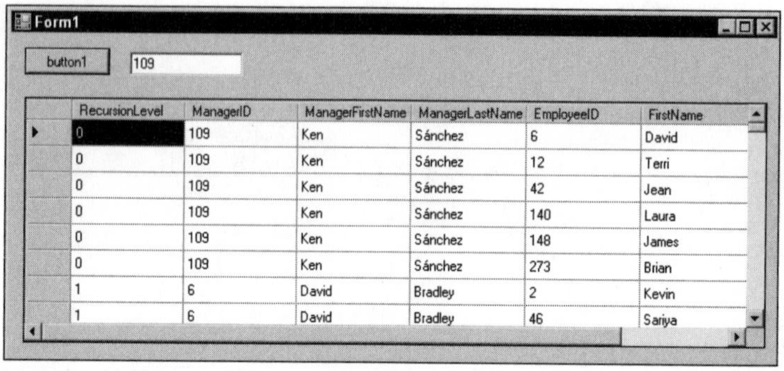

RecursionLevel	ManagerID	ManagerFirstName	ManagerLastName	EmployeeID	FirstName
0	109	Ken	Sánchez	6	David
0	109	Ken	Sánchez	12	Terri
0	109	Ken	Sánchez	42	Jean
0	109	Ken	Sánchez	140	Laura
0	109	Ken	Sánchez	148	James
0	109	Ken	Sánchez	273	Brian
1	6	David	Bradley	2	Kevin
1	6	David	Bradley	46	Sariya

Figure 7-10: Results of entering 109

SOAP endpoints can be created to not only return data, but also to manipulate data in the database. The amount of code required does not change dramatically.

As a database administrator, this may all seem a bit over the top, but it is very important to understand why developers may want to use SOAP endpoints and exactly what they do. As long as the database administrator maintains control of the security and structure of the endpoints and underlying programming objects, there should be no reason why this new powerful feature is not fully supported.

Summary

The SQL Configuration Manager now offers the database administrator a one-stop shop for troubleshooting and configuring SQL Server connection objects and Networking devices. The tools have been consolidated and the protocols simplified. Diagnosing networking problems has never been easier. Using the information in this chapter, you will hopefully be able to configure and secure the network protocols and endpoints that make it possible to make the most of SQL Server 2005 services and features. With the introduction of Service Broker and mirroring, the database administrator's responsibility for network and transport security has never been greater. Be sure to carefully evaluate all the security and configuration options available for each networking object to ensure the highest level of security and functionality.

In Chapter 8, you learn about automating SQL Server 2005 administrative and maintenance processes. You learn to configure jobs and alerts that will keep you informed of SQL Server performance, and keep it performing at peak efficiency.

Automating Administrative Tasks

As nice as it would be to install and configure SQL Server, and then forget about it, that's not a realistic goal for any organization. SQL Server is a product that needs regular maintenance and tender loving care. You're on your own for figuring out how to express your love for your SQL Server, but you can help ensure the health and stability of your server by understanding some of the automation processes that can also make your job easier.

Administrators have better things to do with their time (like playing video games or watching paint dry) than diligently monitor their servers for the slightest hint of trouble. In reality, given the complex nature of our database applications, you need to practice due diligence in keeping the system operational. Here are the topics that this chapter discusses to facilitate that:

❑ Database Mail

❑ Event notifications

❑ SQL Server Agent

❑ SQL Server maintenance plans

So, as you begin this chapter, understand that most of what you will learn will serve as a cornerstone for the topics that are covered in later chapters. Backups, replication, performance monitoring, and the Service Broker are just a few of the topics that can be managed or automated through many of the tools and examples that you will see in this chapter.

The examples in this chapter use the local server configured as both a Simple Mail Transport Protocol (SMTP) server, and a Post Office Protocol (POP3) server. Both features are available out-of-the-box with Windows Server 2003. However, configuration of SMTP and POP3 are beyond the scope of this book. If you choose to use another operating system for your test environment, you may need to refer to an external server name for the SMTP and POP3 services.

Database Mail

Microsoft SQL Server 2005 includes a new and improved method for message delivery to and from the SQL Server. This feature, known as *Database Mail*, allows SQL to send and receive messages through SMTP delivery. One of the many benefits of SQL's Database Mail service is that it will work with any SMTP service, regardless of whether or not it requires authentication. (It should, but that's a topic for another book.)

The Database Mail feature in SQL Server 2005 is a tool that allows you to generate and send email messages from your server. This can provide several advantages, including using an alternate method of returning information to your users, notifying the appropriate personnel that certain events or conditions have been met, or to provide status information about jobs and Integration Services packages. Database Mail was designed with security, scalability, and reliability in mind.

How It Works

Database Mail uses SMTP for message delivery. Messages can be generated from within SQL and can include attachments from outside of the SQL environment. One of the primary benefits of the Database Mail feature is its ability to use any SMTP server to relay messages. This is a significant improvement over prior versions of SQL that use SQLMail and requires a MAPI-compliant mail server (such as Microsoft Exchange) and a MAPI client (such as Microsoft Outlook). Although SQLMail is still available in SQL 2005, it is there for backward compatibility only and will be removed in later versions of SQL.

Another benefit of Database Mail is that it allows you to configure authentication credentials if required by your SMTP server to forward messages and allows you to configure different servers for delivery, in case your preferred server is not available. SQL also uses an external executable, DatabaseMail90.exe, to handle message delivery to an SMTP server. This allows the SQL Server to isolate itself from the process that relays the messages to the SMTP server.

Database Mail uses the msdb database for storing configuration information about Database Mail, controlling access to the feature, and queuing messages until they are ready for delivery. Prior to configuring Database Mail, there are a couple of things you need to consider. A couple of the primary requirements to know are which SMTP servers are available for use, and what credentials are needed. As you'll see in the next section, you can configure multiple servers, with multiple accounts, if necessary. Another consideration is which messages will be retained, and for how long they need to be retained. By default, all sent messages and their attachments are stored in the msdb database. Be aware of your company's security and retention policies for email messages. You may also be under legal obligation to keep messages for a specific amount of time.

> You should be aware that the Database Mail feature is not available in the Express Edition of SQL Server 2005.

The Database Mail feature uses *accounts* to configure access to SMTP servers, and *profiles* to configure access to mail accounts. However, profiles and accounts can be mutually exclusive. You can create accounts without an association with a profile, and you can use the same account with multiple profiles, if necessary.

How to Configure Database Mail

The easiest way to configure SQL Server to use Database Mail is through the Database Mail Configuration Wizard in SQL Server Management Studio. This section steps you through the different pages in the wizard and explains what each page configures.

To launch the wizard, navigate to the Management section of your server in Object Explorer (see Figure 8-1). Expand Management, right-click Database Mail, and select Configure Database Mail.

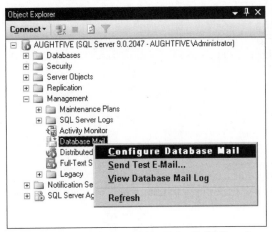

Figure 8-1: Launching the Database Mail Wizard

The first page you will see is simply a start page that explains each of the following steps in the wizard. If you don't want to see this page again, select the checkbox at the bottom of the page indicating you wish to skip this page in the future.

On the next screen, you'll be asked to identify which configuration task you're using the wizard to perform. You can use this to initialize Database Mail for use on this server; or, if it's already configured, you can manage existing mail profiles and configured accounts. You can also change system settings. For this run, select the first option to set up Database Mail (see Figure 8-2).

Database Mail is disabled by default. If this is the first time you've run this wizard, and have not manually enabled Database Mail, you will be prompted to enable it. Once you've enabled Database Mail, the next screen will ask you to provide information for a new Database Mail profile. Enter a name for the profile, and optionally a description to help identify the profile and how it will be used. For this example, enter **AdventureWorksSalesProfile** as the profile name. You can also provide a description, which can be useful for identifying why the profile was created.

Once that information has been entered, you must configure at least one account that this profile will use. The ability to configure multiple accounts under a single profile helps guarantee the availability of the Database Mail feature to users who need to receive information, and path of delivery isn't relevant. The order in which the accounts are listed will determine the order of precedence when sending messages. Accounts listed at the top of the list will be preferred over those listed below them.

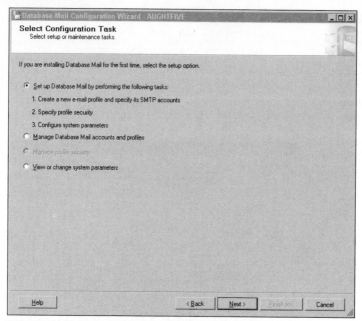

Figure 8-2: Choosing a Database Mail configuration task

To create a new account, click the Add button. In the New Database Mail Account screen (see Figure 8-3), enter in an account name and description, and then information about the account, including the email address that the messages will originate from, the display name for that address, the reply-to address, and the name or IP address of the SMTP server. There is also a box where you can enter the port number used by the SMTP server. Unless you know that your server uses a different port, you should use the standard SMTP port, 25. If your server uses Secure Sockets Layer (SSL) to protect the data in-transit, select the appropriate checkbox.

Also on this screen, you will select the method of authentication the SMTP server requires. By default, Anonymous authentication is selected, but this is not the preferred method for most SMTP servers. If your SMTP server is Windows-based (such as in the case of Microsoft Exchange or IIS), and is a member of the same domain, or a different domain that shares a trust relationship, you may be able to use Windows Authentication using Database Engine service credentials. Otherwise, you can use Basic authentication, providing a username and password manually. Be aware that if SSL is not used between the SQL Server and the SMTP server, the authentication information may be sent in clear text and may be vulnerable to interception.

In this example, use an SMTP service installed on the local machine through IIS. You can use the information in Figure 8-3 to configure your mail account. Once you've entered in the information about the account, click OK to close the New Database Mail Account window. You can enter in more accounts to be used by the same profile, or you can continue on to the next screen by clicking Next.

On the Manage Profile Security screen, you can use the Public Profiles tab (see Figure 8-4) to elect to make the profile public. When a profile is *public*, it means that the profile will be available to all users who are members of the DatabaseMailUsersRole role in the msdb database. You can also define which public profile is the *default public profile*. The default profile is the one that is used when a profile is not specified during the sendmail operation. For private profiles, you can specify (on a per-user basis) which profiles are available to that user (see Figure 8-5). Each user can also have a default profile available to them. The user must already exist in the `msdb` database. For this example, mark the profile as public, and make it the default. Once you've configured the Profile Security options, click Next.

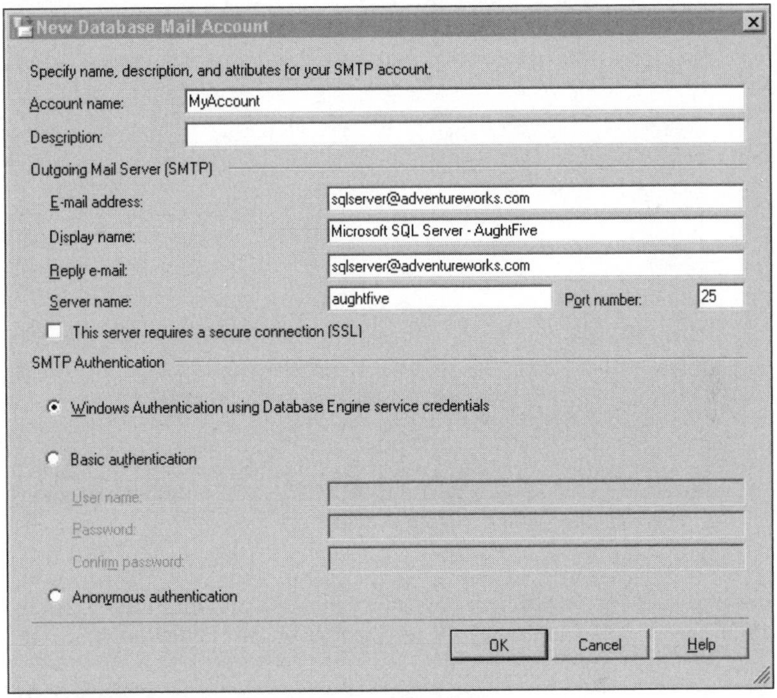

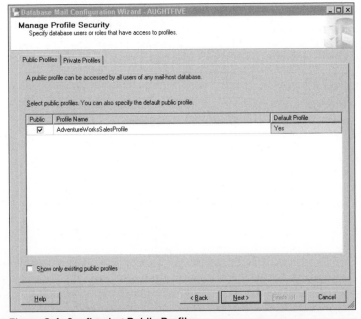

Figure 8-3: New Database Mail Account screen

Figure 8-4: Configuring Public Profiles

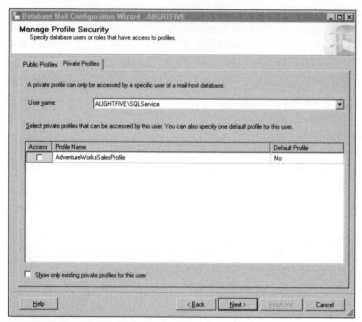

Figure 8-5: Configuring Private Profiles

On the final input page of the wizard, you can change the system configuration values for mail messages sent from the SQL Server. You can identify the information shown in the following table.

Option	Description
Account Retry Attempts	The number of retry attempts SQL Server will make for a mail account within a profile before it moves on to the next account.
Account Retry Delay	The amount of time (in seconds) that the SQL Server will wait between retries.
Maximum File Size	Maximum size (in bytes) of file attachments.
Prohibited Attachment File Extensions	List of file extensions that the SQL Server will not send.
Database Mail Executable Minimum Lifetime	The timeout value for the external executable if there are no more messages in queue.
Logging Level	Choose one of the following:
	Normal — Logs only errors
	Extended — Errors, Warnings, and Informational messages
	Verbose — Extended logging, plus success messages and internal messages

Click Next on the Configure System Parameters page to move to the last page in the wizard. Once you've provided the appropriate values to the wizard, it gives you a summary page with the options you've selected. Clicking Finish will commit your changes, and give you a quick report on the success or failure of each step.

Configuring Database Mail Options

After Database Mail has been enabled, you can use the sysmail_configure_sp stored procedure. The syntax of the sysmail_configure_sp stored procedure is as follows:

```
sysmail_configure_sp [ @parameter_name = ] 'name' , [ @parameter_value = ] 'value'
, [ @description = ] 'description'
```

Similar to the options listed here, you can use the values in the following table for the parameters.

Parameter	Description
AccountRetryAttempts	The number of retry attempts SQL Server will make for a mail account within a profile before it moves on to the next account.
AccountRetryDelay	The amount of time (in seconds) that the SQL Server will wait between retries.
DatabaseMailExeMinimumLifeTime	The timeout value for the external executable if there are no more messages in queue.
DefaultAttachmentEncoding	The default encoding for email attachments.
MaxFileSize	Maximum size (in bytes) of file attachments.
ProhibitedExtensions	List of file extensions that the SQL Server will not send.
LoggingLevel	Choose one of the following numeric values:
	1 — Normal
	2 — Extended
	3 — Verbose

The sysmail_configure_sp stored procedure (as do many of the Database Mail stored procedures) lives in the msdb database. When executing these stored procedures, you'll have to qualify them from within your application or T-SQL statements. Use the following example to set the maximum file size for all attachments sent by Database Mail to 4MB:

```
EXECUTE msdb.dbo.sysmail_configure_sp
    'MaxFileSize', '4194303', 'Max Size 4 MB'
```

Note that the description parameter is optional. Though it may not be required, it is always a good idea to use it to define or explain why a particular configuration value is used.

Managing Profiles and Accounts

Profiles are commonly used as a unit of management for SMTP accounts. However, as mentioned earlier, there is no one-to-one relationship between the two. You can use the Database Mail Configuration Wizard, or you can use a series of stored procedures to create and delete profiles and accounts as needed.

Because you've already been exposed to the different elements of the wizard, you should easily be able to fumble through the different pages to find what you need to configure the accounts and profiles you want. In this section, you learn about the stored procedures used to create and manage Database Mail accounts and profiles.

sysmail_add_profile_sp

The first stored procedure you should know is `sysmail_add_profile_sp`. This stored procedure allows you to create a new profile to be used by the Database Mail service, and uses the following syntax:

```
sysmail_add_profile_sp [ @profile_name = ] 'name' , [ @description = ] 'desc',
[ @profile_id = ] profile_id OUTPUT
```

The following table shows the available options.

Option	Description
profile_name	The name of the profile.
description	An optional description that provides information about the profile.
profile_id	An optional parameter that displays the unique value generated by SQL to identify the profile.
OUTPUT	Keyword used to output the profile_id value.

Try It Out   Create a New Profile

The following example creates a new mail profile, and returns the integer value generated for the profile ID. Begin by declaring the variable for the `profile_id`:

```
DECLARE @profileID INT ;

EXECUTE msdb.dbo.sysmail_add_profile_sp
        @profile_name = 'HumanResourcesMail',
        @description = 'Mail Profile for the Human Resources team.',
        @profile_id = @profileID OUTPUT ;

SELECT @profileID ;
```

Note the ID returned from the SELECT statement. You'll use this in the next example.

The `sysmail_help_profile_sp` stored procedure will return information about the profiles created on the SQL Server. It will return the profile ID, the profile name, and the description, if any. You can also use the `@profile_id` or `@profile_name` variables to limit the results to just the specific profile you're interested in.

```
EXEC msdb.dbo.sysmail_help_profile_sp @profile_id=2
```

You can also query the `sysmail_profile` table in the `msdb` database to return information about the profiles that have been created. In addition to the information returned from the `sysmail_help_profile_sp` stored procedure, you can identify who last modified the account and when.

```
SELECT * FROM msdb.dbo.sysmail_profile
```

sysmail_add_account_sp

To create a new account, use the `sysmail_add_account_sp` stored procedure. This stored procedure will create an account that is not associated with a profile. A different stored procedure can be used to add accounts to a profile, which is discussed later in this chapter.

Creating accounts, as you've seen from the Database Mail Configuration Wizard, is a little more complex than creating profiles, because the accounts may vary from server to server. The following table lists the options you can use with the `sysmail_add_account_sp` procedure.

Parameter	Description
`@account_name = name`	The name of the new account.
`@email_address = address`	The email address associated with the account.
`@display_name = display`	How messages sent from this account display the sender's name.
`@replyto_address = address`	The address that will be used for replies when the client is responding to a message sent to this account.
`@description = desc`	An optional description for this account.
`@mailserver_name = server`	Name or IP address of the SMTP server this account will use.
`@mailserver_type = servertype`	Made available for future technology, SMTP is currently the only value supported, and is the default.
`@port = serverport`	TCP port used by the SMTP server. Default is 25.
`@username = username`	Used if your SMTP server requires authentication.
`@password = password`	The password to be provided for authentication to the SMTP server.
`@use_default_credentials = [0	1]`	A value of 1 indicates that the SQL Server service account will be used for SQL authentication.

Table continued on following page

Parameter	Description
`@enable_ssl = [0	1]`	A value of 1 indicates that SSL will be used between the SQL Server and the SMTP server.
`@account_id = accountID OUTPUT`	Returns the Account ID generated when the account is created.

Try It Out **Create a New Account**

So, take a look at this in action. Use the following example to create a new account:

```
DECLARE @accountID INT;

EXECUTE msdb.dbo.sysmail_add_account_sp
    @account_name = 'Mail Sender',
    @description = 'Generic Account for sending mail',
    @email_address = 'mailsender@adventureworks.com',
    @display_name = 'SQL Database Mail Account',
    @mailserver_name = 'mail.adventureworks.com',
    @username = 'MailSender',
    @password = 'P@ssw0rd',
    @account_id = @accountID OUTPUT ;

SELECT @accountID;
```

Note the account ID returned. You can use this in the next example.

To find out more about the accounts that have been created, use the `sysmail_help_account_sp` stored procedure. This will give you information about the account, such as the ID, the name, and the server options for this account. Use the `@account_id` or `@account_name` variables to limit the results to a specific account.

```
EXECUTE msdb.dbo.sysmail_help_account_sp
```

To limit the output to just the account you're interested in, use the following:

```
EXECUTE msdb.dbo.sysmail_help_account_sp @account_id=2
```

You can also return a simple list of configured accounts by querying the `sysmail_account` table, which includes the `datetime` information of when the account was last modified and who last modified it:

```
SELECT *FROM msdb.dbo.sysmail_account
```

sysmail_add_profileaccount_sp

So, you've created a new profile and a new account. Now you can associate that account with that profile. Remember accounts can be associated with more than one profile, and each profile can be configured to use more that one account.

To create the mapping, you can use the `sysmail_add_profileaccount_sp` stored procedure. This allows you to map an account to a profile using the profile name or profile ID and the account name or account ID. The other option you can specify is the sequence number of the account ID. This is used to determine the order of preference for the account within that profile.

Because this is a fairly simple stored procedure, look at a couple of examples that use the profiles and accounts created previously.

In this first example, you will use the account created during the Database Mail Configuration Wizard, and add it to the profile you created from the `sysmail_add_profile_sp` stored procedure example. This example has you use the `profile_id` of the `HumanResourcesProfile`, and the name of the `MyAccount` account. You can easily mix and match, as long as you declare the correct parameter.

```
EXECUTE msdb.dbo.sysmail_add_profileaccount_sp
    @profile_id = 2,
    @account_name = 'MyAccount',
    @sequence_number = 1;
```

In the next example, add the account created from the `sysmail_add_account_sp` stored procedure to the `HumanResourcesProfile` profile, only this time, you will refer to the profile by name, and the account by ID number.

```
EXECUTE msdb.dbo.sysmail_add_profileaccount_sp
    @profile_name = 'HumanResourcesMail',
    @account_id = 2,
    @sequence_number = 2;
```

To find out what mappings exist between the accounts and profiles, you can use the `sysmail_help_profileaccount_sp` stored procedure. You can limit your results using `@account_id`, `@account_name`, `@profile_id`, or `@profile_name`. Each row returned identifies the profile ID, the profile name, the account ID, the account name, and the sequence number for the account.

```
EXECUTE msdb.dbo.sysmail_help_profileaccount_sp
```

Querying the `sysmail_profileaccount` table in the `msdb` database returns the IDs of profiles and associated accounts, the sequence number for those accounts, and the last modified information, but not the names.

```
SELECT * FROM msdb.dbo.sysmail_profileaccount
```

sysmail_update_profile_sp

Quite simply, you can use this stored procedure to change the name or description of an existing profile. If you're changing the description of the profile, you can refer to it using `@profile_id` or `@profile_name`. If you want to change the name of the profile, you will use `@profile_id`.

Use the following example to change both the name and the description of the `HumanResourcesMail` profile created earlier. Assuming that you did not create any new accounts or profiles other than those used in the examples, the `profile_id` of `HumanResourcesMail` should be 2.

```
EXECUTE msdb.dbo.sysmail_update_profile_sp
    @profile_id = 2,
    @profile_name = 'HRMail',
    @description = 'Human Resources Mail Profile';

EXECUTE msdb.dbo.sysmail_help_profile_sp;
```

This will produce the following output:

```
profile_id   name                        description
-----------  --------------------------  ------------------------------------
1            AdventureWorksSalesProfile   NULL
2            HRMail                       Human Resources Mail Profile
```

sysmail_update_account_sp

This stored procedure can be used to update the properties of a mail account after it has been created. Unlike profiles, accounts have a lot more parameters that can be modified or adjusted as needed. The same parameters from sysmail_add_account_sp procedure can be used, and not unlike the sysmail_update_profile_sp procedure, you can identify the account by account_name or account_id.

In this example, you reconfigure the name, replyto_address, and the description of the MyAccount profile. Unfortunately, with this stored procedure, you cannot cherry-pick which values you want to update. You will have to specify the values for all parameters, as shown here:

```
EXECUTE msdb.dbo.sysmail_update_account_sp
    @account_id = 1,
    @account_name = 'SalesMail',
    @display_name = 'Microsoft SQL Server - Aughtfive',
    @replyto_address = 'administrator@adventureworks.com',
    @description = 'Sales Mail Account',
    @mailserver_name = 'aughtfive',
    @mailserver_type = 'SMTP',
    @port = 25,
    @username = NULL,
    @password = NULL,
    @use_default_credentials = 1,
    @enable_ssl = 0;

EXECUTE msdb.dbo.sysmail_help_account_sp
```

sysmail_update_profileaccount_sp

If you want to change the sequence in which the accounts will be used within a profile, you can use the sysmail_update_profileaccount_sp stored procedure. Specify the profile and the account by either name or ID, and then enter the preferred sequence number. Be aware that more than one account within a profile can have the same sequence number. If this is the case, SQL will arbitrarily decide which one to use. Use the following example to change the sequence numbers of the accounts in the HRMail profile:

```
-- Assigns the Mail Sender account a sequence of 1

EXECUTE msdb.dbo.sysmail_update_profileaccount_sp
    @profile_id = 2,
    @account_id = 2,
```

```
        @sequence_number = 1;

-- Assigns the SalesMail account a sequence number of 2

EXECUTE msdb.dbo.sysmail_update_profileaccount_sp
    @profile_name = 'HRMail',
    @account_name = 'SalesMail',
    @sequence_number = 2;

EXECUTE msdb.dbo.sysmail_help_profileaccount_sp
```

sysmail_add_principalprofile_sp

This stored procedure is used to control access to a mail profile. In order for the profile to be accessible, the profile will be made available to specific database principals within the msdb database. The following table outlines the parameters for the sysmail_add_principalprofile_sp stored procedure.

Option	Description
@principal_id	The ID of the user or role in the msdb database. Use the value *0* to specify the public role. The principal must be specified by either the ID or name.
@principal_name	The name of the user or role in the msdb database. Use the public role if the profile is a public profile.
@profile_id	The ID of the profile. Use either the ID or name to specify the profile.
@profile_name	The name of the profile. Use to identify the profile.
@is_default	Indicates that this profile is the default profile for the specified principal.

Take a look at this stored procedure in action. In this first example, create a new profile with a new account. Then, ensure that the profile is public.

```
-- Create the profile
EXECUTE msdb.dbo.sysmail_add_profile_sp
    @profile_name = 'Purchasing',
    @description = 'Purchasing Mail Profile';

-- Create the account
EXECUTE msdb.dbo.sysmail_add_account_sp
    @account_name = 'PurchasingMail',
    @description = 'Purchasing Mail Account',
    @email_address = 'purchasing@adventureworks.com',
    @display_name = 'AdventureWorks Purchasing Application',
    @mailserver_name = 'localhost',
    @use_default_credentials = 1;

-- Associate the profile and the account
EXECUTE msdb.dbo.sysmail_add_profileaccount_sp
    @profile_name = 'Purchasing',
    @account_name = 'PurchasingMail',
```

```
        @sequence_number = 1;

-- Make the profile public
EXECUTE msdb.dbo.sysmail_add_principalprofile_sp
    @principal_name = 'public',
    @profile_name = 'Purchasing',
    @is_default = 0;
```

To view the security configuration, use the `sysmail_help_principalprofile_sp` stored procedure. You can specify the `principal_id`, `principal_name`, `profile_id`, and/or `profile_name`. Note that you should only provide either the ID or the name for each, not both. For example, if you wanted to see which profiles are available to the `public` role, use the following example:

```
EXECUTE msdb.dbo.sysmail_help_principalprofile_sp
    @principal_name = 'public';
```

If you've been following all the steps in this chapter so far, you should expect to see the following output:

principal_id	principal_name	profile_id	profile_name	is_default
0	public	1	AdventureWorksSalesProfile	1
0	public	3	Purchasing	0

Interestingly enough, if you execute the `sysmail_help_principalprofile_sp` stored procedure without any parameters (such as the `principal_name` as in the previous example), it returns results for the `guest` account, not the `public` role. This is not surprising, though, because the `guest` account, when available, is used when the requestor does not have a user mapping in the `msdb` database.

In the next example, you learn how to create a new profile, account, and new database user named `AWOrderProcessing`. You'll then see how to configure the new profile as the default for that user.

```
-- Create the user
-- In the real world, you would map this to an existing server credential.
USE msdb
CREATE USER AWOrderProcessing
    WITHOUT LOGIN;
GO

-- Create the profile
EXECUTE msdb.dbo.sysmail_add_profile_sp
    @profile_name = 'OrderEntry',
    @description = 'OrderEntry Mail Profile';

-- Create the account
EXECUTE msdb.dbo.sysmail_add_account_sp
    @account_name = 'Orders',
    @description = 'Order Entry Primary Mail Account',
    @email_address = 'orders@adventureworks.com',
    @display_name = 'AdventureWorks Purchasing Application',
    @replyto_address = 'administrator@adventureworks.com',
```

```
        @mailserver_name = 'localhost',
        @use_default_credentials = 1;

    -- Associate the profile and the account
    EXECUTE msdb.dbo.sysmail_add_profileaccount_sp
        @profile_name = 'OrderEntry',
        @account_name = 'Orders',
        @sequence_number = 1;

    --Configure the purchasing account as a backup account
    EXECUTE msdb.dbo.sysmail_add_profileaccount_sp
        @profile_name = 'OrderEntry',
        @account_name = 'PurchasingMail',
        @sequence_number = 2;

    -- Make the profile available to the AWOrderProcessing user
    EXECUTE msdb.dbo.sysmail_add_principalprofile_sp
        @principal_name = AWOrderProcessing,
        @profile_name = 'OrderEntry',
        @is_default = 1;

    -- Show which profiles the AWOrderProcessing user has access to.
    EXECUTE msdb.dbo.sysmail_help_principalprofile_sp
        @principal_name = 'AWOrderProcessing';
```

One thing you should note when you return the list of profiles available to the AWOrderProcessing user is that both of the profiles available to the public role are also available to this user. Also note that the public role and the AWOrderProcessing user each have a default profile. When a database user or a role that is not public has a default profile defined, that profile will be the one used if a profile isn't identified. If the user or role does not have a default profile specified, the default profile of the public role will be used if a profile is not explicitly called.

sysmail_update_principalprofile_sp

Each principal can only have one default profile defined. If you need to change which of the available profiles is the default, use the sysmail_update_principalprofile_sp stored procedure. As with the sysmail_add_principalprofile_sp, you can identify the principal and the profile either by name or ID. The only value you can alter with this stored procedure, though, is the @is_default parameter. Using the last example, if you changed the @is_default option for AWOrderProcessing, then the user would need to manually specify the appropriate profile. Otherwise, in this case, the default profile would come from the public role.

```
    -- Remove the default profile for AWOrderProcessing
    EXECUTE msdb.dbo.sysmail_update_principalprofile_sp
        @principal_name = AWOrderProcessing,
        @profile_id = 4,
        @is_default = 0;

    -- Show which profiles the AWOrderProcessing user has access to.
    EXECUTE msdb.dbo.sysmail_help_principalprofile_sp
        @principal_name = 'AWOrderProcessing';
```

sysmail_delete_principalprofile_sp

If you need to remove the association between a principal and a profile, use the `sysmail_delete_principalprofile_sp` stored procedure. Note that this does not delete the principal or the profile from the database, but rather removes the explicit mapping between the two. You might want to use this if you have to remove the `public` role's access to the specified profile, for example. The syntax is very straightforward, requiring you to identify both the principal and the profile; but again, you can use the name or ID value for either. Use the following example to remove the `Purchasing` profile from the `public` role:

```
EXECUTE msdb.dbo.sysmail_delete_principalprofile_sp
    @principal_name = 'public',
    @profile_name = 'Purchasing';

EXECUTE msdb.dbo.sysmail_help_principalprofile_sp
    @principal_name = 'public';
```

sysmail_delete_profileaccount_sp

If you want to remove an account from a profile, simply use the `sysmail_delete_profileaccount_sp` stored procedure. You need to specify both the profile and the account either by name or ID. The following example removes the Orders account from the `OrderEntry` profile:

```
EXECUTE msdb.dbo.sysmail_delete_profileaccount_sp
    @profile_name = 'OrderEntry',
    @account_name = 'Orders';

EXECUTE msdb.dbo.sysmail_help_profileaccount_sp;
```

sysmail_delete_account_sp

Next, to remove an account from the `msdb` database entirely, use the `sysmail_delete_account_sp` stored procedure. This will not only remove the account, but all references to the account in all profiles where it was configured, as in the following example. If is the only account in the profile, the profile will remain, but will be empty.

```
EXECUTE msdb.dbo.sysmail_delete_account_sp
    @account_name = 'Orders';

EXECUTE msdb.dbo.sysmail_help_account_sp;
```

sysmail_delete_profile_sp

Finally, to remove a profile from the `msdb` database, use the `sysmail_delete_profile_sp` stored procedure. This removes the profile, but will not delete the accounts in the profile. This is because the accounts may be used in other profiles.

```
EXECUTE msdb.dbo.sysmail_delete_profile_sp
    @profile_name = 'OrderEntry';

EXECUTE msdb.dbo.sysmail_help_profileaccount_sp;
```

Guidelines for Deleting Mail Objects

As a general rule, be careful about deleting accounts or profiles. If you are going to delete an account, profile, or account mapping, use the following guidelines:

❑ Deleting a profile/account mapping is non-destructive. It simply removes the relationship between the profile and account. If necessary, this can be easily re-created. If another account is properly configured within the profile, this should not disrupt operations.

❑ Deleting an account removes its availability in all profiles. If the profiles already have another valid account configured, then you (or your users) shouldn't notice any problems. If you are deleting an account that is the only account in one or more profiles, those profiles will not be able to send mail.

❑ Deleting a profile removes a list of configured accounts, not the accounts themselves. If, however, your application is configured to use a mail profile you've recently deleted, once again, your SQL Server will be unable to send messages.

Sending Mail

This chapter has spent a lot of time looking at the elements and configuration of Database Mail, so now let's see where your efforts have gotten you. Sending mail is an easy process. Knowing what to send (or configuring your data for delivery) is another topic entirely. This section introduces the parameters of the `sp_send_dbmail` stored procedure, as well as a couple of useful examples of how to prepare data for sending.

sp_send_dbmail

As mentioned earlier, the stored procedure for sending mail using the Database Mail feature is `sp_send_dbmail`. As with the other Database Mail stored procedures covered earlier in this chapter, this one lives in the `msdb` database; and if you're going to be instantiating it from outside of that database, you'll need to qualify it, as you have been doing throughout the chapter.

Keep in mind that although a mail profile may be made public, and is available to the members of the `public` role, the `sp_send_dbmail` can only be executed by members of the `DatabaseMailUserRole`. Ensure that all logins that need access to the `sp_send_dbmail` stored procedure are mapped to a user in the `msdb` database, and are members of the `DatabaseMailUserRole`.

The following table identifies the different parameters available to `sp_send_dbmail` and their descriptions.

Parameter	Description
@profile_name	Name of the profile the stored procedure will use. If a default profile is specified for the user, or one has been defined for the `public` role, executing the stored procedure, this value is optional.
@recipients	List of email addresses that will receive your message. Use semicolons between values. Although this value is technically optional, you must specify at least one recipient through `@recipients` (To:), `@copy_recipients` (CC:), or `@blind_copy_recipients` (BCC:).

Table continued on following page

Parameter	Description
@copy_recipients	The same as using the CC: (also called Carbon Copy) field in a standard email client. As with the recipients list, you can use semicolons between multiple values.
@blind_copy_recipients	The same as using the BCC: (also known as Blind Carbon Copy) field in a standard email client. This value will indicate a list of recipients for your messages, but the addresses are obfuscated by email clients. Use semicolons between multiple values.
@subject	Subject of the mail message. Defaults to SQL Server Message with no value specified.
@body	Text of the message. Default is NULL.
@body_format	Message delivery format. Choose between TEXT and HTML. Default is TEXT.
@importance	Allows you to specify a value indicating how the client should treat the message. Choose between Low, Normal, and High. Default is Normal.
@sensitivity	Allows you to define a sensitivity level for the message, interpreted by the client. Choose from Normal, Personal, Private, and Confidential. Default is Normal.
@file_attachments	Allows you to provide a list of external files that can be attached to the email message. The user executing the stored procedure must specify (and have access to) the absolute file path where the files reside. Use a semicolon between file paths to specify multiple files.
@query	Identifies a query whose results will be sent as part of the message. The query results can be added to the body of the message, or attached as a file.
@execute_query_database	Identifies the database context in which the aforementioned query will run. This defaults to the current database, and is only used if the @query option is used.
@attach_query_result _as_file	Specifies if the query result is returned as part of the message body or an attached file. It uses a bit value of 0 to append to the body, and a value of 1 to attach a file with the results. Defaults to 0.
@query_attachment _filename	Allows you to define the filename that will be attached if @attach_query_result_as_file is set to 1. If a filename is not provided, SQL will make one up for you.
@query_result_header	Bit value that specifies if column headers are included with the results. Not surprisingly, 0 equals no, and 1 equals yes. Defaults to 1.

Parameter	Description
@query_result_width	Allows you to specify the line width by maximum number of characters. This is an int value with a range between 10 and 32767. Default is 256.
@query_result_separator	Allows you to define a single character delimiter between columns in a query output. The default is a single space (' ').
@exclude_query_output	This option allows you to define (when using a query in a mail message) whether to output the query results to the console. This defaults to 0, which will display the results.
@append_query_error	If an error is returned from a query, setting this value to 1 will include the error in the email message. The default of 0 does not include error information.
@query_no_truncate	Setting the value of this option to 1 will override the default behavior, which is to truncate variable-length columns greater than 256. If you override the default, be aware that columns that store a large amount of data may take longer to process and send.
@mailitem_id id OUTPUT	This option allows you to return the mailitem_id after the message has been generated. You can use this to review or clean up sent messages.

Take a look at some examples of how to send mail messages from within SQL Server.

In this first example, you can create a simple mail message that doesn't rely on any additional data source. This can be executed as a sendmail task upon completion of a job, or through an event notification. This one will send a simple message, indicating that an import task has been successfully completed.

```
EXECUTE msdb.dbo.sp_send_dbmail
    @profile_name = 'HRMail',
    @recipients = 'Michael.Bluth@adventureworks.com',
    @copy_recipients = 'Administrator@adventureworks.com',
    @body = 'Your data has been successfully imported!',
    @subject = 'Import Notification Message - Success';
```

In order for the message to actually be delivered, you must be running SMTP and POP3 services for the adventureworks.com domain, and you must also have Michael.Bluth and the Administrator accounts configured as POP3 recipients. If you have a different SMTP server configured, you can change the @recipients and @copy_recipients parameters to valid mail accounts. The query window will simply return "Mail Queued." The resulting email should look something like Figure 8-6.

Figure 8-6: Simple mail message

Another example uses a query within the sp_send_dbmail stored procedure to send the results to the intended recipient list. In this example, you're going to use a query that returns the first names, last names, and hire dates of all employees hired in the year 2002:

```
EXECUTE msdb.dbo.sp_send_dbmail
    @profile_name = 'HRMail',
    @recipients = 'George.Bluth@adventureworks.com',
    @blind_copy_recipients =
'Michael.Bluth@adventureworks.com;Administrator@adventureworks.com',
    @body = 'Per your request, here are the employees hired in 2002.',
    @query = 'SELECT Person.Contact.FirstName AS First,
          Person.Contact.LastName AS Last,
HumanResources.Employee.HireDate AS [Date of Hire]
        FROM Person.Contact INNER JOIN HumanResources.Employee
          ON Person.Contact.ContactID = HumanResources.Employee.ContactID
        WHERE HireDate > ''2002-01-01'' AND HIREDATE < ''2003-01-01''
        ORDER BY HireDate',
    @execute_query_database = 'AdventureWorks',
    @subject = 'Employees Hired in 2002',
    @attach_query_result_as_file = 1;
```

The result should look something like Figure 8-7.

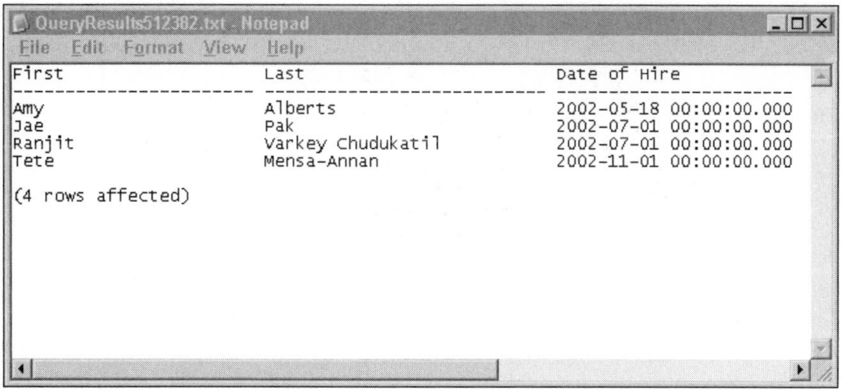

Figure 8-7: Raw output of 2002 New Hires

One more example shows you how to take the information in a query, and prepare it as an HTML document. You can then email the HTML document as the body of the mail message, and as long as the recipient's mail reader can render HTML, the recipient will have a nice-looking display.

```
USE AdventureWorks
DECLARE @tableHTML NVARCHAR(MAX) ;

SET @tableHTML =
    N'<H1>Employees Hired in 2002</H1>' +
    N'<table border="1">' +
    N'<tr><th>First Name</th><th>Last Name</th>' +
    N'<th>Hire Date</th>' +
  CAST ((SELECT td = Person.Contact.FirstName,        '',
                td = Person.Contact.LastName, '',
                td = HumanResources.Employee.HireDate, ''
                FROM Person.Contact INNER JOIN HumanResources.Employee
                ON Person.Contact.ContactID = HumanResources.Employee.ContactID
                WHERE HireDate > '2002-01-01' AND HIREDATE < '2003-01-01'
                Order by HireDate
          FOR XML PATH('tr'), TYPE
        ) AS NVARCHAR(MAX) ) +
    N'</table>';

EXEC msdb.dbo.sp_send_dbmail @recipients='administrator@adventureworks.com',
    @subject = '2002 New Hires',
    @body = @tableHTML,
    @body_format = 'HTML';
```

This will return the output shown in Figure 8-8 to the mail client.

Figure 8-8: HTML document as body of email message

Managing Messages

As mentioned earlier, Database Mail messages are retained on the server. If you want to view which messages have been retained, you can query the sysmail_mailitems table in the msdb database. This returns detailed information about each message, such as who the recipients were, what the body of the message contained, and which profile sent the message.

```
SELECT * FROM msdb.dbo.sysmail_mailitems
```

You can also delete messages from the server by using the using the sysmail_delete_mailitems_sp stored procedure. This will allow you to delete messages that have either failed or succeeded, or delete just messages older than a specific date. Service Pack 1 requires that you provide either the @sent_before or @sent_status option.

To delete messages from before Jan 31st, 2006, use the following example:

```
EXECUTE msdb.dbo.sysmail_delete_mailitems_sp
    @sent_before = 'January 31, 2006' ;
```

To delete messages that show a specific status value, use the following examples:

```
EXECUTE msdb.dbo.sysmail_delete_mailitems_sp
    @sent_status = 'failed';

EXECUTE msdb.dbo.sysmail_delete_mailitems_sp
```

```
    @sent_status = 'retrying';

EXECUTE msdb.dbo.sysmail_delete_mailitems_sp
    @sent_status = 'unsent';

EXECUTE msdb.dbo.sysmail_delete_mailitems_sp
    @sent_status = 'sent';
```

Event Notifications

Event notifications are database objects that send information about server and database events to a Service Broker. They execute in response to data definition language (DDL) statements and SQL Trace events by sending information about these events to a Service Broker service. You can use event notifications to either log activity within a database, or to execute an action asynchronous to an event. They are designed to be an alternative to creating DDL triggers or using SQL Trace functions.

Because event notifications run outside the scope of a transaction, they can be used inside a database application to respond to events without using any resources defined by the immediate transaction. Event notifications operate independently of whether or not the transaction commits. They can also be used to perform an action inside an instance of SQL Server in response to a SQL Trace event.

Every event notification has its own exclusive Service Broker conversation between an instance of SQL Server and the target service you specify. The conversations usually remain open as long as the event notification still exists on the server. Ending a conversation prevents the target service from receiving more messages, and the conversation will not reopen when the event notification fires again.

Event information is an XML data type that provides information about when the event occurs, the object it affects, the batch statement involved, and more. This data can be used by applications that help SQL Server track progress and make decisions.

When designing an event notification, you must define both the scope of the notification and the statement or batch that raises the notification. For example, the event notification can occur as a response to a statement made on all objects in the AdventureWorks database. You can also define the scope as being server-wide, such as triggering event notifications when new databases or logins are created.

More information about the architecture used to create services and queues are covered in Chapter 15. However, you should be aware that some of the mechanisms discussed in this section are also applicable to the next subject, the SQL Server Agent Service. For this reason, you should ensure that the msdb database is configured to manage Service Broker objects and process event notifications. Two important elements of this are ensuring that the SQL Server can trust the database and the object within it, and that the database is configured for Service Broker message delivery. To do this for the msdb database, use the following ALTER DATABASE statement:

```
ALTER DATABASE msdb
SET TRUSTWORTHY ON,
ENABLE_BROKER;
GO
```

Because the SQL Server Agent service may have an active connection to the `msdb` database, it may be necessary to stop the agent service prior to running this statement, and then restarting it once the command has completed successfully.

SQL Server Agent

This section examines how to automate tasks on the SQL Server using the Microsoft SQL Server Agent Service. The SQL Agent service runs as Windows service that is dependent on the SQL Service. Each instance of SQL will have its own Agent service to manage jobs, schedules, operators, and alerts. You learn about the essential components of the Agent service for single and multiple server management configurations.

The primary purpose of the SQL Server Agent is to make your job easier. In a perfect world, you could configure your servers, let them run, and never worry about losing data or the database going offline. But, as is too often the case, this isn't a perfect world. And because you can't realistically monitor every server every minute of every day, you can use the SQL Server Agent to leverage against what you can't do.

> *The SQL Server Agent service is not available in SQL Server 2005 Express Edition.*

Configuring the Agent Service

In Chapter 2, you learned about installing SQL Server, and defining which accounts are used by the SQL Service and the SQL Server Agent Service. A common configuration is to use the same account for both services, but this is not required. In fact, because of certain job or administrative requirements, you may need to use completely different credentials for each. Regardless of whether or not you use the same account, the account used by the SQL Server Agent must be a member of the `sysadmin` fixed server role, and must have the following rights in the Windows operating system where the server is installed:

❑ Adjust memory quotas for a process

❑ Act as part of the operating system

❑ Bypass traverse checking

❑ Log on as a batch job

❑ Log on as a service

❑ Replace a process-level token

These rights can be granted by an administrator editing the Local Security Policy. If the SQL Server Agent will be interacting with services and features outside of the local system, an Active Directory domain account should be used. This allows the SQL Server Agent to use an authenticated account to connect to a remote file system, Web service, or another SQL Server.

An out-of-the-box installation of SQL Server with no changes to the default configuration does not start the SQL Server Agent service, but instead requires manual control over the start and stop behavior of the service. *Don't do this.* If you are going to use the Agent for automation or alerting features, it needs to be running. If the Agent is stopped, no scheduled jobs can run, and no operator will receive notification indicating that a job did or did not run successfully. When installing SQL Server, it is a good practice to configure the Agent to run automatically when Windows starts.

If, however, you did not configure the Agent to start automatically, you'll need to know how to start it manually. There are actually four different ways you can start and stop the SQL Server Agent service. One way is to use the NET START command from a command prompt:

```
NET START SQLSERVERAGENT
```

To stop the service, use the NET STOP command:

```
NET STOP SQLSERVERAGENT
```

You can also use the Services snap-in (see Figure 8-9) from Administrative Tools, or the Computer Management console. From this tool, you can also configure the account that the service runs under, change the startup behavior, choose service recovery options, and view the dependencies of the service.

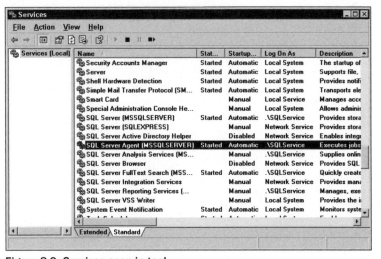

Figure 8-9: Services snap-in tool

In Chapter 3, you learned how to use the SQL Server Configuration Manager. You can similarly use that to configure the account used by the Agent service, the startup behavior, as well as error reporting options.

Finally, you can use SQL Server Management Studio to configure the behavior and properties of the Agent service. This section will spend more time going into depth about configuring the various properties of the service, so you have a good understanding of each of the configurable elements from within a familiar tool. In Object Explorer, you can right-click SQL Server Agent, and either stop or start the service as needed. To configure the service, select Properties from the context menu.

General Properties

From the General Properties sheet (see Figure 8-10), you can see the current state of the service, and you can configure both the SQL Server and SQL Server Agent to automatically restart if they stop unexpectedly. You can also change the location of the error log, and elect to include execution trace messages in the logs for advanced troubleshooting. There is also an option to use an original equipment manufacturer (OEM) file. This allows the log information to store data in a non-Unicode format, which can take up less space on the system. However, if the error logs contain any Unicode data, it may be more difficult to read or interpret. Finally, the NET SEND recipient indicates an operator that can be notified of messages that SQL Server writes to the log file.

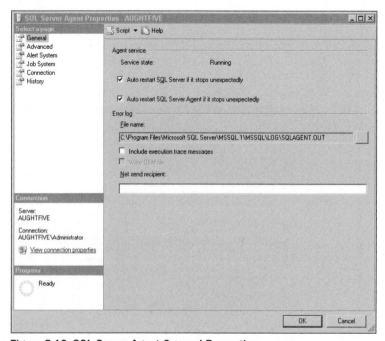

Figure 8-10: SQL Server Agent General Properties

The messenger service is disabled by default in Windows Server 2003. The ability to use NET SEND *may not be available.*

Advanced Properties

In the Advanced Properties sheet (see Figure 8-11), you can enable event forwarding, which will redirect SQL Server events to a different server. To configure this, enable the checkbox next to "Forward events to a different server" and then select an available server or instance from the drop-down list. Once this is configured, you can also determine what type of events will get forwarded. Unhandled events are those that do not have alerts defined by the Agent system, or you can select all events. You can also decide to forward events with a minimum severity level. Severity-level values are discussed in detail later in this chapter.

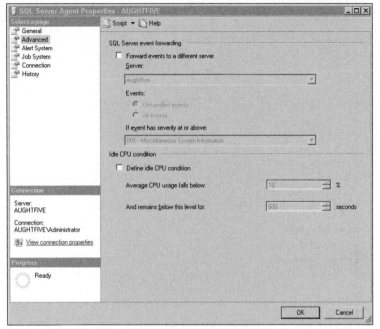

Figure 8-11: SQL Server Agent Advanced Properties

From this window, you can also define the CPU idle threshold. This can be useful if you have any job schedules that define the job should be run when the CPU is idle, such as backing up the transaction log. In this case, the default values indicate that CPU usage must fall below 10 percent for 10 minutes. You can adjust this as necessary to meet your performance needs.

Alert System Properties

You can configure the Alert System properties from this page (see Figure 8-12) by first defining if the SQL Server Agent Mail service is enabled. If you want your operators to receive alert notifications by email, you should enable this feature. You can also decide if you are going to use the Database Mail feature or the SQLMail feature. Remember that SQLMail is provided for backward compatibility only, and should not be used with new applications, because it will be phased out. If you are upgrading from a previous version of SQL, you should try to convert your applications to user Database Mail as soon as possible.

Once you've selected your mail system (Database Mail, preferably), you can then select an appropriate profile to use. If you are using SQLMail, you can test the MAPI connectivity, and allow sent messages to be saved in the Sent Items folder of the Microsoft Outlook profile.

If you will be paging operators, you can configure options for formatting addresses in the To, CC, and subject lines of the message. You can also elect to include the body of the email message in the page. Additionally, you can define a fail-safe operator, and methods for notifying that person. The role of the fail-safe operator is discussed in more detail later in this chapter.

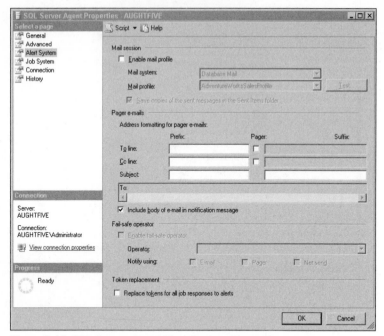

Figure 8-12: SQL Server Agent Alert System Properties

Finally, there is the option to replace tokens for all job responses to alerts. Tokens are a feature (similar to variables) of job steps that are discussed later in this chapter. For now, though, you should understand that this enables token replacement, replacing the variable with an actual value, for any job executed by the alert systems.

Job System Properties

You can specify the time-out value for jobs in the Job System Properties window (see Figure 8-13). This option configures how long the SQL Server Agent will wait for a job to complete before forcefully terminating the job. The default is 15 seconds, but be aware of how long certain jobs may need to take (because of their complexity) or the type of operations being performed.

There is also an option to configure a non-administrative account as a proxy account for job steps. This is only applicable if you are using SQL Server Management Studio to manage an older version of SQL Server and its corresponding Agent service. You can specify the authentication information for the account by providing a username, password, and domain name. Configuring a proxy account for SQL Server 2005 job steps is covered in the section, "Creating Jobs," later in this chapter.

Agent Connection Properties

If you need to connect to an instance of SQL Server that uses a non-standard connection property, you can enter an alias used by the SQL Server to allow the Agent service to establish and maintain a connection (see Figure 8-14). You can also specify whether you require the Agent service to use Windows authentication or SQL authentication. If you select SQL authentication, you must provide a valid login and password for an account that is a member of the sysa5dmin fixed server role.

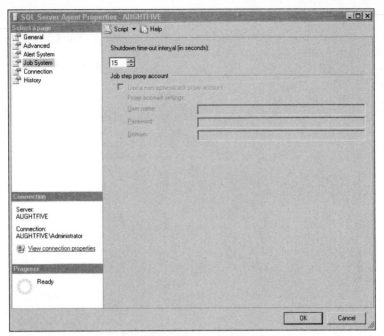

Figure 8-13: SQL Server Agent Job System Properties

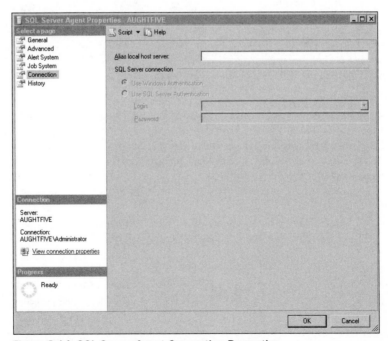

Figure 8-14: SQL Server Agent Connection Properties

Job History Properties

Finally, the History page allows you to configure retention settings for job logs in the msdb database. By default, a maximum of 1,000 rows are stored in the sysjobhistory table, and each job can use no more than 100 rows in that table. You can use this window to remove or change the limit to the size of the job history table (see Figure 8-15).

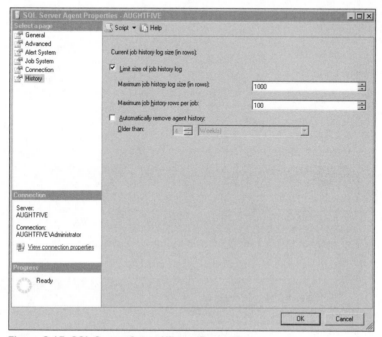

Figure 8-15: SQL Server Agent History Properties

You can also have the Agent service automatically purge old job history rows from the sysjobhistory table. This feature is disabled by default. However, if enabled, it allows you to specify how many days, weeks, or months old a job history record must be before it can be purged from the database. If you need to maintain the job history indefinitely, or need to have greater control over what gets purged, consider creating a custom job that will meet your needs.

Agent Security

When planning to use the SQL Server Agent service, or allowing other users to access it, you need to ensure that appropriate access is granted. By default, only members of the sysadmin fixed server role have complete access to the Agent service. In the msdb database, additional roles are created with varying levels of rights and permissions, but these roles are empty until a user is explicitly added to these roles. In this section, you learn about each of these roles and the permissions assigned to them.

SQLAgentUserRole

The `SQLAgentUserRole` is the most limited of the three Agent roles. Users who are members of this role have the ability to create new jobs and schedules, and can manage only those jobs and schedules they create. However, they cannot view the properties of other jobs on the system, nor can they define operators or proxies. If they need to assign an operator or proxy to a job step, it must have already been defined. Members of this role also cannot delete job history information, even for jobs they own, unless they are granted `EXECUTE` permission on the `sp_purge_jobhistory` stored procedure. Another important limitation on this role is the inability to create or manage multi-server jobs. Any job created by members of this role is limited to the server on which it was created.

SQLAgentReaderRole

As with `SQLAgentUserRole`, `SQLAgentReaderRole` can enable users to create local jobs and schedules, and manage only those that they create. In addition to these permissions, they can also view the properties of other local jobs, as well as multi-server jobs. This gives them the ability to audit the configuration of other jobs on the server, without having any rights to change those settings. Multi-server jobs also cannot be created by members of this role, but the job histories of all local and remote jobs are available for review. Members of this role, too, are prohibited from deleting the history of jobs they own, unless granted `EXECUTE` permission on `sp_purge_jobhistory`

SQLAgentOperatorRole

Members of this role can create local jobs, as well as manage and modify jobs they own. They can also view and delete the job history information for all local jobs. To a limited extent, they can also enable or disable jobs and schedules owned by other users. However, they are still prohibited from creating and managing operators and proxies. They are also limited to read-only access for multi-server jobs, as well. Outside of the `sysadmin` fixed server role, this role is granted the most rights and privileges to the job system in the SQL Server Agent service.

Creating Jobs

Jobs are really at the core of the SQL Server Agent service. *Jobs* are operations that perform through a sequence of steps that run Transact-SQL scripts, launch command-prompt applications, ActiveX script tasks, replication tasks, and a variety of other tasks. Each task is defined as a separate job step. Part of the design of the job system is to build each task so that you can build dependencies and workflows between the job steps. A very simple example of this would be a backup job that ran nightly, and then emailed an administrator to inform him or her that the job was complete. The simplicity and complexity of a job is dependent on what you need it to do. In some cases, you'll want to create multiple jobs, rather than a single, overly complex one, because of the timeout settings mentioned earlier.

Try It Out   Creating a New Job

Begin by creating a new job in SQL Server Management Studio. For this example, you're going to populate only the most basic information about the job from the General properties page. Feel free to browse through the other property pages in this exercise, but be aware that the configurable elements in those pages are covered later in this chapter.

1. In Object Explorer, expand SQL Server Agent.
2. Right-click Jobs and select New Job.

3. In the New Job dialog box (see Figure 8-16), enter **Simple Backup** as the job name.

4. Leave the Owner as the default.

5. Select Database Maintenance in the Category drop-down list.

6. In the description, enter **Simple Backup Job. Test 1.**

7. Remove the check next to Enabled.

8. Click OK.

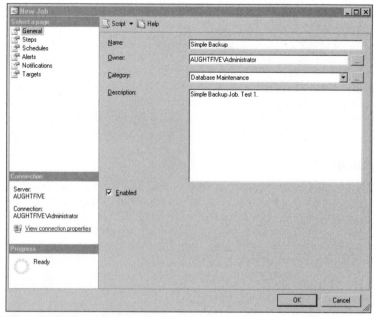

Figure 8-16: New Job Properties

This creates a new job, and prevents the job from running once you close the New Job window. Because the job has no steps, there would have been little harm in letting it run, but it's a habit you will want to get into, until you've tested your jobs to ensure they work as expected.

Now look at how to create a new job using Transact-SQL. The sp_add_job stored procedure allows you to create a new job, and set configurable options on the job. For now, look at a simple example of creating a job, but the following table lists all the options for sp_add_job.

Option	Description
@job_name	The name of the job.
@enabled	The default value of 1 indicated the job is enabled, and a value of 0 means the job is disabled. Disabled jobs can still be manually executed.

Option	Description
`@description`	An optional description of the job. If no value is specified, the field is populated with `No description available`.
`@start_step_id`	In more complex jobs, where you have multiple steps built around dependencies and error handling, you can actually have the job start at a step other than the first one. Use the integer-based job ID value for the initial job step.
`@category_name`	Allows you to type a category name to assign the job. Categories make it easier to group and manage jobs that have similar functions. Be aware that if you misspell an existing job category (as in "Databizase Maintenance") it will return an error. You must use an existing category name.
`@category_id`	Allows you to use the `category_id` value rather than category name. Category names and IDs are stored in `msdb.dbo.syscategories`.
`@owner_login_name`	Allows a system administrator to set a different login as the owner of the job.
`@notify_level_eventlog`	Indicates what information should be added to the Windows Application Log. This is an `int` data type with the following values:
	0 — Never
	1 — On success
	2 — On Failure
	3 — Always
	The default value is 2.
`@notify_level_email`	Indicates when to send email messages regarding this job, using the levels described in `@notify_level_eventlog`. Default is 0.
`@notify_level_netsend`	This value indicates when a NET SEND message should be sent. The Messenger service must be started on both the sender and the recipient machines for this to work. With a default value of 0, the levels for `@notify_level_eventlog` can be used to change its behavior.
`@notify_level_page`	Indicates when to send messages to an SMTP-enabled pager, using the same values as `@notify_level_eventlog`. Default is 0.
`@notify_email_operator_name`	The name of an operator that will receive email messages if email notification is enabled. Do not use the email address, but rather the `sysname` value of the operator.

Table continued on following page

Option	Description
@notify_netsend_operator_name	The name of an operator that will receive NET SEND messages.
@notify_page_operator_name	The name of the operator that will receive SMTP pages.
@delete_level	Indicates when to delete the job, using the values defined in @notify_level_eventlog. If the level is set to 3, the job is deleted upon completion, and no further instances of this job will run. The default is 0.
@job_id job_id OUTPUT	Returns the value of the job_id. The job_id is of the uniqueidentifier data type.

Take a look at using the sp_add_job stored procedure to create a new job with only the basic elements. After creating other elements such as schedules, operators, and alerts, you will add those into the jobs you create in this section. For this example, you will create a new job that will be used for data retrieval tasks:

```
DECLARE @job_id uniqueidentifier;

EXECUTE msdb.dbo.sp_add_job
  @job_name = 'Poor Performers Report',
  @description = 'Monthly task to indicate which sales team members have less
                  than remarkable sales figures over previous year',
  @job_id = @job_id OUTPUT;

SELECT @job_id
```

One thing you should notice about the job_id parameter is that it uses the uniqueidentifier data type. This is also referred to as a Globally Unique Identifier (GUID). GUIDs are used for both jobs and schedules if either will be used for multi-server jobs. Multi-server jobs are covered later in this chapter.

If you're adding a job using the sp_add_job stored procedure, you will also need to ensure that the job can run on the server by using the sp_add_jobserver stored procedure. If the job is going to run on the local server, all you need to define is the job either by job_id or job_name, as in the following example:

```
EXECUTE msdb.dbo.sp_add_jobserver
    @job_name='Poor Performers Report';
```

So, now you have two new jobs available to your Agent service. Neither job has any steps defined, so running them won't accomplish anything, other than receiving a failure message. (But hey, if that's what you're after, go for it.) Before adding steps to your jobs, take a look at how to manage job categories.

Categories

The easiest and preferred method for managing job categories is through SQL Server Management Studio. Though you could directly edit the `syscategories` table, it's not recommended. You can add new categories, and delete user-created categories. Be aware that you cannot delete built-in categories. In this example, you will add a new category called AW - Performance Tasks.

Try It Out   Creating a New Category

1.   From Object Explorer, expand your server, and then expand SQL Server Agent.

2.   Next, right-click Jobs and select Manage Job Categories.

3.   In the Manage Job Categories window (see Figure 8-17), click Add.

4.   For the category name, enter **AW - Performance Tasks**.

5.   Check the box next to "Show all jobs."

6.   Check the box in the row for the Poor Performers Report job.

7.   Click OK.

8.   Click Cancel to close the Manage Job Categories window.

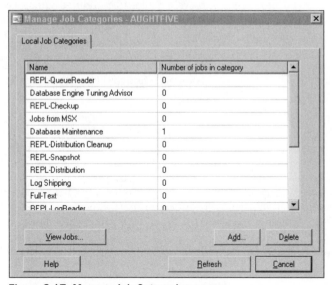

Figure 8-17: Manage Job Categories screen

You have now successfully created the AW - Performance Tasks category and added the Poor Performers Report job to it. This category will also now be available for any new jobs you want to create.

Creating Job Steps

Now that you have a couple of jobs you can work with, add some simple steps to these jobs. Before doing this, though, take a look at the different types of job steps you can define, as shown in the following table.

Step Type	Description
Windows Executable (CmdExec)	This will run Windows executable code, including files with the following extensions: .exe, .bat, .cmd, .com. For fully automated tasks, the executable may contain command-line parameters that can be passed to control execution.
Transact-SQL	Any T-SQL script that will execute in the context of the job owner if not otherwise specified. The Transact-SQL script can contain multiple batches and can include executing stored procedures.
ActiveX Script	Can use any language supported by the Windows Scripting Host. Common examples use VBScript and JavaScript. The script itself is written into the job task.
Replication	Used to initiate replication agents for the different replication types. Chapter 16 introduces replication, and the function of these agents.
Analysis Services	Can be either command steps or queries.
Integration Services	Can execute a SQL Server Integration Services (SSIS) package. For more information about SSIS, see Chapter 13.

For each job step type, you can identify one or more proxy accounts that can be used to execute that step type, in case the owner of the job, or the login under which the job is run, does not have permissions to execute that type of task. It allows you to let users run jobs that contain steps they would not be able to run under their own credentials. You learn about creating and managing proxies later in this chapter.

This first example uses Management Studio again to edit the properties of the Simple Backup job. You're going to add a Transact-SQL step that will perform a full backup of the AdventureWorks database onto the local disk. Before beginning, you should create a folder called dbBackups on your C: drive.

1. From Object Explorer, expand your server, and then expand SQL Server Agent.

2. Expand Jobs.

3. Right-click Simple Backup and select Properties.

4. Under the Select a Page list, select Steps.

5. Click the New button.

6. In the Step Name box, enter **AdventureWorks Backup**.

7. In the Type drop-down list, ensure that Transact-SQL is listed.

8. Leave "Run as" empty.

9. Ensure that master is the selected database.

10. Enter the following code in the command window:

```
BACKUP DATABASE AdventureWorks TO DISK = 'C:\dbBackups\AWFull.bkf';
```

11. Click OK to close the New Job Step window.

12. Click OK to close the Job Properties window.

13. In the SQL Server Management Studio Note, it informs you that the last step will be changed from "Goto Next Step" to "Quit with Success." Click Yes.

You have now created a simple job step. Feel free to enable the job by right-clicking the job and selecting Enable from the context menu. You can also manually run the job at any time, even if it's disabled, by right-clicking and selecting Start Job. The job should execute with success.

If you go back into the job step properties, and look at the Advanced Properties page, you will notice options to configure how the job responds when this step completes. If the job is successful, you can have it perform one of the following tasks:

❑ Go on to the next step.

❑ Quit the job reporting success.

❑ Quit the job reporting failure.

❑ Go to Step: (number).

> *The option to go to a numbered step is only available if you have more than one step in the job. Be careful about creating cyclical jobs where the first step will go to the next step, and the second step will go to the first step.*

On this page, you can also identify the number of retry attempts, and how long (in minutes) the server should wait between retries. If the job step cannot complete successfully, you can also define how the job should behave. You have the same options for defining what to do when the step fails as when it succeeds.

Also, depending on the type of step being executed, you can define additional options or parameters. For example, with Transact-SQL steps, you can specify an output file, log the output to a table, and include output information with the job history. You can also identify who the step should run as.

sp_add_jobstep

You can use the `sp_add_jobstep` stored procedure to add steps to an existing job. Using this procedure allows you to append a step to an existing job, or insert a new step between two existing steps. The following table provides a breakdown of the parameters for `sp_add_jobstep`.

Parameter	Description
@job_id	The uniqueidentifier value of the job. You can use this or job_name to refer to the job to which you are adding the step.
@job_name	The display name of the job. Use either this or the job_id, but not both.

Table continued on following page

Parameter	Description
@step_name	A display name for the step.
@step_id	A unique number indicates where this step should be added into the job step order. If no value is specified, the step_id will auto-increment by one. If the value specified already exists, this will insert this step, and increment the step that previously held this value (and all steps that follow it) by one.
@subsystem	This parameter allows you to identify which subsystem will be used to interpret the step. The available values are:
	ACTIVESCRIPTING — ActiveX script
	CMDEXEC — Windows command or executable
	DISTRIBUTION — Replication Distribution job
	SNAPSHOP — Replication Snapshot job
	LOGREADER — Replication Log Reader Agent job
	MERGE — Replication Merge Agent job
	QueueReader — Replication Queue Reader Agent job
	ANALYSISQUERY — MDX or DMX Analysis Services query
	ANALYSISCOMMAND — XMLA Analysis Services command
	Dts — Integration Services Package
	TSQL — Transact-SQL script. This is the default.
@command	The command that will be executed as the job step. The syntax will vary depending on the subsystem used to process the command.
@on_success_action	Allows you to specify what to do if the step is successful. Use one of the following values: 1 — Quit with success (default)
	2 — Quit with failure
	3 — Go to the next step
	4 — Go to step on_success_step_id
@on_success_step_id	The ID of the step to go to if option 4 is selected above.
@on_fail_action	The same values as on_success_action except on_success_step_id is replaced by on_fail_step_id.
@on_fail_step_id	The ID of the step to go to if option 4 is selected for on_fail_action.
@database_name	The database in which a Transact-SQL step will execute. If no value is specified, the master database is used. If the step is an ActiveX script, this can be used to identify the scripting language.

Parameter	Description
`@database_user_name`	The user account under which the Transact-SQL step will execute.
`@retry_attempts`	The number of attempts a step will make before it fails. Default is `0`.
`@retry_interval`	The number of minutes before `retry_attempts`. Default is `0`.
`@output_file_name`	An external file in which step output is saved. Valid for Transact-SQL and `CmdExec` steps.
`@flags`	Options that control output behavior. Uses the following values:
	`0` — Overwrite output file (default)
	`2` — Append to output file
	`4` — Write T-SQL step output to step history
	`8` — Write log to table, overwriting existing history
	`16` — Write log to table, appending to existing history
`@proxy_id`	The ID of a proxy account that will be used for this job step, if needed.
`@proxy_name`	The name of a proxy account that will be used for this job step, if needed.

There are additional parameters listed in SQL Server Books Online that are identified as "reserved." Because they are not configured, they are not included in this list.

Now take a look at creating a couple of job steps for the Poor Performers Report job. The first step will generate an email message that identifies sales employees that have not exceeded their previous year sales by $200,000 (slackers!). The second step will email an administrator indicating the job has been successful:

```
-- Create the First Step
EXECUTE msdb.dbo.sp_add_jobstep
  @job_name = 'Poor Performers Report',
  @step_id = 1,
  @step_name = 'Send Report',
  @subsystem = 'TSQL',
  @command = 'DECLARE @tableHTML NVARCHAR(MAX) ;
          SET @tableHTML =
              N''<H1>Lowest Sales Increase</H1>'' +
              N''<table border="1">'' +
              N''<tr><th>First Name</th><th>Last Name</th>'' +
              N''<th>Current Year Sales</th>'' +
              N''<th>Previous Year Sales</th>'' +
          CAST ((SELECT td = pC.FirstName,'''',
                     td = pC.LastName, '''',
                     td = sP.SalesYTD, '''',
                   td = sP.SalesLastYear, ''''
                FROM Sales.SalesPerson AS sP INNER JOIN
                HumanResources.Employee AS hrE ON
```

```
                    sP.SalesPersonID = hrE.EmployeeID INNER JOIN
                        Person.Contact AS pC ON hrE.ContactID = pC.ContactID AND
                    hrE.ContactID = pC.ContactID
                    WHERE (sP.SalesYTD - sP.SalesLastYear) < 200000
                FOR XML PATH(''tr''), TYPE
            ) AS NVARCHAR(MAX) ) +
            N''</table>'';

    EXECUTE msdb.dbo.sp_send_dbmail
            @recipients = ''Michael.Bluth@adventureworks.com'',
            @subject = ''First to go...'',
            @body = @tableHTML,
            @body_format = ''HTML'';',
    @database_name = 'AdventureWorks';

-- Create Step 2
EXECUTE msdb.dbo.sp_add_jobstep
 @job_name = 'Poor Performers Report',
 @step_id = 2,
 @step_name = 'Notify Administrator',
 @subsystem = 'TSQL',
 @command = 'EXEC msdb.dbo.sp_send_dbmail
            @recipients = ''administrator@adventureworks.com'',
            @subject = ''Message Sent'',
            @body = ''The Monthly Sales Report has been sent'',
            @body_format = ''HTML'';';
```

Now, you must tell the step that you created earlier to go to the next step once the first step has been completed. For this, use the `sp_update_jobstep` stored procedure, as follows:

```
EXECUTE msdb.dbo.sp_update_jobstep
 @job_name = 'Poor Performers Report',
 @step_id = 1,
 @on_success_action = 3;
```

Remember that when `on_success_action` is set to 3, the step will go to the next step.

Token Replacement

SQL Server 2005 uses tokens in job steps as parameter placeholders. These tokens allow the Agent service to replace the token with an actual value. This is similar to using a variable within a script or an application. When writing jobs, consider using some of these tokens to provide accurate reporting of job status, or to allow your jobs to be more flexible. The following table provides a list of tokens supported by the SQL Server Agent service.

Token	Description
$(A-DBN)	Database name, used in jobs launched by alerts.
$(A-SVR)	Server name, used in jobs launched by alerts.
$(A-ERR)	Error number, used in jobs launched by alerts.

Token	Description
$(A-SEV)	Error severity, used in jobs launched by alerts.
$(A-MSG)	Message text, used in jobs launched by alerts.
$(DATE)	Current date (YYYYMMDD).
$(INST)	Instance name. The default instance returns an empty value.
$(JOBID)	Job ID.
$(MACH)	Computer name.
$(MSSA)	Master SQLServerAgent service name.
$(OSCMD)	Prefix for the program used to run CmdExec steps.
$(SQLDIR)	The SQL Server installation directory.
$(STEPCT)	The number of times this step has executed, excluding retries. Can be used to force a multistep loop to terminate.
$(STEPID)	Step ID.
$(SRVR)	Name of the computer running SQL Server, including the instance name, if any.
$(TIME)	Current time (HHMMSS).
$(STRTTM)	The time (HHMMSS) the job began executing.
$(STRTDT)	The date (YYYYMMDD) the job began executing.
$(WMI(property))	The value of the property specified by property, when the job is launched by a Windows Management Instrumentation (WMI) alert.

Using Tokens in Job Steps

Service Pack 1 for SQL Server 2005 significantly changes the way tokens are used in job steps. With the pre-service pack release, you could simply use a token like a variable, as seen in the following example:

```
PRINT 'The database backup of $(A-DBN) is now complete.'
```

If your job backed up the AdventureWorks database, the job step would have returned the output:

```
'The database backup of AdventureWorks is now complete.'
```

Job steps now require the use of an escape macro to successfully replace the token. The escape macros are used to prevent parsing errors that may exist because of invalid characters in the data that replaces the token. For example, if you installed SQL to a folder called C:\Finance Department's Database and tried to use the $(SQLDIR) token, your job step might fail, believing that the value ended at the word "department." There are four possible escape macros. The following table lists the escape macros and their uses.

Escape Macro	Usage
`$(ESCAPE_SQUOTE(token))`	This allows any single quotation mark in the replacement token string to be replaced by two single quotation marks.
`$(ESCAPE_DQUOTE(token))`	This escape macro replaces a double quotation mark with two double quotation marks.
`$(ESCAPE_RBRACKET(token))`	Use this escape macro to replace a right bracket character with two right bracket characters.
`$(ESCAPE_NONE(token))`	This allows the token to be replaced without escaping any characters. This is designed for backward compatibility.

So, the correct way to use a token is to use the appropriate escape macro when calling the token. For example, the following will prevent a database name that contains a single quote (which is possible) from causing the command to end prematurely:

```
PRINT 'The database backup of $(ESCAPE_SQUOTE(A-DBN)) is now complete.'
```

Creating Schedules

To automate many of the tasks you need to perform to maintain your SQL Server, you must define schedules for when your jobs run. Schedules, not unlike categories, can be created and managed independently of the creation and management of jobs. This allows you to use the same schedule for multiple jobs.

Each job can also use multiple schedules. For example, you may create a job that performs a transaction log backup. If your operation is not a 24_7 business, you might want to create a schedule so that the transaction log is backed up more frequently during business hours. Let's use every two hours as an example. Then, you may want to continue to back up the transaction log after normal business hours, but because there is less activity after hours, you could back up the transaction log every four hours. On the weekends, you may want to back up the transaction logs every eight hours. Not that you would expect a lot of activity, but if someone comes in to work over the weekend, you will want to have a backup of any changes.

You can also enable or disable individual schedules as needed. When a schedule is disabled, any job that uses that schedule will not run under that schedule. However, if a job is configured to use other schedules, the job will run under those schedules. If the job itself is disabled, it will not run under any schedule.

Take a look at the tools used to manage schedules. In this first example, you're going to create a new schedule for your Simple Backup job that will run the job every weekday at noon:

1. From Object Explorer, expand your server, and then expand SQL Server Agent.
2. Right-click Jobs and select Manage Schedules.
3. In the Manage Schedules window, click New...
4. In the New Job Schedule window (see Figure 8-18), enter **Weekdays - Noon** for the schedule name.

5. Ensure that the schedule type is Recurring, and ensure the schedule is Enabled.

6. In the Frequency schedule, make sure that the schedule is set to occur weekly.

7. Select the checkboxes for Monday, Tuesday, Wednesday, Thursday, and Friday.

8. If selected, remove the check in the box next to Sunday.

9. In "Daily frequency," select the radio button marked "Occurs once at:" and set the time to 12:01:00 PM.

10. Leave the "Start date" as the current date, and ensure that "No end date" is selected.

11. Click OK.

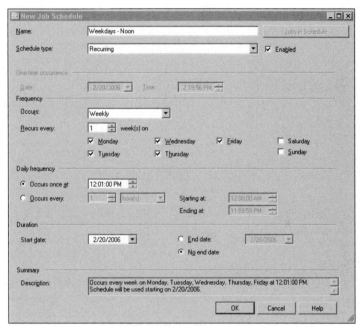

Figure 8-18: New Job Schedule screen

At this point, you can either add the job to the schedule, or you can add the schedule to the job in the properties. Let's look at both methods.

First, in the Manage Schedules window (which should be open, unless you closed it), you should notice that in the "Jobs in schedule" column for the Weekdays - Noon schedule contains the value 0, which is also a hyperlink.

1. Click the number 0 (note that it is a hyperlink) in the "Jobs in schedule" column for the Weekdays - Noon schedule (see Figure 8-19).

2. In the "Jobs Referencing a Schedule" dialog box, click the checkbox in the Selected column for the Simple Backup schedule (see Figure 8-20).

3.   Click OK. Note that the number of jobs in this schedule has incremented.

4.   Click OK to close the Manage Schedules window.

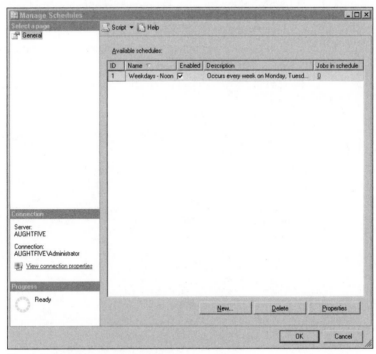

Figure 8-19: Managing Schedules

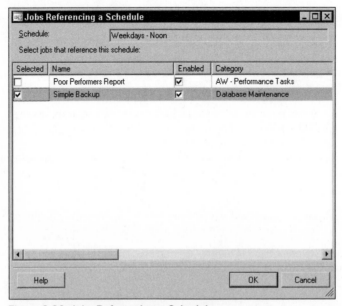

Figure 8-20: Jobs Referencing a Schedule

If you want to add the schedule to the job through the job properties dialog box, follow these instructions:

1. In Object Explorer, expand the Jobs folder.

2. Right-click the Poor Performers Report job and select Properties.

3. Under the "Select a page" section, click Schedules.

4. Under the Schedule list, click Pick (see Figure 8-21).

5. A list of available schedules will appear. Select the Weekdays - Noon schedule and click OK.

6. Click OK to close the Job Properties window.

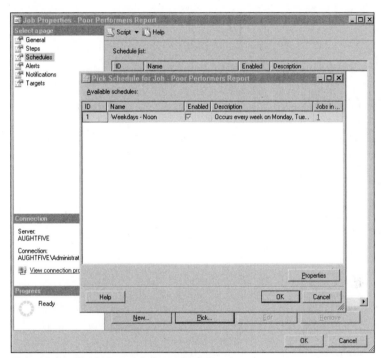

Figure 8-21: Picking an existing schedule

Note that you can also create a new schedule from this window, as well. One of the benefits of SQL Server 2005, and especially of SQL Server Management Studio, is that you usually have more than one option for performing a task. Use whichever tool or method best suits your administrative needs.

sp_add_schedule

You can also create new schedules with the sp_add_schedule stored procedure. When you create the new schedule, you can specify the parameters shown in the following table.

Option	Description
@schedule_name	Friendly name of the schedule.
@enabled	Default value of 1 means the schedule is enabled. A value of 0 will disable the schedule.
@freq_type	Integer value indicating the frequency type of the schedule, using the following values:
	1 — Once
	4 — Daily
	8 — Weekly
	16 — Monthly
	32 — Monthly relative to freq_interval
	64 — Run when the SQL Server Agent starts
	128 — Run when CPU is idle
@freq_interval	The days the job is executed. See the next table for options. This option is not used with all freq_type values.
@freq_subday_type	Identifies the units for freq_subday_interval, with the following values:
	1 — At the specified time
	2 — Seconds
	4 — Minutes
	8 — Hours
@freq_subday_interval	The number of freq_subday_type periods between executions.
@freq_relative_interval	This value is the occurrence of freq_interval in each month if the value of freq_interval is 32. Can use the following values:
	1 — First
	2 — Second
	4 — Third
	8 — Fourth
	16 — Last
@freq_recurrence_factor	Number of weeks or months between executions. Used only of freq_type is 8, 16, or 32. Default is 0.
@active_start_date	Date the job can start. This uses the YYYYMMDD format, and the date must be greater than 19900101. The default is NULL.

Option	Description
@active_end_date	Last date the job will run on this schedule. This also uses the YYYYMMDD format, but has a default of 99991231.
@active_start_time	Time of day on any day between the active_start_date and active_end_date to start a job. The default is 000000, and uses a 24-hour format using HHMMSS.
@active_end_time	Time of day on any day between the active_start_date and active_end_date to end a job. The default is 235959 using a 24-hour HHMMSS format.
@owner_login_name	The name of the login that owns the schedule. By default the creator of the schedule becomes the owner.
@schedule_uid uid OUTPUT	A uniqueidentifier for the schedule.
@schedule_id id OUTPUT	The ID for the schedule using an int data type.

The following table shows the values of freq_type and options for freq_interval.

Value of freq_type	Options for freq_interval
4	Every freq_interval days.
8	Use one or more of the following values. Add the values together to allow multiple days to be selected. For example, to specify the schedule for Tuesday, Wednesday, and Thursday add the values 4 + 8 + 16 for a total value of 24.
	1 — Sunday
	2 — Monday
	4 — Tuesday
	8 — Wednesday
	16 — Thursday
	32 — Friday
	64 — Saturday
16	On the freq_interval day of the month.
32	Uses one of the following values for monthly relative:
	1 — Sunday
	2 — Monday
	3 — Tuesday

Table continued on following page

Value of `freq_type`	Options for `freq_interval`
	4 — Wednesday
	5 — Thursday
	6 — Friday
	7 — Saturday
	8 — Day
	9 — Weekday
	10 — Weekend day

You've probably been able to figure out why SQL Server Management Studio is the preferred method for managing jobs and schedules. But look at an example for creating a new schedule. In this example, you're going to create a new schedule that will run the associated job(s) every eight hours on the weekend. Some comments have been added to help make sense out of some of the values.

```
DECLARE @schguid UNIQUEIDENTIFIER
DECLARE @schid INT

EXECUTE msdb.dbo.sp_add_schedule
  @schedule_name = 'Weekend Schedule',
  @freq_type = 8,   -- Weekly
  @freq_interval = 65,   -- Combination of Saturday(64) and Sunday(1)
  @freq_subday_type = 8,   -- Hours
  @freq_subday_interval = 8,   -- specifies that the job runs every 8 hours
  @freq_recurrence_factor = 1,
  @active_end_date = 20101031,
  @active_end_time = 235959,
  @schedule_uid = @schguid OUTPUT,
  @schedule_id = @schid OUTPUT

SELECT @schguid as GUID,@schid as ID
```

sp_attach_schedule

Creating the schedule will not associate the schedule with any of the jobs you have created, so either you can go back and use Management Studio, or you can use the `sp_attach_schedule` stored procedure. When you created the schedule from the previous example, it should have returned both the GUID and the ID of the schedule.

When creating the mapping between a schedule and a job, you can use either the ID or the name of either element. Note that the `schedule_id` is an `int` value for the local ID, and not the `uniqueidentifier` GUID.

```
EXECUTE msdb.dbo.sp_attach_schedule
@schedule_name = 'Weekend Schedule',
@job_name = 'Simple Backup';
```

Creating Operators

Operators are objects that represent a unit of notification for SQL Server Agent jobs and alerts. Operators can represent an individual person, or a group. Operators are not associated with database or server principals, but are exclusive to the SQL Server Agent service. Earlier in this chapter, you learned how to configure the SQL Server Agent service to use either Database Mail or SQLMail for the alert system. Whichever one you configured, the Agent service will use that to notify the appropriate operators.

When you create a new operator, you assign a name to the operator, and then define the methods for notifying the operator. Your options for notifying an operator include email, NET SEND using the Windows Messenger service, and SMTP-enabled pager.

In this example, you create a new operator for the administrator account. This operator will be available for paging only on the weekend.

1. From Object Explorer, expand your server, and then expand SQL Server Agent.

2. Right-click the Operators folder and select New Operator.

3. In the New Operator window (see Figure 8-23), enter **Server Administrator** in the Name field.

4. Ensure that the Enabled box is checked.

5. In the "e-mail name" field, enter **administrator@adventureworks.com**.

6. Leave the "Net send address" field empty.

7. In the "Pager e-mail name" field, enter **admin-pager@adventureworks.com**.

8. In the "Pager on duty schedule," set the following values:

    a. Friday: 5:00:00 PM — 11:59:59 PM

    b. Saturday: 12:00:00 AM — 11:59:59 PM

    c. Sunday: 12:00:00 AM — 11:59:59 PM

9. Click OK to close the New Operator properties window.

If you open the properties of the properties of the operator you just created, you will notice there are two additional pages. The notification page displays a list of jobs and alerts that have sent notifications to this operator. The history page reports the time of the last notification attempt for each notification type.

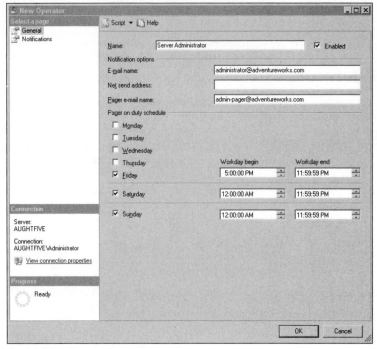

Figure 8-22: Creating a new operator

sp_add_operator

Use the `sp_add_operator` to create a new operator. You can use the values shown in the following table.

Parameter	Description
@name	Name of the operator.
@enabled	Default value is 1. A value of 0 will disable the operator.
@email_address	The email address used to notify the operator.
@pager_address	The SMTP address of the pager.
@weekday_pager_start_time	This value marks the time during the week where the SQL Server Agent will page the operator if necessary. Time is in the 24-hour HHMMSS format.
@weekday_pager_end_time	This value marks the time during the week where the SQL Server Agent will no longer page the operator. Time is in the 24-hour HHMMSS format.
@saturday_pager_start_time	This value marks the time on Saturday where the SQL Server Agent will page the operator if necessary. Time is in the 24-hour HHMMSS format.

Parameter	Description
@saturday_pager_end_time	This value marks the time on Saturday where the SQL Server Agent will no longer page the operator. Time is in the 24-hour HHMMSS format.
@sunday_pager_start_time	This value marks the time on Sunday where the SQL Server Agent will page the operator if necessary. Time is in the 24-hour HHMMSS format.
@sunday_pager_end_time	This value marks the time on Sunday where the SQL Server Agent will no longer page the operator. Time is in the 24-hour HHMMSS format.
@pager_days	Allows you to indicate the days the operator will be available for paging. To enable multiple days, simply add the following values:
	1 — Sunday
	2 — Monday
	4 — Tuesday
	8 — Wednesday
	16 — Thursday
	32 — Friday
	64 — Saturday
@netsend_address	The network address of the operator the Agent will send a message to.

In this example, you create a new operator that represents the Sales Managers group, and enable paging for the group between 8:00 AM and 5:30 PM:

```
EXECUTE msdb.dbo.sp_add_operator
  @name = 'Sales Managers',
  @email_address = 'Sales.Managers@adventureworks.com',
  @pager_address = 'Sales.Managers.Pagers@adventureworks.com',
  @weekday_pager_start_time = 080000,
  @weekday_pager_end_time = 173000,
  @pager_days = 62;
```

To add the operator to an existing job, you can use the sp_update_job stored procedure. You can use this to specify that the operator should be notified using any of the defined methods for that operator. The following example notifies the Sales Managers by email when the Poor Performers report succeeds, and pages them when it job fails:

```
EXECUTE msdb.dbo.sp_update_job
  @job_name = 'Poor Performers Report',
  @notify_email_operator_name = 'Sales Managers',
```

```
@notify_page_operator_name = 'Sales Managers',
@notify_level_email = 1, -- on success
@notify_level_page = 2; -- on failure
```

You can also edit the properties of an existing job to notify an operator when a job fails or succeeds, or both by using the "When the job completes" option. Also on this page, you can configure the job to write an event to the application log, and have the job automatically deleted if one of the completion conditions is met.

The Fail-Safe Operator

After you have created at least one operator, you can designate one as the *fail-safe operator*. The fail-safe operator is an operator whose contact information is cached in memory while the SQL Server is running. This ensures that the operator can still be contacted in case the msdb database becomes unavailable. The fail-safe operator can also be notified if the primary operators for a job or alert cannot be notified. You can define the fail in the SQL Server Agent properties. In the Alert System page, there is a drop-down list allowing you to select an exiting operator as the fail-safe operator, and you can use the checkboxes to determine the methods of notification for this operator.

Creating Alerts

Danger, Will Robinson, Danger! The term "alerts" tends to carry such negative connotation. You may think of loud klaxons going off, the emergency lights turning on, and people shoring up the doors to keep the zombies out. You know, stuff like that. But alerts in SQL Server 2005 don't necessarily mean the end of the world. Alerts can be simply informational, such as letting a manager know that someone on the sales staff is deleting rows from the customers table.

Creating alerts consists of three steps. The first step is to name the alert. You should use a name that will be descriptive, that may also include information about the severity of the event that triggered the alert. The second step is defining the event or performance condition that will trigger the alert. Finally, you must identify what this alert will actually do. Will it notify an operator, or will it run a job?

Alerts typically fall into one of three categories:

❑ *Event-based alerts* are generated on database- or system-level events. These can be system-defined, or you can write your own events.

❑ *Alerts on performance conditions* use SQL Server Performance counters to indicate that a threshold value has been met.

❑ You can also create *alerts based on WMI events*.

SQL Server Event-Based Alerts

SQL Server event-based alerts can be used to execute a task or notify an operator based on a predefined SQL event. These events can be system-created, and usually refer to system-wide activity, or they can be user created, allowing you to define conditions within a specific database. Before looking at creating alerts, take a look at creating events.

SQL Server events are defined as an instance of an action being performed or a condition being met. Although that may sound like a very broad definition, events themselves can be very broad in scope.

SQL Server 2005 has a number of events already defined for you. In fact, the number of events defined is more than 7,500 just for the English language! These events can be generated when a query contains too many referenced tables, or when an index is corrupted. There is also a mechanism for you to create your own events that may be system-wide or database-specific, as needed.

Each event is defined with a unique numerical ID, a severity level, the text of the message, and a language ID number. Severity levels are values between 0 and 25 and are used to categorize the event.

Error messages configured with a severity level of 10 or less will not actually raise a system-level exception. This comes in handy when you want to create an alert on a SQL Server event, but you don't want to throw an exception to the calling application. The following table lists the different severity levels and what they represent.

Severity Level(s)	Description
0–10	Messages with a severity level between 0 and 10 indicate informational messages that do not raise a system error.
11	The object or entity does not exist.
12	Indicates the query does not use locking because of special query hints. Read operations may result in inconsistent data.
13	Deadlock errors.
14	Security errors.
15	Syntax errors.
16	General errors.
17	The SQL Server has run out of resources, or has reached an administrator-defined limit.
18	There is a problem in the database engine, but the statement has been executed and the connection has been maintained.
19	A non-configurable limit has been reached, and the current batch has stopped. Events with a severity level of 19 or higher are automatically logged.
20	A problem has occurred in the current statement.
21	A problem that affects the entire database has occurred, but the database may not have been damaged.
22	A table or index has been damaged by a hardware or software problem.
23	The database has been damaged by a hardware or software problem.
24	General media failure.
25	User-defined.

Querying the `sysmessages` catalog view returns a list of all events defined on the server. To create your own events, you can use the `sp_addmessage` stored procedure. When using `sp_addmessage`, you can use the values shown in following table. All values default to `NULL` unless otherwise stated. The only required values are `@msgnum`, `@severity`, and `@msgtext`.

Option	Description
`@msgnum`	This is the ID number of the message. You must use a value greater than 50,000 for all user-defined messages.
`@severity`	Use an appropriate severity level for this event.
`@msgtext`	This is an `nvarchar(255)` field that contains the message text. You can use parameter placeholders such as `%d` for decimal values and `%s` for string values. When the event is raised, these placeholders are replaced with the actual values.
`@lang`	The language for the message. Each message can be stored for multiple languages, allowing you to localize the message.
`@with_log`	Use `TRUE` to have the event logged in the Windows Application log. `FALSE` is the default.
`@replace`	Use the value `replace` if you are overwriting an existing message.

Take a look at an example of the `sp_addmessage` stored procedure. In this exercise, you create a simple error message that contains notification information whenever a user adds a row to the Credit Card table. In the next step, you'll create a stored procedure that will insert a row into the credit card table, and then you'll execute that stored procedure.

```
-- Create the message
EXECUTE sp_addmessage
@msgnum = 60001,
@severity = 10,
@msgtext = 'Credit Card ID #%d has been added by %s as %s',
@with_log = 'True';
GO

-- Create a stored procedure for inserting credit card data that will raise
-- the error
USE AdventureWorks;
GO

CREATE PROCEDURE AddNewCreditCard
@CardType nvarchar(50),
@CardNumber nvarchar(25),
@ExpMonth tinyint,
@ExpYear smallint
AS
DECLARE @username varchar(60)
DECLARE @loginame varchar(60)
DECLARE @CreditCardInfo Table(CreditCardID INT)
DECLARE @CreditCardID INT
```

```
SET @loginame = suser_sname()
SET @username = user_name()

BEGIN TRANSACTION
INSERT Sales.CreditCard(CardType,CardNumber,ExpMonth,ExpYear)
 OUTPUT INSERTED.CreditCardID
  INTO @CreditCardInfo
 VALUES (@CardType,@CardNumber,@ExpMonth,@ExpYear);

SET @CreditCardID = (Select CreditCardID FROM @CreditCardInfo)

RAISERROR (60001, 10, 1, @CreditCardID, @loginame, @username)
COMMIT TRANSACTION;
GO

-- Run the stored procedure and return the message
EXECUTE AddNewCreditCard
@CardType='Veesa',
@CardNumber='111187620190227',
@ExpMonth='2',
@ExpYear='2009'
```

This should result in the following output:

```
(1 row(s) affected)
Credit Card ID #19238 has been added by AUGHTFIVE\Administrator as dbo
```

Now that you have an event, you should create an alert on that event. In this next exercise, you create an alert that will use the error message created in the previous example, and have a notification sent to the Sales Managers operator:

1. In Object Explorer, expand SQL Server Agent.

2. Right-click Alerts and select New Alert.

3. For the name, enter **NewCCAlert** (see Figure 8-23).

4. Ensure that Type is SQL Server Event Alert.

5. Select AdventureWorks as the database.

6. Under "Alerts will be raised based on," select "Error number."

7. Type **60001** for the error number.

8. Switch to the Response page.

9. Select Notify Operators.

10. Select Email for Sales Managers.

11. Switch to the Options page.

12. Select E-mail under "Include error alert text in:".

13. Click OK.

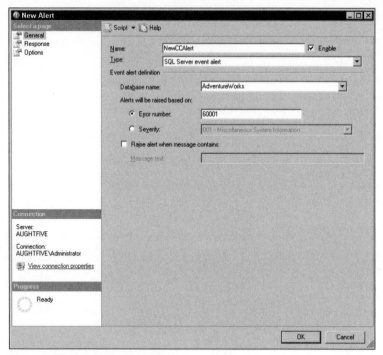

Figure 8-23: Creating a new alert

The following example shows you how to use the sp_add_alert stored procedure to create a new alert, and the sp_add_notification stored procedure to associate the alert with operators that will be notified. Because you cannot have two alerts defined for the same event in the same database, you will need to delete the "NewCCAlert" you created in the previous step first.

```
EXECUTE msdb.dbo.sp_delete_alert
@name = 'NewCCAlert';

EXECUTE msdb.dbo.sp_add_alert
 @name = 'New Credit Card Alert',
 @message_id = 60001,
 @include_event_description_in = 1,
 @database_name = 'AdventureWorks';

EXECUTE msdb.dbo.sp_add_notification
 @alert_name = 'New Credit Card Alert',
 @operator_name = 'Sales Managers',
 @notification_method = 1;
```

The sp_add_alert stored procedure includes a number of options for creating and adding alerts. The following table identifies all the parameters available, but be aware that, depending on the type of alert you are creating, not all options will be used, and, in fact, some cannot be used together.

Option	Description
@name	The name of the alert.
@message_id	The error number of the alert. Only messages written to the application log can cause an alert to be sent.
@severity	The severity level for messages that will generate the alert. If you specify this option, all messages with this severity level will issue this alert.
@enabled	The default value of 1 enables the alert.
@delay_between_responses	The wait period between alert responses in seconds. Raising this value decreases the likelihood of multiple alerts being generated within a short time.
@notification_message	Optional additional message.
@include_event_description_in	The notification type, if any, the message text will be included in. The values here are also used with the sp_add_notification stored procedure. Adding the values indicates multiple notification types:
	0 — None
	1 — E-mail
	2 — Pager
	4 — Net Send
@database_name	Identifies the database for which this alert is active. If you do not specify a database name, the alert will be active for all databases.
@event_description_keyword	This option uses a pattern match to generate the alert only if certain keywords or phrases are present in the error message.
@job_id	ID number of a job that will run as a response to the alert.
@job_name	Name of a job that will run as a response to the alert. Use either job_id or job_name; not both.
@raise_snmp_trap	Default is 1. Changing the value to 0 will not raise an SNMP trap message.
@performance_condition	Allows you to define a performance condition alert in the format of ItemComparatorValue.
	Item — Performance object or counter.
	Comparator — Using greater than (>), less than, (<), or equal to (=).
	Value — Numeric value for the counter.

Table continued on following page

Option	Description
@category_name	Name of the alert category.
@wmi_namespace	Namespace used for WMI queries when using WMI Event alerts.
@wmi_query	A WQL query for WMI providers that report on health or state information.

Performance Condition Alerts

Performance condition alerts use SQL Server performance objects and counters to allow alerts to be defined on server or database activity. For example, you can use this to trigger an alert when the number of transactions per second for the AdventureWorks database rises above a specific value. In this example, you create an alert that will notify you when the transaction log of AdventureWorks is above 85 percent full:

1. In Object Explorer, expand SQL Server Agent.
2. Right-click Alerts and select New Alert.
3. For the name, enter **AWXactLogSpace** (see Figure 8-24).
4. Select SQL Server performance condition alert as the type.
5. From the Object drop-down list, select SQLServer:Databases.
6. From the Counter drop-down list, select Percent Log Used.
7. From the Instance drop-down list, select AdventureWorks.
8. From the "Alert if counter" drop-drop down list, select "rises above."
9. Enter **85** for the value.
10. Select the Response page.
11. Select Notify Operators.
12. Select E-mail and Pager for the Server Administrator.
13. Click OK.

You've now created a new performance alert that will notify an administrator whenever the transaction log for AdventureWorks grows above 85%. Alternatively, you could create a job that would back up and truncate the transaction log. For more information about performance objects and counters, see Chapter 10.

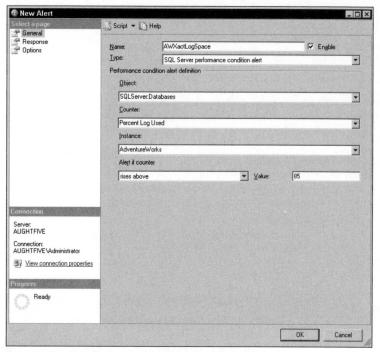

Figure 8-24: Creating a performance condition alert

WMI Event Alerts

SQL Server 2005 can use WMI to collect events for alerting operators. SQL Server uses the WMI Provider for Server Events to make the SQL Server an object manageable by WMI. Any event that can generate event notification can be managed by WMI. SQL Server alerts use WMI Query Language (WQL) to retrieve an event type for a specific database or database object. WQL is similar to SQL, but with extensions specific to WMI. When an alert is created for a WMI event, the WMI Provider for Server Events translates a WMI query into an event notification. The WMI provider will dynamically create a service and queue in the msdb database. The provider reads the data from the queue, and returns it to the application in a managed object format. Event notifications, services, and queues are discussed in more detail in Chapter 15.

To be able to successfully create a WMI event alert, you must ensure that the WMI Performance Adapter service is running. The service is set to be started manually, but if you plan to make WMI event alerts part of your administrative solution, you may want to configure the service to start automatically.

In this example, you create a new alert that uses WMI to record an event when a new table is created in the Person schema of the AdventureWorks database. Before you begin, ensure that the WMI Performance Adapter service is started. Use the following steps to create a new alert:

1. In Object Explorer, expand SQL Server Agent.

2. Right-click Alerts and select New Alert.

3. For the name, enter **Create Table Alert** (see Figure 8-25).

4. Select WMI event alert as the type.

5. Ensure that you are using the default namespace of
   `\\.\root\Microsoft\SqlServer\ServerEvents\MSSQLSERVER`

6. In the query window, enter the following WMI query:

```
SELECT * FROM CREATE_TABLE
WHERE DatabaseName='AdventureWorks' AND SchemaName = 'Person'
```

7. Select the Response page.

8. Select Notify Operators.

9. Select E-mail for the Server Administrator.

10. Click OK.

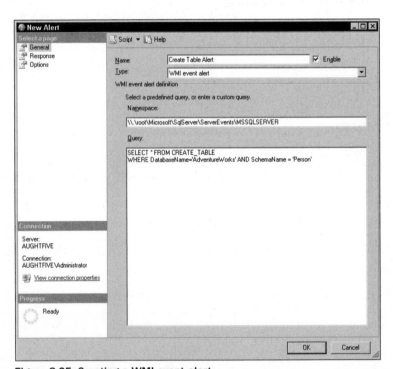

Figure 8-25: Creating a WMI event alert

WMI is a very powerful and complex tool, and with it, there are a number of different Data Definition Language (DDL) and trace events you can watch for with WMI alerts. Read the topic entitled "WMI Provider for Server Events Classes and Properties" in Books Online for a list of available events.

Creating Proxies

SQL Server Agent properties allow you to execute specific job steps with a different security account. This allows you greater flexibility over your application and maintenance designs. It also allows you to create job steps that can be executed by users whose security context would normally prohibit them from running a task. The benefit of this is that the user who creates the job need only have access to the proxy account. The user does not need to create credentials, users, or be given elevated permissions to execute a job step. You can create proxies for the following types of job steps:

❑ ActiveX Script

❑ CmdExec

❑ Replication Distributor

❑ Replication Merge

❑ Replication Queue Reader

❑ Replication Snapshot

❑ Replication Transaction-Log Reader

❑ Analysis Services Command

❑ Analysis Services Query

❑ SSIS Package Execution

There is also a folder for creating and managing unassigned proxies. Note that a single proxy can be used for multiple task types, if needed.

Try It Out Creating a New Proxy

Take a look at the process for creating a new proxy. First of all, proxies use credentials to execute. In Chapter 6, you learned how to create a new credential, but in case you've deleted it, or you're not reading this book from cover-to-cover, you can create a new credential now. Begin by first creating a new Windows user:

1. Go to Start → Control Panel → Administrative Tools → Computer Management.

2. Expand Local Users and Groups, and then expand Users.

3. Right-click the Users folder and select New User (see Figure 8-26).

4. In the username box, enter **ScriptRunner**.

5. Enter **P@ssw0rd** as the password, and remove the check next to "User must change password at next login."

6. Click Create.

7. Click Close.

8. Close Computer Manager.

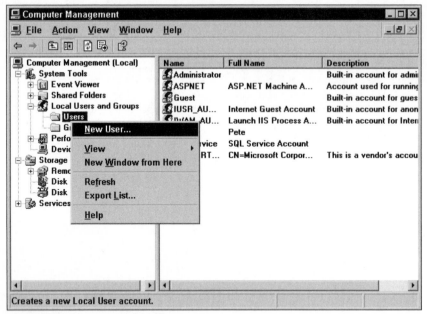

Figure 8-26: Creating a new Windows user

So, now that you have a new user, create a credential for this user:

1. Go back to SQL Server Management Studio.

2. In Object Explorer, expand your server, and expand Security.

3. Right-click Credentials and select New Credential (see Figure 8-27).

4. For the name, enter **ActiveXProxy**.

5. In the identity box enter **Aughtfive\Scriptrunner** (or use your server or domain name in place of Aughtfive).

6. Enter **P@ssw0rd** for the Password and Confirm password fields.

7. Click OK.

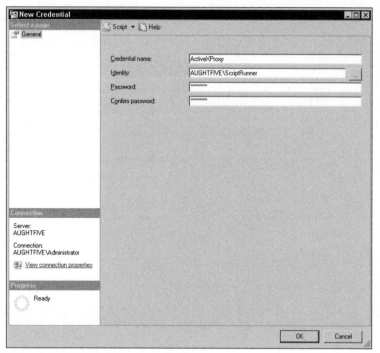

Figure 8-27: Creating a new credential

You now have a new Windows user with an associated credential on your server. Now you can use that credential to create one or more proxies:

1. In Object Explorer, expand SQL Server Agent.

2. Expand Proxies and select ActiveX Script.

3. Right-click ActiveX Script and select New Proxy.

4. Enter **ScriptRunner** as the proxy name (see Figure 8-28).

5. Enter **ActiveXProxy** as the Credential name.

6. Ensure that ActiveX Script is selected under "Active to the following subsystems."

7. Alternately, add additional subsystems, or use the Principals page to identify SQL Logins, server roles, or msdb database roles that can reference this proxy in job creation.

8. Click OK.

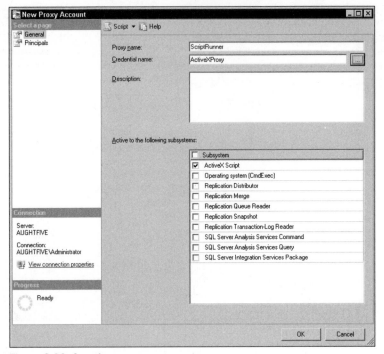

Figure 8-28: Creating a proxy account

Now that you've created a new proxy, let's see how it can be used in a job step. In this next example, you add a new step to your Poor Performers Report job that will contain an ActiveX script. It'll be a fairly useless script, but "Hello World" always makes for great proof of concept!

```
EXECUTE msdb.dbo.sp_add_jobstep
  @job_name = 'Poor Performers Report',
  @step_id = 2,
  @step_name = 'Hello World',
  @subsystem = 'ACTIVESCRIPTING',
  @database_name = 'VBScript',
  @command = 'Sub main()
              Print ("Hello World.")
            End Sub',
  @on_success_action = 3,
  @proxy_name = 'ScriptRunner';
```

Now that this has been added, you can execute the job, and review the job history to see the successful execution of the script as the `ScriptRunner`.

Multi-Server Jobs

SQL Server also supports the ability to create and manage jobs on one server that can be run on multiple SQL Servers. This functionality grants you the ability to administer and control multiple servers at once. This can be beneficial when performing system-level tasks, such as backing up the system databases, or controlling database-level tasks like replication.

Multi-server jobs are configured by first defining a *master server*. This master server acts as the source for all jobs that will be run on multiple *target servers* (see Figure 8-29). When defining a multi-server configuration, be aware that although you can enlist multiple target servers on which remote jobs will run, not every multi-server enabled job will run on all target servers. In fact, you can specify which target servers a multi-server job will run. The downside to this is that each target server can only have one master server. Plan your multi-server job configuration carefully.

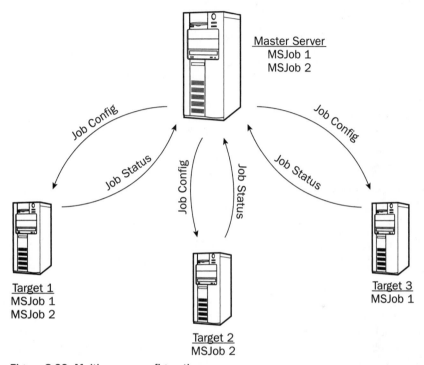

Figure 8-29: Multi-server configuration

There are a few things you need to know about setting up multi-server jobs:

❑ Jobs running on multiple servers that have steps running under a proxy account use the proxy account on the target server. Ensure that you have a proxy server on both the master and target server that has the same access and permissions.

❑ Each target server can have only one server for all jobs.

❑ If you are going to change the name of a target server, you must remove it from the master server, through a process known as *defecting,* and then re-enlist it after the name change.

❑ When removing a multi-server configuration, first defect all target servers before decommissioning the master.

To create multi-server jobs, you must first define the master servers and the target server. You can begin by running the Master Server Wizard in SQL Server Management Studio:

1. In Object Explorer, right-click SQL Server Agent and select Multiserver Administration, then "Make this a master."

2. The wizard begins with an introductory page that informs you of the steps that will be taken in this wizard.

3. The next step creates an MSXOperator account. This operator is used to send information about multi-server jobs. You can provide an email address, pager address, and NET SEND address for message delivery.

4. Then, you will specify at least one server that will be identified as a target server. SQL Server 2005 includes a compatibility check to ensure that the target server will work with the master server.

5. The final step identifies the credentials that will be used to establish authentication and authorization between the two servers. As a best practice, you should use Windows Active Directory domain accounts for the SQL Server Agent service on your master server and all target servers, so that the accounts use the benefit of Active Directory security without having to create duplicate accounts on the servers. If the login for the MSXOperator does not exist on the target server, the wizard will ask you if you want to create it.

Once this has completed, the wizard will perform the following tasks:

❑ Create the MSXOperator.

❑ Ensure that the Agent service is running on the master server.

❑ Ensure that the Agent service account on the target server has rights to log in as a target server.

❑ Enlist the target server into the master server.

Once the wizard has completed successfully, and the server is now configured as a master server, you can create new jobs that will run on the local server, remote servers, or both. You will also be able to go back into an existing job, and specify that job will run as a multi-server job. You can then select on which servers the job will run. This is managed in the Targets property sheet.

Maintenance Plans

SQL Server Management Studio includes a very robust platform for creating and managing maintenance plans. Plans can be created with a wizard, or manually with the Maintenance Plan Designer. Maintenance plans are actually created as Integration Services packages. To create and use Maintenance Plans, Integration Services must be installed.

Maintenance Plan Wizard

Microsoft SQL Server 2005 includes a wizard for checking database integrity, as well as running tasks that help reorganize the data and re-index the data. As you step through the wizard, you are asked to choose which tasks to perform, and then you will provide the configuration options for each task, including which databases to perform the tasks on. The available tasks include the following:

- Checking database integrity
- Shrink the database
- Reorganize indexes
- Rebuild indexes
- Update statistics
- Clean up history
- Executing a SQL Server Agent job
- Backing up databases using full, differential, or transaction log backups

Once you've specified which options to include, and configured them in your maintenance plan, you can also schedule the job to run on a recurring basis. This will create a job that will execute an Integration Service package, which contains each of the steps defined in the maintenance plan. You can execute the maintenance plan from the Maintenance Plan folder under Management, or simply execute the job that was created. You can also modify the maintenance plan at any time, and add or remove tasks as needed.

Maintenance Plan Designer

Although the wizard is an easy way to create a new maintenance plan, it lacks the flexibility that creating a plan with the designer provides. To create a new maintenance plan, right-click the `Maintenance Plans` folder in Management Studio (see Figure 8-31) and click New Maintenance Plan.

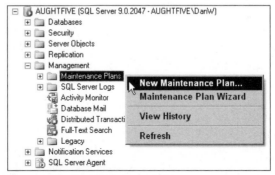

Figure 8-30: New Maintenance Plan

In the resulting New Maintenance Plan dialog, enter a name in the Name field and click OK. This will launch the Maintenance Plan designer, which is based on Integration Services (see Figure 8-31).

To create a maintenance plan, drag the desired tasks from the toolbox on to the design surface. Once the task is on the surface, you can either double-click the task or right-click the task and select Edit from the context menu to configure the task's properties. Additional tasks can be added to the designer and joined by precedence constraints. Each task added is configured with a Success constraint by default. However, right-clicking the constraint (see Figure 8-32) displays a context menu where the constraint can be configured for Success, Failure, or Completion.

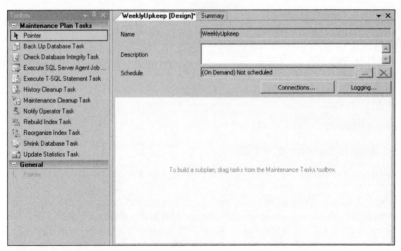

Figure 8-31: Maintenance Plan Designer

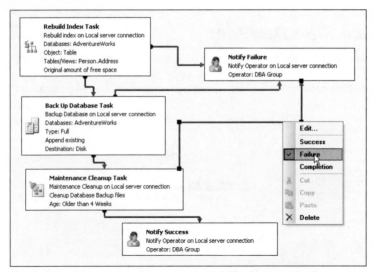

Figure 8-32: Maintenance Plan precedent constraints and tasks

Figure 8-33 shows a Rebuild Index task configured to rebuild the indexes on the `Person.Contact` table. This task will execute a Notify Operator task called "Notify Failure" in the event that it fails and a Backup Database task if it succeeds. The Backup Database task that performs a Full backup of `AdventureWorks` will also execute the Notify Operator task if it fails, but it executes the Maintenance Cleanup task if it succeeds. The Maintenance Cleanup task is configured to delete any backup files over four weeks old, and then to notify an operator that the plan has succeeded if it succeeds, or notify of failure if it fails.

Maintenance plans are configured to run on-demand by default, but they can be configured with a recurring schedule by clicking the ellipses to the right of the Schedule field and setting the properties of the schedule in the resulting schedule screen.

Best Practices

Here are some guidelines that can help you automate administration of your servers:

❑ *Use Database Mail instead of SQLMail* — SQLMail is there for backwards compatibility only, and its dependence on an extended MAPI client and server configuration can make it more cumbersome than it's worth.

❑ *Configure Database Mail to use multiple accounts and multiple SMTP servers for each profile* — This will help increase the ability to deliver messages to the appropriate operators and personnel.

❑ *Configure the* SET TRUSTWORTHY ON *and* ENABLE_BROKER *options for the* msdb *database* — This will help ensure that your event notification messages and alerts can be delivered to the appropriate personnel.

❑ *Configure the SQL Server Agent to start automatically when Windows starts, and configure automatic restart if the service fails* — This helps ensure that scheduled jobs are able to run in case the system is accidentally shut down or restarted.

❑ *Configure the SQL Server Agent to use a domain user account* — This allows you a number of features, including the ability to run and control multi-server jobs using a single account, as well as having better auditing capabilities of how that account is used.

❑ *Configure proxy accounts with only the level of access needed to perform the task they were designed for and nothing else* — Employ the principle of least privilege in all layers of your administrative model.

❑ *Designate groups rather than individuals as operators* — You can specify the email address of a group or distribution list rather than an individual user. This gives you the flexibility of modifying the group membership, and, thereby, changing the target delivery without having to change the job, operator, or notification method.

❑ *Use Maintenance Plans to define a comprehensive set of steps that will check the integrity of your database and help resolve performance issues* — Schedule the maintenance plan to run regularly, but at a time when it least impacts your users.

Summary

In this chapter, you learned about the different tools that can be used to help automate the management of SQL Server 2005. Remember that Database Mail is one of the more essential features to help you administer your server, in that you can use it for notification of both critical and non-critical server events. Its flexibility in its ability to use any standard SMTP server allows you to provide a robust solution without incurring some of the costs of a large-scale enterprise mail solution. You were also introduced to the topic of event notifications, which can provide you with an alternate method of receiving notifications of system or database events.

Finally, you got an exhaustive look at the elements of the SQL Server Agent, including administrative tools for managing jobs, schedules, operators, alerts, and proxy accounts. In the next few chapters, you are going to learn about different tools and resources to manage the SQL Server environment. This chapter should server as a building block for the materials from the next chapters, in that you should be able to take the concepts you've learned here, and apply them to backing up your databases, covered in Chapter 9, and performance monitoring, which you learn about in Chapter 10.

Exercises

1.   Modify the Simple Backup job to notify the administrator by email if the job completes success-
     fully, by pager if the job fails, and have the job write an event to the application log on either
     condition.

2.   Create a new job called AWLogBackup that will back up the transaction log of the
     AdventureWorks database using the following statement:

```
BACKUP LOG AdventureWorks TO DISK = 'C:\dbbackups\AWLog.bak'
```

3.   Ensure that the AdventureWorks database is using the full recovery model. Then configure the
     AWXactLogSpace alert to run the AWLogBackup job when the performance condition is met.

4.   Run the Maintenance Plan Wizard to create a new Maintenance Plan called CheckShrinkNBack
     that will check AdventureWorks' database integrity, shrink the AdventureWorks database, and
     execute your Simple Backup job. Schedule the job to run every Sunday at noon.

Disaster Prevention and Recovery

"There are two things that every database administrator can't live without. The first is an effective backup-and-restore plan. The second is an up-to-date résumé. If you have the first, you may never *need* the second, but if you don't have the first, sooner or later the résumé will be critical to your future employment."

I give that speech to every group of database administrators that I address, and I address a lot of them. It is a fact that disks fail and data gets corrupted. We have all probably suffered from some form of data loss that could have been prevented if the data had been properly backed up. As the individual responsible for the stability and integrity of the organization's data, the database administrator must be diligent and meticulous about planning a database backup strategy so that, in the event of equipment failure, user error, or intentional data corruption, the database can be returned to service in as short as time as possible with minimal loss of data.

This chapter is about the mechanics of database backup and recovery, with a little bit of strategy thrown in for good measure. I will try not to give specific recommendations, because no cookie-cutter recommendation will work for each situation. It is up to you as the database administrator to examine all the possible backup-and-restore operations, and come up with a plan that will prevent data loss and minimize downtime. People are counting on you, and the very organization that you work for may succeed or fail because of your efforts. It is a pretty heavy responsibility to bear, but as more and more lines of business applications are built on top of SQL Server, it is a very real responsibility. So, take a deep breath and learn all that you can about disaster prevention and recovery to ensure you are always the hero, and never the person to blame for lost data.

Preparing the SmallWorks Database

The AdventureWorks database is a fairly large sample database. To reduce the amount of time and disk space required to practice the examples in this chapter, you will first create a smaller version of AdventureWorks. The following script creates a database called SmallWorks made up of a

Primary filegroup and two additional filegroups with one data file each. It then creates a table in each filegroup and populates it with data from the AdventureWorks database. The last action of the script is to set the read-only attribute on the second user-defined filegroup. The script assumes the existence of the C:\SQLData path.

```
CREATE DATABASE SmallWorks ON  PRIMARY
( NAME = 'SmallWorksPrimary'
, FILENAME = 'C:\SQLData\SmallWorks.mdf'
, SIZE = 10MB
, FILEGROWTH = 20%
, MAXSIZE = 50MB)
, FILEGROUP SWUserData1
( NAME = 'SmallWorksData1'
, FILENAME = 'C:\SQLData\SmallWorksData1.ndf'
, SIZE = 10MB
, FILEGROWTH = 20%
, MAXSIZE = 50MB)
, FILEGROUP SWUserData2
( NAME = 'SmallWorksData2'
, FILENAME = 'C:\SQLData\SmallWorksData2.ndf'
, SIZE = 10MB
, FILEGROWTH = 20%
, MAXSIZE = 50MB)
 LOG ON
( NAME = 'SmallWorks_log'
, FILENAME = 'C:\SQLData\SmallWorks_log.ldf'
, SIZE = 10MB
, FILEGROWTH = 10%
, MAXSIZE = 20MB);
GO
USE SmallWorks;
GO
ALTER DATABASE SmallWorks
MODIFY FILEGROUP SWUserData1 DEFAULT;
GO

CREATE TABLE dbo.Contact(
  ContactID int NOT NULL
, FirstName varchar(75) NOT NULL
, LastName varchar(75) NOT NULL
, EmailAddress varchar(255) NULL
, Phone varchar(25) NULL
) ON SWUserData1;

CREATE TABLE dbo.Product(
  ProductID int NOT NULL
, ProductName varchar(75) NOT NULL
, ProductNumber nvarchar(25) NOT NULL
, StandardCost money NOT NULL
, ListPrice money NOT NULL
) ON SWUserData2;

INSERT dbo.Contact
(ContactID, FirstName, LastName, EmailAddress, Phone)
```

```
SELECT ContactID, FirstName, LastName, EmailAddress, Phone
FROM AdventureWorks.Person.Contact
WHERE ContactID < 5000;

INSERT dbo.Product
(ProductID, ProductName, ProductNumber, StandardCost, ListPrice)
SELECT ProductID, Name, ProductNumber, StandardCost, ListPrice
FROM AdventureWorks.Production.Product;

ALTER DATABASE SmallWorks MODIFY FILEGROUP SWUserData2 READONLY;
```

Database Recovery Models

SQL Server has three possible recovery models. However, only two are meant for regular use: the Simple and Full recovery models. The third recovery model, Bulk-Logged, is designed to be an adjunct to the Full recovery model. Each recovery model has its advantages and disadvantages. It is absolutely critical that you have a complete understanding of each model so that you can make an informed and appropriate decision as to what recovery model to operate each database in. Recovery models change the behavior of the transaction log, what backups can be performed, and how data is recovered.

Full Recovery Model

In the Full recovery model, all activity that affects the database is logged in the transaction log in some way or another. Some events are minimally logged such as the TRUNCATE TABLE command, which completely clears the contents of a table. When the TRUNCATE TABLE command is executed, SQL Server logs only the de-allocation of the data pages affected by the truncation. However, all regular database activity is fully logged, including the rebuilding of indexes, bulk copy, SELECT INTO, BULK INSERT, and BLOB (Binary Large Object) updates. The advantage of this full logging is that every transaction can be recovered in the event of a failure. You never have to worry about a lost transaction caused by loss of a data file. With the loss of the actual transaction log, all transactions since the last CHECKPOINT would be lost.

The disadvantage of the Full recovery model is the same as the advantage. Almost everything that affects the database is fully logged. As a result, the transaction log can fill up very quickly. If it is set to auto-grow, it can also get very large, very quickly. Exactly how quick depends on the number of transactions and the size of those transactions. If the log is not carefully monitored and it is left in its default settings of auto-grow and unrestricted file growth, there is a real potential of the transaction log filling up the entire disk. If the transaction log fills to capacity, the database will not accept any modifications. When the database is set to the Full recovery model, it is imperative that an effective plan for backing up the transaction log on a regular basis is developed and implemented. Backing up the transaction log clears it of all old transactions, and makes room for new ones.

In Full recovery model, the transaction log contains a record of all the modifications made to the database since the last BACKUP LOG event. It can be used to recover those transactions, as described later in this chapter.

Bulk-Logged Recovery Model

The Bulk-Logged recovery model, as previously noted, is an adjunct model to the Full recovery model. There are times when the full logging behavior of the Full recovery model can be detrimental to performance and cause unacceptable log file growth. In these situations, the database can be configured to minimally log bulk operations by changing the recovery model to Bulk-Logged. In the Bulk-Logged recovery model, the following database operations are minimally logged:

❑ Index creation

❑ Index rebuild

❑ Bulk copy operations

❑ BULK INSERT

❑ SELECT INTO

❑ BLOB operations

Minimal logging means that the operations listed are logged as having occurred, but the individual rows affected are not logged. In addition to the record of the operation being logged, a record of the physical extents allocated or affected by the operation is recorded in the transaction log. During the next BACKUP LOG event, the affected physical extents are copied to the log backup.

Bulk-Logged recovery keeps the log smaller by minimally logging data-intensive operations, but the log backups can actually be larger. Because the log backups rely on the physical data being intact during the log backup, if the disks are damaged or unavailable, the log backup will fail.

In Bulk-Logged recovery, the transaction log contains a record of all the fully logged modifications made to the database, and the identification of changed extents modified by minimally logged operations since the last BACKUP LOG event. Like the transaction log in the Full recovery model, the transaction log in Bulk-Logged recovery is available to restore transactions in the event of a database failure.

Simple Recovery Model

In the Simple recovery model, the inactive portion of the log is truncated every time SQL Server issues a checkpoint. As explained in Chapter 4, checkpoints are issued periodically by SQL Server to keep the amount of time necessary to recovery a database to a minimum. The inactive portion of the log is essentially the portion of the log from the oldest open transaction to the end of the log.

The Simple recovery model has the advantage of decreasing the administrative overhead of transaction log management. Because the inactive portion of the log is basically cleared of every checkpoint, the log (if planned appropriately) should never grow, and should never need to be managed. However, the transaction log cannot be backed up and used for data recovery, because it does not have a complete record of all the transactions that have modified the database.

SQL Server 2005 Database Backup

SQL Server 2005 backups can be performed during normal database activity. There is no need to disconnect users or shut down any services. Backups can be sent to disk or tape. To send backups to tape, the tape device must be locally attached to the database server. This limitation can be overcome by using third-party products, or mounting the tape device on a Storage Area Network (SAN) that presents the drive as a logical disk device.

Disk destinations are identified by a physical or Universal Naming Convention (UNC) location, as the following examples illustrate:

```
--Full database backup of SmallWorks to a drive location
BACKUP DATABASE SmallWorks
TO DISK = 'C:\SQLBackups\FullSmallWorks.BAK'
WITH DESCRIPTION = 'SmallWorks DB Full Backup';

--Full database backup of SmallWorks to a UNC location
BACKUP DATABASE SmallWorks
TO DISK = '\\AUGHTFIVE\SQLBackups\FullSmallWorks.BAK'
WITH DESCRIPTION = 'SmallWorks DB Full Backup';
```

An important point to remember is that SQL Server will not create the folder specified in a backup destination, only the file. The folder must exist prior to executing the BACKUP command.

Backup Devices

Tape or disk locations can be mapped to a backup device. A *backup device* is an alias to the disk or tape location. The only real advantage of backup devices is that they make the syntax of the backup command simpler. However, because the backup devices are usually created once to hold many backups, the device name will typically be less descriptive than is usually desired.

The following example shows how to create a backup device and then back up the Master database to it:

```
--Create a device for SmallWorks database backups
sp_addumpdevice 'Disk', 'SmallWorksDevice', 'C:\SQLBackups\SmallWorks.BAK';

--Backup the SmallWorks database to the new device
BACKUP DATABASE SmallWorks TO SmallWorksDevice
WITH DESCRIPTION = 'SmallWorks Full Backup';
```

The sp_addumpdevice stored procedure does not verify the existence of the target folder. When using this procedure, to avoid errors, be very sure that the folder exists and that you spelled it correctly before attempting to send a backup to it.

A more foolproof method of creating backup devices is by using Management Studio. To do this, expand the Server Objects node in the Object Explorer of Management Studio, right-click Backup Devices, and select New Backup Device (see Figure 9-1). The Backup Device window will warn you if the folder specified does not exist.

Figure 9-1: New Backup Device screen

How SQL Server Database Backups Work

Regardless of the type of database backup executed, SQL Server performs the following actions:

1. Logs the BACKUP statement in the transaction log.

2. Issues a checkpoint causing all outstanding dirty buffer pages to be written to the disk.

3. Writes all data pages specified by the FULL, DIFFERENTIAL, FILE, or FILEGROUP backup options to the backup media.

4. Writes all data modifications recorded in the transaction log that occurred during the backup to the backup media.

5. Logs the completion of the backup in the transaction log.

Try It Out   Backing Up a Database

Back up the Master database by executing the following command in SQL Server Management Studio:

```
--Full database backup of the Master database
BACKUP DATABASE Master
TO DISK = 'C:\SQLBackups\FullMaster.BAK'
WITH DESCRIPTION = 'MASTER DB FULL Backup';
```

The results of this command should appear something like the following:

```
Processed 360 pages for database 'Master', file 'master' on file 1.
Processed 2 pages for database 'Master', file 'mastlog' on file 1.
BACKUP DATABASE successfully processed 362 pages in 1.431 seconds (2.070 MB/sec).
```

The script performs a Full database backup of the Master database. It assumes you have a folder named SQLBackups. Remember, the backup command will create designated files, but it will not create folders.

Databases can also be backed up using the graphical tools provided with Management Studio. To accomplish the same results as the previous script, follow these steps:

1. Expand the Databases and then the System Databases nodes in the Object Explorer of Management Studio.

2. Right-click the Master database, click Tasks, and click Backup... to launch the Back Up Database dialog (see Figure 9-2).

3. Click the Remove button to remove the default backup location.

4. Click the Add button to specify a new destination for the database backup.

5. In the Select Backup Destination dialog type in a new destination for the backup, such as **C:\SQLBackups\FullMaster.BAK**.

6. Click OK to start the backup.

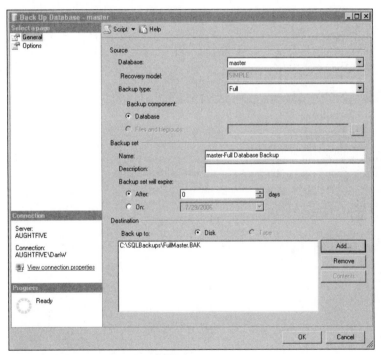

Figure 9-2: Back Up Database dialog

SQL Server 2005 Backup Types

SQL Server 2005 supports several backup types that can be combined or used independently to create backup strategies. This section explores the different types. The next section examines the backup options and how to combine the backup types into an effective backup strategy. Most of the backups are performed the same way using the graphical tools, and the interface is very intuitive. With that in mind, each backup type will only be accompanied by the appropriate Transact-SQL code to use to perform the backup.

Full Backup

Probably the most common and easy-to-implement backup is the Full backup. The Full backup simply backs up all the data in the database and records all database file locations. SQL Server logs the beginning of a Full database backup in the transaction log, and then records all modifications made to the database for the duration of the backup in the transaction log. When all the data pages from the database data files have been transferred to the backup media, SQL Server logs the completion of the backup, and transfers the portion of the transaction log that occurred during the backup to the backup media. Full backups can be used in any recovery model.

The advantage of the Full backup is that it is exceptionally simple. However, Full backups take longer than other backup methods, and typically result in the same unchanged data being backed up over and over again, along with the new and updated data.

```
--Full database backup of SmallWorks
BACKUP DATABASE SmallWorks
TO DISK = 'C:\SQLBackups\SmallWorksFull.BAK'
WITH DESCRIPTION = 'SmallWorks FULL Backup';
```

Differential Backup

Differential backups are used to back up only the data that has changed since the last Full backup. Like the Full backup, the Differential backup also consists of the portion of the transaction log that contains database modifications that occurred during the backup. Because Differential backups only contain the extents of data files that have changed since the last Full backup, they take less time to execute than Full backups. However, each consecutive Differential backup will, in most cases, become progressively larger. If just 1 byte of a 64K extent is modified, the Differential backup will backup the entire extent. The Differential backup is available regardless of the database recovery model, and requires a base Full database backup.

```
--Differential database backup of SmallWorks
BACKUP DATABASE SmallWorks
TO DISK = 'C:\SQLBackups\SmallWorksDiff.BAK'
WITH DIFFERENTIAL, DESCRIPTION = 'SmallWorks Differential Backup';
```

File/Filegroup Backup

When a database is divided across many files and filegroups, these files and filegroups can be backed up individually. This type of backup is particularly useful for very large databases. File and Filegroup backups work similarly as Full and Differential backups in that the data pages of the file, and then all transactions made against the file or filegroup, are added to the backup media. The following is an example of a command that executes a backup of the SWUserData1 filegroup:

```
--Backup of the "SWUserData1" User-Defined Filegroup
BACKUP DATABASE SmallWorks
FILEGROUP = 'SWUserData1'
```

```
TO DISK = 'C:\SQLBackups\SmallWorksUserData1FG.BAK'
WITH DESCRIPTION = 'SmallWorks SWUserData1 Filegroup Backup';
```

To back up a file instead of a filegroup, the logical name of the file is specified in the backup command, as the following example illustrates:

```
--Backup of the SmallWorks data file "SmallWorksUserData1"
--The logical name of the file **NOT the physical file name**
BACKUP DATABASE SmallWorks
FILE = 'SmallWorksData1'
TO DISK = 'C:\SQLBackups\SmallWorksUserData1File.BAK'
WITH DESCRIPTION = 'SmallWorks UserData1 File Backup';
```

File/Filegroup with Differential

An additional option available when backing up files or filegroups is the ability to perform a Differential File or Filegroup backup. This option works exactly like the typical Differential backup; only the changes to the file or filegroup since the last complete File or Filegroup backup are captured, as well as any changes to the files during the backup.

```
--Differential Filegroup Backup of the "SWUserData1" User-Defined Filegroup
BACKUP DATABASE SmallWorks
FILEGROUP = 'SWUserData1'
TO DISK = 'C:\SQLBackups\SmallWorksUserData1FGDIFF.BAK'
WITH DIFFERENTIAL, DESCRIPTION = 'SmallWorks Filegroup Differential Backup';
```

File and Filegroup backups are only available if the database is in Full or Bulk-Logged recovery model, with one exception. If a filegroup is marked as read-only and the database is configured in the Simple recovery model, then that filegroup can be backed up.

Transaction Log Backup

In Full or Bulk-Logged recovery models, it is imperative that periodic Transaction Log backups are completed to both maintain the size of the transaction log within reasonable limits, and to allow for the recovery of data with the least amount of data loss.

Transaction Log backups come in three forms:

❑ *Pure Log backup* — A Pure Log backup contains only transactions and is completed when the database is in Full recovery model or Bulk-Logged recovery model, but no bulk operations have been executed.

❑ *Bulk Log backup* — Bulk Log backups contain both transactional data and any physical extents modified by bulk operations while the database was in Bulk-Logged recovery.

❑ *Tail Log backup* — Tail Log backups are completed when the database is in Full or Bulk-Logged recovery prior to a database restoration to capture all transaction log records that have not yet been backed up. It is possible in some instances to execute a Tail Log backup even if the database is damaged.

```
--Pure or Bulk Log Backup of SmallWorks
BACKUP LOG SmallWorks
TO DISK = 'C:\SQLBackups\SmallWorksLog.TRN'
WITH DESCRIPTION = 'SmallWorks Log Backup';

--Tail Log Backup of SmallWorks
BACKUP LOG SmallWorks
TO DISK = 'C:\SQLBackups\SmallWorksTailLog.TRN'
WITH NO_TRUNCATE, DESCRIPTION = 'SmallWorks Tail Log Backup';
```

Partial Backup

A Partial database backup consists of the Primary filegroup, read-write filegroups, and any read-only filegroup specified. The idea behind the Partial backup is that the Primary filegroup (which contains all the information necessary to bring the database online) and all the filegroups subject to modifications can be backed up together, leaving the filegroups that do not change to be backed up separately (and not as often), saving both time and backup media space.

```
BACKUP DATABASE SmallWorks READ_WRITE_FILEGROUPS
TO DISK = 'C:\SQLBackups\SmallWorksPartial.BAK'
WITH DESCRIPTION = 'Partial Backup of all Read/Write filegroups';
```

Copy Only Backup

Copy Only backups can be performed on database files and transaction logs to create a backup without affecting the chain of backups required to restore a database. They are essentially non-logged backups that can be used outside the maintenance environment. For example, if a copy of the database is needed for test and development, a Copy Only backup can be performed so as not to break the backup chain. Backup chains are discussed in the section "Restoring Databases" later in this chapter.

```
BACKUP DATABASE SmallWorks
TO DISK = 'C:\SQLData\SmallWorksCopyOnly.BAK'
WITH COPY_ONLY, DESCRIPTION = 'Copy only backup';
```

Backup Options

As previously described, backups can be sent to either a disk or tape destination. Another possibility for backup destinations is to send the backups to multiple destinations at the same time. The multiple destinations can be configured as a stripe of the backup or a mirror.

Backup Stripe

Striping a backup across multiple devices may save time in the backup process, because multiple physical devices are being written to simultaneously. To create a backup stripe, simply add multiple destinations to the BACKUP command, as shown in the following code:

```
BACKUP DATABASE SmallWorks
TO DISK='C:\StripedBackupsA\SmallWorksStripe1.bak'
  , DISK='C:\StripedBackupsB\SmallWorksStripe2.bak'
  , DISK='C:\StripedBackupsC\SmallWorksStripe3.bak'
WITH DESCRIPTION = 'Striped Backup';
```

Once a stripe set has been created, each file will only accept backups that also include all the members of the stripe. The three files are now a set made up of three family members. To send a backup to just one of the members, the FORMAT option must be specified. Although the striped backup can improve performance of the backup, a loss or corruption of any file in the stripe will result in a total loss of the backup. Keep in mind that one way to really get a performance advantage from backup stripes is to send the backup to multiple devices with multiple drive controllers.

Mirrored Backup

I received a call late one night from a colleague who had taken over my position after I had moved on to another job. He was desperate. He explained to me that their main database server had suffered a catastrophic failure. They had rebuilt the server, and were in the process of restoring from tape when the tape drive inexplicably decided to devour the tape, and the redundant drive I had set up was out of commission. I listened intently to his story, but in the end, I could only respond with, "If you have another copy of the tape, simply get a different tape drive and restore from the copy. If you don't have another copy, restore from the most recent copy you do have and update your résumé."

I tell this story to every SQL Server Administration class that I teach. I do so to highlight the importance of having redundant backups. It is too easy to feel safe and secure in the knowledge that you are regularly backing up your data. However, your backups are just as vulnerable as the data that they are ostensibly protecting. I have encountered many organizations that wouldn't dream of storing their data on anything but redundant arrays, yet they back up their critical data to a single device and don't make copies of it.

In the past, creating redundant backups meant backing up the database and then backing up the backups, or using a hardware solution that mirrored the backups while they were being created. SQL Server 2005 provides the built-in ability to mirror database backups. However, the mirror option is only available with the Enterprise and Developer editions of SQL Server 2005.

Mirrored backups are not supported through the visual tools. The following code demonstrates how to back up a database to one destination, and mirror the entire backup to another destination simultaneously. The WITH FORMAT option is required to create a new mirrored backup set.

```
BACKUP DATABASE SmallWorks
      TO DISK='C:\MirroredBackupsA\SmallWorksMirror1.bak'
MIRROR TO DISK='C:\MirroredBackupsB\SmallWorksMirror2.bak'
WITH FORMAT, DESCRIPTION = 'Mirrored Backup';
```

WITH Options

The following table lists and briefly describes each option that can be included in the WITH clause of a database backup command.

Option	Description
BLOCKSIZE = integer	Specifies a specific block size. If not specified, SQL Server will attempt to choose a block size that is optimum for the tape or disk destination.
CHECKSUM | NO_CHECKSUM	The CHECKSUM option specifies that SQL Server will validate any page checksum or torn page information when reading the page. SQL Server will also generate page checksum that can be used to validate backups with the RESTORE command. The CHECKSUM option will decrease the speed and performance of the backup. The NO_CHECKSUM setting is the default setting, and configures SQL Server to not generate or validate page checksum data during the backup.
STOP_ON_ERROR | CONTINUE_AFTER_ERROR	The default setting of STOP_ON_ERROR aborts the backup if a bad page checksum or torn page is detected during the backup. The CONTINUE_AFTER_ERROR setting overrides this behavior, allowing the database to be backed up even if there are errors in the database.
DESCRIPTION = string	A description of the database backup is often useful to identify the backup media. The description property supports a description length of 255 characters.
DIFFERENTIAL	Specifies that a Differential backup is to be performed on the associated database or data file/filegroup.
EXPIREDATE = datetime	A date specification used to identify when the backup is no longer required and may be overwritten.
RETAINDAYS = integer	Specifies the number of days the backup is required. This option or the EXPIREDATE option are used to control this behavior.
PASSWORD = string	A password can be assigned to a backup so that the password is required in order to use the backup during a restore operation. The password protection is very weak and should *not* be relied upon to guarantee the security of a backup. The PASSWORD option is deprecated and will be removed in a future release.
FORMAT | NOFORMAT	The FORMAT option is used to create a new backup media set. It will overwrite any existing media set at the destination. NOFORMAT is the default setting, which would prevent an inadvertent overwriting of a backup file that was participating in a backup stripe set.
INIT | NOINIT	The default setting of NOINIT specifies that any backups sent to the destination will be appended to the backup file. INIT specifies that subsequent backups will overwrite the existing backup file contents.

Option	Description
NOSKIP | SKIP	The NOSKIP default setting configures SQL Server to check the backup media's expiration date to prevent inadvertent overwriting of previous backups. The SKIP setting ignores the expiration date information.
MEDIADESCRIPTION = string	A maximum-length string of 255 characters used to describe the backup media.
MEDIANAME = string	The backup media's logical name with a maximum of 128 characters.
MEDIAPASSWORD = string	Like the PASSWORD option that defines a password for an individual backup, the MEDIAPASSWORD sets a password on the backup media set. The MEDIAPASSWORD is also very weak and should not be relied upon for media set security. This option is deprecated.
NAME = string	A maximum length of 128 characters to identify the name of the backup set.
NOREWIND | REWIND	This option is only used when the backup destination is specified as TAPE. The default REWIND option configures SQL Server to rewind the tape when the backup is completed, or the end of the tape is reached during a backup.
NOUNLOAD | UNLOAD	This option is only used with tape backups. The default setting is UNLOAD, which configures SQL Server to rewind and eject the tape when the backup is complete. NOUNLOAD overrides this default behavior, and leaves the tape open and mounted.
RESTART	This option does absolutely nothing. It does not generate an error when used and is included to prevent old scripts from previous releases from failing.
STATS = percentage as integer	Configures SQL Server to return progress information every time the specified percentage is reached. The default is 10.
COPY_ONLY	COPY_ONLY backups do not affect the transaction log sequence. These backups cannot be used for a Differential or Transaction Log backup base.

Backup Strategies

As previously mentioned, the various backup types provided by SQL Server 2005 can be used in different combinations to create a variety of backup strategies. This section covers just a few of the more commonly used backup strategies.

Full Backup Only

The Full backup strategy uses periodic Full database backups with no Log or Differential backups (see Figure 9-3). It is a very useful and simple strategy, but is generally limited to small databases configured in the Simple recovery model and for system databases. This strategy exposes the database to the risk of losing one period of data modifications. For example, if the database is backed up every day at 1:00 a.m. and there is a database failure any time before 1:00 a.m., the most recent restore point will be 1:00 a.m. of the previous day. For small databases with very few daily updates, this may be acceptable.

Full Backup Strategy

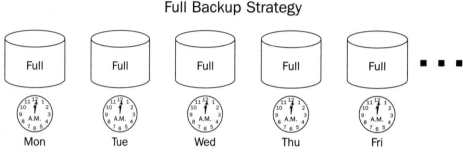

Figure 9-3: Full backup strategy

Full Backup with Differential

Like the Full backup strategy, the Full Backup with Differential strategy is generally limited to databases configured in Simple recovery model, because it does not provide for any management of the transaction log (see Figure 9-4). However, the addition of a periodic Differential backup makes this backup strategy more appropriate for slightly larger changing databases where the management of a transaction log is not desired. Because only data modified since the last Full backup is copied to the backup media, the periodic Differential backups will be smaller when compared to the Full backups and will take less time to execute.

Full Backup with Differential Strategy

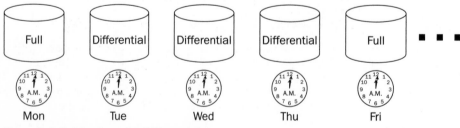

Figure 9-4: Full backup with Differential

Full Backup with Transaction Log

The disadvantage of the Full and Full with Differential plans are that they expose the database to the risk of data loss equal to the periodicity of the backup. By introducing Transaction Log backups into the backup plan, this risk is reduced dramatically (see Figure 9-5). However, the management of transaction logs introduces more complexity to the administration of database files. As previously discussed, when the database is not in Simple recovery mode, the transaction log must be periodically backed up to prevent it from growing too large or filling up. The alternative method of maintaining the log is to periodically clear it, but this is strongly discouraged (as described later).

Full With Log Backup Strategy

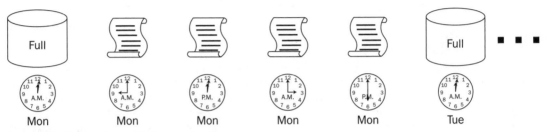

Figure 9-5: Full backup with Transaction Log

In the event of a database failure, the database can be restored up to the moment of failure by performing periodic Transaction Log backups between Full backups. The number of log backups and the periodicity of the backups depend on how busy the database is, and what the acceptable degree of data loss is. In a worst-case scenario, both the database and the transaction log could be lost. If that is the case, then, like the Full and Differential backup plans, the database can only be restored to the end of the previous Transaction Log backup. However, if only the data files are damaged, the database backup, log backups, and online log can be used to restore the database to the moment of failure.

Because Transaction Log backups are typically smaller and faster, they can be scheduled to occur as often as necessary. It is not uncommon to see Transaction Log backups scheduled for every 10 minutes on databases that are subject to very frequent modifications.

Full and Differential Backup with Transaction Log

The disadvantage of performing several Transaction Log backups between Full backups is that, to restore a database, the Full backup and all the logs must be sequentially restored. This can be burdensome if there are a large amount of log backups to restore. To minimize this issue, a Differential backup can be performed to capture all the changes to the database since the last full backup (see Figure 9-6). To restore the database, the log backups between the Full and the Differential can be ignored.

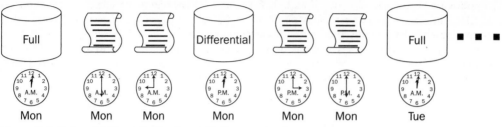

Figure 9-6: Full and Differential backup with Transaction Log

File and Filegroup Backup

With very large databases, it is sometimes more efficient to back up the database in slices. This offers a great deal of flexibility in the backup plan, but it also introduces a proportionate increase in the complexity of the backup plan. Database data files and filegroups can be backed up and restored individually, enabling the administrator to avoid a time-consuming and unnecessary restore of a large database in its entirety. This method is especially useful if some of the filegroups contain read-only data. These filegroups can be backed up once, and then recovered later in the event of a failure with no loss of interim data.

For example, a production database is comprised of four 25GB filegroups. One of the filegroups contains tables that are updated about once every three months. The other three contain transactional data that is updated on a regular basis. The first filegroup can be configured as read-only and backed up. The remaining three can be backed up on a rotating basis, interspersed with Transaction Log backups, as shown in Figure 9-7.

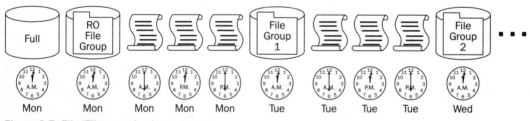

Figure 9-7: File/Filegroup backup strategy

Filegroup with Differential

If the filegroup strategy still backs up too much data that does not change, a File or Filegroup backup can be combined with a File or Filegroup Differential backup. This way, only the changes to the respective file or filegroup will be backed up. However, because the straightforward File/Filegroup backup increases complexity, adding a Differential backup to the mix will complicate things even more, and this strategy will require a great deal of planning and maintenance.

Partial Backup

As previously described, the Partial backup backs up the Primary filegroup and all READ_WRITE configured filegroups by default. In addition, any READONLY configured filegroups desired can be added to the backup set by specifying them in the BACKUP statement (see Figure 9-8). The purpose behind this strategy is to back up the read-only filegroups once, and then to periodically back up only the filegroups subject to modification.

Full and Differential With Log Backup Strategy

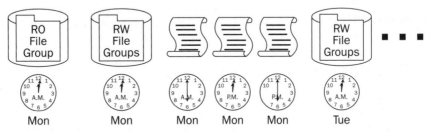

Figure 9-8: Partial backup

Backup Summary

As you can see, there are quite a few different ways to combine backup types to develop an appropriate backup strategy. Each backup type has its advantages and disadvantages. I wish I could give a prescriptive guide to backing up your databases, but I can't. Each environment is unique, from the size of the database and number of transactions per hour to the disk subsystem supporting the database. It is critically important to develop a backup strategy that mitigates the risk of data loss, while at the same time allowing for a realistic and effective data-recovery strategy.

Restoring Databases

I have met with many database administrators who were shocked to discover that their database backup plan did not lend itself to a problem-free recovery. If having an effective backup plan is critical, then having an effective restoration plan is even more critical. SQL Server is very lenient in allowing different backup types at different times, but it is a bit pickier about how those backups are restored. The critical issue in most restoration plans is the sequence of backups. This section describes the restore process, how to prepare a database for restoration, and how to restore databases backed up using the strategies outlined previously.

Restore Process

The restore process is made up of three phases:

- ❏ The *Data Copy phase,* where data pages are copied from the backup media to the data file(s)

- ❏ The *Redo phase,* where the record of committed transactions are restored from a log backup or the log portion of a database backup

- ❏ The *Undo phase,* where uncommitted transactions are rolled back from a log backup or the log portion of a database backup

The Data Copy and Redo phases can span multiple backups. For example, a database is backed up with a Full backup, followed by a Differential backup and then a Transaction Log backup. To restore the database to its most recent state would require restoring the Full backup, then the Differential backup as part of the Data Copy phase. The log portion of the Differential backup would begin the Redo phase, followed by the committed transactions in the Transaction Log backup. After all committed transactions are reapplied to the database, the Undo phase begins, where all uncommitted transactions are rolled back and the database is brought online.

Each phase is linked to the next. If any backup is missing from the sequence, the process stops at the end of the backup preceding the missing sequence. Figure 9-9 illustrates a lost or corrupted log backup. Even though there are an additional two good log backups, they cannot be used because the effects of the transactions recorded in the 12:01 p.m. Transaction Log backup are unknown. The database can only be restored to the end of the 9:00 a.m. Transaction Log backup.

Miss Backup

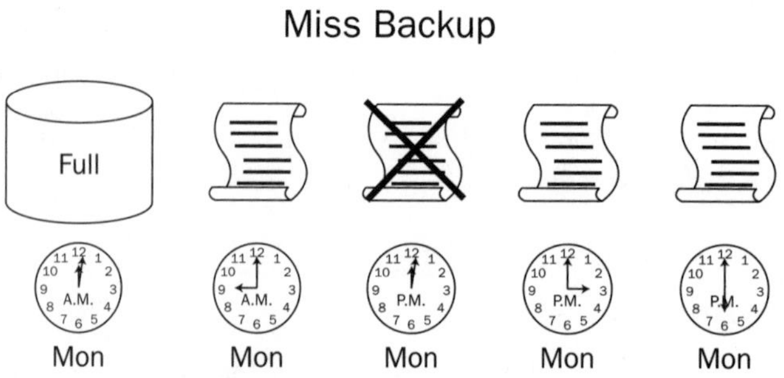

Figure 9-9: Missing backup

Delaying Recovery

When restoring a sequence of backups such as a Full backup and a series of Transaction Log backups as shown in Figure 9-8, the Undo phase and database recovery will have to be delayed so that each additional backup can be restored. Once a database has been recovered, no additional backups can be applied. To delay recovery, the option NO RECOVERY must be specified, along with the RESTORE DATABASE command.

RESTORE Command

Although databases can be restored effectively with the graphical tools provided in Management Studio, there are many advanced restore options that are only available by utilizing Transact-SQL. The simplified RESTORE command syntax is as follows:

```
RESTORE DATABASE | LOG database_name
[File | FileGroup]
[FROM <backup_media> [ ,...n ] ]
[WITH
    [CHECKSUM | NO_CHECKSUM]
    [[,] FILE = file_number]
    [[,] MOVE 'logical_file_name' TO 'operating_system_file_name'] [,...n]
    [[,] RECOVERY | NORECOVERY | STANDBY = standby_file_name]
    [[,] REPLACE]
    [[,] STOPAT = date_time
]
```

For simplicity, let's break down the RESTORE command in to its constituent pieces. The first is the actual RESTORE command, which is typically followed by the argument DATABASE or LOG and then the target database name. However, the RESTORE command can also be used to expose backup media metadata and to verify the integrity of a backup set.

❑   RESTORE HEADERONLY — The RESTORE HEADERONLY command exposes information from the backup media such as the name, description, and type of backup, as well as information about the backed up database.

❑   RESTORE FILELISTONLY — The FILELISTONLY command exposes the name of the files contained in the backup set.

❑   RESTORE LABELONLY — The LABELONLY command retrieves media information, such as the media name and description.

❑   RESTORE VERIFYONLY — The VERIFYONLY command checks the integrity of the backup media. If the backup set was created using the CHECKSUM option, the VERIFYONLY command will read the page checksums, as well as check to make sure the backup set is readable.

RESTORE DATABASE database_name

This specifies that the restore process is for a database, and specifies the name of the target database to restore to. The database name specified does not need to exist or be the same name as the backed up database.

❑   FILE — The RESTORE DATABASE database_name statement can be followed by the logical name of a database data file so that only that file is restored from the backup media. A file can be specified for FULL, FILE, and FILEGROUP backups.

```
RESTORE DATABASE SmallWorks
FILE = 'SmallWorks_Data2'
FROM DISK = 'C:\SQLBackups\SmallWorksFull.BAK';
```

❑   FILEGROUP — The RESTORE DATABASE database_name statement can also be followed by the name of a database filegroup so that only that filegroup is restored from the backup media. A filegroup can be specified for FULL and FILEGROUP backups.

```
RESTORE DATABASE SmallWorks
FILEGROUP = 'SWUserData2'
FROM DISK = 'C:\SQLBackups\SmallWorksFull.BAK';
```

❑   READ_WRITE_FILEGROUPS — The READ_WRITE_FILEGROUPS option only restores those filegroups in the database not marked as read-only. This option can be used with Full and Partial backups.

```
RESTORE DATABASE SmallWorks
READ_WRITE_FILEGROUPS
FROM DISK = 'C:\SQLBackups\SmallWorksFull.BAK';
```

❑   PAGE — To recover from torn page or checksum errors that identify one or more corrupted data pages, the RESTORE DATABASE database_name statement can specify the 8K data page to be restored. The page restore option requires the file ID and page ID to be passed, as the following example illustrates:

```
RESTORE DATABASE SmallWorks PAGE = '1:14'
FROM = 'C:\SQLBackups\SmallWorksFull.BAK';
```

❏   RESTORE LOG database_name—The RESTORE LOG statement specifies that the restore
    process is for a database transaction log. The backup must be from a BACKUP LOG process.
    The restoration of the transaction log must be applied to an existing database. The first Log
    Sequence Number (LSN) of the log backup being restored must be the next consecutive LSN,
    which is the last LSN of the previous log or database backup.

```
RESTORE LOG SmallWorks
FROM DISK = 'C:\SQLBackups\SmallWorksLog.BAK';
```

FROM Options

When restoring a database from either a database backup or a log backup, the RESTORE command
expects a backup media location to be specified in the FROM clause of the RESTORE statement, if no
backup media location is specified, as this example shows:

```
RESTORE DATABASE SmallWorks
```

With this syntax, the database is recovered in place. This may be necessary if the database is left in a
RECOVERING state, but there are no additional backups to be applied.

Other than the recover in place option, the following arguments are valid:

❏   FROM DISK—The FROM DISK = file_location specifies that the backup media resides on
    one or more physical disks identified by a drive letter and location, or a network location identi-
    fied by a UNC, as the following code illustrates:

```
RESTORE DATABASE SmallWorks
FROM DISK = 'C:\SQLBackUps\SmallWorksFull.BAK';

RESTORE DATABASE SmallWorks
FROM DISK = '\\AughtFive\SQLBackUps\SmallWorksFull.BAK';
```

❏   FROM TAPE—The FROM TAPE = tape_device specifies that the backup media resides on one
    or more tapes identified by a tape UNC, as shown in the following code:

```
RESTORE DATABASE Master
FROM TAPE = '\\.\tape1';
```

❏   FROM DATABASE_SNAPSHOT—The DATABASE_SNAPSHOT option specifies that the online
    database will be restored back to the state it was in when the specific database snapshot was
    created. Database snapshots are discussed later in this chapter.

WITH Clause

After the FROM clause and its arguments comes the WITH clause. The WITH clause of the RESTORE command has several options. Following are the most commonly used:

❑ RECOVERY | NORECOVERY — When restoring a database from a sequence of backups, all but the last backup must be restored with the NORECOVERY option. This allows for additional backups to be applied to the database. The RECOVERY option completes the Redo/Undo phase of restoration, as previously described, making the database available to client connections and preventing further restore operations. WITH RECOVERY is the default setting, so it is important to override it until the final backup is being applied. There is no "UnRecover" command that will allow you to restart the restoration process. Once the database is recovered, the entire restore process must be restarted to apply additional backups. However, if all the available backups have been applied, but the database was not recovered, the RESTORE DATABASE command can be specified without designating a source for the restore to invoke the recovery process with the current transaction log.

```
RESTORE DATABASE SmallWorks
FROM DISK = 'C:\SQLBackups\SmallWorksFull.BAK'
WITH NORECOVERY;

RESTORE LOG SmallWorks
FROM DISK = 'C:\SQLBackups\SmallWorksTailLog.BAK'
WITH RECOVERY;
```

❑ STANDBY — The NORECOVERY option leaves the database in a state of recovering and prevents access to the database. The STANDBY option functions much the same way, except it allows for read-only access to the database. It does this through the use of a standby file that stores all the Undo information that would normally be used to recover the database. The STANDBY option allows for a copy of the database to be maintained on a separate server, and periodically updated with additional transaction log restores. This functionality is at the heart of Log Shipping, which is described in Chapter 12.

```
RESTORE DATABASE SmallWorks
FROM  DISK = 'C:\SQLBackups\SmallWorksFull.BAK'
WITH STANDBY = 'C:\SQLBackups\SmallWorksUndoRollback.BAK';
```

❑ CHECKSUM | NO_CHECKSUM — The CHECKSUM option specifies that page checksum information is verified before the data is rewritten to the database during a restore operation. If the backup was not created using the CHECKSUM option, the RESTORE ... WITH CHECKSUM command will fail. It will also throw an error if any checksum errors are encountered during the restore process.

```
BACKUP DATABASE SmallWorks
TO DISK = 'C:\SQLBackups\SmallWorksCheckSumFull.BAK'
WITH CHECKSUM;

--Capture the tail of the log prior to restore operation
BACKUP LOG SmallWorks
TO DISK = 'C:\SQLBackups\SmallWorksTailLog.BAK'
WITH NO_TRUNCATE;

RESTORE DATABASE SmallWorks
FROM DISK = 'C:\SQLBackups\SmallWorkCheckSumsFull.BAK'
WITH CHECKSUM;
```

❑ CONTINUE_AFTER_ERROR | STOP_ON_ERROR — The CONTINUE_AFTER_ERROR option specifies that the restore operation will continue regardless of errors found in the backup media. The default setting of STOP_ON_ERROR will cause the restore operation to fail if any error is encountered.

❑ FILE — One of the more confusing aspects of the RESTORE command is that there is a FILE = *option* in the RESTORE clause that specifies a logical filename, and another FILE = *option* in the WITH clause where an integer value that represents the backup location in the file is specified. Because multiple backups can be stored in a single location identified with a name, it is important to be able to differentiate them. When sending multiple backups to the same file location, it is essentially like storing files within files. To differentiate between the different backups stored in a single file, the FILE = *backup_number* option is specified. The following example shows multiple backups being sent to the same destination. The first is a Full backup, the second is a Differential backup, and the last is a Tail Log backup. The example goes on to show the restoration of the backups from the same file.

```
--Initialize the backup file and backup the SmallWorks database to the file
BACKUP DATABASE SmallWorks
TO DISK = 'C:\SQLBackups\SmallWorksBackups.BAK'
WITH INIT, DESCRIPTION = 'Full Backup of SmallWorks';

--Send an Additional backup to the file
BACKUP DATABASE SmallWorks
TO DISK = 'C:\SQLBackups\SmallWorksBackups.BAK'
WITH DIFFERENTIAL, DESCRIPTION = 'Differential Backup of SmallWorks';

--Capture the tail of the log prior to restore operation
BACKUP LOG SmallWorks
TO DISK = 'C:\SQLBackups\SmallWorksBackups.BAK'
WITH NO_TRUNCATE, DESCRIPTION = 'Tail Log Backup of SmallWorks';

--Restore the Full Backup with NORECOVERY
RESTORE DATABASE SmallWorks
FROM DISK = 'C:\SQLBackups\SmallWorksBackups.BAK'
WITH FILE = 1, NORECOVERY;

--Restore the Differential Backup with NORECOVERY
RESTORE DATABASE SmallWorks
FROM DISK = 'C:\SQLBackups\SmallWorksBackups.BAK'
WITH FILE = 2, NORECOVERY;

--Restore the Tail Log Backup with RECOVERY
RESTORE LOG SmallWorks
FROM DISK = 'C:\SQLBackups\SmallWorksBackups.BAK'
WITH File = 3, RECOVERY;
```

❑ MOVE...TO... — When restoring databases, sometimes it is necessary to change the physical name or location of the database file. The MOVE *logical_filename* TO *operating_system_filename* accomplishes this. For example, a new database server has been installed and you need to move a database from the old server to the new server. The new server's file system is not organized the same as the old server, so new locations must be specified. The following example shows how to move the SmallWorks database from its original location to the new drives identified for data files and log files:

```
RESTORE DATABASE SmallWorks
FROM  DISK = 'C:\SQLBackups\SmallWorksFull.BAK'
WITH MOVE 'SmallWorksPrimary' TO 'S:\SQLData\SmallWorks.mdf'
    , MOVE 'SmallWorks_log' TO 'T:\SQLLogs\SmallWorks_log.ldf'
    , MOVE 'SmallWorksData1' TO 'S:\SQLData\SmallWorksData1.ndf'
    , MOVE 'SmallWorksData2' TO 'S:\SQLData\SmallWorksData2.ndf'
```

❏   PARTIAL — The PARTIAL option specifies that the Primary filegroup and any designated user-defined filegroups will be restored. Partial restores are described later in this chapter.

❏   REPLACE — The REPLACE option overrides the normal database restoration safety checks and specifies that the backup files referenced should replace the existing files. This is sometimes necessary if the transaction log is not available for a Tail Log backup, but the restore operation fails with errors caused by no Tail Log backup existing. The REPLACE option also enables the backup of one database to be restored over an existing database, even if the files and names are different.

Database Restore Preparation

There are a few different reasons to restore a database, and only one of them involves a failure of the database. It may very well be that the only time you will be required to restore a database is to move a database from one server to another, or to restore a test and development database. In any case, there is still some preplanning to do.

Generally, the preparation tasks are as follows:

1.   Isolate the database by placing it in SINGLE_USER mode (if it is accessible).

2.   Back up the tail of the transaction log if in Full or Bulk-Logged recovery mode. This captures all the recent activity.

3.   Gather information about all the backups that are required to restore the database to the most recent consistent state.

Isolate the Database

Isolating the database is typically required because, when restoring a database that is still online, SQL Server essentially drops and then re-creates the database from the backup media. As you learned earlier, a database cannot be dropped if someone is connected to it.

Some documentation specifies that the database should be set to RESTRICTED_USER instead of SINGLE_USER. However, when a database is set to RESTRICTED_USER access, it will still allow multiple connections. SQL Server just limits those connections to privileged users such as dbo or sa. If there are multiple dbo users in your organization RESTRICTED_USER will not prevent them from connecting to the database. RESTRICTED_USER will also not prevent you from opening multiple windows and multiple connections to the database you are trying to restore, thus preventing the restore from occurring. Each query window and the Object Explorer in Management Studio uses its own connection. To ensure that the restore operation will succeed, it is much easier to just place the database in SINGLE_USER access. Ironically, to change the database from MULTI_USER to SINGLE_USER or RESTRICTED_USER access, you must have exclusive access to the database, which equates to SINGLE_USER.

Capture Recent Activity

Backing up the tail of the log ensures that the most recent transactions (since the last backup) are recorded and recoverable. Often, this is not an optional step, and restore operations will not be permitted until the Tail Log backup has been completed.

Gather Backup Information

This last step can be made easier if the entire database server has not suffered a failure. SQL Server records all database backup and restore history in the MSDB database. To see what backups SQL Server Management Studio thinks need to be restored, in the Object Explorer, right-click Databases, click Restore Database, and then choose the database to restore from the Source for Restore database drop-down list.

Management Studio will automatically choose the backups to restore, as shown in Figure 9-10. Keep in mind that this is for a complete restore. If you are restoring a file or filegroup, Management Studio is not as helpful. It will list all the File and Filegroup backups performed, but it will not select any for recovery. You will have to do that manually. Likewise, if the choices made by Management Studio are not what you want, you are able to override the selected backups. If the backup history is not available, the "From device" option can be used to select a file or backup device backup media, and the appropriate backups can be chosen.

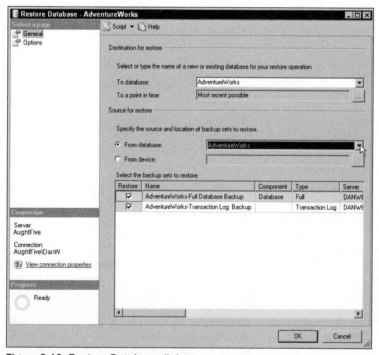

Figure 9-10: Restore Database dialog

As previously described, backup media information can also be retrieved through the use of three `RESTORE` command arguments: `RESTORE HEADERONLY`, `RESTORE FILELISTONLY`, and `RESTORE LABELONLY`.

Restoring User Databases

The backup strategies outlined earlier in this chapter apply mostly to user databases. Although system databases do need to be backed up, the strategy for backing them up is very straightforward and is typically confined to Full database backups only. This is because system databases do not change as often and are typically quite small. This describes the process of restoring user databases from the backup strategies defined earlier.

Full Restore

The periodic Full backup of a database is the simplest of all backup strategies and is also a very simple restore strategy. If the database needs to be restored, simply find the most recent Full backup and use it to restore the database. Figure 9-11 illustrates a database that is damaged at 9:00 a.m. The most recent backup was completed at 12:02 a.m. In this case the 12:02 a.m. backup would be restored with recovery.

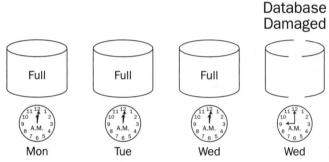

Figure 9-11: Full Restore

```
RESTORE DATABASE SmallWorks
FROM DISK = 'C:\SQLBackups\SmallWorksWed0002.BAK'
WITH RECOVERY;
```

Full with Differential Restore

Differential backups require a Full backup to be applied prior to the restoration of the Differential. Figure 9-12 illustrates a failure of the `SmallWorks` database at 9:00 a.m. on Wednesday. Because a Differential backup was completed at 12:02 a.m. on Wednesday, the Differential backup on Tuesday can be ignored. The recovery process is the Monday Full backup, followed by the Wednesday Differential backup.

347

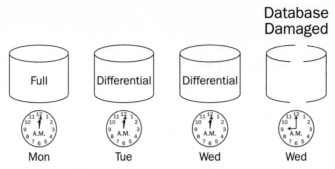

Figure 9-12: Full backup with Differential restore

```
RESTORE DATABASE SmallWorks
FROM DISK = 'C:\SQLBackups\SmallWorksFullMon0002.BAK'
WITH NORECOVERY;

RESTORE DATABASE SmallWorks
FROM DISK = 'C:\SQLBackups\SmallWorksDiffWed0002.BAK'
WITH RECOVERY;
```

Full with Transaction Log Restore

Like the Differential backup restore process, the Transaction Log backup also requires a baseline restore before it can be applied. Figure 9-13 illustrates a SmallWorks database damaged at 3:00 p.m. Because the database is in Simple or Bulk-Logged recovery, the tail of the transaction log may be able to be backed up to capture all the most recent changes to the database. In this way, very little to no data may be lost. The Tail Log backup is completed at 3:10 p.m. After the Tail Log backup is complete, the restoration process can be executed, starting at the Monday Full backup and then proceeding through the remaining Transaction Log backups.

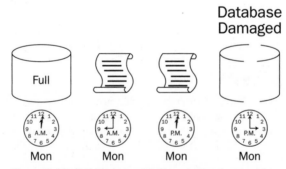

Figure 9-13: Full backup with Transaction Log restore

```
BACKUP LOG SmallWorks
TO DISK = 'C:\SQLBackups\SmallWorksTailLogMon1510.BAK'
WITH NO_TRUNCATE;

RESTORE DATABASE SmallWorks
```

```
FROM DISK = 'C:\SQLBackups\SmallWorksFullMon0002.BAK'
WITH NORECOVERY;

RESTORE LOG SmallWorks
FROM DISK = 'C:\SQLBackups\SmallWorksLogMon0900.BAK'
WITH NORECOVERY;

RESTORE LOG SmallWorks
FROM DISK = 'C:\SQLBackups\SmallWorksLogMon1202.BAK'
WITH NORECOVERY;

RESTORE LOG SmallWorks
FROM DISK = 'C:\SQLBackups\SmallWorksTailLogMon1510.BAK'
WITH RECOVERY;
```

Full and Differential with Transaction Log Restore

When using both Differential and Transaction Log backups to capture changes to the database, the important thing to remember is sequence. Each Differential backup contains the changes made to the database that were recorded in transaction logs during the interval between the Full backup and any Differential backup completed. Figure 9-14 illustrates this behavior. Because the database is damaged at 6:00 p.m., a Tail Log backup is completed to capture all activity between 3:00 p.m. and 6:00 p.m. The database is then restored using the Full, Differential, regular Transaction Log, and Tail Log backups.

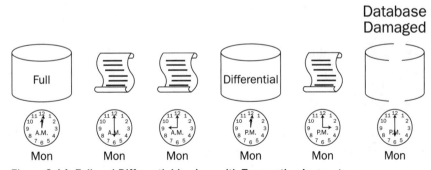

Figure 9-14: Full and Differential backup with Transaction Log restore

```
BACKUP LOG SmallWorks
TO DISK = 'C:\SQLBackups\SmallWorksTailLogMon1810.BAK'
WITH NO_TRUNCATE;

RESTORE DATABASE SmallWorks
FROM DISK = 'C:\SQLBackups\SmallWorksFullMon0002.BAK'
WITH NORECOVERY;

RESTORE DATABASE SmallWorks
FROM DISK = 'C:\SQLBackups\SmallWorksDiffMon1202.BAK'
WITH NORECOVERY;

RESTORE LOG SmallWorks
FROM DISK = 'C:\SQLBackups\SmallWorksLogMon1500.BAK'
```

```
WITH NORECOVERY;

RESTORE LOG SmallWorks
FROM DISK = 'C:\SQLBackups\SmallWorksTailLogMon1810.BAK'
WITH RECOVERY;
```

File and Filegroup Restore

File and filegroup restore processes vary, depending on the recovery model the database is configured for and whether the file or filegroup is marked as read-only. If the database is in Simple recovery, the only files or filegroups that can be restored independently of the complete database are those that are marked as read-only. Because the database is in Simple recovery, no Tail Log backups are allowed, and any restoration of a read-only file or filegroup will result in that file or filegroup being immediately available for queries. The syntax and process for individual file or individual filegroup restores are identical.

File Restore Example 1

This first example shows the process of restoring a single damaged file in the SmallWorks database when it is configured in Full recovery.

The first step is to back up the tail of the active transaction log:

```
--Capture the tail of the transaction log
BACKUP LOG SmallWorks
TO DISK = 'C:\SQLBackups\SmallWorksTailLog.BAK'
WITH INIT, NO_TRUNCATE;
```

The second step is to restore the damaged data file:

```
--Restore the damaged or corrupted file
RESTORE DATABASE SmallWorks FILE = 'SmallWorksData1'
FROM  DISK = 'C:\SQLBackups\SmallWorksFull.BAK';
```

At this point the SmallWorksData1 file is offline, and any queries that reference the dbo.Contact table (which resides on the SmallWorksData1 file) will fail.

The last step is to restore the tail of the log, which returns the SmallWorksData1 file to an online status:

```
--Restore the tail of the log to bring the SmallWorksData1 file online
RESTORE LOG SmallWorks
FROM DISK = 'C:\SQLBackups\SmallWorksTailLog.BAK'
WITH RECOVERY;
```

File Restore Example 2

This second example shows the process of restoring a single damaged data file that resides in a read-only filegroup. In this example, the capture of the tail of the log and the restoration of the tail to bring the file online are unnecessary. This is because the file resides on a read-only filegroup. There are no changes to capture.

```
--Restore the damaged or corrupted file
RESTORE DATABASE SmallWorks FILE = 'SmallWorksData2'
FROM  DISK = 'C:\SQLBackups\SmallWorksFull.BAK';
```

Once the restoration of the SmallWorksData2 file is complete, the database is completely online and accessible.

Partial Restore

The Partial restore process is very similar to the File/Filegroup restoration process. The significant difference is that Partial restores always include the Primary filegroup.

Partial Restore Example 1

The following example shows the SmallWorks database being backed up with a Partial backup, and then the restore process to bring the database back online after suffering a failure of both the SWUserdata1 READWRITE filegroup and the Primary filegroup.

First, perform the Partial backup:

```
BACKUP DATABASE SmallWorks READ_WRITE_FILEGROUPS
TO DISK = 'C:\SQLBackups\SmallWorksFull.BAK'
WITH INIT;
```

Sometime later, the READ_WRITE configured filegroups (including the Primary filegroup) experience a failure. The first step after the failure is to capture all the recent activity and place the database in a mode to recover from the failure:

```
BACKUP LOG SmallWorks
TO DISK = 'C:\SQLBackups\SmallWorksTailLog.BAK'
WITH INIT, NORECOVERY, NO_TRUNCATE;
```

The next step is to restore the READ_WRITE configured filegroups. In the case of the SmallWorks database, that is the Primary and SWUserData1 filegroups:

```
RESTORE DATABASE SmallWorks
FROM  DISK = 'C:\SQLBackups\SmallWorksFull.BAK'
WITH PARTIAL, NORECOVERY;
```

Next, restore the tail of the log and bring the database online:

```
RESTORE LOG SmallWorks
FROM DISK = 'C:\SQLBackups\SmallWorksTailLog.BAK'
WITH RECOVERY;
```

Even though the database is online, the user-defined filegroups are still inaccessible because of the restoring of the Primary filegroup. To bring the user-defined filegroups online you use the RESTORE DATABASE command, but do not specify a source for the restore. This completes the recovery process for the filegroups, and is near instantaneous, because no data is actually being restored.

```
RESTORE DATABASE SmallWorks FILEGROUP = 'SWUserData1'
WITH RECOVERY;

RESTORE DATABASE SmallWorks FILEGROUP = 'SWUserData2'
WITH RECOVERY;
```

The SmallWorks database is now completely online.

Partial Restore Example 2

In this example, only the SWUserdata1 READWRITE filegroup is damaged, so it is unnecessary to restore the Primary database. You start off again with a Partial backup of the SmallWorks database:

```
BACKUP DATABASE SmallWorks READ_WRITE_FILEGROUPS
TO DISK = 'C:\SQLBackups\SmallWorksFull.BAK'
WITH INIT;
```

Sometime later, the file in the SWUserData1 filegroup is damaged. When it is discovered, the tail of the transaction log is captured and the database put in to a state to support recovery.

```
BACKUP LOG SmallWorks
TO DISK = 'C:\SQLBackups\SmallWorksTailLog.BAK'
WITH INIT, NORECOVERY, NO_TRUNCATE;
```

Then restore just the SWUserData1 filegroup and then the tail of the log to bring the database completely online:

```
RESTORE DATABASE SmallWorks FILEGROUP = 'SWUserData1'
FROM  DISK = 'C:\SQLBackups\SmallWorksFull.BAK'
WITH NORECOVERY;

RESTORE LOG SmallWorks
FROM DISK = 'C:\SQLBackups\SmallWorksTailLog.BAK'
WITH RECOVERY;
```

Point-in-Time Restore

SQL Server 2005 supports the recovery of both databases and transaction logs to a specific point in time, but only if the database is configured in the Full or Bulk-Logged recovery models. As previously discussed, the Bulk-Logged recovery model should only be used as an adjunct to the Full recovery model. This is especially true because of the impact of the Bulk-Logged recovery on point-in-time restores. If the database is configured for Bulk-Logged recovery, and the transaction log contains bulk operations, point-in-time recovery is not possible; the transaction log must be restored in its entirety.

Point-in-time database restore operations are useful to restore a database to a point just prior to data corruption because of a malicious or accidental modification of data. For example, an accidental update to the SmallWorks database occurs at 3:00 p.m., but is not detected until 6:15 p.m. A scheduled database backup was completed at 4:00 p.m. and a scheduled Transaction Log backup occurred at 5:00 p.m. To restore the database to just before the accidental update, a point-in-time restore is used. The sequence of events to restore the database is as follows:

```
RESTORE DATABASE SmallWorks
  FROM  DISK = 'C:\SQLBackups\SmallWorksFull1600.BAK'
  WITH STOPAT = '06/05/2006 14:59:00'
 ,NORECOVERY;

RESTORE LOG SmallWorks
  FROM  DISK = 'C:\SQLBackups\SmallWorksLog1700.BAK'
  WITH STOPAT = '06/05/2006 14:59:00'
 ,RECOVERY;
```

Recovering System Databases

System databases are just as vulnerable to failure as user databases, and it is very important to ensure that they are adequately protected. Essentially, you have two choices when it comes to recovering system databases. You can restore them from backup, or you can rebuild them from scratch. I highly recommend the backup-and-restore approach, because rebuilding them from scratch means a ton more work.

Because system databases are usually small, they don't require a great deal of time to back up and they don't take up much space when backed up. How often the structure of your system databases change will determine how often you will need to back them up to minimize the post-restore tasks.

Recovering the Master Database

There are two scenarios for recovering the `Master` database. In the first scenario, the server is accessible. In the second, SQL Server is not accessible.

If SQL Server can be connected to, the server instance must be started in single-user mode to restore and recover the `Master` database. To start an instance of SQL Server in single-user mode, type the following command at the command prompt:

```
sqlservr.exe -m
```

If the server supports multiple instances of SQL Server, be sure to start the right one. The default instance of SQL Server is located in the folder `\Program Files\Microsoft SQL Server\ MSSQL.1\MSSQL\Binn` by default. Each additional instance will have its own `MSSQL.X` folder, but depending on the installation sequence, they may not be in numerical order.

Once the server is started in single-user mode, the `Master` database can be restored. To accomplish this, start another command prompt window and log in to the SQL Server instance with `SQLCMD`. The following example shows a login command to an instance of SQL Server called `AughtFive` (`-S`) using Windows Security (`-E`):

```
C:\>SQLCMD -S AughtFive -E
```

After successfully logging in to the server, the restoration of the `Master` database can be completed through the normal `RESTORE` syntax:

```
1>RESTORE DATABASE MASTER FROM DISK = 'C:\SQLBackups\MasterFull.BAK'
2>GO
Processed 360 pages for database 'Master', file 'master' on file 1.
Processed 2 pages for database 'Master', file 'mastlog' on file 1.
The master database has been successfully restored. Shutting down SQL Server.
SQL Server is terminating this process.
```

As shown in the preceding example, once the `Master` database has been restored, SQL Server will automatically shut down the instance so that it can be restarted with the newly restored `Master` database.

The only database that can be restored in single-user mode is the `Master` database. Once `Master` is restored, restart SQL Server to continue restoring any other system or user databases.

If the instance of SQL Server is not accessible because of a corrupted Master database or total server failure, the Master database will have to be rebuilt. In previous versions of SQL Server, this could be done through a command prompt utility. SQL Server 2005 discontinued support of that utility. To rebuild the Master database, you must re-install SQL Server. Once SQL Server has been re-installed, the most recent backup of the Master database can be used to restore the server using the same procedure outlined previously.

Once the Master database has been restored, and the instance of SQL Server restarted, the remaining system databases and user databases should be remounted automatically. If the backup of the Master database is not up to date or does not exist at all, the remaining system and user databases may not automatically remount, and will have to either be restored or attached. Assuming that the remaining database files are still intact in the file system, it is much faster and easier to attach the databases. The simplest way to attach the existing databases is to use the graphical tools in SQL Server Management Studio.

To attach a database, right-click Databases and click Attach...; the Attach Databases window will appear.

Click the Add button to browse to the location of the database's MDF file and select it.

Each database's MDF file contains the metadata that identifies the location of all the database's constituent files. As long as none of the files are identified with a "Not Found" message, the database should attach with no difficulty. If a data file is missing, the database will not be able to be attached. However, if only the transaction log file is missing, the database can still be successfully attached by selecting the missing log file and clicking Remove. Once the log file is removed from the list, click the OK button to attach the database. SQL Server will re-create a log file using the metadata of the original.

Orphaned Users

After the Master database and all the other databases have been restored or attached, it may be necessary to check the user databases for orphaned users. Orphaned users occur when a SQL Server login has been added to the Master database and granted access to a database, but the backup of the Master database was performed before the Login was created. When the user database was attached or restored, the user database contained the database user, but the Login in the Master database did not exist.

To find and fix orphaned users, the stored procedure sp_change_users_login is used. The sp_change_users_login procedure has three modes defined by the input parameter @Action. The three supported actions are defined in the following table.

Action	Description
'Report'	Returns a list of all database users not associated with a valid SQL Server Login.
'Auto_Fix'	Links the database user to a SQL Server Login with the same name. For example:
	`USE SmallWorks;`
	`GO`
	`sp_change_users_login 'Auto_Fix', 'FredF';`

Action	Description
	This example links the SmallWorks database user "FredF" to a Server Login with the same name if one exists.
'Update_One'	Links a specific database user to a specific SQL Server Login. For example:
	`USE SmallWorks;`
	`GO`
	`sp_change_users_login 'Update_One', 'FredF', 'SQLFredFLogin';`
	This example links the SmallWorks database user "FredF" to a SQL Server Login called "SQLFredFLogin".

Database Restore Summary

Like the backup strategy, it is exceptionally important to have a restore plan. A good restore plan will cover any combination of possible failures and list the steps required to restore the database in the shortest time possible, and with the least amount of data loss. There is no way I could cover every possible combination in the few pages devoted to this topic. It is up to you to analyze your infrastructure and choose the backup-and-restore plan that best fits your environment.

Database Snapshots

Database snapshots can't really be used for disaster recovery in the case of a complete database loss. However, they can be very useful in reversing the effects of database modifications. They are also useful in redirecting queries away from a busy transactional database.

What is a database snapshot? A *snapshot* is a point-in-time, static, read-only view of a database. The creation of a snapshot is instantaneous, because the database that is the source of the snapshot is not actually copied to create the snapshot. Instead, data files are created that will only hold the data pages from the source database that have changed since the snapshot was created. This functionality is called "Copy On Write." When the database snapshot is initially created, near identical data files are created to hold the contents of the snapshot. The difference in the data files is that they have separate physical locations than the source database, and they initially consume very little disk space.

The easiest way to understand database snapshots is to create and use one. Before creating a snapshot of AdventureWorks, create a new test table to manipulate. This makes it a lot easier than using existing tables where pesky constraints can interfere with updates and deletes. The following script creates a new table, and then creates a snapshot of the AdventureWorks database:

```
USE AdventureWorks;
GO
SELECT * INTO dbo.NewContact
FROM Person.Contact
WHERE ContactID < 101;
GO

CREATE DATABASE AdventureWorksSnapShot ON
( NAME = 'AdventureWorks_Data'
, FILENAME = 'C:\SQLSnapShotData\AdventureWorksSnapShot.mdf')
AS SNAPSHOT OF AdventureWorks;
```

A look in the file system reveals that the `AdventureWorksSnapShot.mdf` file is 205,455,360 bytes (your size may vary based on modification made to the `AdventureWorks` database), but it is only consuming 196,608 bytes. SQL Server reserves the same amount of disk space that the database is presently using, but it only allocates enough to store the metadata of the database structure.

Now, take a look at the data in the `AdventureWorks` and `AdventureWorksSnapshot` databases to see what happens to the snapshot database and the data when changes are made to the source database.

First, write a query to return some data from the first three rows of the `dbo.NewContact` table in the `AdventureWorks` database as shown in the following example:

```
USE AdventureWorks;
GO
SELECT ContactID, FirstName, LastName, EmailAddress
FROM dbo.NewContact
WHERE ContactID < 4;
```

The results of this query should look like the following:

```
ContactID   FirstName    LastName     EmailAddress
---------   ---------    ---------    --------------------------------
1           Gustavo      Achong       gustavo0@adventure-works.com
2           Catherine    Abel         catherine0@adventure-works.com
3           Kim          Abercrombie  kim2@adventure-works.com

(3 row(s) affected)
```

Now, write the same query except reference the `AdventureWorksSnapShot` database:

```
USE AdventureWorksSnapShot;
GO
SELECT ContactID, FirstName, LastName, EmailAddress
FROM dbo.NewContact
WHERE ContactID < 4;
```

The results of this second query will be identical:

```
ContactID   FirstName    LastName     EmailAddress
---------   ---------    ---------    --------------------------------
1           Gustavo      Achong       gustavo0@adventure-works.com
2           Catherine    Abel         catherine0@adventure-works.com
```

```
3              Kim            Abercrombie     kim2@adventure-works.com

(3 row(s) affected)
```

Notice that both of the databases return the same results. In actuality, the query to the snapshot database was redirected to the source database, because the data pages containing the contact information had not been changed since the snapshot was created.

Now, update the data in the source database by changing the last name of some contacts. Update all of them so that you can more easily examine the changes to the physical data files hosting the snapshot database.

```
USE AdventureWorks;
GO
UPDATE dbo.NewContact
SET LastName = 'Flintstone';
```

The resulting message lets you know that you successfully updated all 100 rows of data:

```
(100 row(s) affected)
```

The `AdventureWorksSnapShot.mdf` file now consumes 458,752 bytes of data (your results may vary). Updating the 100 rows in the `AdventureWorks` database caused the data pages containing those rows to be copied to the snapshot, resulting in an increase in the size of the snapshot.

Now, query the two databases again to see what the results are:

```
USE AdventureWorks;
GO
SELECT ContactID, FirstName, LastName, EmailAddress
FROM dbo.NewContact
WHERE ContactID < 4;
```

The results of the `AdventureWorks` query show the changes just as expected:

```
ContactID    FirstName     LastName        EmailAddress
---------    ---------     --------        --------------------------------
1            Gustavo       Flintstone      gustavo0@adventure-works.com
2            Catherine     Flintstone      catherine0@adventure-works.com
3            Kim           Flintstone      kim2@adventure-works.com

(3 row(s) affected)
```

However, the snapshot database still reflects the data as it appeared when the snapshot was created. This is what is meant by a "Static, read-only copy" of the database.

```
USE AdventureWorksSnapShot;
GO
SELECT ContactID, FirstName, LastName, EmailAddress
FROM dbo.NewContact
WHERE ContactID < 4;
```

```
ContactID    FirstName     LastName        EmailAddress
---------    ---------     --------        --------------------------------
1            Gustavo       Achong          gustavo0@adventure-works.com
```

```
2          Catherine    Abel         catherine0@adventure-works.com
3          Kim          Abercrombie  kim2@adventure-works.com

(3 row(s) affected)
```

You can create as many snapshots of a database as you want, but keep in mind that each additional snapshot is going to add additional overhead to your source database. The overhead is created because every command that updates or deletes data or objects will cause a write to the snapshot database to record the previous version of the database.

Database Snapshot Limitations

There are some limitations of database snapshots, and limitations on the source database created with the snapshot:

❑ Database snapshots cannot be backed up. Because the snapshot is a combination of data retrieved from the source database and data stored internally, it is impossible to actually back up the snapshot.

❑ Database snapshots cannot be modified.

❑ Source databases cannot be dropped while a snapshot exists.

❑ Source databases cannot be restored to a point in time prior to the creation of the snapshot while the snapshot exists.

Disaster Recovery and Database Snapshots

How exactly do database snapshots fit in to the realm of disaster recovery? That is an excellent question! Snapshots can be used to undo updates to a source database because they have the original copy of the data as it looked prior to the modification.

Undoing Updates

In the previous example, you updated 100 rows with the last name of "Flintstone." To reverse the effects of this frivolous update, the following script can be used:

```
USE AdventureWorks;
GO
UPDATE dbo.New.Contact
SET LastName = SS.LastName
FROM dbo.NewContact NC
JOIN AdventureWorksSnapShot.dbo.NewContact SS
ON SS.ContactID = NC.ContactID
WHERE CC.ContactID < 101;
```

A query of the source database will now reveal that all the last names have been put back to their original values.

Undoing Deletes

Consider the following command that deletes half of the rows from the dbo.NewContact table:

```
USE AdventureWorks;
GO
DELETE dbo.NewContact
WHERE ContactID < 51;
```

If this was a malicious or accidental update, the normal pattern for restoring the data would be to restore the database to a test server, and then copy the data from the test server back to the production database. With a database snapshot, there is no need to involve the database backups.

To restore the data, simply insert the data back in to the source database table by selecting from the snapshot. Because the ContactID column is an IDENTITY column, you must turn off the IDENTITY function prior to inserting the data, and then turn it back on after the data is inserted, as shown in the following example:

```
USE AdventureWorks;
GO
SET IDENTITY_INSERT dbo.NewContact ON;
--Turn off the IDENTITY function to allow
--explicit inserts to the IDENTITY column
INSERT dbo.NewContact
(ContactID, FirstName, LastName, EmailAddress, EmailPromotion, Phone)
SELECT * FROM AdventureWorksSnapShot.dbo.NewContact
WHERE ContactID < 51;
SET IDENTITY_INSERT dbo.NewContact OFF;
--Turn the IDENTITY function back on
```

Undoing Drops

If a database object is dropped from the source database, it can be scripted and re-created from the snapshot database. If it were a table, the table can then be repopulated using the previous method for undoing deletes.

Restoring from Snapshots

If several undesired changes have been made to the source database, it can be restored to the point in time when the snapshot was created by specifying the snapshot as the source of the restore operation. Remember that if multiple snapshots exist, the database cannot be restored to a point in time before a snapshot was created. Those snapshots will have to be dropped first. The following command demonstrates how to restore the AdventureWorks database from a database snapshot:

```
USE MASTER;
GO
RESTORE DATABASE AdventureWorks
FROM DATABASE_SNAPSHOT = 'AdventureWorksSnapShot';
```

Summary

This chapter examined the different ways to back up and restore databases, as well as the different aspects of disaster recovery that are most important to minimizing data loss. You should have concluded that it is all about planning. As database administrators, we are ultimately responsible for maintaining the integrity and security of the data entrusted to us. To accomplish this important goal, it is imperative that we plan for disaster and even more importantly, plan how to recover from any disaster with the absolute minimum amount of data loss and downtime.

In Chapter 10, you learn how to use SQL Server 2005 and Windows operating system tools to monitor SQL Server performance. The goal is to monitor in order to improve performance or prevent degradation of performance. You learn how to leverage the improved and new tools to peek inside SQL Server's insides, and how to use the information gleaned to improve system performance.

Monitoring SQL Server for Performance

One of the primary responsibilities of the database administrator is the ongoing monitoring of SQL Server performance. Much of this monitoring can be automated, but for the most part, the monitoring results must be interpreted and acted upon in a systematic approach by the DBA. The monitoring job never ends, and it can become quite complex. Knowing what to monitor, when to monitor, and what constitutes acceptable and unacceptable behavior can become a full-time job. Making things worse is the fact that each SQL Server installation is different, making a global recommendation about what indicators identify unacceptable and acceptable performance very difficult.

This chapter explains the various tools used to monitor SQL Server and provides guidelines on how to use these tools to identify areas for optimization. Monitoring SQL Server can be a challenging process. SQL Server interacts heavily with every operating system subsystem. Some applications rely heavily on RAM, whereas others are CPU- or disk-intensive. SQL Server can be all three at the same time. SQL Server can also be very network-intensive, especially with distributed applications, replication, or database mirroring. Many database administrators find the whole process of monitoring and optimizing arcane and nebulous. However, it doesn't have to be all that mysterious. A good understanding of the tools, as well as a familiarity with the different objects requiring monitoring, will go a long way to making your optimization process less intimidating.

Whole books have been written on the subject of performance optimization, along with several Web sites dedicated to the subject. I won't attempt to tell you everything you need to know about optimization in this book, but I will describe the fundamentals, which, as in all things, is the best place to start.

Monitoring and Optimization Overview

SQL Server 2005 monitoring can essentially be divided in to five basic areas:

❑ System resources

❑ SQL Server itself

- ❑ The database
- ❑ The database application
- ❑ The network

Before getting in to the specifics of monitoring and optimization, it is very important to understand the methodology of SQL Server monitoring and optimization. Monitoring for the sake of monitoring is useless. You monitor your hardware and SQL Server implementations to anticipate and prevent performance problems. To do this, you must have some kind of plan — a strategy that will enable you to invest the right amount of time and the right amount of resources to maintain and improve the performance of your SQL Servers.

Optimization Strategy

The strategy for monitoring and optimizing SQL Server is fairly straightforward and is made up of the following steps:

1. *Create a performance baseline* — Without a baseline of your database server, it is very unlikely that you will be able to make changes to the server platform with complete confidence that the changes will accomplish the improvements you are looking for. A baseline contains measurements from all the systems previously mentioned (system resources, SQL Server, the database, the database application, and the network). Specific counters and measurements are discussed later in this chapter. When evaluating the baseline, you may identify areas that warrant immediate optimization. If changes are made, a new baseline must be created.

2. *Complete periodic performance audits* — After the baseline is completed, periodic performance audits are performed to ensure that performance has not degraded from when the baseline was created. This step is often supplemented or replaced by reactive audits that are performed in response to complaints of poor server performance. I prefer to be proactive and schedule the audits, but there will invariably be times when a reactive audit will be required because unexpected performance problems arise.

3. *Make changes and evaluate their impact* — After performing audits, you may find areas that require modification. When making these changes, it is important to be meticulous. As a rule, you should not make multiple changes at once. Instead, make one or two changes, and then evaluate the measurements that prompted the changes to be made. This makes it much easier to identify what changes have the greatest impact on performance.

> I work with a colleague that we affectionately call the "Mad Clicker." When something goes wrong in the server room, he invariably gets involved and starts clicking away, making sweeping changes to configuration settings in an attempt to correct the problem. Often, he is successful, but it is next to impossible to duplicate his actions in the future because even he doesn't know everything he changed. Don't be a "Mad Clicker." Complete a modification, and then measure and document the results. This makes it easy to duplicate and easy to rollback if the modifications resulted in a degradation of performance instead of an improvement.

4. *Reset the baseline* — After completing all the modifications, create another baseline to measure future performance trends.

Creating a Baseline

It is very important when creating a baseline that typical activity is monitored. Monitoring performance during a monthly import may give you some interesting data, but it will not help you evaluate and improve overall system performance. There are different ways of creating baselines. Most database administrators have their own preferences on how to gather and compare performance data. They also have their own favorite counters and system views that they feel give them insight into how the database is performing. SQL Server performance monitoring and optimization is more of an art than a science.

I have seen many different recommendations on what System Monitor counters to collect and what SQL Server–specific activity to monitor. All of them were different. Some database administrators recommended monitoring everything, whereas others recommended monitoring a small selection of processes. I support the small selection philosophy for two different reasons. The first is that there is definitely such a thing as "too much information." Collecting every conceivable bit of performance data will most likely result in a case of not seeing the forest because of the trees. There is just too much data to sift through. The second reason (and maybe even more importantly) is the performance factor.

Gathering performance information is not free. The more information you gather, the more it costs in terms of performance. This creates an interesting paradox. To adequately monitor performance, you must introduce performance-degrading actions to the database. The quandary that creates is one where you can never be completely positive that your monitoring actions are not at least marginally responsible for unacceptable performance.

Limiting the data retrieved will reduce this uncertainty, but it is also important to keep in mind that you should not look at any particular counter in isolation. For example, heavy disk activity might be caused by memory limitations, and unsatisfactory CPU performance can be caused by poorly written queries and missing indexes. No one subsystem exists in a vacuum.

So, what should you have in your baseline? Over the years, I have condensed the list of objects and processes that I monitor for baselines and performance audits. Those counters are described in the following pages.

The main tool for creating a performance baseline is Performance Monitor. However, Dynamic Management Views (DMVs) are used as well to give more context to the baseline. After explaining the counters used for a baseline and performance audits, this chapter digs deeper into the SQL Server–specific tools, and explores how to identify misbehaving processes.

Performance Counters

The following are some of the most useful counters to use in creating a baseline and auditing performance after the baseline has been created. This discussion is not meant to be all-inclusive. It is made up of the counters I and a few of my colleagues have come to rely on for a "big picture" view of SQL Server performance. There are many more counters that can be used to diagnose performance issues and to dig deeper into the nuts and bolts of SQL Server activity. But these few will most likely provide the information you need to quickly evaluate the health of your server.

Processor Counters

Processor counters are used in conjunction with other counters to monitor and evaluate CPU performance and identify CPU bottlenecks.

❑ *Processor: % Processor Time* — The % Processor Time counter displays the total percentage of time spent processing non-idle threads. On a multiple-processor machine, each individual processor can be monitored independently. If the CPU affinity settings have been customized, you may want to monitor a specific CPU. Other than that, I normally use the `_total` instance identifier to see the combined processor utilization. CPU activity is a good indicator of SQL Server CPU activity, and is a key way to identify potential CPU bottlenecks. Recommendations on what this counter should look like vary. As a general rule, if total % Processor Time is consistently greater than 70 percent, you probably have a CPU bottleneck, and you should look at either optimizing current application processes, upgrading the CPU, or both. Use this counter along with the Processor Queue Length counter to positively identify CPU bottlenecks.

❑ *Process: % Processor Time (sqlservr)* — The Process: % Processor Time counter (when set to monitor information from the SQL Server process) can be used to determine how much of the total processing time can be attributed to SQL Server.

❑ *System: Processor Queue Length* — The Processor Queue Length counter displays the number of threads waiting to be processed by a CPU. If the average queue length is consistently greater than two times the number of processors, then you may have a CPU bottleneck, because the processors can't keep up with the number of requests.

The Processor Queue Length and the % Processor Time counters together to determine if you have a CPU bottleneck. If both counters are out of acceptable ranges, there is most assuredly a CPU bottleneck.

If the Processor Queue Length is not within acceptable limits, but the % Processor Time is, you may not have a CPU bottleneck, but a configuration problem instead. Ensure that the `max worker threads` server setting has not been set to a value that is too high for your system. The default setting for `max worker threads` is 0 (zero), which configures SQL Server to automatically set `max worker threads` in accordance to the values shown in the following table. However, in addition to 0, it is possible to configure any value between 128 and 32767. SQL Server Books Online gives the acceptable range as 32 through 32767, which is incorrect. The graphical interface *will* accept any value between 0 and 32767, but any value between 1 and 127 results in a setting of 128.

CPUs	32-bit	64-bit
1	256	512
2	256	512
4	256	512
8	288	576
16	352	704
32	480	960

Disk Counters

Several disk counters return disk read and write performance information, as well as data transfer information, for each physical disk or all disks. Physical disk statistics, when combined with memory statistics, give a very accurate view of total IO performance on the server.

❑ *PhysicalDisk: Avg. Disk Queue Length* — As the last mechanical component in modern computer systems, the disk is inherently the slowest, even with the built-in memory cache that virtually all disk controllers are configured with. The Avg. Disk Queue Length counter returns the average number of read and write operations that were queued for an individual disk or all disks. The requests are queued because the disk or disks are too busy, and the controller's onboard memory cache has no space to temporarily store the read or write request. This counter should remain below the number of physical disks multiplied by two. For example, if your database is located on a 10-disk array, the counter should remain below 20.

If this counter is consistently greater than the desired value, the most likely cause is an inadequacy in the disk subsystem, or an inadequate amount of memory on the server. A lack of memory can cause the disk subsystem to be overworked by SQL Server's inability to cache data in memory for long periods of time, resulting in more physical disk reads. Spreading the database across multiple disks and multiple controllers may increase performance. Adding memory, if possible, to the disk controller may also alleviate the disk bottleneck.

❑ *PhysicalDisk: % Disk Time* — This counter measures how busy a physical disk or hardware disk array is. It is the total of read and write activity on the disk or array. The % Disk Time counter shouldn't consistently run at more than 60 percent. If it does, check out the % Disk Read and % Disk Write counters to determine what type of activity the disk is primarily performing. If more than one array is used for the database, this counter can be used to determine if the disk workload is equally divided among all the arrays.

Memory Counters

As previously noted, memory counters (along with disk counters), are used by the DBA to get an overall picture of database I/O. A lack of memory will have a direct impact on disk activity. When optimizing a server, adding memory should always be considered. SQL Server loves memory, and effectively allocates it to minimize the amount of disk access required for database operations. If you are looking for a SQL Server performance panacea, adding memory is as close is you're going to get.

❑ *Memory: Pages/Sec* — The Pages/Sec counter measures the number of pages per second that are paged out of memory to disk, or paged into memory from disk. The official recommendation for this counter is that it should never be consistently greater than zero. In all likelihood, it will regularly spike higher than zero, then return to near zero, and then spike high again, as Figure 10-1 shows. This is perfectly normal, but if the counter is consistently above zero, it indicates a possible memory bottleneck. The solution, of course, is to add memory. However, it may also be that the maximum server memory setting is set too low if there is plenty of memory on the server. The memory counter Available Bytes will show how much memory is available on the system.

Another possible cause of steady memory paging is an application other than SQL Server running on the same server. Ideally, SQL Server should be the only application supported by the server. Sometimes this is not possible, but it is still the ideal configuration.

❑ *Memory: Available Bytes* — The Available Bytes counter indicates how much memory is available to processes. The official recommendation is that there should always be at least 5MB of available memory, but this is a particularly low number, and it should probably be at least 10 times as much.

❑ *Process:Working Set (sqlservr)* — The SQL Server instance of the Working Set counter shows how much memory is in use by SQL Server. If this number is always lower than the minimum server memory setting, or significantly lower than the maximum server memory setting, SQL Server is most likely configured to use too much memory. This is not necessarily a bad thing, as long as it is not interfering with other server processes.

❑ *SQL Server: Buffer Manager: Buffer Cache Hit Ratio* — The Buffer Cache Hit Ratio counter measures the percentage of time that data was found in the buffer without having to be read from disk. This counter should be very high, optimally 90 percent or better. When it is less than 90 percent, disk I/O will be too high, putting added burden on the disk subsystem.

❑ *SQL Server: Buffer Manager: Page Life Expectancy* — The Page Life Expectancy counter returns the number of seconds a data page will stay in the buffer without being referenced by a data operation. The minimum value for this counter is approximately 300 seconds. This counter, along with the Buffer Cache Hit Ratio counter, is probably the best indicator of SQL Server memory health. A higher number for both counters is better.

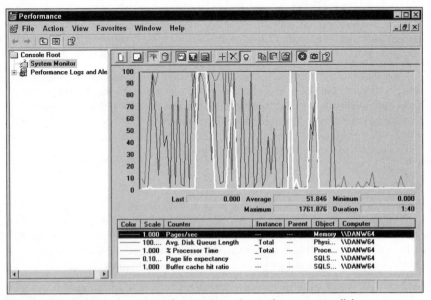

Figure 10-1: Spiking of number of pages in and out of memory to disk

Network Counters

For most network counters, there is no hard-and-fast recommendation for what you should see. The only guidance that can possibly be given is to ensure that the network traffic being generated on the server is well within the capacity of the network connection. Network counters, however, are a good way to measure the network traffic over a period of time to evaluate trends to determine if some type of scaling or load balancing may be in order.

❑ *Network Interface: Bytes Total/Sec* — The Bytes Total/Sec counter measures the total number of bytes that are being sent back and forth between the server and the network. If the server is configured exclusively for SQL Server, almost all of the traffic should belong to SQL Server. As mentioned, this counter is very useful in analyzing network traffic trends. This information is very useful for planning scale-out and upgrade requirements.

SQL Server Counters

After installing SQL Server, a plethora of SQL Server performance objects and counters are configured to assist in the performance monitoring and optimization of SQL Server. If you are like 99 percent of all database administrators, you will most likely never look at a majority of these counters. However, there will be a special few that you will come to completely rely on. The following SQL Server–specific counters are extraordinarily useful in the establishment of a baseline, and comparing activity against the baseline to establish SQL Server performance health:

❏ *SQL Server: General Statistics: User Connections* — The User Connections counter displays the number of user connections that are currently connected to SQL Server. This counter is especially useful in monitoring and tracking connection trends to ensure that the server is configured to adequately handle all connections. Keep in mind that this counter displays the number of user connections, not users. Some applications will create more than one connection per user whereas others may create only one connection, but support multiple users.

❏ *SQL Server: Locks: Average Wait Time* — The Average Wait Time counter is an excellent counter to monitor and track the average amount of time that user requests for data resources have to wait because of concurrent blocks to the data. With the baseline and subsequent audits, this counter will be a leading indicator of database application performance. However, it is just an indicator. Resolving long-term locking requires running traces to record lock information. Traces are discussed later in this chapter.

❏ *SQL Server: Locks: Deadlocks/Sec* — *Deadlocks* occur when two or more transactions hold a lock on different resources and the transactions require access to the resources held by the opposing transaction. If this sounds very confusing, see the sidebar "Sample Events Resulting in a Deadlock" for a simple example illustrating the sequence of events that results in a deadlock.

❏ *SQL Server Access Methods: Page Splits/sec* — As described in Chapter 5, *page splits* occur when SQL Server attempts to insert a row in a clustered or non-clustered index page, but there is not sufficient space available to accommodate the new row. To maintain the contiguousness of the index page, SQL Server splits about half of the data out of the original page and moves it to a free page. This splitting of data is necessary to maintain the indexes, but it causes excessive I/O, because logically contiguous data is no longer physically contiguous. As more and more rows are inserted, the fragmentation of data will become worse.

The Page Splits/sec counter enables the monitoring of page split activity to determine how fast table indexes are becoming fragmented. Though a certain amount of page splitting is normal, excessive page splits will cause a steady deterioration of database performance. Chapter 5 explains how to detect, correct, and mitigate this fragmentation.

When monitoring page split activity, create a baseline shortly after rebuilding the indexes. As subsequent performance audits are completed, compare the page split activity. When the counter begins to spike, it is probably time for the indexes to be rebuilt again with an appropriate fill factor.

Dynamic Management Views

SQL Server 2005 provides many Dynamic Management Views (DMVs) that can be used in the gathering of baseline information, and for diagnosing performance problems. Some of these views offer the same information as performance counters, but in a relational and instantaneous format. Other views provide

Sample Events Resulting in a Deadlock

Two stored procedures are executed at the same time on separate connections. The first stored procedure, `Proc1`, updates one or more rows in `TableA`. The second stored procedure, `Proc2`, updates one or more rows in `TableB`. At this time, `Proc1` has an exclusive lock on the updated rows in `TableA`, and `Proc2` has an exclusive lock on the rows in `TableB`.

Next, `Proc1` attempts to update the same rows in `TableB` that `Proc2` has updated. It will not be able to, because `Proc2` already has an exclusive lock. At this point, `Proc1` is blocked by `Proc2`. `Proc2` then attempts to update the rows that `Proc1` has updated, and is also blocked. This mutual blocking is a *deadlock*.

SQL Server does not allow deadlocks to continue. The database engine monitors for deadlocks and, if one is detected, it will select a victim process and kill that process. The error raised by a terminated deadlock looks like the following message:

```
Msg 1205, Level 13, State 51, Line 6
Transaction (Process ID 53) was deadlocked on lock resources with
another process and has been chosen as the deadlock victim. Rerun
the transaction.
```

The selection process is based on cost. Whichever process would cost the least to rollback is terminated, and the remaining process or processes are allowed to continue. The most significant cause of deadlocks is the updating of tables in an inconsistent process. When database developers are creating procedures for data modification, they should update multiple objects in the same order whenever possible. For example, if `Proc1` and `Proc2` both updated `TableA` first, and then `TableB`, a short-term blocking lock may have occurred, but a deadlock would not have.

Deadlocks may occur occasionally, but they should not be a regular occurrence. Because they are automatically detected and killed, they are sometimes difficult to troubleshoot. The Profiler tool can be used to identify the offending processes involved in a deadlock, as discussed later in this chapter.

more specific database performance information. I won't try to cover all the views in this section, but the following views can prove very helpful in the creation and comparison of performance baselines:

❑ `sys.dm_os_performance_counters` — A very interesting Dynamic Management View as far as operating system information is concerned is `sys.dm_os_performance_counters`. This view provides much the same information as Performance Monitor, except that the information is returned in relational format, and the values returned are instantaneous. Because the data is instantaneous, per second counters will have to be queried at least twice to determine their true value. The columns that are returned by this view are described in the following table.

Column Name	Description
object_name	Counter category, such as `SQLServer:Wait Statistics` or `SQLServer:Buffer Manager`.
counter_name	Name of the counter.

Column Name	Description	
Instance_name	Name of the counter instance, such as database name or instance description. Server-level counters will not have an instance value.	
cntr_value	Instantaneous value of the counter.	
cntr_type	Counter types fall in to the following type categories:	
	65792	Numeric (integer) counter
	1073874176	Average value counter
	1073939712	Base value counter
	272696576	Per second counter
	537003264	Ratio value counter

❏ sys.dm_db_index_physical_stats — As described in Chapter 5, this view returns information about the indexes on a table, including the amount of data on each data page, the amount of fragmentation at the leaf and non-leaf level of the indexes, and the average size of records in an index.

❏ sys.dm_db_index_usage_stats — The sys.dm_db_index_usage_stats view collects cumulative index usage data. This view can be utilized to identify which indexes are seldom referenced and, thus, may be increasing overhead without improving read performance. The following code example demonstrates one possible use of this view by joining it with the sys.indexes system view to return the index name, table name, and index usage information:

```
USE AdventureWorks;
GO
SELECT object_name(S.object_id) AS TableName
,I.name AS IndexName, S.user_seeks AS Seeks
,S.user_scans AS Scans, S.user_updates AS Updates
,S.last_user_seek AS LastSeek, S.last_user_scan AS LastScan
FROM sys.dm_db_index_usage_stats S
JOIN sys.indexes I ON S.object_id = I.object_id
AND S.index_id = I.index_id
WHERE S.object_id > 100000 --Return only user owned index data
ORDER BY Seeks, Scans;
```

Tools and Techniques for Monitoring Performance

Chapter 3 described many of the tools available from a feature point of view. This chapter examines the tools from an implementation point of view, and discusses how to use them to actually perform some key database monitoring tasks. The discussion also examines a couple more tools that were not described in Chapter 3, because they are intricately tied in to the SQL Server Management Studio.

Log File Viewer

The Log File Viewer is an excellent tool for the viewing of SQL Server and operating system logs in a one-time correlated view. For example, memory subsystem errors from the system log can be correlated with SQL Server errors, indicating out-of-memory conditions and allowing you to isolate the problem away from SQL Server. To open the Log File Viewer, expand the Management folder in SQL Server Management Studio, expand SQL Server Logs, right-click the log you want to view, and select View SQL Server Log. Once the Log File Viewer is open, you can choose to open additional SQL Server logs and/or operating system logs by expanding and selecting the logs you want to review (see Figure 10-2). Notice that you can also open up log files for the SQL Server Agent and Database Mail.

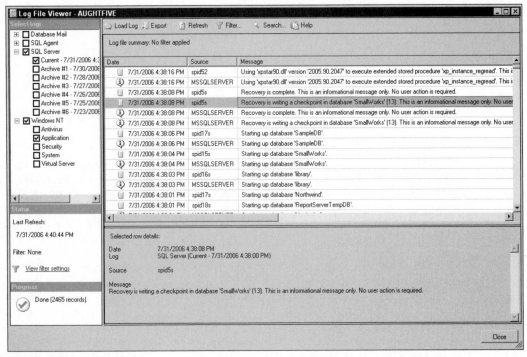

Figure 10-2: Log File Viewer

SQL Server and SQL Server Agent log files are closed and a new log opened every time the respective service is restarted. In a production system, this may not occur very often, resulting in a large log file. To avoid unacceptably large log files, the contents of the log files should be exported and the files cycled. To cycle the SQL Server Log, execute the `sp_cycle_errorlog` stored procedure. To cycle the Agent Log the `sp_cycle_agent_errorlog` stored procedure is used. These procedures clear the contents of the logs without requiring a service restart.

The number of logs that SQL Server keeps can be configured by right-clicking the SQL Server Logs folder and selecting Configure (see Figure 10-3). The minimum and default number of logs is 6, but it can be increased to as many as 99. The number cannot be less than 6.

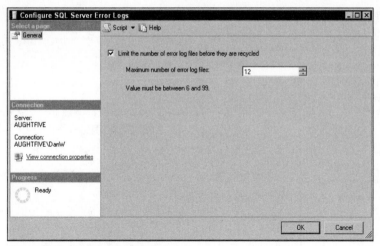

Figure 10-3: Configuring log files

Activity Monitor

Activity Monitor is located in the Management node of SQL Server Management Studio's Object Explorer. The Activity Monitor can be used to identify every current process running on SQL Server and what those processes are doing.

To launch the Activity Monitor, right-click the Activity Monitor node and select one of the view options (or just double-click the Activity Monitor node). The Activity Monitor has three different pages:

❑ *Process Info* — The Process Info page lists a row for every connection to SQL Server, along with several columns describing the process (such as the user associated with the connection, the database context, the command presently running, as well as any wait status and blocking information). Double-clicking a process will bring up the last command executed on that connection, and provide the capability to kill the process, if necessary. Figure 10-4 illustrates this behavior. Also notice in Figure 10-4 that Process 57 is suspended, and is represented with an hour glass because it is waiting on the resource being modified by Process 54.

❑ *Locks by Process* — The Locks by Process page allows for the selection of a specific process by choosing the Process ID in the Selected Process drop-down list. More specific process information is displayed on this page (such as lock types, lock status, and locked resources). Figure 10-5 shows a process that is requesting a shared lock to read a clustered index key. However, the key is being held with an exclusive lock by Process 54.

❑ *Locks by Object* — The Locks by Object page provides even more detailed information about the objects being locked by various processes. Information about the locks being held on any object can be displayed by selecting the object of interest in the Selected Object drop-down list (see Figure 10-6).

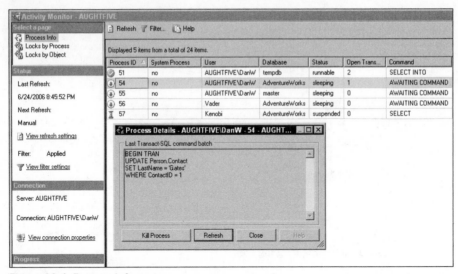

Figure 10-4: Process Info page

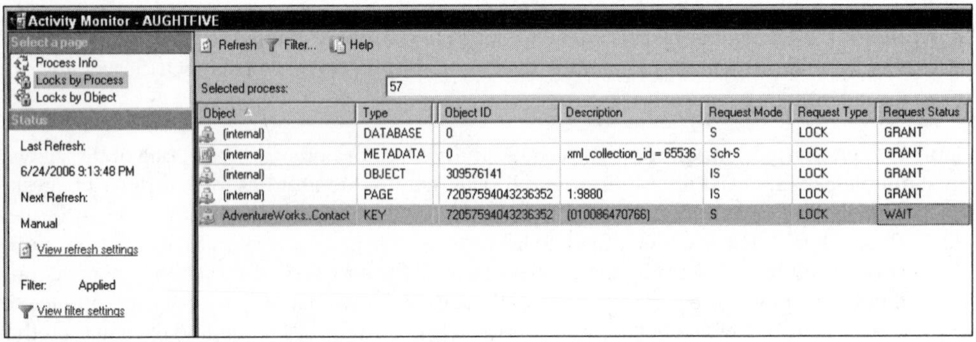

Figure 10-5: Locks by Process page

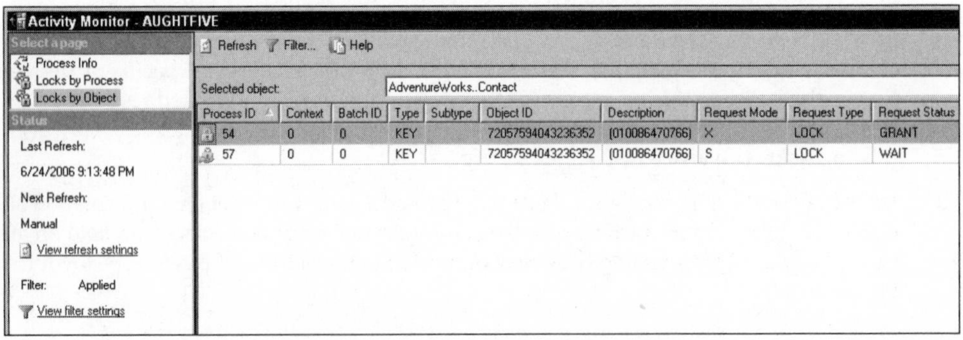

Figure 10-6: Locks by Object page

By default, the Activity Monitor only displays information about the processes and their status when Activity Monitor was opened. To configure Activity Monitor to automatically refresh, click the View Refresh Settings link in the Status pane of Activity Monitor, and configure a refresh period. Keep in mind that frequent refreshing of process information can cause degradation of SQL Server's performance.

System Stored Procedures

Although Activity Monitor is a great graphical tool to view processes and the resources they are using, oftentimes the simpler output of system stored procedures is more appropriate for identifying current processes and identifying any contention.

sp_who and sp_who2

The sp_who2 stored procedure is an undocumented system procedure that offers a distinct advantage over its documented sibling procedure, sp_who. They both return information about current SQL Server processes, but the sp_who2 procedure's information is more comprehensive.

These stored procedures are essentially equivalent to Activity Monitor's Process Info page. The output of sp_who or sp_who2 can be restricted by specifying a process ID as an input parameter. The syntax of the sp_who and sp_who2 procedures is as follows:

```
sp_who [process_ID] | login_name | [ACTIVE]

sp_who2 [process_ID] | [ACTIVE]
```

The sp_who stored procedure returns nine columns described in the following table.

Column Name	Description
spid	Server Process ID. The spid represents the session ID of the connection. Every connection has one spid.
Ecid	Execution Context ID. The ecid value indicates what thread the process was executed on. An ecid of 0 (zero) indicates that the process was executed on the main thread.
Status	The status of the session. Possible status values are as follows:
	Running — The session is performing some work.
	Runnable — The session has performed some work, but it currently has no work to perform.
	Sleeping — The session is waiting to perform work.
	Background — Background processes (typically those owned by the system) that periodically activate to perform an action.
	Suspended — The session has work to do, but has been stopped because it waiting for a process (such as I/O) to complete.
	Dormant — The session is being reset by SQL Server.

Table continued on following page

Column Name	Description
	Rollback — The session is currently rolling back a transaction.
	Pending — The session is waiting on an available thread.
	Spinloop — The session is waiting on a spinlock to become free. Spinlocks are used for fast protection of critical memory regions on multi-CPU machines.
Loginame	The login associated with the session.
Hostname	Host name associated with the session.
Blk	The spid of the session that is blocking the session if one exists. If not, a 0 (zero) is returned.
Dbname	The name of the database connected to by the session.
Cmd	The type of command executing on the session.
request_id	The integer identifier of the request running in the session.

The sp_who2 stored procedure returns 13 columns, although it returns one column, spid, twice; once on the left side of the result set and once on the right to make the result set easier to read. The columns are described in the following table.

Column Name	Description
SPID	Server Process ID. The spid represents the session ID of the connection. Every connection has one spid.
Status	The status information is the same as the sp_who command.
Login	The login associated with the session.
HostName	Host name associated with the session.
BlkBy	The spid of the session that is blocking the session if one exists.
DBName	The name of the database connected to by the session.
Command	The type of command executing on the session.
CPUTime	The cumulative CPU usage for this process.
DiskIO	The cumulative Disk I/O for this process.
LastBatch	The last time the client process executed a remote stored procedure call or an EXECUTE statement. If the process is a system process, the time is the time that SQL Server was last started.
ProgramName	The name of the application (if reported) associated with the session, (for example "Microsoft SQL Server Management Studio").
SPID	Duplicate of the spid recorded in the first column of the results.
RequestID	The integer identifier of the request running in the session.

When the "Active" option is added to sp_who or sp_who2, SQL Server does not return any session that has the Status of "Awaiting Command," which specifies that the session is waiting on input from a user process.

sp_lock

The sp_lock stored procedure returns information similar to Activity Monitor's Locks by Process page, but much more succinct. The object locked or requested to be locked is returned with the lock status, and any identifying information (such as the object's integer identifier), along with the index ID, if any.

SQL Server Locking

To interpret the information returned by sp_lock, it is important to understand the lockable resource types and the modes these locks can take. The possible resource types are described in the following table.

Resource Type	Description
RID	A RID lock is a row lock on a heap. The identifier is in the format FileID:PageNumber:RID, where FileID is the data file containing the row, PageNumber is the integer identifier of the 8K data page, and RID identifies the specific row on the data page.
KEY	A KEY lock is a row-level lock when a clustered index exists. The KEY is a hexadecimal number that the database engine uses internally to track individual clustered index keys.
PAG	PAG indicates that the lock is requested or held on an 8K data page. The value of PAG is the combination of the data file FileID and the integer identifier of the data page.
EXT	An EXT lock is a lock of an entire 64K extent. The value of EXT is the data file FileID and the identifier of the first page on the extent.
TAB	TAB locks are table locks. No resource information is returned for TAB locks because the ObjID column already contains the Object_ID of the table.
DB	DB indicates a database lock. No resource information is returned for DB locks because the dbid column already contains the identifier for the database locked.
APP	APP indicates a lock request held on an application resource. Application locks are issued explicitly through the use of the sp_getapplock stored procedure and are fairly rare.
FIL	A FIL lock is a lock held on a data file. The resource information contains the integer value of the file identifier.
MD	MD locks are metadata locks. MD locks are typically on XML collection data.
HBT	A lock on a Heap or B-Tree index.
AU	A lock on an Allocation Unit.

Locks on resource types are requested and granted by mode. The `sp_lock` stored procedure returns information that identifies the mode of the lock (for example, whether the lock is a shared or exclusive lock). The following table describes the most common modes.

Lock Mode	Description
Sch-S	*Shared schema lock.* Prevents processes from altering the schema of a resource while it is in use. The `Sch-S` lock mode is compatible with other shared locks.
Sch-M	*Schema modification lock.* Required to modify the schema of a resource. This lock mode is not compatible with any other lock mode.
S	*Shared lock.* A shared lock is compatible with all other locks except exclusive locks.
U	*Update lock.* An update lock is used to prevent deadlocks by specifying that a resource is locked for eventual updating.
X	*Exclusive lock.* For any resource that is being modified, created, or dropped, a process will have an exclusive lock during the modification.
IS	*Intent Shared lock.* Intent locks are used on resources higher in the resource hierarchy to prevent more exclusive locks from being issued. For example, an Intent Shared lock can be placed on a data page if an individual row is being read. This prevents an exclusive lock from being placed on the page and trapping the shared process. Intent Shared locks are compatible with all locks except Exclusive.
IU	*Intent Update lock.* These locks function in the same way as Intent Shared locks to prevent more exclusive locks from being granted higher in the resource hierarchy. Intent Update locks are compatible with all locks except Update and Exclusive.
IX	*Intent Exclusive lock.* These locks work the same as the other two intent locks. Intent Exclusive locks are only compatible with other Intent Exclusive locks.
SIU	*Shared Intent Update.* The `SIU` lock mode is a combination of the Shared and Intent Update locks. It is compatible with all other locks except Exclusive, Intent Exclusive, Shared with Intent Exclusive, and Update with Intent Exclusive.
SIX	*Shared with Intent Exclusive.* The `SIX` lock mode is less restrictive than the `IX` lock mode and allows for compatible shared locks higher in the resource hierarchy.
UIX	*Update with Intent Exclusive.* The `UIX` lock mode is a combination of the Update and Intent Exclusive locks. It is only compatible with Intent Shared locks.
BU	*Bulk Update.* Bulk Update locks are issued to bulk load table operation processes when the `TABLOCK` hint is used, or when the `Table Lock On Bulk Load` table option is set. Bulk Update locks are incompatible with all locks except other Bulk Update locks.

KILL

Although not a stored procedure, the KILL command enables the database administrator to kill an offending process just like the Kill Process button on the process property dialog shown in Figure 10-4. The syntax for the KILL command is as follows:

```
KILL spid
```

The KILL command is very useful, but it should be used with great caution. Although it is sometimes necessary to kill a stalled process, it is very important to gather as much information as possible about that process before killing it. For example, killing a transaction that has updated a thousand rows will result in a thousand row rollbacks, resulting in some undesired consequences such as a full transaction log or lost data.

Try it Out   System Stored Procedures

Take a look at what information is returned by the system stored procedures, and how you can use them to isolate troublesome processes.

First, open a query window. Type and execute the following code:

```
USE AdventureWorks;
GO
BEGIN TRAN
UPDATE Person.Contact
SET LastName = 'Gates'
WHERE ContactID = 1;
```

Open a second query window. Type and execute the following code:

```
USE AdventureWorks;
GO
SELECT * FROM Person.Contact
WHERE ContactID = 1;
```

Now, open a third query window and run the sp_who system stored procedure by executing the following command:

```
EXEC sp_who;
```

Notice that one of the processes shows that it is being blocked by another session. In the case shown in Figure 10-7, SPID 53 is being blocked by SPID 52.

Now, execute the sp_who2 stored procedure, but restrict the result set to the Server Process ID (SPID) that is responsible for the block in progress. In my case, the spid is 52.

```
EXEC sp_who2 52;
```

	spid	e...	status	loginame	hostname	blk	dbname	cmd	request_id
9	9	0	background	sa		0	master	BRKR TASK	0
10	10	0	background	sa		0	master	TASK MANAGER	0
11	11	0	suspended	sa		0	master	CHECKPOINT	0
12	12	0	sleeping	sa		0	master	TASK MANAGER	0
13	13	0	sleeping	sa		0	master	TASK MANAGER	0
14	14	0	sleeping	sa		0	master	TASK MANAGER	0
15	15	0	sleeping	sa		0	master	TASK MANAGER	0
16	16	0	background	sa		0	master	BRKR EVENT HNDLR	0
17	17	0	background	sa		0	master	BRKR TASK	0
18	18	0	sleeping	sa		0	master	TASK MANAGER	0
19	19	0	sleeping	sa		0	master	TASK MANAGER	0
20	20	0	sleeping	sa		0	master	TASK MANAGER	0
21	21	0	sleeping	sa		0	master	TASK MANAGER	0
22	23	0	sleeping	sa		0	master	TASK MANAGER	0
23	51	0	sleeping	AUGHTFIVE\DanW	AUGHTFIVE	0	master	AWAITING COMMAND	0
24	52	0	sleeping	AUGHTFIVE\DanW	AUGHTFIVE	0	AdventureWorks	AWAITING COMMAND	0
25	53	0	suspended	AUGHTFIVE\DanW	AUGHTFIVE	52	AdventureWorks	SELECT	0
26	54	0	runnable	AUGHTFIVE\DanW	AUGHTFIVE	0	AdventureWorks	SELECT	0

Figure 10-7: Result of running `sp_who` **system stored procedure**

The more comprehensive results of the `sp_who2` stored procedure execution return very useful information (such as the program and user responsible, as well as when the session executed the command responsible for the lock contention).

Next, identify what object is being contested by the two processes. Execute the `sp_lock` stored procedure. The results of this procedure, like the `sp_who` and `sp_who2` stored procedures, can be restricted by passing in the appropriate process ID.

Type and execute the following command to display the information about the SPID being blocked. This is the SPID that returned a value in the BlkBy column of the `sp_who2` results. For me, it was 53, but remember that your SPID will most likely be different:

```
EXEC sp_lock 53;
```

The results are shown in Figure 10-8.

	spid	dbid	Objld	Indld	Type	Resource	Mode	Status
1	53	6	0	0	DB		S	GRANT
2	53	6	0	0	MD	14(10000:0:0)	Sch-S	GRANT
3	53	6	309576141	0	TAB		IS	GRANT
4	53	6	309576141	1	PAG	1:9688	IS	GRANT
5	53	6	0	0	MD	4(6:0:0)	Sch-S	GRANT
6	53	6	309576141	1	KEY	(010086470766)	S	WAIT

Figure 10-8: `sp_lock` **results**

In Figure 10-8, notice that several locks have been requested and granted, but the shared lock on the clustered index key 010086470766 (which represents the contact in the Person.Contact table with the ID of 1) is in a WAIT status. This is because spid 52 is currently modifying that particular row and has an exclusive lock on that key.

To terminate the blocking process, execute the KILL command specifying the appropriate SPID, which for me, is 52:

```
KILL 52;
```

Use caution when killing a process. SPID 52 is the process on my computer. Your results may vary!

Using Profiler

Chapter 3 described the basic features of Profiler. This section shows you how to gather performance information to isolate and correct database application problems. The guidelines for the traces provided can be combined into a comprehensive trace, or run individually.

Another important consideration for using Profiler is overhead. Running Profiler interactively can create a great deal of server overhead, and create a large uncertainty factor. Profiler is just a graphical interface for viewing the results of a SQL trace. It is an excellent tool, but for large databases with a heavy transaction load, you will probably want to use the sp_trace_setevent, sp_trace_setfilter, sp_trace_setstatus, and sp_trace_create stored procedures to create, configure, and run traces with the trace data collected in files. The data can then be viewed using Profiler straight from the collected files, or you can import the data in to a database for analysis.

Try it Out   Analyzing Deadlocks with Profiler

As mentioned earlier, detecting deadlocks is easy using Performance Monitor. Finding out why deadlocks are happening is more difficult, and requires the running of traces and examining the data collected with Profiler.

Begin by opening SQL Server Management Studio and connecting to a server that hosts the AdventureWorks database. After connecting, launch Profiler and create a new trace based on the Blank template, as shown in Figure 10-9.

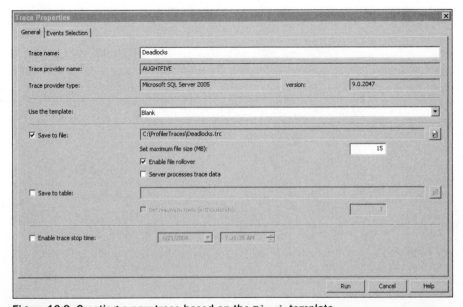

Figure 10-9: Creating a new trace based on the Blank template

On the Events Selection tab, select the Lock events Deadlock graph and Lock:Deadlock Chain, as shown in Figure 10-10. Notice that when Deadlock graph is selected, the Events Extraction Settings tab appears.

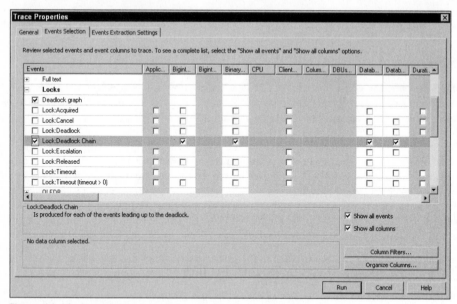

Figure 10-10: Selecting Deadlock graph **and** Lock:Deadlock Chain

To limit the data returned to Profiler, click the Column Filters button and then select Database Name. In the Not Like box, enter **MSDB** to prevent SQL Agent and scheduled monitoring activity from being traced. Click OK.

Figure 10-11 shows the desired configuration. Be careful when filtering databases. It may seem like the best filter would be one that specifies only a particular database by creating the filter where the database ID or database name is like a specific value. However, there are many Profiler events that do not have a specific database context, and these will not display if you set the filter this way. Instead, you must tell the Profiler what databases you don't want to monitor. The deadlock graph is one such event.

In the Event Extraction Settings tab, check the "Save Deadlock XML events separately" checkbox and enter a destination to save the files (see Figure 10-12). Select the option to save "Each Deadlock Batch XML in a distinct file" and click Run.

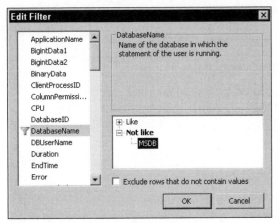

Figure 10-11: Desired configuration

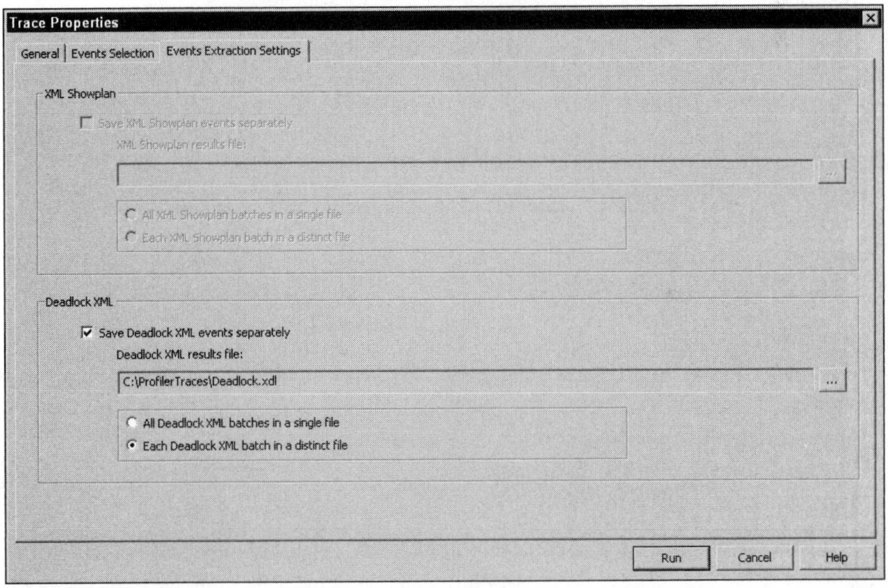

Figure 10-12: Entering a destination to save the files

In SQL Server Management Studio open two new query windows. In the first query window (which is probably called SQLQuery1.sql), type the following code and execute it:

```
--Connection 1
USE AdventureWorks;
GO

BEGIN TRAN

UPDATE Person.Address
SET City = 'Redmond'
WHERE AddressID = 1;
```

In the second query window, type the following code and execute it:

```
--Connection 2
USE AdventureWorks;
GO
BEGIN TRAN
UPDATE Person.Contact
SET LastName = 'Gates'
WHERE ContactID = 1;

UPDATE Person.Address
SET AddressLine1 = '1 Microsoft Way'
WHERE AddressID = 1;
```

This update will not complete because the transaction in Connection 1 has an exclusive lock on the row being updated in the Person.Address table. What is occurring at this point is a blocking lock. The transaction in Connection 2 wants to update the row that is being locked by Connection 1. Blocking locks are allowed, and will continue indefinitely unless a lock timeout has been set, the blocking transaction completes, or an administrator terminates the blocking transaction.

On the first connection, write and execute the following code to update the Person.Contact table:

```
--Connection 1
UPDATE Person.Contact
SET FirstName = 'Bill'
WHERE ContactID = 1;
```

This update causes a deadlock to occur, because both connections hold exclusive locks on resources that the opposing transaction requires to complete. The deadlock is detected and killed.

Return to Profiler, stop the trace, and select the Deadlock graph event class row. The deadlock graph shows the server process IDs and locked resources that were deadlocked. Hovering the mouse over one of the processes will expose the process that participated in the deadlock, as shown in Figure 10-13.

To restore the Person.Contact table to its original state, be sure to execute a ROLLBACK statement on the transaction not killed by the deadlock.

To capture the script that was used to run this trace, click the File menu and select the Export → Script Trace Definition → For SQL Server 2005 (see Figure 10-14). A Save As dialog will be displayed. Save the script as DeadLockTrace.SQL.

Open the DeadLockTrace.SQL file that you just saved with SQL Server Management Studio. This is the script that SQL Server ran to create the trace you just practiced. By saving this script, it can be run at any time without having to launch and run Profiler. For more information about each of the stored procedures, consult SQL Server Books Online, which contains a very thorough description of each procedure.

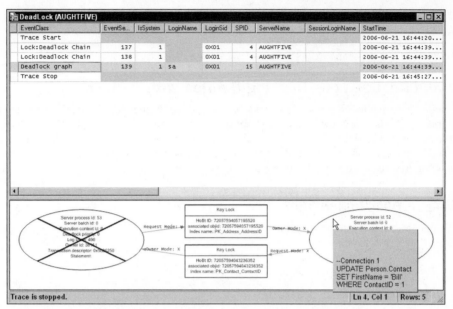

Figure 10-13: Exposing the process that participated in the deadlock

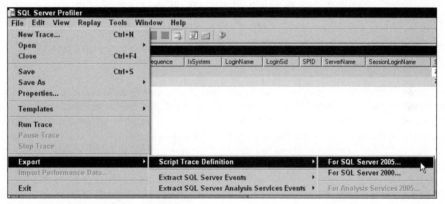

Figure 10-14: Export Trace Definition

Once the trace file is captured, it can either be opened with SQL Profiler or, in the case of larger traces, it can be inserted in to a table for analysis with conventional T-SQL queries. To move the data into a table, the fn_trace_gettable table-valued function can be used. This table-valued function requires two values: the name of the trace file to be imported and the maximum number of rollover files to collect. The default for the number of files is the maximum number of files set with the trace. The following example shows how the trace collected earlier can be added to a table called DeadLockTraceTable in the AdventureWorks database:

```
USE AdventureWorks;
GO
SELECT * INTO DeadLockTraceTable
FROM fn_trace_gettable(C:\ProfilerTraces\DeadLock.trc', NULL);
```

Detect and Analyze Long Running Queries with Profiler

The Profiler is a great tool for analyzing locks, as well as debugging stored procedures and database applications. It is also very useful in the identification and analysis of long running queries that interfere with the performance of SQL Server. The Profiler can return query execution information that can be examined by the database administrator to isolate the cause of the lengthy query. Is it poorly written? Are there no indexes to support the query, or is it just a monster query?

Try it Out   Analyzing Queries

Start Profiler and create a new trace called QueryTuning using the Blank template. Select the following events on the Events Selection tab:

❑   *Performance* — Showplan XML

❑   *Stored Procedures* — SP:Completed

❑   *TSQL* — SQL:BatchCompleted

Click the Column Filters button and create a filter where the database name is like AdventureWorks, and click OK to apply the filter.

Click on the Organize Columns button. Find the Duration column and move it up to the top of the column list to make it easy to read duration data.

On the Events Extraction Settings tab, select the "Save XML Showplan events separately" checkbox. Choose a destination to save the Showplan information, and then choose the option to save each XML Showplan in a separate file. SQLPlan is the file extension given to Showplan data. The Showplan data is stored as XML and can be viewed with Management Studio, as you will see later. When saving query plans in separate files, each file is given the name of the file defined in the destination, along with a numerical identifier appended to the end of the name.

Click Run to start the trace.

Next, open a new Query window in SQL Server Management Studio. Type and execute the following code:

```
USE AdventureWorks;
GO
SELECT P.ProductID, P.name AS Product, TH.TransactionDate, SUM(TH.Quantity),
SUM(TH.ActualCost), SUM(P.StandardCost)
FROM Production.Product P
INNER JOIN Production.TransactionHistory TH
ON P.ProductID = TH.ProductID
GROUP BY P.ProductID, P.Name, TH.TransactionDate;
GO
EXEC dbo.uspGetManagerEmployees 109;
```

```
GO
EXEC dbo.uspGetEmployeeManagers 1;
GO
SELECT P.name AS Product, SUM(SOD.OrderQty) AS SumQty
    , SUM(SOD.UnitPrice) AS SumPrice, SUM(SOD.LineTotal) AS SumTotal
    , CONVERT(char(10), SOH.OrderDate,101) AS orderDate
    , CONVERT(char(10), SOH.ShipDate,101) AS ShipDate
    , CONVERT(char(10), SOH.DueDate,101) AS DueDateFROM Sales.SalesOrderDetail SOD
INNER JOIN Sales.SalesOrderHeader SOH
ON SOH.SalesOrderID = SOD.SalesOrderID
INNER JOIN Production.Product P
ON P.ProductID = SOD.ProductID
GROUP BY P.Name, SOH.OrderDate, SOH.ShipDate, SOH.DueDate;
```

After the query completes, stop the trace and examine the results. Notice that the longest running process is the last one that references the Sales.SalesOrderHeader table, Sales.SalesOrderdetail, and Production.Product tables.

Navigate to the Showplan destination folder and examine the contents. You should see four files named QueryTuning_1.SQLPlan through QueryTuning_4.SQLPlan.

Double-click the QueryTuning_4.SQLPlan file. It will open with SQL Server Management Studio as a graphical execution plan, as shown in Figure 10-15.

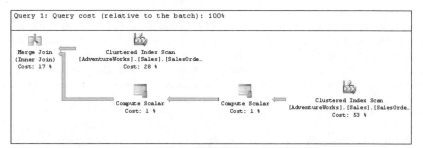

Figure 10-15: SQL Server Management Studio as a graphical execution plan

The information represented in Figure 10-15 is actually saved as XML. This is of particular interest to organizations that want to consume the Showplan data with analysis applications such as the Database Tuning Advisor that are built to analyze query plans and identify areas for improvement.

Change the name of the QueryTuning.SQLPlan to QueryTuning.XML. Right-click the QueryTuning.XML file and choose Open With...Internet Explorer. The Showplan file displayed is rendered with Internet Explorer's built-in XML parser and is readily identified as an XML file.

The Showplan files are very useful in evaluating the actual process that the Database Engine uses to optimize queries and in identifying areas for improvement. The Showplans are read from right to left. Hovering the mouse over an icon will display additional information about the process depicted, often providing insight in how the process can be optimized. For example, if a process shows an unnecessary implied conversion, the data types can be more strictly passed to avoid the implied conversion.

Using the Database Tuning Advisor (DTA)

As described earlier, index usage can be analyzed with DMVs, but the analysis can be a bit tricky and take a great deal of time. Instead of spending hours analyzing index utilization and experimenting with various configurations, the Database Tuning Advisor (DTA) can be utilized to analyze existing indexes. The DTA can return recommendations for the addition of indexes, indexed views, and table partitioning. It can also recommend the dropping of existing data structures where their existence is detrimental to performance.

Try it Out   Using the DTA to Analyze a SQL Script

To try this out, start by creating three new tables to experiment with. Run the following script to create the `NewContact`, `NewSalesOrder`, and `NewTransactionHistory` tables:

```
USE AdventureWorks;
GO
SELECT * INTO dbo.NewContact
FROM Person.Contact;

SELECT * INTO dbo.NewSalesOrder
FROM Sales.SalesOrderDetail;

SELECT * INTO dbo.NewTransactionHistory
FROM Production.TransactionHistory;
```

These tables have no indexes on them, so any query against them will result in a full table scan, which is not the most efficient. You could analyze the queries that will be used to retrieve data from these tables manually and determine what indexes to create, or you can ask the DTA to give you some advice. The DTA can also give recommendations for dropping unneeded indexes, so you will create a nonclustered index on the `NewTransactionHistory` table's `rowguid` column to see what the Advisor thinks of it:

```
USE AdventureWorks;
GO
CREATE NONCLUSTERED INDEX ix_RowGUID ON dbo.NewSalesOrder (rowguid);
```

Now that the tables and an index are in place, analyze a workload to see how queries perform against these tables. The following script flushes all dirty pages to disk, clears out the procedure cache, clears out the buffer cache, and sets `STATISTICS IO` on to capture I/O performance data. Finally, it then queries the three new tables. Write this query in the Query Editor and save it as `AWWorkLoad.SQL`:

```
CHECKPOINT;
DBCC FREEPROCCACHE;
DBCC DROPCLEANBUFFERS;

SET STATISTICS IO ON;
USE AdventureWorks;
GO
   SELECT LastName FROM dbo.NewContact
   WHERE LastName BETWEEN 'A' AND 'C';
```

```
SELECT LastName FROM dbo.NewContact
WHERE LastName LIKE 'M%';

SELECT ProductID, SUM(OrderQty) AS SumQty, SUM(UnitPrice) AS SumPrice
FROM dbo.NewSalesOrder GROUP BY ProductID;

SELECT ProductID, TransactionDate, SUM(Quantity) AS TotalQty
, SUM(ActualCost) AS SumCost
FROM dbo.NewTransactionHistory
WHERE TransactionDate BETWEEN '2003-11-12' AND '2004-01-31'
GROUP BY ProductID, TransactionDate;
```

Before executing the query, select the Include Actual Execution Plan to return the graphical query plan. The message results for this query show a large amount of reads and the creation of work tables for the aggregations:

```
(2116 row(s) affected)
Table 'NewContact'. Scan count 1, logical reads 557, physical reads 0, read-ahead
reads 564, lob logical reads 0, lob physical reads 0, lob read-ahead reads 0.

(1550 row(s) affected)
Table 'NewContact'. Scan count 1, logical reads 557, physical reads 0, read-ahead
reads 0, lob logical reads 0, lob physical reads 0, lob read-ahead reads 0.

(266 row(s) affected)
Table 'Worktable'. Scan count 0, logical reads 0, physical reads 0, read-ahead
reads 0, lob logical reads 0, lob physical reads 0, lob read-ahead reads 0.
Table 'NewSalesOrder'. Scan count 1, logical reads 1495, physical reads 0, read-
ahead reads 1502, lob logical reads 0, lob physical reads 0, lob read-ahead reads
0.

(12849 row(s) affected)
Table 'Worktable'. Scan count 0, logical reads 0, physical reads 0, read-ahead
reads 0, lob logical reads 0, lob physical reads 0, lob read-ahead reads 0.
Table 'NewTransactionHistory'. Scan count 1, logical reads 789, physical reads 0,
read-ahead reads 796, lob logical reads 0, lob physical reads 0, lob read-ahead
reads 0.
```

The execution plan shows the table scans and creation of hash/match working tables to perform the aggregations (see Figure 10-16).

To analyze this query batch, open the DTA and start a new session. In the "Session name" area you can either leave the default value of the logged-in username with date, or type in a descriptive name. In Figure 10-17, the session is called AWWorkLoad Analysis.

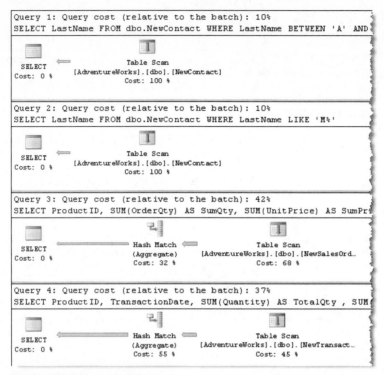

Figure 10-16: Execution plan

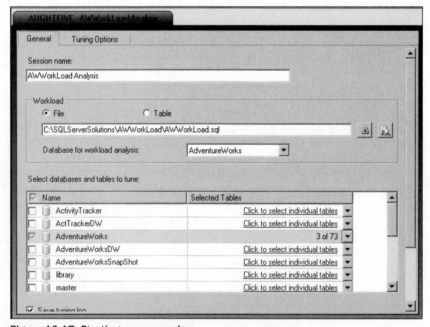

Figure 10-17: Starting a new session

Next, select the `AWWorkLoad.SQL` file as the workload file, set the starting database to `AdventureWorks`, and select just the three tables that are referenced in the file (see Figure 10-17).

On the Tuning Options tab, select the options to use indexes with no partitioning and don't keep existing structures, as shown in Figure 10-18.

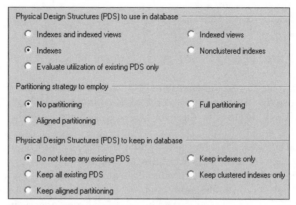

Figure 10-18: Selecting Tuning Options

Click Start Analysis to analyze the `AWWorkLoad.SQL` file. The DTA will collect metadata about the objects and examine possible indexing strategies to improve the performance of the queries. When the analysis is complete, the DTA will return its recommendations. In this case, it shows that by dropping the index on the `rowguid` column and adding indexes to the three tables, it can improve performance by 85 percent, as shown in Figure 10-19.

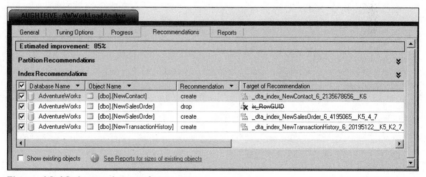

Figure 10-19: Improving performance

The DTA's recommendations can be applied immediately by clicking the Apply Recommendations option in the Actions menu, or they can be saved to a file by clicking the Save Recommendations option. As you can see in Figure 10-19, the names the DTA gives to new objects are not exactly intuitive. I rewrote the recommendations, as the following code illustrates:

```
USE AdventureWorks;
GO
DROP INDEX ix_RowGUID ON dbo.NewSalesOrder;

CREATE NONCLUSTERED INDEX ixProductID ON dbo.NewSalesOrder
(ProductID) INCLUDE ( OrderQty,UnitPrice);

CREATE NONCLUSTERED INDEX ixTranDateProductID ON dbo.NewTransactionHistory
(TransactionDate,ProductID) INCLUDE ( Quantity,ActualCost);

CREATE NONCLUSTERED INDEX ixLastName ON dbo.NewContact (LastName);
```

Take a closer look at the DTA's recommendations. The recommendation for the dropping of the rowguid column index is because that column was never referenced in the work load. Use caution with this behavior of the DTA. The index may be there for a very good reason, but the workload didn't use it.

The next recommendation is for the creation of an index on the ProductID column that includes the OrderQty and UnitPrice columns. This is because of the query that aggregates the two included columns and groups it by the ProductID column. By creating this index, the query optimizer can retrieve all the data to satisfy the query from the index, and no table access will be required. The same behavior is repeated with the NewTransactionHistory table, except that a composite index on the two group-by columns is created, and the aggregated columns are included. With the last recommendation, it is simply a matter of speeding up the search for the LastName column.

Either apply the recommendations, or execute the saved recommendation script to drop the unnecessary index and create the three new indexes. Next, return to the AWWorkLoad.SQL script and re-run it the same as before. Notice the difference in I/O.

```
 (2116 row(s) affected)
Table 'NewContact'. Scan count 1, logical reads 10, physical reads 1,
read-ahead reads 8, lob logical reads 0, lob physical reads 0,
lob read-ahead reads 0.

(1550 row(s) affected)
Table 'NewContact'. Scan count 1, logical reads 9, physical reads 0,
read-ahead reads 7, lob logical reads 0, lob physical reads 0,
lob read-ahead reads 0.

(266 row(s) affected)
Table 'NewSalesOrder'. Scan count 1, logical reads 378, physical reads 1, read-
ahead reads 376, lob logical reads 0, lob physical reads 0,
lob read-ahead reads 0.

(12849 row(s) affected)
Table 'NewTransactionHistory'. Scan count 1, logical reads 118,
physical reads 1, read-ahead reads 115, lob logical reads 0,
lob physical reads 0, lob read-ahead reads 0.
```

The read activity has indeed been reduced by about 85 percent, resulting in a much more efficient query plan. Also notice that the work tables for aggregation were not created at a huge savings. An examination of the query plan shows that no table access was performed. All the data to satisfy the queries was returned from indexes. This is, of course, not always possible, but the DTA will lean toward creating these "Covering Indexes" unless there is a significant amount of data modification on those tables, as well as where the presence of the indexes may be detrimental to performance.

The bottom line is that the DTA can save you valuable time in analyzing table structures, and recommend appropriate indexing strategies to improve performance. Just be sure that the activity that is being analyzed by the DTA is typical of the normal database activity. If the workload being analyzed contains large end-of-quarter analysis queries that are not the typical activity, the DTA may give some recommendations that would be detrimental to normal database operations.

Using the DTA with Profiler

The DTA can also analyze trace data collected by Profiler or the SQL Trace stored procedures to make recommendations. When creating a Profiler trace to use with the DTA, the `Tuning` template can be used, or you can configure your own event settings. However, in order for the DTA to analyze the trace file, performance data must be returned. The events that return data are the "Completed" events such as `SP:Completed` and `SQL:Completed`.

Correlating Database Activity with Performance Counters

Viewing performance counters with System Monitor or viewing SQL Server activity with Profiler can help monitor and detect high-cost activity. But until SQL Server 2005 was released, correlating data from the two tools was not possible except with third-party software. Profiler now has the capability to import and correlate performance data based on time. This is extraordinarily useful in finding out what processes are causing system bottlenecks.

Try it Out   **Correlating Performance Data with Profiler Data**

With the three tables created in the previous section and a new working script, try out this new feature. First, open a new query window. Type the following code and save it as `AWPerformance.SQL`:

```
USE AdventureWorks;
GO
DECLARE @Iterations AS int;
SET @Iterations = 0;
WHILE @Iterations < 10
BEGIN
  SELECT ProductID, SUM(OrderQty) AS TotalProduct, SUM(UnitPrice)
  FROM dbo.NewSalesOrder GROUP BY ProductID
    WAITFOR DELAY '00:00:02'
  UPDATE dbo.NewSalesOrder SET UnitPrice = UnitPrice * 1.25
  WHERE ProductID % 2 = 0
  SET @Iterations = @Iterations + 1
END
  WAITFOR DELAY '00:00:02';

IF EXISTS (SELECT * FROM sys.indexes
WHERE name = 'ix_TransactionID')
DROP INDEX ix_TransactionID ON dbo.NewTransactionHistory
CREATE NONCLUSTERED INDEX ix_TransactionID ON dbo.NewTransactionHistory
(TransactionID);

SET @Iterations = 0;
```

```
WHILE @Iterations < 5
BEGIN
  INSERT dbo.NewTransactionHistory
  (ProductID, ReferenceOrderID, ReferenceOrderLineID, TransactionDate
  , TransactionType, Quantity, ActualCost, ModifiedDate)
  SELECT ProductID, ReferenceOrderID, ReferenceOrderLineID, TransactionDate
  , TransactionType, Quantity, ActualCost, ModifiedDate
  FROM dbo.NewTransactionHistory WHERE TransactionID % 21 = 1
    WAITFOR DELAY '00:00:02'
  UPDATE dbo.NewSalesOrder SET UnitPrice = UnitPrice / 1.25
  WHERE ProductID % 2 = 0
  SET @Iterations = @Iterations + 1
END
  WAITFOR DELAY '00:00:02';
ALTER INDEX ix_TransactionID
ON dbo.NewTransactionHistory REBUILD;
```

Now, open Performance Monitor and create a new Counter Log. For now, include a few counters to make it easier to see how to use the tools. Add the Pages/sec, Avg. Disk Queue Length, %Processor Time, and Page Splits/sec counters to the counter log, and change the sampling interval to every 1 second, as shown in Figure 10-20. Click OK to save the Counter Log and start the sampling.

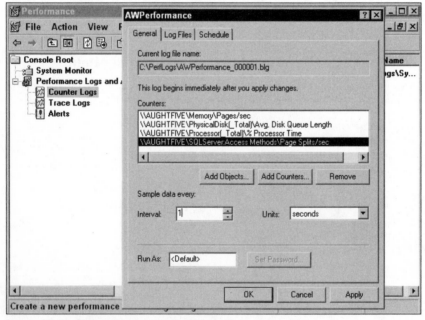

Figure 10-20: Changing the sampling interval

Next, open SQL Server Profiler and create a new trace called AWPerformance using the Blank template. Save the trace to a file called AWPerformance.trc with a maximum size of 15MB. On the Events Selection tab, select the SQL:BatchCompleted and SQL:StmtCompleted events. Click the Organize Columns button and move the Text Data column up just below Application Name, click OK, and then click Run.

Return to the AWPerformance script created earlier and run it. After the script completes (it will take a couple of minutes), stop the Profiler trace and the counter log.

In Profiler, open the AWPerformance.trc trace file that was created by Profiler. Then, import the performance counter log by selecting the Import Performance Data option on the File menu. Notice that the Profiler events and Performance Monitor events are now time-correlated. By selecting a peak value in the performance data window, the corresponding trace event is highlighted in the trace window. Selecting a particular trace event will cause the associated performance data to be highlighted. Figure 10-21 shows the correlation between a spike in the Performance Counter Log and an INSERT operation in the Profiler results.

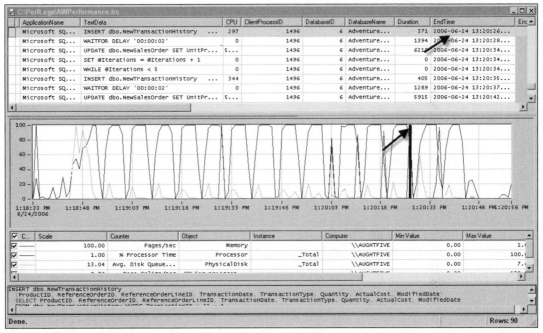

Figure 10-21: Highlighting of the associated performance data

Monitoring Files

One of the more mundane (but imminently important) monitoring tasks for every database administrator is that of monitoring and managing file sizes. The default setting for both data files and log files is to grow automatically with no maximum size. This is probably not the most ideal configuration. Generally, during the database design and planning phase, a determination of database size is made. This determination should identify the starting size of the database files and the anticipated rate of growth of each file type. However, unexpected growth, especially with the log file, is very typical. This makes the monitoring of file sizes especially important. If a data file fills to capacity, no data modifications will be allowed. The same goes for the log files.

Disk Usage Report

There are a number of ways to monitor database file sizes. The Disk Usage report in SQL Server Management Studio (see Figure 10-22) is one. This report is very informative and can be used to find the tables that are consuming the most space, as well as index structures and files. The disadvantage of the Disk Usage report is that you have to run the report to get it.

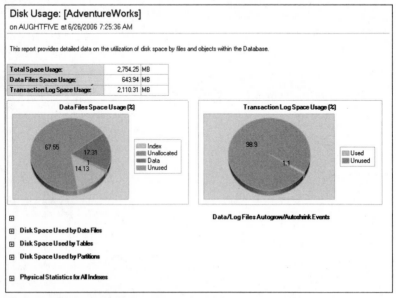

Figure 10-22: Disk Usage report

sp_spaceused

The `sp_spaceused` stored procedure can also be used to return some of the same information as the Disk Usage report, but the `sp_spaceused` stored procedure will only return space information for the entire database if no object name parameter is passed with it or a single object. The following example shows how to run `sp_spaceused` to retrieve information from the `AdventureWorks` database and a table in the `AdventureWorks` database:

```
SET NOCOUNT ON;
USE AdventureWorks;
GO
SELECT 'AdventureWorks Space Used Data'
EXEC sp_spaceused; --Return total database size and available disk spave

SELECT 'Person.Contact Space Used Data'
EXEC sp_spaceused 'Person.Contact'; --Return allocation data for Person.Contact
```

The results of this script are as follows (your results will look a little different, because I formatted the results to fit on the page):

```
------------------------------
AdventureWorks Space Used Data

database_name      database_size      unallocated space
-------------      -------------      -----------------
AdventureWorks     695.13 MB          475.20 MB

reserved           data               index_size         unused
----------------   ----------------   ----------------   ----------------
172784 KB          87616 KB           78776 KB           6392 KB


------------------------------
Person.Contact Space Used Data

name        rows       reserved    data        index_size     unused
---------   --------   ---------   ---------   ------------   -----
Contact     19972      11304 KB    8920 KB     2032 KB        352 KB
```

sys.sysfiles

The system view `sys.sysfiles` is another great way to retrieve information about files in the database, but the default data returned is not the most intuitive. For example, the `size` attribute is not a file size, but the number of 8K data pages and the `maxsize` attribute returns –1 if no maximum size is specified. To make the results more concise and readable, you can create a script like the one that follows:

```sql
SELECT Name, FileName
, CAST((Size * 8192 / 1048576) AS varchar(10)) + 'MB' AS FileSize
, MaxSize =
    CASE MaxSize
        WHEN -1 THEN 'Unlimited'
        ELSE CAST((Maxsize / 128) AS varchar(10)) + 'MB'
    END FROM sys.sysfiles;
```

The results of this query are simple and easy to understand (see Figure 10-23). They can also be consumed by an application and programmatic decisions made based on the results.

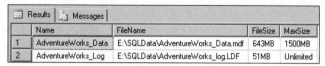

Figure 10-23: Query results

Monitoring Files with Performance Monitor

Probably the most efficient way of keeping abreast of the amount of free space in data and log files is to use performance counters. The `SQL Server:Databases` performance object has several counters that can be used to monitor disk and log file sizes. You can use these counters to create alerts as described in Chapter 8. This way, SQL Server does the monitoring for you, and sends you notifications when a data file has exceeded a preconfigured size or the transaction log has filled to a percentage greater than a certain value.

Monitoring Database Modifications

Like many people in the information technology field, I cut my teeth in desktop support, then moved on to network support, and finally settled in with SQL Server. I can't begin to count how many times I began a support conversation with, "Have you changed anything recently?" only to hear the canned response, "No, I haven't done anything. It just stopped working." I bet you can relate. As a database administrator, your audience has changed a bit, but when a database application suddenly quits working, I can almost guarantee that you will hear the same answer from database and application developers, "I didn't do anything, it just stopped working."

A very powerful new feature in SQL Server 2005 gives the DBA the ability to debunk that claim with solid audit evidence that, indeed, something was changed to break the database. This new feature is the ability to monitor and even prevent database modifications through the use of Data Definition Language (DDL) triggers and event notifications.

Data Definition Language (DDL) Triggers

DDL triggers can be defined at the database and server scope. Like traditional Data Modification Language (DML) triggers, DDL triggers fire *after* the event that the trigger is defined on. If a trigger is defined to prevent the dropping of a database, the database will be dropped first, and then put back when the trigger fires with ROLLBACK statement in it. This can prove to be very costly, but may be less costly than having to restore the database from scratch.

Unlike traditional triggers, DDL triggers are defined on a particular statement or group of statements, regardless of the object that the statement is directed to, and are not assigned to a particular object. As a result, a DROP_DATABASE trigger will fire no matter what database is dropped.

In traditional DML triggers, a great deal of the functionality of the trigger is gained from access to the Deleted and Inserted tables that exist in memory for the duration of the trigger. DDL triggers do not use the Inserted and Deleted tables. Instead, if information from the event needs to be captured, the EVENTDATA function is used.

SQL Server Books Online contains a complete hierarchical listing of server- and database-level events that can used with DDL triggers. You can find the list under the topic "Event Groups for Use with DDL Triggers."

EVENTDATA Function

The EVENTDATA function returns an XML document that contains predefined data about the event that caused the trigger to execute. The type of data largely depends on the event that caused the trigger to execute, but all triggers return the time the trigger was fired, the ID of the process that caused the trigger to execute, and the type of event.

The following example creates a server-scoped DDL trigger that will execute any time a database is created, altered, or dropped:

```
USE Master;
GO
CREATE TRIGGER ServerDBEvent
ON ALL SERVER
```

```
FOR CREATE_DATABASE, DROP_DATABASE, ALTER_DATABASE
AS
DECLARE @Data AS xml
DECLARE @EventType AS nvarchar(25)
DECLARE @PostTime AS nvarchar(25)
DECLARE @ServerName AS nvarchar(25)
DECLARE @DBName AS nvarchar(25)
DECLARE @Login AS nvarchar(25)
DECLARE @TSQLCommand AS nvarchar(MAX)

    SET @Data = EVENTDATA()
    SELECT @EventType =
      @Data.value('(/EVENT_INSTANCE/EventType)[1]','nvarchar(25)')
    , @PostTime = @Data.value('(/EVENT_INSTANCE/PostTime)[1]','nvarchar(25)')
    , @ServerName =
      @Data.value('(/EVENT_INSTANCE/ServerName)[1]','nvarchar(25)')
    , @Login = @Data.value('(/EVENT_INSTANCE/LoginName)[1]','nvarchar(25)')
    , @DBName =
      @Data.value('(/EVENT_INSTANCE/DatabaseName)[1]','nvarchar(25)')
    , @TSQLCommand =
      @Data.value('(/EVENT_INSTANCE/TSQLCommand)[1]','nvarchar(max)')

    PRINT @EventType
    PRINT @PostTime
    PRINT @ServerName
    PRINT @login
    PRINT @DBName
    PRINT @TSQLCommand;
GO
```

To test the trigger, execute the following code and examine the output:

```
USE Master;
GO
CREATE DATABASE SampleDB;
GO
ALTER DATABASE SampleDB SET RECOVERY SIMPLE;
```

```
RESULTS:
---------------------------------------------------------
CREATE_DATABASE
2006-06-26T20:29:27.670
AUGHTFIVE
AUGHTFIVE\DanW
SampleDB
CREATE DATABASE SampleDB

ALTER_DATABASE
2006-06-26T20:29:27.750
AUGHTFIVE
AUGHTFIVE\DanW
SampleDB
ALTER DATABASE SampleDB SET RECOVERY SIMPLE
```

Try it Out   Database Scoped DDL Trigger

In this exercise you create a DDL trigger that prevents modifications to the database, and records information about who tried to modify the database and how they tried to modify it in an audit table.

First, you must create a table that will contain the auditing information gathered from the DDL trigger. To do that, type and execute the following code:

```
USE AdventureWorks;
GO
CREATE TABLE DatabaseDDLAudit
(AuditID int IDENTITY(1,1) NOT NULL
,PostTime datetime NOT NULL
,LoginName nvarchar(128) NULL
,Command nvarchar(MAX) NULL
,EventData xml NULL);
```

Now that you have an audit table, you can create the DDL database trigger that will insert into the table and prevent any modifications to the database. To create the trigger, type and execute the following code:

```
USE AdventureWorks;
GO
CREATE TRIGGER NoDDLAllowed
ON DATABASE
FOR DDL_DATABASE_LEVEL_EVENTS
AS
SET NOCOUNT ON
DECLARE @data AS xml, @PostTime AS datetime, @HostName AS nvarchar(128)
DECLARE @LoginName AS nvarchar(128), @Command AS nvarchar(MAX)

SET @data = EVENTDATA()

SELECT
@PostTime =
  CAST(@Data.value('(/EVENT_INSTANCE/PostTime)[1]','nvarchar(25)')AS datetime)
,@HostName =
  @Data.value('(/EVENT_INSTANCE/HostName)[1]','nvarchar(25)')
,@LoginName =
  @Data.value('(/EVENT_INSTANCE/LoginName)[1]','nvarchar(25)')
,@Command =
  @Data.value('(/EVENT_INSTANCE/TSQLCommand)[1]','nvarchar(max)')

RAISERROR ('What?! Are you nuts? Modifications to this database are not allowed!
You can expect a visit from human resources shortly.', 16, 1)
ROLLBACK
INSERT DatabaseDDLAudit
  (PostTime, LoginName, Command, EventData)
VALUES    (@PostTime, @LoginName, @Command, @Data)
RETURN;
GO
```

To test the trigger and review the data collected, execute the following code:

```
USE AdventureWorks;
GO
ALTER TABLE Person.Contact
ADD NewColumn varchar(10) NULL;
```

Your results should look like the following:

```
Msg 50000, Level 16, State 1, Procedure NoDDLAllowed, Line 21
What?! Are you nuts? Modifications to this database are not allowed! You can expect
a visit from human resources shortly.
Msg 3609, Level 16, State 2, Line 1
The transaction ended in the trigger. The batch has been aborted.
```

Now, query the audit table to see the data collected by executing the following command:

```
USE AdventureWorks;
GO
SELECT * FROM DatabaseDDLAudit;
```

When it comes time to make authorized changes to the database, the trigger will have to be disabled or dropped (preferably disabled). The following script demonstrates how to disable the DDL trigger, make changes, and re-enable the trigger when complete:

```
USE AdventureWorks;
GO
DISABLE TRIGGER NoDDLAllowed
ON DATABASE;
GO
CREATE TABLE TestTable
(Column1 int
,Column2 int);
GO
ENABLE TRIGGER NoDDLAllowed
ON DATABASE;
```

Summary

As you can see, monitoring the database server can become a full-time job. This chapter only scratched the surface when it comes to the events that can be monitored. However, this chapter should give you a very good start on designing a monitoring strategy, and determining what events are the most important for your particular environment. Keep in mind that all monitoring will have a certain amount of impact on SQL Server's overall performance. The more you monitor, the more the cost. Monitor in small slices, but be sure to get the big picture by putting all the slices together. Then, when it comes to making changes to the system, make small changes and measure your results.

Having a hot or warm standby server (or some other failover solution) is critical to maintaining a highly available server platform. Chapter 11 discusses how to use Windows Clustering, SQL Server Log-Shipping, and SQL Server Mirroring configurations to maximize the availability of your database.

SQL Server High Availability

Picture this. You're sitting at your desk, reading your favorite tech blog, when all of a sudden, the phone rings. It's the help desk. "The server's down," the help desk technician informs you. It's the finance database server — your server.

The problem could be any number of things. A failed disk, network problems, or power outages are among the many things that can plague you as a database administrator. However, with the right combination of hardware and software, many of these outages can be avoided.

This chapter should provide you with a basic understanding of the topic of high availability, and the tools provided to help improve the availability of your databases. This chapter covers the following topics:

❑   Availability

❑   Clustering

❑   Log shipping

❑   Database mirroring

Unless otherwise stated, the high-availability topics covered in this chapter are available only in the Standard, Enterprise, and Developer Editions of SQL Server 2005.

Introduction to Availability

The definition of *high availability* is subjective. This is because you may have some applications that need to be available 24 hours a day, seven days a week; and you may have other database applications that only need to be available during business hours. High availability isn't always about full-time operations, but rather about services being accessible to your users when they need them.

High availability is also about being able to meet Service Level Agreements (SLAs), which define your requirements for maintaining application and service availability in order to meet user demand and keep services online. For example, there is a concept known as the *rule of nines*. The rule of nines is based on the realization that 100 percent availability may be a pipe dream. It identifies a more realistic series of uptime requirements based on percentage values just shy of 100 percent. The following table lists the number of minutes per year based on the rule of nines.

Percentage of Uptime per Year	Downtime per Year in Minutes
99%	5259.6
99.9%	525.96
99.99%	52.596
99.999%	5.259

As you can see, the ultimate goal for any high-availability solution is the *five nines* rule, which provides you with a little more than 5 minutes of downtime per year. Again, you might not be supporting an application that needs to be running for all but an hour a year, so plan your availability solutions accordingly.

High availability may also be dictated by your budget. To achieve the "five nines" of availability, you might have to maintain multiple data centers around the world, with redundancy built in at each location. While a full list of options for a true "five nines" environment are outside of the scope of this book, this chapter will educate you about the features inherent to Microsoft SQL Server 2005 that allow you to improve your application availability.

Failover Clustering

When it comes to high availability with instant or near-instant failover, clustering provides an invaluable service. SQL Server Clustering is based on the Windows Clustering service, and is only available in Windows 2000 Advanced Server and Datacenter editions, and Windows Server 2003 Enterprise and Datacenter editions. Clustering works by using two or more servers (referred to as *nodes*) to act as a single virtual server for your end users. Each edition of Windows has its own limitations regarding the number of servers that can participate in a cluster. The following table lists the supported editions of Windows and the maximum number of nodes available to each.

Windows Server Edition	Maximum Nodes Supported
Windows 2000 Advanced Server Edition	2
Windows 2000 Datacenter Edition	4
Windows Server 2003 Enterprise Edition	8
Windows Server 2003 Datacenter Edition	8

When reviewing high-availability options for SQL, an understanding of how Windows Clustering works, as well as how SQL can use clustering, will help you make an informed decision. In this section, you learn about the basics of Windows Clustering, and the pros and cons of how it works with SQL.

Windows Clustering—A Quick Primer

Microsoft offers two ways to introduce high availability into the Windows Server operating system: Network Load Balancing and Windows Clustering. *Network Load Balancing* (NLB) is based around the premise of several different servers operating somewhat independently, but acting as a single unit. One of the best examples of an implementation of NLB is a Web farm. As you can see in Figure 11-1, each server that participates in a Web farm operates its own Web services and usually has its own copy of the Web pages that will be served to the public. When all members of the Web farm are participating to provide a highly available Web application, they appear to your clients as a single unified Web site. For example, when UserA connects to `www.yoursite.you`, he or she might actually connect to server 37; but when UserB connects to `www.yoursite.you`, he or she might be connecting to server 42.

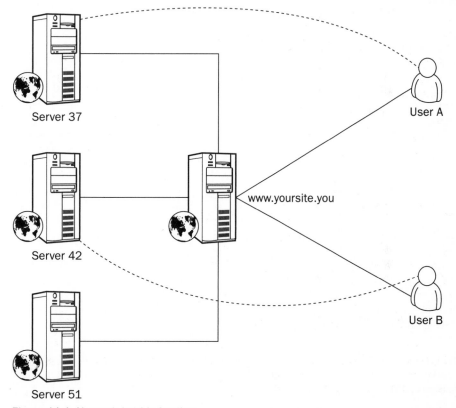

Figure 11-1: Network load balancing

With *Windows Clustering* (shown in Figure 11-2), cluster-aware applications access data on a shared volume known as a *quorum*. The quorum is responsible for storing the shared data that will be accessed by the cluster nodes, as well as identifying which node is the primary node for the application. In many Windows Clustering scenarios, the quorum device is a single shared storage unit that requires each node have a connection to it, using either Small Computer Systems Interface (SCSI) or Fibre Channel. Unfortunately, this single storage model allows for a single point of failure should the quorum device no longer be available.

Enhancements in the Windows Clustering service, however, can allow the quorum data to be replicated, so that each node can have a copy of the quorum data connected locally. This allows clusters to be used over wide area networks (WANs) or virtual private networks (VPNs). This is also referred to as a *majority node cluster*.

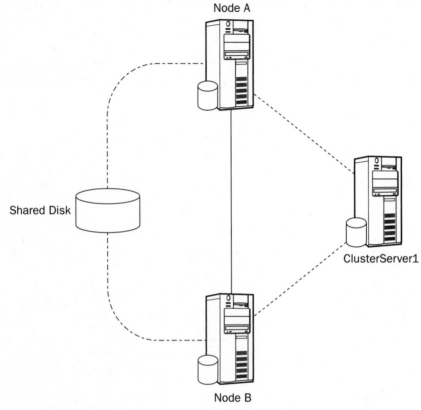

Figure 11-2: Windows clustering

When building highly available applications, many organizations employ a model when NLB is used on the front-end, for firewall and Web services; and clustering is used on the back end, for database applications.

Clustering Components

So, what do you need to begin clustering? Well, you'll need a couple of servers. Each server must also have two network interface cards (NICs). One NIC in each server will be connected to your network and will be used to listen for client requests, and the other will be used only between cluster nodes to share *heartbeat* information between the primary node and the secondary nodes. This heartbeat information is what will be used to provide failover when it becomes necessary. You must also specify the storage device that will be used for storing quorum data and your application data. Your operating system (OS) will not be installed on the quorum device, but your applications and data will use it.

Clustering works by configuring a virtual server for the cluster. This virtual server appears to be a single server to your clients and end-user applications. It is given a name and IP address, and, as explained in Chapter 2, SQL Server can then be installed on it.

Active/Passive Clustering

Most applications (and SQL is no exception) use what is known as *Active/Passive clustering*. In the Active/Passive clustering model, for a single application, one node is designated as the *primary node*. All requests that come in to the cluster virtual server are directed to this *primary cluster*. *Secondary nodes* are *failover nodes* and only become active when the primary node is unavailable, and no heartbeat exists for that node. When this happens, a secondary node begins taking over the work for the cluster, allowing applications to continue running with little noticeable interruption. Figure 11-2 is an example of an Active/Passive cluster. Because your client applications always use the virtual server, and not the primary server, they are oblivious to the work that goes on behind the scenes.

Active/Active Clustering

Active/Active clustering is rarely employed, and with good reason. First of all, the term "active/active" can be a little misleading. You would think that unlike an active/passive cluster (in which one node does all the work, while the other nodes hang back and wait for something interesting to happen), an active/active cluster would ensure that everyone is playing an equal part in making this application highly available. This, however, is not the case. An active/active cluster usually describes a scenario in which more than one cluster-aware application is running, and each application has a different node configured as the primary node for that application. The primary reason for this is mainly because of the technical limitations of how databases and other application services work. Focusing just on SQL, for example, only one server can write to the active transaction log at a time. Because the other nodes are not able to write to the same transaction log, what else is there for them to do?

Well, you could configure a second virtual server using one of the existing standby nodes as the primary for this new server, and install another instance of SQL on that one. For example, suppose you have two servers, Node A and Node B, that are configured so that Node A is the primary node and Node B is the secondary node for ClusterServer1. You then decide to use these two servers to create a second virtual server named ClusterServer2, only this time Node B is the primary node, and Node A is the secondary node, as shown in Figure 11-3.

You *could* do that. But in order for Active/Active clustering to work, the standby servers must be able to handle the combined workload for both virtual servers should they fail. So, if Server A comes to a screeching halt, Server B has to be able to respond to client requests for both virtual servers. Now, in a two-node environment, this is probably not an optimal solution. However, because Windows Server 2003 can support up to eight nodes in a cluster, it may be more feasible.

Technically, this is really more of an (Active/Passive)/(Active/Passive) implementation, but that's just splitting hairs.

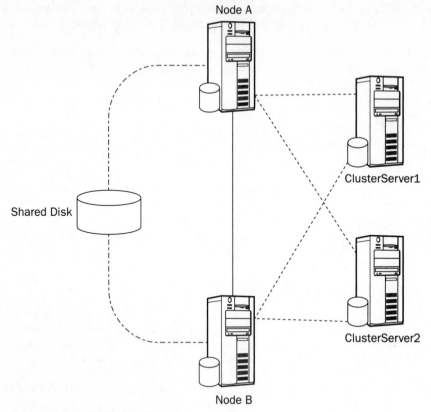

Figure 11-3: Active/Active clustering

Considering Clustering

Now that you're familiar with how Windows Clustering works, you can see that it offers you some significant benefits. It can provide instant or near-instant failover with no client reconfiguration required, because they point to the cluster name, not individual nodes. It is also a high-availability solution that provides failover of the entire instance of SQL, not just a specific database. However, clustering can be cost-prohibitive with the software and hardware cost requirements for some.

Log Shipping

Log shipping is another method by which a SQL database can be made highly available. Unlike failover clustering, log shipping is managed on a per-database basis. It provides you with the ability to designate one or more servers to hold a secondary copy of the database in question. It does this by making regular backups of the transaction log and then restoring the backups onto a secondary server. This section explains how to configure log shipping, and how to perform failover for a database. Log shipping is also available in the Workgroup edition of SQL Server 2005.

Preparing for Log Shipping

Before you can configure log shipping, you will want to ensure that a few things have been correctly configured. First of all, ensure that reliable network connectivity exists between the primary server and the standby server. When using the wizard, you can make a full backup of the current server, and restore that backup on the standby server. If your database is particularly large, a full backup from the wizard may not be possible, so you may need to manually configure the backup and restore for the source database.

Next, ensure that your database is using the Full recovery model. This is required, because the log shipping process must make regular backups of the transaction log. Using the Bulk-Logged recovery model prevents data entered at the primary server using a non-logged bulk operation from being applied to the secondary servers, as well.

You will also want to ensure that the target database doesn't already exist on the standby server. Typically, in production environments, this isn't a problem. However, sometimes a server that had been primarily used for testing gets "promoted" into the production environment. If this is the case, ensure that the server is clean, and if it does have a copy of the production database, it is from a recent backup.

Configuring Log Shipping with SQL Management Studio

You can configure log shipping for a database at any time by viewing the Properties sheet of the database, or by right-clicking the database and selecting Tasks → Ship Transaction Logs from the Object Explorer, as shown in Figure 11-4.

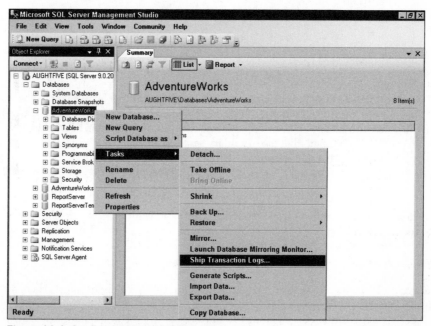

Figure 11-4: Configuring log shipping

In the Transaction Log Shipping page, you can configure the required options for backing up the database, designating secondary servers, and a monitoring server. To begin, you will need to enable this database as the primary server for log shipping. Figure 11-5 shows a database that has already been configured for log shipping and monitoring. Notice the checkbox that indicates this server is the primary server.

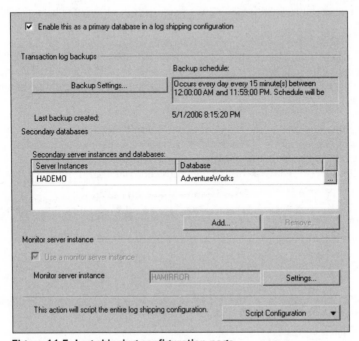

Figure 11-5: Log shipping configuration page

If you click the Backup Settings button, a new window will appear that allows you to specify the location and frequency for the backup operations. Assuming the secondary servers will be on different physical servers (which they should be — otherwise, you really don't gain much benefit from log shipping), you will need to provide a UNC path that the secondary servers can use to retrieve the backups generated by the log shipping process. The transaction logs will be copied from this location to a local file system path on each secondary server. You can also specify a local file system path where the initial full backup and subsequent transaction log backups will be located.

If you are going to have multiple secondary servers, and you want to be able to continue using the alternate secondary servers after one of them has been promoted to the new primary server, consider placing the backup folder on a share that is accessible to all servers and will not be impacted if there is a general server failure on the primary server.

Notice in Figure 11-6 that you can also specify automatic cleanup behavior for files generated by log shipping. The default configuration deletes files older than 72 hours and will generate an alert when a backup hasn't been performed for an hour. You can also specify the frequency of the backup operation, and change the default name assigned to the backup job.

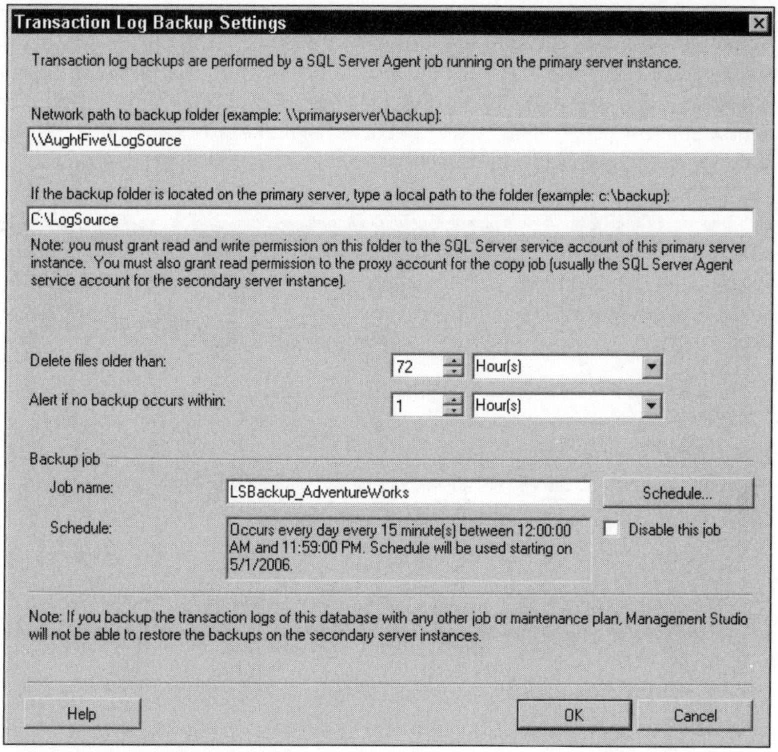

Figure 11-6: Backup options

One thing you will want to be careful about, especially with environments that have a heavy transaction processing load, is how often the transaction log backup runs. A student of mine once ran into an issue where they had configured the backup job to run every 5 minutes because of the large number of transactions being processed. Unfortunately, at roughly the same time every week, another maintenance task would run that would cause the backup job to take longer than expected. This meant that the restore operation on the standby server was still waiting for the new log before the backup had been moved over. The remedy I suggested to this student was to specify a different schedule that would backup and restore the transaction log less frequently while this other maintenance task ran. It resulted in a larger file being copied over, but the backup and copy were able to complete before the next restore job.

Once you've configured the backup job settings, you can configure one or more secondary servers. Secondary servers can be configured as a hot standby that will sit in a NO RECOVERY state until failover is initiated, or they can also be configured as a read-only copy of the database (which may be helpful for querying data for reporting and analysis services).

To configure a new secondary server, from the Transaction Log Shipping page, click Add. This also brings up a new window with three option screens. From the header section of the window, you can specify the name of the secondary server and the name of the standby database. If used for failover, the name of the secondary database should be the same as the primary to minimize application reconfiguration on your client applications.

As you can see from Figure 11-7, you can configure the options for performing the initial restore of the database. You can have the restore begin immediately after configuring the log shipping options; you can specify an existing backup file to use for building a new standby server; or, if the standby server already has a restored copy of the database, you can select that option, as well. If you have restored the database on a new standby server using existing backups, make sure you apply all transaction log back-ups to ensure that the database is in a consistent state.

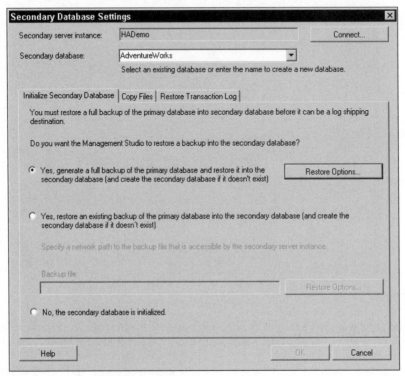

Figure 11-7: Configuring standby servers

The Copy Files tab allows you to configure options for the file copy task (see Figure 11-8). A new job will be created that copies the files created by the backup operation to the destination folder on the secondary server. As with the backup job, you can specify the frequency of this job, and also the options for cleaning up older files.

The Restore Transaction Log tab allows you to configure the restore operation. As you can see in Figure 11-9, you can choose to have the destination database use the NO RECOVERY mode (which prevents client access) or the STANDBY mode (which allows read-only access to the database). Depending on the frequency of the restore operations and the tasks that will use the standby database, you may need to disconnect users when restoring the database backups. So, enable that checkbox if necessary. You can also configure the restore operation to be delayed to help guarantee that the backup and copy operations have a chance to complete, and specify how long the server should wait without performing a restore before an alert is fired. Finally, you can configure the appropriate schedule for the restore tasks. As with the other scheduled oper-ations, the transaction log restore will run every 15 minutes.

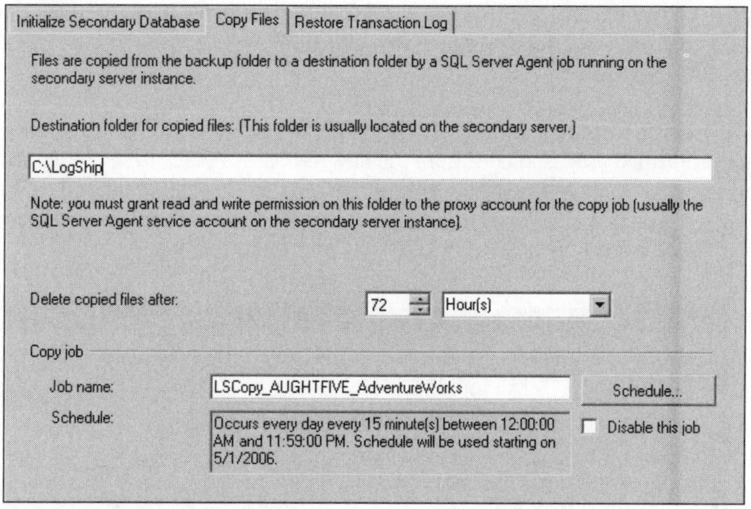

Figure 11-8: Copy Files options

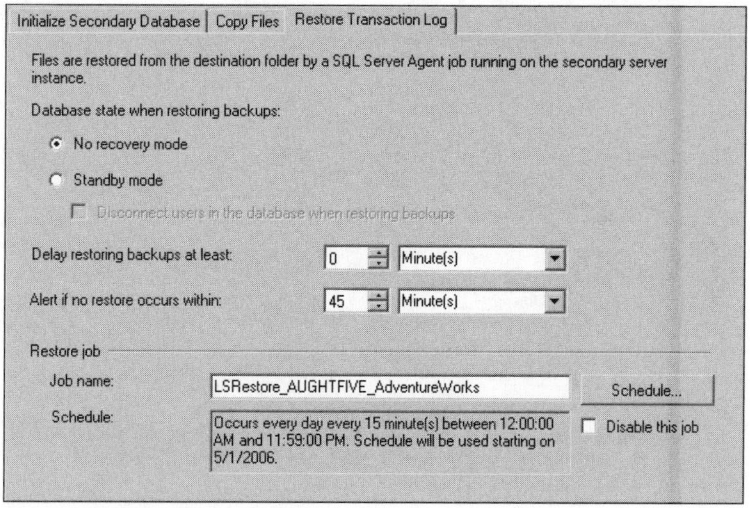

Figure 11-9: Restoring the logs

Optionally, you can also configure a server to monitor log shipping operations. This server should be a SQL Server that doesn't directly participate in the log shipping process. Although you could potentially use the primary server or one of the secondary servers as the log shipping monitor, it may be counter-productive, because you want to be able to validate the status of the log shipping operation between the primary and standby servers. Because the purpose of log shipping is to create a standby server that could be used if the primary fails, it makes little sense to put the monitor on the server that is more likely to fail, or will be the one to handle the additional workload if the primary does fail.

The purpose of the log shipping monitor is simply to track the details of the log shipping process for that database. It will keep track of primary server backups, copy operations, and secondary server restore operations. It will also generate alert information for failed backups. Although this data is recorded on each of the respective servers, having a single repository for this data may make it easier to track and monitor the log shipping process.

To add a monitor server, from the Transaction Log Shipping page, select "Use a monitor server instance," and then click Configure to add and configure the new server. As you can see in Figure 11-10, you can specify the server that will act as the monitoring server, and the login that is used as the proxy account of the log shipping job. You can also configure the history retention value, and the name for the job that will generate alerts if there is a problem with the backup, copy, or restore jobs.

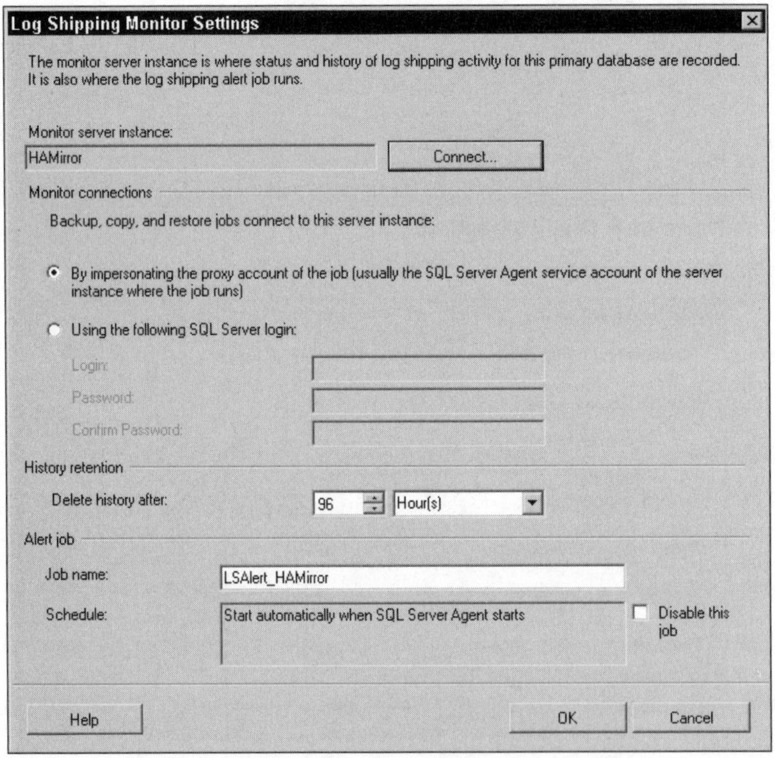

Figure 11-10: Log shipping monitor

Once the log shipping monitor is configured, you can also use it to view reports about any and all log shipping databases that this server monitors. Do this by selecting the server name from the Object Browser, and then selecting Transaction Log Shipping Status from the list of available reports in the Summary tab. Whereas the primary and secondary servers will let you view report information about the configuration on the servers themselves, using a monitoring server allows you to view the status of the primary and secondary servers from just the one report. You can also use this server to monitor multiple instances of log shipping for all your databases, and keep track of them through this reporting tool.

Once you have your log shipping options configured, you can apply them to the database, and if everything is configured properly, the backups should begin right away. Unless you've changed the schedule for the jobs, they should run every 15 minutes.

Configuring Log Shipping with Transact-SQL

Optionally, you can use a series of stored procedures to configure log shipping, as well. This may make it easier for you to streamline the log shipping configuration process, especially if you will be configuring multiple secondary servers. A number of stored procedures are available that will help automate the process of configuring log shipping.

The following table lists primary server stored procedures.

Stored Procedure	Description
sp_add_log_shipping_primary_database	Use this to configure the primary database for log shipping.
sp_add_log_shipping_primary_secondary	This will add a secondary database to an existing primary.
sp_change_log_shipping_primary_database	This stored procedure changes the primary database settings.
sp_cleanup_log_shipping_history	You can use this to clean up local job history.
sp_delete_log_shipping_primary_database	When you want to stop log shipping, you can use this stored procedure.
sp_delete_log_shipping_primary_secondary	If you want to remove a secondary server from the primary, use this stored procedure.
sp_help_log_shipping_primary_database	This will display primary database settings for the local server.
sp_help_log_shipping_primary_secondary	This will display secondary server names for a specified primary database.
sp_refresh_log_shipping_monitor	This will update the monitor with the latest data.

The following table lists secondary server stored procedures.

Stored Procedure	Description
sp_add_log_shipping_secondary_database	This will add a secondary database.
sp_add_log_shipping_secondary_primary	Use this to specify the primary server and database information for the secondary server.
sp_change_log_shipping_secondary_database	This allows you to change settings on the secondary database.

Table continued on following page

Stored Procedure	Description
sp_change_log_shipping_secondary_primary	This allows you to change additional settings such as destination folder and file retention.
sp_cleanup_log_shipping_history	This will clean up local history.
sp_delete_log_shipping_secondary_database	Use this to remove a secondary database.
sp_delete_log_shipping_secondary_primary	This will remove information about the primary from the secondary server.
sp_help_log_shipping_secondary_database	Use this to retrieve secondary database settings.
sp_help_log_shipping_secondary_primary	This allows you to view the settings for the primary database.
sp_refresh_log_shipping_monitor	Update the monitor with the latest information about the secondary database.

The following table lists monitor server stored procedures.

Stored Procedure	Description
sp_add_log_shipping_alert_job	Creates an alert job if one doesn't already exist.
sp_delete_log_shipping_alert_job	Removes the alert job if there are no primary databases listed.
sp_help_log_shipping_alert_job	This will return the job ID of the alert job.
sp_help_log_shipping_monitor_primary	Use this to display monitor records about the specified primary database.
sp_help_log_shipping_monitor_secondary	Use this to display monitor records about the specified secondary database.

If you want to see some of these stored procedures in action, rather than immediately applying the log shipping changes to the primary database, you can choose to script the commands to a file. You can then alter the file or copy its contents to automate the creation of multiple secondary databases. Following is the script that was generated from the example configuration presented earlier. Note that there are several elements that must be configured on both the primary and secondary servers. If you want to run the script to configure your servers, be sure to replace the server names Aughtfive and HADemo with your primary and secondary server names as needed.

```
-- Execute the following statements at the Primary to configure Log Shipping
-- for the database [AUGHTFIVE].[AdventureWorks],
-- The script needs to be run at the Primary in the context of the [msdb]
-- database.
```

```
--------------------------------------------------------------------------------
Adding the Log Shipping configuration

-- ****** Begin: Script to be run at Primary: [AUGHTFIVE] ******

DECLARE @LS_BackupJobId      AS uniqueidentifier
DECLARE @LS_PrimaryId        AS uniqueidentifier
DECLARE @SP_Add_RetCode      AS int

EXEC @SP_Add_RetCode = master.dbo.sp_add_log_shipping_primary_database
        @database = N'AdventureWorks'
        ,@backup_directory = N'C:\LogSource'
        ,@backup_share = N'\\AughtFive\LogSource'
        ,@backup_job_name = N'LSBackup_AdventureWorks'
        ,@backup_retention_period = 4320
        ,@monitor_server = N'HAMirror'
        ,@monitor_server_security_mode = 1
        ,@backup_threshold = 60
        ,@threshold_alert_enabled = 1
        ,@history_retention_period = 5760
        ,@backup_job_id = @LS_BackupJobId OUTPUT
        ,@primary_id = @LS_PrimaryId OUTPUT
        ,@overwrite = 1

IF (@@ERROR = 0 AND @SP_Add_RetCode = 0)
BEGIN

DECLARE @LS_BackUpScheduleUID      As uniqueidentifier
DECLARE @LS_BackUpScheduleID       AS int

EXEC msdb.dbo.sp_add_schedule
        @schedule_name =N'LSBackupSchedule_AUGHTFIVE1'
        ,@enabled = 1
        ,@freq_type = 4
        ,@freq_interval = 1
        ,@freq_subday_type = 4
        ,@freq_subday_interval = 15
        ,@freq_recurrence_factor = 0
        ,@active_start_date = 20060501
        ,@active_end_date = 99991231
        ,@active_start_time = 0
        ,@active_end_time = 235900
        ,@schedule_uid = @LS_BackUpScheduleUID OUTPUT
        ,@schedule_id = @LS_BackUpScheduleID OUTPUT

EXEC msdb.dbo.sp_attach_schedule
        @job_id = @LS_BackupJobId
        ,@schedule_id = @LS_BackUpScheduleID

EXEC msdb.dbo.sp_update_job
        @job_id = @LS_BackupJobId
        ,@enabled = 1

END
```

```
-- ****** End: Script to be run at Primary: [AUGHTFIVE]  ******


-- Execute the following statements at the Secondary to configure Log Shipping
-- for the database [HADemo].[AdventureWorks],
-- the script needs to be run at the Secondary in the context of the [msdb]
-- database.
-------------------------------------------------------------------------------

-- Adding the Log Shipping configuration

-- ****** Begin: Script to be run at Secondary: [HADemo] ******

DECLARE @LS_Secondary__CopyJobId     AS uniqueidentifier
DECLARE @LS_Secondary__RestoreJobId    AS uniqueidentifier
DECLARE @LS_Secondary__SecondaryId     AS uniqueidentifier
DECLARE @LS_Add_RetCode     As int

EXEC @LS_Add_RetCode = master.dbo.sp_add_log_shipping_secondary_primary
        @primary_server = N'AUGHTFIVE'
        ,@primary_database = N'AdventureWorks'
        ,@backup_source_directory = N'\\AughtFive\LogSource'
        ,@backup_destination_directory = N'C:\LogShip'
        ,@copy_job_name = N'LSCopy_AUGHTFIVE_AdventureWorks'
        ,@restore_job_name = N'LSRestore_AUGHTFIVE_AdventureWorks'
        ,@file_retention_period = 4320
        ,@monitor_server = N'HAMirror'
        ,@monitor_server_security_mode = 1
        ,@overwrite = 1
        ,@copy_job_id = @LS_Secondary__CopyJobId OUTPUT
        ,@restore_job_id = @LS_Secondary__RestoreJobId OUTPUT
        ,@secondary_id = @LS_Secondary__SecondaryId OUTPUT

IF (@@ERROR = 0 AND @LS_Add_RetCode = 0)
BEGIN

DECLARE @LS_SecondaryCopyJobScheduleUID     As uniqueidentifier
DECLARE @LS_SecondaryCopyJobScheduleID     AS int

EXEC msdb.dbo.sp_add_schedule
        @schedule_name =N'DefaultCopyJobSchedule'
        ,@enabled = 1
        ,@freq_type = 4
        ,@freq_interval = 1
        ,@freq_subday_type = 4
        ,@freq_subday_interval = 15
        ,@freq_recurrence_factor = 0
        ,@active_start_date = 20060501
        ,@active_end_date = 99991231
        ,@active_start_time = 0
        ,@active_end_time = 235900
        ,@schedule_uid = @LS_SecondaryCopyJobScheduleUID OUTPUT
        ,@schedule_id = @LS_SecondaryCopyJobScheduleID OUTPUT

EXEC msdb.dbo.sp_attach_schedule
```

```
        @job_id = @LS_Secondary__CopyJobId
        ,@schedule_id = @LS_SecondaryCopyJobScheduleID

DECLARE @LS_SecondaryRestoreJobScheduleUID      As uniqueidentifier
DECLARE @LS_SecondaryRestoreJobScheduleID       AS int

EXEC msdb.dbo.sp_add_schedule
        @schedule_name =N'DefaultRestoreJobSchedule'
        ,@enabled = 1
        ,@freq_type = 4
        ,@freq_interval = 1
        ,@freq_subday_type = 4
        ,@freq_subday_interval = 15
        ,@freq_recurrence_factor = 0
        ,@active_start_date = 20060501
        ,@active_end_date = 99991231
        ,@active_start_time = 0
        ,@active_end_time = 235900
        ,@schedule_uid = @LS_SecondaryRestoreJobScheduleUID OUTPUT
        ,@schedule_id = @LS_SecondaryRestoreJobScheduleID OUTPUT

EXEC msdb.dbo.sp_attach_schedule
        @job_id = @LS_Secondary__RestoreJobId
        ,@schedule_id = @LS_SecondaryRestoreJobScheduleID


END

DECLARE @LS_Add_RetCode2      As int

IF (@@ERROR = 0 AND @LS_Add_RetCode = 0)
BEGIN

EXEC @LS_Add_RetCode2 = master.dbo.sp_add_log_shipping_secondary_database
        @secondary_database = N'AdventureWorks'
        ,@primary_server = N'AUGHTFIVE'
        ,@primary_database = N'AdventureWorks'
        ,@restore_delay = 0
        ,@restore_mode = 0
        ,@disconnect_users      = 0
        ,@restore_threshold = 45
        ,@threshold_alert_enabled = 1
        ,@history_retention_period      = 5760
        ,@overwrite = 1

END

IF (@@error = 0 AND @LS_Add_RetCode = 0)
BEGIN

EXEC msdb.dbo.sp_update_job
        @job_id = @LS_Secondary__CopyJobId
        ,@enabled = 1

EXEC msdb.dbo.sp_update_job
```

```
                @job_id = @LS_Secondary__RestoreJobId
                ,@enabled = 1

END

-- ****** Begin: Script to be run at Primary: [AUGHTFIVE] ******

EXEC master.dbo.sp_add_log_shipping_primary_secondary
            @primary_database = N'AdventureWorks'
            ,@secondary_server = N'HADemo'
            ,@secondary_database = N'AdventureWorks'
            ,@overwrite = 1

-- ****** End: Script to be run at Primary: [AUGHTFIVE]  ******
```

Configuring Failover

To configure failover between a primary and a secondary server, use the following procedure:

1. If there are any uncopied backup files from the backup share, copy them to the copy destination on each secondary server.

2. Apply all remaining transaction logs in sequence to each secondary database.

3. Perform a backup of the active transaction log on the primary database, if possible. Copy the backup and apply to each standby database.

4. If the primary server is still operational, you may be able to configure the primary database as a new secondary database once the failover has been completed. You can facilitate this by backing up the transaction log on the primary database using the NO RECOVERY option. This allows you to apply transaction log backups from the replacement database.

5. Select one of the secondary servers to host the new primary database by placing the database in recovery mode. As you learned in Chapter 9, this will bring the database to an operational state.

If you have additional secondary servers, you can configure the newly recovered database to act as the primary for additional secondary databases, and make the original primary database a new secondary. Perform the following steps to swap roles:

1. Disable the backup job on the original primary server.

2. Disable the copy and restore jobs on the original secondary server.

3. Use the same share created for the original primary for backups of the new primary database.

4. Add the original database as a secondary database.

5. In the secondary database options on the original database, specify that the database is already initialized. This will save you from having to do a full restore.

Because log shipping is configured on a per-database basis, you may need to perform some additional tasks to ensure that your users can maintain consistent access to the database, even in the event of a failover. First of all, the applications your clients are using must be aware of the change. This may require the application be manually configured to use the new primary server. Also, to ensure consistent access to the database from your application, you will want to ensure that all associated metadata for that database is migrated over. This includes SQL Logins, jobs and alerts, to name a few. Because of some of the limitations of log shipping, it is great for creating read-only standby servers, but a moderate solution for failover considerations.

Database Mirroring

Database mirroring is a new feature introduced in SQL 2005 as an additional high-availability offering. Although initially disabled when SQL 2005 was first launched, the release of Service Pack 1 for SQL 2005 in April of 2006 enabled it for production use. The basic concept is very similar to log shipping in that transaction log records are sent from a source database (known as the *principal* database) to a destination database (known as the *mirror* database). However, instead of a transaction log being copied on a file basis, individual log records are sent on a transaction-by-transaction basis. While database mirroring is also a database-level redundancy solution, it relies on constant communication between servers to maintain transactional integrity. Database mirroring also offers the added advantage of automatic and almost instantaneous failover when configured with a third witness server.

Database mirroring is configured by establishing a partnership between the server hosting the principal database and the server hosting the mirror database. Rather than using the file system as the method of maintaining consistency between the two servers, communications are established and maintained using SQL Server endpoints. Another key difference between log shipping and database mirroring is that database mirroring restricts you to one principal and one mirror for each database.

Database mirroring requires the use of at least two instances of SQL Server. Although these instances could conceivably be on the same physical server, it makes much more sense to have them on separate servers to protect against server failure (see Figure 11-11).

The three server roles in a database mirroring configuration are as follows:

- ❑ *Principal Server* — The principal server hosts the copy of the database that clients connect to and interact with. As transactions occur on the principal database, the transaction log records are forwarded to the mirror database.

- ❑ *Mirror Server* — The mirror server hosts a copy of the principal database and applies the transaction log records sent by the principal database to keep the mirrored database in sync with the principal database.

- ❑ *Witness Server* — The witness server is optional. It is only needed if automatic failover to the mirror server is required in the case of a principal database failure. The witness server monitors the status of the principal and mirror servers in a high-availability configuration, which is described in the section "Database Mirroring Modes," later in this chapter.

When using database mirroring, the mirror database is not directly accessible for client requests, because it is in the constant state of recovering transaction log records. However, indirect access can be configured by creating a database snapshot of the mirrored database. Keep in mind that database snapshots are a point-in-time view of the database and will not reflect the ongoing modifications to the mirror.

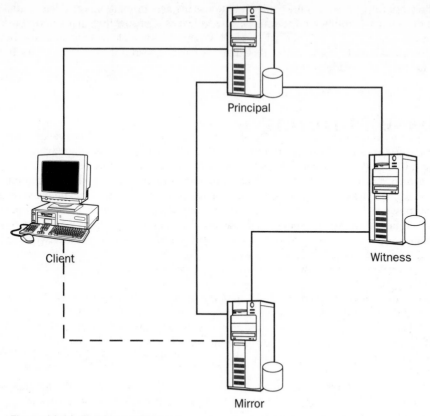

Figure 11-11: Database mirroring

Client Redirection

One of the big advantages of database mirroring is that clients can automatically be redirected to the mirror server in the case of a principal database failure. However, the automatic redirection is not a server-based feature. The connection string of clients are configured to work with a mirrored database by adding the `Failover Partner` attribute, as shown in the following example:

```
Server=AughtFive; Failover Partner=Dagobah; Database=AdventureWorks
```

If the client's attempt to connect to the server identified by the `Server` attribute fails, it will try the server identified by the `Failover Partner` attribute. The opposite is also true. If the client attempts to connect to the failover partner and it is not available, it will try the original server.

Database Mirroring Modes

When building a mirroring solution, you can choose between three operating modes. The database can be configured to use *high-performance mode, high-safety without automatic failover mode,* and *high-safety with automatic failover mode.* Each operating mode has its advantages and disadvantages. It is important to understand exactly what each mode provides, and how it affects your high-availability solution.

High-Performance

High-performance mode uses asynchronous processing. In this mode the principal server sends an acknowledgment to the client application of a successful transaction as soon as it sends the corresponding log record to the mirror server, but it does not wait for acknowledgment from the mirror server that the log record was received. Under normal workload conditions, the latency between the principal and the mirror is relatively small. However, if the principal server is under heavy workload, this can increase the gap between the two partners.

In high-performance mode, there is no automatic failover and no witness server is required. A witness server can be configured, but there is absolutely no advantage to this arrangement, because a failure of the principal will still require a forcing of the database service on the mirror. Once the original principal is restored to service, it will configure itself as a mirror, but the mirroring session will remain in a SUSPENDED state until explicitly resumed by the administrator. Resuming and forcing the mirroring service is described later in this chapter.

High-Safety without Automatic Failover

In this mode, the principal server does not send an acknowledgment to the client of a successful transaction until the mirror server acknowledges the receipt of the corresponding transaction log record. Although this helps protect against data loss in the case of a failure, it can add latency to your transaction processing. There is no automatic failover in this mode and no witness server. Failure of the principal database will require manually forcing the service on the witness server to promote its principal. The process of forcing the service is described later in this chapter. In the case of a mirror server failure, the principal will remain available to clients, but the mirroring session will be in a disconnected state.

High-Safety with Automatic Failover

With the high-safety with automatic failover mode, a witness server is used to provide automatic failover. The witness server does not directly participate in the mirroring process but acts as an overseer between the two servers. As long as two of the three servers participating in this mode can vouch for connectivity, and participation in the mirror session, a database will be available to client requests. When two of the servers agree on the status of the mirroring session, it is called a *quorum*.

If quorum is lost by the mirror or principal server, the mirroring configuration will change. The following table describes some possible scenarios.

Mirror Configuration	Description
Loss of the principal server	If the mirror server and the witness server agree that the principal server is no longer available, the witness server will promote itself to principal and begin accepting client requests. Once the principal server is returned to service, it will contact the witness and original mirror server to discover the status of the mirror configuration, demote itself to mirror status, and synchronize with the new principal.

Table continued on following page

Mirror Configuration	Description
Loss of the mirror server	When the principal server and the witness server agree that the mirror server is no longer available, the principal server will remain online and service client requests, but the mirroring state will be changed to disconnected. Once the mirror server becomes available again, it will synchronize itself with the principal and the mirror session will continue.
Loss of the witness server	As long as the principal and mirror server can establish a quorum, the principal database will remain online and available to client requests. However, no automatic failover will be available as long as the witness server is out of commission.
Loss of the principal and witness server	Without the possibility of a quorum, the mirror server will also be unavailable, because it cannot verify the status of the principal or witness server. To restore the mirror database to service, it will be necessary to remove mirroring from the mirror and manually recover it.
Loss of the mirror and witness server	If the principal server loses contact with both the witness and the mirror server, it will take its database offline and change the database's status to RESTORING. This is to avoid the possibility that the mirror server and witness server have established a quorum and the mirror server is answering client requests, preventing a "dual brain" scenario where both the mirror and principal are responding to client requests. To bring the principal database back online, database mirroring must be removed and the principal manually restored.

Configuring Database Mirroring

This section explains how to configure database mirroring between two servers, with an optional witness server to monitor the mirror. I'll begin by showing you how to set up database mirroring from SQL Server Management Studio, and then showing you a Transact-SQL alternative. Before you use either, though, you must perform a full backup of your database, and restore it on the mirror server using the NO RECOVERY option. Refer to Chapter 9 for the backup-and-restore process.

Using SQL Server Management Studio

To set up mirroring, begin by opening the Mirroring page on the Properties sheet of the database. You can also get to this page by selecting Mirroring from the Tasks menu of the database. As you can see in Figure 11-12, the first step you will need to execute is configuring security for database mirroring. Clicking the Configure Security button will launch a wizard that will ask you to provide the connection options for the principal, mirror, and witness server endpoints.

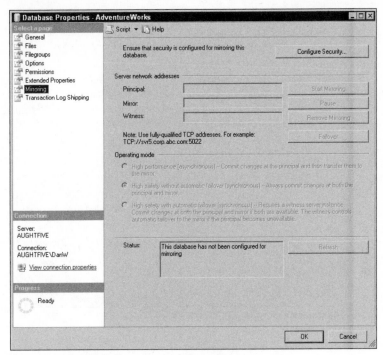

Figure 11-12: Database mirroring Properties page

The first page of the wizard, like many other wizards, includes a summary of the tasks that will be completed when the wizard is complete. Click Next to move to the next page, which will ask you if you will be configuring a witness server. While the witness is certainly optional, it's a good idea to have one for applications that need automatic failover.

The next page of the wizard asks you to identify which servers will be configured through this wizard. You will want to check all participating servers, including the witness server if one is being used.

Moving on to the next page of the wizard, you can configure the options for the principal server, including the TCP port and name that will be used by the endpoint on the principal server. (Refer to Chapter 7 for a more detailed explanation of endpoints.) You can also specify whether or not the endpoint will use encryption. The default values for all endpoints use 5022 as the port number, mirroring as the name, and encryption is enabled, but you can change these values as necessary.

Next, you will configure the same information for the mirror server. Figure 11-13 shows an example of the page you will see when configuring the endpoints. Note that when you are creating the endpoints on each of the servers, you must have the appropriate permissions to create and configure security on endpoints.

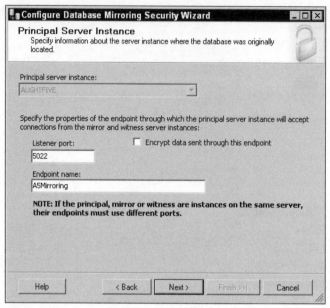

Figure 11-13: Configuring the mirror server

If configuring a witness server, the next page will ask you to provide the server name and endpoint configuration for the witness. If you look at Figure 11-13, there is a note that specifies that if more than one role is on the same physical server, the port numbers must be different. For example, if you install another instance of SQL on the same server as your mirror database to act as the witness, when you create the witness endpoint, you will have to use a different port number.

If a SQL Server has more than one database that will participate in database mirroring, all databases can share the same endpoint. This prevents you from having to create five endpoints for the same purpose, but for five different databases. Make sure, however, that endpoint security is properly configured, especially if the databases are owned by different users.

Because database mirroring is designed to work without requiring all machines be identically configured, or even members of the same domain, the wizard then allows you to specify the account information for each server (see Figure 11-14). Note that the wizard informs you that if the SQL Servers all use the same account, local accounts, or domain accounts in non-trusting domains to leave the values blank.

Once you have entered this information, the summary page of the wizard allows you to review your configuration. If you are satisfied with your settings, click Finish to create the endpoints, and, if necessary, apply the appropriate permissions. Figure 11-15 shows a sample summary page. Note that the two endpoints that participate in the actual mirroring process have their roles identified as *partners*, whereas the witness server is simply identified as *witness*.

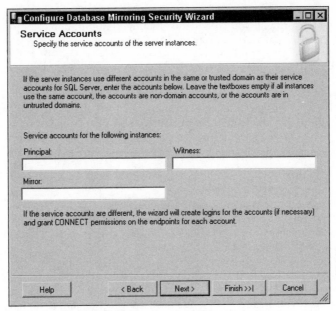

Figure 11-14: Specifying service accounts

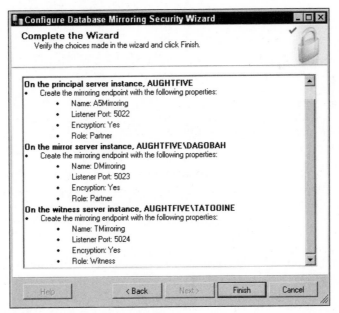

Figure 11-15: Wizard summary

Now that you've completed the wizard, SQL Server will prompt you to see if you want to start mirroring now, or to delay mirroring. If you are satisfied that the configuration is correct, and the mirror server is consistent with the principal server, and then click the button to begin mirroring.

Using Transact-SQL

The T-SQL commands for configuring database mirroring are easy to use and understand. Creating an endpoint for database mirroring is often a lot less complex than other endpoints you might create. Again, refer to Chapter 7 for a more detailed explanation on what endpoints are and how they work.

For database mirroring, execute the following to create an endpoint that does not use encryption:

```
USE Master;
GO
CREATE ENDPOINT MirroringEndPoint
    STATE = STARTED
    AS TCP ( LISTENER_PORT = 5022 )
    FOR DATABASE_MIRRORING (ROLE=PARTNER)
GO
```

Executing this statement on both the principal and mirrored servers creates identical endpoints that can be used for mirroring. If you are just testing mirroring for practice, and don't have a separate physical server to use, installing another instance will allow you to mirror databases, as long as the endpoints use different port numbers.

When using a witness server, execute the following command on the witness instance to create the appropriate endpoint:

```
USE Master;
GO
CREATE ENDPOINT WitnessEndPoint
    STATE = STARTED
    AS TCP ( LISTENER_PORT = 5022 )
    FOR DATABASE_MIRRORING (ROLE=WITNESS)
GO
```

Note that the only things different are the endpoint name and the role, and of those two, only one is required to be different (that would be the role; the name is irrelevant to the process).

Additional options for creating database mirroring endpoints allow you to specify authentication and encryption options. Authentication allows you to choose from the following authentication methods:

❑ Windows NT LAN Manager (NTLM)

❑ Windows Kerberos

❑ Windows Negotiate (Kerberos, if available; if not, fall back to NTLM)

❑ Certificate certificate_name

You can also specify to try certificate authentication first, and failing that, using Windows authentication, or vice versa. Additionally, you can specify that encryption is disabled, supported, or required, and, if supported or required, which encryption algorithm to use, Advanced Encryption Standard (AES) or

RC4. If you specify both AES and RC4, you can choose the preferred order for each. For more on encryption and certificates, refer to Chapter 6.

So, if you were to create a new endpoint that used Windows authentication and AES encryption, you might use the following code:

```
USE Master;
GO
CREATE ENDPOINT WitnessEndPoint
    STATE = STARTED
    AS TCP ( LISTENER_PORT = 5022 )
    FOR DATABASE_MIRRORING (AUTHENTICATION = WINDOWS NEGOTIATE,
    ENCRYPTION = REQUIRED ALGORITHM AES, ROLE = PARTNER);
GO
```

Now that you have your endpoints created, the next step is to establish the mirror. This is done simply by pointing the database on each server to the target partner. You will use an ALTER DATABASE statement to accomplish this, as in the following example (you may need to change the URLs to match your server names):

```
-- Execute this statement on the principal server
-- to specify the endpoint for the mirror

USE Master;
GO
ALTER DATABASE AdventureWorks
SET PARTNER = 'TCP://HAMirror.adventureworks.com:5022';


-- Execute this statement on the mirror server
-- to specify the endpoint for the principal

USE Master;
GO
ALTER DATABASE AdventureWorks
SET PARTNER = 'TCP://Adventureworks.adventureworks.com:5022';

-- Execute this statement on the principal server
-- to specify the endpoint for the witness

USE Master;
GO
ALTER DATABASE AdventureWorks
SET WITNESS = 'TCP://HADemo.adventureworks.com:5022';
```

When both the principal and mirror servers have been configured to recognize one another, the mirroring process begins. By default, database mirroring is configured to use synchronous mode, but you can change this after mirroring has begun by executing the following statement at the principal server:

```
USE Master;
GO
ALTER DATABASE AdventureWorks
SET PARTNER SAFETY OFF;
```

To turn synchronous mode back on, use the SET PARTNER SAFETY FULL option.

Monitoring Database Mirroring

Monitoring your mirrored database can give you an idea of how well your mirroring solution is working, and whether or not there are latency or consistency issues that must be addressed. On both the principal and mirror servers, you can query the following system catalog views to view the status and configuration of all mirrors on that server:

❑   sys.database_mirroring

❑   sys.database_mirroring_endpoints

You can also query the sys.database_mirroring_witnesses on the witness server (if there is one) to view the witness server's summary of the mirrors it is aware of. Microsoft also provides a nice UI tool that can be launched from the context menu of any user database on any SQL Server. You will need to provide the appropriate connection options to either the principal or the mirror to register a particular database, but the fact that you can launch the tool from anywhere makes it a handy resource. Just choose the option to Launch Database Mirroring Monitor from the Tasks menu of a database, and a new window appears (see Figure 11-16).

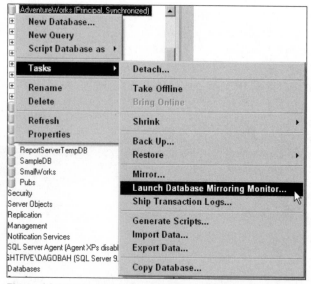

Figure 11-16: Launching the Database Mirroring Monitor

In the details pane, click the link to register a new mirrored database that will be monitored by this tool (see Figure 11-17). In the registration page, click the Connect button to connect to either the principal or the mirror server, using the appropriate authentication and connection options. You are then presented with a list of mirrored databases on that instance. Select the appropriate database(s) to register, and click OK. If you need to use different authentication credentials between the principal and the mirror, you can also select the "Show the Manage Server Connections dialog box when I click OK" option to specify per-server connection options.

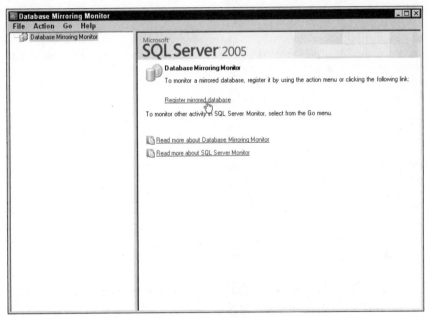

Figure 11-17: The Database Mirroring Monitor

Once you've registered your database, you will be able to expand the list in the tree pane, and select the database to see the status of the mirror. Figure 11-18 shows an example of the status screen, which includes identifying the servers, their roles, the mirroring state, and their connection to the witness server.

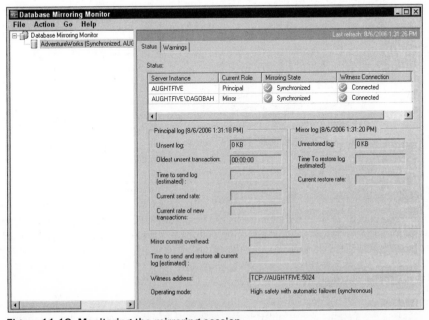

Figure 11-18: Monitoring the mirroring session

Additional information is available that will help you identify potential latency properties by showing the stats for the principal and mirror logs.

Clicking the Warnings tab allows you to view or configure the current settings for generating alerts based on mirroring conditions. The warnings can be generated on the following conditions:

- ❏ Threshold in kilobytes for the unsent log
- ❏ Threshold in kilobytes for the unrestored log
- ❏ Oldest unsent transaction in minutes
- ❏ Mirror commit overhead in milliseconds

As you can see from Figure 11-19, the thresholds can be defined on both the principal and the mirror, and you can, in fact, use different values on each. Your warning threshold should be based on known and expected performance values, and may need to be adjusted to accommodate changes to your mirroring system. In any event, it's a good idea to make sure that you use consistent values between the principal and the mirror, so that you can respond appropriately to the alert.

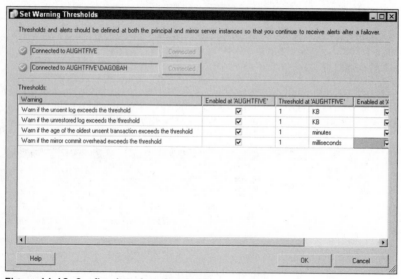

Figure 11-19: Configuring alert thresholds

Managing Database Mirroring

Among the maintenance tasks associated with database mirroring are pausing a session, resuming a paused session, initiating mirror failover, forcing principal service, and removing mirroring for the database.

Pausing a Mirror Session

If there is a significant delay in database responsiveness that may be caused by the additional work of having to maintain constant communications between the principal and its mirror, you may want to consider temporarily suspending the communications. To pause the session using SQL Server Management Studio, navigate to the Mirroring page on the database Properties sheet, and simply click Pause (see Figure 11-20).

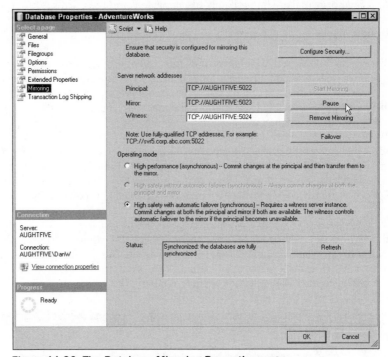

Figure 11-20: The Database Mirroring Properties page

Using Transact-SQL, execute an ALTER DATABASE statement with the SET PARTNER SUSPEND option, as in the following example:

```
USE Master;
ALTER DATABASE AdventureWorks SET PARTNER SUSPEND;
GO
```

Resuming a Mirror Session

Although pausing the session will allow you to later resume the session with no data loss, the transaction log cannot be truncated until the mirror has been resumed. For this reason, it is a good idea to resume the mirroring session as quickly as possible. To resume mirroring from SQL Server Management Studio, simply click the Resume button, which replaced the Pause button when the session was suspended.

Use the SET PARTNER RESUME option for the ALTER DATABASE statement to resume the mirror from Transact-SQL, as in the following example:

```
USE Master;
ALTER DATABASE AdventureWorks SET PARTNER RESUME;
GO
```

Manual Failover

Regardless of the operating mode of the mirror, you can manually initiate failover at any time from SQL Server Management Studio or T-SQL. When initiating failover, be aware that any clients that are connected to the original principal are immediately disconnected, and the mirror is brought online. The original principal, if online, is then converted to a mirror, and will remain in the NO RECOVERY state until failover is executed again.

Be aware of the effects failover will have on your clients. Client applications that use the SQL Native Client or the .NET Framework Data Provider for SQL Server can be configured to use database mirroring, allowing clients to be redirected to a mirror server in the event of a failover. Users may notice a slight delay or interruption after a failover, but, for the most part, operations should continue as normal, as long as a few precautions are in place.

Because database mirroring only copies the contents of a specific database, specific server-wide resources (such as logins) must be available on the mirror either prior to or immediately after the failover. For this reason, when using database mirroring, it's a good idea to create and schedule an Integration Services package, which will regularly copy additional objects. See Chapter 13 for an introduction to the Integration Services tools.

To initiate failover from SQL Server Management Studio, click the Failover button in the Mirroring Properties page of the principal database. That's it. SQL handles the rest (see Figure 11-21). If you need to restore a former principal back to its "principalian" state, you must connect to the *new* principal, the original mirror, and click the Failover button on that database's properties.

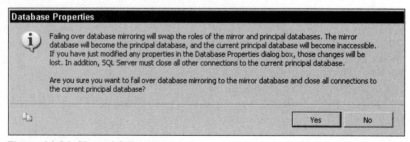

Figure 11-21: Manual failover

To manually initiate failover using Transact-SQL, again, you must be connected to the principal server, then execute the following:

```
USE Master;
ALTER DATABASE AdventureWorks SET PARTNER FAILOVER;
GO
```

This will immediately bring the principal down as a mirror, and promote the original mirror to the principal database.

Forcing Service on the Mirror

As previously described, the mirror server is not automatically available in the case of a principal server failure when operating in high-performance or high-safety without automatic failover modes. To force the mirror server to promote itself and service client requests, the following command must be issued on the mirror server:

```
USE Master;
ALTER DATABASE AdventureWorks SET PARTNER FAILOVER;
GO
```

Removing a Database Mirror

Once you no longer need a database mirroring session, you can break the mirror. Breaking the mirror allows both participating servers to maintain a copy of the database. The principal will remain online, and the mirror will remain in the recovery mode.

Breaking the mirror will not delete, remove, or alter the endpoints, which is a very good thing, because they may still be used by other databases that are using database mirroring.

To break the mirror from SQL Server Management Studio, click the Remove Mirror button on the mirroring Properties page of the principal database. Using Transact-SQL, use the SET PARTNER OFF option for the ALTER DATABASE statement, as shown here:

```
USE Master;
ALTER DATABASE AdventureWorks SET PARTNER OFF;
```

Optionally, you can then bring the mirror server online by using RESTORE DATABASE AdventureWorks WITH RECOVERY option. Just ensure that your clients know which one is the real database, and which one is the imposter!

Summary

The reality is that there is no one-size-fits-all solution to high availability. The best way to provide for a highly available and highly reliable solution is to use a combination of tools and techniques to allow your database to stay operational, even during the most serious outages.

In this chapter, you learned how SQL Clustering uses redundant hardware to provide quick failover with no loss of data or services for an entire server. You also learned about the database-level redundancy provided by both log shipping and database mirroring, and the benefits of each.

The next few chapters let you explore some of the additional features of SQL Server 2005. In Chapter 12, you learn about Common Language Runtime (CLR) built into SQL Server 2005, for integration with your .NET applications.

Administering SQL CLR Programming Objects

The objective of this chapter is to show you, the system administrator, how to manage the configuration and the settings related to maintaining the security and stability of SQL Common Language Runtime (CLR) database objects. The discussion presents you with some simple examples of CLR program code, but because this is not a programming book, I will use very basic code examples that you can obtain from Books Online and the Microsoft Web site. The purpose is to show you how to manage these objects after they have been created.

Databases and Programming

When Dan asked me to write this chapter, I immediately asked him how he intended for this topic to fit neatly into a book about database administration. You see, I'm a programmer primarily, and database administration has always been the thing that the other guys at the other end of the IT shop did.

If you're a career database administrator, then you probably know that I represent the contingent of unruly coders who often want to deploy precarious, custom-built applications on your servers. In the process of finding new and creative ways to solve problems with program code, programmers tend to break things. Because the administrator's job is to maintain a stable and secure server environment, it would naturally make sense to keep programmers (and their pesky program code) as far away from the servers as possible.

If you are a developer and you are reading this, you may think that I am making a lot of to do about nothing, but most of the seasoned database administrators in the enterprise space (especially those with development skills) have learned to be very cautious of custom code and assemblies that could bring their servers down or cause hard-to-solve performance problems. I fully acknowledge the fact that many of you wear both a programming hat and an administrator hat from time to time, and, as you read this chapter, I may seem to present a single-minded view of the DBA role. This is to simply keep us focused on our purpose, which is database administration. Therefore, I ask that if you consider yourself to be a programmer/DBA, please place your DBA hat only squarely on your head and read on.

So, why in the world would you consider allowing new program code to run on your database server? I have good news. Managing custom code can now be completely secure, stable, and fully integrated into the SQL Server database server environment. Best of all, the control over these components is completely in the hands of our esteemed database administrators.

In past versions of SQL Server, database programming objects (mainly stored procedures) could be extended using custom programming technologies. Even before Microsoft began to extend the original Sybase SQL Server product, extended stored procedures could be written using complex C and C++ programming. In later versions, a set of system stored procedures were added, allowing COM components to be called. Many production SQL Server–based applications use these procedures to send email, automate Windows services, and to interact with the file system. Relying on extended stored procedures and custom-written COM objects can be risky business, because these technologies provide no built-in protection from memory leaks, buffer overruns, and unstable operations. By contrast, the .NET Framework run-time provides a rigid layer of protection of both stability and security.

In my mind, this is the most compelling new feature that SQL Server 2005 has to offer. Transact-SQL has been pushed to and beyond its limits for a long time now. Not too many years ago, the words *database* and *programming* were rarely used in the same sentence, especially when discussing work performed in a database, rather than in a separate application. However, these two words are commonly juxtaposed today, and are often used to describe the day-to-day activities of a new breed of IT professionals who write stored procedures, user-defined functions, triggers, types, and aggregations for database solutions. The two isolated worlds of database management and programming began to collide about the time that the SQL Server product began to mature.

I recall attending the launch event for SQL Server 7.0. Stave Ballmer, now the CEO of Microsoft, presented after a series of new feature demonstrations. He asked all of the DBAs in the audience to stand up. Out of about 1,500 people in attendance, about 100 DBAs rose to their feet. He said that he was going to offer some career advice to this group. He said *"learn Visual Basic."* After this short message, 100 DBAs sat down, some confused and some angry.

It hasn't taken many years to see Steve's prediction fulfilled in a few different ways. After emerging from the economic decline at the turn of the century, many IT shops have been restructured with some technical professionals filling multiple roles. Although it's still true in larger companies that programmers are programmers and administrators are administrators, now it's not uncommon to find seasoned programmers who often build and configure development servers. It's also not uncommon to find administrators who write script and program code to perform automated administrative tasks. And in smaller shops, it's quite common to find one person who does both.

Is the SQL Language a Relic?

The Transact-SQL language is a very effective tool for retrieving and manipulating data stored in a relational database. The main purpose of SQL is to return results from one or many tables combined by using joins and unions, to insert new rows, and to update and delete rows in a table. SQL may be used to efficiently perform common value comparisons, mathematical operations, numeric aggregation, string parsing, and concatenation. When it comes to processing complex business logic, SQL has its limits.

By design, it was not intended to perform looping and enumeration. Conditional branching capabilities are very limited and, even with the new structured error handling in SQL Server 2005, exception handling is still a matter of failing gracefully, rather than recovering from, and managing the program logic following an exception. Transact-SQL remains the best language choice for standard data-retrieval and data-manipulation operations. However, for implementing complex business rule logic requiring row-by-row operations, loops and counters, decision structures, and including values from sources outside of SQL databases, extending database programming through the CLR may offer many advantages. Cursor operations are particularly taxing on the database engine, and simply cannot be optimized.

Is SQL a relic? No. It has certainly been around longer than some modern object-oriented programming languages such as C# and Java, but for its purpose, SQL is by no means antiquated. It will be around for a long time, and should be used to perform the day-to-day administrative, management, and programming tasks in SQL Server. The Transact-SQL language has been enhanced for SQL Server 2005. It's lean and efficient, and is the easiest way to get the best performance out of your SQL Server databases for most types of operations.

.Net and the CLR

Software developers know that the Microsoft .NET CLR is at the core of an entire application development platform. In simple terms, the CLR is really just a set of installed components that allow software and custom-built components to run on a computer. In addition to this capability, the CLR also provides a safety net to ensure that software runs safely and securely, and that it doesn't misuse or waste system resources.

Assemblies

A .NET *assembly* is the executable form of program code. An assembly that is used to contain SQL CLR objects is typically built as a class library with a DLL file extension. A newly built assembly actually contains semi-compiled Microsoft Intermediate Language (MSIL) code. An assembly is stored in this intermediate, semi-compiled state so that it can be fully compiled into the most optimal form when it runs on the target computer, rather than the computer where it was developed.

SQL CLR object assemblies are stored in the database rather than as EXE or DLL files in the file system and are fully manageable objects that can be secured and controlled just like all other database objects. It is a defined programming object organized into a simple hierarchy, consisting of namespaces, classes, and methods. A single assembly may host many SQL Server objects (such as functions, stored procedures, aggregates, and data types).

Namespaces

A *namespace* is an organizational structure used to group classes into manageable categories. A namespace may contain any number of subordinate namespaces that are used to group and manage similar object classes. The .NET Framework consists of scores of nested namespaces, which in turn contain thousands of classes. A namespace provides no inherent functionality, other than to be a container for classes. In the case of SQL Server assemblies, the namespaces contained in the assemblies help organize the functionality of the assembly by using descriptive names to specify each embedded procedure or function contained in the assembly.

Classes

A *class* defines a programming object and is typically used to group program logic for an entity or functional unit. For example, a `Customer` class may be used to encapsulate all of the programming logic related to customers. Beyond the scope of database objects, classes are used to define object-oriented programming structures for collections and hierarchies of objects. A class provides the definition for an object created by program code (known as an *instance* of a class) at run-time. If you were learning to program with objects, this would be a very long and tedious, perhaps even philosophical, discourse about how you should use classes to implement object-oriented design patterns for architecting software solutions. Luckily for you, as a database administrator or designer using SQL CLR, you won't be required to use classes at this level of depth. For our purposes, a class is merely a logical container for related program code.

Methods

Within classes, program code may define several things such as *members, properties, structures, enumerations, events,* and *methods*. Although these programming constructs may be used internally by a SQL CLR object, the only thing of consequence exposed to SQL Server are methods. In simple terms, a *method* is a function or procedure used to return values or structured data to its calling object. Just like a user-defined function in Transact-SQL, a method may accept any number of input parameters, and return a value or some type of object.

SQL Server CLR Objects

So, what's all the hoopla about using .NET assemblies in databases? We've survived for a long time without combining programming with databases. Business has driven technology (and, to some degree perhaps, technology has driven business) to the point where it's necessary to raise the bar. Business applications now require more than just the capability to put information into a database so that you can take it back out. Complex business processes require complex program logic, which goes beyond the scope of simple CRUD (Create, Read, Update, and Delete) database operations.

For this reason, SQL Server 2005 allows five types of database objects (traditionally defined either internally or in Transact-SQL code) to be created with .NET program code. This gives programmers and solution architects the ability to control the behavior of database operations, and to provide advanced capabilities in the data storage layer of a solution.

SQL Server CLR objects (or SQL CLR) are programming routines built into .NET assemblies that are stored and managed within a database. The execution of the objects occurs within the SQL Server process space, according to the rules and security context of the database and SQL Server. To behave well in this environment, certain restrictions apply:

❑ All assembly code must be type-safe. This means that all values exchanged between objects conform to standard data types and must be explicitly declared. The run-time will not perform any implicit type conversion from one object to another if the types are not already compatible.

❑ Several class and method attributes have been added to support SQL CLR functionality, security, and features. Using unrelated attributes may render the assembly incompatible and not allow it to execute.

❏ All static (or shared) data members must be read-only.

❏ SQL CLR doesn't support code with `Finalizer` methods. Assemblies containing this code will not be allowed to execute.

Some Transact-SQL statements have been added to support new SQL CLR capabilities, and other statements have been updated. Generally, the `CREATE` and `ALTER` statements have been extended with provisions for the new programming paradigm. Some of these changes are noted in the following sections for the database objects supported by SQL CLR.

Enabling SQL CLR

The SQL CLR feature is disabled by default, and must be explicitly enabled on the database server. This is done using the `sp_configure` system stored procedure. Pass the character value `CLR ENABLED` in the first argument and the numeric value `1` (for `True`) in the second argument. The setting is then applied by executing the `RECONFIGURE` command after changing this setting. The following script demonstrates how this is done:

```
USE Master
GO
sp_configure 'CLR ENABLED', 1;
RECONFIGURE WITH OVERRIDE;
GO
```

The results of this command should look something like this:

```
Configuration option 'clr enabled' changed from 0 to 1. Run the RECONFIGURE
statement to install.
```

Creating a SQL CLR Assembly

Before creating a SQL CLR assembly, it would be helpful to have one to work with. The following exercise guides you through the process of creating a simple function that will return the message "Hello World" when called from a T-SQL command. To follow along with this exercise, you must have Visual Studio 2005 installed with Visual Basic.

Try It Out   Building a CLR User-Defined Function

Open Visual Studio 2005 and create a new project by selecting New → Project on the File menu (see Figure 12-1).

In the resulting New Project window (see Figure 12-2), choose Database as the project type and give the project and solution a name. By default, the solution has the same name as the project, but I changed it to make it a bit less redundant. Assign the project the name `SayHello`, the solution the name `SayHelloSolution`, and click OK.

Figure 12-1: Starting a new project

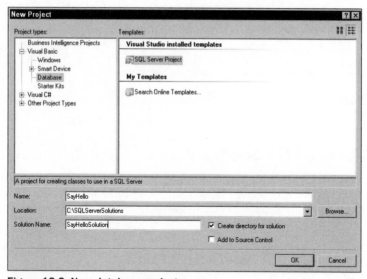

Figure 12-2: New database project

Visual Studio will prompt you for a database reference. This will establish the database connection used to deploy the objects. If a connection object to the AdventureWorks database appears in the Add Database Reference dialog (as shown in Figure 12-3), choose it.

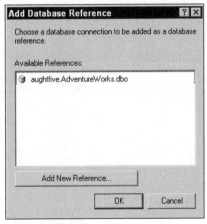

Figure 12-3: Add Database Reference

If no connection to AdventureWorks exists, you will need to create one by clicking the Add New Reference button and supplying the appropriate values for a connection to the database, as shown in Figure 12-4.

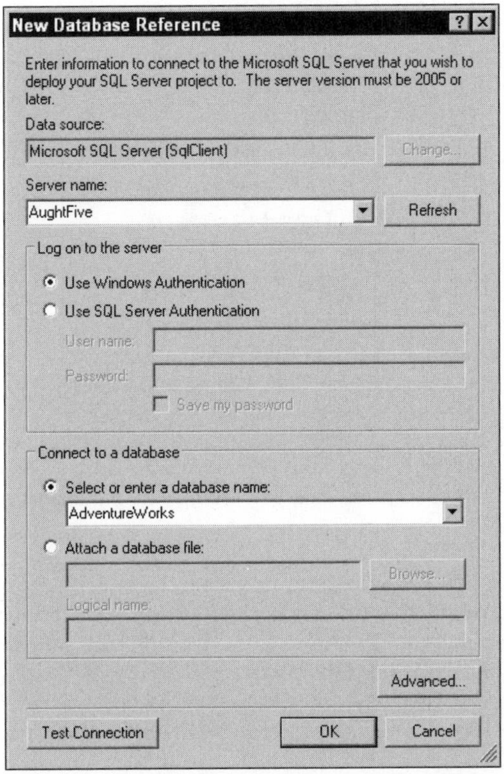

New Database Reference   ? X

Enter information to connect to the Microsoft SQL Server that you wish to deploy your SQL Server project to. The server version must be 2005 or later.

Data source:

Microsoft SQL Server (SqlClient)   Change...

Server name:

AughtFive   ▼   Refresh

Log on to the server

● Use Windows Authentication

○ Use SQL Server Authentication

    User name:

    Password:

    ☐ Save my password

Connect to a database

● Select or enter a database name:

AdventureWorks   ▼

○ Attach a database file:

              Browse...

    Logical name:

Advanced...

Test Connection   OK   Cancel

Figure 12-4: New Database Reference

If SQL/CLR debugging has not been enabled previously on this development computer, the message box shown in Figure 12-5 will appear. Click Yes to enable this feature.

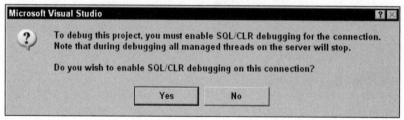

Figure 12-5: Enable SQL/CLR debugging

After adding a database reference, an empty project is created with no objects. Database objects are added by either right-clicking the project in the Solution Explorer and choosing an object from the Add context menu, or by choosing an Add option from the Project menu (see Figure 12-6).

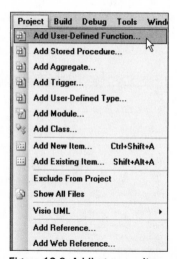

Figure 12-6: Adding a new item

Clicking any of the choices in the Add menu will launch the Add New Item window (see Figure 12-7). Ensure that User-Defined Function is selected in the template pane, and give the function the name fnHello.

Creating any of the objects will generate the appropriate class or structure file in the designer with a set of skeleton code to get you started. In the case of the function you just created, a simple class module will be added to the project. Figure 12-8 shows a new user-defined function code module added to a Visual Basic database project. Note the namepaces referenced in the Imports statements. These namespaces are either required or typically used in database projects. Also note the method attribute (that is, <Microsoft.SQLServer.Server.SQLFunction()>) that marks this part of the assembly as a SQL CLR user-defined function.

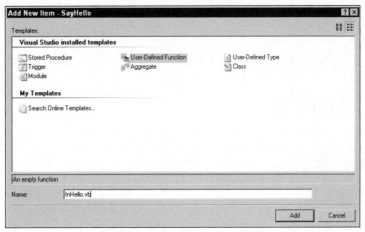

Figure 12-7: New user-defined function

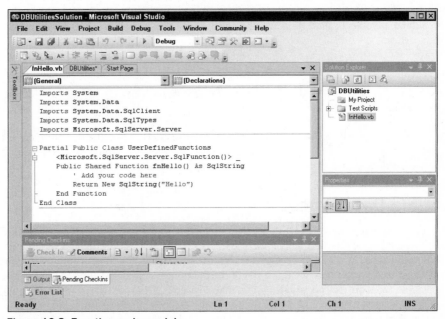

Figure 12-8: Function code module

Change the string in the fnHello code module so that it says "Hello World", because it is an established tradition that Hello World is always the first application.

On the Build menu, click the Build SayHello option to create the DLL that you will use in the next exercises. Note that the other option is Deploy SayHello. Deploying the project will create the assembly and the function in the AdventureWorks database. Because you want to explore this process more systematically, just build it for now. When I created the solution, I saved it to the C:\SQLServerSolutions folder and had Visual Studio create a new solution folder upon creation. As a result, the built SayHello DLL file is now located in the C:\SQLServerSolutions\SayHelloSolution\SayHello\bin folder.

Next you'll explore how to add this assembly to the AdventureWorks database and manage it.

Adding an Assembly

Prior to defining any SQL CLR object, the .NET assembly containing the executable code must be loaded into the database. This is performed with the CREATE ASSEMBLY statement. Note that the ALTER ASSEMBLY and DROP ASSEMBLY statements were also added for managing these objects. In its simplest form, the CREATE ASSEMBLY statement syntax is as follows:

```
CREATE ASSEMBLY <assembly name>
FROM <source file path>
WITH PERMISSION_SET = <permission set>
```

The following example shows this statement used to load the SayHello assembly file into the database. After this statement is executed, this file is no longer necessary because the executable code will be contained in a database object called HelloWorld.

```
USE AdventureWorks;
GO
CREATE ASSEMBLY HelloWorld
FROM 'C:\SQLServerSolutions\SayHelloSolution\SayHello\bin\SayHello.dll'
WITH PERMISSION_SET = SAFE
```

After the assembly has been loaded in this manner, you can add the specific function that is contained in it. Remember that assemblies can actually contain many objects, so one imported assembly can be referenced to create new functions, stored procedures, aggregates, and types.

Compatible Data Types

As .NET programming procedures are defined and then integrated with SQL Server CLR objects, it is crucial that all data types be matched with compatible types. Most SQL Server data types have compatible equivalent native types in the .NET Framework. Note that variables, method arguments, and return values may be defined using either native .NET types or the data types defined within the SqlClient namespace. The SqlClient types are exact equivalents that map to each SQL Server type through internal wrapper code. Not all SQL Server types have compatible equivalents, though. If execution fails, reporting a type mismatch or invalid cast, you likely have an incompatible data type issue. The following table shows common SQL Server types with .NET equivalent types.

SQL Server Type	.NET Framework Type
bigint	int64
binary	byte
bit	boolean

SQL Server Type	.NET Framework Type
datetime	datetime
decimal	decimal
float	double
int	int32, integer
money	decimal
nchar	string, char()
numeric	decimal
nvarchar	string, char()
real	single
rowversion	byte()
smalldatetime	datetime
smallInt	int16
smallmoney	decimal
sql_variant	object
tinyint	byte
uniqueIdentifier	guid
varbinary	byte

User-Defined Functions

When a standard Transact-SQL user-defined function executes, SQL Server uses a work table to store intermediate values while a table-valued function executes. By contrast, a SQL CLR function will use only available memory on the server to stored intermediate rows and values. This doesn't necessarily mean that a SQL CLR function will always be faster because of the added overhead of calling into the .NET CLR. However, for complex operations and especially for larger result sets, using CLR-based functions may provide a significant performance edge over traditional functions.

These statements in Transact-SQL have been extended to support SQL CLR functions:

❑   CREATE FUNCTION

❑   ALTER FUNCTION

Because the purpose of a function is to return a value, the CREATE FUNCTION statement should include the RETURNS keyword followed by a SQL data type, as you can see in the following example:

```
USE AdventureWorks;
GO
CREATE FUNCTION dbo.fnHello()
RETURNS nvarchar(20)
AS
EXTERNAL NAME HelloWorld.[SayHello.UserDefinedFunctions].fnHello;
```

Scalar and Computational Functions

Outside of data access, there are some things that Transact-SQL just doesn't do very effectively. The mathematical, computational, and string-manipulation functions in Transact-SQL are very basic when compared with classes in the .NET Framework.

Once the SQL CLR class has been loaded into memory and the necessary objects have been instantiated, the .NET function code should execute considerably faster than Transact-SQL. The performance improvement isn't as apparent in a simple demonstration because SQL CLR functions typically excel when used to perform complex operations on a large volume of data.

Table-Valued Functions

User-defined functions may be used to return table-valued result sets, much like a stored procedure or parameterized view. The implementation code for this type of function is quite a bit different from a standard .NET function or method routine. The following example comes right out of the SQL Server Books On Line. Because I'm not providing a comprehensive programming reference, this should serve to give you a starting point and introduce the concepts necessary to support this type of programming effort.

Two procedures are required to return a table-type output. The first code procedure initializes the result set and specifies a procedure to use to fill each row. Note the `FillRowMethodName` attribute in the required `<SqlFunction>` attribute tag. This method must implement the `IEnumerable` interface. Any discussion beyond this is out of scope for this book. In other words, creating table-valued user-defined functions requires a bit of programming effort and must conform to a very specific predefined pattern to generate an appropriate table-type result set.

CLR Stored Procedures

Many systems today use a variety of extended stored procedures that call into COM components and other forms of unmanaged code. Extended stored procedures have been used to perform operations that SQL Server doesn't provide right out-of-the-box. Following are examples of operations that may have been performed using extended stored procedures and custom program code:

- ❑ Reading, writing, and manipulating files in the files system
- ❑ Interacting with the system event log
- ❑ Consuming data or services from a Web service
- ❑ Interacting with the system registry

Aside from the issues of security risk and system stability, some of these stored procedures may not be supported in future releases of SQL Server. I don't suggest that you rush to replace all of your existing code, unless, of course, it's not working well or you have some other compelling reason to do so.

However, you should make it a point to review these options, and begin planning to make appropriate changes before you get stuck.

The Transact-SQL standard for SQL Server 2005 has been extended for the CREATE and ALTER statements to support SQL CLR stored procedures.

The syntax for creating a stored procedure from a CLR assembly, in its simplest form, is as follows:

```
CREATE PROCEDURE <procedure name>
(<parameter list i.e. @Param1, @Param2...>)
AS EXTERNAL NAME <namespace.class.method>
WITH PERMISSION_SET = <permission set>
```

The following example shows a stored procedure defined from a SQL CLR assembly called CLR_Library:

```
CREATE PROCEDURE GetSalesOrderHeader()
AS EXTERNAL NAME CLR_Library.Sales.GetOrderCount
```

A method can accept any number of parameters (often referred to as *arguments* in the programming world). The following code example shows the same CLR stored procedure definition for a method with two input parameters:

```
CREATE PROCEDURE CountSalesOrderHeader(@StartDate DateTime, @EndDate DateTime)
AS EXTERNAL NAME CLR_Library. Sales.GetOrderCount
```

Triggers

Triggers are really just special stored procedures that execute automatically when certain database object actions occur. A trigger can be designated to execute when an object is created or altered. For tables, related triggers may execute when a record is inserted, updated, or deleted. Objects may have multiple triggers defined as well. Since SQL Server 2000, extensions have been made to the Transact-SQL standard for these statements to support SQL CLR triggers:

```
CREATE TRIGGER
ALTER TRIGGER
```

The CREATE and ALTER TRIGGER Transact-SQL statements for SQL CLR triggers are nearly identical to the traditional Transact-SQL counterparts, with the addition of the EXTERNAL NAME statement:

```
CREATE TRIGGER TR_Customer_Ins_Upd
ON Customer
FOR INSERT, UPDATE
AS
EXTERNAL NAME CLR_Library.CLRTriggers.TrCustomerInsUpd
```

A notable feature (added for trigger support) is the SqlTriggerContext object, which provides a variety of useful metadata about the current trigger call. This object's properties include event data (such as the time, process ID, and event type), the trigger action (such as Insert, Update, or Delete), specific column update flags, and the count of affected columns.

```
Imports System
Imports System.Data.Sql
Imports Microsoft.SqlServer.Server
Imports System.Collections
Imports System.Data.SqlTypes
Imports System.Diagnostics
Imports System.Runtime.InteropServices

Public Class TabularEventLog
    <SqlFunction(FillRowMethodName:="FillRow")> _
    Public Shared Function InitMethod(ByVal logname As String) _
        As IEnumerable
        Return New EventLog(logname, Environment.MachineName).Entries
    End Function

    Public Shared Sub FillRow(ByVal obj As Object, _
        <Out()> ByRef timeWritten As SqlDateTime, _
        <Out()> ByRef message As SqlChars, _
        <Out()> ByRef category As SqlChars, _
        <Out()> ByRef instanceId As Long)
        Dim eventLogEnTry As EventLogEntry = CType(obj, EventLogEntry)
        timeWritten = New SqlDateTime(eventLogEnTry.TimeWritten)
        message = New SqlChars(eventLogEnTry.Message)
        category = New SqlChars(eventLogEnTry.Category)
        instanceId = eventLogEnTry.InstanceId
    End Sub
End Class
```

User-Defined Types

User-defined types (UDTs) in Transact-SQL are generally simple wrappers around standard SQL Server data types. A UDT may be used to apply the correct data type and behaviors to many tables and columns in a database, but the Transact-SQL version of UDTs is very simple and equally limited. User-defined types implemented through SQL CLR can be much more than just an aliased data type. They can enforce business logic rules and restrictions on data values. You can now apply a UDT to complex, structured data rather than just simple, scalar values.

Unlike the previous database objects you have looked at, a UDT is implemented as a structure or class, rather than as a method, in program code. The recommended technique is to use a .NET standard structure, rather than as a class. Structures are similar to classes, but don't have to be instanced in the same way that objects are created from classes. Following is the auto-generated Visual Basic code for a new UDT created by adding a new UDT in a Visual Studio Database project. Note that several standard properties and methods are defined.

```
Imports System
Imports System.Data
Imports System.Data.SqlClient
Imports System.Data.SqlTypes
Imports Microsoft.SqlServer.Server

<Serializable()> _
<Microsoft.SqlServer.Server.SqlUserDefinedType(Format.Native)> _
```

```vb
Public Structure PhoneNumber
    Implements INullable

    Public Overrides Function ToString() As String
        ' Put your code here
        Return ""
    End Function

    Public ReadOnly Property IsNull() As Boolean _
          Implements INullable.IsNull
        Get
            ' Put your code here
            Return m_Null
        End Get
    End Property

    Public Shared ReadOnly Property Null As PhoneNumber
        Get
            Dim h As PhoneNumber = New PhoneNumber
            h.m_Null = True
            Return h
        End Get
    End Property

    Public Shared Function Parse(ByVal s As SqlString) As PhoneNumber
        If s.IsNull Then
            Return Null
        End If

        Dim u As PhoneNumber = New PhoneNumber
        ' Put your code here
        Return u
    End Function

    ' This is a place-holder method
    Public Function Method1() As String
        ' Put your code here
        Return "Hello"
    End Function

    ' This is a place-holder static method
    Public Shared Function Method2() As SqlString
        ' Put your code here
        Return New SqlString("Hello")
    End Function

    ' This is a place-holder field member
    Public m_var1 As Integer
    ' Private member
    Private m_Null As Boolean
End Structure
```

This is very similar to defining the class members for a class in object-oriented application development. In this example, the PhoneNumber type is used to manage a scalar value. The PhoneNumber structure contains a property with the same name. A number of standard methods are used to provide common functionality. For example, the `ToString()`, `IsNull()`, and `Parse()` methods are common for many .NET types and provide the means for interrogating and returning a value.

Specific implementation code should be added to give this UDT its appropriate behavior. In this example, for a phone number, the `Parse()` method might be used to return part of the phone number. You could require a single argument to indicate what part of the phone number to return (the area code, prefix, or postfix of the entire phone number value).

Following is the final, working code for the `PhoneNumber` UDT:

```vb
Imports System
Imports System.Data
Imports System.Data.SqlClient
Imports System.Data.SqlTypes
Imports Microsoft.SqlServer.Server

<Serializable()> _
<Microsoft.SqlServer.Server.SqlUserDefinedType( _
        Format.UserDefined, IsByteOrdered:=True, IsFixedLength:=False, _
        MaxByteSize:=14)> _
    Public Structure PhoneNumber

    Implements INullable

    Private Shared sPhoneIn As String
    Private Shared sPhoneOut As String
    Private Shared sAccessDigit As String
    Private Shared sAreaCode As String
    Private Shared sPrefix As String
    Private Shared sPostfix As String
    Private m_Null As Boolean

    '-- The ToString method returns a character
    '-- representation of the UDT value...
    Public Overrides Function ToString() As String
        Select Case sPhoneIn.Length
            Case 7
                sPhoneOut = sPrefix & "-" & sPostfix
            Case 10
                sPhoneOut = "(" & sAreaCode & ") " & sPrefix & "-" & sPostfix
            Case 11
                sPhoneOut = sAccessDigit & " (" & sAreaCode & ") " & _
                sPrefix & "-" & sPostfix
            Case Else
                Throw New ApplicationException( _
                    "Not the correct length for a phone number.")
        End Select
        Return sPhoneOut
    End Function

    '-- IsNull and Null custom properties support nullability...
```

```vbnet
        Public ReadOnly Property IsNull() As Boolean Implements INullable.IsNull
            Get
                If sPhoneIn = "" Then
                    Return m_Null
                End If
            End Get
        End Property

        Public Shared ReadOnly Property Null() As PhoneNumber
            Get
                Dim pn As PhoneNumber = New PhoneNumber
                pn.m_Null = True
                Return pn
            End Get
        End Property

        '-- The Parse method returns an appropriately typed value from the UDT...
        Public Shared Function Parse(ByVal s As SqlString) As PhoneNumber
            If s.IsNull Then
                Return Null
            End If

            Dim Phone1 As PhoneNumber = New PhoneNumber
            sPhoneIn = Phone1.ToString.Replace("(", "").Replace(")", _
                    "").Replace("-", "").Replace(" ", "").Replace(".", "")
            '-- Validate entry:
            If IsNumeric(sPhoneIn) Then
                Select Case sPhoneIn.Length
                    Case 7
                        sPrefix = sPhoneIn.Substring(0, 3)
                        sPostfix = sPhoneIn.Substring(3, 4)
                    Case 10
                        sAreaCode = sPhoneIn.Substring(0, 3)
                        sPrefix = sPhoneIn.Substring(3, 3)
                        sPostfix = sPhoneIn.Substring(6, 4)
                    Case 11
                        sAccessDigit = sPhoneIn.Substring(0, 1)
                        sAreaCode = sPhoneIn.Substring(1, 3)
                        sPrefix = sPhoneIn.Substring(4, 3)
                        sPostfix = sPhoneIn.Substring(7, 4)
                    Case Else
                        Throw New ApplicationException( _
                                "Not the correct length for a phone number.")
                End Select
                Return Phone1
            Else
                Throw New ApplicationException( _
                        "Phone number value contains some funky characters.")
            End If
        End Function

        '-- Custom properties used to return attributes of the UDT...
        Public ReadOnly Property AccessDigit() As SqlString
```

```
            Get
                Return sAccessDigit
            End Get
        End Property

        Public ReadOnly Property AreaCode() As SqlString
            Get
                Return sAreaCode
            End Get
        End Property


        Public ReadOnly Property Prefix() As SqlString
            Get
                Return sPrefix
            End Get
        End Property

        Public ReadOnly Property Postfix() As SqlString
            Get
                Return sPostfix
            End Get
        End Property

End Structure
```

User-Defined Aggregates

Custom aggregation code is relatively complex, because multiple program routines are called to build aggregate values as a result set is populated. Throughout this process, the aggregate structure is initialized, values are added and may be merged with those previously collected, and then, finally, the resulting value is calculated and the structure is terminated.

After the user-defined aggregate (UDA) assembly has been programmed, tested, and deployed to an external assembly, the database aggregation is defined using the following Transact-SQL syntax:

```
CREATE AGGREGATE [ schema_name . ] aggregate_name
        (@param_name <input_sqltype> )
RETURNS <return_sqltype>
EXTERNAL NAME assembly_name [ .class_name ]
```

Using the automated UDA feature in a Visual Studio SQL CLR project produces the following starting code:

```
Imports System
Imports System.Data
Imports System.Data.SqlClient
Imports System.Data.SqlTypes
Imports Microsoft.SqlServer.Server

<Serializable()> _
```

```vbnet
<Microsoft.SqlServer.Server.SqlUserDefinedAggregate(Format.Native)> _
Public Structure RMS

    Public Sub Init()
        ' Put your code here
    End Sub

    Public Sub Accumulate(ByVal value As SqlString)
        ' Put your code here
    End Sub

    Public Sub Merge(ByVal value as RMS)
        ' Put your code here
    End Sub

    Public Function Terminate() As SqlString
        ' Put your code here
        Return New SqlString("")
    End Function

    ' This is a place-holder field member
    Private var1 As Integer

End Structure
```

As you see, four methods and one variable are defined by the template. Each of these procedures has a specific purpose and may be called multiple times under certain conditions as a query is executed.

In SQL CLR UDAs, you define an initializing method that occurs on the start of a query's grouping (initiated by the SQL GROUP BY clause), an Accumulate method to aggregate new values within the grouping, and a Terminate method to return the final result. In addition, UDAs have a Merge method that the SQL Server engine may use when the optimizer chooses to implement the UDA with multiple threads. The Merge method combines the results of multiple instances of the UDA back into the parent thread to return a unified result. If we were to rewrite our own version of the standard Transact-SQL SUM() aggregate function for SQL CLR using Visual Basic.NET, it might look like this:

```vbnet
Imports System
Imports System.Data
Imports System.Data.SqlClient
Imports System.Data.SqlTypes
Imports Microsoft.SqlServer.Server


<Serializable()> _
<Microsoft.SqlServer.Server.SqlUserDefinedAggregate(Format.Native)> _
Public Structure SumAmt
    Private m_TotalAmt As SqlMoney

    '-- Init is called once per aggregate use...
    Public Sub Init()
        m_TotalAmt = 0
    End Sub
```

```
    '-- Accumulate is called once per value input...
    Public Sub Accumulate(ByVal myAmt As SqlMoney)
        If Not myAmt.IsNull Then
            m_TotalAmt += myAmt
        End If
    End Sub

    '-- Merge is called if the SQL optimizer decides to
    '-- spawn multiple threads and needs to combine the results...
    Public Sub Merge(ByVal ThreadedTotAmt As SumAmt)
        If Not ThreadedTotAmt.m_TotalAmt.IsNull Then
            m_TotalAmt += ThreadedTotAmt.m_TotalAmt
        End If
    End Sub

    '-- Returns result...
    Public Function Terminate() As SqlMoney
        If m_TotalAmt.IsNull Then
            Return SqlMoney.Null
        Else
            Return m_TotalAmt
        End If
    End Function

End Structure
```

This code provided courtesy of Douglas Hinson, who was a member of the author team on the book Professional SQL Server 2005 Integration Services *(Indianapolis: Wiley, 2006).*

Code-Generation Features in Visual Studio

In a previous exercise, you saw how to create a simple user-defined function using Visual Studio, and how to add that assembly to SQL Server using the CREATE ASSEMBLY command. In the following sections, you will build on that exercise, and explore additional features and capabilities of the Visual Studio Database Project.

Although it's important to understand how to import assemblies and create programming objects in SQL Server by referencing those assemblies, all of the SQL CLR objects can be developed, debugged, tested, and deployed from the Visual Studio development environment. I'll take you on a brief tour and step through this process. Once again, remember that this is not a book on programming, so I'm simply introducing the basic features. There are many elements to a complete solution, and considerations depend upon the security restrictions and required access to external resources.

The first step is to drop the assembly and function created in earlier exercises. To do this, execute the following command:

```
USE AdventureWorks;
GO
DROP FUNCTION dbo.fnHello;
DROP ASSEMBLY HelloWorld;
```

Open the previous `SayHello` solution.

You can set a number of optional properties for a project using the project property pages. For example, a digital signature can be added to the assembly. To view these tabbed dialogs, right-click the `SayHello` project in the Solution Explorer tree and select Properties. The Properties page has several tabs that enable the configuration of the project. The number of tabs will vary, depending on the installation of Visual Studio and add-ins such as Visual Source Safe 2005 or Visual Studio Team System. A fairly typical arrangement is shown in Figure 12-9.

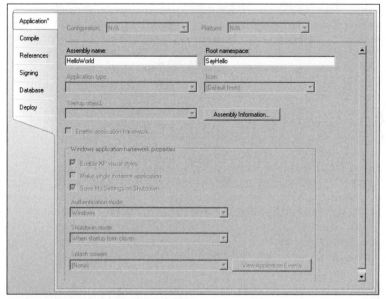

Figure 12-9: Project Properties page

On the Application tab, change the assembly name to "HelloWorld." Finally, to deploy the finished stored procedure directly to the database, you can right-click the project in the Solution Explorer and select Deploy from the menu or choose Deploy from the Build menu.

This action saves the project, builds the assembly DLL file, and then executes the necessary CREATE ASSEMBLY and CREATE FUNCTION Transact-SQL script on the database server. After deploying the project, open SQL Server Management Studio to examine the newly created function and assembly.

Expand the `AdventureWorks` database, then the `Programmability` folder and `Assemblies` folder. Note that the `HelloWorld` assembly has been added (see Figure 12-10). Expanding the `Functions` and `Scalar-Valued Functions` folder in the `Programmability` folder will expose several functions, of which one is the `fnHello` function just created by deploying the project with Visual Studio (see Figure 12-10).

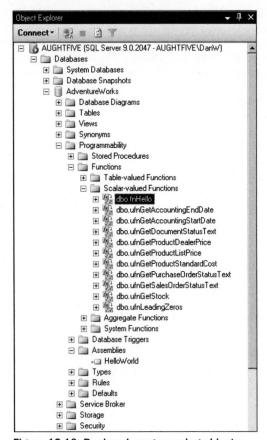

Figure 12-10: Deployed programming objects

Test the function to make sure it works. Open a new query window in Management Studio and execute the following command:

```
USE AdventureWorks;
GO
SELECT dbo.fnHello() AS Greeting;
```

You should see the following results:

```
Greeting
---------------------------------------------------------------------
Hello World

(1 row(s) affected)
```

That was easy! Now I admit that you probably won't have much use for a Hello World function in your database, but it is not much more difficult to create very robust functions that execute complex mathematical calculations or complex string manipulation. Offloading these types of processes to the CLR will result in a great improvement over executing them with T-SQL.

As you can see, in an integrated environment where a developer has connectivity to the database server, Visual Studio can be used to manage the entire development, debugging, testing, and deployment cycle. As an administrator, you will need to decide what level of access developers should have, which will determine just how simple and convenient this process may be for your development staff.

In a formal production environment, you may elect to set up a development database server and allow rights and connectivity for the developers to this machine. After objects have been properly tested and validated using the development server, you can either use these Visual Studio projects for deployment to production from the integrated development environment, or execute Transact-SQL scripts manually. The object scripts can also be generated from the development server and then executed on the production server, saving you much of the manual scripting effort.

Now that you know how the SQL CLR object development process works, I'll to spend the remainder of this chapter dealing with the common administrative tasks that you will need to understand to support these features in a production environment. I'll show you how to perform some of the same actions manually, and discuss some of the decisions you will need to make to maintain a safe and secure server to host SQL CLR objects and assemblies.

Programming Support

Taking database objects beyond the capabilities of Transact-SQL will require that your team understands the advantages afforded by using the .NET Framework and CLR. SQL Server already has strong features built-in to take advantage of performance-enhancing features such as parallel code execution and explicit memory management. Solution designers and administrators see these capabilities as "black box features" and can do little to control the Database Engine's behavior. Programmers have the ability to work at a much lower level, and can determine how program code utilizes system resources under very specific conditions. The .NET CLR contains several security options. For example, program methods can be explicitly tagged to use external code known to be safe that might not otherwise be permitted to execute. Following are just a few common capabilities offered by custom code written for the .NET CLR.

Threading

The .NET Framework supports both implicit and explicit multithreading. A *thread* is a distinct unit of execution that shares memory with the other threads in a process space. By spawning multiple threads of execution within an application, long-running code will not block the execution of another thread. Under the right conditions, this enables a component to perform multiple tasks in parallel with improved efficiently.

The SQL Server database engine is inherently multithreaded, but threads are managed only by internal logic without input from the user or query designer. You can see evidence of this by viewing the execution plan for a complex query. Some steps in the plan will execute simultaneously. Buffers and in-memory tables may be used to synchronize the results of parallel operations. Again, this is a decision the database engine makes for you that may be influenced by the syntax of a query, but cannot be declared explicitly.

In .NET program code, threads may be created either implicitly by using delegates, callbacks and events, or explicitly by declaring and managing thread objects. Multithread programming can be a tricky business, and often requires a high level of programming expertise.

Advanced programmers may use multithreading to launch simultaneous operations. The results may be queued and then combined after all threads report completion. Because threads execute independently, some form of synchronization code must be used to determine when a threaded routine has completed and its result. The overall effect, when used appropriately, may be a much faster set of coordinated operations.

Impersonation

Identity impersonation causes the security context for one object to be passed to another object. Simply put, this allows access to multiple objects (which may exist in multiple components) after authenticating only one time. Say that a CLR stored procedure is executed (either interactively or by an automated process) and the procedure calls into an external assembly. Impersonation would copy the user context for the database object, and apply it to the assembly and other related running code. This requires that the CLR object user has authenticated using SQL Server authentication.

Security Options

As a database system administrator, one of your primary concerns should be the safety and security of your server infrastructure. The very thought of allowing custom code to run on a production server may be enough to keep system administrators up at night. As an application developer, I've sat with many a database administrator, asking to have components installed, jobs scheduled, and script enabled to perform some task on a live server. In nearly every case, my code was viewed as a threat and the administrator's job was to prevent *my* alien code from opening security holes on *his* server. I understand and fully embrace this as a working system of checks and balances. This works as long as coders understand the need for security restrictions and administrators appreciate the need to extend database and application functionality.

One of the first things you should know about .NET security from the beginning is that it is inherently designed to be safe right out-of-the-box, and without additional configuration. Unlike many programming models in the past, default settings are restrictive and set to protect code from accessing volatile system resources and to prevent system invasion. That said, it is important that you understand what settings are necessary for program code to run and to have access to only the resources it needs to get the job done. You will likely be required to enable specific capabilities in order for CLR code to run on your servers. In addition to standard SQL Server permissions, there are two separate security measures that affect .NET code running within SQL CLR objects: one applied by SQL Server to restrict an assembly's freedom and one applied by the .NET run-time itself.

.NET Security

Before any custom code can execute, the request must pass through three separate layers of authentication and permissions, as shown in Figure 12-11.

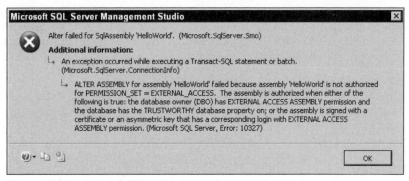

Figure 12-11: Layers of authentication and permissions

First, any user request must be authenticated by Windows (assuming you are using Windows-integrated security in SQL Server), and then SQL Server must authenticate the user and grant object-level permission for the request. These measures apply to any database object and are not specific to an assembly. Next, the specific SQL CLR permission set is checked. This permission set was applied when the SQL CLR object was created. It will determine whether SQL Server grants the assembly permission to use certain features of the .NET run-time classes, and whether it can access any external resources. Finally, the assembly must satisfy the rules of code access security, enforced by the .NET CLR. This security layer may also determine whether the assembly or certain class methods within the assembly can have access to external resources.

In Figure 12-11, note the two layers of permissions for the two arrows associated with the .NET Runtime. SQL CLR Permission Sets (managed by SQL Server) allow access to the .NET assembly, which resides within the database and encapsulates SQL CLR database objects. This permission set controls access to these objects because they are perceived to be safe. The second arrow, showing the internal assembly accessing external resources (such as the file system, external data sources, and external managed or unmanaged components) will utilize .NET's own Code Access Security. To allow this code to execute, a SQL CLR permission set other than Safe must be specified, and then appropriate measures are taken to make this code assessable to the internal assembly. This is the point of greatest potential risk, and should be carefully planned and coordinated with application developers.

Securing SQL CLR

SQL CLR objects may be secured at different levels. After considering a user's access to the database server and permissions granted or denied within SQL Server to any objects, special execution permissions are set for SQL CLR objects. This gives an administrator a simple (but effective) blanket of control over each CLR object in the database. Without contending with the complexities of programming objects, SQL CLR permission sets simply allow you enable varying levels of access to managed assemblies.

SQL Server CLR Permission Sets

To simplify the security model for assemblies added to a database, a set of three permission levels are defined within SQL Server. These are used to allow assemblies to have access to resources known to be safe or otherwise. These settings are implemented by restricting the assembly's access to specific .NET

Framework run-time system class libraries. For the Safe permission setting, some of the .NET classes have had some functionality disabled to prevent security work-arounds. The permission set is applied when a SQL CLR object is created or altered. For example, the following code is used to create a SQL CLR stored procedure with the External Access SQL CLR permission set:

```
USE AdventureWorks;
GO
CREATE ASSEMBLY HelloWorld
FROM 'C:\SQLServerSolutions\SayHelloSolution\SayHello\bin\SayHello.dll'
WITH PERMISSION_SET = External_Access
```

The preceding command will fail with a "Assembly not authorized for PERMISSION_SET = EXTERNAL_ACCESS" *error if certain criteria are not met, as described in the end of this section.*

Safe Permission

This setting only allows safe .NET code to run in SQL CLR assemblies. You should use this setting when an assembly doesn't require the use of external data, or components outside of the SQL Server database server environment.

The Safe permission set allows an assembly to execute with minimal permissions, and to have access to only internal database resources and .NET classes that are known to be safe. In other words, the code can perform internal logic and access data from the local database server. The Safe setting does not allow access to external data, nor to external resources (such as the file system, executables, or the system registry). Even though the use of this setting is fairly restrictive, this may be advantageous, because the code has access to most of the .NET system classes and can process program logic beyond the capabilities of objects written in Transact-SQL. Beyond this, the Safe permission setting will allow the code to perform most any task that would normally be granted to a SQL stored procedure or user-defined function.

External Access Permission

This setting is more permissive than the Safe setting, yet doesn't allow some of the more risky capabilities of the Unsafe setting described later. Using the External_Access setting will allow an assembly to use .NET Framework class libraries to gain access to external system and network resources. These may include the local or remote file system, Active Directory, the system registry, logs, files, and external data sources. This setting will allow the code send email, use the Internet, and consume Web services. The External_Access setting doesn't allow an assembly to call unmanaged code in any form, such as COM-based DLLs, ActiveX controls, and VBScript.

This is a useful and reasonably safe setting when used along with disciplined programming practices and thorough testing. Because the stability of .NET code is generally not a concern, an administrator's attention should be focused on ensuring that solution developers are accessing only essential resources, and that all code is tested and verified prior to being deployed to production servers.

Unsafe Permission

The Unsafe permission setting is at the opposite end of the permission spectrum, and allows complete access to all of the .NET Framework classes. As such, code may access the file system, the system registry, network resources, and even the Internet. This setting also allows the assembly code to execute unmanaged components and executables.

Looking beyond security concerns for the moment, .NET code is generally stable because of the CLR's isolated process space and exception-handling model. Even if bugging code were to crash, the CLR will shut down the process gracefully without taking system processes with it. This built-in stability all changes, however, when .NET code calls into older, unmanaged code.

Before you get excited about using terms like "Unsafe," let's put this into perspective. We have had the capability to extend SQL Server's reach using external applications and components for several years in the form of command-line executables and extended stored procedures. Many trustworthy SQL Server solutions send email messages using COM-based Collaboration Data Object (CDO) code or interact with the file system using external VBScript. Older custom, extended stored procedures are written in C++ and may use the MFC libraries. The point is that these are all examples of what is now called "unmanaged code" and falls into the category of "Unsafe" code from the perspective of a SQL Server CLR object.

Using the Unsafe setting to enable access to external resources isn't necessarily a bad thing. This just means that the .NET CLR can't guarantee that it's safe — you and your developers have to do that, just like many of us have been doing for the past 10 or 12 years. If you have existing components that your solution relies upon, that have been tested and verified to be safe, you can use the Unsafe setting to call them from a CLR stored procedure, trigger, or user-defined function.

Enabling External Access and Unsafe Permissions

In order to set an assembly's permission level to External Access or Unsafe, one of two conditions must be met. Either the database Trustworthy attribute must be True and the database owner has the EXTERNAL ACCESS ASSEMBLY or UNSAFE ASSEMBLY permission (sa does by default), or the assembly must be signed with a certificate or asymmetric key and that key is mapped to a login with the EXTERNAL ACCESS ASSEMBLY or UNSAFE ASSEMBLY permission. If either of these conditions is not met, any attempt to change the permission set of the assembly will fail with the error shown in Figure 12-11. Following the principle of least privilege, the recommended configuration is the use of a certificate or key and not to set the Trustworthy attribute to True if the only requirement is to allow CLR objects greater access. See Chapter 6 for more information on SQL Server certificates and asymmetric keys.

Summary

As a system administrator, you probably have your hands full with servers and databases that need to be stable and secure. Adding custom programming components to the mix has always been risky business, not to mention one more thing to worry about affecting your corporate infrastructure. Your task should be to minimize this risk and support only components that are easy to manage, and those that will play fairly with other applications. The .NET-managed Common Language Runtime (CLR) offers greater peace-of-mind with little risk of affecting anything else running on your servers.

Adding custom-programmed objects to your database opens a whole new world of opportunity for SQL Server users, developers, and administrators. SQL CLR takes database object security to the next level with a simple, integrated model. Executable assemblies reside in a SQL Server database rather than the file system. Database programming objects (such as stored procedures, triggers, types, user-defined functions, and aggregates) run as compiled .NET program code within the SQL Server processing space.

Applications developed with .NET-managed code are inherently secure and offer many choices for component configuration and flexibility, but along with these options comes a great deal of complexity. The SQL CLR security model makes security very simple by distilling the task of securing an object to three basic settings. As an administrator, you decide whether to allow an object to execute only code known to be absolutely safe to access external resources, or whether to let down your defenses to let potentially unsafe code run. The latter choice allows you to depend on and trust the capable (but more complicated) features of .NET code access security. For most objects, trusting only safe code will be sufficient, and your task remains simple and uncomplicated. However, more sophisticated custom code objects may require a greater investment of knowledge and skill. In such cases, you will likely need to work closely with application developers to make appropriate trade-off decisions to provide the right functionality for your users, along with a manageable level of security for your peace-of-mind.

In Chapter 13, you learn about another new and powerful part of SQL Server 2005: SQL Server Integration Services (SSIS). SSIS replaces the old Data Transformation Services (DTS) and adds new power and functionality that DTS never had. Chapter 13 explores the basics of SSIS and gives you a good head start on building custom data transformations.

Introduction to SQL Server 2005 Integration Services

With the release of SQL Server 2005, Microsoft introduced a replacement to its Data Transformation Services (DTS) known as SQL Server Integration Services (SSIS). Familiarity with DTS, fortunately, is not prerequisite knowledge for understanding the concepts in this chapter. This chapter is designed to help you understand the features and management of SSIS. Although this chapter will not (and realistically *cannot*) be an exhaustive review of SSIS, it should give you a good foundation of understanding how data can be moved between various sources and destinations, and how it can be modified in the process. This chapter covers the following topics:

❑   A general introduction to SSIS and its features

❑   The import and export tools used to move data around

❑   The different options for transforming data using SSIS

About SSIS

As mentioned earlier, SSIS is designed to be a replacement for DTS. Although many database administrators found DTS to be an extremely useful tool for manipulating and automating the transfer of data from one source to another, it was prohibitively difficult for many administrators who lacked significant programming or scripting skills to be able to perform complex transformations. SSIS, or simply Integration Services, changes all that.

Integration Services is part of a suite of tools included in the Business Intelligence (BI) Development Studio. The BI Development Studio is an instance of Visual Studio 2005, which includes the add-ins for designing solutions for Integration Services, Analysis Services, and Reporting Services. One of the benefits of using the BI Development Studio is that it allows you to develop Integration Services solutions without having to maintain an active connection to an existing SQL Server. This gives you the ability to design solutions that can run on multiple servers, or can be executed from a file system.

Integration Services is an Extract, Transform, and Load (ETL) tool. This means that with Integration Services, you define a data source, and, from that data source, you define which data you are interested in copying to a new destination. After having extracted the data, you then perform any optional transformations on the data to prepare it for its destination. For example, you may want to take a column that stores a string value that is either "True" or "False" into a Boolean value, "1" or "0," respectively. This allows you to match the current data type of the destination. Finally, the load sequence takes the transformed data and injects it into the appropriate destination.

SQL Server Integration Services is actually made up of four different components:

❑ Integration Services itself

❑ Integration Services object model

❑ Integrated Services run-time

❑ Integrated Services data flow

Each of these components is used to create a robust experience for designing, managing, and executing packages built for SSIS. In the next few sections, you learn about each of these components.

Integration Service

The Integration Service itself is actually managed through SQL Server Management Studio, not unlike many of your other server components. This component is used to handle the management and monitoring of both stored and running packages. Packages can be stored either in the file system or they can be stored in the msdb database on a running instance of SQL Server 2005.

> Integration Services, when installed, assumes that the local default instance contains the msdb database that will be used for the package repository. However, because SQL Server 2005 and SQL Server 2000 can both be installed on the same machine, it is possible that your default instance is running a legacy version of SQL Server. If this is the case, you must manually edit the <ServerName> element in the MSDtsSrvr.ini.xml file. This file is in the 90\DTS\Binn directory of your SQL Server installation folder.

You can use SQL Server Management Studio to connect to an instance of SSIS, as shown in Figure 13-1. The following is a list of manageable features of the Integration Service in SQL Server Management Studio:

❑ Connect to multiple Integration Services servers

❑ Manage package storage

❑ Customize storage folders

❑ Import and export packages

❑ Start local and remote stored packages

❑ Stop local and remote running packages

❑ Monitor local and remote running packages

❑ View the Windows Event log

Figure 13-1: Connecting to Integration Services

Once you've connected to the Integration Service, you can manage packages using Object Explorer, as shown in Figure 13-2.

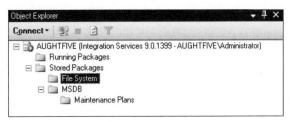

Figure 13-2: The Integration Services package store

From the Object Explorer, you can create additional folders for organizing your packages, you can import or export packages to the package stores, and you can execute packages or stop packages.

Integration Services Object Model

Integration Services includes a new object model for including both native and managed application programming interfaces (APIs) for customizing the behavior of your Integration Services solutions. You can use these APIs for accessing SSIS tools, command-line functions, or custom applications. You can also use the object model for executing SSIS tools and packages from within your own applications.

Integration Services Run-time

The Integration Services Run-time engine is responsible for saving the control flow logic and execution of SSIS packages. Integration Services run-time executables include packages, containers, predefined and custom tasks, and event handlers. The run-time handles execution order, logging, variables, and event handling. Programming the Integration Services Run-time engine allows you to automate the creation, configuration, and execution of packages through the object model.

Integration Services Packages

Packages are units of execution that are composed of a series of other elements, including containers, tasks, and event handlers. You can create and manage packages through the BI Development Studio, or programmatically, using the Integration Services object model. Each package contains a *control flow*, which is a series of tasks (related or not) that will execute as a unit. Similar to jobs in the SQL Server Agent service (see Chapter 8), Integration Services packages use a customizable logic flow that controls the timed or constrained execution of individual tasks.

Integration Services Tasks

Tasks are the basic unit of work within an Integration Services package. Each task defines an action that will be taken as part of the execution of this package. Some of the basic task types include Execute SQL tasks, in which a T-SQL script will be executed; file system tasks, which interact with a local or remote file system; and data flow tasks, which control how data is copied between a source and destination. Many other types of tasks are discussed later in this chapter.

Integration Services Containers

Containers are objects that exist within the Integration Services environment to allow you to define one or more tasks as a unit of work. You can use containers to define parameters for the execution of these tasks. Four types of containers are available, and you learn more about them later in this chapter.

Integration Services Event Handlers

Event handlers are similar to packages, in that within them, you can define tasks and containers. One major difference, though, is that event handlers are reactionary. This means that the tasks defined within an event handler will only be executed when a specific event occurs. These events are defined on tasks, containers, or the package itself, and include events that are fired before, during, and after the execution of the package.

Integration Services Data Flow

One of the most significant benefits of the SSIS features is the separation of the control flow from the *data flow*. Each package that contains a data flow task (such as an import or export) identifies the data flow task to the run-time engine, but then a separate data flow engine is invoked for that operation. The data flow engine manages what is typically the whole point of an SSIS package, and that is extracting, transforming, and loading data. The data flow engine will extract data from data files or relational databases, manage any and all transforms that manipulate that data, and then provide that transformed data to the destination. A package may have more than one data flow task, and each task will execute its own data flow process for moving and manipulating data.

Importing and Exporting Data

One of the easiest ways to understand SSIS, and to see it in action, is through the Import/Export Wizard, which can be run from the Management Studio. The process is essentially the same for both operations. The primary difference between the import operation and the export operation is whether your SQL Server is the source or the destination. It should be noted, however, that SSIS doesn't need to use a SQL Server as either the source or the destination! You can use SSIS to import data from a flat-file source (such a comma-separated value file) into a Microsoft Access database.

In this example, you use a simple comma-separated value (CSV) file that contains a list of additional promotions the Adventure Works sales team will use for 2007. The contents of this file will then be imported into the `Sales.SpecialOffer` table. Begin by creating a folder on the root of your `C:` drive called `SSISDemos`. Create a new text file in this folder, and enter the following data into the text file.

```
Description,DiscountPct,Type,Category,StartDate,EndDate
President's Day Sale,0.1,Holiday Promotion,Customer,2/16/2007,2/19/2007
Memorial Day Madness,0.25,Holiday Promotion,Customer,5/28/2007,5/28/2007
Fourth of July Sale,0.05,Holiday Promotion,Customer,7/1/2007,7/7/2007
Seasonal Discount,0.075,Seasonal Discount,Reseller,10/1/2007,10/31/2007
```

Save the file as `Promos.csv`, and then follow these steps:

1. Start or open SQL Server Management Studio.

2. In the Object Explorer, select your server and expand Databases.

3. Right-click AdventureWorks and select Tasks → Import Data. This will launch the SQL Server Import and Export Wizard. As with many other wizards in SQL Server Management Studio, you can elect to not see the introductory page of the wizard in the future.

4. Click Next to move to the Data Source selection page.

On this page, you can select the data source that will be used for the import process. Figure 13-3 shows the data source as you will configure it for this exercise. You should note that the options in the window will change to reflect the parameters of whichever data source you choose. Also note that a number of connection providers are already available out-of-the-box from SQL Server 2005, including the SQL Native Client, OLE DB providers for Analysis Services and Oracle, and Microsoft Office Excel and Access file formats.

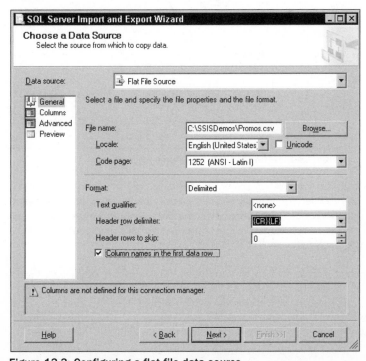

Figure 13-3: Configuring a flat file data source

Now, follow these steps:

1. Select Flat File Source as your data source.

2. In the "File name" box, you can enter the path to the file you created earlier (C:\SSISDemos\ Promos.csv), or you can use the Browse button to find the file. Note that if you use the Browse button, it defaults to the .txt file extension, and you must select .csv from the drop-down list.

3. Based on the contents of the file, it should recognize the correct locale, code page, and format. You should select the "Column names in the first data row" checkbox, because you have included the header row in your file.

4. Click Next on the Data Source selection page to take you to the Columns page.

This page, as shown in Figure 13-4, allows you to configure the row and column delimiters that are used in your flat file source. For example, if you used a pipe character (|) instead of a comma, you could enter that into the "Column delimiter" field.

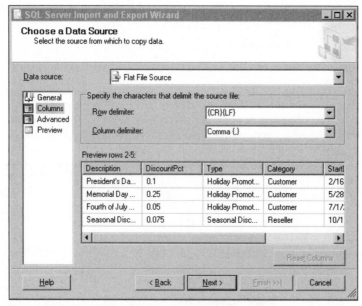

Figure 13-4: Setting the flat file source options

This window also provides you with a columnized preview window of the data source, so that you can verify the configuration of the data source provider. If the columns appear to be misaligned, or the data does not appear in the correct format, you may be using a different column or row delimiter, and will need to adjust your settings accordingly.

Before clicking Next, choose the Advanced window. This window, represented in Figure 13-5, allows you to view or configure the properties of each column. This can be helpful when preparing data for the destination, and ensuring that it is in the correct format. You also have the ability to add or remove columns as needed and can use the Suggest Types button to evaluate the data in the file, and provide recommendations for the data types prior to importing the data.

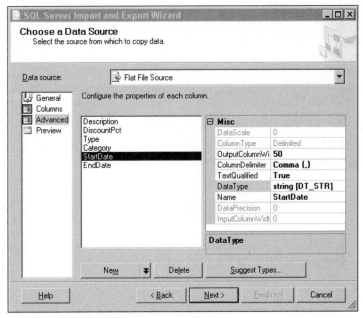

Figure 13-5: Setting the data type option

Click Next without making any changes on the Advanced page. The next step in the wizard asks you to provide configuration information for the data destination. As mentioned to earlier, you can use any of the available providers for both source and destination, and neither of them has to be a SQL Server. You could, in fact, use this import wizard to import the flat file into a Microsoft Excel spreadsheet, a Microsoft Access database, an Oracle database, or even another flat file. This functionality allows you to use SSIS to build complex packages that may have very distinct data migration paths before the execution can complete.

For this example, though, you're going to make it easy on yourself, and choose the SQL Native Client as your destination provider (this should be the default). When choosing the SQL Native Client, follow these steps:

1.   Select your server name from the drop-down list if it is not already provided.

2.   Choose Windows Authentication.

3.   Ensure that `AdventureWorks` is selected as the target database.

The New button on this screen allows you to create a new database on this server for your data import. Figure 13-6 displays the configuration information you should use.

The next page in the wizard allows you to define the specific views or tables that will be used as the destination for the data in your file. The default behavior of the wizard is to create a new table based on the name of the file, using the data types that were specified in the source configuration. You can use the drop-down list to select the correct table, as shown in Figure 13-7.

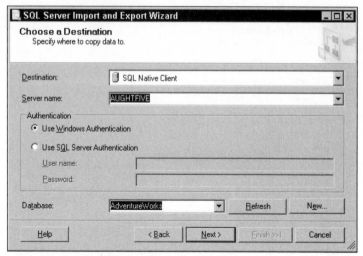

Figure 13-6: Choosing the destination

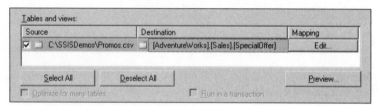

Figure 13-7: Creating the destination table

Clicking the Edit button under the Mapping column activates the Column Mapping window. This displays the column name in the data source, and allows you to match it to a column name in the destination. Fortunately, the file you created earlier happens to use the exact same column names as the destination table, so there is no guesswork as to where the data will go. However, you can use this utility to specify that certain columns will be ignored, or simply mapped to a different target column.

You can also see in Figure 13-8 that there are options to delete or append rows in the destination table. In some cases, you may want to drop the table and then re-create it. This can be especially helpful if you want to completely purge the table, and there are no foreign-key constraints on it.

The next page in the wizard allows you to define the specific views or tables that will be used as the destination for the data in your file. The default behavior of the wizard is to create a new table based on the name of the file, using the data types that were specified in the source configuration. You can use the drop-down list to select the correct table, as shown in Figure 13-7.

Once you have provided all the information about the source and destination, the wizard will ask if you want to execute the package immediately, and if you want to save your configuration as an SSIS package in either the msdb database or the file system (see Figure 13-9). For now, just choose to execute the package immediately, and don't worry about saving the package. You can either click Finish on this page to begin package execution, or you can click Next to view the summary information about the package before executing.

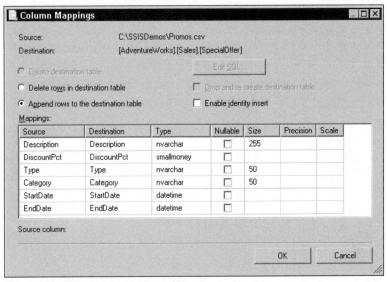

Figure 13-8: Destination table options

Figure 13-9: Execute the package without saving

As long as all the steps have been followed as indicated, your data should now be imported success-fully! You can execute a simple SELECT * FROM Sales.SpecialOffer query to see the imported data. If there was a problem with the execution of the package, use the error report information to pinpoint where the problem occurred, and what could be done to resolve it.

Now that you've had a chance to see the import wizard at work, you should see the export wizard in action! It's actually pretty much more of the same. This time, however, you can export data using a query and save the results as a Microsoft Excel file. Follow these steps:

1. Begin by right-clicking the AdventureWorks database and selecting Tasks → Export Data.

2. In the Choose a Data Source page, ensure that the SQL Native Client is specified as the Data Source, Windows Authentication is selected, and the database is AdventureWorks.

3. Once you've configured or confirmed as necessary, click Next.

4. In the Choose a Destination page, choose Microsoft Excel as the destination.

5. Enter 'C:\SSISDemos\EmployeeData.xls' as the filename, and use the default Excel version (it should be 97-2005).

6. Ensure that "First row has column names" is selected and click Next.

7. In the next window, you will be asked if you want to select data from existing tables and views, or if you want to specify a query to find the data to transfer. Choose the second option, "Write a query to specify the data to transfer," and click Next.

8. In the Source Query window, enter the following query and click Next:

```
USE AdventureWorks;
GO
SELECT PC.FirstName, PC.LastName, PC.EmailAddress, HRE.MaritalStatus,
HRE.Gender, HRE.VacationHours, HRE.SickLeaveHours, HRE.SalariedFlag,
HREP.Rate, HREP.ModifiedDate
FROM  Person.Contact AS PC
INNER JOIN HumanResources.Employee AS HRE
  ON PC.ContactID = HRE.ContactID
INNER JOIN HumanResources.EmployeePayHistory AS HREP
  ON HRE.EmployeeID = HREP.EmployeeID
ORDER BY PC.LastName;
```

9. In the Select Source Tables and Views window, you can change the column mapping options, or rename the destination worksheet for the new file. Feel free to explore the different options, but do not change the defaults.

10. Once you're finished, click Next, and then click Finish on the next page to execute the package immediately.

Your results should look something like Figure 13-10.

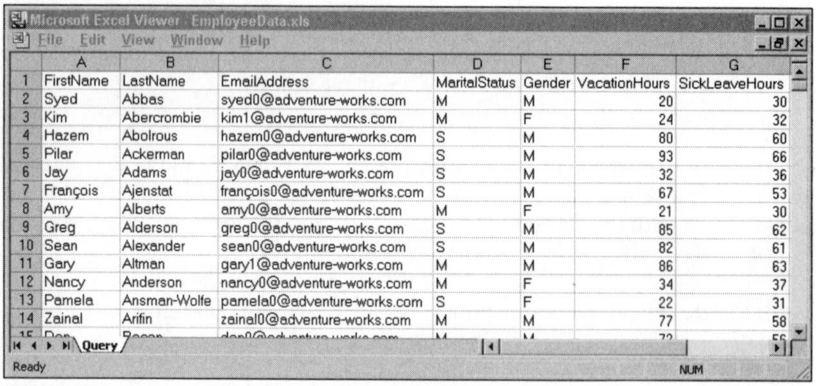

Figure 13-10: Viewing the exported Excel data

Transforming Data with SSIS

Now the fun really begins. By now you should have a pretty good understanding of the concepts of how Integration Services can manage control and data flow, and you've seen a simple example of how to get data into and out of the SQL Server using the basic tools. In this section, you're going to see how those components can be expanded on to provide a more complete scenario for working with Integration Services.

You should first become familiar with the Integrated Development Environment (IDE). Integration Services, along with Analysis Services and Reporting Services, relies heavily on the BI Development Studio. The BI Development Studio is really just a fancy name for Visual Studio, and is, in fact, the Visual Studio 2005 IDE, but it includes only those add-ins for SQL-based services. If you install the full version of Visual Studio 2005, or just language add-ins like Visual Basic and C#, you'll find that it starts the same environment. For the sake of simplicity, let's just refer to the IDE as Visual Studio.

To begin creating a new SQL Server Integration Services packages, simply launch Visual Studio and create a new project. Of the types of projects available, Integration Services is available under Business Intelligence Projects (see Figure 13-11). Once you've created your new project, notice that, like other Visual Studio projects, you have a toolbox that contains controls and resources for your projects. The development environment is broken up into four different sections, each of which allows you to control different aspects of your project. These sections include a management area for the Control Flow, management of the Data Flow, Event Handlers, and a Package Explorer. During the execution or debugging of a package, a fifth tab appears, allowing you to view package execution progress. In the next few sections, you learn about each of the different management areas, how they're used, and what options are available when working in those areas.

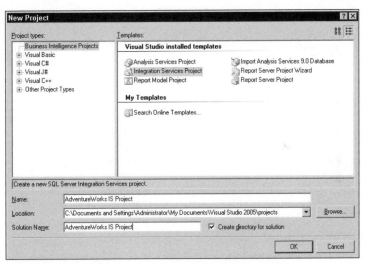

Figure 13-11: Creating a new Integration Services project

Understanding the Development Environment

As mentioned earlier, the development environment includes a number of tools and features that will allow to you have complete control over your Integration Services packages. In this section, you learn how to navigate your way through the different resources available to you. Chapter 3 covered the different tools and features of the SQL Server Management Studio development environment. The environment used by Integration Services is very similar. As with SQL Server Management Studio, you can pin and unpin different control boxes as needed to customize the look and feel of your workspace. Figure 13-12 shows an example of a typical development environment for Integration Services.

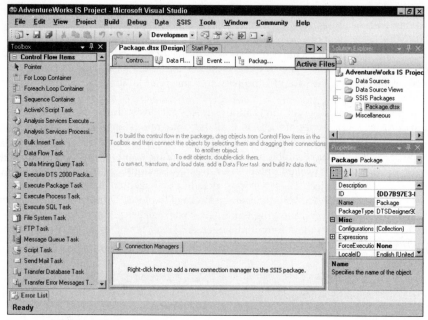

Figure 13-12: The Integration Services designer IDE

Toolbox

As with many other Visual Studio projects, the Toolbox is invaluable for finding the controls and features you need to make your project easy to design and configure. Integration Services packages are no exception, and can provide you a host of different elements. For the most part, you have two main toolboxes. The main Toolbox window contains control flow and maintenance plan tasks, and is your primary toolbox. The other contains data flow items such as sources, transforms, and destinations; it is only available while configuring a data flow task. You learn more about the items in these toolboxes later.

Solution Explorer

The Solution Explorer (shown on the right side of the screen) is a repository that allows you to manage multiple Integration Services packages and related resources. It is broken down into four main sections. The first section, Data Sources, allows you to create Data Source objects that can be used by multiple packages in the same project. You can create a new data source or choose an existing one using a wizard.

Data Source Views (DSVs) are objects that refer to a configurable subset of objects in your database, and provide benefits such as caching metadata, or defining relationships. These DSVs can also be used by multiple packages.

You then have the packages themselves, and then finally, any miscellaneous files that are used by your Integration Services packages. Note that the package names end with a .dtsx file extension. This is the default extension for Integration Services packages that is kind of a hold-over from when it was still called Data Transformation Services.

Properties

The Properties tab is a dynamically updating box that allows you to view or update the properties of the currently selected item. You can sort the list of property elements alphabetically or categorically.

Connection Managers

The Connection Managers tab (at the bottom of the screen) contains a list of connection objects specific to the package you are currently editing. Connections can be based on existing data sources, or you can create unique connections for only that package. Connections can use OLE DB, ADO.NET, Flat File, and other connection types. Connections can also be made on-the-fly, such as when defining a data flow task that uses a Microsoft Excel data source for an import operation. You will not need to create the connection to the Excel file beforehand, but once you define the source, it will be added to the list of connections.

Package Elements

When creating a new SSIS package, it's important that you be familiar with the different elements available. Familiarizing yourself with the variety of tools available will help you create more robust packages, which can execute a complex series of tasks. This section introduces you to these resources.

Control Flow

Your main environment is the Control Flow section, shown on the left side of Figure 13-12. The control flow environment allows you to define one or more tasks that will be executed for this Integration Services project, and specify the order in which those tasks are executed (hence the term "Control Flow"). You can choose to define tasks that are serialized, meaning that one task must reach a completion state before the next task begins. You can also execute tasks in parallel, allowing multiple operations to be executed simultaneously. As long as there are no dependencies between these tasks, this can take advantage of your system resources, and dramatically decrease the execution time of your packages. You can reduce the total time the package takes to execute significantly with parallel execution.

To add items to your package's control flow, simply choose the appropriate item and drag it into the Control Flow pane, which is the first tab on the left in the middle of Figure 13-12. Once you've dragged an item into the Control Flow pane, you can then configure that item. Some tasks may display with an error symbol (the red circle with the white X) or a warning symbol (the yellow triangle with the black exclamation point) to indicate that further configuration is needed for that task to be able to execute properly. In some cases, simply configuring the task can "fix" the problem. You can also view the Error List (by pressing Ctrl+E or selecting View → Error List) and review the available errors and warnings. You can also double-click on an error or warning to have the IDE take you straight to where you need to go to fix the event.

Control Flow Tasks

This section briefly identifies each of the control flow tasks that can be used to build your packages. Also listed are Database Maintenance tasks that may be useful to you as well. (Refer to the left side of Figure 13-12.)

❑ *For Loop Container* — Containers are interesting in that they are both a task and collection of tasks at the same time. In this case, the For Loop container allows you to execute one or more tasks that will continually execute until the result of the executed task returns a Boolean "false" value.

❑ *ForEach Loop Container* — Similar to the For Loop container, ForEach Loop containers allow you to execute tasks for each instance of a type of object. The ForEach loop includes enumerators for files, items, ADO record sets, ADO.NET schemas, variables, XML nodes, or SQL Management Objects.

❑ *Sequence Container* — These containers allow you to define a series of tasks that will execute in sequence. It is similar in many regards to simply grouping tasks, which is covered later in this section, but allows additional functionality (such as limiting the scope of a variable to only the tasks within this container).

Each of the following tasks is also a container unto itself. This is referred to as the Task Host Container, and is not a container type you need to separately manage or add to your package.

❑ *ActiveX Script Task* — The ActiveX script task allows you to run scripts that use VBScript or JavaScript as a step in your process flow. This has been largely superseded by the Script task, which uses VisualBasic.Net scripts. ActiveX scripts are primarily used with older packages that have been upgraded from DTS 2000.

❑ *Analysis Services Execute DDL Task* — This task allows you to execute a Data Definition Language (DDL) statement in Analysis Services.

❑ *Analysis Services Processing Task* — This task contains configuration options for processing Analysis Services objects.

❑ *Bulk Insert Task* — This task is used to import a large amount of data from a flat file source.

❑ *Data Flow Task* — This task is pretty much the bread and butter of Integration Services. It allows you to define how data is processed as it moves from source to destination.

❑ *Data Mining Query Task* — You can use the Data Mining Query task to run prediction queries using a Data Mining Extension (DMX) statement.

❑ *Execute DTS 2000 Package Task* — This task is used to execute packages created in DTS from SQL 2000, but have not yet been upgraded or migrated to Integration Services.

❑ *Execute Package Task* — This task can be used to launch another Integration Services task.

❑ *Execute Process Task* — You can use this to execute a Windows application or batch file.

❑ *Execute SQL Task* — Use this task to execute a SQL script. Second only to the Data Flow task, this is probably one of the more commonly used tasks.

❑ *File System Task* — File system tasks are used to interact with the file system, such as creating files and directories.

❑ *FTP Task* — You can use the File Transfer Protocol (FTP) to upload or download files to FTP servers.

❑ *Message Queue Task* — Using this task allows you to configure your package to interact with Microsoft Message Queuing (MSMQ) services.

❑ *Script Task* — This task is used to execute a Microsoft Visual Basic.Net script.

❑ *Send Mail Task* — Use this task to send email messages during the execution of a package.

❑ *Transfer Database Task* — This task is used to transfer entire databases between different instances of SQL Server.

❑ *Transfer Error Messages Task* — This task allows you to copy user-defined error messages (with an error number above 50,000) between instances of SQL Server. The data is stored in the `sysmessages` table of the `Master` database.

❑ *Transfer Jobs Task* — This task is used to copy jobs between instances of SQL Server.

❑ *Transfer Logins Task* — Use the Transfer Logins task to copy logins between SQL Servers. This can be useful when creating a redundant server for fault-tolerance.

❑ *Transfer Master Stored Procedures Task* — You can use this task if you've created user-defined stored procedures in the `Master` database that you want to copy to another instance of SQL Server.

❑ *Transfer SQL Server Object Task* — Use this task to transfer other SQL objects such as tables, views, stored procedures, and triggers between instances.

❑ *Web Service Task* — The Web Service task is used to initiate a connection to a Web site, and can be used to return information to a variable or file.

❑ *WMI Data Reader Task* — The WMI Data Reader task can be used to query Windows Management Instrumentation (WMI) namespaces to return information about the computer system.

❑ *WMI Event Watcher Task* — This task can be used to query WMI for events relating to system behavior or performance.

❑ *XML Task* — You can add XML tasks to work with XML files and data sets.

❑ *Back Up Database Task* — The Back Up Database task does exactly what the name suggests, and allows you to configure a database backup as part of a package.

❑ *Check Database Integrity Task* — Use the Check Database Integrity task to check the structural integrity and space allocation of all objects within a specified database.

❑ *Execute SQL Server Agent Job Task* — You can also configure an Integration Services package to launch a SQL Server Job as part of its process flow.

❑ *Execute T-SQL Statement Task* — Similar to the Execute SQL task, this requires that you specifically use the Transact-SQL dialect of the SQL language.

❑ *History Cleanup Task* — This task can be used to remove extemporaneous data from the `msdb` database, specifically historical information about backups, restores, jobs, and maintenance plans.

❑ *Maintenance Cleanup Task* — Use this task to remove leftover data from maintenance plans, such as backup files or text reports.

❑ *Notify Operator Task* — During the execution of a package, you may want to notify an operator that a certain step has completed or failed.

❑ *Rebuild Index Task* — You can use this task to rebuild an index during the execution of your package.

❑ *Reorganize Index Task* — Rather than rebuilding, you can also reorganize one or more indices from one or more databases.

❑ *Shrink Database Task* — Use this task to shrink one or more databases.

❑ *Update Statistics Task* — This task allows you to execute a controlled `UPDATE STATISTICS` task for one or more databases.

Precedence Constraints

Now that you've been introduced to the different tasks available for your control flow, you must understand how you can arrange or use these tasks together. When you add tasks to the control flow, you must specify how and when to execute these tasks. If you were to just add a bunch of tasks into the control flow, and then run the package, all of the tasks would try to execute at the same time. That may be desirable in some instances, but in most cases, you want to ensure that there is a defined logic to how and when the different tasks will execute. In more complex packages, some steps may not be executed at all unless there is a problem.

Precedence constraints are used to control the order in which tasks are executed, and whether or not they are executed based on the prior task failing, succeeding, or either. Tasks may also have more than one precedence constraint defined. When defining multiple precedence constraints on a task, you can also specify whether they are evaluated using the AND operator, which requires both constraints to evaluate to true; or the OR operator, which will execute the task as long as one of the constraints is met.

Remember that using multiple precedence constraints on a task means that either all conditions must be met, or just one. The conditions, however, could be completely different. For example, Task C has two precedence constraints defined. The first one requires that Task A succeeds, and the second one requires that Task B fails. If the AND operator is specified, then Task A *must* succeed, and Task B *must* fail. If Task B executes successfully, Task C will not run. If the OR operator is used, then Task C will run if Task A succeeds, regardless of the outcome of Task B, or if Task B fails, regardless of the outcome of Task A.

Figure 13-13 shows three tasks included in the control flow of a package. The first task will execute a SQL statement, and if it succeeds, the data flow task will execute. If the SQL task fails, then the Send Mail task will execute, and notify the appropriate personnel.

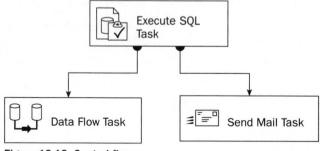

Figure 13-13: Control flow

Task Grouping

There is also a feature in Integration Services that allows you to add multiple tasks and containers to a group (see Figure 13-14). Unlike containers, groups are not treated as a unit of execution, but they can help clean up the logic flow. As a UI enhancement more than anything else, when you group tasks together, you can "hide" the tasks from view by collapsing the group. This can be helpful when you have a complex package, and want to simplify the view. Also, note that precedence constraints cannot be defined on a group, but are defined on the tasks within that group.

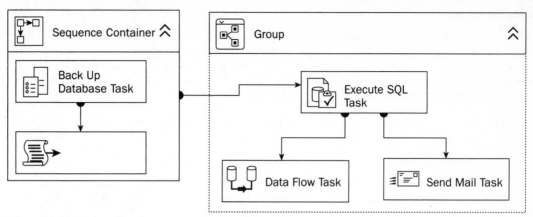

Figure 13-14: Control flow between a container and group

Data Flow

As mentioned earlier, one of the biggest improvements to managing Integration Services packages was removing the data flow logic from the control flow. This allows you to create more complex transformations that are easier to design and are more manageable. Data flow tasks appear as a single unit of execution in the control flow, but may have many complex steps in the data flow view.

When you switch to the data flow view, a drop-down list appears with all data flow tasks in the package. Each data flow task will allow you to configure at least a source and destination. You can optionally apply one or more transforms that can modify or prepare the data before it reaches its destination.

Data Sources

Out of the box, SQL Server 2005 includes six data sources you can use in your data flow. You can, in fact, use multiple data sources in your task. This allows you to use a merge transformation to join the data sets before it reaches the destination. The following data sources are available:

❑ *Data Reader Source* — Use the Data Reader Source with an ADO.NET connection manager to connect to a .NET provider.

❑ *Excel Source* — Use with Microsoft Excel spreadsheets.

❑ *Flat File Source* — This allows you to import from a variety of flat file formats (such as comma-separated, tab-separated, and fixed-length fields).

❑ *OLE DB Source* — Use with any OLE DB data source.

❑ *Raw File Source* — This is a specialized flat file format that is optimized for quick use. This is typically created by Raw File destinations to allow fast processing of the data, because minimal translation is required.

❑ *XML Source* — This allows you to use an XML file as a data source. You must ensure that elements within your XML file can be mapped to SQL fields. You can do this by creating a schema mapping file, using an inline schema within the file, or allowing Integration Services to try to create an XSD mapping file for this data source.

Transformations

Integration Services includes a number of built-in transforms to help modify or improve your data during the transfer process. With DTS 2000, many of these transforms had to be built programmatically, making the process of performing complex transformations burdensome. Although there are still programmatic options that let you build your own custom transforms, you can use the following transforms to create complex packages with minimal programming ability:

❑ *Aggregate* — This transform is used to perform aggregate calculations, such as AVERAGE, GROUP BY, and COUNT.

❑ *Audit* — Use the Audit transform to output additional data about the environment.

❑ *Character Map* — The Character Map transform lets you transform string data. You can use this to convert uppercase to lowercase, and traditional Chinese to simplified Chinese, for example.

❑ *Conditional Split* — The conditional split transform is used to send different data sets from the same source to different destinations.

❑ *Data Conversion* — Use the Data Conversion transform when you need to change the data type between source and destination.

❑ *Data Mining Query* — This can be used to perform prediction queries against data mining models.

❑ *Derived Column* — Derived Columns can be used to modify the data itself during transformation.

❑ *Export Column* — This transform imports data into a file.

❑ *Fuzzy Grouping* — You can use this transform to help standardize your data. It allows you to look for string data that is similar, and replaces the variants with a standard value.

❑ *Fuzzy Lookup* — Similar to the lookup transform, the fuzzy lookup uses values in a reference table, but accepts variants on the data.

❑ *Import Column* — This transform reads data from a file, and adds it to the data flow.

❑ *Lookup* — With a Lookup transform, existing data is joined to data being imported. This references values in a lookup table, but with an exact match.

❑ *Merge* — As the name suggests, the Merge transform merges data between two data sets. Use the Union All transform to join more than two data sources.

❑ *Merge Join* — Similar to the Merge transform, this transform uses JOIN statements to combine the data.

❑ *Multicast* — This transform allows the data to be sent to multiple destinations.

❑ *OLE DB Command* — Use this to execute a SQL command for each row in the input flow.

❑ *Percentage Sampling* — You can use this transform to return a random sampling of data from the input. When using this transform, specify a percentage of the total rows that will be sent to the output.

❑ *Pivot* — This can be used to denormalize data.

❑ *Row Count* — Use this transform to return a count of the total number of rows passed through, and return the count to a variable.

❑ *Row Sampling* — Similar to Percentage Sampling, Row Sampling outputs random rows, but you specify the total number of rows to be returned.

❑ *Script Component* — This transform allows you to execute a custom script task that will transform the data.

❑ *Slowly Changing Dimension* — Used with dimension tables to perform changing attribute, historical attribute, fixed attribute, and inferred member changes.

❑ *Sort* — This transform allows you to sort the data on one or more import columns.

❑ *Term Extraction* — You can use this transform to extract English nouns or noun phrases and redirect the terms to the output.

❑ *Term Lookup* — This transform uses a reference table and returns a count of the items in the reference table that appear in the data flow.

❑ *Union All* — This transform can be used to merge multiple data sets.

❑ *Unpivot* — Use the Unpivot transform to normalize data.

Data Destinations

Integration Services allows you to specify one or more destinations in a data flow task. The following is a list of data flow destinations that are available with SQL Server out-of-the-box:

❑ *Data Mining Model Training* — This destination passes data through data mining model algorithms to train the data mining model.

❑ *DataReader Destination* — This uses the DataReader interface in ADO.NET.

❑ *Dimension Processing* — This destination loads data into an Analysis Services dimension.

❑ *Excel Destination* — Use this to output your data to a Microsoft Excel file.

❑ *Flat File Destination* — This can be used to output the data to comma-separated, tab-separated, or fixed-length file.

❑ *OLE DB Destination* — This destination uses an OLE DB provider.

❑ *Partition Processing* — This destination is used to output the data to an Analysis Services partition.

❑ *Raw File Destination* — Used as an intermediary output between data flow tasks, this format allows for quick processing as minimal formatting options need to be defined.

❑ *Recordset Destination* — This outputs the data to an ADO recordset.

❑ *SQL Server Destination* — This inserts data into a Microsoft SQL Server destination.

❑ *SQL Server Mobile Destination* — This destination is used for SQL Server Mobile Edition clients.

Event Handling

Event handling is another feature of Integration Services that provides more granular control over the execution of your packages, and the tasks within them. Frequently associated with error handling, event handling allows you to execute additional tasks before a task executes, during task execution, and after task execution.

Any well-designed package includes the ability to control or monitor the execution of the tasks within. Using efficient error handling and event handling is the cornerstone for creating packages that require minimal maintenance and hands-on execution. The Event Handling tab includes options for configuring tasks that execute for the following 12 package- or task-level events:

- ❑ OnError
- ❑ OnExecStatusChanged
- ❑ OnInformation
- ❑ OnPostExecute
- ❑ OnPostValidate
- ❑ OnPreExecute
- ❑ OnPreValidate
- ❑ OnProgress
- ❑ OnQueryCancel
- ❑ OnTaskFailed
- ❑ OnVariableValueChanged
- ❑ OnWarning

Configuring additional tasks on these events can improve error handling and provide you with more precise control over execution of your packages. Be careful, though. Too much granularity can cause more administrative work than necessary.

Package Explorer

The Package Explorer is a useful utility that allows you to view the different elements of your package in an organized, hierarchical structure. Though this view isn't representative of the control or data flow, it can help you quickly find an element of either. You can view or modify the properties, or delete unused elements from your package.

Creating a Simple Package

So, now that you have a fairly good understanding of the different elements of an Integration Services package, it's time to put it to use. In this scenario, the employees at AdventureWorks have decided to pool some of their resources and decided to keep a DVD library of titles in the office to share among themselves. Anyone is welcome to participate, but if you're going to borrow, you're going to contribute!

Up until now, one of the employees had been keeping track of their collection using an InfoPath form. However, over the last couple of months, the collection has grown significantly, and the core group who started the library wants a better way to manage it. They've decided to store the data in SQL, but rather than having to re-enter all the data by hand, they would prefer to import the XML file into the database.

For this example, you can download an XML file from http://p2p.wrox.com/ (search for the ISBN — 04700047046 — or title of this book), or you could build your own sample file. The one provided uses the following format:

```
<?xml version="1.0" standalone="yes"?>
<DVDs>
  <Table>
    <Title>Movie Title</Title>
    <Year>YYYY</Year>
    <Run-time>hh:MM</Run-time>
    <Rating>XX</Rating>
  </Table>
</DVDs>
```

Save the file as `C:\SSISDemos\DVDLib.xml`.

Create the Connection

You'll begin by creating a new Integration Services project called AdventureWorks IS Project. When you create the project, a new package named `Package.dtsx` is created. Rename the package `XMLImport.dtsx`.

Follow these steps:

1. Although you'll only be creating one package in this exercise, create a new Data Source that will be available to all packages that are part of this project. Right-click Data Sources and select New Data Source to launch the Wizard.

2. In the Wizard, click Next on the introduction page. Then, on the next page, "Select how to define the connection," click New. In the Connection Manager dialog box, either enter your server name, or select it from the drop-down list. Use Windows Authentication, and select AdventureWorks as the database. Click OK when these options have been selected.

3. Click Next to go to the Completing the Wizard page, and leave the default Data Source name. Click Finish to complete the wizard.

4. Now, below the Control Flow pane, you should see the Connection Managers pane. Right-click anywhere in the pane and select New Connection from Data Source.

5. Select Adventure Works and click OK.

Create the Data Flow Task

Now it's time to put the package to work. The first thing to do is create a new Data Flow task. From your Toolbox, drag the Data Flow task into the control flow window, and rename it XML Transfer.

Click the Data Flow tab. You should see XML Transfer in the drop-down list. If you had more than one data flow task in your package, you could navigate through them without having to go back to the control flow task to manage it.

The first thing to do to build the data flow is to specify the source. Drag the XML Source from the Toolbox into the data flow pane, and then double-click it to open up the XML Source Editor.

For the Data Access mode, ensure that XML file location is selected. Type the path or browse to the `DVDLib.xml` file. Because there is no schema mapping file, you can have the SQL Server generate one. Click the Generate XSD button, and use the default filename and location.

You can navigate to the Columns page to view the columns that will be imported into your database, but you should not need to change anything in there. Click OK to exit the editor.

Because the table you are going to create will store the Year column as a `smallint` value, you can change the output of the XML file to use a signed 2-byte integer, rather than the default of a 2-byte unsigned integer. This also gives you an opportunity to see the Advanced Editor. Right-click the XML Source object and select Show Advanced Editor.

Click the "Input and Output Properties" tab and expand Output Columns. Select Year, and, in the right pane, under Data Type Properties, change the value two-byte unsigned integer [DT_UI2] to two-byte signed integer [DT_I2]. See Figure 13-15 for an example.

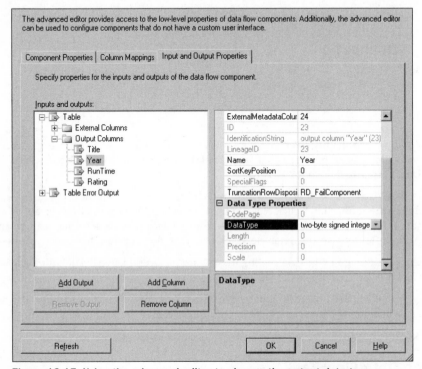

Figure 13-15: Using the advanced editor to change the output data type

At this point, you could simply provide the data to a destination, but that wouldn't be much fun. To see how transforms work, you can apply a simple transform to your data before it reaches the destination. In this example, you'll use the Sort transform to sort based on the title. Drag the Sort transform from the Toolbox into the Data Flow pane.

Two things must happen next in order for the sort to work:

❑ You must configure the output of your XML source to go to the Sort transform. Select the XML Source, and then click and drag the green arrow to the Sort transform.

❑ You must tell the transform which column or columns to sort on. Double-click the Sort transform to open the editor.

In the Sort Transformation editor, the top pane lists the available fields, and the bottom shows you which ones have been selected for sorting. Select the Title column from the top pane. In the bottom pane, rename the output alias to Sort Title. Your configuration should look like Figure 13-16.

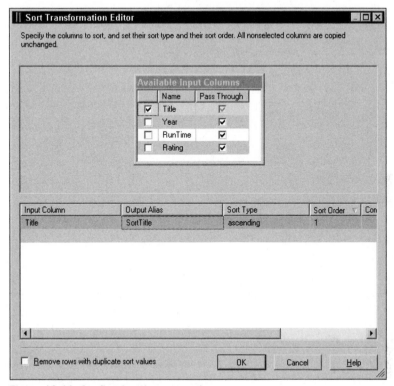

Figure 13-16: Configuring the sort options

Now it's time to define the destination. Drag the SQL Server Destination object from the Toolbox into the Data Flow. Before you configure the destination options, select the Sort transform, and drag the green output arrow to the SQL Server Destination object (see Figure 13-17).

Double-click the SQL Server Destination to open the editor. Because you've already defined a connection manager, Adventure Works should already be populated. Under "Use a table or view," click New, and replace the existing SQL code with the following:

```
CREATE SCHEMA DVD

CREATE TABLE [DVD].[Library] (
    [ID] int IDENTITY NOT NULL,
    [Title] NVARCHAR(255),
    [Year] SMALLINT,
    [Run-time] NVARCHAR(255),
    [Rating] NVARCHAR(255)
)
```

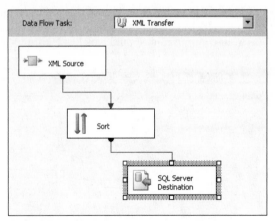

Figure 13-17: Data flow from XML to SQL

> *Because the schema did not exist before you clicked OK, an error message will appear informing you that the table couldn't be created. Click OK, and just select the new* DVD.Library *table from the drop-down list.*

Select the Mappings page. Create a mapping to the destination Title column from the SortTitle column. You can do this either by clicking the SortTitle field and dragging it over to the title field, or by using the drop-down list in the Input Column column. Ensure that the ID column has <ignore> mapped to it. Click OK to close the editor.

So That's It, Right?

You *could* save and execute the package now, and you'd have a new table with some movie data in it. But I'm not really happy with this data. The person who was adding the titles to the InfoPath form had no consideration for how to sort titles. When you execute this task, all of the movies that begin with articles like "The," "An," and "A" will be grouped together. For example, "The Black Hole" should be sorted alphabetically under "B," not under "T."

You could always fix this after the fact, but one of the requirements of being an effective database administrator is that you understand your data, and how it will be used. So, before you can consider this package a success, you need to fix someone else's mistake.

Go back into the Control Flow Items list and drag an Execute SQL task into your Control Flow. Double-click the Execute SQL task to open the task editor. On the General page, find the Connection parameter, and select Adventure Works from the drop-down list.

Then, find the SQL Statement parameter and click the "..." button. Enter the following code in the SQL query window:

```
Update DVD.Library
Set Title = CASE
    When Title like 'The %' THEN (SUBSTRING(Title, 5, 255) + ', The')
    When Title like 'An %' THEN (SUBSTRING(Title, 4, 255) + ', An')
```

```
When Title like 'A %' THEN (SUBSTRING(Title, 3, 255) + ', A')
Else Title
END;
```

Click OK to exit the query window, and then OK again to exit the task editor.

Save your package and then right-click the package name from the Solution Explorer. Select "Execute package." All steps should execute successfully. When they do, select Stop Debugging from the debug menu. Open SQL Server Management Studio, and execute the following query:

```
USE AdventureWorks;
GO
SELECT * FROM DVD.Library
ORDER BY Title;
```

The query should return the data sorted by title, without articles like "the" being grouped together.

Summary

In summary, SQL Server 2005 Integration Services is a very powerful tool for controlling data transformation operations between SQL Servers and other data stores. It allows you to create very simple data flow models, or very complex ones. It is also extensible, allowing you to programmatically build additional transformations and controls. This chapter provided you with a high-level overview of how the Integration Service works, how to use the Import and Export wizards, and how to build simple packages using the SSIS designer. If you would like to learn more about Integration Services, check out *Professional SQL Server 2005 Integration Service* (Indianapolis: Wiley, 2006).

In Chapter 14, you learn about Notification Services and how you can use it to help build relationships between your data and your customers.

Introduction to SQL Server 2005 Notification Services

In this day and age of rapid communication and instant gratification, it's important to be able to provide dynamic services to meet customer demands and to stay competitive. Notification Services is a feature of SQL Server 2005 that helps you build relationships with your customers by providing a mechanism for them to receive updated information about your products and services. You can use it to let customers know when a price drops, or when new inventory arrives. You can use Notification Services to communicate with a handful of customers, or with thousands.

This chapter provides you with an overview of how Notification Services works, and how to manage both instances and applications that can help create a robust application environment. Although this chapter does not get into the nuts and bolts of building a complex Notification Services application, you will learn some key administrative concepts when managing notification services.

Many of the examples in this chapter are used for demonstration purposes only, because building a Notification Services solution falls outside of the scope of this book. However, the sample code and application are available for download at `http://p2p.wrox.com/download`. Instructions on configuring and installing the Notification Services application are included in the download.

Overview

Without flooding you with marketing terms extolling the virtues of Notification Services, the bottom line is that it's a pretty darned cool feature. Notification Services is not part of the core functionality of SQL Server 2005, but it's an excellent ancillary feature. Many applications can benefit from automation, and Notification Services provides a framework for building robust application services.

So, how does it work? The basic design of a Notification Services application begins with a customer who wants information. The customer requests information through an application, which could be a Web site or a Windows application. The application generates the necessary subscription components and sends it to the Notification Services solution, which interacts with your database to keep track of activity related to the request. When an event that meets the customer's request occurs, your Notification Services application takes the necessary steps to ensure the customer is notified as requested. The versatility of Notification Services allows you to use out-of-the-box features and tools and/or create customized application solutions that fit your specific needs.

Introduction to the Notification Services Architecture

Now, it's time to take some of the ambiguity out of the process. First of all, Notification Services uses two components to build an application solution. There components are known as instances and applications. An *instance*, as the name might suggest, is representative of the service itself, and is used to control access to applications. *Applications* are bound to instances and are used to control and store information about subscriptions. Each instance and application has its own database that stores information about subscribers and subscriptions. Installing and registering instances is covered later in this chapter.

In this section, you learn about the framework of a Notification Services solution and the process flow used by these applications. The Notification Services architecture can be broken down into four logical components. Each component defines part of the overall solution that collects information about subscribers, subscriptions, events, formatting, and distribution of notifications. These components include the following:

- ❑ Subscription management
- ❑ Event collection
- ❑ Subscription processing
- ❑ Notification formatting and delivery

While these components provide you with a solid framework for building applications, Notification Services also allows you to create custom event collection and formatting components.

Subscription Management

Your Notification Services application is worthless without subscribers. Subscribers, the data they're interested in, and the method of delivery are all part of the subscription management architecture. When subscribers use the applications you've provided to create a subscription, the application is known as the *subscription management interface* (SMI). Through the SMI, three objects are created: the subscriber object, the subscriber device object, and the subscription object. The *subscriber object* represents the user who is requesting the subscription. The *subscriber device object* represents the method in which the subscriber expects to be notified. The *subscription object* represents the relationship between the subscriber, the subscription device, and the data.

The subscriber object and subscriber device object are stored in the instance database, and the subscription object is stored in the application database. This model allows the same subscriber to have subscriptions to multiple applications and data sets without having to re-create the subscriber and subscription device for each application.

When building a Notification Services–enabled application, the application developer can define how the information is defined and collected. For example, you could provide a Web page that allows users to input their names and email addresses to request notification when a certain product becomes available. Chapter 13 described a scenario where the employees of AdventureWorks have access to a DVD library that they can borrow from and contribute to. In some cases, a user may want to know when a particular title is available to check out. Figure 14-1 shows a sample SMI, where users can input their name and email address, and then click the Subscribe button. This creates the subscriber (User Name), the subscriber device (email address), and subscription (the request to be notified when this title is available).

Figure 14-1: The Subscription Management Interface (SMI)

Event Collection

The event collection process monitors the different sources that participate in the Notification Services architecture. This could include files, applications, or databases. Each source type will use the appropriate API for submitting data to the application. The following APIs can be used to collect event information:

❑   *Event Object API* — This tracks information submitted by an application to the database. In this case, the data is intercepted as an *event feed* and passed to the event collector as the data is being updated.

❑   *XML API* — This collects XML event data from the event source (such as an XML bulk load or XML file stream) into the event table.

❑   *SQL Server API* — This can use stored procedures to query database objects to look for changes to the data that would qualify as a *database table event*. These procedures can be executed manually or on a predefined schedule.

In the earlier example, the DVD Library application uses the SQL Server API to look for changes to specific database tables. When a user returns a DVD to the library by clicking the "Check In" button on the Web application, a stored procedure is executed that updates the loan status of the DVD. A trigger is fired when the UPDATE statement is executed to alter the loan status. This trigger stores event data in a separate collection table. The following code includes the contents of the Preinstall.sql file, used to build the Notification Services application, and illustrates the creation of a table to store event collection data, and the trigger that populates the event collection table. Note that before executing this code, you must have created and populated the DVD.Library table from Chapter 13.

```
/* If you have already executed the Preinstall.sql file, you can comment out the
code between the begin preinstall.sql and end preinstall.sql comment lines. */

-- begin preinstall.sql

/* This script will create the necessary components for the DVD Library application
   Run this script before installing the Notification Services application */

/* This will add the status column to the DVD.Library table from Chapter 13
   and designate the ID column as the primary key if you did not create the table
and schema in Chapter 13 you can uncomment out the following CREATE statements to
create them now. */

--USE AdventureWorks;
--GO
--CREATE SCHEMA DVD;
--GO
--CREATE TABLE [DVD].[Library] (
--      [ID] int IDENTITY NOT NULL,
--      [Title] NVARCHAR(255),
--      [Year] SMALLINT,
--      [Run-time] NVARCHAR(255),
--      [Rating] NVARCHAR(255)
--);

USE AdventureWorks;
GO
ALTER TABLE DVD.Library
      ADD CONSTRAINT pkid PRIMARY KEY CLUSTERED(ID),
      Status BIT NOT NULL DEFAULT(0);
GO

-- Adds two new error messages to the sysmessages table
EXECUTE sp_addmessage @msgnum=60501, @severity=16, @msgtext='This DVD has already
been checked out!';
EXECUTE sp_addmessage @msgnum=60502, @severity=16, @msgtext='You can't check in
something you didn't check out!';
```

```
GO

-- Creates a new table to track loan history
CREATE TABLE DVD.LoanHistory
 (LoanID INT IDENTITY NOT NULL,
  DVDID INT NOT NULL REFERENCES DVD.Library(ID),
  BorrowedBy NVARCHAR(30) NOT NULL,
  LoanDate DateTime NOT NULL,
  ReturnDate DateTime NULL);
GO

-- Creates a stored procedure that will be called by the application to check out a
-- movie
CREATE PROCEDURE Dvd.Checkout
    @DVDID int
AS
    SELECT * FROM DVD.LoanHistory WHERE DVDID=@DVDID AND ReturnDate IS NULL
    IF @@ROWCOUNT > 0 RAISERROR (60501,16,1)
    ELSE BEGIN
        INSERT DVD.LoanHistory (DVDID,BorrowedBy,LoanDate)
        VALUES(@DVDID,suser_sname(),GETDATE())
        UPDATE DVD.Library
        SET Status = 1
        WHERE ID=@DVDID;
    END;
GO

-- Creates a stored procedure that will be called by the application to return a
--movie
CREATE PROCEDURE Dvd.Checkin
    @DVDID int
 AS
    SELECT * FROM DVD.LoanHistory WHERE DVDID=@DVDID AND ReturnDate IS NULL
    AND BorrowedBy=Suser_Sname()
    IF @@ROWCOUNT = 0 RAISERROR (60502,16,1)
    ELSE BEGIN
            UPDATE DVD.LoanHistory
                Set ReturnDate=GetDate()
                Where DVDID = @DVDID AND
                BorrowedBy = Suser_Sname()AND
                ReturnDate IS NULL
            UPDATE DVD.Library
                SET Status = 0
                WHERE ID=@DVDID;
    END;
GO

-- end preinstall.sql

USE AdventureWorks;
GO

-- Creates the a table for the Notification Services application to store
-- pending notifications
```

```
CREATE TABLE dbo.PendingCheckInNotifications
(PendingCheckInID integer IDENTITY PRIMARY KEY,
 DVDID INT,
 Title NVARCHAR(255),
 Status BIT);
GO

-- Creates a trigger that executes when the loanhistory table is updated
CREATE TRIGGER DVD.CheckInTrigger
ON DVD.loanhistory
FOR UPDATE
AS
INSERT INTO dbo.PendingCheckInNotifications
SELECT i.DVDID, l.Title, l.status
FROM INSERTED i JOIN DVD.Library l
ON i.DVDID = l.ID;
GO
```

When the events have been collected by the appropriate provider, they are stored in an Events table, which is used by the subscription processing architecture. In Figure 14-2, a user checks the title back into the library. This executes the stored procedure that updates the LoanHistory table, which in turn will fire the trigger to record the event in the PendingCheckInNotifications table.

Figure 14-2: Generating the event

494

Subscription Processing

The goal of the subscription processing architecture can be simply defined as matching events to subscriptions. This is performed by the *notification generator*, which uses rules in the application architecture that define the relationship between events and subscriptions. It also defines what other conditions must be met before a notification is generated. Again, flexibility is given to the application developer to create either very general "catch-all" rules, or very complex, granular matching requirements.

When the notification generator has matched an event to an existing subscription, a notification is generated and stored in a notifications table. The generator uses an application-defined schedule known as the *quantum duration*, which is a fixed value that defines the how often the generator will run. The generator is also capable of storing historical data in an optional *chronicle* table that can be defined as part of the application framework.

In the following script, a stored procedure is created in the AdventureWorks database that executes another stored procedure in the application database itself. This stored procedure collects the event data for the application so that it can be used for subscription matching.

```
USE AdventureWorks;
GO
CREATE PROCEDURE dbo.ProcessPendingCheckins
AS
EXECUTE AWInstanceDVDLibrary.dbo.NSEventSubmitBatchDVDCheckInEvent
'DVDCheckInEventProvider',
    'SELECT DVDID, Title, Status FROM
    AdventureWorks.dbo.PendingCheckInNotifications',
    'TRUNCATE TABLE AdventureWorks.dbo.PendingCheckInNotifications';
GO
```

Keep in mind that not every event will have a subscription associated with it, and some events may have multiple subscriptions. Only those events that match to one or more subscriptions can generate notifications.

Notification Formatting and Delivery

The next step in the Notification Services application workflow is the message formatting and delivery process. After notifications have been generated and stored in the notifications table, the *distributor* (which is responsible for the final stages) prepares the data in the format required by the delivery method. By default, Notification Services uses XML Stylesheet (XLST) files to define how the data will look when sent to the appropriate output device. You can create a different XLST for each device type to ensure the data will be displayed properly on that device.

Once the notification has been prepared, a *delivery channel* is used to provide the notification to the subscriber. Delivery channels are defined in the instance, not the application, and are used to define how the message will be delivered to the subscriber. An instance of Notification Services supports multiple delivery channels, each using a specific protocol to reach the subscriber:

❑ *SMTP* — Allows messages to be sent via email.

❑ *File* — Sends notification services to the file system.

❑ *HTTP* — Can be used for as a transport for other protocols such as Simple Object Access Protocol (SOAP) and Short Message Service (SMS).

The SMTP and File protocols are considered standard protocols, meaning that once the formatting process is complete, little else needs to be done to prepare the notification for delivery. The HTTP protocol is considered a custom protocol, in that the HTTP protocol is simply a wrapper for another protocol, and the application developer must define the custom protocol. The extensibility of Notification Services is again evident by allowing you (or your application developer) to create custom delivery channels and custom protocols as needed.

In Figure 14-3, you can see the notification message that was sent to Chris@adventureworks.com, informing him that the title he was interested in has been returned to the library. The delivery channel used the SMTP protocol, and formatted the message using UTF-8 encoding (mainly because Outlook Express doesn't display UTF-16 properly by default).

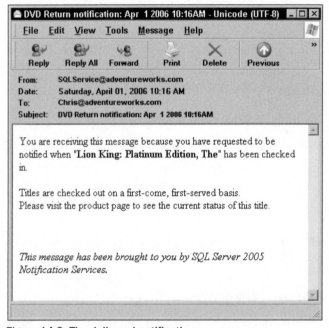

Figure 14-3: The delivered notification

Now that you understand the process flow, you can see how applications use Notification Services to provide a mechanism for creating responsive and automated applications. In the next section, you learn more about building and installing Notification Services applications.

Installing a Notification Services Application

To provide a more complete picture of how Notification Services works and can be managed, you will learn about the process of creating an instance and an associated application. In this section, you will be exposed to the configuration options for both instances and applications, using the DVD Library scenario. You will learn about creating a Notification Services instance and a dependent application.

The Notification Services Instance

As mentioned earlier, Notification Services instances are used to control and manage Notification Services applications. Instances share subscriber and subscription delivery objects among applications, and can either be installed as server-side hosted components or client-side non-hosted components. When registering hosted Notification Services instances, you will install the Notification Services engine as a Windows service, which will be used for event collection applications, subscriber collection, and delivery notification. With non-hosted instances, external applications can use event-collection APIs to report to the instance, without having to create a Windows service.

Notification Services instances can be built using either the `Microsoft.SqlServer.Management.Nmo` namespace or an Instance Configuration File (ICF). The ICF is an XML file that uses specific elements to define the instance to the SQL Server. Regardless of the method used to build the instance, the following information can be provided when building the application:

- ❑ Instance name
- ❑ Name of the SQL Server used to host the instance and application databases
- ❑ Optional instance description
- ❑ All applications hosted by the instance
- ❑ Information about any custom delivery protocols available to all applications
- ❑ Information about all delivery channels used by any application
- ❑ Encryption options
- ❑ Optional history and version information

These options provide information about the configuration and behavior of the Notification Services instance. The following table shows a list of the specific sections for the instance configuration.

Section	Description
Parameters	This section allows you to specify values for placeholders that can be used throughout your configuration file.
File Documentation	This section stores version and history information about the instance.
Instance Settings	Use this to store information about the instance, including the name of the instance, the name of the SQL Server on which the instance will run, and database configuration for the instance database.
Application Settings	This section is used to list all attached applications, and the location of the Application Definition File (ADF).
Protocol Settings	Each custom protocol that will be used must be defined in this section. Standard protocols do not need to be listed.
Delivery Channels	Each delivery channel and its configuration settings must be listed in this section.
Encryption Arguments	This section can be used to specify that sensitive information in the instance be encrypted.

In most cases, as a database administrator, you won't be responsible for building a Notification Services solution, but you may be responsible for installing and managing Notification Services applications. To install the sample Notification Services solution, you will need an ICF. If you downloaded the samples listed at the beginning of the chapter, you can use the ICF named `Config.XML`. The file contents are as follows:

```xml
<?xml version="1.0" encoding="utf-8"?>
<NotificationServicesInstance xmlns:xsd="http://www.w3.org/2001/XMLSchema"
xmlns:xsi="http://www.w3.org/2001/XMLSchema-instance"
xmlns="http://www.microsoft.com/MicrosoftNotificationServices/ConfigurationFileSche
ma">


<ParameterDefaults>
     <Parameter>
          <Name>BaseDirectoryPath</Name>
          <Value>C:\NSDemos</Value>
     </Parameter>
     <Parameter>
          <Name>SqlServer</Name>
          <Value>AughtFive</Value>
     </Parameter>
</ParameterDefaults>
<InstanceName>AWInstance</InstanceName>
<SqlServerSystem>%SQLServer%</SqlServerSystem>
<Applications>
     <Application>
          <ApplicationName>DVDLibrary</ApplicationName>
          <BaseDirectoryPath>%BaseDirectoryPath%</BaseDirectoryPath>
     <ApplicationDefinitionFilePath>ADF.xml</ApplicationDefinitionFilePath>
          <Parameters>
               <Parameter>
                    <Name>_DBSystem_</Name>
                    <Value>%SqlServer%</Value>
               </Parameter>
               <Parameter>
                    <Name>_NSSystem_</Name>
                    <Value>%SqlServer%</Value>
               </Parameter>
               <Parameter>
                    <Name>_BaseDirectoryPath_</Name>
                    <Value>%BaseDirectoryPath%</Value>
               </Parameter>
          </Parameters>
     </Application>
</Applications>
<DeliveryChannels>
     <DeliveryChannel>
          <DeliveryChannelName>EmailChannel</DeliveryChannelName>
          <ProtocolName>SMTP</ProtocolName>
          <Arguments>
               <Argument>
                    <Name>SMTPServer</Name>
                    <Value>localhost</Value>
```

```
            </Argument>
            <Argument>
                    <Name>BodyEncoding</Name>
                    <Value>utf-8</Value>
            </Argument>
        </Arguments>
    </DeliveryChannel>
</DeliveryChannels>
</NotificationServicesInstance>
```

Examining the contents of this file reveals a couple of things to note. In the `<ParameterDefaults>` section, the values for variables used throughout the ICF are specified. In this case, the base directory path is `C:\NSDemos`, and the SQL Server is identified as `AughtFive`. These values are designed to be defaults used when no other value is specified. They can be modified in the file itself or can be changed when creating the instance. This makes it easier to deploy the same Notification Services solution on multiple servers. When specifying a value for `<SQLServer>`, you cannot use "." or "localhost," or an IP address. The `<InstanceName>` section creates a name for the Notification Services instance, and the `<Applications>` section provides configuration options for the DVD Library application, which uses a configuration file name `ADF.XML`, which is covered in the next section. Finally, in the `<DeliveryChannel>` section, the SMTP protocol is used, and will use the local server as the SMTP relay. Messages will be encoded using the UTF-8 format.

The Notification Services Application

Each Notification Services application maintains its own event schemas, subscriptions schemas, and notification schemas. Each application may also have specific operational parameters that are unique to the application itself. Applications are still dependent on the parent instance for subscriber, delivery channel, and delivery protocol information. This data may be shared with other applications that are part of the same instance.

Notification Services applications can also be built using the Notification Services Management Objects namespace or an XML file known as an Application Definition File (ADF), which may contain the following information:

- ❑ The structure of application events
- ❑ The structure of application subscriptions
- ❑ Queries that join event data and subscription data to create notifications
- ❑ The structure and content format of the resulting notifications
- ❑ Delivery protocols and delivery options used
- ❑ Event providers that collect data and submit the event to the application
- ❑ Generator execution frequency
- ❑ Formatting and distribution options
- ❑ The application database structure
- ❑ Operational settings for the application

Similar to the ICF, the ADF shares many of the same sections, but also contains additional elements that help control the execution of the application. The following table shows a list of the main elements of the application definition file.

Section	Description
Parameters	As with the ICF, you can specify parameter defaults used throughout the definition file.
File Documentation	This section is also used for version and history information.
Database Settings	This allows customization of the application database.
Event Classes	Use this section to define event tables and views that will be used in the application.
Subscription Classes	This section will create tables and views for each subscription class that will be used by your application.
Notification Classes	Another part of the application architecture that will create the necessary database objects.
Provider Settings	Information about hosted and non-hosted providers are listed here.
Generator Settings	Settings for the notification generator (including the name of the server running the generation process) are listed here.
Distributor Settings	This section identifies which server runs the distributor component, and its related settings.
Application Execution Settings	This controls the application execution, including defining the *quanta* of the application. The quanta setting is used to identify how frequently Notification Services processes data, and how far back behind the system clock the application can fall before skipping rules.

The `Config.xml` file displayed earlier refers to an ADF named (appropriately) `ADF.xml` that will create an application named `DVDLibrary`. The contents of the `ADF.xml` file are as follows:

```xml
<?xml version="1.0" encoding="utf-8" ?>
<Application xmlns:xsd="http://www.w3.org/2001/XMLSchema"
xmlns:xsi="http://www.w3.org/2001/XMLSchema-instance"
xmlns="http://www.microsoft.com/MicrosoftNotificationServices/ApplicationDefinition
FileSchema">
<Version>
    <Major>1</Major>
    <Minor>0</Minor>
    <Build>0</Build>
    <Revision>0</Revision>
</Version>
<History>
    <CreationDate>2006-04-01</CreationDate>
    <CreationTime>11:12:52.0000000-08:00</CreationTime>
```

```
            <LastModifiedDate>2006-04-12</LastModifiedDate>
            <LastModifiedTime>11:54:13.3261327-08:00</LastModifiedTime>
    </History>
    <EventClasses>
        <EventClass>
            <EventClassName>DVDCheckInEvent</EventClassName>
            <Schema>
                <Field>
                    <FieldName>DVDID</FieldName>
                     <FieldType>Int</FieldType>
                    <FieldTypeMods>not null</FieldTypeMods>
                </Field>
                <Field>
                    <FieldName>Title</FieldName>
                    <FieldType>nvarchar(255)</FieldType>
                    <FieldTypeMods>not null</FieldTypeMods>
                </Field>
                <Field>
                    <FieldName>CheckinStatus</FieldName>
                    <FieldType>bit</FieldType>
                    <FieldTypeMods>not null</FieldTypeMods>
                </Field>
            </Schema>
            <IndexSqlSchema>
                <SqlStatement>CREATE INDEX dvdlibindex ON DVDCheckInEvent
                    (DVDID)</SqlStatement>
            </IndexSqlSchema>
        </EventClass>
    </EventClasses>
    <SubscriptionClasses>
        <SubscriptionClass>
            <SubscriptionClassName>DVDCheckinSubscription</SubscriptionClassName>
            <Schema>
                <Field>
                    <FieldName>DeviceName</FieldName>
                    <FieldType>nvarchar(255)</FieldType>
                    <FieldTypeMods>not null</FieldTypeMods>
                </Field>
                <Field>
                    <FieldName>SubscriberLocale</FieldName>
                    <FieldType>nvarchar(10)</FieldType>
                    <FieldTypeMods>not null</FieldTypeMods>
                </Field>
                <Field>
                    <FieldName>DVDID</FieldName>
                    <FieldType>int</FieldType>
                    <FieldTypeMods>not null</FieldTypeMods>
                </Field>
            </Schema>
            <IndexSqlSchema>
                <SqlStatement>ALTER TABLE DVDCheckinSubscription ADD
                    CONSTRAINT UniqueSub UNIQUE(SubscriberID,DVDID)
                </SqlStatement>
            </IndexSqlSchema>
```

```xml
        <EventRules>
           <EventRule>
             <RuleName>DVDCheckinSubscriptionsEventRule</RuleName>
             <Action>INSERT INTO DVDCheckInNotification
                 (SubscriberID, DeviceName, SubscriberLocale,
                 DVDID, Title, CheckInStatus)
                 SELECT s.SubscriberID, s.DeviceName,
                 SubscriberLocale, e.DVDID,e.Title,e.CheckInStatus
                 FROM DVDCheckInEvent e
                 JOIN DVDCheckinSubscription s
                 ON e.DVDID = s.DVDID
             </Action>
             <EventClassName>DVDCheckInEvent</EventClassName>
           </EventRule>
        </EventRules>
      </SubscriptionClass>
   </SubscriptionClasses>
<NotificationClasses>
   <NotificationClass>
      <NotificationClassName>DVDCheckInNotification</NotificationClassName>
         <Schema>
             <Fields>
                 <Field>
                     <FieldName>DVDID</FieldName>
                     <FieldType>Int</FieldType>
                 </Field>
                 <Field>
                     <FieldName>Title</FieldName>
                     <FieldType>nvarchar(255)</FieldType>
                 </Field>
                 <Field>
                     <FieldName>CheckinStatus</FieldName>
                     <FieldType>bit</FieldType>
                 </Field>
             </Fields>
         </Schema>
      <ContentFormatter>
          <ClassName>XsltFormatter</ClassName>
          <Arguments>
              <Argument>
                  <Name>XsltBaseDirectoryPath</Name>
                  <Value>%_BaseDirectoryPath_%</Value>
              </Argument>
              <Argument>
                  <Name>XsltFileName</Name>
                  <Value>DVDCheckin.xslt</Value>
              </Argument>
          </Arguments>
      </ContentFormatter>
<Protocols>
   <Protocol>
     <ProtocolName>SMTP</ProtocolName>
     <Fields>
        <Field>
```

```xml
            <FieldName>Subject</FieldName>
            <SqlExpression>&apos;DVD Return notification:
            &apos;+CONVERT(NVARCHAR(30), GETDATE())</SqlExpression>
        </Field>
        <Field>
            <FieldName>BodyFormat</FieldName>
            <SqlExpression>&apos;html&apos;</SqlExpression>
        </Field>
        <Field>
            <FieldName>From</FieldName>
            <SqlExpression>&apos;SQLService@adventureworks.com&apos;
            </SqlExpression>
        </Field>
        <Field>
            <FieldName>Priority</FieldName>
            <SqlExpression>&apos;Normal&apos;</SqlExpression>
        </Field>
        <Field>
            <FieldName>To</FieldName>
            <SqlExpression>DeviceAddress</SqlExpression>
        </Field>
      </Fields>
    </Protocol>
  </Protocols>
<ExpirationAge>PT2H</ExpirationAge>
</NotificationClass>
</NotificationClasses>
<Providers>
    <NonHostedProvider>
        <ProviderName>DVDCheckinEventProvider</ProviderName>
    </NonHostedProvider>
</Providers>
<Generator>
    <SystemName>%_NSSystem_%</SystemName>
</Generator>
<Distributors>
    <Distributor>
        <SystemName>%_NSSystem_%</SystemName>
    </Distributor>
</Distributors>
<ApplicationExecutionSettings>
    <QuantumDuration>P0DT0H0M30S</QuantumDuration>
    <ChronicleQuantumLimit>0</ChronicleQuantumLimit>
    <SubscriptionQuantumLimit>0</SubscriptionQuantumLimit>
    <ProcessEventsInOrder>true</ProcessEventsInOrder>
</ApplicationExecutionSettings>
</Application>
```

Examining this file shows you that several database objects will be created (including tables, views, an index, and a unique constraint on the subscription table). Also note the format of the `<QuantumDuration>` element. This is what is known as a *primitive duration* format, where you define the number of years, months, days, hours, minutes, and seconds that will be used. In this case, the quantum value for the application is 30 seconds. This means that the generator will process data every 30 seconds.

Creating the Instance

Now that you have an ICF and ADF, you are ready to create the instance on your local server. Note that if your server is not named `AughtFive`, you will need to change the value of the `<SQLServer>` parameter to reflect your actual server name. You can do this by editing the ICF, or specifying a different value when creating the instance during the creation process.

Follow these steps:

1. If it's not already running, open SQL Server Management Studio, and ensure that the Object Explorer is visible and has your server listed.

2. Expand your server and right-click the Notification Services folder. Select New Notification Services Instance.

3. Specify the path to the configuration file, then confirm or change the values for the parameters specified in your file. Figure 14-4 shows a sample configuration.

4. Ensure that "Enable instance after it is created" is selected and click OK.

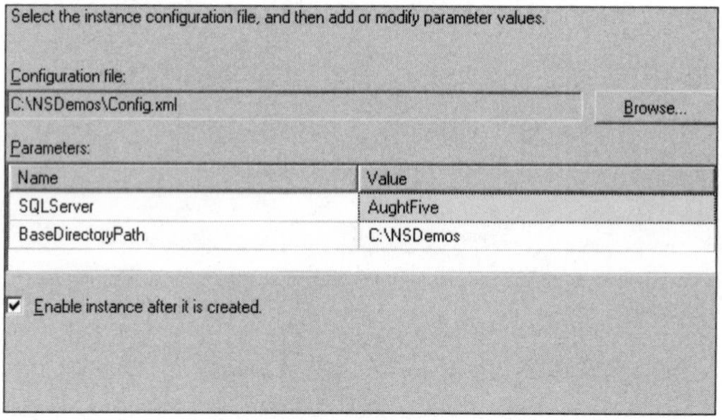

Select the instance configuration file, and then add or modify parameter values.	

Configuration file:

C:\NSDemos\Config.xml   Browse...

Parameters:

Name	Value
SQLServer	AughtFive
BaseDirectoryPath	C:\NSDemos

☑ Enable instance after it is created.

Figure 14-4: Creating the Notification Services Instance

The new instance should now be created. At this point, the application, subscriptions, and event provider should be enabled. However, the generator and the distributor cannot be enabled until the service is registered. Figure 14-5 shows the application properties window. Note that if you have more than one application associated with this instance, you can view each application's properties by selecting the application from the drop-down list.

The next step for this example is to register the instance as a Windows service. From the Object Explorer, ensure that Notification Services is expanded and right-click your instance name. Select Tasks → Register.

Ensure that the Instance Name is correct, and select the option to Create Windows Service. Enter a valid username and password for the Windows service, and ensure that Windows Authentication is selected. Click OK to register the service.

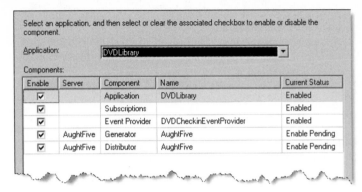

Figure 14-5: Confirming the application status

Once the instance has been registered and the Windows service created, right-click the instance name and select Start. After the service has successfully started, the Generator and Distributor status should change to Enabled. The service can also be controlled using the Services console or through the SQL Server Configuration Manager. With the Notification Services application in place, you can develop or modify your applications to take advantage of its features.

Summary

This chapter introduced you to Notification Services for SQL Server 2005. While you probably will not be able to go out and design enterprise-level solutions from this information, you should be able to understand the process flow for Notification Services applications, and be able to install a new Notification Services instance if asked to do so. This chapter provided you with a brief introduction to the Notification Services architecture, and described how to install a Notification Services application.

In Chapter 15, you learn about another new feature in SQL Server 2005, the Service Broker, and how you can use it with your applications to provide more accurate and reliable asynchronous message delivery.

Introduction to the Service Broker

SQL Server 2005 introduces a new feature known as the Service Broker that allows you to build more robust applications without having to rely on external technologies. Similar in concept to the Microsoft Message Queuing Service (MSMQ), Service Broker allows you to define services within one or more SQL databases that can all interact with one another, and build communication paths for more complete end-to-end connectivity using native SQL features.

This chapter examines the basics of how the Service Broker features operate, and how they can be leveraged to provide you with a mechanism for building inclusive application solutions. This chapter covers the following topics:

- ❑ Service-Oriented Architecture
- ❑ Service Broker overview
- ❑ Service Broker elements
- ❑ Service Broker security
- ❑ A Sample Service Broker application

Service-Oriented Architecture

In SQL Server 2005, Service Broker employs a model that uses Service-Oriented Architecture (SOA) for defining how data is treated by the variety of applications that will interact with it. SOA is based on the idea of separating data from the different processes that will view or manipulate that data. This allows you to build applications that do one thing, and do it well, without having to format the data to fit the application.

A good example of SOA in action is email. Many of us use email every day without thinking about what happens behind the scenes when we send an electronic message to someone. When I open up my Microsoft Outlook client, I need to specify to whom the message will be delivered, and what the message will say. I can also set other options, such as formatting the message as HTML, or requiring a read-receipt be sent so I know when my boss has been notified that I'm coming into work late today.

Now, just because I've set these options in my client doesn't mean that my boss has to conform to them. He could be using another mail client that is configured to display all messages in plain text, regardless of source formatting. He can also explicitly specify not to return read-receipt messages to the originator.

Regardless of how we each have our respective clients configured, email is doing exactly what it is supposed to, by providing an asynchronous message delivery that allows me to convey my tardiness, which can be read at my boss's leisure.

Service Broker Overview

Service Broker behaves similarly to the email example in the earlier section. Applications can use the features of Service Broker to create loosely coupled applications and services that provide asynchronous, ordered delivery of messages for efficient and appropriate processing. That sounds good, but what does it mean?

Well, it means that when your developers are building applications that use SQL, they can take advantage of features that allow them to submit updates without waiting for a response. It also means that when certain conditions are met, users can be notified that the data has changed, or requires their attention. Service Broker provides you with the tools and the framework to build these types of solutions without having to purchase costly third-party projects.

Because there are already external and third-party solutions that provide some (if not all) of the features the Service Broker offers, you may wonder why you would use Service Broker. The best advice is to weigh the benefits of Service Broker against your other options, and decide which works best for you. One of the most touted benefits, from an administrative standpoint, is that the configuration of Service Broker can be easily backed up when you perform regular backups of your user and system databases.

The decision to use Service Broker will be made by your application developers, but as a SQL Server 2005 administrator, you will be responsible for knowing what this Service Broker is and how to manage it. Many of the features of Service Broker you learn about in this chapter build on an understanding of other topics covered elsewhere in this book. For example, you can refer to Chapter 6 for more information about creating certificates, and Chapter 7 to learn more about creating endpoints.

Service Broker Elements

Service Broker employs a framework that uses messages as a unit of work. However, the handling and processing of these messages are defined by a variety of elements, including the conversation architecture, delivery contracts, queues, and services. In this section, you learn about the components that are used in a Service Broker solution.

Conversations

Service Broker uses *conversations* to define a persistent communication architecture that is reliable and asynchronous. The conversation architecture uses messages, dialogs, and conversation groups to control the flow of data in a Service Broker application.

Messages

Messages are the unit of information in a conversation. When Service Broker applications communicate with one another, they must agree on what type of data will be passed between them, and what formatting and data validation (if any) are required. Each message is tagged with the conversation identity, as well as a sequence number so that the messages can be processed in sequential order.

The content and formatting of the message is defined by the application. When a message is received by Service Broker, the message content is validated against the message type. Although the messages are stored as `varbinary(max)`, a *message type object* defines the message type and stores the type information as a database object. The message type object must be created on any SQL Server that will use that message type.

Creating a message type requires that you supply a validation parameter for the message to be considered correctly formatted. Message types are usually validated by using well-formed XML or XML defined by a specific schema, but you can also define that the message type is empty, meaning that the message body is `NULL`. You can also choose to forgo message validation altogether. Other data types can be used in Service Broker messages as long as SQL does not need to validate the message contents.

Dialog Conversations

When messages are sent between two instances of Service Broker, a *dialog conversation* (or simply *dialog*) is established. Dialogs use message delivery that is defined as *exactly-once-in-order* (EOIO). The conversation identifier and sequence numbers for each message are used to identify related messages to ensure that they are delivered in the correct order. Dialogs, therefore, establish a long-running stream of messages that exist between two services.

For each dialog, one service acts as the *initiator*, which establishes the conversation. The *target* is the service that will accept the conversation. A contract for the conversation, described later in this chapter, determines the messages each participant can send.

Dialogs automatically generate *acknowledgments* when receiving a message to guarantee reliable delivery. Each outgoing message is stored in a transmission queue until the acknowledgment is received. Automating this process prevents the application from needing a separate, explicit acknowledgment mechanism for each message. These acknowledgment messages are part of the internal functions of Service Broker, and are not part of the official application message stream.

Because Service Broker is designed for asynchronous communications, if a remote service is unavailable, the messages will be stored in a queue until the service is again available, or the lifetime for the dialog has ended.

The *lifetime of a dialog* is dependent on several factors. The dialog can be ended when an application either explicitly terminates it, or receives an associated error message. Each participant is equally responsible for ending the dialog when one of those two conditions is met. Common scenarios for ending a dialog conversation require one of the participants to specify the dialog will be ending without error, and notifying the other participant.

When designing Service Broker applications, the application developer can also specify a maximum lifetime for the dialog. When this dialog lifetime is reached, a time-out error message is placed on the service queue, and new messages for that dialog are refused. Messages that were generated prior to the end of the conversation can still be received after the conversation has ended, but no new messages can be sent or received after the conversation has ended.

Conversation Groups

Conversation groups are used to identify conversations that are related and typically part of the same business logic. Conversation groups are associated with a specific service. Conversations that are members in a conversation group are either sent to or received from that particular service. For each service, SQL will associate the message to an appropriate conversation group, which guarantees the messages received by the application for each conversation are processed exactly in order. This allows applications to receive messages from multiple sources, but process-related messages from those sources in the order that they are received by all services.

Conversation groups are subjective, meaning that the initiator may treat a message as belonging to Conversation Group A, whereas the target may treat the message as belonging to Conversation Group 24. This allows each participant to treat the message in a way that is appropriate for what it knows about the application.

For example, a sales tracking application may receive messages from a service that manages pricing information, as well as messages from an inventory service that tracks the availability of products in stock. This sales tracking application can tag messages from the independent conversations of the pricing and inventory services as being part of the same conversation group, which can be used to identify sales trends of products based on whether the price goes up or down. Neither the inventory service nor the pricing service is aware of this relationship, because it is irrelevant to how they send messages to the sales tracking application.

Contracts

Contracts are agreements between services about which messages each server will send to accomplish certain tasks. For each message type, a contract is defined to specify who can send that message type. Three types of contracts can be created:

- ❑ *Initiator Only* — Only the service initiator will be able to send messages of the type defined in this contract.
- ❑ *Target Only* — The service target will be the only one sending this type of message.
- ❑ *Any* — Allows either the target or the initiator to send this type of message.

In SQL Server 2005, a default contract is created and configured to use the default message type. This contract uses the SENT BY ANY statement to allow either the initiator or target to send the default message type.

Queues

Queues are a major component in the Service Broker architecture. They are used to provide the asynchronous processing of data between applications and services as needed. Service Broker uses queues to store messages. When a message is sent or received by a service, the messages are inserted into the appropriate incoming or outgoing queue. Queues are managed by the Service Broker, and the contents of the queues can be queried like a table or view object.

When viewing a queue, each row contains the content of the message, the message type, the target service, validation, contract, and conversation information for the message. Your application uses this information to identify and process the message as expected. Queues are also used to help guarantee the messages are processed in the order they were sent, not the order they were received.

In SQL Server 2005, you can use stored procedures to process the messages in the queue when there is work to do. Service Broker also allows you to execute multiple instances of the same stored procedure to more efficiently process the messages in the queue.

Services

The term *service* when used in the Service Broker context refers to a software component that performs a specific business task or set of tasks. Conversations, as noted earlier, are defined between services. The service name is used as an addressable endpoint to deliver messages to the appropriate queue within the context of a database, to route messages to the appropriate service, as well as to enforce contracts and remote security requirements for a new conversation.

Services each use a specific queue for storing incoming messages, and the contracts used by the service define which tasks are accepted for new conversations.

Routes

Routes are used to indicate where messages should be delivered. When messages are sent by an initiator, Service Broker must be able to find the target service. Just as you might use a map to find the nearest Italian restaurant, Service Broker must find a way to contact the target for a conversation. Routes are composed of three components to help uniquely identify the correct target:

❑   *Service name* — The name must exactly match the target service.

❑   *Broker instance identifier* — A value of the GUID data type used to identify the database that holds the queue for the service.

❑   *Network Address* — Usually a hostname or IP address of the system that hosts the target service. Optionally, this can instead be the address of a forwarding broker, which knows how to forward the message to the appropriate target.

When finding the appropriate route for a conversation, SQL Server must match the name and broker instance identifier specified in a BEGIN DIALOG CONVERSATION statement with the service name and broker instance identifier in the route. If the route does not provide a service name or broker identifier, any service name or broker identifier can be matched. SQL Server will choose the appropriate route based on a list defined in the sys.routes table of the database that contains the initiator service. If the service broker cannot find the correct route for the message, the message is dropped.

Each database contains a route named `AutoCreatedLocal`, which will match any service name and broker instance. Message delivery is restricted to the current instance, however. Although this might be acceptable for applications that use services that are all stored in the same SQL Service instance, it is generally a good idea to manually create a route for each service to help guarantee the availability of the service. This also prevents the `AutoCreatedLocal` route from being modified to the point of being unusable for its intended purpose.

You can use the `CREATE ROUTE` statement to specify the connection option for the remote service. This is typically the address and port number used to connect to an endpoint on the target server.

Security Considerations for Service Broker

Security, of course, is a concern when building Service Broker solutions. Whether your application is completely localized to a single database, or will span multiple databases on multiple servers, you need to have an understanding of the impact that security will play on your Service Broker applications.

Service Broker uses two security models to determine how to secure communications for Service Broker applications. Dialog security is used to handle encryption, remote authentication, and remote authorization for conversations. Transport security, on the other hand, handles security between two server instances.

Dialog Security

Dialog security focuses on securing individual conversations between services. If the initiator and target services exist in the same database, encryption is automatically enabled, and a session key is used to encrypt the communications. Encryption can also be turned off for intra-database service communications, but it's generally not recommended. Dialog security also provides two modes in which to operate when communicating between servers: full security and anonymous security.

Full Security

Full security requires that a mutual trust relationship be established between the initiator and target services. This is accomplished through the use of Public Key Certificates. When the target service resides on a remote server, a user with `SEND` permissions to the Service Broker service must own a certificate and the corresponding private key. The user and certificate information (but not the private key) must be defined on the database that holds the initiator service in a *remote service binding*. The remote service binding ties the username, certificate, and remote target service together to find and establish a trusted connection. The certificate that is used in the full security model must have the options to begin service broker dialogs. This is done by using the `ACTIVE FOR BEGIN_DIALOG = ON` option in the `CREATE CERTIFICATE` statement.

Anonymous Security

Anonymous security authenticates the target service to the initiator, but not the other way around. Unlike the full security model, this does not require a certificate mapping for the remote user, but the user specified in the remote service binding must be a member of the public role in the target database. This also requires that the public role in the target database be granted `SEND` permission on the target service. Messages using anonymous security are encrypted using a session key generated by the database that contains the initiating service.

Transport Security

Transport security is managed by controlling access to the endpoints that are used to connect to a remote service. When creating the endpoint, you can specify the authentication options, using Kerberos, NTLM, or certificate-based authentication. You can also specify encryption options for the connection, using AES or RC4. Again, remember that transport security is defined for the entire server instance, which includes all services in all databases. Chapter 7 provides greater detail on creating endpoints.

Creating a Sample Application

This section provides some sample code that can help clarify some of the ambiguities in how Service Broker works. In this example, AdventureWorks has a `helpdesk` application they use to allow users to submit trouble tickets using a Web application. Service Broker will automate the process of inserting the data into a table used by the `helpdesk` application, as well as sending the user a confirmation that the support request has been received.

Figure 15-1 is a rough map of the sample application you will be using in this exercise. The intent is to allow you to follow the path the application will take.

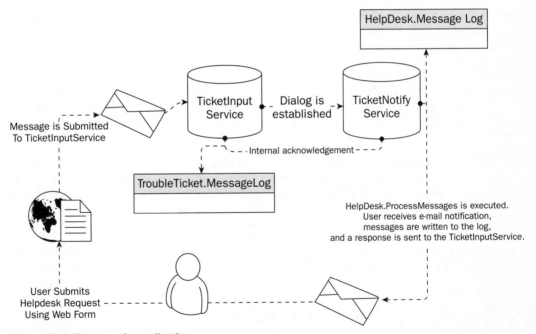

Figure 15-1: The sample application

It begins with the end user submitting a service request through a Web form. The request is then sent to the `TicketInputService`, which establishes a dialog with the `TicketNotifyService`. The message will be immediately delivered to the `TicketNotifyService`, which stores the information in the service queue until the `HelpDesk.ProcessMessages` stored procedure is executed. When the stored procedure executes, an email is sent to the person who submitted the request, the message is logged to the HelpDesk.MessageLog table, and a response is automatically sent back to the TicketInputService. The response messages are held in the queue for the TicketInputService until the TroubleTicket .ProcessMessages stored procedure is executed, at which time the messages are logged, and the queue is cleared.

Preparing the Database

You need to begin by taking a couple of steps prior to building your Service Broker solution. The absolute first thing you must do is to create a database master key. There is actually one case in which you can get away without using a database master key, but it requires that your services all live in the same database, and you explicitly set ENCRYPTION = OFF when starting a conversation. You can find more information about creating and using the database master key in Chapter 6. If you did not read through Chapter 6, and have not already created a database master key, you can use the following code to create one:

```
USE AdventureWorks;
GO
CREATE MASTER KEY
ENCRYPTION BY PASSWORD = 'P@ssw0rd';
GO
```

One interesting thing about Service Broker services and the database master key is that if encryption is enabled, and no database master key exists, you can continue to submit messages to your services until you're blue in the face, and they never show up in the queue. However, if you later realize your mistake, and *then* create the master key, the next time you submit a message, all of the previous messages that seemed to have disappeared into the ether will now be added to the service queue! I actually encountered this when preparing some demonstrations using a beta build of SQL Server 2005. I had even deleted and re-created the queues and services several times before realizing my mistake. When I finally got the service to receive messages into the queue, I had 10 sample messages from previous attempts in addition to the one I had just submitted.

The next step is to ensure that the ENABLE_BROKER option has been set for the database. You can do this by using an ALTER DATABASE statement. Also, if your application will also be accessing services or resources outside of the local database, you may need to set the TRUSTWORTHY setting to ON. The following example configures the database with both settings:

```
USE Master;
GO
ALTER DATABASE AdventureWorks SET ENABLE_BROKER, TRUSTWORTHY ON;
GO
```

Creating the Service Broker Objects

Now that you've prepared the AdventureWorks database for your Service Broker application, it's time to begin creating the Service Broker objects. For this example, you are going to create two queues, two services, one message type, and one contract to use that message type between the services.

Begin by creating two new schemas for the objects you will create. Using different schemas helps define a separation of the resources used by each service. In this example, you are going to create a Helpdesk schema and a TroubleTicket schema. Use the following code to create the schemas:

```
USE AdventureWorks;
GO

CREATE SCHEMA TroubleTicket;
GO
CREATE SCHEMA HelpDesk;
GO
```

The next step is to create the message type and validation (if any) that will be used by the Service Broker application. Because both of the services you will create exist in the `AdventureWorks` database, you will only need to define the message type once. Remember that if the initiator and target services exist in different databases, you will need to create the same message type in both databases. Use the `CREATE MESSAGE TYPE` statement to create a new message. This statement uses the following syntax:

```
CREATE MESSAGE TYPE message_type_name
    [ AUTHORIZATION owner_name ]
    [ VALIDATION = validation_method ]
```

The `message_type_name` value must be unique within the database, and commonly uses a URL (or URL-like) convention that allows you to create a hierarchical namespace for creating multiple message types for different services. The `AUTHORIZATION` option allows the creator to specify a different database user as the owner of the message type, provided the creator has `IMPERSONATE` permissions, and the `VALIDATION` option can be one of the following choices:

❏   `NONE` — No validation of the data is performed by Service Broker.

❏   `EMPTY` — The message body contains no data.

❏   `WELL_FORMED_XML` — The message body must use well-formed XML.

❏   `VALID_XML WITH SCHEMA COLLECTION` schema_collection — The message body must contain XML data that conforms to a specific schema document, which must be supplied separately. You can create a new schema collection using the `CREATE XML SCHEMA COLLECTION` statement, providing the name and the schema definition.

For this example, you will create a new message type called `//AdventureWorks.com/Helpdesk/SupportTicket` that uses well-formed XML, as seen in the following code:

```
CREATE MESSAGE TYPE [//AdventureWorks.com/Helpdesk/SupportTicket]
    VALIDATION = WELL_FORMED_XML;
```

Next, you need to create the contract that will call this message type and specify who can send messages of this type. The `CREATE CONTRACT` statement can contain multiple message types, each one having a different `SENT BY` clause. Because this example only defines one message type that will be sent by the initiator service (which you have yet to create), you can use the following example:

```
CREATE CONTRACT [//AdventureWorks.com/HelpDesk/SubmitSupportTicket]
(
    [//AdventureWorks.com/Helpdesk/SupportTicket]
    SENT BY INITIATOR
);
```

The next step is to create the queues that will be used by the services. The first queue will be used by the service that will receive the messages from the Web application. This is the queue for the initiator service. The second queue, for the target service, will be used to receive the messages from the initiator, and then automatically notify the end user that the support ticket has been created. Use the following to create the queues:

```
CREATE QUEUE TroubleTicket.TicketInputQueue;
GO


CREATE QUEUE HelpDesk.UserNotifyQueue;
GO
```

The final step in this phase is to create the services. When creating a service, use the following syntax for the CREATE SERVICE statement:

```
CREATE SERVICE service_name [ AUTHORIZATION owner_name ]
    ON QUEUE [ schema_name. ]queue_name
    [ contract_name ]
```

When you create a new service, the required parameters are at least the service name, and the queue for the service. If the service will be a target for an existing contract, you must specify the contract name.

For this demonstration, you will create two services. The first one, the initiator, will receive data from a Web application, which calls a stored procedure to insert the required values. The second service, acting as the target, will be used to notify the end user that the submission has been received. Execute the following code to create the required services:

```
-- Creating the Initiator Service
CREATE SERVICE [//AdventureWorks.com/HelpDesk/TicketInputService]
ON QUEUE TroubleTicket.TicketInputQueue;

-- Creating the Target Service
CREATE SERVICE [//AdventureWorks.com/Helpdesk/TicketNotifyService]
ON QUEUE HelpDesk.UserNotifyQueue
([//AdventureWorks.com/HelpDesk/SubmitSupportTicket]);
```

Creating Objects for the TicketInputService

In this section, you create several objects used by the TicketInputService to receive and process the messages, allowing them to move on to the next service. You will begin by creating a new table that will be used to store the incoming data, so that it can be used by the helpdesk application. This table will not actually be used by Service Broker, but will demonstrate how Service Broker can be implemented along with other features and objects in SQL Server. Use the following code to create the table that will store the data input by the user:

```
USE AdventureWorks;
GO

-- Create a table to store Helpdesk Information

Create Table HelpDesk.TroubleTickets(
```

```
ID INT IDENTITY,
firstName Name,
lastName Name,
Issue nvarchar(max)
);
GO
```

Note that the `Name` data type is a user-defined data type that already exists in the `AdventureWorks` database.

In the next step, you create a stored procedure that will take data from the Web form. The stored procedure will then insert the data into the table you just created, and will create a well-formed XML message with the same data that will be added to the queue for the `TicketInputService`. This stored procedure also establishes the dialog between the initiator and target services.

```
USE AdventureWorks;
GO
-- stored procedure to send issues to the ticket submission Service
CREATE PROCEDURE TroubleTicket.AddNewTicket
@firstName Name,
@lastName Name,
@emailAddress Name,
@issue nvarchar(max)
AS
BEGIN

    Insert HelpDesk.TroubleTickets (firstname, lastname, issue) VALUES
(@firstname, @lastname, @issue)
    DECLARE @message NVARCHAR(MAX)
    SET @message = NCHAR(0xFEFF)
        + '<Customer>'
            + '<CustomerName>' + @firstName + ' ' + @lastName +
'</CustomerName>'
            + '<EmailAddress>' + @emailAddress + '</EmailAddress>'
            + '<issue>' + @issue + '</issue>'
        + '</Customer>'

    DECLARE @conversationHandle UNIQUEIDENTIFIER

    BEGIN DIALOG CONVERSATION @conversationHandle
    FROM SERVICE [//AdventureWorks.com/HelpDesk/TicketInputService]
    TO SERVICE '//AdventureWorks.com/Helpdesk/TicketNotifyService', 'CURRENT
DATABASE'
    ON CONTRACT [//AdventureWorks.com/HelpDesk/SubmitSupportTicket]

    ;SEND ON CONVERSATION @conversationHandle
    MESSAGE TYPE [//AdventureWorks.com/Helpdesk/SupportTicket]
    (@message)

END;
GO
```

Note that, in the BEGIN DIALOG CONVERSATION statement, the TO SERVICE parameter uses single quotes rather than brackets to encapsulate the target service. You should also provide routing information for the target service. As you can see, because this service exists within the same database as the initiator, you can use 'CURRENT SERVICE'. If the target service exists in another database, you can use the remote service's GUID.

Next, you create a table that will log the activity of the TicketInputService. Do this by executing the following code:

```
USE AdventureWorks;
GO
-- log table for received messages
CREATE TABLE TroubleTicket.MessageLog(
    messageID int IDENTITY PRIMARY KEY,
    queueName nvarchar(25),
    message nvarchar(max),
    conversationID uniqueidentifier);
GO
```

Now, create a stored procedure that will write to the TroubleTicket.MessageLog table:

```
USE AdventureWorks;
GO
-- stored procedure to log messages
CREATE PROCEDURE TroubleTicket.LogMessage
(@queuename nvarchar(25), @message nvarchar(max), @conversation_id
uniqueidentifier=NULL)
AS
    IF (@conversation_id IS NULL)
        PRINT 'Queue: ' + @queuename
            + ' Message: ' + @message
    ELSE
        PRINT 'Queue: ' + @queuename
            + ' Message: ' + @message
            + ' Conversation: ' + CAST(@conversation_id AS NVARCHAR(MAX))

    INSERT INTO TroubleTicket.MessageLog (queueName, message, conversationID)
    VALUES (@queuename, @message, @conversation_id);
GO
```

The final step in creating the objects for the TicketInputService is creating a stored procedure that will execute the stored procedure listed earlier, write the queued messages to the log (if any), and write a notice indicating that no further messages have been found once the queue has been cleared:

```
USE AdventureWorks;
GO
-- stored procedure to read and process messages from queue
CREATE PROCEDURE TroubleTicket.ProcessMessages
AS
    WHILE (1 = 1)
```

```
        BEGIN
            DECLARE @conversationHandle UNIQUEIDENTIFIER,
                    @messageTypeName NVARCHAR(256)

            ;RECEIVE TOP(1)
                @conversationHandle = conversation_handle,
                @messageTypeName = message_type_name
            FROM TroubleTicket.TicketInputQueue

            IF @@ROWCOUNT = 0
            BEGIN
                EXEC TroubleTicket.LogMessage 'TicketInputQueue', 'No further
messages found.'
                RETURN
            END

            END CONVERSATION @conversationHandle
            EXEC TroubleTicket.LogMessage 'TicketInputQueue', @messageTypeName,
@conversationHandle
        END;
GO
```

Creating Objects for the TicketNotifyService

Now, you need to create the supporting objects for the target service. Remember that this service will be used to notify the end user that the submission has been received, and a trouble ticket has been generated. Your first object is a stored procedure that will extract the details of the message from the XML data, so that it can be used in the notification message. Create the stored procedure using the following code:

```
USE AdventureWorks;
GO

CREATE PROCEDURE HelpDesk.ExtractXML
(@XMLstring NVARCHAR(MAX), @customerName Name OUTPUT, @emailAddress Name OUTPUT,
@issue nvarchar(max) OUTPUT)
AS
    DECLARE @idoc int
    EXEC sp_xml_preparedocument @idoc OUTPUT, @XMLstring

    SELECT    @customerName = CustomerName,
              @emailAddress = EmailAddress,
              @issue = issue
    FROM OPENXML (@idoc, '/Customer',2)
    WITH (CustomerName Name, EmailAddress Name, issue nvarchar(max))

    EXEC sp_xml_removedocument @idoc;
GO
```

The next step, just like you did with the last service, is to create a log table, and a stored procedure that writes to the log table. The commands are essentially the same as for the TicketInputService, but these objects are located in the Helpdesk schema:

```
USE AdventureWorks;
GO
CREATE TABLE HelpDesk.MessageLog(
     messageID int IDENTITY PRIMARY KEY,
     queueName nvarchar(25),
     message nvarchar(max),
     conversationID uniqueidentifier) ;
GO

-- stored procedure to log messages
CREATE PROCEDURE HelpDesk.LogMessage
(@queuename nvarchar(25), @message nvarchar(max), @conversation_id
uniqueidentifier=NULL)
AS
     IF (@conversation_id IS NULL)
          PRINT 'Queue: ' + @queuename
               + ' Message: ' + @message
     ELSE
          PRINT 'Queue: ' + @queuename
               + ' Message: ' + @message
               + ' Conversation: ' + CAST(@conversation_id AS NVARCHAR(MAX))

     INSERT INTO HelpDesk.MessageLog (queueName, message, conversationID)
     VALUES (@queuename, @message, @conversation_id) ;
GO
```

The final step for this service is to create a stored procedure that will read and process messages in the queue:

```
USE AdventureWorks;
GO
CREATE PROCEDURE HelpDesk.ProcessMessages
AS
     WHILE (1 = 1)
     BEGIN
          DECLARE @conversationHandle UNIQUEIDENTIFIER,
               @messageTypeName NVARCHAR(256),
               @messageBody NVARCHAR(MAX);

          RECEIVE TOP(1)
               @conversationHandle = conversation_handle,
               @messageTypeName = message_type_name,
               @messageBody = message_body
          FROM UserNotifyQueue

          IF @@ROWCOUNT = 0
          BEGIN
               EXEC HelpDesk.LogMessage 'UserNotifyQueue',
                    'No further messages found.'
               RETURN
          END
```

```
        IF
         @messageTypeName =
           'http://schemas.microsoft.com/SQL/ServiceBroker/Error'
        OR
         @messageTypeName =
                'http://schemas.microsoft.com/SQL/ServiceBroker/EndDialog'

        BEGIN
            END CONVERSATION @conversationHandle
            EXEC HelpDesk.LogMessage 'UserNotifyQueue',
            @messageTypeName, @conversationHandle
            CONTINUE
        END

        IF @messageTypeName <>
            '//AdventureWorks.com/Helpdesk/SupportTicket'
        BEGIN
            END CONVERSATION @conversationHandle
                WITH ERROR = 500
                DESCRIPTION = 'Invalid message type.'
            EXEC HelpDesk.LogMessage 'UserNotifyQueue',
            'Invalid message type found.', @conversationHandle
            CONTINUE
        END

        DECLARE @customerName Name, @emailAddress Name, @issue nvarchar(max)
        EXEC HelpDesk.ExtractXML @messageBody, @customerName OUTPUT,
            @emailAddress OUTPUT, @issue OUTPUT

    /*          Send an Email using Database Mail
    This section has been commented out so that the values may be substituted with
your own, if you have a valid database mail profile, you can configure the stored
proc to use it instead.  Leaving these lines commented out will not impact the
operation of the queues.

        EXEC msdb.dbo.sp_send_dbmail
            @profile_name = 'HelpDesk',
            @recipients= @emailAddress,
            @subject='Trouble Ticket Issued',
            @body='Your support call has been logged,
            and someone will be contacting you soon.'
    */

        DECLARE @output NVARCHAR(MAX)
        SET @output = 'A HelpDesk support ticket has been created for '
                + @customerName + '. '
                + 'Email sent to ' + @emailAddress +
                ', regarding ' + @issue + '.'

    EXEC HelpDesk.LogMessage 'UserNotifyQueue', @output, @conversationHandle

        END CONVERSATION @conversationHandle
    END;
GO
```

Testing the Application

Now, it's time to see Service Broker in action. Because building a Web-based front-end for your application falls well outside of the scope of this book, you can just execute the stored procedures manually. The effect is still the same, and the results are no different.

So, begin by creating a couple of trouble tickets (from a couple of troublemakers):

```
USE AdventureWorks;
GO
EXEC TroubleTicket.AddNewTicket
     'George',
     'Costanza',
     'George@adventureworks.com',
     'My monitor display is fuzzy';
GO

EXEC TroubleTicket.AddNewTicket
     'Comso',
     'Kramer',
     'Cosmo@adventureworks.com',
     'The nnnnnnnnn key onnnn my keyboard sticks.';
GO
```

Because you have not configured the stored procedures that will process the messages to run automatically, or through any other invocation method, you will have to manually execute them as you step through this exercise. Before you process the messages, you can query the queue directly to see the messages that are queued up. Because the conversation is established when the AddNewTicket stored procedure is executed, messages are delivered immediately to the queue for the TicketNotifyService. You can query its queue with the following statement:

```
SELECT * FROM HelpDesk.UserNotifyQueue;
```

This should result in output similar to Figure 15-2.

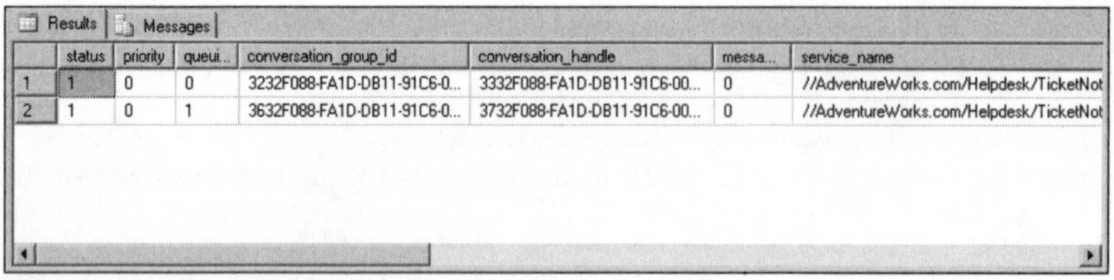

	status	priority	queui...	conversation_group_id	conversation_handle	meesa...	service_name
1	1	0	0	3232F088-FA1D-DB11-91C6-0...	3332F088-FA1D-DB11-91C6-00...	0	//AdventureWorks.com/Helpdesk/TicketNot
2	1	0	1	3632F088-FA1D-DB11-91C6-0...	3732F088-FA1D-DB11-91C6-00...	0	//AdventureWorks.com/Helpdesk/TicketNot

Figure 15-2: The User Notify queue

To process the messages and deliver notification to end user, execute the Helpdesk.ProcessMessages stored procedure:

```
EXEC HelpDesk.ProcessMessages;
```

After executing this stored procedure, the following messages should be returned:

```
(1 row(s) affected)
Queue: UserNotifyQueue Message: A HelpDesk support ticket has been created for
George Costanza. Email sent to George@adventureworks.com, regarding My monitor
display is fuzzy. Conversation: 3332F088-FA1D-DB11-91C6-0003FF232532

(1 row(s) affected)

(1 row(s) affected)
Queue: UserNotifyQueue Message: A HelpDesk support ticket has been created for
Comso Kramer. Email sent to Cosmo@adventureworks.com, regarding The nnnnnnnnn key
onnnn my keyboard sticks. Conversation: 3732F088-FA1D-DB11-91C6-0003FF232532

(1 row(s) affected)

(0 row(s) affected)
Queue: UserNotifyQueue Message: No further messages found.

(1 row(s) affected)
```

This will generate the messages, as well as write to the message log you created in the last exercise. You can view the log contents by using the following query:

```
SELECT * FROM HelpDesk.MessageLog;
```

You should see results similar to Figure 15-3.

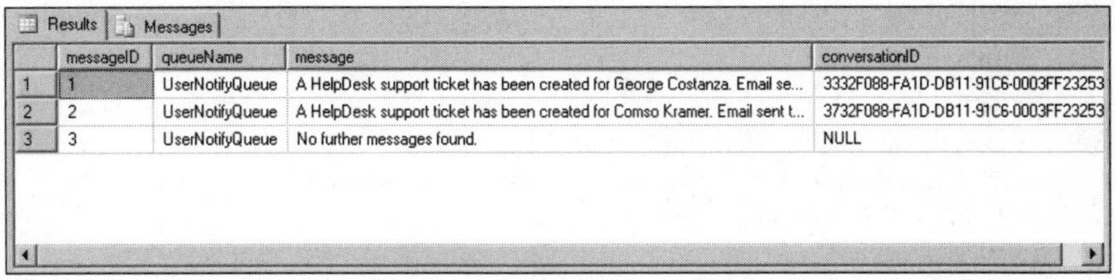

Results | Messages

	messageID	queueName	message	conversationID
1	1	UserNotifyQueue	A HelpDesk support ticket has been created for George Costanza. Email se...	3332F088-FA1D-DB11-91C6-0003FF23253
2	2	UserNotifyQueue	A HelpDesk support ticket has been created for Comso Kramer. Email sent t...	3732F088-FA1D-DB11-91C6-0003FF23253
3	3	UserNotifyQueue	No further messages found.	NULL

Figure 15-3: The `HelpDesk` message log

Additionally, when the messages were processed by the `TicketNotifyService`, response messages were generated for the `TicketInputService`. You can view the queued messages for the `TicketInputService` by querying its queue, also.

```
SELECT * FROM TroubleTicket.TicketInputQueue;
```

This should return output similar to that shown in Figure 15-4.

	status	priority	queu...	conversation_group_id	conversation_handle	message_sequence_number	service_name
1	1	0	0	3132F088-FA1D-DB11-91C6-0003FF232532	3032F088-FA1D-DB11-91C6...	0	//AdventureWo
2	1	0	1	3532F088-FA1D-DB11-91C6-0003FF232532	3432F088-FA1D-DB11-91C6...	0	//AdventureWo

Figure 15-4: The Ticket Input queue

To write the queued responses to the log for the `TicketInputService`, execute the `TroubleTicket.ProcessMessages` stored procedure as listed here:

```
EXEC TroubleTicket.ProcessMessages;
```

As the messages get processed and logged, you should get messages similar to the following:

```
(1 row(s) affected)
Queue: TicketInputQueue Message:
http://schemas.microsoft.com/SQL/ServiceBroker/EndDialog Conversation: 3032F088-
FA1D-DB11-91C6-0003FF232532

(1 row(s) affected)

(1 row(s) affected)
Queue: TicketInputQueue Message:
http://schemas.microsoft.com/SQL/ServiceBroker/EndDialog Conversation: 3432F088-
FA1D-DB11-91C6-0003FF232532

(1 row(s) affected)

(0 row(s) affected)
Queue: TicketInputQueue Message: No further messages found.

(1 row(s) affected)
```

Now that the queue has been cleared, you can view the response messages in the log.

```
SELECT * FROM TroubleTicket.MessageLog;
```

The response messages confirm the dialog for each message has ended, as shown in Figure 15-5.

	messageID	queueName	message	conversationID
1	1	TicketInputQueue	http://schemas.microsoft.com/SQL/ServiceBroker/EndDialog	3032F088-FA1D-DB11-91C6-0003FF232532
2	2	TicketInputQueue	http://schemas.microsoft.com/SQL/ServiceBroker/EndDialog	3432F088-FA1D-DB11-91C6-0003FF232532
3	3	TicketInputQueue	No further messages found.	NULL

Figure 15-5: The `TroubleTicket` message log

Summary

Now that you've now seen end-to-end delivery of messages using Service Broker, it should be easier for you to envision how it can be implemented with other applications. It is yet another feature that has been built in to SQL Server 2005 to create a more application-friendly architecture to meet the needs of many organizations, both large and small.

In this chapter, you learned about the concepts of SOA, what Service Broker is, what components are used in a Service Broker solution, and options for securing your Service Broker communications. You also had an opportunity to see Service Broker in action by building a simple application that shows you the process flow of Service Broker messages between services.

Chapter 16 gives you an introduction to SQL Server 2005 replication. You will learn about the different replication models, types, and options available for providing a distributed database solution.

Introduction to Replication

The world is getting smaller. When it comes to communications, faraway places don't seem so far away anymore. Many of us work for companies that have a global presence, or a mobile sales force. We need to be able to provide access to data and services wherever our users are. SQL Server can provide a way to increase the availability of your data and applications through the use of replication.

This chapter presents an overview of how replication works. You will learn about the different SQL Server replication components, as well as learning about the physical and logical design options for replication.

Replication Overview

SQL Server replication operates similarly to print media. In fact, many of the terms used in replication are also used with newspaper and magazine distribution. Replication begins at the server known as the *publisher*. Just as a newspaper collects articles its readership is interested in, the publisher compiles and arranges data into *articles*, and one or more articles are included in a *publication*. To get data to *subscribers*, the newspaper needs to employ a *distributor*.

In SQL Server replication, just as in the newspaper business, the subscribers can choose to have the distributor deliver the publication to them, or they can go to the distributor to pick up the publication. This is not unlike going to a newsstand or your favorite coffee shop and picking up a newspaper. SQL Server also allows you to specify whether the publisher is also the distributor, or if another server is used as an intermediary distributor. This is not unlike the newspaper hiring carriers directly, versus outsourcing the work to a third party.

Here's a review of some of the key terms used in the last paragraph, and a preview of some in the SQL Server Replication Agents section, to help provide a clearer understanding of the way replication works:

❑ *Publisher*—The server providing the source data that will be made available to subscribers.

❑ *Article*—A collection of data that exists as part of a replication publication.

- ❑ *Publication* — One or more articles that act as a unit of replication.

- ❑ *Distributor* — The server that is responsible for providing data to subscribers.

- ❑ *Subscriber* — A server or client that receives a publication.

- ❑ *Push Replication* — A method of replication whereby the distributor delivers the data to the subscriber.

- ❑ *Pull Replication* — A method of replication whereby the subscriber requests the data from the distributor.

- ❑ *Publisher/Distributor* — A publishing server that acts as its own distributor.

SQL Server replication can be used to provide data to another database (which can be used for Analysis and Reporting Services), to a remote office for local application use, or to client applications for offline or asynchronous use. When choosing a replication strategy, you must have a solid understanding of how the data will be used.

Consider the following questions:

- ❑ Do the users need access to up-to-the-minute data, or can they work with data that is provided on a regular schedule?

- ❑ Do the users need to be able to make changes to the data, and should those changes be synchronized with the original source material?

- ❑ Will the data originate from a single source, or will multiple sources be used to provide data to a centralized database?

Finding answers to these questions (and more) can help you make the appropriate decisions about your replication topology. You can use this information to help build solutions to make your database applications more responsive and more useful to your users.

Also note that when replication is configured, a new system database named `distribution` is created. This database is used for storing metadata and history information about your replication topology. One distribution database is created for a single instance of SQL Server and is shared among all databases.

SQL Server Replication Agents

Now that you've got the terminology down, and have an idea of what your users' needs are, it's time to take a look at the mechanics behind replication. This section introduces the various replication agents that are available for your solution. *Replication agents* are programs that run certain tasks to control preparation and distribution of your data. The agents that are used depend on the type of replication used in your solution. Some of these agents are available to all replication types, and some are specific to just one type of replication.

Replication relies on the SQL Server Agent service when the server is a publisher or distributor to automate the replication process. Though it is *possible* to manually execute the replication agents, it would be more work than it's probably worth. Ensure that your SQL Server Agent service is running, and, in most cases, it should be configured to start when the server starts.

Snapshot Agent

With SQL Server replication, the Snapshot Agent is used for almost all replication types. The Snapshot Agent is executed at the distributor, and is responsible for preparing the initial data files and schema information about the articles that will be published. The data is written to a snapshot folder on the file system and synchronization data is written to the distribution database. It often acts as the baseline for other replication agents. In this way, it's not unlike the way a full backup works when using differential or transaction log backups.

Log Reader Agent

The Log Reader Agent is used specifically with *transactional replication*. When a transaction that is part of a publication is written to the transaction log, the Log Reader Agent copies those transactions from the publisher to the distribution database on the distributor. This allows those transactions to then be executed on the subscriber databases. Each database that participates in transactional replication has its own Log Reader Agent.

Distribution Agent

Used with both snapshot and transactional replication, the Distribution Agent applies snapshots to subscribers, and, in the case of transactional replication, moves the transactions to the subscribers. If *pull replication* is used, the Distribution Agent is executed at the subscriber. If *push replication* is used, it is run at the distributor.

Merge Agent

When *merge replication* is used, the Merge Agent provides the initial snapshot to the subscriber, not unlike the Distribution Agent. Each subscription has its own Merge Agent that handles the reconciliation of data between the publisher and the subscriber. Another similarity it shares with the Distribution Agent is that it runs at the distributor for push subscriptions, and at the subscriber for pull subscriptions. When communicating between publishers and the subscribers, the Merge Agent typically downloads the changes to the subscriber, and uploads changes to the publisher.

Queue Reader Agent

The Queue Reader Agent is used with a specific type of transactional replication that allows updatable subscriptions. When updates from the subscriber are provided to the publisher, these updates can be queued, and then processed as a unit. This agent runs at the distributor, and only one instance is required for all publications in the distribution database.

SQL Server Replication Types

The term *replication type* refers to the logical model of a replication topology, and although there are only three main types (transactional, snapshot, and merge), each one offers additional configuration options that allow you to have more granular control over how data gets from source to destination, and what happens to it when it gets there. Consideration for the different replication types is based on the way the data is going to be used, and how important it is that the data be current.

Two key terms to remember when choosing a replication type are autonomy and latency. *Autonomy* refers to the amount of "hands-off-ness" of the data. *Latency* refers to the amount of time that elapses between when a change is made to the data and when the data is replicated to the subscriber. In the different replication types available, there is a direct correlation between autonomy and latency.

For example, AdventureWorks has a regional office that uses quarterly updates on sales figures for an employee incentive program. Because this program is only in place at the regional office, there's no need to provide updates back to the home office. Once the home office provides the data to the regional office, they don't do anything else with it. Any changes to the data will not be reflected back in the corporate database, much to the relief of the company's corporate auditors. In this scenario, a high amount of autonomy and latency are evident. The regional office gets the updated data once every three months; and once they get it, they own the data for their own needs.

Conversely, a retail chain that requires real-time inventory tracking from their Point-of-Sale system that would not only update the local inventory database, but also ensure that each retail and warehouse location are aware of the product inventory at the other locations. This is an example of an application that requires very low latency. In this scenario, when a customer is looking for a DVD player that's out of stock at the Seattle location, a sales clerk can inform the customer of the availability of that model at the Bellevue and Tacoma locations.

Distributed Transactions

Although distributed transactions aren't part of SQL Server replication, per se, it's important to know how distributed transactions fit into the distributed data model. First and foremost, any transaction that executes across more than one database, even if it is attached to the same instance, is considered a distributed transaction. This is because the scope of the transaction exists outside of the context of the current database.

For example, the following SQL script executes in the context of the AdventureWorks database, but only one of the tables is actually created in the tempdb database. Because both CREATE TABLE statements are wrapped in the BEGIN TRANSACTION and COMMIT TRANSACTION statements, they must both execute, or the entire transaction fails.

```
USE AdventureWorks;
GO
BEGIN TRANSACTION;
CREATE TABLE dbo.MyDTTable(col1 INT, col2 VARCHAR(10));
CREATE TABLE tempdb.dbo.MyOtherDTTable (col1 INT, col2 VARCHAR(10));
COMMIT TRANSACTION;
```

This is a very simplified example of how distributed transactions are designed to work, but you get the idea. When an application executes distributed transactions against multiple servers, an additional step may be taken in order to ensure the availability of the target servers. This is what's knows as a *two-phase commit* (2PC).

The first phase is the preparation phase. This step prepares the destination servers, known as *resource managers*, by sending out a command to inform them that a transaction is coming. The resource managers take every possible precaution to ensure that when the transaction is received, it can be processed without failure. This helps ensure the stability and reliability of the distributed transaction. The resource manager then informs the *transaction manager*, usually the Microsoft Distributed Transaction Coordinator (MS DTC), whether or not the preparations were successful.

The second phase is executed when all the resource managers have reported successful preparation. In this phase, the transaction manager expects to receive a successful commit from each of the resource managers. When it does, then it can report the transaction as having been committed to the application. If just one of the resource managers reports failure, the transaction must be rolled back from all resource managers, and the transaction manager reports the failure to the application.

Distributed transactions can also be executed directly from stored procedures, or other Transact-SQL methods. You can use the BEGIN DISTRIBUTED TRANSACTION statement to explicitly invoke a distributed transaction.

Distributed transactions do not define a publisher, distributor, and subscriber the way replication does. Instead, it relies on the application design to control how data is processed across multiple servers. It does offer the least amount of autonomy and latency, because the transactions are immediately processed on destination servers.

Transactional Replication

Transactional replication has the lowest latency and autonomy of the three standard replication types. With transactional replication, you begin with a snapshot of the data that will be used as a baseline for further transactions to be applied against. As transactions are committed, those that apply to data that participates in transactional replication are copied to the distribution database on the distributor. Then the subscribers can receive the transactions and apply the changes to the copied data.

Standard Transactional Publication

Standard transactional publication replication is used when the subscriber accepts the publication for read-only use. This prevents the subscriber from being able to update the data on the publisher, but does not prevent clients from updating data on the subscriber itself. For example, a remote server may use the replicated data in conjunction with SQL Reporting Services to provide access to historical and trend data, and modifications may be made locally, but no changes can be submitted at the remote server that will be accepted at the original publisher.

Transactional Publications with Updatable Subscriptions in a Hierarchical Topology

This implementation of transactional replication allows a model where you have a single publisher with multiple subscribers. Periodically, the subscribers may need to make changes to the replicated data, in which case, the update is sent back to the original publisher. The original publisher provides those updates (through the distributor) to all the subscribers. This can be helpful in an environment where a remote site receives corporate sales data but occasionally submits updates regarding their local sales department.

Updatable subscriptions in a hierarchical topology allow both immediate and queued updates to be submitted from the subscribers. Immediate updates are processed similarly to distributed transactions, in that a two-phase commit is used. If immediate updates are not necessary, subscriber updates can be stored in a queue, and then applied asynchronously whenever the publisher is available.

Transactional Publications in a Peer-to-Peer Topology

New to SQL Server with SQL Server 2005, *peer-to-peer transactional replication* creates an environment where all participants are both publishers and subscribers. This implementation allows you to create a distributed database environment where all SQL Servers can provide and receive updates with low latency. This further lowers the autonomy previously offered by transactional replication, by allowing any data to be changed on any server, and all participating servers will receive the updates. When using peer-to-peer transactional replication, use SQL security features to take appropriate precautions to ensure that data can only be updated from approved locations.

Snapshot Replication

Snapshot replication can be used in replication topologies where there can be significant latency between when changes are committed on the publisher, and when they are received by the subscriber. Rather than providing updates on a transaction-by-transaction basis, snapshots of the entire article are taken at the publisher periodically, and then applied to the subscriber as a unit.

When a snapshot is generated, it is saved as a file to a file system that must be accessible to the publisher, the distributor, and the subscriber. If one or more of these are on different physical servers, you should specify a Universal Naming Convention (UNC) path for the snapshot folder location. If all the components reside on the same server (which can be the case if you're using replication to populate a separate database on the same server for Reporting Services or Analysis Services), you can use a local file system path. The files generated by snapshot replication are files that can be easily applied to the subscriber using BCP.

The obvious benefit of snapshot replication is for asynchronous environments where there can be a delay between the publisher and subscriber. However, because the snapshots are copied and applied each time replication occurs, it can be prohibitively resource-consuming for large amounts of data. There are options that can allow you to compress the snapshot files, as well as to help reduce disk usage and transfer times between the distributor and subscriber, though.

As with transactional replication, snapshot replication also supports the use of immediate or queued updating subscriptions.

Merge Replication

Merge replication is used in environments where clients and servers may be working independently of one another, but they periodically need to connect to synchronize data. Merge replication is often used in client and server environments. For example, if you have a mobile sales force where all members of the sales team need access to customer information, but will not always have connectivity to your server, an application that replicates data relevant to their customers can provide them access to the information they need. They can also use the application to submit orders, track invoices, and keep notes about their clients. When they are back in the office, or can connect to the corporate network remotely, they can synchronize their changes with their home servers.

Merge replication introduces a number of changes to your publishing databases that are used for tracking and synchronization. This includes adding a column to published tables used for tracking, as well as additional tables and triggers that are used to store row history data for published rows. These elements are designed to be unobtrusive, and the triggers created by replication will not affect any user-defined triggers that you have created.

Merge replication offers both a blessing and a curse with its ability to handle synchronizations from multiple subscribers. Its blessings come from the ability to grant users offline access to data sets that are critical to their needs. Its curse comes from the fact that multiple offline subscribers may be trying to synchronize changes to the same data.

The change-tracking mechanism employed by merge replication allows you define how conflicts are resolved between multiple subscribers. For example, a particular subscriber may be given more weight than others, and, therefore, its changes should be considered authoritative. There are also mechanisms to programmatically build more complex resolvers. This allows you to create more granular rules about conflict resolution, giving priority to certain subscribers only if specific criteria are met.

Oracle Replication

No, that's not a typo. Microsoft SQL Server 2005 supports replication of Oracle objects. To expect that this works perfectly out-of-the-box with no additional configuration is a bit naïve, but you should be familiar with some of the concepts and caveats of using SQL Server for Oracle replication. For example, SQL Server requires that your Oracle server be running at least version 8.0.5. Configuration of your Oracle server as the publisher may depend on the specific version you are using and the tools available for that version. Refer to the topic "Oracle Publishing Overview" in Books Online for a more complete list of requirements.

Snapshot replication from an Oracle database operates similarly to SQL Server snapshots. The Snapshot Agent connects to the Oracle publication, and retrieves rows and creates schema scripts for each published table. As with SQL snapshot replication, the entire dataset is created each time the table is run.

Unlike homogenous SQL Server transactional replication (which monitors the transaction log for changes), transactional replication for Oracle requires that changes be made to the Oracle database by creating tracking tables and triggers. When changes to a published Oracle table are made, the triggers fire and insert the changes into the tracking table. This is not unlike the behavior seen in merge replication. SQL Server, again acting as the distributor, executes the Log Reader Agent to move the changes from the tracking table to the distribution database. The distributor then provides the changes to the subscribers as would be expected.

SQL Server Replication Models

Now that you have an understanding of the different types of replication available, the next consideration in building your replication topology is to identify the model that will be used. Whereas the type defined the logical flow of data, the *model* defines the physical implementation of how the data will be distributed. Any of the aforementioned SQL Server replication types can use any of the SQL Server replication models. The overall design and topology for replication should be built around how the data is used, and the accessibility requirements for your users and your applications.

Another consideration when choosing an appropriate replication model is whether to have the publisher and the distributor on the same instance. Geographical distribution and network availability may influence your decision to use a local distributor versus a remote one.

Single Publisher / Multiple Subscribers

In cases where the data should originate from only location only, a *single publisher / multiple subscriber model* can be used to provide access to data for remote locations. For example, AdventureWorks has offices across the United States. The corporate office, headquartered in Tacoma, might need to make its sales data available to its remote offices in Omaha, Baton Rouge, and Rochester for a reporting application. In this case, the company may want to use a single distributor in the Tacoma office to provide updates using snapshot replication to each of the field offices.

In this scenario, the AdventureWorks field office will get sales data updates through an asynchronous delivery method. Because they will not be changing the data that is replicated, there is no need for updatable subscriptions, and each office will receive the same data.

Multiple Publishers / Single Subscriber

The *multiple publishers / single subscriber model* can be used where multiple servers will track and update data, but that data will need to be consolidated on a single server. Let's look at a retail chain as an example of how this can work.

An electronics retailer uses an inventory-tracking database to keep track of product stock at each location. Each store maintains its own inventory through its shipping department and point of sale application. Each location uses transactional replication to provide changes to its local stock to a regional warehouse, which holds the subscriber database. This helps the regional inventory manager keep track of when a specific store is running low on a certain product, and she can make arrangements to provide the items to the store. Because transactional replication is used in this topology, the inventory database at the regional warehouse gets updated with minimal delay.

Multiple Publishers / Multiple Subscribers

The *multiple publishers / multiple subscribers model* works well for environments where data must be shared among peers. This can be useful in applications where the local database stores information about local and remote operations. Each publisher can provide updates made locally to all other replication partners that participate in this model, and receive the updates in turn.

For example, three friends decide to get into the fast-food business, and each buys several franchises within their cities. Each restaurant keeps track of its own inventory, as well as being able to see the inventory at the other locations. This is so that the local manager can call another store for spare ingredients, just in case the supplier cannot deliver in time. To prevent having a separate inventory table for each location, merge replication can be used. Each store updates its own inventory values daily and then synchronizes with the other locations so that each store is aware of the inventory at the other locations.

Replication Tools

When reviewing the options provided for designing the replication topology, additional considerations may be evaluated for determining what data is replicated and how. This section provides an overview of some of the available tools and procedures that can help provide a more robust replication architecture.

Filtering

It is not always appropriate to replicate entire tables from one server to another. You can, in fact, use filtering at the publisher to limit what will be available to the subscribers. Subscriptions can also employ filters at the subscriber to ensure that only data relevant to that subscriber is received and processed. Four types of filters are available:

- ❏ Static row filters
- ❏ Column filters
- ❏ Parameterized row filters
- ❏ Join filters

Static Row Filters

Static row filters can be used with all types of replication. They are defined at the publisher, and allow you to limit which rows will be made available in a publication by simply using a WHERE clause. For example, you could provide regional managers with Human Resources data about the employees at only their respective locations by using a row filter based on the employee's city field, or another location-identifying column.

Column Filters

Column filtering can be used to remove certain columns from all rows in a publication. For example, if you have Human Resources data that will be made available to multiple databases for different applications, it may not always be appropriate to include confidential data such as salary information or the employees' Social Security numbers. In this case, you can create publications that eliminate the unnecessary data from the publication without removing it from the base table.

Column filtering can be used with all types of replication. However, certain types of columns may be excluded from filtering depending on which replication type you are using. You can use both column filters and row filters in a single publication to narrow the scope of the published data.

Parameterized Row Filters

Parameterized row filters are available only with merge replication, and are similar in concept to static row filters. In execution, though, they are significantly different. The purpose of parameterized row filters is to be able to create multiple data partitions that will be replicated without having to create multiple publications. For example, if you use the same base table, and you have two different subscribers that each need a different subset of that same table, using standard row filters would require you to create two publications, one for subscriber A, and the other for subscriber B.

With parameterized row filters, you can specify that for subscriber A, you are interested in rows that have the values WA, NE, and OK in the state field. For subscriber B, you are interested in providing rows that contain the values CA, OR, and AK in the state field. Each of these data sets exists as part of the same publication.

The partitions created by parameterized row filters can also overlap. Using the preceding example, if a new subscriber wanted all the rows with the values WA, OR, NV, and TX in the state column, then that is an example of an *overlapping partition*. You can configure overlapping partitions to allow updates from the subscriber to any column, or only any non-shared column. *Nonoverlapping partitions* can be made available to multiple subscribers, preventing the subscriber from updating the changes. If a nonover-lapping partition is available to only one subscriber, then that subscriber can make changes to all columns in that partition.

Join Filters

Join filters are also limited to merge replication, and are commonly used to extend the data in a publication that uses parameterized row filters. This operates similarly to a JOIN statement in Transact-SQL to combine the data from one or more tables. The data in the related tables is published only if it meets the condition of the JOIN FILTER clause.

New Publication Wizard

Once the design of your replication topology has been decided on, and you know what type of replication you will be using, you can use the New Publication Wizard to create a new replication publication. To launch the wizard, start SQL Server Management Studio and expand the replication folder. Right-click the Local Publications folder and choose New Publication.

Click Next on the New Publication Wizard introduction page. On the next page, you can select which server will act as the distributor. As you can see in Figure 16-1, if you have not already configured a server to be the distributor, you can use the local server. In this case, it will create the distribution database and transaction log files. Click Next once you've selected your distributor.

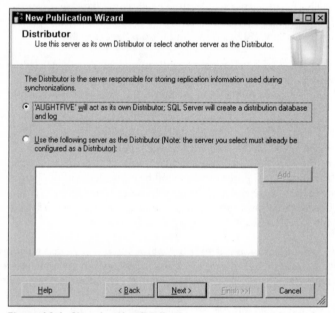

Figure 16-1: Choosing the distributor

On the next page, you must specify the location that will be used to store the snapshot files. Remember that if your subscriber is a remote client or server, you should specify a UNC path instead of a local file system path to enable pull subscriptions.

Next, choose the database that will be providing the publication. For this example, select the Adventure Works database from the list. After selecting the appropriate database, click Next to move on to the next page, which will ask you about the type of replication you will use.

When presented with the list of available replication options, note that a brief description of each replication type is available to help you review which type is the appropriate selection for your application. For this example, select "Transactional publication" and click Next.

On the next page, you can select which objects will be available for replication to the subscribers. Figure 16-2 shows an example where the Sales.CreditCard table is selected. A single publication can include multiple articles, which may be tables, views, or other SQL objects.

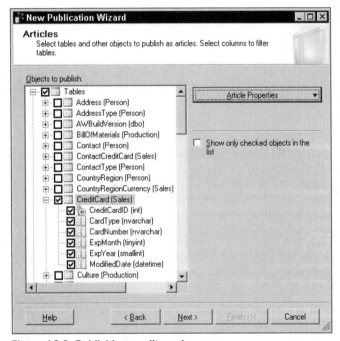

Figure 16-2: Publishing credit cards

The next page in the wizard gives you the option of filtering the rows that will be included in the publication. Clicking the Add button allows you to create a new filter. Note that the filter statement is prepared as a simple SELECT statement, where you can provide the value for the WHERE clause.

Next, you have the option to generate the snapshot immediately, and/or generate the snapshot on a schedule. Select the option to create the snapshot immediately and click Next.

You can then select the accounts the Snapshot Agent and Log Reader Agent will run as. Although you can use the SQL Server Agent account (which makes for an easier demo), it is not a best security practice, and the wizard will warn you of that. You can specify a Windows account to run the agent under, and a SQL account used to connect to publisher as. Because this is only a demonstration, go ahead and select the SQL Server Agent option, and ensure that both the Snapshot Agent and Log Reader Agent are configured with the same credentials.

Next, you can choose to create the publication immediately, or simply generate a script that can be used to create the publication later. Choose the option to create the publication now and click Next.

Finally, on the summary page, give the new publication a name (such as AWCCPub) and click Finish to create the new publication. Figure 16-3 shows a summary of the options selected in this example.

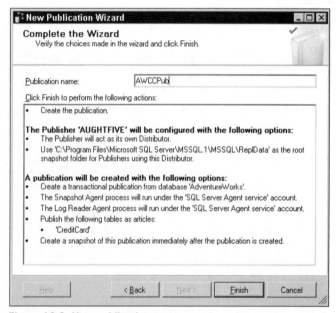

Figure 16-3: New publication summary

New Subscription Wizard

Now that you have a source, it's time to create a destination. To prepare for this example, you will need to create a target database that will act as the subscriber. Execute the following code to create a new database called AWReplicationDemo. Because no options are specified when you create the target database, its configuration is based on your model database, and should only contain system objects.

```
USE master
CREATE DATABASE AWReplicationDemo;
GO
```

Once the database has been created, right-click the Local Subscriptions folder and select New Subscriptions. Click Next to get past the introduction page of the wizard, and move on to the list of publications (see Figure 16-4). Note that the publications are listed by server, and you can use the drop-down list to find another SQL or Oracle publisher. Select the AWCCPub publication and click Next.

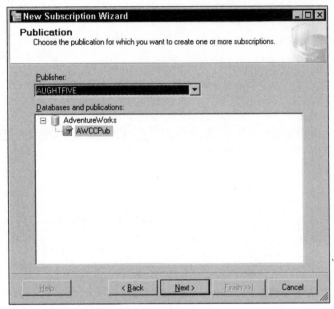

Figure 16-4: Choosing a publication

On the next page, specify whether this will be a push subscription or a pull subscription. Select "Push subscription" and click Next. You will then be asked to specify the target database. Choose the AWReplicationDemo database created earlier and click Next.

You must then choose the security context the Distribution Agent will run under. Again, against better judgment, select the SQL Server Agent option, and click Next.

Next, specify an appropriate schedule for the Distribution Agent. Choose the default of Run Continuously and click Next. You will then be asked to specify when to initialize the subscription. Choose the default option to initialize immediately.

On the next page, choose to create the subscription immediately, and click Next to see a summary of your selections. Figure 16-5 shows an example summary page.

Figure 16-5: Creating the subscription

Replication Monitor

SQL Server 2005 includes an improved Replication Monitor that can be used to track the status of your publications and subscriptions. It can provide information on latency, replication history, warnings, and alerts. You can view the Replication Monitor by right-clicking the replication folder and selecting Launch Replication Monitor. Figure 16-6 shows you an example of the interface for the Replication Monitor.

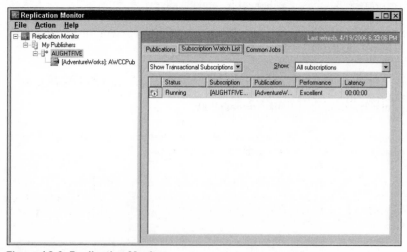

Figure 16-6: Replication Monitor

If you double-click a subscription, you can view the details of the subscription, including the history between the publication and distributor, and also between the distributor and subscriber. Figure 16-7 shows an example of the subscription details window. To test both the replication and see the Replication Monitor in action, begin by enabling Auto Refresh from the Action menu of the Subscription history window. Then, execute the following code to insert a new row in the `Sales.CreditCard` table on the `AdventureWorks` database, which should get replicated to the subscriber:

```
USE AdventureWorks;
GO
INSERT Sales.CreditCard (CardType, CardNumber, ExpMonth, ExpYear)
VALUES ('MisterClub','1234876510190210',12,2025);
```

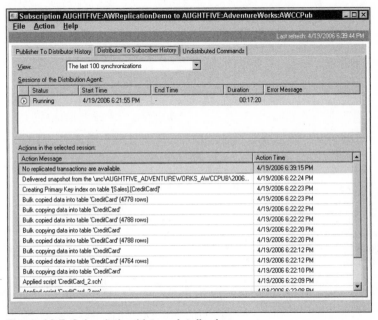

Figure 16-7: Subscription history details view

Within a short period of time, you should see that the transaction was delivered from the publisher to the subscriber from the distributor.

Summary

Replication is a topic that every database administrator should be familiar with. Although one chapter can't provide you with an exhaustive examination to the finer points of replication, you should have obtained a good feel for what options SQL Server replication offers. This chapter looked at the following topics:

❑ An overview of how SQL Server replication works

❑ The agents used by SQL Server replication

❑ The different replication types

❑ The different physical replication models

❑ Some of the tools used in SQL Server replication

Exercise Answers

This appendix provides the answers to Exercises appearing earlier in the book.

Chapter 6

Exercise 1

```
CREATE LOGIN James
WITH PASSWORD='MyP@ssw0rd',
DEFAULT_DATABASE=AdventureWorks,
CHECK_POLICY=ON,
CHECK_EXPIRATION=OFF;
GO

USE AdventureWorks
CREATE USER Jimbo FROM LOGIN James
WITH DEFAULT_SCHEMA = HumanResources;
GO

GRANT SELECT,UPDATE ON SCHEMA :: HumanResources TO Jimbo
```

Exercise 2

```
USE AdventureWorks;
CREATE CERTIFICATE HRCert
    ENCRYPTION BY PASSWORD = 'HRPassw0rd'
    WITH SUBJECT = 'HR Certificate',
    EXPIRY_DATE = '1/31/2016';
GO

USE AdventureWorks
CREATE SYMMETRIC KEY HRDataKey
    WITH ALGORITHM = AES_128
    ENCRYPTION BY CERTIFICATE HRCert;
```

```
GO

GRANT CONTROL ON CERTIFICATE :: HRCert to Jimbo
GRANT ALTER ON SYMMETRIC KEY :: HRDataKey to Jimbo

ALTER TABLE HumanResources.Employee
    ADD EncryptedSSN varbinary(128)
```

Exercise 3

```
OPEN SYMMETRIC KEY HRDataKey
 DECRYPTION BY CERTIFICATE HRCert
 WITH PASSWORD = 'HRPassw0rd'

UPDATE HumanResources.Employee
SET EncryptedSSN
    = EncryptByKey(Key_GUID('HRDataKey'), NationalIDNumber);
GO

CLOSE SYMMETRIC KEY HRDataKey;
GO
```

Exercise 4

```
OPEN SYMMETRIC KEY HRDataKey
 DECRYPTION BY CERTIFICATE HRCert
 WITH PASSWORD = 'HRPassw0rd'

SELECT *,CONVERT(nvarchar, DecryptByKey(EncryptedSSN))
    AS 'DecryptedSSN'
    FROM HumanResources.Employee;
GO

CLOSE SYMMETRIC KEY HRDataKey;
GO
```

Chapter 8

Exercise 1

1. In Object Explorer, expand your server.
2. Expand SQL Server Agent, and expand Jobs.
3. Right-click the Simple Backup job and select Properties.
4. Select the Notifications Page.
5. Check E-mail, select Server Administrator and select "When the job succeeds."
6. Check Page, select Server Administrator and select "When the job fails."
7. Check Write to the Windows Application event log and select "When the job completes."
8. Click OK to close the job properties.

Exercise 2

1. In Object Explorer, expand your server.

2. Expand SQL Server Agent, and expand Jobs.

3. Right-click Jobs and select New Job...

4. On the General page, enter the **AWLogBackup** for the job name.

5. Select Database Maintenance for the category.

6. Select the Steps page.

7. Press New.

8. Enter **Backup Log** for the step name.

9. Enter the following in the command box: **BACKUP LOG AdventureWorks TO DISK = 'C:\dbbackups\AWLog.bak'.**

10. Click OK to close the job properties.

11. Expand Alerts.

12. Right-click the AWXactLogSpace Alert and select Properties.

13. Select the Response page and check Execute job.

14. Enter **AWLogBackup** as the job name.

15. Press OK to close the alert properties.

16. Execute the following statement in a query window.

```
ALTER DATABASE AdventureWorks
  SET RECOVERY FULL;
```

You must make a complete backup of the database after changing the recovery mode before you can successfully back up the transaction log.

Exercise 3

1. In Object Explorer, expand your server, and expand Management.

2. Right-click Maintenance Plans and select Maintenance Plan Wizard.

3. Click Next at the intro page.

4. Enter **CheckShrinkNBack** as the Name and click Next.

5. Select Check Database Integrity.

6. Select Shrink Database.

7. Select Execute SQL Server Agent Job.

8. Click Next.

9. Click Next on the Select Maintenance Task Order.

10. In the Define Database Check Integrity Task page select These Databases: AdventureWorks

11.   Click OK, and then click Next.

12.   In the Define Shrink Database Task page select These Databases: AdventureWorks.

13.   Click OK, and then click Next.

14.   Select Simple Backup and click Next.

15.   In the Select Plan Properties page, Click Change.

16.   In the New Job Schedule, enter **Every Sunday** as the name, and click OK.

17.   In the Select Report Options page, click Next.

18.   Click Finish to create the new maintenance plan.

19.   Click Close when the wizard completes.

Index

SYMBOLS AND NUMERICS

| (pipe character), 468
2PC (two-phase commit), 530–531

A

-A argument, SQLCMD utility, 90
access sensitivity, collation settings, 36
accounts
  Database Mail feature
    creating, 256
    deletion guidelines, 268
    retry attempts, 258
    sysmail_add_account_sp stored procedure, 261–262
    sysmail_add_profileaccount_sp stored procedure, 262–263
    sysmail_delete_account_sp stored procedure, 268
    sysmail_update_account_sp stored procedure, 264
  security, 224
acknowledgment, dialog conversations, 509
active/active clustering, 405
active/passive clustering, 405
ActiveX script Task, control flow, 476
Activity Monitor tool, 371–373
Add button (New Database dialog box), 118
Add New Derived Table feature, Query Designer toolbar, 63
Add Related Tables feature, Database Diagram tool, 60

Add Table feature
  Database Diagram toolbar, 60
  Query Designer toolbar, 63
Add to Help Favorites command, Help toolbar, 61
Add/Remove Group By feature, Query Designer toolbar, 63
addresses, IP, 231
ADF (Application Definition File), 499
Advanced Properties sheet (Agent Service), 278–279
AES (Advanced Encryption Standard), 214
After triggers, 163
Agent Connection Properties, 280–281
Agent Service
  Advanced Properties sheet, 278–279
  Agent Connection Properties, 280–281
  Alert Systems properties, 279–280
  alerts
    creation, 304
    event-based, 304–308
    performance condition, 310
    sp_add_alert stored procedure, 308
    sp_addmessage stored procedure, 306
    WMI event, 311–312
  configuration, 276–277
  General Properties sheet, 278
  Job System Properties window, 280
  jobs
    adding to schedules, 295–297
    categories, 287
    creation, 283–286
    data retrieval tasks, 286
    defined, 283
    history properties, 282
    job step creation, 288–292

Agent Service (continued)

  logins, 285

  multi-server, 316–317

  names, 284

  sp_add_jobstep stored procedure, 289–290

  token replacement, 292–293

  operators

    creation, 301

    fail-safe, 304

    sp_add_operator stored procedure, 302–304

  proxies, 313–316

  schedules

    adding jobs to, 295–297

    creation, 294

    sp_add_schedule stored procedure, 297–300

    sp_attach_schedule stored procedure, 300–301

  security, 282–283

  SQLAgentOperatorRole permission, 283

  SQLAgentReaderRole permission, 283

  SQLAgentUserRole permission, 283

agents, replication, 529

aggregate functions, 167, 209

Alert Systems properties (Agent Service), 279–280

alerts

  creation, 304

  event-based, 304–308

  performance condition, 310

  sp_add_alert stored procedure, 308

  sp_addmessage stored procedure, 306

  WMI event, 311–312

aligned indexes, 146

aligned partitioning, 86

All Languages area, Text Editor configuration, 72

ALTER APPLICATION **statement, 197**

ALTER CERTIFICATE **statement, 220**

ALTER CREDENTIAL **statement, 186**

ALTER DATABASE **statement, 431**

ALTER INDEX **statement, 153**

ALTER LOGIN **statement, 183**

ALTER ROLE **statement, 194**

ALTER SCHEMA **statement, 135**

ALTER TABLE **statement, 156**

American National Standards Institute. *See* **ANSI**

AMOs (Analysis Management Objects), 9

Analysis Designers area, Designers configuration, 76

Analysis Services

  Analysis Services DMX Query feature, Standard toolbar, 68

  Analysis Services Execute DDL Task, control flow, 476

  Analysis Services MDX Query feature, Standard toolbar, 68

  Analysis Services Project template, BI Studio, 79

  mined data, 3

  toolbar, 68

Analysis XMLA Query feature, Standard toolbar, 68

Analyze Query in Database Engine Tuning Advisor feature, SQL Editor toolbar, 67

anonymous authentication, 256

anonymous dialog security, 512

ANSI (American National Standards Institute)

  ANSI NULL Default settings, 123–124

  ANSI NULLS Enabled settings, 124

  ANSI Padding Enabled settings, 124

  ANSI Warnings Enabled settings, 124

  discussed, 2

answers to exercises, 543–546

APIs (application programming interfaces), 465

Application Definition File (ADF), 499

applications

  Notification Service

    definition file elements, 499–500

    discussed, 490

    primitive duration format, 503

  removing unused, 225

  roles, fixed database roles, 195

arguments, SQLCMD utility, 89–90

Arithmetic Abort Enabled option (New Database dialog box), 125

arithmetic overflow, 125

Arrange Selection feature, Database Diagram toolbar, 60

Arrange Tables feature, Database Diagram toolbar, 60

Ask a Question command, Help toolbar, 62

assemblies

  Assembly Assisted Editor, 169

  CLR (Common Language Run-Time)

    adding, 444

    CREATE ASSEMBLY statement, 444

    creation, 439–442, 444

    discussed, 169, 437

  defined, 167, 169

  New Assembly dialog box, 169–170

  permissions, 170

asymmetric keys, 218

audits

  results, triggers, 169

  security, 225

authentication

  anonymous, 256

  AUTHENTICATION argument, 242

bad login/password error message, 34
Database Mail feature, 256
discussed, 175
Mixed Mode configuration, 33–34
mode configuration, SQL Server 2005 installation, 33–34
overview, 18
trusted connection error message, 34
Windows Authentication mode changes, 176–178
Windows Only configuration, 33–34
AUTH_REALM argument, 242
Auto Close option (New Database dialog box), 125
Auto Create Statistics option (New Database dialog box), 125
Auto Shrink option (New Database dialog box), 125
Auto Update Statistics option (New Database dialog box), 125
Auto-Commit transactions, 106–107
auto-grow transaction log behavior, 110
automatic cleanup behavior, log shipping, 408
automation techniques, best practices, 321
auto-start feature, SQL Server 2005 installation, 28
availability. See high-availability
Available Databases feature, SQL Editor toolbar, 66

B

Back Up Database Task, control flow, 477
backups. See also restoration
Bulk Log, 331
Copy Only, 332
devices, 327
Differential, 330
file/filegroup, 330–331
Full
with Differential strategy, 336
overview, 330
with Transaction Log strategy, 337–338
functionality, 328–329
log shipping, 408
Maintenance Plan wizard, 319
mirrored, 333
Partial, 332, 339
Pure Log, 331
restore preparation, 345–347
scheduled, 352
stripes, 332–333
Tail Log, 331
transaction log, 110, 331
WITH clause and, 333–335
Backward Compatibility System views, 165

Ballmer, Steve (Microsoft CEO), 436
baseline creation, performance optimization, 361–362
basic information retrieval, databases, 117–118
BATCHES argument, 243
BCM (Bulk Changed Map) pages, 105
BCP utility
export table to flat file example, 93
import flat file example with format file, 93
non-XML format file example, 92
syntax, 91
XML format file example, 92–93
best practices
automation techniques, 321
security, 224–226
BI Studio (Business Intelligence Development Studio)
Analysis Services Project template, 79
Import Analysis Services 9.0 template, 79
integration services, 463
Integration Services Project template, 79
New Project screen, 78–79
packages, 78
Report Model Project template, 80
Report Server Project template, 79
Report Server Project Wizard template, 80
bigint data type, 98
binary data type, 100
binary sorting, collation settings, 36
bit data type, 98
Bookmarks window (SQL Server Management Studio), 53
Bryant, Todd (*Professional SQL Server 2005 Reporting Services*), 3, 11
buffer cache
hit ratio measures, performance optimization, 366
overview, 23
Bulk Change Map (BCM) pages, 105
Bulk Insert Task, control flow, 476
Bulk Log backups, 331
bulk update locks, 376
bulkadmin fixed security role, 187
Bulk-Logged recovery model, 122–123, 325
Business Intelligence Development Studio. See BI Studio
bytes counters, performance optimization, 365

C

CA (Certification Authority), 219
cache
buffer, hit ratio measures, 366
log, 23
procedure, 23

Cancel Executing Query feature, SQL Editor toolbar, 66

capacity planning, database, 114–115

cascading constraints, 160–161

case-sensitivity

  collation settings, 36

  SQLCMD utility, 89

catalog. See databases

categories, Agent Service jobs, 287

CDO (Collaboration Data Object), 461

certificates, public key, 218–221

Certification Authority (CA), 219

Change Connection feature, SQL Editor toolbar, 66

Change Source Control feature, Source Control
    toolbar, 65

Change Type feature, Query Designer toolbar, 63

char **data type, 99**

CHARACTER_SET **argument, 244**

check constraints, 161

Check Database Integrity Task, control flow, 477

Check In feature, Source Control toolbar, 65

Check Out for Edit feature, Source Control toolbar, 65

Check Question Status command, Help toolbar, 62

CHECKPOINT **event, 109–110**

classes, 438

Clear all bookmarks in all files, Text Editor toolbar, 70

CLEAR_PORT **argument, 242**

client redirection, database mirroring, 420

closed cursor commands, databases, 126

CLR (Common Language Run-Time)

  assemblies

    adding, 444

    CREATE ASSEMBLY statement, 444

    creation, 439–442, 444

    discussed, 169, 437

  compatible data types, 444–445

  defined, 435

  enabling, 439

  functionality, 438

  improvements to, 3

  safe permission setting, 460

  security, 458–461

  stored procedures, 446–447

  triggers, 447–448

  UDAs (user-defined aggregates), 452–454

  UDTs (user-defined types), 448–452

  user-defined functions, 445–446

clustered indexes, 136–137

clustering

  active/active, 405

  active/passive, 405

cluster groups

  defined, 39

  Domain Groups, 41

components, 404–405

failover

  discussed, 402

  log shipping and, 418–419

  manual, 432

majority node, 404

quorum, 403

recommendations, 406

Windows, 402–403

Code Editor (SQL Server Management Studio), 50

code generation features, Visual Studio, 454–457

Collaboration Data Object (CDO), 461

collation settings

  database creation, 122

  language, 141

  SQL Server 2005 installation

    accent sensitivity, 36

    binary sorting, 36

    case sensitivity, 36

    default collation, 35

    discussed, 34

    non-compatible collation issues, 37

    width sensitivity, 36

  table functions, 141

colors, Environment configuration, 71

column filtering, replication tools, 536

Comingore, Derek (*Professional SQL Server 2005 CLR***
    *Stored Procedures, Functions, and Triggers***), 3**

command-line tools

  BCP utility

    export table to flat file example, 93

    import flat file example with format file, 93

    non-XML format file example, 92

    syntax, 91

    XML format file example, 92–93

  DACs (Dedicated Administrator Connections), 91

  SQLCMD utility

    arguments, 89–90

    case-sensitivity, 89–91

commands

  KILL, 377

  RECONFIGURE, 438

  SETVAR, 90–91

Comment Out Selected Lines feature

  SQL Editor toolbar, 67

  Text Editor toolbar, 70

Common Language Run-Time. See CLR

Common Table Expressions (CTE), 2
communication support
  language support, 8–9
  object models, 9
Compare feature, Source Control toolbar, 65
Compatibility level drop-down list (New Database dialog
    box), 123
compliance, ANSI, 2
COMPRESSION argument, 242
computational functions, 446
Concatenate Null Yields Null option (New Database
    dialog box), 126
configuration
  Agent Service, 276–277
  Database Mail feature, 255–259
  database mirroring, 422–426
  ICF (Instance Configuration File), 497
  log shipping, 407–411
  Reporting Services Configuration Manager, 87–89
  SQL Server Configuration Manager, 87, 232
  SQL Server Management Studio
    Designers section, 76–77
    Environment section, 71–72
    Query Execution section, 72–74
    Query Results section, 74–76
    Source Control section, 72
    Text Editor section, 72
conformity, key, 159
Connect feature, SQL Editor toolbar, 66
Connections project folder, 52
constraints
  cascading, 160–161
  check, 161
  default, 162–163
  schema scope permissions, 209
containers, control flow tasks, 475
Contents command, Help toolbar, 61
contracts, Server Broker service, 510
control flow, integration services, 465, 475–477
conversations, Server Broker service, 509–510
Copy Only backups, 332
Counihan, James (Professional SQL Server 2005
    Reporting Services), 3, 11
CREATE APPLICATION statement, 196
CREATE ASSEMBLY statement, 444
CREATE CERTIFICATE statement, 220
CREATE CREDENTIAL statement, 186
CREATE ENDPOINT statement, 241

CREATE FUNCTION statement, 445
CREATE INDEX statement, 153
CREATE LOGIN statement, 181, 183–184
CREATE ROLE statement, 194
CREATE SCHEMA statement, 134
CREATE TABLE statement, 155–156
CREATE USER statement, 190, 192
creation scripts, database, 131–132
credentials, 185–186
cross-database ownership, 126
CTE (Common Table Expressions), 2
cursor
  closed cursor commands, 126
  cursor data type, 102

D

DACs (Dedicated Administrator Connections)
  endpoints, 236
  overview, 91
Data Copy phase, restoration, 339
Data Definition Language (DDL)
  database creation scripts, 132
  event notifications, 275
  performance optimization, 396, 398–399
  trigger functions, 2
Data Encryption Standard (DES), 214
data files
  primary, 17–18
  storage architecture, 102–104
data flow, integration services
  data destinations, 481
  overview, 465
  sources, 479
  transformations, 480–481
Data Flow Task, control flow, 476
data manipulation data types, physical database
    structure, 101–102
Data Manipulation Language (DML) triggers,
    163, 167–169
Data Mining Query Task, control flow, 476
data pages, 103–104
Data Protection API (DPAPI), 214
data retrieval tasks, Agent Service jobs, 286
Data Source Views (DSVs), 474
data tier
  objects, 4
  Web services, 246

data transformation, integration services, 472–475

Data Transformation Services (DTS), 4

data types

  `bigint`, 98

  `binary`, 100

  `bit`, 98

  `char`, 99

  CLR compatible, 444–445

  `cursor`, 102

  data manipulation, 101–102

  `datetime`, 99

  `decimal`, 98

  fixed-length, 98–100

  `float`, 99

  `image`, 101

  improvements to, 2

  `int`, 98

  large object, 100–101

  `money`, 99

  `nchar`, 99

  `ntext`, 101

  `numeric`, 98

  `nvarchar`, 100

  `real`, 99

  `rowversion`, 100

  `smalldatetime`, 99

  `smallint`, 98

  `smallmoney`, 99

  `sql_varian`, 101

  `table`, 101

  `text`, 100

  `timestamp`, 100

  `tinyint`, 98

  `uniqueidentifier`, 100

  user-defined, 170–171

  `varbinary`, 100

  `varchar`, 100

  variable-length, 100–101

  XML, 101

database administrators (DBAs), 45

`DATABASE` **argument, 244**

Database Consistency Checker (DBCC)

  fragmented indexes, 151–152

  overview, 97

Database Diagram toolbar, 59–60

Database Engine components, 2–3

Database Engine Query feature, Standard toolbar, 68

Database files section (New Database dialog box), 118–119

Database Mail feature

  accounts

    creating, 256

    deletion guidelines, 268

    retry attempts, 258

    `sysmail_add_account_sp` stored procedure, 261–262

    `sysmail_add_profileaccount_sp` stored procedure, 262–263

    `sysmail_delete_account_sp` stored procedure, 268

    `sysmail_update_account_sp` stored procedure, 264

  advantages of, 254

  authentication method selection, 256

  configuration, 255–259

  enabling, 255

  file attachment size, 258

  functionality, 254

  logging levels, 258

  mail message example, 272–273

  MAPI-compliant mail server, 254

  message queue, timeout value, 258

  messages, managing, 274–275

  overview, 5

  port numbers, 256

  private profiles, 256

  profiles

    creation, 260

    deletion guidelines, 268

    naming, 255

    `sysmail_add_principalprofile_sp` stored procedure, 265–267

    `sysmail_add_profile_sp` stored procedure, 260

    `sysmail_delete_principalprofile_sp` stored procedure, 268

    `sysmail_delete_profileaccount_sp` stored procedure, 268

    `sysmail_delete_profile_sp` stored procedure, 268

    `sysmail_update_principalprofile_sp` stored procedure, 267

    `sysmail_update_profileaccount_sp` stored procedure, 264–265

    `sysmail_update_profile_sp` stored procedure, 263–264

  public profiles, 256–257

  sending mail, 269–271

Database Read Only option (New Database dialog box), 126
database scope permissions, 206–209
Database Setup area, Reporting Services Configuration Manager, 88
Database State option (New dialog box), 126–127
Database Tuning Advisor (DTA)
  end-of-quarter analysis, 391
  General tab, 84–85
  Profiler tool and, 391–392
  recommendations, 389
  script analysis, 386–387
  session creation, 84
  sessions, starting new, 387–388
  tuning option selection, 389
  Tuning Options tab, 86–87
database_id parameter, 149
databases. See also New Database dialog box; tables
  ALTER DATABASE statement, 431
  arithmetic overflow, 125
  basic information retrieval, 117–118
  capacity planning, 114–115
  closed cursor commands, 126
  collation settings, 122
  creation scripts, 131–132
  cross-database ownership, 126
  date statistics, 127
  defaults, 172
  diagrams, 163–164
  distribution, 16–17, 113
  file growth, 120–121
  file size considerations, 120
  filegroups, 118
  file-shrink operations, 125
  isolating, 345
  maintenance, 120
  names, 116
  numeric rounding, 128
  page write verification, 128–129
  performance, 120
  rules, 172
  scope, 12
  Shiloh, 20
  size requirement calculation, 115
  Sphinx system, 20
  state, 126–127
  statistics, missing, 125
  system
    default location, 17
    distribution databases and, 113

    Master, 14
    Model, 14–15
    MSDB, 15
    recovery, 353–354
    restricted activity, 17
    TempDB, 15–16
  system views, 164–165
  test, 115
  user, 16, 113, 347–349
  user security
    CREATE USER statement, 190, 192
    default schemas, 188–189
    guest accounts, 190
    naming conventions, 188
  views, 164
Date Correlation Optimization Enabled option (New Database dialog box), 127
date statistics, database, 127
datetime data type, 99
DBAs (database administrators), 45
DBCC (Database Consistency Checker)
  fragmented indexes, 151–152
  overview, 97
dbcreator fixed security role, 187
DCM (Differential Changed Map) pages, 105
DDL (Data Definition Language)
  database creation scripts, 132
  event notifications, 275
  performance optimization, 396, 398–399
  trigger functions, 2
deadlocks
  analyzing with Profiler tool, 379
  exposing process participated in, 383
  performance optimization, 367–368
decimal data type, 98
Decrease feature, SQL Editor toolbar, 67
Decrease Indent feature, Text Editor toolbar, 70
Dedicated Administrator Connections (DACs)
  endpoints, 236
  overview, 91
default collation, 35
default constraints, 162–163
Default Cursor option (New Database dialog box), 127
default instances, SQL Server 2005 installation, 31
DEFAULT_LOGON_DOMAIN argument, 242
defaults, standalone, 172
Delete Tables From Database feature, Database Diagram toolbar, 60
deletes, undoing, 359

deleting
  Database Mail accounts and profiles, 268
  Database Mail messages, 274
delivery channels, Notification Services, 495–496
denying permissions, 198–200
DES (Data Encryption Standard), 214
Design Query in Editor feature, SQL Editor toolbar, 67
Designers section, SQL Server Management Studio configuration, 76–77
Developer Edition, software requirements, 27–28
development environment, integration services, 473–475
diagrams, database, 163–164
dialog boxes
  Concatenate Null Yields Null option, 126
  New Assembly, 169–170
  New Database
    accessing, 116
    Add button, 118
    ANSI NULL Default settings, 123–124
    ANSI NULLS Enabled settings, 124
    ANSI Padding Enabled settings, 124
    ANSI Warnings Enabled settings, 124
    Arithmetic Abort Enabled option, 125
    Auto Close option, 125
    Auto Create Statistics option, 125
    Auto Shrink option, 125
    Auto Update Statistics Asynchronously option, 125–126
    Auto Update Statistics option, 125
    Compatibility level drop-down list, 123
    Database files section, 118–119
    Database Read Only option, 126
    Database State option, 126–127
    Date Correlation Optimization Enabled option, 127
    Default Cursor, 127
    discussed, 49
    Numeric Round-Abort option, 128
    Owner field, 117
    Page Verify option, 128–129
    Parameterization option, 129
    Path column, 121
    Quoted Identifiers Enabled option, 130–131
    Recovery model section, 122–123
    Recursive Triggers Enabled option, 131
    Restrict Access option, 131
    Script Action options, 131–132
    Select a page section, 121
    Trustworthy option, 131
  New Database Reference, 441
  New Login, 180
  New Maintenance Plan, 319–320
  Restoration, 346
  Trace Properties
    discussed, 80
    Events Extraction Settings tab, 83
    Events Selection tab, 82–83
    General tab, 81–82
dialog conversations, Server Broker service, 509
dialog security, Server Broker service, 512
Differential backups, 330
Differential Changed Map (DCM) pages, 105
Differential strategy, Full backups with, 336
digital signatures, 223–224
Disconnect feature, SQL Editor toolbar, 66
disk counters, performance optimization, 364–365
Disk Usage report, 394
`diskadmin` **fixed security role, 187**
Display Estimated Execution Plan feature, SQL Editor toolbar, 66
Display on Object Member List feature, Text Editor toolbar, 70
Display Parameter Info feature, Text Editor toolbar, 70
Display Quick Info feature, Text Editor toolbar, 70
Display Word Completion feature, Text Editor toolbar, 70
distributed transactions, replication, 530–531
Distribution Agent, 529
distribution databases
  overview, 16–17
  system databases and, 113
DML (Data Manipulation Language) triggers, 163, 167–169
DMVs (Dynamic Management Views), 367–368
dockable windows, 47
Domain Groups, cluster groups, 41
DPAPI (Data Protection API), 214
dragging windows, 47
`DROP APPLICATION ROLE` **statement, 197**
`DROP CERTIFICATE` **statement, 220**
`DROP ROLE` **statement, 194**
`DROP_EXISTING` **statement, 153–154**
DSVs (Data Source Views), 474
DTA (Database Tuning Advisor)
  end-of-quarter analysis, 391
  General tab, 84–85
  Profiler tool and, 391–392
  recommendations, 389
  script analysis, 386–387

session creation, 84
sessions, starting new, 387–388
tuning option selection, 389
Tuning Options tab, 86–87
DTS (Data Transformation Services), 4
DuVarney, Dave (*Professional SQL Server 2005 Reporting Services*), 3, 11
Dynamic Management Views (DMVs), 367–368
Dynamic System views, 165
dynamic views and functions, Resource **database, 97**

E

-E **argument, SQLCMD utility, 89**
EFS (Encrypting File System), 219
email. See Database Mail feature
Email Settings area, Reporting Services Configuration Manager, 89
Enabled **property, TCP/IP protocol, 230**
encryption
 AES (Advanced Encryption Standard), 214
 asymmetric keys, 218
 certificates, 218–221
 data columns, 221–222
 DES (Data Encryption Standard), 214
 discussed, 213
 EFS (Encrypting File System), 219
 hierarchy, 215
 symmetric keys, 216–217
Encryption Keys area, Reporting Services Configuration Manager, 88
end-of-quarter analysis, DTA, 391
endpoints
 CREATE ENDPOINT statement, 241
 creation, 246–250
 DAC, 236
 Local Machine, 236
 mirroring, 238–239
 Named Pipes, 236
 security, 246
 Service Broker, 245–246
 SOAP, 240–244
 started state, 234
 stopped state, 234
 TSQL Default TCP, 234–235
 TSQL TCP, 236–237
 types, 233
 VIA, 236
Enterprise Data Platform, 1

Enterprise Edition
 features, 5–6
 flexibility in, 7
 software requirements, 27–28
enumerations, 438
Environment section
 Source Control configuration, 72
 SQL Server Management Studio configuration, 71–72
errors
 bad login/password message, 34
 error handling, improvements to, 2
 error reporting screen, SQL Server 2005 installation, 37
 trusted connection message, 34
ETL (Extract-Transform-Load) solutions, 79
event collection process, Notification Services
 code, 492–494
 discussed, 491
 generation, 494
 SQL Server API, 492
 XML API, 492
event handlers, integration service, 465, 481
event notifications, 275–276
Event Object API, event collection process, 491
event-based alerts, 304–308
EVENTDATA **function, 396–397**
Events Extraction Settings tab (Trace Properties dialog box), 83
Events Selection tab
 Profiler tool, 380
 Trace Properties dialog box, 82–83
exclusive locks, 376
Execute DTS 2000 Package Task, control flow, 476
Execute feature, SQL Editor toolbar, 66
Execute Package Task, control flow, 476
Execute Process Task, control flow, 476
Execute SQL feature, Query Designer toolbar, 63
Execute SQL Server Agent Job Task, control flow, 477
Execute SQL Task, control flow, 476
Execute T-SQL Statement Task, control flow, 477
Execution Account area, Reporting Services Configuration Manager, 89
exercises, answers to, 543–546
explicit permissions, 211–213
Explicit transactions, 108–109
Express Edition
 features, 6–7
 software requirements, 27–28
Extensible Markup Language (XML)
 discussed, 2
 overview, 9

Extensible Markup Language (XML) (continued)

XML API, event collection process, 492

XML data type, 101

XML indexes

primary, 138–140

secondary path, 140

secondary property, 141

secondary value, 141

XML Schema Definition (XML), 244

XML section, Text Editor configuration, 72

XML Task, control flow, 477

Extensible Markup Language for Analysis (XMLA), 9

extents, mixed/uniform, 102

external access permission setting, CLR, 460

Extract-Transform-Load (ETL) solutions, 79

F

failover clustering

discussed, 402

log shipping and, 418–419

manual, 432

fail-safe operators, 304

Features tool, SQL Server Surface Area Configuration feature, 43

File extensions area, Text Editor configuration, 72

file growth, database, 120–121

File System Task, control flow, 476

filegroups

advantages of, 119

backups, 330–331

names, 119

primary, 17–18, 119

read-only, 119

restoration, 350–351

table partitions, 143

user-defined, 119

files

attachment size, Database Mail feature, 258

backups, 330–331

monitoring, 393–395

restoration, 350–351

size considerations, databases, 120

file-shrink operations, database, 125

fill factor, mitigating fragmentation with, 152–153

filters

filtering tools, replication, 535–536

settings, Log File Viewer, 77

traced events, 83

five nines rule, high-availability concept, 402

fixed database roles

ALTER APPLICATION statement, 197

ALTER ROLE statement, 194

application roles, 195

built-in principals, 193

CREATE APPLICATION statement, 196

CREATE ROLE statement, 194

creation, 193

DROP APPLICATION ROLE statement, 197

DROP ROLE statement, 194

list of, 192–193

fixed-length data types, 98–100

float **data type, 99**

floating windows, 47

fonts

Environment configuration, 71

Font Size command, Help toolbar, 61

forced services, database mirroring, 433

foreign keys, 158–160

formatting, Notification Services, 495–496

fragmentation

checking for, 148–149

leaf-level, 150–151

mitigating with fill factor, 152–153

page splits, 147

removing, 153

free space, in transaction logs, 110–111

FROM **clause, restoration and, 342**

FTP Task, control flow, 476

Full backups

with Differential strategy, 336

overview, 330

with Transaction Log strategy, 337–338

full dialog security, 512

full partitioning, 86

Full recovery model, 122, 325

functions

aggregate, 167, 209

computational, 446

CREATE FUNCTION statement, 445

EVENTDATA, 396–397

LTrim, 15

RTrim, 15

scalar, 167, 446

schema scope permissions, 210

system, 167

table-valued, 167, 446

Trim, 15

user-defined, 167, 445–446

G

GAM (Global Allocation Map) pages, 105
general area, Environment configuration, 71
General Properties sheet (Agent Service), 278
General tab
  DTA, 84–85
  Trace Properties dialog box, 81–82
Generate Change Script feature
  Database Diagram toolbar, 60
  Table Designer toolbar, 69
Get feature, Source Control toolbar, 65
Get Latest Version feature, Source Control toolbar, 65
Global Allocation Map (GAM) pages, 105
GRANT SELECT **statement, 134–135**
granting permissions, 198–200
guest accounts, database user security, 190

H

hardware considerations, SQL Server 2005 installation, 22
Harinath, Sivakumar (*Professional SQL Server Analysis Services 2005 with MDX*), 3
hashing logarithm, 181–182
HEADER_LIMIT **argument, 244**
help options
  Help area, Environment configuration, 72
  Help Favorites command, Help toolbar, 61
  Help toolbar, 61–62
high-availability
  clustering
    active/active, 405
    active/passive, 405
    components, 404–405
    failover, 402
    majority node, 404
    recommendations, 406
    Windows, 402–403
  database mirroring
    client redirection, 420
    configuration, 422–426
    failover, manual, 432
    forced services, 433
    high-performance mode, 421
    high-safety with/without automatic failover, 421
    monitoring, 428–430
    partner roles, 424
    removing, 433
    server roles, 419
    service account specification, 424–425
    sessions, pausing, 430–431
    sessions, resuming, 431
    T-SQL commands, 426–427
    witness roles, 424
  five nines rule, 402
  log shipping
    automatic cleanup behavior, 408
    backup settings, 408
    discussed, 406, 409
    failover considerations, 418–419
    heavy transaction processing load caution, 409
    history retention value configuration, 412
    preparation for, 407
    secondary server configuration, 409–411
    T-SQL and, 413–417
  rule on nines, 401–402
  SLAs (Service Level Agreements), 401
high-performance database mirroring mode, 421
high-safety with/without automatic failover mode, database mirroring, 421
History Cleanup Task, control flow, 477
history of SQL Server, 19–20
history retention value configuration, log shipping, 412
How Do I command, Help toolbar, 61

I

-i **argument, SQLCMD utility, 89**
IAM (Index Allocation Map) pages, 105
ICF (Instance Configuration File), 497
IDE (Integrated Development Environment), 45
identity impersonation, programming support, 458
IIS (Internet Information Services), 3
image **data type, 101**
image pages, 105
impersonation, programming support, 458
Implicit transactions, 107–108
Import Analysis Services 9.0 template (BI Studio), 79
Include Actual Execution Plan feature, SQL Editor toolbar, 67
Increase Indent feature
  SQL Editor toolbar, 67
  Text Editor toolbar, 70
Index Allocation Map (IAM) pages, 105
Index command, Help toolbar, 61
index pages, 105
indexes
  aligned, 146
  clustered, 136–137

indexes (continued)

fragmentation
checking for, 148–149
leaf-level, 150–151
mitigating with fill factor, 152–153
page splits, 147
removing, 153
non-clustered, 137
rebuilding, 153–154
reorganization, 154
XML
primary, 138–140
secondary path, 140
secondary property, 141
secondary value, 141
index_id **parameter, 149**
Information Schema views, 164
**Initialization tool, Reporting Services Configuration
Manager, 88**
Initiator Only contract, 510
initiators, dialog conversations, 509
in-row data, physical database structure, 101
installation, SQL Server 2005
authentication mode configuration, 33–34
auto-start feature, 28
collation settings
accent sensitivity, 36
binary sorting, 36
case sensitivity, 36
default collation, 35
discussed, 34
non-compatible collation issues, 37
width sensitivity, 36
error reporting screen, 37
hardware considerations, 22
inspecting/reviewing, 43
instance options, 31
memory considerations, 23
planning considerations, 21–22
post-installation considerations, 41–43
processor considerations, 23
SCC (System Configuration Checker), 29–30
service options, 32–33
setup progress screen, 38
SETUP.EXE file, 28
software requirements, 27
storage considerations
discussed, 23
efficiency, maximizing, 24
local attached disk array, 26

optimal installation, 23–24
SAN and NAS versus local disk storage, 25
Virtual Server name configuration, 39–41
to Windows cluster, 38
Instance Configuration File (ICF), 497
instance of classes, 438
instance options, SQL Server 2005 installation, 31
instances, Notification Service
configuration and behaviors, 497–498
discussed, 490
multiple services, 499
Instead Of triggers, 163
int **data type, 98**
Integrated Development Environment (IDE), 45
integration services
control flow, 465, 476–477
data, importing/exporting, 466–470
data flow
data destinations, 481
overview, 465
sources, 479
transformations, 480–481
data transformation, 472–475
data type option, setting, 469
destination table creation, 470
development environment, 473–475
event handlers, 465, 481
object model, 465
packages
control flow, 475
discussed, 465
execution, 486–487
simple package creation, 482–485
precedence constraints, 478
run-time, 465
SSIS (SQL Server Integration Services)
components, 463–464
MSDB database, 15
overview, 4
tasks, 465, 475–478
Integration Services Project template (BI Studio), 79
integrity checks, Maintenance Plan wizard, 319
intent exclusive locks, 376
intent shared locks, 376
intent update locks, 376
interface
Reporting Services Configuration Manager, 87
SQL Server Management Studio, 46
Internet Information Services (IIS), 3
IP addresses, 231

IPC (Inter-Process Communication) channels, **230**
ISO (Organization for International Standards), **35**

J

jobs, Agent Service
adding to schedules, 295–297
categories, 287
creation, 283–286
data retrieval tasks, 286
defined, 283
history properties, 282
job step creation, 288–292
Job System Properties window, 280
logins, 285
multi-server, 316–317
names, 284
sp_add_jobstep stored procedure, 289–290
token replacement, 292–294
join filters, replication tools, 536

K

Keep Alive **property, TCP/IP protocol, 230**
keyboards, Environment configuration, 72
keys
conformity, 159
foreign, 158–160
primary, 155–156
unique, 156–158

L

language collation settings, 141
large object data types, 100–101
leaf-level fragmentation, 150–151
Listen All **property, TCP/IP protocol, 230**
local attached disk array, storage considerations, 26
local disk storage, 25–26
Local Machine endpoint, 236
lockable resource type stored procedures, 375–378
Locks by Object page (Activity Monitor tool), 371
Locks by Process page (Activity Monitor tool), 371
log cache, 23
Log File Viewer tool. *See also* **transaction logs**
filter settings, 77
opening, 77
performance optimization, 370
Log Reader Agent, 529
Log Sequence Number (LSN), 110, 342

log shipping
automatic cleanup behavior, 408
backup settings, 408
configuration, 407–411
discussed, 406
failover considerations, 418–419
heavy transaction processing load caution, 409
history retention value configuration, 412
preparation for, 407
secondary server configuration, 409–411
T-SQL and, 413–417
logging levels, Database Mail feature, 258
logins
adding to fixed server role, 187
Agent Service jobs, 285
ALTER LOGIN statement, 183
CREATE LOGIN statement, 181, 183
creation, 180, 182–183
managing, 183
New Login dialog box, 180
password name criteria, 179–180
stored procedures for, 184
LOGIN_TYPE **argument, 244**
LSN (Log Sequence Number), 110, 342
LTrim **function, 15**

M

mail. *See* **Database Mail feature**
maintenance
database, 120
schema, 135
table, 147
Maintenance Cleanup Task, control flow, 477
Maintenance Plan wizard, 318–319
Maintenance Plans area, Designers configuration, 76
majority node clustering, 404
Manage Check Constraints feature
Database Diagram toolbar, 60
Table Designer toolbar, 69
Manage Full-Text Indexes feature
Database Diagram toolbar, 60
Table Designer toolbar, 69
Manage Indexes and Keys feature
Database Diagram toolbar, 60
Table Designer toolbar, 69
Manage XML Indexes feature
Database Diagram toolbar, 60
Table Designer toolbar, 69
manual failover, 432

MAPI (Messaging Application Programming Interface)
Database Mail feature and, 254
discussed, 5
MARS (Multiple Active Result Sets)
functionality, 2
TempDB database, 16
Master **database, 14**
master server, 317
**MCBA (Microsoft Certified Database Administrator)
certification, 45**
MDX (Multidimensional Expressions), 9
memory
hardware considerations, 22
SQL Server 2005 installation, 23
memory counters, performance optimization, 365–366
Merge Agent, 529
merge replication, 532–533
message conversations, Server Broker service, 509
message queue
Message Queue Task, control flow, 476
timeout value, 258
messages
Database Mail feature, 274–275
SOAP, 240
Messaging Application Programming Interface (MAPI)
Database Mail feature and, 254
discussed, 5
methods, 438
Microsoft CEO (Ballmer), 436
**Microsoft Certified Database Administrator (MCBA)
certification, 45**
Microsoft Desktop Edition (MSDE), 6
**Microsoft Distributed Transaction Coordinator
(MS DTC), 530**
Microsoft Management Console (MMC)
discussed, 45
SQL Server Configuration Manager, 87
Microsoft Message Queuing (MSMQ), 4
mined data, Analysis Services, 3
mirrored backups, 333
mirroring
client redirection, 420
configuration, 422–426
endpoints, 238–239
failover, manual, 432
forced services, 433
high-performance mode, 421
high-safety with/without automatic failover mode, 421
monitoring, 428–430
partner roles, 424

removing, 433
server roles, 419
service account specification, 424–425
sessions
pausing, 430–431
resuming, 431
T-SQL commands, 426–427
witness roles, 424
Miscellaneous project folder, 52
mixed extents, 102
Mixed Mode
authentication, 33–34
server security, 19
MMC (Microsoft Management Console)
discussed, 45
SQL Server Configuration Manager, 87
Mobile Edition features, 6
Mobile Editor toolbar options, 67
mode **parameter, 149**
Model **database, 14–15**
money **data type, 99**
Move the caret features, Text Editor toolbar, 70
**MS DTC (Microsoft Distributed Transaction
Coordinator), 530**
MSDB **database, 15**
MSDE (Microsoft Desktop Edition), 6
MSDTC **service, 12**
MSDTSServer **service, 11**
MSFTESQL **service, 11**
MSMQ (Microsoft Message Queuing), 4
MSSQLServer **service, 9**
MSSQLServerADHelper **service, 10**
MSSQLServerOLAPService **service, 10**
Multidimensional Expressions (MDX), 9
multidimensional queries, 50
Multiple Active Result Sets (MARS)
functionality, 2
TempDB database, 16
multiple instances, 5
**multiple publishers/multiple subscribers replication
model, 534**
**multiple publishers/single subscriber replication
model, 534**
multi-server Agent Service jobs, 316–317

N

name resolution, schemas and, 133
named instances, SQL Server 2005 installation, 31
Named Pipes protocol, 230, 236

names

Agent Service jobs, 284

database, 116

Database Mail profiles, 255

filegroup, 119

object, 13–14

password, 179–180

session, 84–85

namespaces

defined, 437

NAMESPACE argument, 244

schema, 133

URL, 245

naming conventions, database user security, 188

NAS (Network Attached Storage), 25–26

native client configuration

Native Client Configuration node (SQL Server Configuration Manager), 87

overview, 232

nchar **data type, 99**

NET SEND **statement, 301**

NET STOP **statement, 277**

Network Attached Storage (NAS), 25–26

Network Configuration node (SQL Server Configuration Manager), 87

network counters, performance optimization, 366

network interface cards (NICs), 404

network protocols, removing unused, 225

New Assembly dialog box, 169–170

New Database dialog box

accessing, 116

Add button, 118

ANSI NULL Default settings, 123–124

ANSI NULLS Enabled settings, 124

ANSI Padding Enabled settings, 124

ANSI Warnings Enabled settings, 124

Arithmetic Abort Enabled option, 125

Auto Close option, 125

Auto Create Statistics option, 125

Auto Shrink option, 125

Auto Update Statistics Asynchronously option, 125–126

Auto Update Statistics option, 125

Compatibility level drop-down list, 123

Concatenate Null Yields Null option, 126

Database files section, 118–119

Database Read Only option, 126

Database State option, 126–127

Date Correlation Optimization Enabled option, 127

Default Cursor option, 127

discussed, 49

Numeric Round-Abort option, 128

Owner field, 117

Page Verify option, 128–129

Parameterization option, 129

Path column, 121

Quoted Identifiers Enabled option, 130–131

Recovery model section, 122–123

Recursive Triggers Enabled option, 131

Restrict Access option, 131

Script Action options, 131–132

Select a page section, 121

Trustworthy option, 131

New Database Reference dialog box, 441

New Login dialog box, 180

New Maintenance Plan dialog box, 319–320

New Project screen, BI Studio, 78–79

New Query feature, Standard toolbar, 68

New Subscription Wizard, 538–540

New Table feature, Database Diagram toolbar, 60

New Text Animation feature, Database Diagram toolbar, 60

NICs (network interface cards), 404

No Delay **property, TCP/IP protocol, 230**

non-clustered indexes, 137

Notification Services

applications

definition file elements, 499–500

overview, 490

primitive duration format, 503

architecture, 490

delivery channels, 495–496

event collection process

code, 492–494

Event Object API, 491

generation, 494

SQL Server API, 492

XML API, 492

formatting, 495–496

instances

configuration and behaviors, 497–498

creation, 504–505

discussed, 490

multiple services, 499

overview, 4, 489

SMI (subscription management interface), 490–491

subscription processing, 495

Notify Operator Task, control flow, 477

ntext **data type, 101**

NTFS (NT File System), 102

NTLM (NT Lan Manager), 176
`numeric` **data type, 98**
Numeric Round-Abort option (New Database dialog box), 128
`nvarchar` **data type, 100**

O

`-o` **argument, SQLCMD utility, 90**
Object Explorer (SQL Server Management Studio)
  functionality, 48
  script creation, 49
object models
  communication support, 9
  integration services, 465
object names, 13–14
`object_id` **parameter, 149**
OEM (original equipment manufacturer) file, 278
OLTP (Online Transaction Processing), 2
`ON DELETE CASCADE` **statement, 160**
`ON DELETE SET DEFAULT` **statement, 161**
`ON DELETE SET NULL` **statement, 160**
`ON UPDATE CASCADE` **statement, 160**
`ON UPDATE SET DEFAULT` **statement, 161**
`ON UPDATE SET NULL` **statement, 160**
Online Transaction Processing (OLTP), 2
operators, Agent Service
  creation, 301
  fail-safe, 304
  `sp_add_operator` stored procedure, 302–304
optimization strategies, performance, 361–362
Oracle replication, 533
organization, index, 154
Organization for International Standards (ISO), 35
original equipment manufacturer (OEM) file, 278
orphaned users, recovery, 354
Owner field (New Database dialog box), 117
ownership, schema, 133

P

`-P` **argument, SQLCMD utility, 89**
packages, integration services
  control flow, 475
  discussed, 465
  execution, 486–487
  simple package creation, 482–486
Page Free Space (PFS) pages, 105
page life expectancy measures, performance optimization, 366

page splits
  fragmentation, 147
  performance optimization, 367
Page Verify option (New Database dialog box), 128–129
pages
  BCM, 105
  data, 103–104
  DCM, 105
  GAM, 105
  IAM, 105
  image, 105
  index, 105
  PFS, 105
  SGAM, 105
  storage architecture, 103–105
  text, 105
Parameterization option (New Database dialog box), 129
parameterized row filters, replication tools, 535–536
parameters, sending mail, 269–271
Parse feature, SQL Editor toolbar, 66
Partial backups, 332, 339
partitioning
  aligned, 86
  full, 86
  improvements to, 2
  table
    discussed, 141
    filegroup creation, 143
    multiple files, 142
    Partition Functions, 144–145
    Partition Schemes, 145–146
    statistic reporting, 143
`Partition_number` **parameter, 149**
partner roles, database mirroring, 424
passwords
  hashing logarithm, 181–182
  name criteria, 179–180
  policies, 225
`PATH` **argument, 242**
Path column (New Database dialog box), 121
pausing mirror sessions, 430–431
PDS (Physical Design Structure), 86
peer-to-peer transactional replication, 532
performance condition alerts, 310, 389
performance optimization
  Activity Monitor tool, 371–373
  available bytes counters, 365
  baseline creation, 361–362

buffer cache hit ratio measures, 366

DDL (Data Definition Language) triggers, 396, 398–399

deadlocks, 367–368

disk counters, 364–365

Disk Usage report, 394

DMVs (Dynamic Management Views), 367–369

DTA (Database Tuning Advisor)

  end-of-quarter analysis, 391

  Profiler tool and, 391–392

  recommendations, 389–390

  script analysis, 386–387

  sessions, starting new, 387–388

EVENTDATA function, 396–397

files, monitoring, 393–395

KILL command, 377

lockable resource types stored procedures, 375–378

Log File Viewer tool, 370

memory counters, 365–366

modifications, monitoring, 395

network counters, 366

optimization strategies, 361–362

page life expectancy measures, 366

page splits, 367

performance counters, 395

processor counters, 363–364

Profiler tool

  deadlock graph, 382

  deadlocks, exposing process participated in, 383

  discussed, 377

  DTA and, 391–392

  Events Selection tab, 380

  limiting data returned to, 380

  query analysis, 384–385

  query windows, 381

  transaction load considerations, 379

queue length counters, 364

sp_lock stored procedure, 375

sp_spaceused stored procedure, 394–395

sp_who stored procedure, 373–375

sp_who2 stored procedure, 373–375

SQL Server-specific counters, 367

sys.sysfiles parameter, 395

user connection counters, 367

wait time counters, 367

working sets counters, 365

permissions

  Agent Service, 283

  assembly, 170

  CLR (Common Language Run-Time), 460

  database scope, 206–209

  denying, 198–200

  explicit, 211–213

  granting, 198–200

  managing, 211–213

  principle of least privilege, 200

  revoking, 198–200

  schema scope, 209–210

  security levels, 201

  server, 202–206

PFS (Page Free Space) pages, 105

physical database structure

  data manipulation data types, 101–102

  discussed, 97

  fixed-length data types, 98–100

  in-row data, 101

  large object data types, 100

  variable-length data types, 100–101

Physical Design Structure (PDS), 86

physical disk statistics, disk counters, 365

pipe character (|), 468

PKI (Public Key Infrastructure), 219

Plain Text area, Text Editor configuration, 72

planning considerations, SQL Server 2005 installation, 21–22

Plug-In Selection area, Source Control configuration, 72

point-in-time restoration, 352

policies, password, 225

POP3 (Post Office Protocol) server, 253

port numbers, Database Mail feature, 256

PORTS **argument, 242**

post-installation considerations, SQL Server 2005, 41–43

precedence constraints, 478

primary data files, 17–18

primary filegroups, 17–18, 119

primary keys, 155–156

primary XML indexes, 138–140

primitive duration format, applications, 503

principals, security, 178

principle of least privilege, permissions, 200

private profiles, Database Mail feature, 256

procedure cache, 23

procedures, schema scope permissions, 210

Process Info page (Activity Monitor tool), 371

processadmin **fixed security role, 187**

processor considerations, SQL Server 2005 installation, 23

processor counters, performance optimization, 363–364

Professional SQL Server Analysis Services 2005 with MDX (Harinath and Quinn), 3

Professional SQL Server 2005 CLR Stored Procedures, Functions, and Triggers (Comingore), 3

Professional SQL Server 2005 Reporting Services (Turley, Bryant, Counihan, and DuVarney), 3, 11

Profiler tool

deadlocks

analyzing, 379

exposing process participated in, 383

graph, 382

DTA and, 391–392

Events Selection tab, 380

limiting data returned to, 380

query analysis, 384–385

query windows, 381

transaction load considerations, 379

profiles, Database Mail feature

creation, 260

deletion guidelines, 268

naming, 255

`sysmail_add_principalprofile_sp` stored procedure, 267

`sysmail_add_profile_sp` stored procedure, 260

`sysmail_delete_principalprofile_sp` stored procedure, 268

`sysmail_delete_profileaccount_sp` stored procedure, 268

`sysmail_delete_profile_sp` stored procedure, 268

`sysmail_update_principalprofile_sp` stored procedure, 267

`sysmail_update_profileaccount_sp` stored procedure, 264–265

`sysmail_update_profile_sp` stored procedure, 263–264

programming support

impersonation, 458

threading, 457–458

project and solution association, 51

project folders, Solution Explorer, 52

properties, 438

Properties feature, Source Control toolbar, 65

Properties Window feature, Standard toolbar, 68

Properties window (SQL Server Management Studio), 52

proxies, Agent Service, 313–316

public key certificates, 218–221

Public Key Infrastructure (PKI), 219

public profiles, Database Mail feature, 256–257

publication, New Publication Wizard, 536–538

Pure Log backups, 331

Q

queries

analysis, Profiler tool, 384–385

multidimensional, 50

Queries project folder, 52

Query Designer toolbar, 50, 62–63

Query Execution section, SQL Server Management Studio configuration, 72–74

Query Results section, SQL Server Management Studio configuration, 74–76

Queue Reader Agent, 529

queues

length counters, performance optimization, 364

schema scope permissions, 210

Server Broker service, 511

Quinn, Stephen R. (*Professional SQL Server Analysis Services 2005 with MDX*), 3

quorum, cluster-aware applications, 403

Quoted Identifiers Enabled option (New Database dialog box), 130–131

R

RAID (Redundant Array of Inexpensive Disks), 120

RDBMS (Relational Database Management System), 1

read-only filegroups, 119

`real` **data type, 99**

Rebuild Index Task, control flow, 477

Recalculate Page Breaks feature, Database Diagram toolbar, 60

recommendations, DTA, 389

`RECONFIGURE` **command, 438**

recording transactions, 109–110

recovery. *See also* **snapshots**

Bulk-Logged model, 122–123, 325

Full model, 122, 325

orphaned users, 354

Simple model, 123, 326

snapshots and, 358–359

system databases, 353–354

Recovery model section (New Database dialog box), 122–123

Recursive Triggers Enabled option (New Database dialog box), 131

Redo phase, restoration, 339

Redundant Array of Inexpensive Disks (RAID), 120

Refresh Status feature, Source Control toolbar, 65

Registered Servers feature

SQL Server Management Studio, 52

Standard toolbar, 68

Relational Database Management System (RDBMS), 1

Relationships feature

Database Diagram toolbar, 60

Table Designer toolbar, 69

remote connections, enabling/disabling, 41

Remove From Diagram feature, Database Diagram toolbar, 60

Reorganize Index Task, control flow, 477

reorganizing indexes, 154

replication

column filtering, 535

distributed transactions, 530–531

Distribution Agent, 529

filtering tools, 535–536

join filters, 536

Log Reader Agent, 529

merge, 532–533

Merge Agent, 529

multiple publishers/multiple subscribers model, 534

multiple publishers/single subscriber model, 534

New Publication Wizard, 536–538

New Subscription Wizard, 538–540

Oracle, 533

overview, 4, 527

parameterized row filters, 535–536

peer-to-peer transactional, 532

Queue Reader Agent, 529

Replication Monitor service, 540–541

replication type, 529

single publisher/multiple subscribers model, 534

snapshot, 532

Snapshot Agent, 529

standard transactional publication, 531

static row filters, 535

strategies, 528

transactional, 531–532

Replication Management Objects (RMOs), 9

Report Manager Virtual Directory area, Reporting Services Configuration Manager, 88

Report Model Project template (BI Studio), 80

Report Server Project template (BI Studio), 79

Report Server Project Wizard template (BI Studio), 80

Report Server Virtual Directory area, Reporting Services Configuration Manager, 88

Reporting Services Configuration Manager

configuration areas, 88–89

interface, 87

reports, Disk Usage, 394

ReportServer **service, 11**

Resource **database**

dynamic views and functions, 97

SYS schema, 96

resource managers, distributed transactions, 530

restoration. See also **backups**

Data Copy phase, 339

database name specified, 341–342

database preparation, 345–347

files and filegroups, 350–351

FROM clause and, 342

point-in-time, 352

Redo phase, 339

Restoration dialog box, 346

RESTORE command, 340–341

from snapshots, 359

Undo phase, 339

user databases, 347–349

WITH clause and, 342–345

Restrict Access option (New Database dialog box), 131

Results to File feature, SQL Editor toolbar, 67

Results to Grid feature, SQL Editor toolbar, 67

Results to Text feature, SQL Editor toolbar, 67

resuming mirror sessions, 431

retry attempts, Database Mail accounts, 258

revoking permissions, 198–200

RMOs (Replication Management Objects), 9

routes, Server Broker service, 511–512

rowversion **data type, 100**

RTrim **function, 15**

rule of nines, high-availability concept, 401–402

rules, database, 172

run-time integration services, 465

S

-S **argument, SQLCMD utility, 89**

safe permission setting, CLR, 460

SAM (Security Accounts Manager), 176

SAN (Storage Area Network)

communication support, 8

local disk storage versus, 25–26

network infrastructure, 25

Save All feature, Standard toolbar, 68

Save feature, Standard toolbar, 68

Save Search command, Help toolbar, 61
scalar functions, 167, 446
SCC (System Configuration Checker), 29–30
scheduled backups, 352
schedules
  adding jobs to, 295–297
  creation, 294
  `sp_add_schedule` stored procedure, 297–300
  `sp_attach_schedule` stored procedure, 300–301
SCHEMA **argument, 244**
schema modification locks, 376
schema scope permissions, 209–210
schemas
  creation, 134–135
  defined, 13, 132
  maintenance, 135
  name resolution and, 133
  namespaces, 133
  ownership, 133
  security scope, 133
Script Action options (New Database dialog box),
  131–132
Script Task, control flow, 476
scripts
  analysis, performance optimization, 386–387
  creation, 49
SCSI (Small Computer Systems Interface), 25, 403
Search command, Help toolbar, 61
Secondary Global Allocation Map (SGAM) pages, 105
secondary server configuration, log shipping, 409–411
secondary XML path indexes, 140
secondary XML property indexes, 141
secondary XML value indexes, 141
Secure Sockets Layer (SSL), 225
security
  account, 224
  Agent Service, 282–283
  applications, removing unused, 225
  audits, 225
  authentication
    anonymous, 256
    AUTHENTICATION argument, 242
    bad login/password error message, 34
    Database Mail feature, 256
    discussed, 175
    Mixed Mode configuration, 33–34
    mode configuration, SQL Server 2005 installation,
      33–34
    overview, 18
    trusted connection error message, 34

    Windows Authentication mode changes, 176–178
    Windows Only configuration, 33–34
  best practices, 224–226
  CA (Certification Authority), 219
  CLR (Common Language Run-Time), 458–461
  credentials, 185–186
  database users
    CREATE USER statement, 190, 192
    default schemas, 188–189
    guest accounts, 190
    naming conventions, 188
  digital signatures, 223–224
  DPAPI (Data Protection API), 214
  encryption
    AES (Advanced Encryption Standard), 214
    asymmetric keys, 218
    certificates, 218–221
    data columns, 221–222
    DES (Data Encryption Standard), 214
    discussed, 213
    EFS (Encrypting File System), 219
    hierarchy, 215
    symmetric keys, 216–217
  endpoints, 246
  fixed database roles
    ALTER APPLICATION statement, 197
    ALTER ROLE statement, 194
    application roles, 195
    built-in principals, 193
    CREATE APPLICATION statement, 196
    CREATE ROLE statement, 194
    creation, 193
    DROP APPLICATION ROLE statement, 197
    DROP ROLE statement, 194
    list of, 192–193
  improvements to, 2
  logins
    adding to fixed server role, 187
    ALTER LOGIN statement, 183
    CREATE LOGIN statement, 181, 183–184
    creation, 180, 182–183
    managing, 183
    password name criteria, 179–180
    stored procedures for, 184
  Mixed Mode, 19
  network protocols, removing unused, 225
  permissions
    database scope, 206–209
    denying, 198–200
    explicit, 211–213

granting, 198–200
managing, 211–213
principle of least privilege, 200
revoking, 198–200
schema scope, 209–210
security levels, 201
server, 202–206
PKI (Public Key Infrastructure), 219
principals, 178
SAM (Security Accounts Manager), 176
schemas, 133
Server Broker service, 512
server roles, 186–187
SID (Security Identifier), 182
SSL (Secure Sockets Layer), 225
Security Accounts Manager (SAM), 176
Security Identifier (SID), 182
`securityadmin` **fixed server role, 186**
Select a page section (New Database dialog box), 121
Send Feedback command, Help toolbar, 62
Send Mail Task, control flow, 476
sending mail, parameters associated with, 269–271
Server Management Studio
Activity Monitor tool, 371–373
Bookmarks window, 53
Code Editor, 50
configuration
Designers section, 76–77
Environment section, 71–72
Query Execution, 72–74
Query Results section, 74–76
Source Control section, 72
Text Editor section, 72
Database Diagram node, 163–164
default view, 46
dockable windows, 47
Help toolbar, 61–62
interface, 46
Object Explorer
functionality, 48
New Database dialog box, 49
script creation, 49
Properties window, 52
Registered Servers window, 52
Solution Explorer
discussed, 50
project and solution association, 51
project folders, 52
solution folders, 52
`ssmssln` extension, 51

Summary window, 54
Template Explorer, 55–56
toolbars
Analysis Services, 68
custom creation, 58–59
Database Diagram, 59–60
Mobile Editor, 67
Query Designer, 62–63
Source Control, 63–65
SQL Editor, 66–67
Standard, 68
Table Designer, 69
Text Editor, 69–70
Toolbars menu, 56–57
View Designer, 71
Toolbox windows, 53
Web browser window, 54
Server Network Interface (SNI), 8
server roles, security, 186–187
Server Status area, Reporting Services Configuration Manager, 88
`serveradmin` **fixed server role, 186**
servers
master, 317
permissions, 202–206
Registered Servers window, 52
scope, 12
target, 317
service account specification, database mirroring, 424–425
Service Broker
contracts, 510
conversation groups, 510
dialog conversions, 509–510
dialog security, 512
message conversations, 509
overview, 4, 508
queues, 511
routes, 511–512
sample application
database preparation, 514
discussed, 513
object creation, 514–516
stored procedures, 519–521
table creation, 516–519
testing, 522–524
services, 511
transport security, 513

Service Broker endpoints, 245–246

Service Level Agreements (SLAs), 401

service options, SQL Server 2005 installation, 32–33

Service Oriented Architecture (SOA)

  overview, 4, 507–508

  Service Broker endpoints, 245

Services and Connections tool, 41–42

Services node (SQL Server Configuration Manager), 87

services, Server Broker service, 511

sessions

  database mirroring

    pausing, 430–431

    resuming, 431

  DTA, 387–388

  names, 84–85

  SESSIONS argument, 244

  SESSION_TIMEOUT argument, 244

Set Primary Key feature, Database Diagram toolbar, 60

Set/Remove Primary feature, Table Designer toolbar, 69

setup progress screen, SQL Server 2005 installation, 38

setupadmin fixed security role, 187

SETUP.EXE file, SQL Server 2005 installation, 28

SETVAR command, 90–91

SGAM (Secondary Global Allocation Map) pages, 105

Share feature, Source Control toolbar, 65

shared intent locks, 376

shared locks, 376

Shared Memory protocol, 230

shared schema locks, 376

shared with intent exclusive locks, 376

Shiloh database version, 20

Show Criteria feature, Query Designer toolbar, 63

Show Diagram Pane feature, Query Designer toolbar, 63

Show Relationship Labels feature, Database Diagram toolbar, 60

Show Results Pane feature, Query Designer toolbar, 63

Show SQL Pane feature, Query Designer toolbar, 63

Shrink Database Task, control flow, 477

SID (Security Identifier), 182

Simple Mail Transfer Protocol (SMTP), 5, 253

Simple Object Access Protocol (SOAP)

  communication support, 8

  endpoints, 240–244

  messages, 240

Simple recovery model, 123, 326

single publisher/multiple subscribers replication model, 534

SITE argument, 242

size requirement calculation, database, 115

SLAs (Service Level Agreements), 401

Small Computer Systems Interface (SCSI), 25, 403

small works database example, 323–325

smalldatetime data type, 99

smallint data type, 98

smallmoney data type, 99

SMI (subscription management interface), 490–491

SMOs (SQL Management Objects), 9

SMTP (Simple Mail Transfer Protocol), 5, 253

Snapshot Agent, 529

snapshot replication, 532

snapshots. See also recovery

  creation, 355–357

  defined, 355

  deletes, undoing, 359

  drops, undoing, 359

  limitations, 358

  recovery and, 358–359

  restoring from, 359

  updates, undoing, 358

SNI (Server Network Interface), 8

SOA (Service Oriented Architecture)

  overview, 4, 507

  Service Broker endpoints, 245

SOAP (Simple Object Access Protocol)

  communication support, 8

  endpoints, 240–244

  messages, 240

software requirements, SQL Server 2005 installation, 27

Solution Explorer (SQL Server Management Studio)

  discussed, 50

  project and solution association, 51

  project folders, 52

  solution folders, 52

  .ssmssln extension, 51

Source Control Manager feature, Source Control toolbar, 65

Source Control section, SQL Server Management Studio configuration, 72

Source Control toolbar, 63–65

sp_add_alert stored procedure, 308

sp_addmessage stored procedure, 306

sp_add_operator stored procedure, 302–304

sp_add_schedule stored procedure, 297–300

sp_addumpdevice stored procedure, 327

sp_attach_schedule stored procedure, 300–301

Specify Values for Template Parameters feature, SQL Editor toolbar, 67

Sphinx database system, 20
sp_lock **stored procedure, 375**
sp_spaceused **stored procedure, 394–395**
sp_who **stored procedure, 373–375**
sp_who2 **stored procedure, 373–375**
SQL Editor toolbar, 66–67
SQL Management Objects (SMOs), 9
SQL Server Agent Service
  Advanced Properties sheet, 278–279
  Agent Connection Properties, 280–281
  Alert Systems properties, 279–280
  alerts
    creation, 304
    event-based, 304–308
    performance condition, 310
    sp_add_alert stored procedure, 308
    sp_addmessage stored procedure, 306
    WMI event, 311–312
  configuration, 276–277
  General Properties sheet, 278
  Job System Properties window, 280
  jobs
    adding to schedules, 295–297
    categories, 287
    creation, 283–286
    data retrieval tasks, 286
    defined, 283
    history properties, 282
    job step creation, 288–292
    logins, 285
    multi-server, 316–317
    names, 284
    sp_add_jobstep stored procedure, 289–290
    token replacement, 292–293
  operators
    creation, 301
    fail-safe, 304
    sp_add_operator stored procedure, 302–304
  proxies, 313–316
  schedules
    adding jobs to, 295–297
    creation, 294
    sp_add_schedule stored procedure, 297–300
    sp_attach_schedule stored procedure, 300–301
  security, 282–283
  SQLAgentOperatorRole permission, 283
  SQLAgentReaderRole permission, 283
  SQLAgentUserRole permission, 283
SQL Server API, event collection process, 492

SQL Server Configuration Manager
  client protocol configuration, 232
  nodes, 87
SQL Server history, 19–20
SQL Server Integration Services (SSIS)
  components, 463–464
  MSDB database, 15
  overview, 4
SQL Server Management Studio
  Activity Monitor tool, 371–373
  Bookmarks window, 53
  Code Editor, 50
  configuration
    Designers section, 76–77
    Environment section, 71–72
    Query Execution, 72–74
    Query Results section, 74–76
    Source Control section, 72
    Text Editor section, 72
  Database Diagram node, 163–164
  default view, 46
  dockable windows, 47
  Help toolbar, 61–62
  interface, 46
  Object Explorer
    functionality, 48
    New Database dialog box, 49
    script creation, 49
  Properties window, 52
  Registered Servers window, 52
  Solution Explorer
    discussed, 50
    project and solution association, 51
    project folders, 52
    solution folders, 52
    .ssmssln extension, 51
  Summary window, 54
  Template Explorer, 55–56
  toolbars
    Analysis Services, 68
    custom creation, 58–59
    Database Diagram, 59–60
    Mobile Editor, 67
    Query Designer, 62–63
    Source Control, 63–65
    SQL Editor, 66–67
    Standard, 68
    Table Designer, 69
    Text Editor, 69–70

SQL Server Management Studio (continued)
- Toolbars menu, 56–57
- View Designer, 71
- Toolbox windows, 53
- Web browser window, 54

SQL Server Mobile Query feature, Standard toolbar, 68

SQL Server Profiler
- SQL Server Traces, 80
- Trace Properties dialog box
  - discussed, 80
  - Events Extraction Settings tab, 83
  - Events Selection tab, 82–83
  - General tab, 81–82

SQL Server Resolution Protocol (SSRP), 11

SQL Server Surface Area Configuration feature
- Features tool, 43
- Services and Connections tool, 41–42

SQL Server-specific counters, performance optimization, 367

`SQLAgentOperatorRole` **permission, 283**

`SQLAgentReaderRole` **permission, 283**

`SQLAgentUserRole` **permission, 283**

`SQLBrowser` **service, 10–11**

SQLCMD utility
- arguments, 89–90
- case-sensitivity, 89

SQLCMID Mode feature, SQL Editor toolbar, 67

`SQLServerAgent` **service, 10**

`sql_variant` **data type, 101**

`SQLWriter` **service, 11**

SSIS (SQL Server Integration Services)
- components, 463–464
- MSDB database, 15
- overview, 4

SSL (Secure Sockets Layer), 225

`SSL_PORT` **argument, 242**

`.ssmssln` **extension, 51**

SSRP (SQL Server Resolution Protocol), 11

standalone defaults, 172

Standard Edition
- availability and scalability enhancements, 7
- features, 5–6
- software requirements, 27–28

Standard toolbar, 68

standard transactional publication replication, 531

started endpoint state, 234

statements
- `ALTER APPLICATION`, 197
- `ALTER CERTIFICATE`, 220
- `ALTER CREDENTIAL`, 186

- `ALTER DATABASE`, 431
- `ALTER INDEX`, 153
- `ALTER LOGIN`, 183
- `ALTER ROLE`, 194
- `ALTER SCHEMA`, 135
- `ALTER TABLE`, 156
- `CREATE APPLICATION`, 196
- `CREATE CERTIFICATE`, 196
- `CREATE CREDENTIAL`, 196
- `CREATE ENDPOINT`, 196
- `CREATE FUNCTION`, 445
- `CREATE INDEX`, 153
- `CREATE LOGIN`, 181, 183–184
- `CREATE ROLE`, 194
- `CREATE SCHEMA`, 134
- `CREATE TABLE`, 155–156
- `CREATE USER`, 190, 192
- `DROP APPLICATION ROLE`, 197
- `DROP CERTIFICATE`, 220
- `DROP EXISTING`, 153–154
- `DROP ROLE`, 194
- `GRANT SELECT`, 134–135
- `NET SEND`, 301
- `NET STOP`, 277
- `ON DELETE CASCADE`, 277
- `ON DELETE SET DEFAULT`, 161
- `ON DELETE SET NULL`, 160
- `ON UPDATE CASCADE`, 160
- `ON UPDATE SET DEFAULT`, 161
- `ON UPDATE SET NULL`, 160
- `UPDATE STATISTICS`, 168

static row filters, replication tools, 535

Static System views, 164

statistic reporting, table partitions, 143

statistics
- Maintenance Plan wizard, 319
- missing, 125
- schema scope permissions, 210

stopped endpoint state, 234

storage
- data files, 102–104
- pages, 103–105
- Resource database, 96
- SQL Server 2005 installation
  - discussed, 23
  - efficiency, maximizing, 24
  - local attached disk array, 26
  - optimal installation, 23–24
  - SAN/NAS versus local disk storage, 25–26

Storage Area Network (SAN)
communication support, 8
local disk storage versus, 25–26
network infrastructure, 25
stored procedures
CLR (Common Language Run-Time), 446–447
lockable resource type, 375–378
login, 184
purpose of, 167
system, 167
user-created, 167
stripes, backup, 332–333
structures, 438
subscription management interface (SMI), 490–491
subscription processing, Notification Services, 495
Summary feature, Standard toolbar, 68
Summary window (SQL Server Management Studio), 54
symmetric keys, 216–217
Sync With Table of Contents command, Help toolbar, 61
synonyms
creating, 165–166
schema scope permissions, 210
`SYS` **schema, 96**
`sysadmin` **fixed server role, 186**
`sysmail_add_account_sp` **stored procedure,
261–262**
`sysmail_add_principalprofile_sp` **stored
procedure, 265–267**
`sysmail_add_profileaccount_sp` **stored
procedure, 262–263**
`sysmail_add_profile_sp` **stored procedure, 260**
`sysmail_delete_account_sp` **stored
procedure, 268**
`sysmail_delete_principalprofile_sp` **stored
procedure, 268**
`sysmail_delete_profileaccount_sp` **stored
procedure, 268**
`sysmail_delete_profile_sp` **stored procedure, 268**
`sysmail_update_account_sp` **stored procedure, 264**
`sysmail_update_principalprofile_sp` **stored
procedure, 267**
`sysmail_update_profileaccount_sp` **stored
procedure, 264–265**
`sys.sysfiles` **parameter, 395**
System Configuration Check (SCC), 29–30
system databases
default location, 17
distribution databases and, 113
`Master`, 14

`Model`, 14–15
`MSDB`, 15
recovery, 353–354
restricted activity, 17
`TempDB`, 15–16
system functions, 167
system views, 164–165
system-stored procedures, 167

T
**Table and Database Designers area, Designers section
configuration, 76**
`table` **data type, 101**
Table Designer toolbar, 69
Table View feature, Database Diagram toolbar, 60
tables. *See also* **databases**
architecture, 136
cascading constraints, 160–161
check constraints, 161
collation support, 141
CTE (Common Table Expressions), 2
default constraints, 162–163
discussed, 136
DML triggers, 163
indexes
clustered, 136–137
non-clustered, 137
XML, 138–141
keys
conformity, 159
foreign, 158–160
primary, 155–156
unique, 156–158
maintenance, 147
opening, 62
partitions
discussed, 141
filegroup creation, 143
multiple files, 142
Partition Functions, 144–145
Partition Schemes, 145–146
statistic reporting, 143
schema scope permissions, 210
`TRUNCATE TABLE` command, 325
table-valued functions, 167, 446
Tabular Data Stream (TDS), 8, 234
Tail Lob backups, 331
Target Only contract, 510
target server, 317

tasks, integration service, 465, 475–478
TB (terabytes), 7
TCP/IP protocol
Enabled property, 230
IP addresses, 231
Keep Alive property, 230
Listen All property, 230
No Delay property, 230
TDS (Tabular Data Stream), 8, 234
TempDB database, 15–16
Template Explorer feature
SQL Server Management Studio, 55–56
Standard toolbar, 68
templates, 79–80
terabytes (TB), 7
test databases, 115
testing triggers, 168–169
text data type, 100
Text Editor section, SQL Server Management Studio
configuration, 72
Text Editor toolbar, 69–70
text pages, 105
threading, 457–458
timeout value, message queue, 258
timestamp data type, 100
tinyint data type, 98
Toggle a Bookmark on the Current Line feature, Text
Editor toolbar, 70
token replacement, Agent Service jobs, 292–294
toolbars, SQL Server Management Studio
Analysis Services, 68
custom toolbar creation, 58–59
Database Diagram, 59–60
Help, 61–62
Mobile Editor, 67
Query Designer, 62–63
Source Control, 63–65
SQL Editor, 66–67
Standard, 68
Table Designer, 69
Text Editor, 69–70
Toolbars menu, 56–57
View Designer, 71
Toolbox window (SQL Server Management Studio), 53
Trace Properties dialog box
discussed, 80
Events Extraction Settings tab, 83
Events Selection tab, 82–83
General tab, 81–82

traced events, 82–84
transaction load considerations, Profiler tool, 379
transaction logs
Auto-Commit transactions, 106–107
auto-grow behavior, 110
backups, 110, 331
CHECKPOINT event, 109–110
Explicit, 108–109
free space in, 110–111
Implicit transactions, 107–108
inactive portion of, 110
LSN (Log Sequence Number), 110
physical characteristics, 110
purpose of, 105
recording transactions in, 109–110
transactional consistency, 18
transactional replication, 531–532
Transact-Structured Query Language. See T-SQL
Transfer Database Task, control flow, 476
Transfer Error Messages Task, control flow, 477
Transfer Job Task, control flow, 477
Transfer Logins Task, control flow, 477
Transfer Master Stored Procedures Task, control
flow, 477
transformations, data flow integration services,
480–481
transport security, Server Broker service, 513
triggers
After, 163
audit results, 169
CLR (Common Language Run-Time), 447–448
DML, 163, 167–169
Instead Of, 163
testing, 168–169
Trim function, 15
TRUNCATE TABLE command, 325
trusted connection error message, authentication, 34
Trustworthy option (New Database dialog box), 131
TSQL Default TCP endpoints, 234–235
TSQL TCP endpoints, 236–237
T-SQL (Transact-Structured Query Language)
database mirroring, 426–427
log shipping and, 413–417
multidimensional queries, 50
overview, 8
Tuning Options tab (DTA), 86–87
Turley, Paul (Professional SQL Server 2005 Reporting
Services), 3, 11

two-phase commit (2PC), 530–531

types

defined, 170

UDTs, 171–172

U

-U **argument, SQLCMD utility, 89**

UDAs (user-defined aggregates), 452–454

UDTs (user-defined types)

CLR (Common Language Run-Time), 448–452

overview, 171–172

UNC (Universal Naming Convention), 25–26

Uncomment Selected Lines feature

SQL Editor toolbar, 67

Text Editor toolbar, 70

Undo Checkout feature, Source Control toolbar, 65

Undo phase, restoration, 339

uniform extents, 102

unique keys, 156–158

uniqueidentifier **data type, 100**

Universal Naming Convention (UNC), 25–26

unsafe permission settings, CLR, 460–461

update locks, 376

UPDATE STATISTICS **statement, 168**

Update Statistics Task, control flow, 477

update with intent exclusive locks, 376

updates, undoing, 358

URL namespace, reserving, 245

user connection counters, performance optimization, 367

user databases

discussed, 113

overview, 16

restoration, 347–349

user security. See security

user-created stored procedures, 167

user-defined aggregates (UDAs), 452–454

user-defined data types

CLR (Common Language Run-Time), 448–452

overview, 170–171

user-defined filegroups, 119

user-defined functions, 167, 445–446

user-defined types (UDTs), 171–172

V

-v **argument, SQLCMD utility, 90**

varbinary **data type, 100**

varchar **data type, 100**

variable-length data types, 100–101

Verify SQL Syntax feature, Query Designer toolbar, 63

VIA (Virtual Interface Adapter) protocol, 8

VIA endpoints, 236

View Designer toolbar, 71

View History feature, Source Control toolbar, 65

View Page Breaks feature, Database Diagram toolbar, 60

views

Backward Compatibility System, 165

database, 164

Dynamic System, 165

Information Schema, 164

schema scope permissions, 210

Static System, 164

system, 164–165

Virtual Interface Adapter (VIA) protocol, 8

Virtual Server name configuration, SQL Server 2005 installation, 39–41

Visual Source Safe Explorer, Source Control toolbar, 64

Visual Studio, code generation features, 454–457

VPNs (virtual private networks), 404

W

wait time counters, performance optimization, 367

WANs (wide area networks), 404

WDSL (Web Service Descriptive Language), 241

Web Browser Refresh command, Help toolbar, 61

Web Browser Search command, Help toolbar, 61

Web Browser Stop command, Help toolbar, 61

Web browser window (SQL Server Management Studio), 54

Web Service Descriptive Language (WSDL), 241

Web services

data tier, 246

Web Service Identity area, Reporting Services Configuration Manager, 88

Web Service Task, control flow, 477

WEBMETHOD **argument, 243**

wide area networks (WANs), 404

width sensitivity, collation settings, 36

window properties, 47

Windows Authentication mode changes, 176–178

Windows cluster

overview, 402–403

SQL Server 2005 installation, 38

Windows Only configuration, authentication, 33–34

Windows Service Identity area, Reporting Services Configuration Manager, 88

WITH **clause**

backups and, 333–335

restoration and, 342–345

witness roles, database mirroring, 424

WMI event alerts, 311–312

Workgroup Edition

features, 5–6

flexibility in, 7

software requirements, 27–28

working sets counters, performance optimization, 365

WSDL **argument, 243**

X

XLST (XML Stylesheet), 495

XML (Extensible Markup Language)

discussed, 2

overview, 9

XML API, event collection process, 492

XML data type, 101

XML indexes

primary, 138–140

secondary path, 140

secondary property, 141

secondary value, 141

XML Schema Definition (XML), 244

XML section, Text Editor configuration, 72

XML Task, control flow, 477

XML Stylesheet (XLST), 495

XMLA (Extensible Markup Language for Analysis), 9

xp_instance_regwrite **extended stored procedure, 177**

XSD (XML Schema Definition), 244

Z

Zoom feature, Database Diagram toolbar, 60